Computer Animation

Algorithms and Techniques
Fourth Edition

Rick Parent

Professor Emeritus, Computer Science and Engineering,
Ohio State University

Andrew Hogue

Associate Professor, Game Development and Interactive Media,
Faculty of Business and IT, Ontario Tech University,
Oshawa, Ontario, Canada

ELSEVIER

MK
MORGAN KAUFMANN PUBLISHERS
AN IMPRINT OF ELSEVIER

Morgan Kaufmann is an imprint of Elsevier
50 Hampshire Street, 5th Floor, Cambridge, MA 02139, United States

ISBN: 978-0-443-13512-5

For information on all Morgan Kaufmann publications visit our website at https://www.elsevier.com/books-and-journals

Publisher: Peter Linsley
Acquisitions Editor: Stephen Merken
Editorial Project Manager: Helena Beauchamp
Production Project Manager: Nayagi Anandan
Cover Designer: Greg Harris

Typeset by TNQ Tech

To Kim and John, for teaching me to keep things in perspective.
And to my wife, Arlene, for her attention-to-detail approach to life, especially when juxtaposed to my 'big picture' way of doing things.
– Rick

To my kids Suzy, Maddie, Zoe for listening to my crazy ideas.
My parents, for giving me a strong foundation that encouraged both computer science and creativity. Last but not least, to my wife Jess, for putting up with my ADHD, always keeping me on track, and enabling me to turn my creative ideas into reality, you are my rock.
– Andrew

Contents

About the Authors

Rick Parent is a professor emeritus in the Computer Science and Engineering Department of Ohio State University (OSU). As a graduate student, Rick worked at the Computer Graphics Research Group (CGRG) at OSU under the direction of Charles Csuri. In 1977, he received his PhD from the Computer and Information Science (CIS) Department, majoring in artificial intelligence. For the next three years he worked at CGRG, first as a research associate and then as associate director. In 1980 he cofounded and was president of The Computer Animation Company. In 1985, he joined the faculty of the CIS Department (now the Department of Computer Science and Engineering [CSE]) at Ohio State. Rick's research interests include various aspects of computer animation with special focus on animation of the human figure. He is the author of *Computer Animation: Algorithms and Techniques,* published by Morgan Kaufmann. The first edition came out in 2001, and the second edition was published in September 2007 The third edition was published in 2012. The book has been translated into Russian, Polish, French, and Chinese, and over 10,000 copies have been sold. Since retirement, Rick has been advising his few remaining PhD students to see them through to their degrees.

Andrew Hogue is an associate professor at Ontario Tech University in the Game Development and Interactive Media program within the Faculty of Business and Information Technology. He has served as Program Director and Area Lead (informally and formally) since he joined Ontario Tech in 2007–2022. Dr. Hogue has developed and maintained a number of fundamental courses for the Game Development program, and he currently teaches Essential Math for Games 1, AI and Animation, Programming in C/C++, and Advanced Computer Graphics. His research encompasses a variety of disciplines, including the creation of new virtual reality (VR) interfaces for traditional artists and the application of volumetric video (VV) in healthcare education. His main research interests currently revolve around the development of new technologies and experiences that use VV and is exploring the current state of visual realism in VR, the impact of varying realism on the user experience, and implications on self-efficacy and knowledge retention in virtual learning environments. Working with industry and artistic partners, Dr. Hogue is pushing the boundaries of digital media and transforming the way we create animation in games, enhance realism, and engage users in training and simulation environments. He is committed to improving the way we create animation in games and enhance realism in training and simulation environments in meaningful ways. Dr. Hogue's passion for innovation and new technologies positions him at the forefront of advancing the field of digital media.

Preface

Overview

Computer animation is big business: in the United States alone, the film/television entertainment industry totaled $36.8 billion in 2021 [1] [2]. The vast majority of films use some form of computer animation in their visual effects (VFX), and it is commonplace for animation and VFX to play a large role in many television shows. Additionally, the video game industry has leveraged computer animation technology and is a burgeoning industry. According to the Entertainment Software Association, in 2022 the US video game industry had a revenue of $60.4 billion [3].

This highly dynamic field spans the entire spectrum from art, to film, to computer science and beyond. The past few years have seen huge changes in how computer animation is designed, created, and deployed in various industries. Fundamental advances from academic research have enabled the development of animation tools that leverage artificial intelligence and computer vision to allow for high-quality motion capture of human performances in real time.

In this book, we aim to arm the reader with knowledge of the fundamentals of computer animation that can empower them to create new ideas, new tools, and new techniques and to critically investigate new directions that inspire the next generation of animators and programmers.

Ancillary materials for this book can be found here: https://github.com/syberhogue/Book-Computer-Animation-Algorithms-Techniques.

Who is this book for?

When embarking on writing this new edition, we thought carefully about the audience on whom we are focused and the various contextual lenses with which these individuals may view the book. We focus on three primary lens archetypes for the content in this book: the Student, the Educator, and the Professional.

The student

Although the book is primarily focused on undergraduates in technical fields such as computer science and game development, we aim to provide enough detail to engage nonprogrammers and artists in the fundamentals to enhance their creative practice in ways we have not seen previously. We assume a few things about this student archetype: that they have an introductory grasp of computer programming knowledge or scripting (i.e., they have either taken an introductory programming course or have some basic experience with Python, c#, or C/C++ or have a good grasp of Unity/Unreal/Godot or similar modern game engines). Basic knowledge of computer graphics techniques and introductory linear algebra (vectors and matrices) are helpful but not essential, as we review the fundamentals required. Wherever possible, we will provide references to further your knowledge in areas we can only touch upon for further reading.

The educator

Fundamentally, this textbook is intended to be used in technical computer animation–focused courses at an intermediate/advanced level (i.e., second-, third-, and fourth-year undergraduate college/university). The previous editions of this text have been used effectively by Dr. Andrew Hogue in his second-year animation course in a game development and interactive media program at Ontario Tech University since 2008. To better map to existing curricula, the content has been reordered and revised such that educators can more easily adopt the content as a primary resource. Guided by Bloom's taxonomy, we provide categorical exercises that can be used either directly or as a template for your particular coursework/assignments as described below:

Beginner level

- Beginner exercises are intended to introduce students to the topics. *Bloom Verbs:* Remember (Define, State, List), Understand (Classify, Describe, Discuss).

Intermediate level

- Intermediate exercises are intended to build a foundation. *Bloom Verbs:* Apply (Implement, Solve, Demonstrate), Analyze (Compare, Contrast, Experiment).

Advanced level

- Advanced exercises are intended to encourage a deep understanding that uses the foundation to innovate or think creatively and critically. *Bloom Verbs:* Evaluate (Defend, Critique, Argue), Create (Design, Develop, Investigate).

The professional

We aim to provide enough detail on the mathematical and algorithmic fundamentals for professional programmers, technical artists, and animators to be able to use this book as a helpful reference for building animation systems, game engines, and tools for the nonprogrammers in your teams. We hope you find the discussions, pseudocode, and math useful for your professional practice.

Who is this book NOT for?

This book is focused on the fundamentals (algorithms, and techniques) and applications (film, games, tools) related to Computer Animation. This text is *not* intended to provide detailed instructions on how to use a particular off-the-shelf animation software package or game engine, as there are other very good resources that are constantly changing. We will provide references when possible for the interested reader throughout. This book does not attempt to cover the *theory* of computer animation, address the aesthetics of computer animation, or discuss the artistic issues involved in designing animations (unless it is pertinent to the discussion). It does not detail the production issues in the actual commercial enterprise of producing a finished piece of animation. And, finally, it does not address the issue of *computer-assisted animation,* which, for our purposes, is taken to mean the computerization of conventional hand-drawn techniques; for the most part, that area has its own set of separate issues [4], [5].

Artists, animators, programmers

A common misconception for students is that there is little to no overlap between the necessary knowledge between artists, animators, and programmers as it pertains to computer animation. In our experience over the past decades, it has become clear that there is much overlap between these professions and although each obviously has a different set of skills needed to perform their jobs, knowledge of the fundamentals of all professions only serves to enhance your craft. Artists with a programming background are highly sought after as technical artists, and they often work to develop tools between the art and programming teams. Similarly, animators with fundamental knowledge of how motion capture, performance capture, or 3D animation software works can optimize their capture sessions and push the boundaries of their craft further and faster.

Differences from the previous editions

The previous edition (published in 2012) was geared primarily toward an advanced undergraduate (or graduate) student in computer science (a programmer) interested in developing computer animation algorithms. Since then, over a decade of technical and creative advances have been made in computer animation, and we felt that it was time to update the content to reflect these advances while retaining the strong technical fundamentals and foundations of the previous edition. We have also seen the rise of new undergraduate programs in game development and interactive media, where students are exposed to these ideas earlier and are highly interested in both the tools and algorithms involved in creating interesting characters that are interactive and use new animation capture techniques to bring a level of realism to them that has never been seen before. This required us to reorder and revise the content in a way that maps to these new styles of curricula more effectively and provide exercises for students to challenge themselves (and others) while also providing educators with a template for coursework/exercises to enhance their offerings.

Practical techniques

This book addresses practical issues, provides accessible techniques, and offers straightforward implementations. Purely theoretical discussions have been avoided except to point out avenues of current and future research. In some cases, programming examples are complete working code segments in C, which can be copied, compiled, and run to produce basic examples of the algorithms discussed; other programming examples are C-like *pseudocode* that can straightforwardly be translated into working code. C was chosen because it forms the common basis for languages such as C++ and it lends itself to illustrating the step-by-step nature of algorithms. The appendices cover basic material that the reader may find useful as a refresher, as well as specific algorithms for use in implementations. In the spirit of practicality, we note that one fundamental need for those developing animation tools and algorithms is to be able to evaluate techniques and tools that enable animators and artists appropriate levels of expressiveness, yet at the same time allow for high computational performance and ensure animators have an appropriate amount of control. Obviously, no one tool is going to be right for every animator, for every animation, or even for every scene. The appropriateness of a particular animation tool depends on the effect desired and the control required by the animator. In this spirit, alternative approaches are presented whenever possible.

Organization of the book

This book is organized into four sections: Section 1: The Fundamentals; Section 2: Locomotion; Section 3: Animation; and Section 4: Advanced Algorithms and Techniques.

Section 1: The Fundamentals (Chapters 1–2) presents the foundation and fundamentals of computer animation from historical, mathematical, and algorithmic perspectives. The goal is to provide the reader with enough foundational knowledge that they can implement the techniques presented in later chapters. Chapter 1 discusses general issues related to animation, including motion perception, the heritage of conventional animation paying particular attention to its technological innovations, overviews of animation production and computer animation production, and a snapshot of the ever-evolving history of computer animation. These provide a broad perspective of the art and craft that is animation from its humble beginnings until today.

Chapter 2 presents background material and reviews the basics of computer graphics necessary for animation. It reviews computational issues in computer graphics to ensure a solid background in the techniques that are important in understanding the remainder of the book.

Section 2: Locomotion (Chapters 3–6) builds on the foundation and describes how we represent objects, how we can move these objects in a virtual environment and build systems to control them effectively. Chapter 3 discusses how we represent 3D objects in space for various needs and purposes ranging from basic primitives to volumetric signed distance fields.

Chapter 4 covers the basics of interpolation introducing how we can move these objects smoothly on curves: time-space curves, arc-length parameterization of a curve, and speed control along a curve. Interpolation of orientation with an emphasis on using quaternions is covered, and various ways to work with paths are then presented. Chapter 5 covers physics and simulation-based animation method including rigid bodies, particles, and springs. Chapter 6 is focused on controlling objects, building upon previous chapters, and introduces the concept of paths, keyframing, state machines, and steering.

Section 3: Animation (Chapters 7—10) focuses on techniques for bringing life to our objects, simulating human movements, and technology for motion/performance capture. Chapter 7 discusses sprite flipbooks, morphing, and humanoid character representation and animation techniques. Chapter 8 introduces techniques for acquiring animation data from motion capture, to authoring tools and how to work with animation data. Chapter 9 discusses animation systems, combining previous algorithms to enhance character animations using blending, animation-driven locomotion, motion graphs and motion-matching techniques. Chapter 10 discusses facial animation: facial modeling, expressions, and lip-synch animation and modern ways to think about and manipulate faces.

Section 4: Advanced Algorithms and Techniques (Chapters 11—12) focuses on advanced techniques, recent research results looking to the future of animation. Chapter 11 discusses fluids, liquids, and gases, and Chapter 12 explores recent advances in animation and looks at the future of animation using artificial intelligence techniques.

Acknowledgments

From Rick Parent: Many people contributed in various ways to this book. First and foremost, I'd like to thank my wife, Arlene, who both tolerated my preoccupation with this project and greatly increased the readability of the book. In general, I owe much to the students I have had the pleasure of knowing and/or working with over the years and whose collective interest in, knowledge of, and enthusiasm for the field has fueled my own. Their contributions cannot be overstated. These include Doug Roble, John Chadwick, Dave Haumann, Dave Ebert, Matt Lewis, Karan Singh, Steve May, James Hahn, Ferdi Scheepers, Dave Miller, Beth Hofer, Madhavi Muppala, Domin Lee, Kevin Rogers, Brent Watkins, Brad Winemiller, Meg Geroch, Lawson Wade, Arun Somasundaram, Scott King, and Scott (Slim) Whitman (apologies to anyone left out).

I would also like to thank the readers who, over the years, have given me feedback (both good and bad) concerning the book. In particular, I would like to note the critical contributions of Dr. Philip Schlup of Colorado State University, Dr. Brian Wyvill of the University of Calgary, and Dr. Przemyslaw Kiciak of the University of Warsaw. And finally, I would like to acknowledge the support of the Department of Computer Science and Engineering at Ohio State (Xiaodong Zhang, Chair), as well as the support of the Advanced Computing Center for Art and Design (Maria Palazzi, Director).

From Andrew Hogue: This book could not have been written without the support of a number of individuals. Rick Parent, for believing in me and allowing my vision for editing and refining the book content to thrive. My wife, Jess, who has supported me in my teaching, curriculum development, dealing with student crises, finding solutions to my wackiness and creativity and keeping me grounded and centered. My colleagues in the Game Development and Interactive Media program at Ontario Tech and specifically Alvaro Quevedo, Bill Kapralos, James Robb, and Gavin Ball for your insight, mentorship, and guidance for curriculum development, former Dean Michael Bliemel and Dean Carolyn McGregor, who were completely supportive of me embarking on this during my research leave and beyond. All of my current and former graduate and undergraduate students have been integral and inspiring with the passion they've had during our courses and research.

We would also like to thank Elsevier's reviewers and multiple editors for seeing this project through.

References

[1]. https://www.forbes.com/sites/bradadgate/2022/03/17/overview-of-the-entertainment-market-in-2021-coming-out-of-covid-19/?sh=3d8b6d49519c.

[2]. All time grossing movies. In: The internet movie database (IMDB). IMDb.com, Inc; 2012. Web, http://www.imdb.com/boxoffice/alltimegross.

[3]. ESA 2022 essential facts games industry https://www.theesa.com/wp-content/uploads/2022/06/2022-Essential-Facts-About-the-Video-Game-Industry.pdf

[4]. Catmull E. The problems of computer-assisted animation. In: Computer graphics. Proceedings of SIGGRAPH 78. 12(3). Atlanta, Ga; 1978. p. 348−53.

[5]. Levoy M. A color animation system based on the multiplane technique. In: George J, editor. Computer graphics. Proceedings of SIGGRAPH 77. 11(2). San Jose, Calif; 1977. p. 65−71.

CHAPTER

1 Introduction

Computer animation, for many people, is synonymous with big-screen productions such as *Star Wars*, *Toy Story*, and *Avatar*. But not all, or arguably even most, computer animation is done in Hollywood. Television shows, video games, mobile apps, and web pages now commonly employ animation techniques in a variety of ways. Video games take advantage of state-of-the-art computer graphics techniques and have been a major motivating force driving research in computer animation. Real-time performance-driven computer animation has appeared at SIGGRAPH[1] and even *Sesame Street*. With the advent of real-time volumetric video and motion-capture technologies, capturing live 4D performances is now possible! Desktop computer animation software is now available at a reasonable and low cost (or free, i.e. Blender), and computer animation on the Web is ubiquitous. Computer animation techniques are present and commonplace in serious games and training simulators for pilots, SWAT teams, and nuclear reactor operators. The distinguishing characteristics of these applications are the costs required, the image quality desired, and the amount and type of interaction afforded. Because computer animation is everywhere, in this book we do not focus on a single specific application of animation but rather present the fundamental algorithms and techniques applicable to all (or most) of them.

Computer animation, as used here, refers to any computer-driven computation used in producing images intended to create the perception of motion. The emphasis in this book is on algorithms and techniques that create and process three-dimensional graphical motion data. While related to the ever-changing field of computer graphics and rendering, computer animation is less about the visual rendering and more about the algorithms and techniques of representing and manipulating the motion of "moving" objects. Generally, any value that can be changed in a digital simulation can be "animated." For example, an object's position and orientation are obvious candidates for animation. If animation was limited to simply the position and orientation of an object, though, we would create very uninteresting stories. Animation encompasses the manipulation of *all* dynamic data pertaining to the system, and as such we can develop techniques that animate the following (but not limited

[1] SIGGRAPH is the Association for Computing Machinery's (ACM) special interest group on computer graphics. The ACM is the main professional group for computer scientists.

Computer Animation. https://doi.org/10.1016/B978-0-443-13512-5.00001-X

to): an object's shape, its shading parameters, its texture coordinates, the lighting parameters, and the camera parameters.

This book is organized into four main sections: (1) the fundamentals, (2) locomotion, (3) animation, and (4) advanced techniques. **Section 1** lays the foundations, with the remainder of this chapter providing a historical overview of the computer animation field. Chapter 2 focuses on the mathematical foundations necessary for understanding the rest of the book including the fundamental geometric transformations and associated representations of graphical data. **Section 2: Locomotion** comprises Chapters 3–6, where we build on the fundamentals and define algorithms that enable us to move objects programmatically, deterministically, and reliably. These will cover how we represent objects, different ways we can control these objects and manipulate their data, and how we can animate their movement through space smoothly and efficiently.

Section 3: Animation comprises Chapters 7–10 and builds on the previous concepts and applies them to groups of objects, scenes, and characters. Concepts covered are how we can deform and skin objects, define and animate relationships and hierarchies of objects (e.g., skeletons/rigs/scene graphs) and use this to create interesting character movements, facial animations, exploring methods to acquire this data (i.e., motion-capture) and defining systems that transition smoothly between multiple animation clips.

Section 4: Advanced Techniques comprises Chapters 11 and 12 and explores concepts related to animating fluids, gases, and implicit surfaces, and looks at the future of computer animation and the implications of artificial intelligence algorithms on the field.

The appendices provide ancillary material that are useful for the advanced reader to provide details that would otherwise derail from the discussion in various chapters. The appendices cover additional concepts and mathematical details that are relevant for animation but could not be included so as to not impede the flow of the discussions but are included as reference.

In considering computer animation techniques, there are three general approaches to motion control. The first is *artist-driven animation*, in which the animator/artist has the prime responsibility for crafting the motion. The foundation of artistic animation is interpolation, which is presented in Chapter 4. Various animation techniques that use interpolation foundationally in different ways are introduced throughout **Section 2** to control individual objects and expanded upon in **Section 3** to create more interesting character animations. The second is *data-driven animation*, where live motion and performance is captured and mapped onto graphical objects. Generally referred to as *motion capture*, various sensors and techniques have historically been applied to capture human motion, and we explore this in Chapter 8. The third is *algorithm-driven* or *procedural animation*, in which there is a computational model that is used to control the motion. Usually, this is in the form of setting initial conditions for some type of physical or behavioral simulation. Procedural animation is discussed throughout this book and specifically in Chapters 5, 11, and 12.

To set the context for computer animation, it is important to understand its heritage, its history, and certain relevant concepts. The remainder of this chapter discusses motion perception, the technical evolution of animation, animation production, and notable works in computer animation. It provides a grounding in computer animation as a field of endeavor and inquiry.

1.1 Motion perception

The adage "a picture is worth a thousand words" means that a single image can quickly convey a large amount of information because the human visual system is a sophisticated information processor. It follows, then, that moving images (or sequences of images of changing subjects) have the potential to convey an immense amount of information in a short time. Indeed, the human visual system has evolved to quickly notice and interpret movement, a fundamental requirement for survival in an ever-changing world.

It is widely recognized that a series of images, when displayed in rapid succession, are perceived by an observer as a single moving image. This is possible because the eye–brain complex has the ability, under sufficient viewing conditions and within certain playback rates, to create a sensation of continuous imagery from such a sequence of still images. A commonly held view is that this experience is due to *persistence of vision*, whereby the eye retains a visual imprint of an image for a brief instant once the stimulus is removed. It is argued that these imprints, called *positive afterimages* of the individual stills, fill in the gaps between the images to produce the perception of a continuously changing image. Peter Roget (of *Roget's Thesaurus* fame) presented the idea of impressions of light being retained on the retina in 1824 [1]. But persistence of vision is not the same as perception of motion. Rotating a white light source fast enough will create the impression of a stationary white ring. Although this effect can be attributed to persistence of vision, the result is static. The sequential illumination of a group of lights typical of a movie theater marquee produces the illusion of a lighted object circling the signage. Motion is perceived, yet persistence of vision does not appear to be involved because no individual images are present. The causality of the (physiological) persistence of vision mechanism, however, has been called into question and the perception of motion has been attributed to a (psychological) mechanism known as the *phi phenomenon* (as is the case in the movie marquee example). A related phenomenon, for example the apparent motion of a disk traveling between two flickering disks, is referred to as *beta movement* [2–5].

Whatever the underlying mechanism is, the result is that in both film and video, a sequence of images can be displayed at rates fast enough to fool the eye into interpreting it as continuous imagery. When the perception of continuous imagery fails to be created, the display is said to *flicker*. In this case, the animation appears as a rapid sequence of still images to the eye–brain complex. Depending on conditions such as room lighting and viewing distance, the rate at which individual images must be played back in order to maintain the perception of continuous imagery varies. This rate is referred to as the *critical flicker frequency* [6].

While perception of motion addresses the lower limits for establishing the perception of continuous imagery, there are also upper limits to what the eye can perceive. The receptors in the eye continually sample light in the environment. The limitations on motion perception are determined, in part, by the reaction time of those sensors and by other mechanical limitations such as blinking and tracking. If an object moves too quickly with respect to the viewer, then the receptors in the eye will not be able to respond fast enough for the brain to distinguish sharply defined, individual detail; *motion blur* results [7]. In a sequence of still images, motion blur is produced by a combination of the object's speed and the time interval over which the scene is sampled. In a still camera, a fast-moving object will not blur if the shutter speed is fast enough relative to the object's speed. Motion blur is part of our everyday experience, and when images are presented in sequence without motion blur, they tend to result in odd or unnatural looking movement. An example of this is the use of "motion smoothing" in modern televisions that upscale and interpolate the incoming video signal from 30 frames per second (fps) to 60 or 120 fps resulting in a subtle but noticeable uncanniness. In computer graphics, motion blur can be computed using postprocessing techniques or through clever sampling tricks with ray tracing, as the system can sample the scene at any precise instant in time. To compute motion blur, the scene is sampled over an interval of time, and the resulting pixel colors averaged to produce the *blur*, or cleverly manipulated to appear as though it were [8,9]. If motion blur is not calculated, then images of a fast-moving object can appear unnatural or disjointed, similar to viewing live action under the effects of a strobe light; often referred to as *strobing*. In hand-drawn animation, fast-moving objects are typically stretched in the direction of travel so that the object's images in adjacent frames overlap [10], reducing the strobing effect.

There are actually two rates of concern, one is the *playback* (or *refresh*) rate—the number of images per second displayed in the viewing process and is related to flicker. The other is the *sampling* (or *update or frame*) rate—the number of different images that occur per second—which determines how jerky or smooth the motion appears. For example, historically an analog television signal conforming to the National Television Standards Committee (NTSC) format displays images at a rate of roughly 30 frames per second (fps),[2] but because it is *interlaced*,[3] *fields* are played at 60 frames per second to prevent flicker under normal viewing conditions [11]. In some programs (e.g., some Saturday morning cartoons) there may be only six different images per second, with each image repeatedly displayed five times. Often, lip-sync animation is drawn *on twos* (every other frame) because drawing it *on ones*

[2] More accurately, the format for broadcast television system, established by the NTSC, specifies a frame rate of 29.97 fps [50].

[3] An *interlaced* display is one in which a frame is divided into two *fields*. Each field consists of odd or even numbered scanlines. The odd and even fields are displayed in alternate scans of the display device [6].

(animating it in every frame) makes it appear too hectic. Film is typically shown in movie theatres at playback rates of 24 fps (in the United States) but, to reduce the flicker, each frame is actually displayed twice (*double-shuttered*) to obtain an effective refresh rate of 48 fps. On the other hand, because an NTSC television signal is interlaced, smoother motion can be produced by sampling the scene every 60th of a second even though the complete frames are only played back at 30 fps [6]. Nowadays, computer displays and televisions are progressive scan (*noninterlaced*) devices with refresh rates far exceeding 70 fps [11]. Video games have pushed this even further with monitors that advertise refresh rates of 240Hz and beyond that intend to provide smoother and more responsive gaming in fast-paced first-person shooter or racing games, which is especially important to professional gamers.

The display and perception of animation using a sequence of still images imposes certain requirements on how those images are computed and displayed effectively. Understanding the operation, limits, and trade-offs of the human visual system are essential when making intelligent decisions about designing any type of visual and auditory content, including computer animation. Kuroki et al. [12] showed that blur and jerkiness in film can be eliminated at 250 fps but the perceptual system saturates at 240 fps. Recent work also demonstrated that observers perceived enhanced detail at higher frame-rates [13].

1.2 The heritage of animation

In the most general sense, *animate*[4] means "give life to" and includes live-action puppetry such as that found on *Sesame Street* and the use of electromechanical devices to move puppets, such as *animatronics*. History is replete with attempts to bring objects to life. This history is a combination of myth, deception, entertainment, science, and medicine. Many of the references to animation are in the form of stories about conjuring a life force into some humanoid form: from Pygmalion to Prometheus to Wagner's homunculus in Goethe's *Faust* to Shelley's Dr. Frankenstein. Some of the history is about trying to create mechanical devices that mimic certain human activity: from Jacque Vaucanson's mechanical flute player, drummer, and defecating duck in the 1730s to Wolfgang von Kempelen's chess player in 1769 to Pierre Jaquet-Droz's writing automaton of 1774 to the electromechanical humanoid robots (*animatronics*) popular today. The early mechanisms from the 1700s and 1800s were set in the milieu of scientific debate over the mechanistic nature of the human body (e.g., *L'Homme Machine*, translated as *Man a Machine*, was written by Julien Offray de La Mettrie in 1747 and was quite controversial). This activity in humanoid mechanical devices was propelled by a confluence of talents contributed

[4] A more restricted definition of *animation*, also found in the literature, requires the use of a sequence of stills to create the visual impression of motion. The restricted definition does not admit techniques such as animatronics or shadow puppets under the rubric animation.

by magicians, clock makers, philosophers, scientists, artists, anatomists, glove makers, and surgeons (see Gaby Wood's book for an entertaining survey on the quest for mechanical life [14]). Here, however, the focus is on devices that use a sequence of individual still images to create the effect of a single moving image, because these devices have a closer relationship to hand-drawn animation.

1.2.1 Early devices

Persistence of vision and the ability to interpret a series of stills as a moving image were actively investigated in the 1800s [15], well before the film camera was invented. The recognition and subsequent investigation of this effect led to a variety of devices intended as parlor toys [16,17]. Perhaps the simplest of these early devices is the *thaumatrope*, a flat disk with images drawn on both sides with two strings connected opposite each other on the rim of the disk (see Figure 1.1). The disk could be quickly flipped back and forth by twirling the strings. When flipped rapidly enough, the two images appear to be superimposed. The classic example uses the image of a bird on one side and the image of a birdcage on the other; the rotating disk visually places the bird inside the birdcage. An equally primitive technique is the *flip book*, a tablet of paper with an individual drawing on each page. When the pages are flipped rapidly, the viewer has the impression of motion.

FIGURE 1.1

A thaumatrope.

Image adapted from "Taumatropio topo e gabbia, 1825.gif", Public domain, via Wikimedia Commons

One of the most well-known early animation devices is the *zoetrope*, or wheel of life. The zoetrope has a short, fat cylinder that rotates on its axis of symmetry. Around the inside of the cylinder is a sequence of drawings, each one slightly different from the ones next to it. The cylinder has long vertical slits cut into its side between each adjacent pair of images so that when it is spun on its axis each slit allows the eye to see the image on the opposite wall of the cylinder (see Figure 1.2). The sequence of slits passing in front of the eye as the cylinder is spun on its axis presents a sequence of images to the eye, creating the illusion of motion.

Related gizmos that use a rotating mechanism to present a sequence of stills to the viewer are the *phenakistoscope* and the *praxinoscope*. The phenakistoscope also uses a series of rotating slots to present a sequence of images to the viewer by positioning two disks rotating in unison on an axis; one disk has slits, and the other contains images facing the slits. One sights along the axis of rotation so the slits pass in front of the eye, which can thus view a sequence of images from the other disk. The praxinoscope uses a cylindrical arrangement of rotating mirrors inside a large cylinder of images facing the mirrors. The mirrors are angled so that as the cylinders rotate in unison, each image is successively reflected to the observer.

Just before the turn of the century, the moving image began making its way on stage. The *magic lantern* (an image projector powered by candle or lamp) and shadow puppets became popular theater entertainment [18]. On the educational front, Etienne-Jules Marey [19] and Eadweard Muybridge [20,21] investigated the motions of humans and animals. To show image sequences during his lectures, Muybridge invented the *zoopraxiscope*, a projection device also based on rotating slotted disks. Then, in 1891, the seed of a revolution was planted: Thomas Edison invented the motion picture viewer (the *kinetoscope*), giving birth to a new industry [17].

FIGURE 1.2

A zoetrope.

1.2.2 The early days of "conventional" animation

Animation in America exploded in the twentieth century in the form of filming hand-drawn, two-dimensional images (referred to here also as *conventional* or *traditional* animation). Studying the early days of conventional animation is interesting in itself [17,22–24], but the purpose of this overview is to provide an appreciation of the technological advances that drove the progress of animation during the early years.

After Edison's kinetoscope, there were several rapid developments in film technology. One of the most notable developments was the motion picture projector by the Lumiere brothers, Auguste and Louis, in France. They are credited with the first commercial, public screening of film in Paris on December 28, 1895. They called their device the *cinematograph*. It is a camera that could both project and develop film. They used it to film everyday events including a train coming into a train station; this footage, when shown to the audience, sent everyone scrambling for cover. It was also used for aerial photography (years before the airplane took to the skies).

The earliest use of a camera to make lifeless things appear to move occurred in 1896 by Georges Méliès. Méliès used simple camera tricks such as multiple exposures and stop-motion techniques to make objects appear, disappear, and change shape [25]. His best known trick film is *A Trip to the Moon* (1902). One of the earliest pioneers in film animation was J. Stuart Blackton, an American who animated "smoke" in a scene in 1900, ushering in the field of *visual effects*. Blackton is credited with creating the first animated cartoon, *Humorous Phases of Funny Faces* (1906), by drawing and erasing on a chalkboard between takes. Emile Cohl, a Frenchman, produced several vignettes including *Fantasmagorie* (1908), which is considered to be the first fully animated film ever made. The American Winsor McCay is the first celebrated animator, best known for his works *Little Nemo* (1911) and *Gertie the Dinosaur* (1914). McCay is considered by many to have produced the first popular animations [22].

Like many of the early animators, McCay was an accomplished newspaper cartoonist. He redrew each complete image on rice paper mounted on cardboard and then filmed them individually. He was also the first to experiment with color in animation. Much of his early work was incorporated into vaudeville acts in which he "interacted" with an animated character on a screen. Similarly, early cartoons often incorporated live action with animated characters. To appreciate the impact of such a popular entertainment format, keep in mind the relative naïveté of audiences at the time; they had no idea how film worked, much less what hand-drawn animation was. As Arthur C. Clarke stated about sufficiently advanced technology, it must have been indistinguishable from magic.

The first major technical developments in the animation process can be traced to the efforts of John Bray, one of the first to recognize that patenting aspects of the animation process would result in a competitive advantage [22]. Starting in 1910, his work laid the foundation for conventional animation as it exists today. Earl Hurd, who joined forces with Bray in 1914, patented the use of translucent *cels*[5] in the compositing of multiple layers of drawings into a final image and also patented gray-scale drawings as opposed to black and white. Later developments by Bray and others enhanced the overlay idea to include a peg system for registration and the drawing of the background on long sheets of paper so that *panning* (translating the background relative to the camera, perpendicular to the view direction) could be performed more easily. Out of Bray's studio came Max Fleischer (Betty Boop), Paul Terry (Terrytoons), George Stallings (Tom and Jerry), and Walter Lantz (Woody Woodpecker). In 1915, Fleischer patented *rotoscoping* (drawing images on cells by tracing over previously recorded live action). Several years later, in 1920, Bray experimented with color in the short *The Debut of Thomas Cat*.

While the technology was advancing, animation as an art form was struggling. The first animated character with an identifiable personality was Felix the Cat, drawn by Otto Messmer of Pat Sullivan's studio [22]. Felix was the most popular and most financially successful cartoon of the mid-1920s. In the late 1920s, however, new forces had to be reckoned with: sound and Walt Disney.

1.2.3 Disney

Walt Disney was, of course, the overpowering force in the history of conventional animation. Not only did his studio contribute several technical innovations, but Disney, more than anyone else, advanced animation as an art form [24]. Disney's innovations in animation technology included the use of a storyboard to review the story and pencil sketches to review motion. In addition, he pioneered the use of sound and color in animation (although he was not the first to use color). Disney also studied live-action sequences to create more realistic motion in his films. When he used sound for the first time in *Steamboat Willie* (1928), he gained an advantage over his competitors.

One of the most significant technical innovations of the Disney studio was the development of the multiplane camera [22,23]. The multiplane camera consists of a camera mounted above multiple planes, each of which holds an animation cell. Each of the planes can move in six directions (right, left, up, down, in, out), and the camera can move closer and farther away (see Figure 1.3).

Multiplane camera animation is more powerful than one might think. By moving the camera closer to the planes while the planes are used to move foreground images out to the sides, a more effective zoom can be performed. Moving multiple planes at different rates can produce the *parallax effect*, which is the visual effect of closer objects apparently moving faster across the field of view than objects farther away, as an observer's view pans across an environment. This is very effective in

---

[5] Cel is short for *celluloid*, which was the original material used in making the translucent layers. Currently, cels are made from acetate.

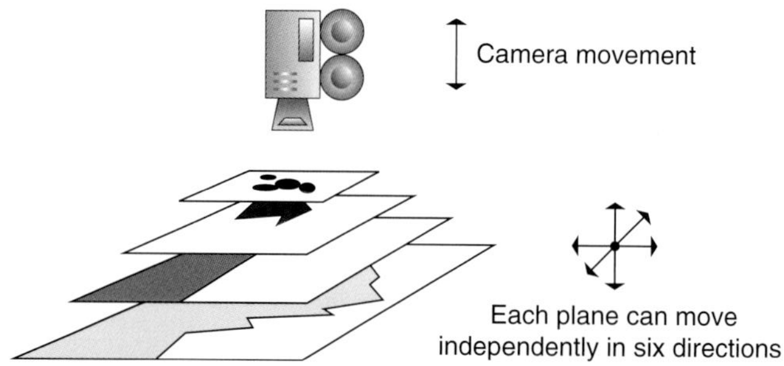

FIGURE 1.3

Directional range of the multiplane camera, inside of which the image is optically composited.

creating the illusion of depth and an enhanced sensation of three dimensions. Keeping the camera lens open during movement can produce several additional effects: figures can be extruded into shapes of higher dimension, depth cues can be incorporated into an image by blurring the figures on more distant cels, and a blurred image of a moving object can be produced.

With regard to the art of animation, Disney perfected the ability to impart unique, endearing personalities in his characters, such as those exemplified in Mickey Mouse, Pluto, Goofy, the Three Little Pigs, and the Seven Dwarfs [23,24]. He promoted the idea that the mind of the character was the driving force of the action and that a key to believable animated motion was the analysis of real-life motion. He also developed mood pieces, for example, *Skeleton Dance* (1929) and *Fantasia* (1940).

1.2.4 Contributions of others

The 1930s saw the proliferation of animation studios, among them Fleischer, Iwerks, Van Beuren, Universal Pictures, Paramount, MGM, and Warner Brothers. The technological advances that are of concern here were mostly complete by this period. The differences between, and contributions of, the various studios have to do more with the artistic aspects of animation than with the technology involved in producing animation [22]. Many of the notable animators in these studios were graduates of Disney's or Bray's studio. Among the most recognizable names are Ub Iwerks, George Stallings, Max Fleischer, Bill Nolan, Chuck Jones, Paul Terry, and Walter Lantz.

1.2.5 Other media for animation

The rich heritage of hand-drawn animation in the United States makes it natural to consider it the precursor to computer animation, which also has strong roots in the

United States. However, computer animation has a close relationship to other animation techniques as well.

A good comparison can be made between computer animation and some of the stop-motion techniques, such as clay and puppet animation. Typically, in three-dimensional computer animation, one of the first steps is the object modeling process. The models are then manipulated to create the three-dimensional scenes that are rendered to produce the images of the animation. In much the same way, clay and puppet stop-motion animation use three-dimensional figures that are built and then animated in separate, well-defined stages [16]. Once the physical three-dimensional figures are created, they are used to lay out a three-dimensional environment. A camera is positioned to view the environment and record an image. One or more of the figures are manipulated, and the camera may be repositioned. The camera records another image of the scene. The figures are manipulated again, another image is taken of the scene, and the process is repeated to produce the animated sequence.

Willis O'Brien of *King Kong* fame is generally considered the dean of this type of stop-motion animation. His understudy, who went on to create an impressive body of work in his own right, was Ray Harryhausen (*Mighty Joe Young*, *Jason and the Argonauts*, and many more). More recent impressive examples of three-dimensional stop-motion animation are Nick Park's *Wallace and Gromit* series and *Chicken Run* and Tim Burton's projects such as *The Nightmare Before Christmas*, *James and the Giant Peach*, *Corpse Bride*, and *Alice in Wonderland*.

Because of computer animation's close association with video technology, it has also been associated with video art, which depends largely on the analog manipulation of the video signal in producing effects such as colorization and warping [26]. Because creating video art is inherently a two-dimensional process, the relationship is viewed mainly in the context of computer animation post-production techniques. Even this connection has faded because the popularity of recording computer animation by digital means has eliminated most analog processing.

1.2.6 Animation in video games and interactive media

Video games have influenced the development of computer animation as much as (if not more than) film and television. Possibly the first video game, "Tennis for Two" [27] (and clearly a precursor to Pong) was introduced in 1958 at the Brookhaven National Laboratory by William Higinbotham, an American physicist. Tennis for Two used an oscilloscope display and an analog computer circuit to enable two players to serve and hit a ball drawn as a bright dot and moved across the screen subject to gravity. From an animation perspective, the movement of the ball across the screen must be calculated using physical equations of movement taking into account gravity (and possibly other forces). This was clearly a form of procedural physics-based animation and is fundamental to modern video games. The evolution of early game systems and game animation was rapid, from the Atari 2600 (1977) to more sophisticated 8-bit Super Mario Bros in the Nintendo Entertainment System (NES) in

1983, to 16-bit images with the TurboGrafx-16 (1987), the Sega Genesis (1988), and the Super Nintendo (SNES, 1990). In all of these game systems, game animation can be separated into (1) the movement of the character/objects' position on the screen (i.e., locomotion), and (2) changes in appearance of the character/object due to the action they are performing (i.e., walking, crouching, jumping). The movement of object position can be defined procedurally using physics as before, but the change in appearance utilized a digital version of the traditional analog animation technique: the flip-book. Artists would define/draw key frames and subsequently draw in-between images to ensure smooth, continuous, and interesting dynamics when played back in succession. Many modern games still use this method. The 1990s computational advancements and the introduction of 3D games such as Virtua Fighter (1993, Sega), Doom (1993, id Software), Quake (1996, id Software), and Super Mario 64 (1996, Nintendo) successively defined a new paradigm for animation and employed a combination of 2D sprite-based animation and expanded this technique to 3D polygons to define more complex character movement. Half-Life (1998, Valve Software) was the first to employ a skeletal animation and rigging technique leading to easier animation authoring and efficient memory storage. This technique has since become a foundational technique for animation in modern games as it lends itself easily to the use of motion capture, blending, and procedurally driven animation rigs. We will explore each of these techniques in detail in subsequent chapters.

1.3 Animation production

Although producing a final animated film is not the subject of this book, the production process merits some discussion in order to establish the context in which an animator works. It is useful for technical animators to have some familiarity with how a piece of animation is broken into parts and how a finished piece is produced. Much of this is taken directly from conventional animation and is directly applicable to any type of animation.

A piece of animation is usually discussed using a four-level hierarchy, although the specific naming convention for the levels may vary.[6] Here, the overall animation—the entire project—is referred to as the *production*. Typically, productions are broken into major parts referred to as *sequences*. A sequence is a major episode and is usually identified by an associated staging area; a production usually consists of one to a dozen sequences. A sequence is broken down into one or more *shots*; each shot is the recording of the action from a single point of view. A shot is broken down into the individual *frames* of film. A frame is a single recorded image. This results in the hierarchy shown in Figure 1.4.

[6] Live-action film tends to use a five-level hierarchy: film, sequence, scene, shot, and frame [51]. Here, the terminology, which is often used in feature-length computer animation, is presented.

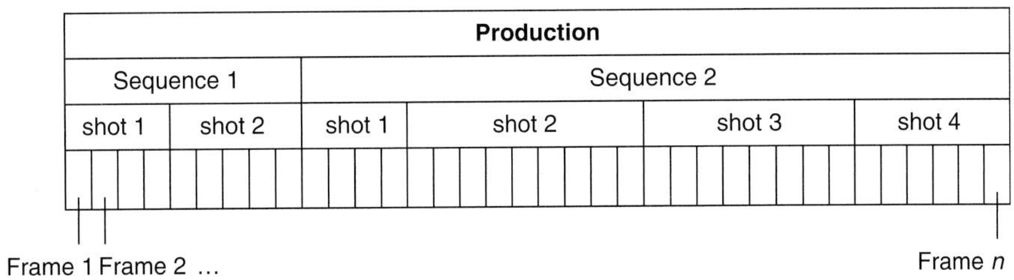

FIGURE 1.4

Sample hierarchy of a simple animation production.

Several steps are required to successfully plan and carry out the production of a piece of animation [16,23]. Animation is a trial-and-error process that involves feedback from one step to previous steps and usually demands several iterations through multiple steps at various times. Even so, the production of animation typically follows a standard pattern. First, a *preliminary story* is decided on, including a *script*. A *storyboard* is developed that lays out the action scenes by sketching representative frames. The frames are often accompanied by text that sketches out the action taking place. This is used to present, review, and critique the action, as well as to examine character development.

A model sheet is developed that consists of a number of drawings for each figure in various poses and is used to ensure that each figure's appearance is consistent as it is repeatedly drawn during the animation process. The exposure sheet records information for each frame such as sound track cues, camera moves, and compositing elements. The *route sheet* records the statistics and responsibility for each scene.

An *animatic*, or *story reel*, may be produced in which the storyboard frames are recorded, each for as long as the sequence it represents, thus creating a rough review of the timing. Often, a *scratch track*, or *rough sound track*, is built at the same time the storyboard is being developed and is included in the animatic. Once the storyboard has been decided on (see Figure 1.5), the *detailed story* is worked out to identify the actions in more detail. *Key frames* (also known as *extremes*) are then identified and produced by master animators to aid in confirmation of timing, character development, and image quality. Associate and assistant animators are responsible for producing the frames between the keys; this is called *in-betweening*. *Test shots*, short sequences rendered in full color, are used to test the rendering and motions. To completely check the motion, a *pencil test* may be shot, which is a full-motion rendering of an extended sequence using low-quality images such as pencil sketches. Problems identified in the test shots and pencil tests may require reworking of the key frames, detailed story, or even the storyboard.

Inking refers to the process of transferring the penciled frames to cels. *Opaquing*, also called *painting*, is the application of color to these cels.

FIGURE 1.5

Sample storyboard panels, 4 sequences shown as columns with 4 shots each. Column 1 (Sequence 1/Left), Story/shot flow: Establish tone, Confirm social connection, Build dialogue energy, Payoff in a lively group moment. (Shot 1-top) Host raises a glass (welcome): A medium welcoming shot; slight push-in to set tone and invite the audience into the space. (Shot 2) Handshake (first agreement/intro): Cut on action; hands land center-frame to punctuate the beat. (Shot 3): Animated conversation by the bar. Two-shot with expressive hand gestures; alternating eyelines for natural rhythm.(Shot 4-bottom): Group toasting/laughing. Energy peak; overlapping motion and quick reaction cuts sell warmth and volume.

ATTRIBUTION: Rodrigo Ferrusca, CC BY-SA 3.0 https://creativecommons.org/licenses/by-sa/3.0, via Wikimedia Commons

1.3.1 Principles of animation

To study various techniques and algorithms used in computer animation, it is useful to first understand their relationship to the animation principles used in hand-drawn animation. In an article by Lasseter [28], the principles of animation, articulated by some of the original Disney animators [24], are related to techniques commonly used in computer animation. The principles are squash and stretch, timing, secondary action, slow in and slow out, arcs, follow through and overlapping action, exaggeration, appeal, anticipation, staging, solid drawing, and straight ahead and pose to pose. Lasseter is a conventionally trained animator who worked at Disney before going to Pixar. At Pixar, he was responsible for many celebrated computer animations including *Tin Toy* that, in 1989, was the first computer animation to win an Academy Award. Whereas Lasseter discusses each principle in terms of how it might be implemented using computer animation techniques, the principles are organized here according to the type of motion quality they contribute to in a significant way. Because several principles relate to multiple qualities, some principles appear under more than one heading.

Simulating physics

Squash and stretch, *timing*, *secondary action*, *slow in and slow out*, and *arcs* establish the physical basis of objects in the scene. A given object possesses some degree of rigidity and should appear to have some amount of mass. This is reflected in the distortion (squash and stretch) of its shape during an action, especially a collision. More importantly, squash and stretching of the object can be used to exaggerate the movement of the object allowing its motion to "feel" smoother. For example, in Figure 1.6 you can see the ball flattens as it leaves and hits the ground plane (note that this is highly exaggerated for illustration purposes). This squashing and stretching of the object imbues the object with a small amount of character rather than a stiff, lifeless animation that would result without. This is a simple yet valuable tool for those wishing to bring life to an object and can be applied in all aspects of the character (e.g., portions of their face, clothing, and limbs can all stretch at different rates to produce different effects and evoke different emotions). Some great examples of this can be found in Overwatch and demonstrated in [29]. The animation must support these notions consistently for a given object throughout the animation. Timing has to do with how actions are spaced according to the weight, size, and personality of an object or character and, in part, with the physics of movement and the artistic aspects of the animation. Secondary action supports the main action, possibly supplying physically based reactions to an action that just occurred.

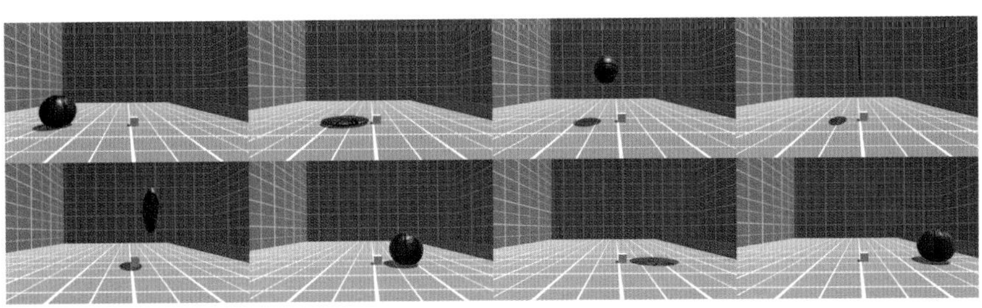

FIGURE 1.6

Simple squash & stretch example. Starting from the top row, this shows an extremely exaggerated example of a ball anticipating a jump, stretching during the jump, landing and flattening and rolling away.

Slow in and slow out and arcs are concerned with how things move through space. Objects slow in and slow out of poses. When speaking of the actions involved, objects are said to "ease in" and "ease out." Such speed variations model inertia, friction, and viscosity. Objects, because of the physical laws of nature such as gravity, usually move not in straight lines but rather in arcs.

Designing aesthetically pleasing actions

Appeal, *solid drawing*, and *follow through/overlapping action* are principles that address the aesthetic design of an action or action sequence. To keep the audience's attention, the animator needs to make it enjoyable to watch (appeal). In addition, actions should flow into one another (follow through/overlapping action) to make the entire shot appear to continually evolve instead of looking like disjointed movements. Solid drawing refers to making the character look pliable and not stiff or wooden. Squash and stretch can also be used in this regard. Secondary actions and timing considerations also play a role in designing pleasing motion.

Effectively presenting action

Often the animator needs to employ *exaggeration* so a motion cannot be missed or so it makes a point (Tex Avery is well known for this type of conventional animation). *Anticipation* and *staging* concern how an action is presented to the audience. Anticipation dictates that an upcoming action is set up so that the audience knows it (or something) is coming. Staging expands on this notion of presenting an action so that it is not missed by the audience. *Timing* is also involved in effective presentation to the extent that an action has to be given the appropriate duration for the intended effect to reach the audience. *Secondary action* can also be used to create an effective presentation of an action.

Production technique

Straight ahead versus *pose to pose* concerns how a motion is created. Straight ahead refers to progressing from a starting point and developing the motion continually along the way. Physically based animation could be considered a form of straight-ahead processing. Pose to pose, the typical approach in conventional animation, refers to identifying key frames and then interpolating the intermediate frames, an approach the computer is particularly good at.

1.3.2 Principles of filmmaking

Basic principles of filmmaking are worth reviewing in order to get a sense of how effective imagery is constructed. Several of the basic principles are listed in the following sections, although more complete references should be consulted by the interested reader (e.g.,[30]). Some of the following principles are guidelines that should be followed when composing a single image; others are options of how to present the action.

Three-point lighting

There is a standard set of three lights that are used to illuminate the central figure in a scene. These are the *key light*, the *fill light*, and the *rim light*. The key light is often positioned up and to the side of the camera, pointing directly at the central figure. This focuses the observer's attention on what is important. The rim light is positioned behind the central figure and serves to highlight the rim, thus outlining the figure and making the figure stand out from the background. The fill light is a flood light typically positioned below the camera that fills the figure with a soft light bringing out other details in the figure's appearance. See Figure 1.7 (Color Plate 1) for an example.

180 degree rule

When filming a line of action, for example the conversation between two figures, it is common to show each figure in isolation during the action. The camera is positioned in front of a figure but a little off to the side. The 180 degree rule states that when showing the two figures, one after the other, in isolation, the camera should stay on the same side of the line of action. Thus, the camera's orientation should stay within the 180 degrees that is on one side of the line between the figures.

Rule of thirds

The rule of thirds says that the interesting places to place an object in an image are one-third along the way, either side to side or up and down or both. In particular, don't center your subject in the image, and don't put your subject at the edge of the image.

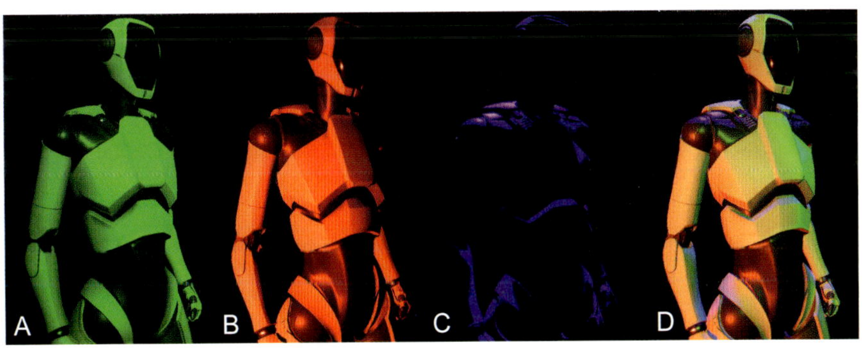

FIGURE 1.7

(a) Key light. The 'key', or main light (shown here in green), is placed at 45 degrees from the camera on the right. This light has the highest intensity in the setup and is responsible for the cast shadows of the objects. (b) Fill light. The 'fill' light (shown here in red) is placed the left (opposite side of the 'key' light) and is used to illuminate the dark areas unlit by the key light. This light is less intense and does not cast shadows or highlights on the objects. (c) Rim light. A 'rim' light (shown here in blue) is placed above and behind the objects to highlight their edges which are otherwise in shadow. These highlights help separate the objects from the background and from other overlapping objects in the scene. (d) All lights. This is the final lighting setup combining the key, fill, and rim lights.

Types of shots

Types of camera shots are categorized based on the distance from the camera to the subject and the angle at which the shot is taken. The distance-based shots are *extreme long range*, *long range*, *medium range* or *bust shot*, *close-up*, and *extreme close-up*. Which type of shot to use depends on the amount and location of detail that is to be shown and how much environmental context is to be included in the shot.

A *low angle shot*, meaning the camera is low shooting up at the subject, imparts a feeling of power or dominance to the subject. Conversely, a *high angle shot*, in which the camera shoots down on the subject, presents a feeling that the subject is insignificant or subordinate.

Tilt

Tilting the camera (rotating the camera about its view direction) can convey a sense of urgency, strangeness, or fear to the shot.

Framing

Framing refers to allowing enough room in the image for the action being captured. In a relatively static view, allow enough room so the subject does not fill the frame (unless there is a reason to do so). Allow enough room for motion. If your subject is walking, frame the motion so there is room in front of the subject so the subject does not appear to be walking out of the frame.

Focus the viewer's attention

Draw the viewer's attention to what's important in the image. Use color, lighting, movement, focus, and so forth to direct the attention of the viewer to what you want the viewer to see. For example, the eye will naturally follow converging lines, the gaze of figures in the image, a progression from dark to light or dark to bright, and an identifiable path in the image.

1.3.3 Sound

Sound is an integral part of almost all animation, whether it's hand-drawn, computer based, or stop-motion [16,22]. Up through the 1920s, the early "silent films" were played in theaters with live mood music accompaniment. That changed as sound recording technology was developed for film and, later, for video.

Audio recording techniques had been around for 30 years by the time moving images were first recorded on film. It took another 30 years to develop techniques for playing a sound track in sync with recorded action. Since then, various formats have been developed for film sound tracks. Most formats record the audio on the same medium that records the images. In most of the various formats for film, for example, audio is recorded along the side of the images or between the sprocket holes in one to six tracks. Early formats used optical or magnetic analog tracks for sound, but more recent formats digitally print the sound track on the film. By recording the audio on the same stock as the film, the timing between the imagery and the audio is physically enforced by the structure of the recording technology. In some formats, a separate medium, such as a CD, is used to hold the audio. This allows more audio to be recorded, but it creates a synchronization issue during playback. In the case of video, audio tracks are recorded alongside the tracks used to encode the video signal.

In the early film and video formats, audio was recorded as a low bandwidth analog signal resulting in very low-quality sound. Today's film and video technology acknowledges the importance of sound and provides multiple, high-quality digital audio tracks. Sound has four roles in a production: voice, body sounds, special effects, and background music.

In live action, voice is recorded with the action because of timing considerations while most of the other sounds are added in a post-processing phase. In animation, voices are recorded first and the animation made to sync with it. In addition, recording visuals of the voice talent during the audio recording can be used to guide the animators as they create the facial expressions and body language that accompanies the speech.

Nonspeech sounds made by the actors, such as rustling of clothes, footsteps, and objects being handled, are called body sounds. The recorded body sounds are usually replaced by synthesized sounds, called *foley*, for purposes of artistic control. These synthesized sounds must be synced with the motions of the actors. The people responsible for creating these sounds are called *foley artists*.

Special effects, such as door slams and the revving of car engines, must also be synced with the action, but with lesser precision than voice and foley sounds.

Recording background and mood music can be added after the fact and usually require no precise timing with the action. All the sounds other than voice are added after the live action or animation is recorded.

1.3.4 Principles of animation for games and interactive media

Animation in video games can often be thought of as an extension of filmmaking with some very specific constraints and differences. As in filmmaking, game development typically employs many of the same design concepts, such as the use of storyboarding to define the story beats ensuring proper game and story flow, concept art for environments and characters, animatics and temporary animations to demonstrate and critique the art direction, and final polish to ensure aesthetically pleasing character movement and cut-scenes. As in film, motion capture is used in many modern games to bring "life" and more natural motion to the characters. However, there are a number of constraints that make games fundamentally different than film, which in turn has significant impact on the animations and expressiveness that are possible.

Real-time rendering requirements

Film is largely a static medium. Once released, it is not changed (although after-release editing is becoming more common on streaming platforms). Because of the complexity of objects and scenes in computer-animated films, a single frame of computer generated imagery can take hours to render. This is not possible for games as they require a *minimum* of 30 frames per second to be rendered. Because there are 1000 ms per second, a single frame must take a *maximum* of 33.33 ms to render. This includes all game computations and includes game logic, input, visual effects, character movement, character animation, and post-processing shader effects. This imposes real constraints on the type of algorithm and size of data that can be employed for animation. Generally, games favor simple approximate algorithms instead of complex physical simulations for the most part.

Interactivity

Games are inherently interactive, which means that objects and characters must react to the player input. This has several implications on game animation. Imagine a third-person game like Lara Croft or Uncharted, in which the player uses a game controller to control their avatar. The system translates the buttons and controller axes into actions such as walk forward, turn left, and so on. These actions result in a triggering of a new animation clip to be played, and the character should move appropriately. Preferably, however, the animations should transition smoothly and not abruptly from the current frame of animation to the intended clip. This requires careful thought and crafting of a large number of animations that are then cycled through or a system that can procedurally ensure smooth transitions at the expense of potential input lag. Characters typically interact with the environment (e.g., trip over rocks, stop at walls, run into another player). Thus a set of animations must be authored or defined to enable such interactions. Depending on the game context, failure to adequately represent the space of animations "realistically" will negatively impact player immersion. Thus, there are tradeoffs in terms of the choice of data, the number of clips and transitions, and the algorithm used for animation.

Platform computational constraints impact animation

Fixed hardware platforms like a game console (e.g., Sony PlayStation 5, Nintendo Switch, Microsoft Xbox) impose computational and memory limits on the game itself. Given the nature of these games, the animation processing time and memory budget is lower than other gameplay assets. Games that target mobile devices (e.g., smartphones) have significantly stricter constraints. This means that the choice of platform impacts which algorithms we can or should use and what types of data can be supported, which in turn has an impact on how expressive our characters can be.

1.4 Computer animation production

Computer animation production has borrowed most of the ideas from conventional animation production, including the use of a storyboard, test shots, and pencil testing. The storyboard has translated directly to computer animation production, although it may be done on-line. It still holds the same functional place in the animation process and is an important component in planning animation. The use of key frames, and interpolating between them, has become a fundamental technique in computer animation.

While computer animation has borrowed the production approaches of conventional animation, there are significant differences between how computer animation and conventional animation create an individual frame of the animation. In computer animation, there is usually a strict distinction among creating the models; creating a layout of the models including camera positioning and lighting; specifying the motion of the models, lights, and camera; and the rendering process applied to those models. This allows for reusing models and lighting setups. In conventional animation, all of these processes happen simultaneously as each drawing is created; the only exception is the possible reuse of backgrounds, for example, with the multilayer approach.

The two main evaluation tools of conventional animation, test shots and pencil tests, have counterparts in computer animation. A speed/quality trade-off can be made in several stages of creating a frame of computer animation: model building, lighting, motion control, and rendering. By using high-quality techniques in only one or two of these stages, that aspect of the presentation can be quickly checked in a cost-effective manner. A test shot in computer animation is produced by a high-quality rendering of a highly detailed model to see a single frame, a short sequence of frames of the final product, or every *n*th frame of a longer sequence from the final animation. The equivalent of a pencil test can be performed by simplifying the sophistication of the models used, by using low-quality and/or low-resolution renderings, by eliminating all but the most important lights, or by using simplified motion.

Often, it is useful to have several representations of each model available at varying levels of detail. For example, placeholder cubes can be rendered to present the gross motion of rigid bodies in space and to see spatial and temporal relationships among objects. "Solids of revolution" objects (objects created by rotating a silhouette edge at certain intervals around an axis and then defining planar surfaces to fill the space between these silhouette slices) lend themselves quite well to multiple levels of detail for a given model based on the number of slices used. Texture maps and displacement maps can be disabled until the final renderings.

To simplify motion, articulated figures[7] can be kept in key poses as they navigate through an environment in order to avoid interpolation or inverse kinematics. Collision detection and response can be selectively "turned off" when not central to the effect created by the sequence. Complex effects such as smoke and water can be removed or represented by simple geometric shapes during testing.

Many aspects of the rendering can be selectively turned on or off to provide great flexibility in giving the animator clues to the finished product's quality without committing to the full computations required in the final presentation. Often, the

[7] *Articulated figures* are models consisting of rigid segments usually connected together in a tree-like structure; the connections are revolute or prismatic joints, allowing a segment to rotate or translate relative to the segment to which it is connected.

resulting animation can be computed in real time for very effective motion testing before committing to a full anti-aliased, transparent, texture-mapped rendering. Wire-frame rendering of objects can sometimes provide sufficient visual cues to be used in testing. Shadows, smooth shading, texture maps, environmental maps, specular reflection, and solid texturing are options the animator can use for a given run of the rendering program.

Even in finished pieces of commercial animation, it is common practice to take computational shortcuts when they do not affect the quality of the final product. For example, the animator can select which objects can shadow which other objects in the scene. In addition to being a compositional issue, selective shadowing saves time over a more robust approach in which every object can shadow every other object. In animation, environmental mapping is commonly used instead of ray tracing; photorealistic rendering is typically avoided.

Computer animation is well suited for producing the equivalent of test shots and pencil tests. In fact, because the quality of the separate stages of computer animation can be independently controlled, it can be argued that it is even better suited for these evaluation techniques than conventional animation.

1.4.1 Computer animation production tasks

While motion control is the primary subject of this book, it is worth noting that motion control is only one aspect of the effort required to produce computer animation. The other tasks (and the other talents) that are integral to the final product should not be overlooked. As previously mentioned, producing quality animation is a trial-and-error, iterative process wherein performing one task may require rethinking one or more previously completed tasks. Even so, these tasks can be laid out in an approximate chronological order according to the way they are typically encountered. The order presented here summarizes an article that describes the system used to produce Pixar's *Toy Story* [31]. See Figure 1.8.

- The *Story Department* translates the verbal into the visual. The screenplay enters the Story Department, the storyboard is developed, and the story reel leaves. These visuals then go to the Art Department.
- The *Art Department*, working from the storyboard, creates the designs and color studies for the film, including detailed model descriptions and lighting scenarios. The Art Department develops a consistent look to be used in the imagery. This look guides the Modeling, Layout, and Shading Departments.
- The *Modeling Department* creates the characters and the world in which they live. Every brick and stick to appear in the film must be handcrafted. Often, figures with jointed appendages, or other models with characteristic motion, are created as parameterized models. Parameters that control standard movements of the figure are defined. This facilitates the ability of animators to *stay on the model*, ensuring that the animation remains consistent with the concept of the model. The models are given to Layout and Shading.

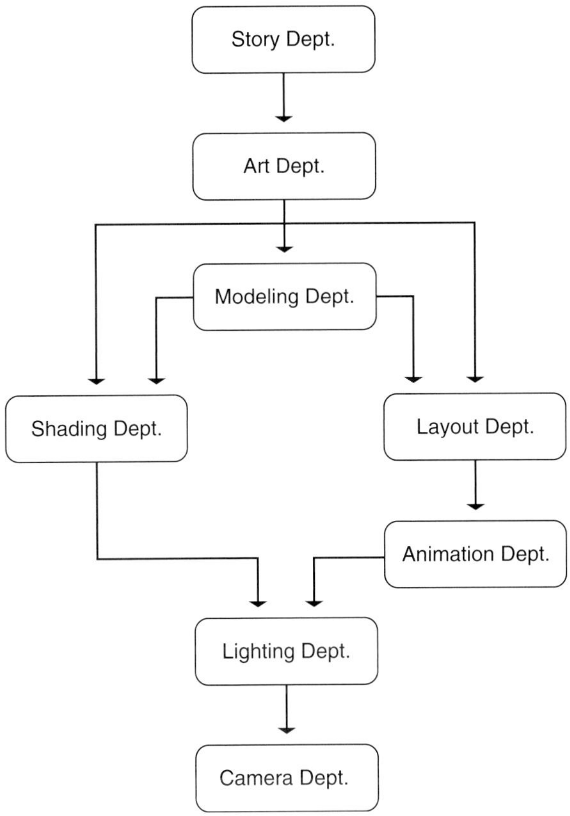

FIGURE 1.8

Traditional computer animation production pipeline.

- On one path between the Modeling Department and Lighting Department lies the *Shading Department.* Shading must translate the attributes of the object that relate to its visual appearance into texture maps, displacement shaders, and lighting models. Relevant attributes include the material the object is made of, its age, and its condition. Much of the effective appearance of an object comes not from its shape but from shading—the visual qualities of its surface.
- On the other path between Modeling and Lighting lies the *Layout Department*, followed by the Animation Department. Layout is responsible for taking the film from two dimensions to three dimensions. To ensure good flow, Layout implements proper *staging* (designing the space for the action to take place in) and *blocking* (planning out the general movements of the actors and camera). This guides the Animation Department.
- Working from audio, the story, and the blocking and staging produced by Layout, the *Animation Department* is responsible for bringing the characters to life. As mentioned, complex figures are often parameterized by the Model Department

so that a character's basic movements (e.g., smiling, taking a step) have already been defined. Animation uses these motions and creates the subtler gestures and movements necessary for the "actor" to effectively carry out the scene.
- The *Lighting Department* assigns to each sequence a team that is responsible for translating the Art Department's vision into digital reality. At this point the animation and camera placement have been done. Key lights are set to establish the basic lighting environment. Subtler lighting particular to an individual shot refines this in order to establish the correct mood and bring focus to the action.
- The *Camera Department* is responsible for actually rendering the frames. During *Toy Story*, Pixar used a dedicated array of hundreds of processors called the *Render Farm.* The term render farm is now commonly used to refer to any such collection of processors for image rendering.

1.4.2 Digital editing

A revolution swept the film and video industries in the 1990s: the digital representation of images. Even if computer graphics and digital effects are not a consideration in the production process, it has become commonplace to store program elements in digital form instead of using the analog film and videotape formats. Digital representations have the advantage of being able to be copied with no image degradation. So, even if the material was originally recorded using analog means, it is often cost-effective to transcribe the images to a digital image store. And, of course, once the material is in digital form, digital manipulation of the images is a natural capability to incorporate in any system.

In the old days ...

The most useful and fundamental digital image manipulation capability is that of editing sequences of images together to create a new presentation. Originally, film sequences were edited together by physically cutting and splicing tape. This is an example of *nonlinear editing*, in which sequences can be inserted in any order at any time to assemble the final presentation. However, splicing is a time-consuming process, and making changes in the presentation or trying different alternatives can place a heavy burden on the stock material as well.

Electronic editing[8] allows the manipulation of images as electronic signals rather than using a physical process. The standard configuration uses two source videotape players, a switching box, and an output videotape recorder. More advanced configurations include a character generator (text overlays) and special effects generator (e.g., wipes, fades) on the input side, and the switching box is replaced by an editing station (see Figure 1.9). The two source tapes are searched to locate the initial

---

[8] To simplify the discussion and make it more relevant to the capabilities of the personal computer, the discussion here focuses on video editing, although much of it is directly applicable to digital film editing, except that film standards require much higher resolution and therefore more expensive equipment.

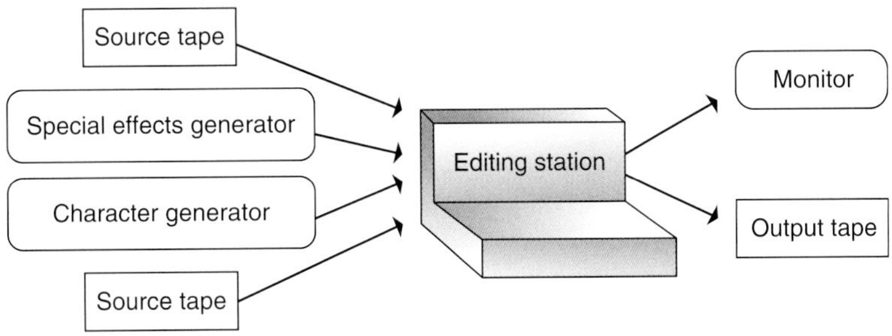

FIGURE 1.9

Linear editing system.

desired sequence; the tape deck on which it is found is selected for recording on the output deck; and the sequence is recorded. The tapes are then searched to locate the next segment, the deck is selected for input, and the segment is recorded on the output tape. This continues until the new composite sequence has been created on the output tape. The use of two source tapes allows multiple sources to be more easily integrated into the final program. Because the output is assembled in sequential order, this is referred to as *linear editing*. The linear assembly of the output is considered the main drawback of this technique. Electronic editing also has the drawback that the material is copied in the editing process, introducing some image degradation. Because the output tape is commonly used to master the tapes that are sent out to be viewed, these tapes are already third generation. Another drawback is the amount of wear on the source material as the source tapes are repeatedly played and rewound as the next desired sequence is searched for. If different output versions are required (called *versioning*), the source material will be subjected to even more wear and tear because the source material has to undergo more handling as it is processed for multiple purposes.

Often, to facilitate the final assemblage of the output sequence and avoid excessive wear of the original source material, copies of the source material are used in a preprocessing stage in which the final edits are determined. This is called *off-line editing*. The result of this stage is an *edit decision list* (EDL), which is a final list of the edits that need to be made to assemble the final piece. The EDL is then passed to the *on-line editing* stage, which uses the original source material to make the edits and create the finished piece. This process is referred to as *conforming*.

To keep track of edit locations, control track pulses can be incorporated onto the tape used to assemble the 30 fps NTSC video signal. Simple editing systems count the pulses, and this is called *control track editing*. However, the continual shuffling of the tape back and forth during the play and rewind of the editing process can result in the editing unit losing count of the pulses. This is something the operator must be aware of and take into account. In addition, because the edit counts are relative to the current tape location, the edit locations are lost when the editing station is turned off.

The Society of Motion Picture and Television Engineers time code is an absolute eight-digit tag on each frame in the form of HHMMSSFF, where HH is the hour, MM is the minute, SS is the second, and FF is the frame number. This tag is calculated from the beginning of the sequence. This allows an editing station to record the absolute frame number for an edit and then store the edit location in a file that can be retrieved for later use.

The process described so far is called *assemble editing*. *Insert editing* is possible if a control signal is first laid down on the output tape. Then sequences can be inserted anywhere on the tape in forming the final sequence. This provides some nonlinear editing capability, but it is still not possible to easily lengthen or shorten a sequence without repositioning other sequences on the tape to compensate for the change.

Digital on-line nonlinear editing

To incorporate a more flexible nonlinear approach, fully digital editing systems have become more accessible [32]. These can be systems dedicated to editing, or they can be software systems that run on standard computers. Analog tape may still be used as the source material and for the final product, but everything between is digitally represented and controlled[9] (see Figure 1.10).

After a sequence has been digitized, an icon representing it can be dragged onto a timeline provided by the editing system. Sequences can be placed relative to one another; they can be repeated, cut short, overlapped with other sequences, combined with transition effects, and mixed with other effects. A simplified example of such a timeline is shown in Figure 1.11.

The positioning of the elements in the timeline is conceptual only; typically the data in the digital image store is not actually copied or moved. The output sequence can be played back in real time if the disk random access and graphics display are fast enough to fetch and compile the separate tracks on the fly. In the case of overlapping sequences with transitions, the digital store must support the access of multiple tracks simultaneously so a transition can be constructed on the fly or the transition sequence needs to be precomputed (sometimes referred to as *rendering*) and explicitly stored for

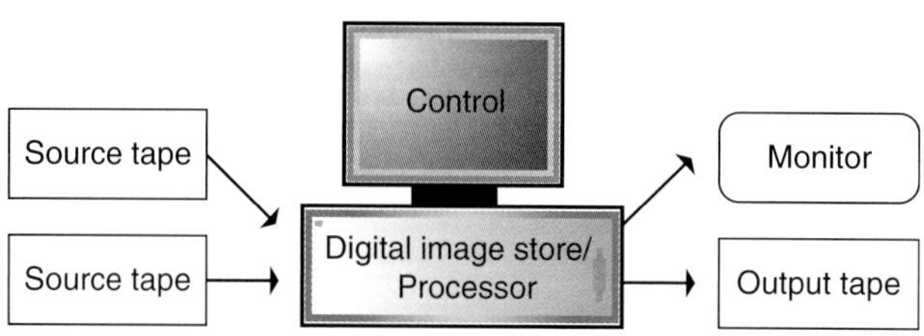

FIGURE 1.10

Online non-linear editing system.

[9] It is interesting to note that the whole process from recording to projection can now be done digitally.

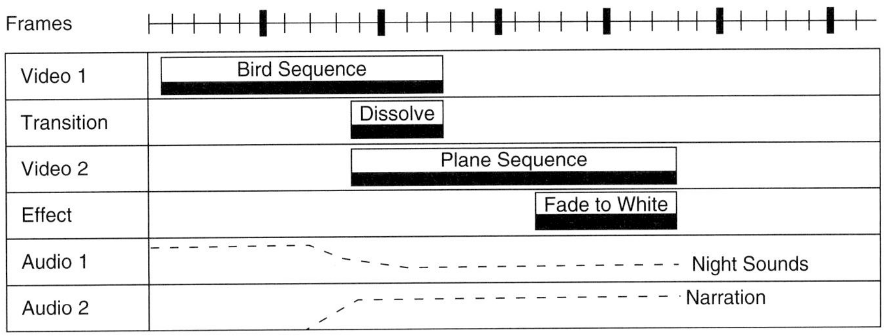

FIGURE 1.11

Simplified example of a timeline used for nonlinear digital editing.

access during playback. When the sequence is finalized it can be assembled and stored digitally or recorded on video. Whatever the case, the flexibility of this approach, with the ability to change edits and try alternatives without generational degradation, makes nonlinear digital editing systems very powerful.

1.4.3 Digital video

As the cost of computer memory decreases and processor speeds increase, the capture, compression, storage, and playback of high-quality digital video is ubiquitous. This has several important ramifications. First, desktop animation has become inexpensive enough to be within the reach of the consumer. Second, in the film industry it has meant that compositing is no longer optical. Optically compositing each element in a film meant another pass of the negative through an optical film printer, which meant additional degradation of image quality. With the advent of digital compositing, the limit on the number of composited elements is removed. Third, once films are routinely stored digitally, digital techniques can be used for wire removal and to apply special effects. These digital techniques have become the bread and butter of computer graphics in the film industry.

When one works with digital video, there are several issues that need to be addressed to determine the cost, speed, storage requirements, and overall quality of the resulting system. Compression techniques can be used to conserve space or reduce transmission time, but some compression compromises the quality of the image, and the speed of compression/decompression may restrict a particular technique's suitability for a given application. During video capture, any image compression must operate in real time. Formats used for storage and playback can be encoded off-line, but the decoding must support real-time playback. Video resolution, video frame rates, and full-color imagery require that 27 MB/sec be supported for video playback.[10] An hour of uncompressed video requires just under 100 GB of storage.[11] While lossless compression (the original data can be exactly reconstructed) is possible, most video compression is lossy (not all of the original signal is recoverable) because of the favorable quality/space trade-off. There are several digital video formats used by different manufacturers of video equipment for various applications, as well as video formats for streaming video and storage; these formats include D1, D2, D3, D5, miniDV, DVC, Digital8, MPEG-4, digital Betacam, H.261, and H.263. Better signal quality can be attained with the use of component instead of composite signals. Discussion of these and other issues related to digital video is beyond the scope of this book.

1.4.4 Digital audio

Audio is just as important to computer animation as it is to traditional animation. Over the years, audio technology, like image technology, has gone digital. Early audio recordings used an electromechanical stylus to etch representations of the signal into wax drums or plastic platters. Later, the signal was used to modulate the magnetization of some type of ferromagnetic material on plastic tape. Digital audio has since taken over. Digital audio has the same advantages as digital imagery when it comes to duplicating and editing. Digital audio can be copied, cut and pasted, transitioned, and looped over without any degradation in signal quality—a distinct advantage over its analog counterpart. The sound capability in personal computers has dramatically improved over the years so that now high-quality sound capability is standard. As with digital imagery, there are file formats and compression standards to consider when dealing with digital audio. In addition, there is a standard for digitally controlling musical devices.

Digital musical device control

Musical instrument digital interface (MIDI) is a standard developed in 1983 to control musical instruments without being tied to any one instrument in particular. MIDI commands are keynote commands to musical devices and are intended to represent a musical performance. Mostly, the commands take the form of "note x on" and "note x off," where x is any of the standard musical notes. There are also control commands to set pitch, loudness, and so forth. Some devices can also send out MIDI commands as they are played in order to record the performance as keys are depressed and released. MIDI supports up to 16 channels, and devices can be daisy-chained so that, for example, a device can be set up to respond only to a particular track.

---

[10] 640 pixels/scanline $\times$ 480 scanlines/frame $\times$ 3 bytes/pixel $\times$ 30 fps $=$ 27,630,000 bytes/sec.

[11] 27,630,000 bytes/sec $\times$ 3600 sec/hour $=$ 99,468,000,000 bytes/hour.

Digital audio sampling

Sounds are pressure waves of air. In audio recording, the pressure waves are converted to some representation of the waveform. When it is recorded digitally, the wave is sampled at certain intervals—the sampling rate—with a certain number of bits per sample—the sample size—using a certain number of tracks. The sampling rate determines the highest frequency, called the Nyquist frequency, which can accurately be reconstructed. A voice signal can be sampled at a much lower rate than CD-quality music because the highest frequency of a voice signal is much lower than the highest frequency that might occur in a piece of music. The number of bits per sample determines how much distortion there is in the recorded signal. The number of tracks is how many independent signals make up the music—one for mono, two for stereo, more for various "surround sound" recordings or for later editing. A voice signal and AM radio are sampled at approximately 10K samples per second with 8 bits per sample using one track. CD-quality music is sampled at 44.1K samples per second with 16 bits per sample using two tracks.

Similar to digital imagery, the digital recording can then be compressed for more efficient storage and transmission. The compression can either be lossless (the original signal can be reconstructed exactly) or lossy (some of the original signal is lost in the compression/decompression procedure—usually the very high frequencies). General data compression techniques can be used, but don't do as well on audio data as the compression schemes that use the fact that the file contains audio, referred to as being *perceptually based*. Compression of speech can use techniques that are less sensitive to preserving all of the frequency components of the sound. Common audio data compression techniques include MP3, MPEG-4 ALS, TTA, and FLAC.

1.5 A brief history of computer animation

1.5.1 Early activity (pre-1980)

The earliest computer animation of the late 1960s and early 1970s was produced by a mix of researchers in university labs and individual visionary artists [33–35]. At the time, raster displays driven by frame buffers were just being developed, and digital output to television was still in the experimental stage. The displays in use were primarily storage tubes and refresh vector displays. Storage tubes retain an image indefinitely because of internal circuitry that continuously streams electrons to the display. However, because the image cannot be easily modified, storage tubes were used mainly to draw complex static models. Vector (calligraphic) displays use a display list of line- and arc-drawing instructions that an internal processor uses to repeatedly draw an image that would otherwise quickly fade on the screen. Vector displays can draw moving images by carefully changing the display list between refreshes. These displays were popular for interactive design tasks.

During this time period, static images were often recorded onto film by placing a camera in front of the display and recording an image of vectors on the screen. In this way, shaded images could be produced by opening the shutter of the film camera and essentially scan converting the elements (e.g., polygons) by drawing closely spaced horizontal vectors to fill the figure; after scan conversion was completed, the shutter was closed to terminate the image recording. The intensity of the image could be regulated by using the intensity control of the vector display or by controlling other aspects of the image recording such as by varying the density of the vectors. An image of a single color was generated by placing a colored filter in front of the camera lens. A full-color image could be produced by breaking the image into its red, green, and blue components and triple exposing the film with each exposure using the corresponding colored filter. This same approach could be used to produce animation as long as the motion camera was capable of single-frame recording. Single-frame recording required precise frame registration, usually available only in expensive film equipment. Animated sequences could be colored by triple exposing the entire film. The programmer (animator) was fortunate if both the camera and the filters could be controlled by computer.

The earliest research in computer graphics and animation occurred at the Massachusetts Institute of Technology in 1963 when Ivan Sutherland developed an interactive constraint satisfaction system on a vector refresh display [36]. The user could construct an assembly of lines by specifying constraints between the various graphical elements. If one of the graphical elements moved, the system calculated the reaction of other elements to this manipulation based on satisfying the specified constraints. By interactively manipulating one of the graphical elements, the user could produce complex motion in the rest of the assembly. Later, at the University of Utah, Sutherland helped David Evans establish the first significant research program in computer graphics and animation.

As early as the early 1960s, computer animation was produced as artistic expression. The early artistic animators in this period included Ken Knowlton, Lillian Schwartz, S. Van Der Beek, John Whitney, Sr., and A. M. Noll. Typical artistic animations consisted of animated abstract line drawings displayed on vector refresh displays. Chuck Csuri, an artist at Ohio State University, produced pieces such as *Hummingbird* (1967) that were more representational.

In the early 1970s, computer animation in university research labs became more widespread. Computer graphics, as well as computer animation, received an important impetus through government funding at the University of Utah [37]. As a result, Utah produced several groundbreaking works in animation: an animated hand and face by Ed Catmull (Hand/Face, 1972), a walking and talking human figure by Barry Wessler (*Not Just Reality*, 1973), and a talking face by Fred Parke (*Talking Face*, 1974). Although the imagery was extremely primitive by today's standards, the presentations of lip-synced facial animation and linked-appendage figure animation were impressive demonstrations well ahead of their time.

In 1972, Chuck Csuri founded the Computer Graphics Research Group (CGRG) at Ohio State with the focus of bringing computer technology to bear on creating animation [38]. Tom DeFanti produced the Graphics Symbiosis System (GRASS) in the early 1970s that scripted interactive control of animated objects on a vector display device. Later in the 1970s, CGRG produced animations using a real-time video playback system developed at North Carolina State University under the direction of John Staudhammer. Software developed at CGRG compressed frames of animation and stored them to disk. During playback, the compressed digital frames were retrieved from the disk and piped to the special-purpose hardware, which took the digital information, decompressed it on the fly, and converted it into a video signal for display on a standard television. The animation was driven by the ANIMA II language [39]. In the mid-1980s, Julian Gomez developed TWIXT [40], a track-based key-frame animation system.

In 1973, the first computer language–based key-frame animation system, ANTICS, was developed by Alan Kitching at the Atlas Computer Laboratory under the auspices of the Royal College of Art in the United Kingdom [41,42]. ANTICS is a Fortran software package specifically designed for animators and graphic designers. It is a two-dimensional system that provides capabilities analogous to traditional cel animation.

In the mid-1970s, Norm Badler at the University of Pennsylvania conducted investigations into posing a human figure. He developed a constraint system to move the figure from one pose to another. He has continued this research and established the Center for Human Modeling and Simulation at the University of Pennsylvania. *Jack* is a software package developed at the center that supports the positioning and animation of anthropometrically valid human figures in a virtual world [43].

In the late 1970s, the New York Institute of Technology (NYIT) produced several computer animation systems, thanks to individuals such as Ed Catmull and Alvy Ray Smith [33]. At the end of the 1970s, NYIT embarked on an ambitious project to producc a wholly computer generated feature film using three-dimensional computer animation, titled *The Works*. While the project was never completed, excerpts were shown at several SIGGRAPH conferences as progress was made. The excerpts demonstrated high-quality rendering, jointed figures, and interacting objects. The system used at NYIT was BBOP, a three-dimensional key-frame figure animation system [44].

In 1974, the first computer animation nominated for an Academy Award, *Hunger*, was produced by Rene Jodoin; it was directed and animated by Peter Foldes. This piece used a 2½ D system that depended heavily on object shape modification and line interpolation techniques [45]. The system was developed by Nestor Burtnyk and Marceli Wein at the National Research Council of Canada in conjunction with the National Film Board of Canada. *Hunger* was the first animated story using computer animation.

In the early 1980s Daniel Thalmann and Nadia Magnenat-Thalmann started work in computer animation at the University of Montreal [33]. Over the years, their labs have produced several impressive animations, including *Dream Flight* (N. Magnenat-Thalmann, D. Thalmann, P. Bergeron, 1982), *Tony de Peltrie* (P. Bergeron, 1985), and *Rendez-vous à Montréal* (N. Magnenat-Thalmann and D. Thalmann, 1987).

Others who advanced computer animation during this period were Ed Emshwiller at NYIT, who demonstrated moving texture maps in *Sunstone* (1979); Jim Blinn, who produced the *Voyager* flyby animations at the Jet Propulsion Laboratory (1979); Don Greenberg, who used architectural walkthroughs of the Cornell University campus (1971); and Nelson Max at the Education Development Center, who animated space-filling curves (1972).

Commercial efforts at computer animation first occurred in the late 1960s with Lee Harrison's SCANIMATE system based on analog computing technology [46]. Digital technology soon took over, and the mid- to late-1970s saw the first serious hints of commercial three-dimensional digital computer animation. Tom DeFanti developed the GRASS at Ohio State University (1976), a derivative of which was used in the computer graphics sequences of the first *Star Wars* film (1977). In addition to *Star Wars*, films such as *Future World* (1976), *Alien* (1979), and *Looker* [26][12] (1981) began to incorporate simple computer animation as examples of advanced technology. This was an exciting time for those in the research labs wondering if computer animation would ever see the light of day. One of the earliest companies to use three-dimensional computer animation was the Mathematical Application Group Inc. (MAGI), which used a ray-casting algorithm to provide scientific visualizations. MAGI also adapted its technique to produce early commercials for television.

1.5.2 The middle years (the 1980s)

The 1980s saw a more serious move by entrepreneurs into commercial animation. Computer hardware advanced significantly with the introduction of the VAX computer in the 1970s and the IBM PC at the beginning of the 1980s. Hardware z-buffers were produced by companies such as Raster Tech and Ikonas, Silicon Graphics was formed, and flight simulators based on digital technology were taking off because of efforts by the Evans and Sutherland Corporation. These hardware developments were making the promise of cost-effective computer animation to venture capitalists. At the same time, graphics software was getting more sophisticated: Turner Whitted introduced anti-aliased ray tracing (*The Compleat Angler*, 1980), Loren Carpenter produced a flyby of fractal terrain (*Vol Libre*, 1980), and Nelson Max produced several films about molecules and one of the first films animating waves (*Carla's Island*, 1981). Companies such as Alias, Wavefront, and TDI were starting to produce sophisticated software tools making advanced rendering and animation available off the shelf for the first time.

[12] The film *Looker* is interesting as an early commentary on the potential use of digital actors in the entertainment industry.

Animation houses specializing in three-dimensional computer animation started to appear. Television commercials, initially in the form of flying logos, provided a profitable area where companies could hone their skills. Demo reels appeared at SIGGRAPH produced by the first wave of computer graphics companies such as Information International Inc. (III, or triple-I), Digital Effects, MAGI, Robert Abel and Associates, and Real Time Design (ZGRASS).

The first four companies combined to produce the digital imagery in Disney's TRON (1982), which was a landmark movie for its (relatively) extensive use of a computer-generated environment in which graphical objects were animated. Previously, the predominant use of computer graphics in movies had been to show a monitor (or simulated projection) of something that was supposed to be a computer graphics display (*Futureworld*, 1976; *Star Wars*, 1977; *Alien*, 1979; *Looker*, 1981). Still, in *TRON*, the computer-generated imagery was not meant to simulate reality; the action takes place inside a computer, so a computer-generated look was consistent with the story line.

At the same time that computer graphics were starting to find their way into the movies, it was becoming a more popular tool for generating television commercials. As a result, more computer graphics companies surfaced, including Digital Pictures, Image West, Cranston-Csuri Productions, Pacific Data Images, Lucasfilm, Marks and Marks, Digital Productions, and Omnibus Computer Graphics.

Most early use of synthetic imagery in movies was incorporated with the intent that it would appear as if computer generated. The other use of computer animation during this period was to "do animation." That is, the animations were meant not to fool the eye into thinking that what was being seen was real but rather to replace the look and feel of two-dimensional conventional animation with that of three-dimensional computer animation. Of special note are the award-winning animations produced by Lucasfilm and, later, by Pixar:

The Adventures of Andre and Wally B. (1984)—first computer animation demonstrating motion blur
Luxo Jr. (1986)—nominated for an Academy Award
Red's Dream (1987)
Tin Toy (1988)—first computer animation to win an Academy Award
Knick Knack (1989)
Geri's Game (1997)—Academy Award winner

These early animations paved the way for three-dimensional computer animation to be accepted as an art form. They were among the first fully computer-generated three-dimensional animations to be taken seriously as animations, irrespective of the technique involved. Another early piece of three-dimensional animation, which integrated computer graphics with conventional animation, was *Technological Threat* (1988, Kroyer Films). This was one of three films nominated for an Academy Award as an animated short in 1989; *Tin Toy* came out the victor.

One of the early uses of computer graphics in film was to model and animate spacecraft. Working in (virtual) outer space with spacecraft has the advantages of simple illumination models, a relatively bare environment, and relatively simple animation of rigid bodies. In addition, spacecraft are usually modeled by relatively simple geometry—as is the surrounding environment (planets)—when in flight. *The Last Starfighter* (1984, Digital Productions) used computer animation instead of building models for special effects; the computer used, the Cray X-MP, even appeared in the movie credits. The action takes place in space and on planets; computer graphics were used for the scenes in space, and physical models were used for the scenes on a planet. Approximately twenty minutes of computer graphics was used in the movie. While it is not hard to tell when the movie switches between graphical and physical models, this was the first time graphics were used as an extensive part of a live-action film in which the graphics were supposed to look realistic (i.e., *special effects*).

1.5.3 Animation comes of age (the mid-1980s–2010s)

As modeling, rendering, and animation became more sophisticated and the hardware became faster and inexpensive, quality computer graphics began to spread to the Internet, television commercials, computer games, and stand-alone game units. In film, computer graphics help to bring alien creatures to life. Synthetic alien creatures, while they should appear to be real, do not have to match specific audience expectations. *Young Sherlock Holmes* (1986, ILM) was the first to place a synthetic character in a live-action feature film. An articulated stained glass window comes to life and is made part of the live action. The light sources and movements of the camera in the live action had to be mimicked in the synthetic environment, and images from the live action were made to refract through the synthetic stained glass. In *The Abyss* (1989, ILM), computer graphics are used to create an alien creature that appears to be made from water. Other notable films in which synthetic alien creatures are used are *Terminator II* (1991, ILM), *Casper* (1995, ILM), *Species* (1995, Boss Film Studios), and *Men in Black* (1997, ILM).

A significant advance in the use of computer graphics for the movies came about because of the revolution in cheap digital technology, which allowed film sequences to be stored digitally. Once the film is stored digitally, it is in a form suitable for digital special effects processing, digital compositing, and the addition of synthetic elements. For example, computer graphics can be used to remove the mechanical supports of a prop or to introduce digital explosions or laser blasts. For the most part, this resides in the two-dimensional realm, thus it is not the focus of this book. However, with the advent of digital techniques for two-dimensional compositing, sequences are more routinely available in digital representations, making them amenable to a variety of digital postprocessing techniques. The first digital blue screen matte extraction was in *Willow* (1988, ILM). The first digital wire removal was in *Howard the Duck* (1986, ILM). In *True Lies* (1994, Digital Domain), digital techniques inserted atmospheric distortion to show engine heat.

In *Forrest Gump* (1994, ILM), computer graphics inserted a ping-pong ball in a sequence showing an extremely fast action game, inserted a new character into old film footage, and enabled the illusion of a double amputee as played by a completely able actor. In *Babe* (1995, Rhythm & Hues), computer graphics were used to move the mouths of animals and fill in the background uncovered by the movement. In *Interview with a Vampire* (1994, Digital Domain), computer graphics were used to curl the hair of a woman during her transformation into a vampire. In this case, some of the effect was created using three-dimensional graphics, which were then integrated into the scene by two-dimensional techniques. More recently, the *Matrix* series (*The Matrix*, 1999; *The Matrix Reloaded*, 2003; *The Matrix Revolutions*, 2003, Groucho II Film Partnership) popularized the use of a digital visual effect used to show characters dodging bullets—slow motion was digitally enhanced to show unfilmable events such as a flying bullets.

A popular graphical technique for special effects is the use of particle systems. One of the earliest examples is in *Star Trek II: The Wrath of Khan* (1982, Lucasfilm), in which a wall of fire sweeps over the surface of a planet. Although by today's standards the wall of fire is not very convincing, it was an important step in the use of computer graphics in movies. Particle systems are also used in *Lawnmower Man* (1992, Angel Studios, Xaos), in which a character disintegrates into a swirl of small spheres. The modeling of a comet's tail in the opening sequence of the television series *Star Trek: Deep Space Nine* (1993, Paramount Television) is a more recent example of a particle system. In a much more ambitious and effective application, *Twister* (1996, ILM) uses particle systems to simulate a tornado.

More challenging is the use of computer graphics to create realistic models of creatures with which the audience is intimately familiar. *Jurassic Park* (1993, ILM) is the first example of a movie that completely integrates computer graphics characters (dinosaurs) of which the audience has fairly specific expectations. Of course, there is still some leeway here, because the audience does not have precise knowledge of how dinosaurs look. *Jumanji* (1995, ILM) takes on the ultimate task of modeling creatures for which the audience has precise expectations (various jungle animals). Most of the action is fast and blurry, so the audience does not have time to dwell on the synthetic creatures visually, but the result is very effective. To a lesser extent, *Batman Returns* (1995, PDI) does the same thing by providing "stunt doubles" of Batman in a few scenes. The scenes are quick and the stunt double is viewed from a distance, but it was the first example of a full computer graphics stunt double in a movie. More recently, the Spider-Man movies (2002–present, Sony) make extensive use of synthetic stunt doubles. Use of synthetic stunt doubles in film is now commonplace.

Computer graphics show much potential for managing the complexity in crowd scenes. PDI used computer graphics to create large crowds in the Bud Bowl commercials of the mid-1980s. In feature films, some of the well-known crowd scenes occur in the wildebeest scene in *Lion King* (1994, Disney), the alien charge in *Starship Troopers* (1997, Tippet Studio), synthetic figures populating the deck of the ship in *Titanic* (1998, ILM), and various crowds in the *Star Wars* films

(1977–2005, Lucasfilm) and *The Lord of the Rings* trilogy (2001–2003, New Line Cinema).

A holy grail of computer animation is to produce a synthetic human characters indistinguishable from a real person. Early examples of animations using "synthetic actors" are *Tony de Peltrie* (1985, P. Bergeron), *Rendez-vous à Montréal* (1988, D. Thalmann), *Sextone for President* (1989, Kleiser-Walziac Construction Company), and *Don't Touch Me* (1989, Kleiser-Walziac Construction Company). However, it is obvious to viewers that these animations are computer generated. Recent advances in illumination models and texturing have produced human figures that are much more realistic and have been incorporated into otherwise live-action films.

Synthetic actors have progressed from being distantly viewed stunt doubles and passengers on a boat to assuming central roles in various movies: the dragon in *Dragonheart* (1996, Tippett Studio, ILM); the Jello-like main character in *Flubber* (1997, ILM); the aliens in *Mars Attacks* (1996, ILM); and the ghosts in *Casper* (1995, ILM). The first fully articulated humanoid synthetic actor integral to a movie was the character Jar-Jar Binks in *Star Wars: Episode I* (1999, ILM). More recently, Gollum in the *Lord of the Rings: The Return of the King* (2004, New Line Cinema[13]) and Dobby in the Harry Potter series (2001–2011, Warner Bros.) display actor-like visual qualities and the personality of a live actor not previously demonstrated in computer-generated characters.

However, a revolution is brewing in the realistic digital representation of human actors. At this point, we are not quite to the place where a digital human is indistinguishable from a live actor, but that time is drawing nearer. An early attempt at such realism was undertaken by *Final Fantasy: The Spirits Within* (2001, Chris Lee Productions), which incorporated full body and facial animation of human figures. The hair animation was particularly convincing; however, the facial animation was stiff and unexpressive. Several films effectively manipulated the appearance of facial features as a special effect including *The Curious Case of Benjamin Button* (2008, Paramount Pictures) and *Alice in Wonderland* (2010, Walt Disney Pictures). *Avatar* (2009, 20th Century Fox) with full body/face motion captures animated human-like creatures by mapping the performance of actors to the synthetic creatures. However, the most ambitious attempt at a synthetic actor is in the film *TRON: Legacy* (2010, Walt Disney Pictures), which animates a computer graphics version of a young Jeff Bridges. In this case, the audience (at least those of us old enough to remember what Jeff Bridges looked like when he was young) have a specific expectation of what a young Jeff Bridges should look like. The representation is effective for the most part; however, the film editing prevents the audience from closely inspecting the young Jeff Bridges and even so, there is an unreal eeriness about

[13] For brevity, only the first production company itemized on the Internet Movie Database website (www.imdb.com) is given when more than one production company is listed.

the figure. But this shows that synthetic actors are on their way to a theater near you. Advances in hair, clothes, and skin have paved the way, but facial animation has still not been totally conquered.

Of course, one use of computer animation is simply to "do animation"; computer graphics are used to produce animated pieces that are essentially three-dimensional cartoons that would otherwise be done by more traditional means. The animation does not attempt to fool the viewer into thinking anything is real; it is meant simply to entertain. The film *Hunger* falls into this category, as do the Lucasfilm/Pixar animations. *Toy Story* is the first full-length, fully computer-generated three-dimensional animated feature film. Other feature-length three-dimensional cartoons soon emerged, such as *Antz* (1998, PDI), *A Bug's Life* (1998, Pixar), *Toy Story 2* (1999, Pixar), *Shrek* (2001, PDI), and *Shrek 2* (2004, PDI). In 2002, *Shrek* won the first-ever Academy Award for Best Animated Feature.

Many animations of this type have been made for television. In an episode of *The Simpsons* (1995, PDI), Homer steps into a synthetic world and turns into a three-dimensional computer-generated character. There have been popular television commercials involving computer animation—too many to mention at this point. Many Saturday morning cartoons are now produced using three-dimensional computer animation. Because many images are generated to produce an animation, the rendering used in computer-animated weekly cartoons tends to be computationally efficient.

An example of rendering at the other extreme is *Bunny* (1999, Blue Sky Productions), which received an Academy Award for animated short. *Bunny* uses high-quality rendering in its imagery, including ray tracing and radiosity, as does *Ice Age* (2002, Blue Sky Productions). *The Incredibles* (2004, Disney/Pixar), which garnered another Academy Award for Pixar, included hair animation, subsurface scattering for illuminating skin, cloth animation, and skin-deforming muscle models. *Polar Express* (2004, Warner Bros.) advanced the use of motion capture technology to capture full body and face motion in animating this children's story.

Computer animation is now well established as a (some would say "the") principal medium for doing animation. Indeed, at one time, both *Jurassic Park* and *Shrek 2* were on the top ten list of all-time worldwide box office grossing movies [47].

Three-dimensional computer graphics are also playing an increasing role in the production of conventional hand-drawn animation. Computer animation has been used to model three-dimensional elements in hand-drawn environments. The previously mentioned *Technological Threat* (1988) is an early animation that combined computer-animated characters with hand-drawn characters to produce an entertaining commentary on the use of technology. Three-dimensional environments were constructed for conventionally animated figures in *Beauty and the Beast* (1991, Disney) and *Tarzan* (1999, Disney); three-dimensional synthetic objects, such as chariots, were animated in conventionally drawn environments in *Prince of Egypt* (1998, DreamWorks). Because photorealism is not the objective, the rendering in such animation is done to blend with the relatively simple rendering of hand-drawn animation.

Finally, morphing, even though it is a two-dimensional animation technique, should be mentioned because of its use in some films and its high impact in television commercials. This is essentially a two-dimensional procedure that warps control points (or feature lines) of one image into the control points (feature lines) of another image while the images themselves are blended. In *Star Trek IV: The Voyage Home* (1986, ILM), one of the first commercial morphs occurred in the back-in-time dream sequence. In *Willow* (1988, ILM), a series of morphs changes one animal into another. This technique is also used very effectively in *Terminator II* (1991, ILM). In the early 1990s, PDI promoted the use of morphing in various productions. Michael Jackson's music video *Black or White*, in which people's faces morph into other faces, did much to popularize the technique. In a Plymouth Voyager commercial (1991, PDI) the previous year's car bodies and interiors morph into the new models, and in an Exxon commercial (1992, PDI) a car changes into a tiger. Morphing remains a useful and popular technique.

1.5.4 Modern animation (2010s and beyond)

Since 2010, many animated films have captured the hearts of audiences and garnered critical acclaim. Particular attention should be paid to those films that have pushed the medium forward, challenging our perceptions of what is possible. One such film is *The Lego Movie* (2014), which pays homage to the days of stop-motion animation while utilizing completely digital techniques to create an authentic and deliberate stop-motion feel. *Spider-Man: Into the Spiderverse* (2018), which won an Academy Award for Best Animated Feature, has a unique visual style that looks like the art was ripped directly out of a comic book.

Meanwhile, significant advances in animation techniques can be seen in the video game industry. Amnesia: The Dark Descent (2010, Frictional Games) demonstrated that photorealism is not necessary to tell an engaging horror narrative, while Minecraft (2011) captured the attention of the world with simple blocks and sprite-based animations. Hellblade: Senua's Sacrifice (2017, Ninja Theory) raised the bar for character design, bringing a level of believable photorealism never seen before. Overwatch (2016, Blizzard) employs amazing animation that leverages the principles of animation in a way that is subtle yet effective. The current trend in game animation is to use motion capture for realistic motion, with Ubisoft pioneering the development of data-driven motion-matching algorithms [48]. Just recently, in 2023, the highly anticipated Hellblade 2 was demoed to showcase the use of mobile phones and Unreal Engine 5 to quickly produce highly realistic facial animations within seconds of capture [49].

1.6 Summary

Computer graphics and computer animation have created a revolution in visual effects and animation production. Advances are still being made, and new digital techniques are finding a receptive audience. Yet there is more potential to be realized as players in the entertainment industry demand their own special look and each company tries to establish a competitive edge in the imagery it produces.

Computer animation has come a long way since the early days of Ivan Sutherland and the University of Utah. Viewed in the context of the historical development of animation, the use of digital technology is indeed both a big and an important step. Low-cost computing and inexpensive (and free) 3D modeling and animation software has democratized computer animation, bringing it within reach of more people than ever. It remains to be seen how the limits of the technology will be pushed as new and interesting ways to create moving images are explored. Of particular importance is the use of motion and performance capture, which bring a high degree of realism to digital characters; the use of inexpensive mobile phones to capture facial animations in real time (i.e. Unreal Engine 5 demo); the evolution of 3D scanning; and volumetric video technologies that can capture photorealistic 4D recordings. Moreover, the rapid uptake of artificial intelligence techniques are enabling the development of animation tools that will revolutionize the special effects and animation industries in the coming decades. While the tools of the trade may rapidly change, knowledge of the fundamentals of animation will empower artists and software developers to design and create dazzling visuals that continually astound and amaze us.

Exercises

1. **Beginner**
   a. List the major players in the early days of computer animation.
   b. Identify the first feature-length film to use CGI.
   c. List the timeline of significant milestones in the development of computer animation.
   d. Describe the differences between 2D and 3D animation.
   e. Explain key frames and in-betweens in an animation.
   f. Compare and contrast artist-driven, data-driven, and algorithm-driven animation.
   g. From your perspective (the viewer), compare animation for film and video games. Think about the similarities and differences in terms of technology and constraints, and describe a unique experience in which you had an emotional reaction. What aspects of the animation led to this reaction?

2. **Intermediate**
   a. Explore predefined characters and animations in Adobe Mixamo. Select three animations that interest you. Draw a timeline and define areas on the timeline of interest in terms of changes in tempo/speed, start/end of an event, follow-through, and any squashing/stretching. Can you observe any differences in terms of these qualities between the animations you chose? Can you identify any impact these qualities may have on you as a viewer?
   b. Analyze a scene from a film or video game in terms of animation style and discuss how it affects the storytelling or immersion. Break down the clip into its components: list all objects you observe throughout; are they animated or static? What actions do they perform and when? How do they move? When/why do they move? Draw a timeline-breakdown chart for the clip.
3. **Advanced**
   a. Critique a computer-animated film or game and discuss its strengths and weaknesses in terms of animation quality and storytelling. Develop a simple storyboard for the film that provides a concise overview of the major story elements.
   b. Pick two scenes from an animated film or video game. Identify, compare, and contrast the animation techniques used and evaluate their effectiveness. Think about the constraints of the medium and describe how these constraints may have affected the animation.
   c. Create a short traditional flip-book animation on paper that demonstrates timing, squashing, and stretching of a bouncing ball. Using your phone (and a tripod), take images of each page in your flip-book and assemble them as an image sequence into a video.
   d. Imagine you are a character in your favorite 2D sprite-based video game. Capture a few short videos (1–2 seconds maximum) of you or your friend performing one of the basic actions for the game (i.e. jumping, punching, kicking, crouching, walking forward/backward).
      i. Extract the frames from the video at a low framerate (e.g., 5 fps) and identify the *key* frames that are visually important to define the action and put them in a directory. Draw a timeline for the animation and label the key frames you identified. Create two or three different potential timing charts for these key frames.
      ii. Using these images as reference, draw a character in each key pose or use an AI tool like Stable Diffusion + ControlNet to generate the same character in each pose. Tip: if you want the animation to be smoother, use a tool like Flowframes to automatically interpolate in-betweens.
      iii. For each of the image sequences, create a sprite animation using Unity or Unreal.

References

[1] Roget P. Explanation of an optical deception in the appearance of the spokes of a wheel seen through vertical apertures. Philos Trans R Soc Lond 1825;115:131–40. presented in 1824.

[2] Anderson J, Anderson B. The myth of persistence of vision revisited. J Film Video 1993;45(1):3–12.

[3] Anderson J, Fisher B. The myth of persistence of vision. J Univ Film Assoc 1978; XXX(4):3–8.

[4] Ehrenstein WH. Basics of seeing motion. Arq Bras Oftalmal 2003;66(5):44–53.

[5] Steinman R, Pizlo Z, Pizlo F. Phi is not beta, and why Wertheimer's discovery launched the Gestalt revolution. Vis Res 2000;40(17):2257–64.

[6] Conrac Corp. Raster graphics handbook. New York: Van Nostrand Reinhold; 1985.

[7] Cutting J. Perception with an eye for motion. Cambridge, Mass: MIT Press; 1986.

[8] Korein J, Badler N. Temporal anti-aliasing in computer generated animation. In: Computer graphics (Proceedings of SIGGRAPH 83), 17(3); 1983. p. 377–88. Detroit, Mich.

[9] Potmesil M, Chadkravarty I. Modeling motion blur in computer generated images. Computer graphics (Proceedings of SIGGRAPH 83) 1983;17(3):389–400. Detroit, Mich.

[10] Williams R. The animator's survival kit. New York: Faber and Faber; 2002.

[11] Poynton C. Digital video and HDTV algorithms and interfaces. San Francisco, Calif.: Morgan-Kaufmann; 2003.

[12] Kuroki Y. Improvement of 3D visual image quality by using high frame rate. J Soc Info Dis 2012;20. https://doi.org/10.1002/jsid.107.

[13] Allison R, Fujii Y, Wilcox L. Effects of motion picture frame rate on material and texture appearance. J Vis 2017;17(10):418. https://doi.org/10.1167/17.10.418.

[14] Wood G. Living dolls—a magical history of the quest for mechanical life. London: Faber and Faber Limited; 2002.

[15] Burns P. The complete history of the discovery of cinematography, http://www.precinemahistory.net/introduction.htm (accessed Apr. 06, 2023).

[16] Laybourne K. The animation book: a complete guide to animated filmmaking—from flip-books to sound cartoons to 3-D animation. New York: Three Rivers Press; 1998.

[17] Solomon C. The history of animation: enchanted drawings. New York: Wings Books; 1994.

[18] Balzer R. Optical amusements: magic lanterns and other transforming images; a catalog of popular entertainments. Richard Balzer; 1987.

[19] Marey E. Animal mechanism: a treatise on terrestrial and aerial locomotion. New York: Appleton and Co; 1874.

[20] Muybridge E. Animals in motion. New York: Dover Publications; 1957.

[21] Muybridge E. The human figure in motion. New York: Dover Publications; 1955.

[22] Maltin L. Of Mice and Magic: a history of American animated cartoons. New York: Penguin Books; 1987.

[23] Thomas B. Disney's art of animation from Mickey Mouse to "Beauty and the Beast. New York: Hyperion; 1991.

[24] Thomas F, Johnson O. The illusion of life. New York: Hyperion; 1981.

[25] Wikipedia contributors. Georges Méliès. Wikipedia; 2023. https://en.wikipedia.org/wiki/Georges_M%C3%A9li%C3%A8s. (accessed 6 April 2023).

[26] Davis D. Art and the future: a history/prophecy of the collaboration between science, technology, and art. New York: Praeger Publishers; 1973.
[27] Brookhaven National Laboratory, "The first video game?", https://www.bnl.gov/about/history/firstvideo.php. Retrieved March 20, 2023.
[28] Lasseter J. Principles of traditional animation applied to 3D computer animation. In: Stone MC, editor. Computer graphics (Proceedings of SIGGRAPH 87), 21(4); 1987. p. 35–44. Anaheim, Calif.
[29] VIK7ORIO. Funny animations in slow motion [overwatch]. YouTube; 2018. https://www.youtube.com/watch?v=Lk4coGVVfVU. (accessed 6 April 2023).
[30] Mascelli J. The five C's of cinematography. Hollywood, Calif: Cine/Grafic Publications; 1965.
[31] Henne M, Hickel H, Johnson E, Konishi S. The making of *Toy Story*. In: Proceedings of Comp Con 96; 1996. p. 463–8. San Jose, Calif.
[32] A guide to non-linear video editing," Adobe. https://www.adobe.com/creativecloud/video/hub/ideas/what-is-non-linear-editing (accessed Apr. 06, 2023).
[33] Magnenat-Thalmann N, Thalmann D. Computer animation: theory and practice. New York: Springer-Verlag; 1985.
[34] Magnenat-Thalmann N, Thalmann D. New trends in animation and visualization. New York: John Wiley & Sons; 1991.
[35] Siegel H. An overview of computer animation & modelling. In: Computer animation proceedings of the conference held at computer graphics 87. London; 1987. p. 27–37.
[36] Sutherland I. SKETCHPAD: a man-machine graphical communication system. Ph.D. dissertation, MIT; 1963.
[37] Geometric design and computation. GDC: History, http://www.cs.utah.edu/gdc/history (accessed Apr. 06, 2023).
[38] Charles Csuri," Charles Csuri. https://www.charlescsuri.com/bio (accessed Apr. 06, 2023).
[39] Hackathorn R. Anima II: a 3-D color animation system. In: George J, editor. Computer graphics (Proceedings of SIGGRAPH 77), 11(2); 1977. p. 54–64. San Jose, Calif.
[40] Tajchman EJ. The incredible electronic machine. 1977. p. 22–4. Videography.
[41] Kitching A. Computer animation—some new ANTICS. British Kinematography Sound and Television; 1973. p. 372–86.
[42] Chilton::ACL::ANTICS: computer animation system. http://www.chilton-computing.org.uk/acl/applications/graphics/p003.htm (accessed Apr. 06, 2023).
[43] The center for human modeling and simulation. "CG@Penn | HMS Center." http://cg.cis.upenn.edu/hms.html (accessed Apr. 06, 2023).
[44] Stern G Bbop. A program for 3-dimensional animation83. Nicograph; 1983. p. 403–4.
[45] Burtnyk N, Wein M. Computer animation of free form images. In: Proceedings of the 2nd annual conference on computer graphics and interactive techniques, SIGGRAPH 75 (Bowling Green, Ohio, June 25– 27, 1975). New York: ACM Press; p. 78–80.
[46] Sieg D. Welcome to the SCANIMATE site—history of computer animation—early analog computers, http://scanimate.net (accessed Apr. 06, 2023).
[47] Box Office Mojo. All time worldwide box office grosses, http://www.boxofficemojo.com/alltime/world (accessed Apr. 06, 2023).
[48] Michael Büttner and Simon Clavet. Motion matching - the road to next gen animation. Proc Nucl Ai 2015. https://www.youtube.com/watch?v=z_wpgHFSWss&t=658s. (accessed 6 April 2023).

[49] IGN. MetaHuman - real-time facial model animation demo | State of Unreal 2023. YouTube; 2023 [Online]. Available: https://www.youtube.com/watch?v=pnaKyc3mQVk. (accessed 6 April 2023).
[50] Wikipedia contributors. NTSC. Wikipedia; 2023. https://en.wikipedia.org/wiki/NTSC. (accessed 6 April 2023).
[51] Coynik D. Film: real to reel. Evanston, Ill: McDougal, Littell; 1976.

CHAPTER 2

Math foundations

2.1 Scalars and vectors

Scalars

Scalars are 1D quantities such as speed, length, distance, or weight. You can think of them as representing just a magnitude of a particular measurable quantity. For example, you might describe a character as being 6 feet tall or weighing 150 pounds. These are scalar quantities.

Notation: A scalar is simply denoted as a numerical value and unit (e.g., weight, 5 kg; height, 180 cm).

Basic operations: $+$, $-$, $*$

Addition $(+)$, $a+b=b+a$, **e.g.** $2+5=5+2=7$
Subtraction $(-)$, $a-b$, **e.g.** $2-7=-5$
Multiply $(*)$, $a*b=b*a$, **e.g.** $-2*5=5*(-2)=-10$

Vectors

You can think of vectors as simply a collection of scalars that are related to a particular quantity. Vectors have a number of components that determine their dimension, we call these "N-tuples." In 2D, we use two-values (two-tuple), and in 3D we need three-values (three-tuple). For example, a pixel location on a 2D image can be denoted by two distances from the top left corner of the image (i.e., the horizontal distance x and the vertical distance y). We would group these together as a single vector (i.e., $\vec{v}=(x,y)$). Vectors are a fundamental unit of how we talk about animation concepts … so get used to them! We will use them extensively throughout, and you will require a basic understanding of their operations and geometric interpretation for almost everything related to animation, games, and artificial intelligence/machine learning.

There are two fundamental properties of vectors:

1. Vectors have a length (or scale), and length is always a scalar value.
2. Vectors have direction. Direction for our purposes will *always* be defined as a unit vector $\rightarrow$ that means it has length of 1.

Computer Animation. https://doi.org/10.1016/B978-0-443-13512-5.00002-1

Notation: In 2D, vectors have two components and would consist of a two-tuple (x, y).

We use the notation $\overrightarrow{v} = (x, y)$ to denote a vector; note the arrow on top of the v. Sometimes we use parentheses, $(\cdot)$, which defines the ordering of the values in a set, or matrix notation using brackets, $[\cdot]$, which means that we should think of the vector as a column as it can be handy when we start rotating and transforming objects in space. $\overrightarrow{v} = (x, y) = \begin{bmatrix} x \\ y \end{bmatrix} = [x \quad y]^T$

Generally,
$\overrightarrow{v}_{2D} = (x, y)$, $\overrightarrow{v}_{3D} = (x, y, z)$, $\overrightarrow{v}_{4D} = (x, y, z, w)$, $\overrightarrow{v}_{nD} = (x_0, x_1, \ldots x_n)$.

Aside

We will see the square bracket notation $[\cdot]$ again when we discuss matrices as this is the notation we adopt, hence we will see later that a vector is always thought of as a column of a matrix. We can convert column vectors to rows using the notation $\overrightarrow{v} = [x, y, z]^T$, which will allow us to be concise. The operator $[\cdot]^T$ is what we call the *transpose* operator that just reorders rows to be columns and vice versa.

Basic vector toolbox

Here we briefly define the basic vector operations, how to compute them, and discuss a few examples of where in animation they are used explicitly/often. Think of this section as describing the tools in a toolbox for animation. We will make use of these concepts in future chapters.

Addition (+)

Interpretation/application: Addition of two vectors is used to move objects in space. That is, if your object is located at position $\overrightarrow{a} = (-1, 2)$ and you wish to move it by a particular amount such as $b = (2, 3)$, then the new position, $\overrightarrow{a}'$, of the object can be described using vector addition as
$\overrightarrow{a}' = \overrightarrow{a} + b = (-1, 2) + (2, 3) = (-1 + 2, 2 + 3) = (1, 5)$ (see Figure 2.1b).
Requirements: Both vectors must have the same dimension.
Operation:

- $\overrightarrow{v}_1 = (x_0, x_1, x_n)$, $\overrightarrow{v}_2 = (y_0, y_1, y_n)$
- $\overrightarrow{v}_1 + \overrightarrow{v}_2 = (x_0 + y_0, x_1 + y_1, \dot{c}x_n + y_n)$

Result: Vector of same dimension as input
Examples:

- $\overrightarrow{v}_1 = (2, 3)$, $\overrightarrow{v}_2 = (5, 6) \rightarrow \overrightarrow{v}_1 + \overrightarrow{v}_2 = (2, 3) + (5, 6) = (2 + 5, 3 + 6) = (7, 9)$
- $\overrightarrow{v}_1 = (1, 2, 3)$, $\overrightarrow{v}_2 = (4, 5, 6)$, $\overrightarrow{v}_1 + \overrightarrow{v}_2 = (1 + 4, 2 + 5, 3 + 6) = (5, 7, 9)$

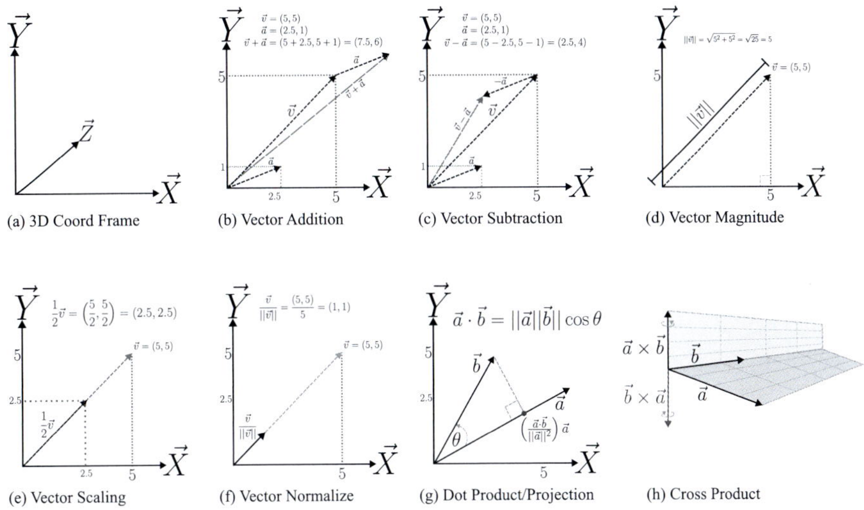

FIGURE 2.1

Geometry of the basic vector operations in our toolbox.

Subtraction (−)

Interpretation/application: Subtraction of two vectors can be used to move objects similarly to addition, and it can also be used to find the change between two vector quantities (i.e., the difference between them) (see Figure 2.1c).

Requirements: Both vectors must have the same dimension.

Operation:

- $\vec{v}_1 = (x_0, x_1, x_n), \vec{v}_2 = (y_0, y_1, y_n)$
- $\vec{v}_1 - \vec{v}_2 = (x_0 - y_0, x_1 - y_1, \cdot\, x_n - y_n)$

Result: Vector of same dimension as input

Examples:

- $\vec{v}_1 = (2,3), \vec{v}_2 = (5,6)$
  $\rightarrow \vec{v}_1 - \vec{v}_2 = (2,3) - (5,6) = (2-5, 3-6) = (-3-6)$
- $\vec{v}_1 = (1,2,3), \vec{v}_2 =$
  $(4,5,6), \vec{v}_1 - \vec{v}_2 = (1-4, 2-5, 3-6) = (-3, -3, -3)$

Magnitude/length

Interpretation/application: This tool gives us the ability to determine many geometric aspects about length/distance. For example, we may require the distance between two points to see if they are close or if one object needs to behave differently, we may need to know how big an object is or how tall an object is. For these (and others) we use this operation to compute the length of a vector (see Figure 2.1d).

Notation: $\text{Length}\left(\vec{v}\right) = \left\|\vec{v}\right\|$.

Operation:

- $\vec{v} = (x_0, x_1, \ldots x_n)$
- $\text{Length}\left(\vec{v}\right) = \left\|\vec{v}\right\| = \sqrt{x_0^2 + x_1^2 + +x_n^2}$

Result: Scalar value denoting the length of the vector.
Examples:

- $\vec{v} = (1,2); \text{Length}\left(\vec{v}\right) = \sqrt{1*1+2*2} = \sqrt{1+4} = \sqrt{5}$

Multiply by scalar

Interpretation/application: Scaling a vector does not change its direction, only its magnitude/length. In computer graphics, one application of this is in ray casting/ray tracing; that is, given a particular direction vector you can simply scale the direction vector to sample a new position in space (see Figure 2.1e).
Operation/notation:

- $\vec{v} = (x,y,z),\ \vec{v}a = a\vec{v} = (ax, ay, az)$

Result: Vector with same direction but scaled length
Examples:

- $\vec{v} = (1,2,3); 2\vec{v} = \vec{v}*2 = (2*1, 2*2, 2*3) = (2,4,6)$

Normalize

Interpretation/application: Used to convert a vector into a *unit direction*, useful for determining the direction of movement so we can move objects one step at a time smoothly along a given path (see Figure 2.1f).
Operation/notation: Compute the length of the vector and divide each vector component by this value.

$$\text{Normalize}\left(\vec{v}\right) = \frac{\vec{v}}{\left\|\vec{v}\right\|}$$

Result: Vector with unit length
Examples:

$$\text{Given } \vec{v} = (1,2) \text{ Normalize}\left(\vec{v}\right)$$

$$\text{Length}\left(\vec{v}\right) = \sqrt{1^2+2^2} = \sqrt{5}$$

Thus,

$$\vec{v}' = \frac{\vec{v}}{\|\vec{v}\|} = \left(\frac{1}{\sqrt{5}}, \frac{2}{\sqrt{5}}\right)$$

Dot product (a.k.a scalar product)

Interpretation/application: One of the most versatile of the vector operations, the dot product has many different uses in computer animation and graphics. One interpretation is to consider this operation as a measure of alignment of two vectors. When they are aligned, the dot product of the two vectors results in the product of the two vector lengths; when the vectors are perpendicular, the dot product results in a value of zero. Also, the sign of the dot product indicates if the two vectors are pointing generally in the same direction (positive) or opposite directions (negative). Another useful interpretation is that it is proportional to the cosine of the angle between two vectors, enabling us to easily determine the angle between two vectors. We will use both of these extensively when determining whether an object/character can "see" an object, detecting collisions of two objects, or projecting one object onto another (see Figure 2.1g).

Requirements: Operates on two vectors of same dimension, resulting in a scalar value.

Notation/operation:

$$\vec{a} = (a_0, a_1, .., a_n), \vec{b} = (b_0, b_1, .., b_n)$$

$$\text{dot}\left(\vec{a}, \vec{b}\right) = \vec{a} \cdot \vec{b} = (a_0 b_0, a_1 b_1, .., a_n b_n) = \sum_i^n a_i b_i$$

$$\text{dot}\left(\vec{a}, \vec{b}\right) = \left\|\vec{a}\right\| \left\|\vec{b}\right\| \cos\theta$$

Result: Scalar value

Examples:

- $\vec{a} = (1,2), b = (3,4)$
- $\text{dot}\left(\vec{a}, b\right) = \vec{a} \cdot b = (1,2) \cdot (3,4) = 1 * 3 + 2 * 4 = 3 + 8 = 11$

Cross product (a.k.a. vector product)

Interpretation/application: The cross product is used to determine a direction that is perpendicular to two other vectors. We use this when constructing a coordinate frame in 3D when we know the direction and one other approximate direction (i.e., the up direction or the left/right direction). We will use this to move objects/cameras along curves and splines smoothly (see Figure 2.1h).

Notation:

- Cross $\left(\vec{v}_1, \vec{v}_2\right)$
- Given $\vec{v}_1 = \left(x_1, y_1, z_1\right)$ and $\vec{v}_2 = \left(x_2, y_2, z_2\right)$, the cross product can be computed as

$$\text{Cross}\left(\vec{v}_1, \vec{v}_2\right) = \begin{bmatrix} x \\ y \\ z \end{bmatrix} = \begin{bmatrix} y_1 z_2 & - & z_1 y_2 \\ z_1 x_2 & - & x_1 z_2 \\ x_1 y_2 & - & y_1 x_2 \end{bmatrix}$$

Requirements:

- Two vectors of same dimension, which results in a vector orthogonal to both.
- Order matters!

Result: Vector of same dimension as input perpendicular to input vectors

Examples:

- $$\vec{v}_1 = (1,0,0), \vec{v}_2 = (0,1,0) \rightarrow \vec{v}_1 \times \vec{v}_2 = \begin{bmatrix} 0(0) & - & 0(1) \\ 0(0) & - & 1(0) \\ 1(1) & - & 0(0) \end{bmatrix} = (0,0,1)$$
- $$(1,2,3) \times (-1, -4, -5) = \begin{bmatrix} 2(-5) & - & 3(-4) \\ 3(-1) & - & 1(-5) \\ 1(-4) & - & 2(-1) \end{bmatrix} = (2, 2, -2)$$

2.2 Matrices

Matrices allow us to more succinctly write down and manipulate relationships between vectors and objects. A matrix can be thought of as a table of scalars with a number of rows and columns.

Note that the number of rows and columns need *not* be the same in general!

However, some operations have a few requirements regarding the shape/size of the matrix. For example, some operations such as the determinant are only defined on square matrices (where the number of rows and columns have the same number of elements).

Generally, we define our scalar elements in the matrix by a two-tuple (i.e., row, column), make use of square brackets $[\cdot]$ to denote a matrix, and use capital bold letters to denote matrices such as:

$$\mathbf{M} = \begin{bmatrix} a & b & c \\ d & e & f \end{bmatrix}$$

We call this matrix a 2×3 matrix as it has two rows (horizontal) and three columns (vertical) and may also refer to it as $\mathbf{M}_{2\times3}$.

More generally, a matrix has N rows and M columns and we would say that it is a $N \times M$ matrix.

Here, A is an $N \times M$ matrix and would look like the following (Eq. 2.1):

$$\mathbf{A_{N\times M}} = \begin{bmatrix} a_{00} & a_{01} & \cdots & a_{0M} \\ a_{10} & a_{11} & \cdots & a_{0M} \\ \vdots & \vdots & \ddots & \vdots \\ a_{N0} & a_{N1} & \cdots & a_{NM} \end{bmatrix} \tag{2.1}$$

In computer animation, we see matrices when specifying transformations on objects such as rotation, skew, affine deformations, and even as a succinct way of denoting coordinate frames.

One special matrix to look out for is the 4×4 *homogeneous* matrix, which will allow us to simplify our notation for general transformations of objects.

Basic matrix toolbox

Here we briefly define the basic matrix operations and how to compute them.

Addition (+)

Notation:

- Given two matrices, **A** and **B**, addition is specified as $\mathbf{A} + \mathbf{B}$.

Requirements:

- Two matrices, $\mathbf{A}_{M\times N}$ and $\mathbf{B}_{M\times N}$, with the same number of rows (M) and columns (N).

Operation:

- Performed by adding the elements in the same locations in both matrices

Result: Matrix with same size/shape as input

Examples:

$$\text{Given } \mathbf{A} = \begin{bmatrix} 1 & 2 \\ 3 & 4 \end{bmatrix}, \mathbf{B} = \begin{bmatrix} 5 & 6 \\ 7 & 8 \end{bmatrix}$$

$$\mathbf{A} + \mathbf{B} = \begin{bmatrix} 1+5 & 2+6 \\ 3+7 & 4+8 \end{bmatrix} = \begin{bmatrix} 6 & 8 \\ 10 & 12 \end{bmatrix}$$

Subtraction (−)

Notation:

- Given two matrices, **A** and **B**, subtraction is specified as $\mathbf{A} - \mathbf{B}$.

Requirements:

- Two matrices, $\mathbf{A}_{M\times N}$ and $\mathbf{B}_{M\times N}$, with the same number of rows (M) and columns (N).

Operation:

- Performed by subtracting the elements in the same locations in both matrices.

Result: Matrix with same size/shape as input

Examples:

$$\text{Given } \mathbf{A} = \begin{bmatrix} 1 & 2 \\ 3 & 4 \end{bmatrix}, \mathbf{B} = \begin{bmatrix} 5 & 6 \\ 7 & 8 \end{bmatrix}$$

$$\mathbf{A} - \mathbf{B} = \begin{bmatrix} 1-5 & 2-6 \\ 3-7 & 4-8 \end{bmatrix} = \begin{bmatrix} -4 & -4 \\ -4 & -4 \end{bmatrix}$$

Scalar multiply

Notation:

- Given a matrix (**A**) and a scalar (s), scalar multiply is specified as $s\mathbf{A}$.

Requirements:

- A matrix (**A**) and a scalar (s).

Operation:

- This is performed by multiplying *all* elements of the matrix by the specified scalar.

Result: Matrix with same size/shape as input matrix

Examples:

$$\text{Given } \mathbf{A} = \begin{bmatrix} 1 & 2 \\ 3 & 4 \end{bmatrix}, s = 2$$

$$s\mathbf{A} = 2\begin{bmatrix} 1 & 2 \\ 3 & 4 \end{bmatrix} = \begin{bmatrix} 2*1 & 2*2 \\ 2*3 & 2*4 \end{bmatrix} = \begin{bmatrix} 2 & 4 \\ 6 & 8 \end{bmatrix}$$

Diagonal

Notation:

- Given a matrix (**A**), the diagonal operator is specified as $diag(\mathbf{A})$.

Requirements:

- A matrix (**A**).

Operation:

- The diagonal or $diag(\cdot)$ is an operation that simply lists the main diagonal elements starting at the first element.

Result: Vector (or set of scalars) with dimension of $\min(N_{rows}, N_{cols})$

Examples:

$$\mathbf{B} = \begin{bmatrix} 3 & -2 & 4 \\ 2 & -1 & 3 \\ 7 & 10 & -5 \end{bmatrix}, \ diag(\mathbf{B}) = (3, -1, -5)$$

Matrix multiply

Interpretation/application:

- We use matrix multiplication to combine sequences of transformations, rotations, and apply transformations to vectors. If two matrices encode rotations, then multiplying them will encode a single matrix that represents the two rotations concatenated (one after the other).

Notation:

- Given two matrices, $\mathbf{A}_{i\times j}, \mathbf{B}_{m\times n}$, then we specify matrix multiplication as $\mathbf{A}_{i\times j} \times \mathbf{B}_{m\times n}$.

Requirements:

- Two matrices with dimensions $\mathbf{A}_{i\times j}, \mathbf{B}_{m\times n}$, where $j == m$ resulting in a matrix $\mathbf{C}_{i\times n}$.
- The number of columns in the first matrix *must* be equal to the number of rows in the second matrix.
- *Order matters!* Generally, $\mathbf{A}_{i\times j} \times \mathbf{B}_{m\times n} \neq \mathbf{B}_{m\times n} \times \mathbf{A}_{i\times j}$.

Operation:

- The simplest way to think of matrix multiplication is to think in terms of vector dot products. Think of the rows in **A** as vectors and the columns in **B** as vectors. Let's call the i-th row in **A**, $\vec{a}_i$ and the j-th column in **B** as b_j. Then in the resulting matrix, the ij-th element can be computed as the dot product $\vec{a}_i \cdot b_j$.

Result: Matrix with dimension $i \times j$

Example:

$$
\begin{aligned}
\mathbf{A}_{3\times 2} \times \mathbf{B}_{3\times 2} &= \begin{bmatrix} 1 & 2 \\ 3 & 4 \\ 5 & 6 \end{bmatrix}_{3\times 2} \times \begin{bmatrix} -1 & -2 \\ -3 & -4 \end{bmatrix}_{2\times 2} \\
&= \begin{bmatrix} \vec{a}_1 \\ \vec{a}_2 \\ \vec{a}_3 \end{bmatrix} \times \begin{bmatrix} \vec{b}_1 & \vec{b}_2 \end{bmatrix} \\
&= \begin{bmatrix} \vec{a}_1 \cdot \vec{b}_1 & \vec{a}_1 \cdot \vec{b}_2 \\ \vec{a}_2 \cdot \vec{b}_1 & \vec{a}_2 \cdot \vec{b}_2 \\ \vec{a}_3 \cdot \vec{b}_1 & \vec{a}_3 \cdot \vec{b}_2 \end{bmatrix}_{3\times 2} \\
&= \begin{bmatrix} 1(-1) + 2(-3) & 1(-2) + 2(-4) \\ 3(-1) + 4(-3) & 3(-2) + 4(-4) \\ 5(-1) + 6(-3) & 5(-2) + 6(-4) \end{bmatrix}_{3\times 2} \\
&= \begin{bmatrix} -7 & -10 \\ -15 & -22 \\ -23 & -34 \end{bmatrix}_{3\times 2}
\end{aligned}
$$

Vector multiply

Interpretation/application:

- A special case of matrix multiplication because we can write a vector as a single column of a matrix. We use this to apply a transformation to a vector (i.e., place a model in the world and/or rotate/scale the model).

Notation:

- Given matrix ($\mathbf{A}$) and column vector ($\vec{v}$), we denote their multiplication as $\mathbf{A}\vec{v}$.

Requirements:

- A vector ($\vec{v}$) of dimension n and a matrix ($\mathbf{A}_{m \times n}$).

Operation:

- Write the vector as a column matrix and perform matrix multiplication.

Examples:

$$
\begin{aligned}
\mathrm{A}\vec{v} &= \begin{bmatrix} 1 & 2 \\ 3 & 4 \end{bmatrix} \begin{bmatrix} 5 \\ 6 \end{bmatrix} \\
&= \begin{bmatrix} \vec{a}_1 \\ \vec{a}_2 \end{bmatrix} \begin{bmatrix} \vec{v} \end{bmatrix} = \begin{bmatrix} \vec{a}_1 \cdot \vec{v} \\ \vec{a}_2 \cdot \vec{v} \end{bmatrix} \\
&= \begin{bmatrix} 1(5) + 2(6) \\ 3(5) + 4(6) \end{bmatrix} = \begin{bmatrix} 17 \\ 39 \end{bmatrix}
\end{aligned}
$$

Transpose

Interpretation/application:

- The transpose converts all rows of a matrix into columns. We use the transpose often; for example, if a vector is written as a column matrix, then the transpose of this is a row. This allows us to more succinctly write equations. It also is related to inverse transformations, specifically when we discuss rotations we will see that the transpose of a rotation matrix defines a rotation in the *opposite* direction. This works on any matrix and leaves the main diagonal in the same locations in the result.

Notation:

- Given a matrix ($\mathbf{A}$) we denote its transpose as $transpose(\mathbf{A}) = \mathbf{A}^T$.

Requirements:

- A matrix ($\mathbf{A}_{m \times n}$).

Operation:

- For each row in the input matrix, write it as the corresponding column in the output matrix.

Result: Matrix with swapped dimensions

Examples:

Given a 2×2 matrix

$$\mathbf{B} = \begin{bmatrix} 4 & -6 \\ 1 & -2 \end{bmatrix}$$

its transpose is computed as:

$$\text{transpose}(\mathbf{B}) = \mathbf{B}^T = \begin{bmatrix} 4 & 1 \\ -6 & -2 \end{bmatrix}.$$

Similarly,

$$\mathbf{C} = \begin{bmatrix} -1 & 2 & 4 \\ 7 & 10 & 2 \end{bmatrix} \mathbf{C}^T = \begin{bmatrix} -1 & 7 \\ 2 & 10 \\ 4 & 2 \end{bmatrix}.$$

Special matrices

We must identify a few special types of matrices as they have specific uses and may be referred to by these names in further sections and chapters.

Square matrix

A square matrix is a matrix containing the same number of rows and columns.

$$\mathbf{A}_{2\times 2} = \begin{bmatrix} a_{00} & a_{01} \\ a_{10} & a_{11} \end{bmatrix} \mathbf{B} = \begin{bmatrix} 4 & -6 \\ 1 & -2 \end{bmatrix}$$

Identity matrix

An identity matrix is a square matrix where the main diagonal are all values of 1 and every other element in the matrix is 0. Multiplying any matrix (or vector) by an identity matrix does not change the matrix. It is like multiplying any number by 1: it doesn't change the values.

$$\mathbf{A} = \begin{bmatrix} 1 & 0 \\ 0 & 1 \end{bmatrix} \mathbf{B} = \begin{bmatrix} 1 & 0 & 0 \\ 0 & 1 & 0 \\ 0 & 0 & 1 \end{bmatrix}$$

Homogeneous matrix

A homogeneous matrix is the name we give to a specific type of 4×4 matrix where the upper 3×3 sub-matrix denotes a 3D rotation matrix $\mathbf{R}_{3\times 3}$, the last column denotes a translation vector ($\vec{t}_{3\times 1}$), and the last row is always $(0, 0, 0, 1)$. This is used extensively in computer animation and computer graphics in rendering systems, character rigging, and kinematics.

Notation:
We often denote this type of matrix as in Equation 2.2:

$$T_{4\times4} = \begin{bmatrix} \mathbf{R}_{3\times3} & \vec{t}_{3\times1} \\ 0_{1\times3} & 1 \end{bmatrix}_{4\times4} \tag{2.2}$$

Other operations: determinant, inverse, and beyond

It is beyond the scope of this chapter to discuss these concepts in depth; however, we will provide their high-level definitions as needed by an animation developer.

Determinant

The determinant ($\det(\mathbf{M})$) is an operation that can be used to see if an inverse is possible. Another use is to determine if the matrix is indeed a rotation matrix as the determinant of a rotation has to be positive and have a value of 1.

Inverse

The inverse of a matrix, $\mathbf{M}^{-1}$, is used extensively to solve equations. Although we cannot divide with matrices, the inverse allows us a similar relationship: $\mathbf{A}\mathbf{A}^{-1} = \mathbf{A}^{-1}\mathbf{A} = \mathbf{I}$, where $\mathbf{I}$ is the identity matrix. This is used extensively to rearrange transformations to determine the opposite transformation.

For example, imagine we have two objects (Dog, Cat), and let's say we have defined a transformation ($\mathbf{T}$) that describes how to transform points from the Dog coordinate frame (d) into the Cat coordinate frame (c). We would then be able to describe the following relationship for any point, $\vec{p}_{\mathrm{d}}$ as $\vec{p}_{\mathrm{c}} = \mathbf{T}\vec{p}_{\mathrm{d}}$. If however, we want to describe points from the Cat relative to the Dog, then we must rearrange the equation and solve for the point in the Dog's coordinate frame by multiplying both sides of the equation by the inverse of the transform:

$$\begin{aligned} \mathbf{T}^{-1}\vec{p}_{\mathrm{c}} &= \mathbf{T}^{-1}\mathbf{T}\vec{p}_{\mathrm{d}} \\ \mathbf{T}^{-1}\vec{p}_{c} &= \mathbf{I}\vec{p}_{d} \\ \vec{p}_{d} &= \mathbf{T}^{-1}\vec{p}_{c} \end{aligned}$$

2.3 Coordinate systems and transformations

Much of computer graphics and computer animation involves transforming data (e.g., [2], [7]). In fact, one can think of the entire graphics pipeline as taking the input data stream from its geometric definitions and through the application of a series of transformations results in a set of pixels drawn to the screen. Imagine a virtual object we wish to animate and draw to the screen. We first define the geometry data of the object in a "canonical" coordinate frame relative to the object itself. Next, we transform this data from the object-centered frame into a world coordinate frame common to all other objects, virtual cameras, lights, and so on. This data must be transformed over time in order to produce animation. In each frame, data transformations are used to animate, deform, and move/pose objects, projected onto an image plane, clipped to fit into the "window," and finally scaled to the desired resolution. The workhorse transformational representation of computer graphics is the 4×4 homogeneous transformation matrix, which can be used to represent combinations of 3D rotations, translations, and scales, as well as perspective projection. In this section we will provide an overview of the common conventions related to defining data within computer graphics and computer animation. Chapter 3 will formalize these concepts in the context of representing objects.

Coordinate spaces and common conventions

A coordinate space can be defined by using a left- or a right-handed coordinate system (see Figure 2.2). Left-handed coordinate systems have the x-, y-, and z-coordinate axes aligned as the thumb, index finger, and middle finger of the left hand are arranged when held at right angles to each other in a natural pose: extending the thumb out to the side of the hand, extending the index finger coplanar with the palm, and extending the middle finger perpendicular to the palm. The right-handed coordinate system is organized similarly with respect to the right hand. These configurations are inherently different; there is no series of pure rotations that transforms a left-handed configuration of axes into a right-handed configuration. Which configuration to use is a matter of convention. It makes no difference as long as everyone knows and understands the implications. Another arbitrary convention is the axis to use as the *up vector*. Some applications assume that the y-axis is "up." Other applications assume that the z-axis is "up." As with handedness, it makes no difference as long as everyone is aware of the assumption being made. In this book, the y-axis is considered "up" (see Table 2.1).

General affine transforms

Moving objects and characters throughout space can be performed with a series of "transformations." Specifically, we want to be able to specify translation, rotation, and scale transformations and define the language/notation we will use to specify

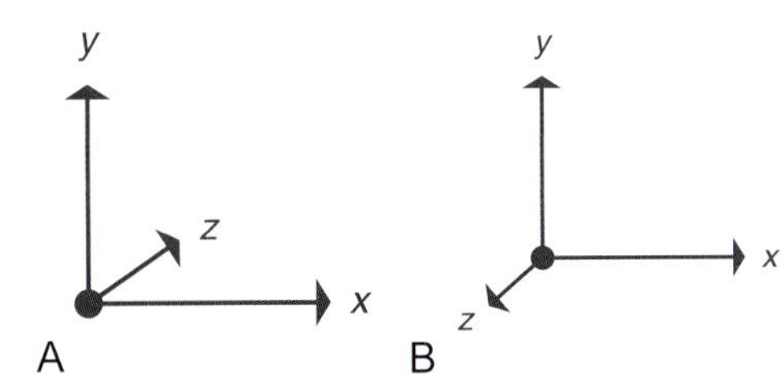

FIGURE 2.2

(a) Left-handed and (b) right-handed coordinate systems.

Table 2.1 Common coordinate system conventions for popular software/APIs

API	Handedness	Up	Engine	Handedness	Up	Software	Handedness	Up
OpenGL	Right	+Y	Unity	Left	+Y	Blender	Right	+Z
DirectX	Left	+Y	Unreal	Left	+Z	Maya	Right	+Y
Vulkan	Right	+Y	Godot	Right	+Y	3DS Max	Right	+Z

sequences of transformations. To simplify matters, our discussion here is focused on transforming a point in space that will be extended to other types of geometric primitives and objects in the next chapter. Unless stated otherwise, the space is assumed to be 3D and right-handed.

Translation

Translation is defined simply as the vector addition of two vectors. Translation offsets the given vector by a defined displacement vector ($\vec{t}$) where the amount of displacement is $\|\vec{t}\|$ and direction of displacement is $\frac{\vec{t}}{\|\vec{t}\|}$. Given a vector ($\vec{v}$), and a displacement vector ($\vec{t}$) of the same dimension, translation is performed as $\vec{v}' = \vec{v} + \vec{t}$.

Translations allow us to move objects through our coordinate space, incorporate additional displacement to vertices to deform objects over time, and provide a systematic way to take steps in a particular direction.

Scale

Scaling transformations are performed often to change the size of objects when positioning them and when performing squash/stretch to create more interesting elastic deformations. Scaling changes the length of the input vector. Because we are defining points here, the length of the line connecting the point to the origin is what is actually being scaled. This operation allows us to make objects bigger/smaller along all (or some) of their dimensions.

We perform a scaling transformation by specifying an $n \times n$ square diagonal matrix where the diagonal values represent the amount to scale the respective dimensions $\mathbf{S}$ and multiplying any vector of dimension n, $\vec{v}' = \mathbf{S}\vec{v}$. There are two types of scaling matrices, where S is either a *uniform* or *nonuniform* scaling operation. A *uniform* transformation matrix scales *all* dimensions *equally* by the same amount. Given the amount of scaling to perform, s, we would define the scaling matrix in 3D as a 3×3 square matrix:

$$\mathbf{S} = \mathrm{diag}(s, s, s) = \begin{bmatrix} s & 0 & 0 \\ 0 & s & 0 \\ 0 & 0 & s \end{bmatrix}$$

Scaling each axis by a potentially different scale requires a *nonuniform* transformation matrix. Given the amount of scaling to perform on each axis, s_x, s_y, s_z, we would define the scaling matrix as:

$$\mathbf{S} = \text{diag}(s_x, s_y, s_z) = \begin{bmatrix} s_x & 0 & 0 \\ 0 & s_y & 0 \\ 0 & 0 & s_z \end{bmatrix}$$

Rotation

Rotations can be defined in a variety of ways (e.g., using matrices, quaternions, or scalar Euler angles). In 3D, we might employ a 3×3 transformation matrix, whereas in 2D we might use a 2×2 transformation matrix. We will go into more detail as to the various representations of rotations later (Euler angle, axis-angle, quaternion, exponential map), but for the time being, imagine a 3×3 matrix $\mathbf{R}$ that when applied (multiplied by a vector) will rotate an input vector by some amount resulting in a rotated vector. Operationally, this is performed as a matrix multiplication of the rotation with the vector as $\vec{v}' = \mathbf{R}\vec{v}$. How we compute the values of $\mathbf{R}$ will come shortly.

General transformations

We can define a formula that encapsulates all three of these transformations as $\vec{v}' = \mathbf{SR}\vec{v} + \vec{t}$, where $\vec{v}$ is the vector we wish to transform, $\vec{t}$ is the translation vector, $\mathbf{R}$ is the rotation matrix, and $\mathbf{S}$ is the scaling matrix and applies to 2D and 3D representations.

Homogeneous representation of points

We often use a *homogeneous representation* of a point in space in computer animation and graphics. This means that a 3D point is represented by a four-element vector.[1] The coordinates of the represented point are determined by dividing the fourth component into the first three (Eq. 2.3).

$$\left(\frac{x}{w}, \frac{y}{w}, \frac{z}{w}\right) \equiv [x, y, z, w] \tag{2.3}$$

Typically, when transforming a point in world space, the fourth component will have a value of 1. This means a point in space has a very simple homogeneous representation (Eq. 2.4).

$$\vec{v} = (x, y, z) \equiv [x, y, z, 1]^T \tag{2.4}$$

Why would we do this? Representing points in this manner gives us a notational trick we can use to simplify and keep track of transformations a bit more easily (this

---

[1] Note the potential source of confusion in the use of the term *vector* to mean (1) a direction in space or (2) a $1 \times n$ or $n \times 1$ matrix. The context in which *vector* is used should make its meaning clear.

becomes important when you start applying multiple transformations to move points from one coordinate frame to another, such as for character rigging or kinematics).

Homogeneous transformations

The word *homogeneous* refers to things that are the same by nature. For example, homogenized milk is milk that is of all the same form and does not separate into its components. In our context we want to have the same representation for *all* types of transformations. Notably, from the general equation $\vec{v}' = \mathbf{SR}\vec{v} + \vec{t}$, we see that we have two matrices (scale, rotate), and a vector addition (translate). If we can specify all of these in a single matrix, then it will be simpler to refer to and use leading to fewer mistakes in the long run. To do so, the basic transformations (rotate, translate, and scale) can be stored as 4×4 transformation matrices. The 4×4 matrix is the smallest matrix that can represent all of the basic transformations. Because it is a square matrix, it has the potential for having a computable inverse, which is important for texture mapping and illumination calculations. In the case of rotation, translation, and nonzero scale transformations, the matrix always has a computable inverse (and this has a specific form that is simpler to think about than a general matrix inverse). These transformation matrices can be multiplied with other transformation matrices to produce compound transformations while still maintaining the 4×4 structure. The 4×4 identity matrix has zeros everywhere except along its diagonal; the diagonal elements all equal 1 (Eq. 2.5).

$$\begin{bmatrix} x' \\ y' \\ z' \\ 1 \end{bmatrix} = \begin{bmatrix} 1 & 0 & 0 & 0 \\ 0 & 1 & 0 & 0 \\ 0 & 0 & 1 & 0 \\ 0 & 0 & 0 & 1 \end{bmatrix} \begin{bmatrix} x \\ y \\ z \\ 1 \end{bmatrix} \tag{2.5}$$

Typically, a point is represented as a 4×1 column matrix (also known as a *column vector*) and is transformed by multiplying by a 4×4 matrix on the left (also known as *premultiplying* the column vector by the matrix), as shown in Equation 2.5 in the case of the identity matrix. This is the convention we adopt throughout this book. However, it is worth noting that some texts represent points as a 1×4 matrix (also known as a *row vector*) and thus transform it by multiplying it by a matrix on its right (the matrix *postmultiplies* the row vector). For example, postmultiplying a point by the identity transformation would appear as in Equation 2.6.

$$[x' \quad y' \quad z' \quad 1] = [x \quad y \quad z \quad 1] \begin{bmatrix} 1 & 0 & 0 & 0 \\ 0 & 1 & 0 & 0 \\ 0 & 0 & 1 & 0 \\ 0 & 0 & 0 & 1 \end{bmatrix} \tag{2.6}$$

Because the conventions are equivalent, it is immaterial which is used as long as consistency is maintained. Important note: the 4×4 transformation matrix used in one of the notations is the transpose of the 4×4 transformation matrix used in the other notation.

Transformation sequences

One of the main advantages of representing basic transformations as homogeneous matrices is that when they are multiplied together, the transformations easily concatenate, producing a compound transformation. This enables a series of transformations, $\mathbf{M}_{\mathrm{i}} = \mathbf{M}_0 \cdots \mathbf{M}_{\mathrm{n}}$, to be premultiplied so that a single compound transformation matrix, $\mathbf{M}$, can be applied to a point $\overrightarrow{p}$ (see Aside 1) rather than applying the first transformation to the point and subsequently applying the next to the result and so on. This is especially useful (i.e., computationally efficient) when applying the same series of transformations to a multitude of points (and it improves numerical stability).

Aside 1:

Imagine we have six transformations to apply to a particular point, the transformation could be described as: $\overrightarrow{p}' = \mathbf{M}_5\mathbf{M}_4\mathbf{M}_3\mathbf{M}_2\mathbf{M}_1\overrightarrow{p}$, requiring us to iteratively multiply each matrix by the result of the previous multiplication. By combining the matrix multiplications into a single premultiplied matrix such as $\mathbf{M} = \mathbf{M}_6\mathbf{M}_5\mathbf{M}_4\mathbf{M}_3\mathbf{M}_2\mathbf{M}_1$, we can simplify the transformation equation as

$$\overrightarrow{p}' = \mathbf{M}\overrightarrow{p}. \tag{2.7}$$

It is important to note the ordering here of the transformations (the subscripts denote the order in which the transformations apply to the point. For beginners, this always seems counterintuitive as you are used to seeing list orderings from left to right. For transformations, always look at the vector you are transforming, the matrix to its immediate left will apply first, then the next one to the result of that transformation, and so on.

Redefining SRT (scale/rotate/translate) as homogeneous operations

For now, we consider only the basic SRT transformations (scale, rotate, and translate). These transformations, and any combination of these, are *affine transformations* [4]. It should be noted that the transformation matrices are the same whether the space is left- or right-handed. Restricting discussion to the basic transformations allows the fourth element of each point vector to be assigned the value of 1 and the last row of the transformation matrix to be assigned the value [0 0 0 1] (Eq. 2.8).

$$\begin{bmatrix} x' \\ y' \\ z' \\ 1 \end{bmatrix} = \begin{bmatrix} a & b & c & d \\ e & f & g & h \\ i & j & k & l \\ 0 & 0 & 0 & 1 \end{bmatrix} \begin{bmatrix} x \\ y \\ z \\ 1 \end{bmatrix} \tag{2.8}$$

If you were to expand Equation 2.8 using matrix multiplication you would see the following system of equations emerge:

$$\begin{aligned} x' &= ax + by + cz + d \\ y' &= ex + fy + gz + h \\ z' &= ix + jy + kz + l \\ 1 &= 0x + 0y + 0z + 1 \end{aligned}$$

This means that the quantity represented by the vector (d, h, l) is added to the other elements through vector addition! The x, y, and z translation values of the transformation are the first three values of the fourth column (d, h, and l in Eq. 2.9). The upper left 3×3 submatrix coefficients $(a, b, c, e, f, g, i, j, k)$ represent a combination of rotation and scaling. Setting the upper left 3×3 submatrix to an identity transformation and specifying only translation produces Equation 2.9.

$$\begin{bmatrix} x+t_x \\ y+t_y \\ z+t_z \\ 1 \end{bmatrix} = \begin{bmatrix} 1 & 0 & 0 & t_x \\ 0 & 1 & 0 & t_y \\ 0 & 0 & 1 & t_z \\ 0 & 0 & 0 & 1 \end{bmatrix} \begin{bmatrix} x \\ y \\ z \\ 1 \end{bmatrix} \tag{2.9}$$

Equivalently, this can also be written as $\vec{v}' = \mathbf{I}\vec{v} + \vec{t}$.

As before, we can define a uniform or nonuniform scaling transformation. Let's assume a nonuniform scaling of s_x, s_y, s_z (uniform scaling is a special case where $s_x = s_y = s_z$ and can be defined in this way as Equation 2.10:

$$\begin{bmatrix} s_x x \\ s_y y \\ s_z z \\ 1 \end{bmatrix} = \begin{bmatrix} s_x & 0 & 0 & 0 \\ 0 & s_y & 0 & 0 \\ 0 & 0 & s_z & 0 \\ 0 & 0 & 0 & 1 \end{bmatrix} \begin{bmatrix} x \\ y \\ z \\ 1 \end{bmatrix} \tag{2.10}$$

Rotations can also be set using the upper left 3×3 submatrix (a, b, c, e, f, g, i, j, and k of Eq. 2.9). Rotation matrices around the x-, y-, and z-axis are shown in Equations 2.11–2.13, respectively. In a right-handed coordinate system, a positive angle of rotation produces a counterclockwise rotation as viewed from the positive end of the axis looking toward the origin (the right-hand rule). In a left-handed (right-handed) coordinate system, a positive angle of rotation produces a clockwise (counterclockwise) rotation as viewed from the positive end of an axis. This can be remembered by noting that when pointing the thumb of the left (right) hand in the direction of the positive axis, the fingers wrap clockwise (counterclockwise) around the closed hand when viewed from the end of the thumb.

$$\begin{bmatrix} x' \\ y' \\ z' \\ 1 \end{bmatrix} = \begin{bmatrix} 1 & 0 & 0 & 0 \\ 0 & \cos\theta & -\sin\theta & 0 \\ 0 & \sin\theta & \cos\theta & 0 \\ 0 & 0 & 0 & 1 \end{bmatrix} \begin{bmatrix} x \\ y \\ z \\ 1 \end{bmatrix} \tag{2.11}$$

$$\begin{bmatrix} x' \\ y' \\ z' \\ 1 \end{bmatrix} = \begin{bmatrix} \cos\theta & 0 & \sin\theta & 0 \\ 0 & 1 & 0 & 0 \\ -\sin\theta & 0 & \cos\theta & 0 \\ 0 & 0 & 0 & 1 \end{bmatrix} \begin{bmatrix} x \\ y \\ z \\ 1 \end{bmatrix} \tag{2.12}$$

$$\begin{bmatrix} x' \\ y' \\ z' \\ 1 \end{bmatrix} = \begin{bmatrix} \cos\theta & -\sin\theta & 0 & 0 \\ \sin\theta & \cos\theta & 0 & 0 \\ 0 & 0 & 1 & 0 \\ 0 & 0 & 0 & 1 \end{bmatrix} \begin{bmatrix} x \\ y \\ z \\ 1 \end{bmatrix} \tag{2.13}$$

Combinations of rotations and translations are usually referred to as *rigid transformations* because distance is preserved and the spatial extent of the object does not change; only its position and orientation in space are changed. *Similarity transformations* also allow uniform scale in addition to rotation and translation. These transformations preserve the object's intrinsic properties[2] (e.g., dihedral angles[3]) and relative distances but not absolute distances. Nonuniform scale, however, is usually not considered a similarity transformation because object properties such as dihedral angles are changed. A *shear* transformation is a combination of rotation and nonuniform scale and creates columns (rows) that might not be orthogonal to each other. Any combination of rotations, translations, and (uniform or nonuniform) scales still retains the last row of three 0s followed by a 1. Notice that any affine transformation can be represented by a multiplicative 3×3 matrix (representing rotations, scales, and shears) followed by an additive three-element vector (translation).

General homogeneous transform structure

Combining these into a singular notation, we can restructure our original transformation equation as:

$$\vec{v}' = \mathbf{SR}\vec{v} + \vec{t} \rightarrow \mathbf{T}\vec{v}' \tag{2.14}$$

where

$$\begin{bmatrix} x' \\ y' \\ z' \\ 1 \end{bmatrix} = \begin{bmatrix} \mathbf{S}_{3\times3}\mathbf{R}_{3\times3} & t \\ \mathbf{0}_{1\times3} & 1 \end{bmatrix} \begin{bmatrix} x \\ y \\ z \\ 1 \end{bmatrix}. \tag{2.15}$$

Now, simply by multiplying transformations together we end up concatenating the entire transform (scale, rotation, translation) all at once. Namely, if we had two transformations applied one after the other (e.g., $\mathbf{T}_0, \mathbf{T}_1$), we can define the relationship as $\vec{v}' = \mathbf{T}_2\vec{v} = \mathbf{T}_1\mathbf{T}_0\vec{v}$. Here it is important to note the ordering of the transformations.

---

2 An object's intrinsic properties are those that are measured irrespective of an external coordinate system.

3 The dihedral angle is the interior angle between adjacent polygons measured at the common edge.

2.4 Orientation representation

A common issue that arises in computer animation is deciding the best way to represent the position and orientation of an object in space and how to interpolate the represented transformations over time to produce motion. A typical scenario is one in which the user specifies an object in two transformed states and the computer is used to interpolate intermediate states, thus producing animated *keyframe* motion. Another scenario is when an object is to undergo two or more successive transformations and it would be efficient to concatenate these transformations into a single representation before applying it to a multitude of object vertices. This section discusses possible orientation representations and identifies strengths and weaknesses; the next chapter addresses the best way to interpolate orientations using these representations. In this discussion, it is assumed that the final transformation applied to the object is a result of rotations and translations only, so that there is no scaling involved, nonuniform or otherwise; that is, the transformations are considered *rigid*.

As discussed previously, we can represent the orientation and position of an object using a 4×4 transformation matrix. For example, a user may specify a series of rotations and translations to apply to an object. This series of transformations is compiled into 4×4 matrices and is multiplied together to produce a compound 4×4 transformation matrix. In such a matrix, the upper-left 3×3 submatrix represents a rotation to apply to the object, whereas the first three elements of the fourth column represent the translation. No matter how the 4×4 transformation matrix was formed, the final 4×4 transformation matrix produced will result in a matrix that specifies the final "pose" of the object as a 3×3 rotation matrix and a translation vector.

Let's define a pose of an object as a particular rigid body transformation from a given coordinate system (i.e., the world frame), thus Pose; $P = \left\{\mathbf{R}, \vec{t}\right\}$. Now imagine we have two poses that define the start and end, respectively, $P_1 = \left\{\mathbf{R}_1, \vec{t}_1\right\}, P_2 = \left\{\mathbf{R}_2, \vec{t}_2\right\}$. What if we wanted to smoothly animate an object from one of these poses to another? Well, we could assume a few things; for instance, because we only have two poses, the best we can do is assume they are connected by a straight line. This would make it easy to determine a set of evenly spaced points between $\vec{t}_1$ and $\vec{t}_2$. We will see in later chapters that this is called *linear interpolation*. However, it isn't so easy to determine what happens to the two rotation matrices.

How can we determine a set of rotation matrices that define intermediate poses between these two given orientations? The naïve way would be to simply apply the same linear interpolation to all nine elements of the rotation matrices. However this would be a *very, very bad* idea. Very quickly you would find out that the resulting intermediate rotations would not actually represent a valid rotation! Moreover, even if it did, errors from the subsequent computation would creep into each calculation causing further problems and instability. Thus we must find a better way to

$$\begin{bmatrix} 0 & 0 & 1 \\ 0 & 1 & 0 \\ -1 & 0 & 0 \end{bmatrix} \qquad \begin{bmatrix} 0 & 0 & -1 \\ 0 & 1 & 0 \\ 1 & 0 & 0 \end{bmatrix}$$

Positive 90-degree *y*-axis rotation   Negative 90-degree *y*-axis rotation

$$\begin{bmatrix} 0 & 0 & 0 \\ 0 & 1 & 0 \\ 0 & 0 & 0 \end{bmatrix}$$

Interpolated matrix halfway between the orientation representations above

FIGURE 2.3

Direct interpolation of transformation matrix values can result in nonsense transformations.

represent rotations that allow us to more easily compute these intermediate orientations.

Interpolation of orientations is not nearly as straightforward as interpolation of translation vectors. An essential property of 3×3 rotation matrices is that it represents a coordinate frame. This means that the rows and columns are orthonormal (unit length and perpendicular to each other). Simple linear interpolation between the nine pairs of numbers that make up the two 3×3 rotation matrices to be interpolated will *not* produce intermediate 3×3 matrices that preserve this property and as such are not actually rigid body rotations. It should be easy to see that interpolating from a rotation of $+90$ degrees about the y-axis to a rotation of -90 degrees about the y-axis results in intermediate transformations that are nonsense (see Figure 2.3).

Luckily for us all, there are alternative representations that are more useful than transformation matrices in performing such interpolations including fixed angle, Euler angle, axis–angle, quaternions, and exponential maps.

Fixed-angle representation

A *fixed-angle* representation[4] really refers to "angles used to rotate about fixed axes." A fixed order of three rotations is implied, such as x-y-z. This means that orientation is given by a set of three ordered parameters that represent three ordered rotations about fixed axes: first around x, then around y, and then around z. There are many possible orderings of the rotations, and, in fact, it is not necessary to use all three

[4] Terms referring to rotational representations are not used consistently in the literature. This book follows the usage found in *Robotics*[1], where *fixed angle* refers to rotation about the fixed (global) axes and *Euler angle* refers to rotation about the rotating (local) axes.

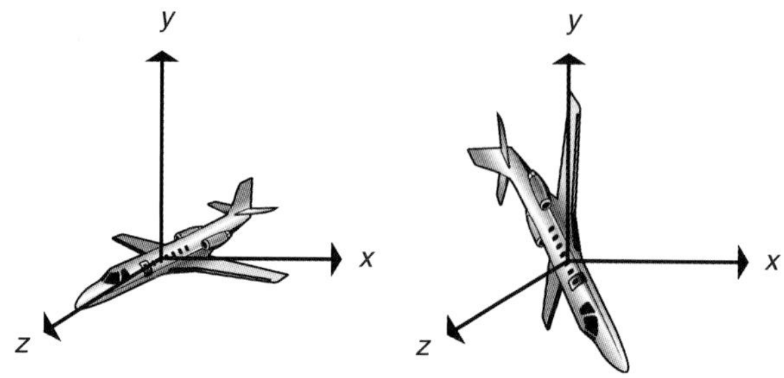

FIGURE 2.4

Fixed-angle representation.

coordinate axes. For example, *x-y-x* is a feasible set of rotations. The only orderings that do not make sense are those in which an axis immediately follows itself, such as in *x-x-y*. In any case, the main point is that the orientation of an object is given by three angles, such as (10, 45, 90). In this example, the orientation represented is obtained by rotating the object first about the *x*-axis by 10 degrees, then about the *y*-axis by 45 degrees, and then about the *z*-axis by 90 degrees. In Figure 2.4, the aircraft is shown in its initial orientation and in the orientation represented by the values of (10, 45, 90).

The following notation will be used to represent such a sequence of rotations: $R_z(90)R_y(45)R_x(10)$ (in this text, transformations are implemented by premultiplying column vectors by transformation matrices; thus the rotation matrices appear in right to left order).

From this orientation, changing the *x*-axis rotation value, which is applied first to the data points, will make the aircraft's nose dip more or less in the *y-z* plane. Changing the *y*-axis rotation will change the amount the aircraft, which has been rotated around the *x*-axis, rotates out of the *y-z* plane. Changing the *z*-axis rotation value, the rotation applied last, will change how much the twice-rotated aircraft will rotate about the *z*-axis.

The problem with using this scheme is that two of the axes of rotation can effectively line up on top of each other when an object can rotate freely in space (or around a joint with 3 degrees of freedom[5] joint). Consider an object in an orientation represented by (0, 90, 0), as shown in Figure 2.5. Examine the effect a slight change in the first and third parametric values has on the object in that orientation. A slight change of the third parameter will rotate the object slightly about the global *z*-axis because that is the rotation applied last to the data points. However, note that the effect of a slight change of the first parameter, which rotates the original data points around the *x*-axis, will also have the effect of rotating the transformed object slightly about the *z*-axis (Figure 2.6). This results because the 90-degree *y*-axis rotation has

[5] The degrees of freedom that an object possesses is the number of independent variables that have to be specified to completely locate that object (and all of its parts).

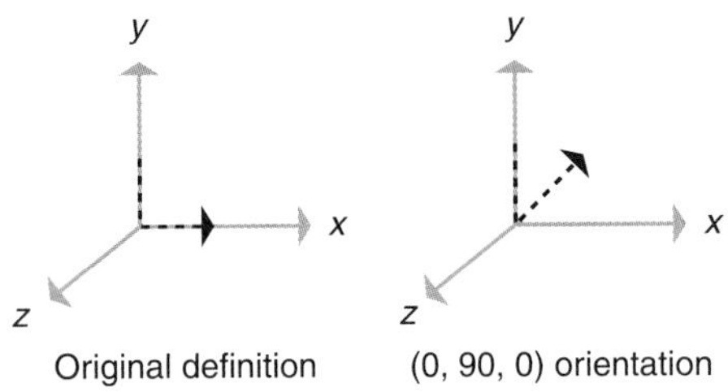

FIGURE 2.5

Fixed-angle representation of (0, 90, 0).

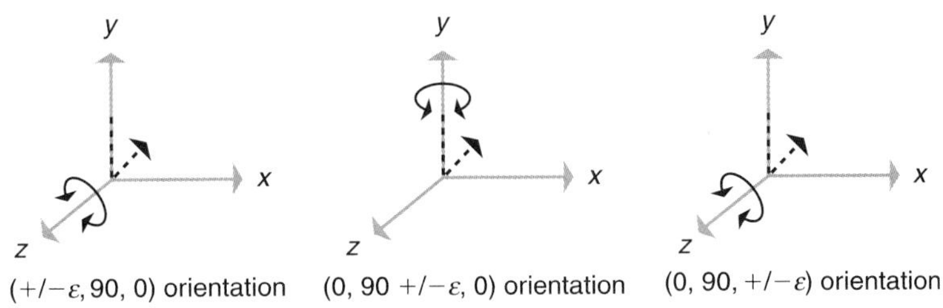

FIGURE 2.6

Effect of slightly altering values of fixed-angle representation (0, 90, 0).

essentially made the first axis of rotation align with the third axis of rotation. The effect is called *gimbal lock*. From the orientation (0, 90, 0), the object can no longer be rotated about the global x-axis by a small change in its orientation representation. Actually, the representation that will perform an incremental rotation about the x-axis from the (0, 90, 0) orientation is (90, 90 + ε, 90), which is not very intuitive.

The cause of this problem can often make interpolation between key positions problematic. Consider the key orientations (0, 90, 0) and (90, 45, 90), as shown in Figure 2.7. The second orientation is a 45-degree x-axis rotation from the first position. However, as discussed above, the object can no longer directly rotate about the x-axis from the first key orientation because of the 90-degree y-axis rotation. Direct interpolation of the key orientation representations would produce (45, 67.5, 45) as

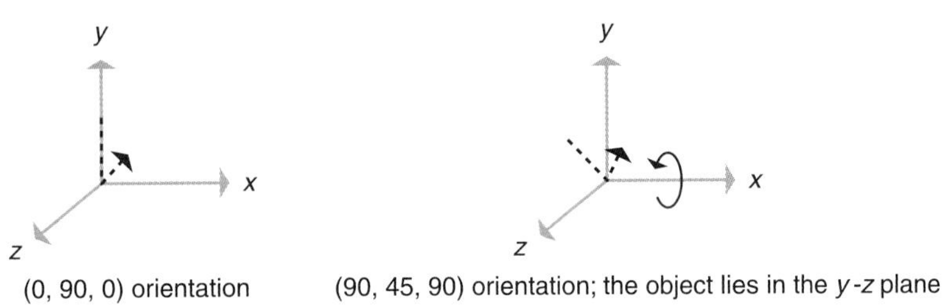

FIGURE 2.7

Example orientations to interpolate.

the halfway orientation, which is very different from the (90, 22.5, 90) orientation that is desired (because that is the representation of the orientation that is intuitively halfway between the two given orientations). The result is that the object will swing out of the *y-z* plane during the interpolation, which is not the behavior one would expect.

In its favor, the fixed-angle representation is compact, fairly intuitive, and easy to work with because the implied operations correspond to what we know how to do mathematically—rotate data around the global axes. However, it is often not the most desirable representation to use because of the gimbal lock problem.

Euler angle representation

In a *Euler angle* representation, the axes of rotation are the axes of the local coordinate system that rotate with the object, as opposed to the fixed global axes. A typical example of using Euler angles is found in the roll, pitch, and yaw of an aircraft (Figure 2.8).

As with the fixed-angle representation, the Euler angle representation can use any of various orderings of three axes of rotation as its representation scheme. Consider a Euler angle representation that uses an *x-y-z* ordering and is specified as (α, β, γ). The *x*-axis rotation, represented by the transformation matrix $\mathbf{R}_x(\alpha)$, is followed by the *y*-axis rotation, represented by the transformation matrix $\mathbf{R}_y(\beta)$, around the *y*-axis of the local, rotated coordinate system. Using a prime symbol to represent rotation about a rotated frame and remembering that points are represented as column vectors and are premultiplied by transformation matrices, one achieves a result of $\mathbf{R}_y{}'(\beta)\mathbf{R}_x(\alpha)$. Using global-axis rotation matrices to implement the transformations, the *y*-axis rotation around the rotated frame can be affected by $\mathbf{R}_x(\alpha)\mathbf{R}_y(\beta)\mathbf{R}_x(-\alpha)$. Thus the result after the first two rotations is shown in Equation 2.16.

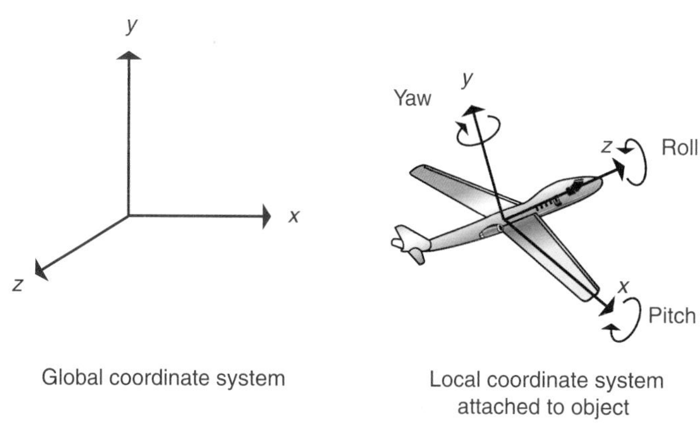

FIGURE 2.8

Euler angle representation.

$$\mathbf{R}_y{}'(\beta)\mathbf{R}_x(\alpha) = \mathbf{R}_x(\alpha)\mathbf{R}_y(\beta)\mathbf{R}_x(-\alpha)\mathbf{R}_x(\alpha) = \mathbf{R}_x(\alpha)\mathbf{R}_y(\beta) \tag{2.16}$$

The third rotation, $\mathbf{R}_z(\gamma)$, is around the now twice-rotated frame. This rotation can be affected by undoing the previous rotations with $\mathbf{R}_x(-\alpha)$ followed by $\mathbf{R}_y(-\beta)$, then rotating around the global z-axis by $\mathbf{R}_z(\gamma)$, and then reapplying the previous rotations. Putting all three rotations together, and using a double prime to denote rotation about a twice-rotated frame, results in Equation 2.17.

$$\begin{aligned}\mathbf{R}_z{}''(\gamma)\mathbf{R}_y{}'(\beta)\mathbf{R}_x(\alpha) &= \mathbf{R}_x(\alpha)\mathbf{R}_y(\beta)\mathbf{R}_z(\gamma)\mathbf{R}_y(-\beta)\mathbf{R}_x(-\alpha)\mathbf{R}_x(\alpha)\mathbf{R}_y(\beta) \\ &= \mathbf{R}_x(\alpha)\mathbf{R}_y(\beta)\mathbf{R}_z(\gamma)\end{aligned} \tag{2.17}$$

Thus this system of Euler angles is precisely equivalent to the fixed-angle system in reverse order. This is true for any system of Euler angles. For example, z-y-x Euler angles are equivalent to x-y-z fixed angles. Therefore, the Euler angle representation has exactly the same advantages and disadvantages (i.e., gimbal lock) as those of the fixed-angle representation.

Angle and axis representation

In the mid-1700s, Leonhard Euler showed that one orientation can be derived from another by a single rotation about an axis. This is known as the Euler rotation theorem [1]. Thus any orientation can be represented by three numbers: two for the axis, such as longitude and latitude, and one for the angle (see Figure 2.9). The rotational axis can also be represented (somewhat inefficiently) by a unit three-dimensional vector $\vec{a}$ and angle, θ, that rotates around this axis. Interpolation between representations $\left(\vec{a}_1, \vec{\theta}_1\right)$ and $\left(\vec{a}_2, \vec{\theta}_2\right)$ can be implemented by interpolating the axes of rotation and the angles separately (see Figure 2.10). An intermediate axis can be determined by rotating one axis part way toward the other. The axis for this rotation is formed by taking the cross product of two axes, $\vec{a}_1 \times \vec{a}_2$. The angle between the two axes is determined by taking the inverse cosine of the dot product of normalized versions of the axes. An interpolant, k, can then be used to form an intermediate axis

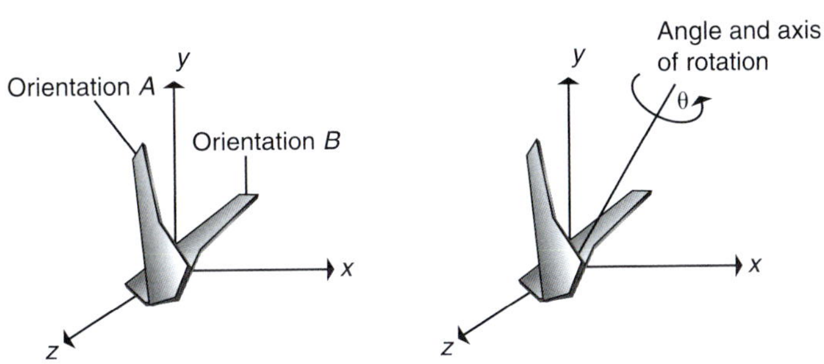

FIGURE 2.9

Euler's rotation theorem implies that for any two orientations of an object, one can be produced from the other by a single rotation about an arbitrary axis.

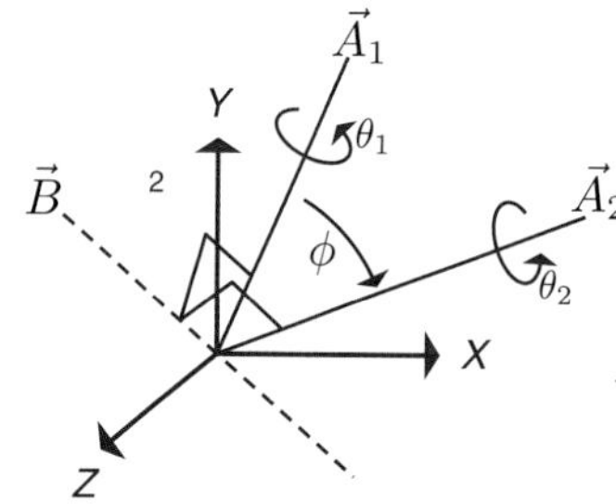

$$\vec{B} = \vec{A}_1 \times \vec{A}_2$$
$$\phi = \cos^{-1}\left(\frac{\vec{A}_1 \cdot \vec{A}_2}{||\vec{A}_1||||\vec{A}_2||}\right)$$

$$\vec{A}_k = \mathbf{Rotate}(\vec{B}, k\phi, \vec{A}_1)$$
$$\theta_k = (1-k)\theta_1 + k\theta_2$$

FIGURE 2.10

Interpolating axis-angle representations of (A_1, θ_1) and (A_2, θ_2) by k to get (A_k, θ_k), where "Rotate(a,b,c)" rotates "c" around "a" by "b" degrees.

and angle pair. Note that the axis—angle representation does not lend itself to easily concatenating a series of rotations. However, the information contained in this representation can be put in a form in which these operations are "easily" implemented: *quaternions*.

Quaternion representation

As discussed earlier, the representations covered so far have drawbacks when interpolating intermediate orientations when an object or joint has 3 degrees of rotational freedom. A better approach is to use *quaternions* to represent orientation [5]. A quaternion, denoted as $\widehat{q}$ (we use the hat symbol to ensure we know this is a special type of vector with specific properties), is a four-tuple of real numbers, $\widehat{q} = [w, x, y, z,]$, or, equivalently, $\left[w, \vec{v}\right]$, consisting of a scalar, w, and a three-dimensional vector, $\vec{v}$. Because of its ease of use and efficiency for rotations, the quaternion has become the de facto standard for representing rotation in computer graphics and game engines.

The quaternion is an alternative to the axis and angle representation in that it contains the same information in a different, but *mathematically* convenient, form. Importantly, it is in a form that can be interpolated and also used in concatenating a series of rotations into a single representation. The axis and angle information of a quaternion can be viewed as an orientation of an object relative to its initial object frame, or it can be considered as the representation of a rotation to apply to an object. In the former view, being able to interpolate between represented orientations is important in generating keyframe animation. In the latter view, concatenating a series of rotations into a simple representation is a common and useful operation to apply a single, compound transformation to an object. Here we discuss quaternion operations as we did with vectors and matrices, from a functional perspective. We do not need to delve too deep into the mathematical (... mystical?) nature of four-dimensional complex numbers in order to use them effectively.

Basic quaternion toolbox

Quaternions are essentially vectors with four dimensions, $\widehat{q} = [w, x, y, z,]$. We use the hat notation to distinguish it between vectors as there are a couple of things we can do with them that we cannot do with vectors. They obey the same vector rules regarding magnitude ($\|\cdot\|$), addition (+), subtraction (−), dot product, and scalar multiply.

One major difference is that it is possible to multiply two quaternions together (you cannot with vectors). Multiplying two quaternions together is a special operation that we will cover as it relates to concatenating transformations.

Quaternion magnitude/length

Interpretation/application:

- Defined the same way as for vectors and is used to normalize the quaternion.

Notation:

- Like vectors, we denote the magnitude/length as $\|\widehat{q}\|$.

Requirements: A quaternion $\widehat{q} = [w, x, y, z]$.

Operation: $\|\widehat{q}\| = [w, (x, y, z)] = \sqrt{w^2 + x^2 + y^2 + z^2}$

Result: A scalar value denoting the length of the quaternion

Quaternion addition/subtraction

Interpretation/application:

- Defined the same way as for vectors and is used to normalize the quaternion. Note that this operation does *not* compound rotations. You must use quaternion multiply for that.

Notation:

- As with vectors, addition/subtraction of two quaternions is denoted as $\widehat{q}_1 + \widehat{q}_2$, $\widehat{q}_1 - \widehat{q}_2$.

Requirements: Two quaternions $\widehat{q}_1 = [w_1, x_1, y_1, z_1]$, $\widehat{q}_2 = [w_2, x_2, y_2, z_2]$.

Operation:

Addition: $\widehat{q}_1 + \widehat{q}_2 = \left[w_1, \vec{v}_1\right] + \left[w_2, \vec{v}_2\right] = \left[w_1 + w_2, \vec{v}_1 + \vec{v}_2\right]$

Subtraction: $\widehat{q}_1 - \widehat{q}_2 = \left[w_1, \vec{v}_1\right] - \left[w_2, \vec{v}_2\right] = \left[w_1 - w_2, \vec{v}_1 - \vec{v}_2\right]$

Result: A quaternion

Dot product

Interpretation/application:

- Defined the same way as for vectors.

Notation:

- As with vectors, the dot product of two quaternions is denoted as $\widehat{q}_1 \cdot \widehat{q}_2$, $\widehat{q}_1 - \widehat{q}_2$.

Requirements: Two quaternions $\widehat{q}_1 = [w_1, x_1, y_1, z_1]$, $\widehat{q}_2 = [w_2, x_2, y_2, z_2]$.

Operation: $\widehat{q}_1 \cdot \widehat{q}_2 - \left[w_1, \vec{v}_1\right] \cdot \left[w_2, \vec{v}_2\right] - \left[w_1 w_2 + \vec{v}_1 \cdot \vec{v}_2\right]$

Result: A scalar value

Quaternion multiplication

Interpretation/application:

- Quaternion multiplication is used to compound two rotations in sequence. We do not derive the formula (Eq. 2.18) here as it will scare the non-mathematically minded readers. Note that similar to matrices, quaternion multiplication is *associative*, $(\widehat{q}_1\widehat{q}_2)\widehat{q}_3 = \widehat{q}_1(\widehat{q}_2\widehat{q}_3)$, but is *not commutative*, $\widehat{q}_1\widehat{q}_2 \neq \widehat{q}_2\widehat{q}_1$.

Notation:

- As with vectors, the dot product of two quaternions is denoted as $\widehat{q}_1 \otimes \widehat{q}_2$.

Requirements: Two quaternions $\widehat{q}_1 = [w_1, x_1, y_1, z_1], \widehat{q}_2 = [w_2, x_2, y_2, z_2]$

Operation:

$$\widehat{q}_1\widehat{q}_2 = \widehat{q}_1 \otimes \widehat{q}_2 = \left[w_1, \vec{v}_1\right] \otimes \left[w_2, \vec{v}_2\right] = \left[w_1 w_2 - \vec{v}_1 \cdot \vec{v}_2, w_1 \vec{v}_2 + w_2 \vec{v}_1 + \vec{v}_1 \times \vec{v}_2\right] \tag{2.18}$$

Result: A scalar value

> **Aside (for the more mathematically minded reader):**
>
> A quaternion can be considered a *complex number* with imaginary parts i, j, k and the relationship $i^2 = j^2 = k^2 = ijk = -1$. Imagine you have two quaternions $\widehat{q}_1 = w_1 + x_1 i + y_1 j + z_1 k, \widehat{q}_2 = w_2 + x_2 i + y_2 j + z_2 k$. Just like with any polynomial, you can multiply them together: $\widehat{q}_1\widehat{q}_2 = (w_1 + x_1 i + y_1 j + z_1 k)\ (w_2 + x_2 i + y_2 j + z_2 k)$. Expanding this completely will result in a number of terms including those that can be simplified using the properties $i^2 = j^2 = k^2 = ijk = -1$. The simplified form will result in an equivalent expression to Equation 2.18. We leave it up to the reader to prove it to themselves that this is true.

Pure quaternions

Interpretation/application: A point in space, $\vec{v}$, (rather a vector from the origin to that point), is represented as a special "pure quaternion," that is a quaternion with scalar value of zero. It is easy to see that quaternion multiplication of two orthogonal vectors $\vec{v}_1 \cdot \vec{v}_2 = 0$ computes the cross-product of those vectors (Eq. 2.19). This is used when rotating a vector by a quaternion as we need to operate completely within quaternion mathematics, thus we need to represent the vector as a type of quaternion without changing its geometric interpretation.

Notation: $\widehat{v} = \left[0, \vec{v}\right]$.

Requirements: A 3D vector, $\widehat{v} = [x, y, z]$.

Operation:

$$\left[0, \vec{v}_1\right] \otimes \left[0, \vec{v}_2\right] = \left[0, \vec{v}_1 \times \vec{v}_2\right] \text{if } \vec{v}_1 \cdot \vec{v}_2 = 0 \tag{2.19}$$

Result: A quaternion with no value on the w axis

Identity quaternion

Interpretation/application: The identity quaternion is the multiplicative identity and does not modify the values of the quaternion it is applied to. Similar to the value 1 or the identity matrix.
Notation: $\hat{q}_{\mathbf{I}} = [1, (0, 0, 0)]$
Example:

$$\hat{q}\hat{q}_{\mathbf{I}} = \left[w, \vec{v}\right] \otimes [1, (0, 0, 0)] = \left[w, \vec{v}\right] \tag{2.20}$$

Quaternion inverse/conjugate

Interpretation/application: The *inverse of a quaternion*, $\hat{q}^{-1} = \left[w, \vec{v}\right]^{-1}$, is obtained by negating its vector part and dividing both parts by the magnitude squared (the sum of the squares of the four components), as shown in Equation 2.21. Note that for unit quaternions this is also called the *conjugate* and denoted sometimes as $\hat{q}^{c} = \hat{q}^{-1}$, where$\|\hat{q}\| = 1$.
Properties:

- Multiplication of a quaternion, by its inverse, results in the multiplicative identity.

Notation: $\hat{q}^{-1} = \left[w, \vec{v}\right]^{-1}, \hat{q}^{c} = \hat{q}^{-1}$, where $\|\hat{q}\| = 1$

Requirements: A quaternion $\hat{q} = \left[w, \vec{v}\right] = [w, x, y, z]$

Operation:

$$\hat{q} = \left[w, \vec{v}\right] \rightarrow \hat{q}^{-1} = \frac{\left[w, -\vec{v}\right]}{\|\hat{q}\|} = \frac{1}{\|\hat{q}\|}\left[w, -\vec{v}\right] \tag{2.21}$$

Result: A quaternion; in the case of a rotation quaternion, this represents a rotation in the opposite direction.

Normalizing quaternions

Interpretation/application:

- Given any quaternion, this operation ensures that its length is 1, resulting in a unit-length quaternion (also referred to as a unit quaternion).

Requirements: A quaternion $\hat{q} = \left[w, \vec{v}\right] = [w, x, y, z]$.

Operation:

$$Normalize(\hat{q}) \rightarrow \hat{q}' = \frac{\hat{q}}{\|\hat{q}\|} \tag{2.22}$$

Result: A unit-length quaternion

Representing rotations using quaternions

Interpretation/application: A rotation represented in quaternion form can be achieved with a specific encoding of the axis you want to rotate around and the angle denoting how much you want to rotate.

Notation: $QuatRot\left(\theta, \overrightarrow{a}\right)$ or sometimes $\widehat{q}_\theta$.

Requirements: A scalar angle, θ, and a normalized axis, $\overrightarrow{a} = \left[a_x, a_y, a_z\right]$ where $\left\|\overrightarrow{a}\right\| = 1$.

Operation:

$$QuatRot\left(\theta, \overrightarrow{a}\right) \rightarrow \left[\cos\left(\frac{\theta}{2}\right), \sin\left(\frac{\theta}{2}\right)\overrightarrow{a}\right] \tag{2.23}$$

Result: A quaternion that represents the intended axis-angle rotation

Rotating vectors using quaternions

Interpretation/application: To rotate a vector using a rotation quaternion, we first represent the vector as a pure quaternion. The vector is then rotated according to Equation 2.24. Note that this requires two quaternion multiplications.

Notation: $Rot_{\hat{q}\theta}\left(\overrightarrow{v}\right)$.

Requirements: A unit quaternion representing a rotation of θ around axis $\overrightarrow{a}$, $\widehat{q}_\theta = \left[\cos\frac{\theta}{2}, \sin\frac{\theta}{2}\overrightarrow{a}\right]$, and a vector to rotate, $\overrightarrow{v} = [x, y, z]$ represented as a pure quaternion $\widehat{v} = \left[0, \overrightarrow{v}\right]$.

Operation:

$$Rot_{\hat{q}\theta}\left(\overrightarrow{v}\right) \equiv \widehat{q}_\theta \widehat{v} \widehat{q}_\theta^{-1} = \widehat{v}' \tag{2.24}$$

Result: A pure quaternion representing the rotated vector, $\widehat{v}' = \left[0, \overrightarrow{v}'\right]$

Rotation sequences

A sequence of rotations can be concatenated into a single representation using quaternion multiplication. Consider a rotation represented by a quaternion, $\widehat{p}$, followed by a rotation represented by a quaternion, $\widehat{q}$, on a vector, $\overrightarrow{v}$ (Eq. 2.25).

$$\mathrm{Rot}_{\hat{q}}\left(\mathrm{Rot}_{\hat{p}}\left(\overrightarrow{v}\right)\right) = \widehat{q}\left(\widehat{p}\widehat{v}\widehat{p}^{-1}\right)\widehat{q}^{-1} = \left(\widehat{q}\widehat{p}\right)\widehat{v}\left(\widehat{q}\widehat{p}\right)^{-1} = \mathrm{Rot}_{\hat{q}\hat{p}}\left(\overrightarrow{v}\right) \tag{2.25}$$

The inverse of a quaternion represents rotation about the same axis by the same amount but in the reverse direction. Equation 2.26 shows that rotating a vector by a quaternion, $\hat{q}$, followed by rotating the result by the inverse of that same quaternion produces the original vector.

$$\mathrm{Rot}_{\hat{q}^{-1}}\left(\mathrm{Rot}_{\hat{q}}\left(\vec{v}\right)\right)=\hat{q}^{-1}(\hat{q}\hat{v}\hat{q}^{-1})\hat{q}=(\hat{q}^{-1}\hat{q})\hat{v}(\hat{q}^{-1}\hat{q})=\hat{v} \tag{2.26}$$

Also, notice that in performing rotation, $\hat{q}\hat{v}\hat{q}^{-1}$, all effects of magnitude are divided out due to the multiplication by the inverse of the quaternion. Thus, any scalar multiple of a quaternion represents the same rotation as the corresponding unit quaternion (similar to how the homogeneous representation of points is scale invariant).

Exponential map representation

Exponential maps, similar to quaternions, represent an orientation as an axis of rotation and an associated angle of rotation as a single vector [3]. The direction of the vector is the axis of rotation, and the magnitude is the amount of rotation. In addition, a zero rotation is assigned to the zero vector, making the representation continuous at the origin. Notice that an exponential map uses three parameters instead of the quaternions' four. The main advantage is that it has well-formed derivatives, which becomes important, for example, when dealing with angular velocity. This representation does have some drawbacks. Similar to Euler angles, it has singularities. However, in practice, these can be avoided. Also, it is difficult to concatenate rotations using exponential maps and is best done by converting to rotation matrices.

2.5 Chapter summary

In this chapter, we summarized the basic mathematical foundations required for computer animation. We covered the basics of vectors, matrices, and transformations, and we depicted rotations using various representations. Linear transformations represented by 4 × 4 matrices are a fundamental operation in computer graphics and animation. Our focus here was a high-level summary of the "tools" of the trade from the perspective of a technical artist and/or animation programmer, and as such we did not cover the underlying theoretical underpinnings of linear algebra. For this, we recommend that readers see [6] for a more mathematically rigorous theoretical understanding. Understanding how to use these tools and how to manipulate them is a great first step into the world of computer animation. You should be proud of yourself if you have understood these concepts so far. The interested reader should delve into this material, perform the exercises below, and refer to this chapter as you practice the techniques described in later chapters.

2.6 Exercises

Setup

Vectors: $\vec{a} = (1,0,1)$, $\vec{b} = (2,0,-1)$, $\vec{c} = (0,0,2)$, $\vec{d} = (-1,-1,-1)$

Matrices:

$$A = \begin{bmatrix} 1 & 2 \\ 3 & 4 \end{bmatrix} B = \begin{bmatrix} -1 & 20 \\ 7 & -3 \end{bmatrix} C = \begin{bmatrix} 0 & -2 \\ 2 & 9 \end{bmatrix} D = \begin{bmatrix} 1 & 0 & 0 \\ 3 & 4 & 0 \\ 6 & 7 & 8 \end{bmatrix}$$

$$E = \begin{bmatrix} 0 & -2 & -3 \\ 4 & 0 & 5 \\ 2 & -7 & 0 \end{bmatrix} F = \begin{bmatrix} 1 & 3 & 3 \\ 0 & 1 & -2 \\ 0 & 0 & -8 \end{bmatrix} G = \begin{bmatrix} 1 & 7 & 6 \\ -2 & 4 & 2 \end{bmatrix} H = \begin{bmatrix} 1 & 3 \\ 8 & -1 \\ 5 & 72 \end{bmatrix}$$

2D transformations:

$$\mathbf{J} = \begin{bmatrix} -2 & 0 \\ 0 & -2 \end{bmatrix}, \mathbf{K} = \begin{bmatrix} 1 & 0 \\ 0 & 2 \end{bmatrix}, \mathbf{L} = \begin{bmatrix} -2 & 0 \\ 0 & 3 \end{bmatrix}, \mathbf{M} = \begin{bmatrix} 2 & 5 \\ -6 & 2 \end{bmatrix}$$

$\vec{v}_1 = (1,1)$, $\vec{v}_2 = (-1,1)$, $\vec{v}_3 = (2,0)$, $\vec{v}_4 = (3,-2)$

Beginner

B1. For each of the vectors above, plot them on a graph drawing an arrow from the origin to the point specified.

B2. Perform the following operations and draw both vectors and the result on a graph:

a. $\vec{a} + \vec{b}$, $\vec{a} - \vec{b}$

b. $\vec{b} + \vec{c}$, $\vec{b} - \vec{c}$

c. $\vec{a} + \vec{d}$, $\vec{a} - \vec{d}$

B3. Perform the following operations:

a. $\vec{a} \cdot \vec{b}$, $\vec{a} \cdot \vec{d}$

b. $\vec{d} \cdot \vec{d}$, $2\vec{a} + 3\vec{d}$

c. $\vec{b} + \frac{1}{2}\left(\vec{b} - \vec{d}\right)$, $\vec{b} + 2\frac{\vec{b}}{\|\vec{b}\|}$, $\vec{b} + 3\frac{\vec{b}}{\|\vec{b}\|}$, $\vec{b} + 4\frac{\vec{b}}{\|\vec{b}\|}$

B4. Perform the following operations, plot each of the following and the resulting vector on a graph. Can you infer anything geometric from the results?

a. $\vec{a} \times \vec{b}$, $\vec{b} \times \vec{c}$, $\vec{a} \times \vec{d}$

B5. Compute the angle between the following pairs of vectors:

a. $\vec{a}, \vec{b}, \quad \vec{c}, \vec{a}, \quad \vec{b}, \vec{d}$

b. $\vec{a}, (\vec{b} \times \vec{c}), \quad \vec{d}, (\vec{b} \times \vec{d})$

B6. Perform the following operations:

a. $\|\vec{a}\|, \|\vec{b}\|, \|\vec{c}\|, \|\vec{d}\|$

b. Normalize each of the vectors

c. Compute the length between $\vec{a}$ and $\vec{d}$, $\vec{a}$ and $\vec{b}$, and $\vec{c}$ and $\vec{d}$

B7. Write the number of rows and columns for each matrix above.

B8. Identify the main diagonal of each matrix above.

B9. Write a 2×2, 3×3, and a 4×4 identity matrix.

B10. Where possible, perform the following operations:

a. $\mathbf{A} + \mathbf{B}$, $\mathbf{A} - \mathbf{C}$, $\mathbf{E} + \mathbf{F}$, $\mathbf{D} - \mathbf{E}$

b. Give the transpose of each matrix above.

c. $\mathbf{AB}$, $\mathbf{AB}^T$, $(\mathbf{AB}^T)$, $\left(\mathbf{A}^{\mathbf{T}}\mathbf{B}^T\right)$, $\mathbf{B}^T\mathbf{A}^T$

d. $\mathbf{CD}$, $\mathbf{FE}$, $\mathbf{EF}$

e. $\mathbf{E}\vec{a}$, $\mathbf{E}\vec{b}$

f. $10\mathbf{D}$, $2\mathbf{E} + 4\mathbf{E}^T$

B11. Apply the transformation above and interpret the results:

a. $\mathbf{J}\vec{v}_1, \mathbf{J}\vec{v}_2, \mathbf{J}\vec{v}_3, \mathbf{J}\vec{v}_4$

b. $\mathbf{K}\vec{v}_1, \mathbf{K}\vec{v}_2, \mathbf{K}\vec{v}_3, \mathbf{K}\vec{v}_4$

c. $\mathbf{L}\vec{v}_1, \mathbf{L}\vec{v}_2, \mathbf{L}\vec{v}_3, \mathbf{L}\vec{v}_4$

B12. Determine a homogeneous transformation matrix with the following properties:

a. Translation of $\vec{a}$ and a rotation of 90 degrees around the x-axis

b. Translation of $\vec{b}$ and a rotation of 45 degrees around the y-axis

c. Translation of $\vec{c}$ and a rotation of -20 degrees around the y-axis

B13. Compute the rotation quaternion for the following axis-angle pairs:

a. $\hat{q}_1 : \theta = 20^o, \ \overrightarrow{axis} = \frac{\vec{a}}{\|\vec{a}\|}$

b. $\hat{q}_2 : \theta = 90^o, \ \overrightarrow{axis} = \frac{\vec{c}}{\|\vec{c}\|}$

c. $\hat{q}_3 : \theta = -90^o, \ \overrightarrow{axis} = \frac{\vec{c}}{\|\vec{c}\|}$

d. $\hat{q}_4 : \theta = 90^o, \ \overrightarrow{axis} = -\frac{\vec{c}}{\|\vec{c}\|}$

Intermediate

I1. Show that the dot product of two perpendicular vectors is zero. Similarly, show how the dot product is at a maximum value for two vectors when they are aligned and at a minimum when they are pointing away from each other.

I2. A triangle is defined by the points $\vec{p}_1 = (1, 1, 0)$, $\vec{p}_1 = (1, 2, 3)$, $\vec{p}_1 = (0, 2, -1)$. Plot this triangle on a graph. Calculate and label the vectors that denote its three edges $\vec{e}_1 \cdot \vec{e}_2, \vec{e}_3$. Compute *all* of the possible perpendicular vectors by taking the cross product of edge-pairs. What are the relationships between the results?

I3. Come up with a set of random 2D and 3D vectors and determine if they are linearly independent by checking if they are perpendicular.

I4. Show that the composition of two rotation matrices results in another rotation matrix using a purely symbolic approach and also by developing a complete example.

I5. Show that quaternion multiplication is associative but not commutative through an example.

I6. Rotate the vector $\vec{a}$ by the quaternion $\widehat{q}_1$ above resulting in $\vec{a}'$.

I7. Rotate $\vec{a}'$ above by the quaternion $\widehat{q}_2$ above.

I8. Compute $\widehat{q}_{12} = \widehat{q}_2 \widehat{q}_1$.

I9. Rotate $\vec{a}'$ above by $\widehat{q}_{12}$ and show that it is equivalent to the previous result both numerically and symbolically.

Advanced

A1. Develop a vector class in your programming language of choice that implements the operations listed. Provide a set of unit-tests that demonstrate the accuracy of your implementation.

A2. Develop a 3D and 4D homogeneous matrix class in your programming language of choice that implements the operations listed. Provide a set of unit-tests that demonstrate the accuracy of your implementation.

A3. Develop a quaternion class in your programming language of choice that implements the operations listed. Provide a set of unit-tests that demonstrate the accuracy of your implementation.

A4. Determine a method of computing a quaternion that represents a fraction of the angle between two quaternions. Think about how you might parameterize this problem, what are the parameters, what is changing, and what is fixed.

References

[1] Craig J. Robotics. New York: Addison-Wesley; 1989.

[2] Foley J, van Dam A, Feiner S, Hughes J. Computer graphics: principles and practice. 2nd ed. New York: Addison-Wesley; 1990.

[3] Grassia FS. Practical parameterization of rotations using the exponential map. J Graph Tool 1998;3(3).
[4] Mortenson M. Geometric modeling. New York: John Wiley & Sons; 1997.
[5] Shoemake K. Animating rotation with quaternion curves. In: Barsky BA, editor. Computer graphics. Proceedings of SIGGRAPH 85, 19(3). San Francisco, Calif; 1985. p. 143–52.
[6] Strong G. Linear algebra and its applications. New York: Academic Press; 1980.
[7] Watt A, Watt M. Advanced animation and rendering techniques. New York: Addison-Wesley; 1992.

CHAPTER

Objects in Space

3

Before we get to objects, we have to first think about how the environment is set up for our objects/characters. By *environment*, we mean the digital environment in which our characters will animate, play, or dance in our video game or animation. For simplicity, let's focus on an example of an environment, such as a simple apartment (see Figure 3.1). In this bare apartment we have a few rooms, a doorway, some windows, and basic furniture. How do we define such an apartment? We need to define the overall size of the room, the thickness of the walls/doors, size of the windows, location of the furniture, and orientation of the furniture as a starting point. Moreover, for rendering purposes we would need to define other aspects of the room such as materials, lighting, location/orientation of the virtual camera, and so forth. We need to denote aspects of this room that are static (e.g., walls, floor, ceiling, cupboards) and which are dynamic (e.g., movable furniture, doors that can open).

Imagine now, we are developing an animation where the non-player-characters (NPCs) are on patrol and your job is to get to the door without being *seen*. How would we set up the scene?

First off, we need to define *WHERE* the objects are in the room. This requires us to define positions of each object relative to a common *GLOBAL* coordinate frame. We can then move these objects simply by adding/subtracting appropriate values in the direction of movement of each character. While they are in *patrol mode*, they follow a predefined path and we simply draw the current frame of their animation. Now, how do we define the notion of being "seen"? One simple way to do it is to define a sphere (called a *bounding volume*) centered around each enemy. If the player character is within this bounding volume, the enemy can *see* you. We can use a geometric primitive (sphere in 3D, circle in 2D) to define this volume. Every time we need to update the positions or behaviors of our system, we simply need to compute the distance between this geometric primitive and a similarly defined primitive surrounding the player! If the distance between these primitives indicates that the two volumes are intersecting, the system needs to take action and some behavior must be invoked (e.g., physics update, deformation, artificial intelligence behavior change, animation clip change).

Luckily, the geometry we use is simple, so we can perform many calculations quickly. Where possible, the concepts in this chapter will be presented with video game examples, examples showing how to do the calculations, and code that implements them in order for you to gain an appreciation for them.

Computer Animation. https://doi.org/10.1016/B978-0-443-13512-5.00003-3

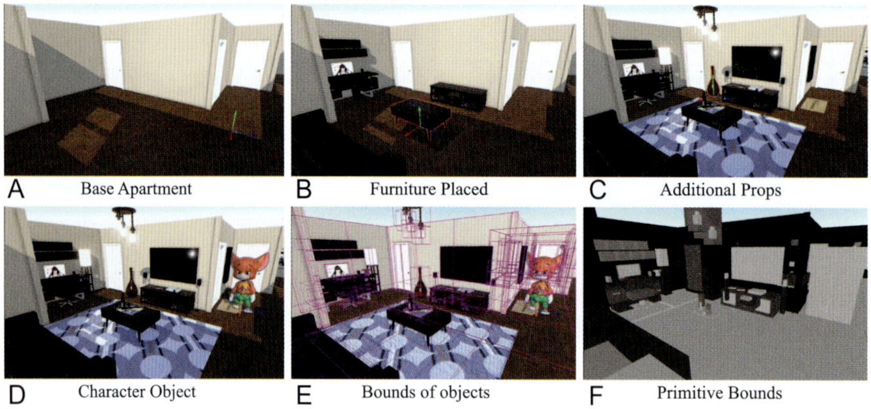

FIGURE 3.1

A simple apartment in Unity showing object placement and primitive boundary volumes.

3.1 Basic primitives

Let's be a bit more formal and start defining these ideas more concretely with the notation we will use throughout this book.

3.1.1 Coordinate systems

To define the location of any object, we need to specify where we are measuring the object relative from and the distances along each of the directions/dimensions of the space. For example, in the room described above, we cannot just say that the main character starts at the location of 2 m; this wouldn't make any sense as it is ambiguous—2 m relative to … where? We could say 2 m in front of the door, which is better but still ambiguous—where is the door, or how far left or right of the door? We could say 2 m in front and 1 m left of the middle of the doorway, which is more specific, but ambiguity remains due to the unspecified height—the location at floor level or closer to the middle of the door?

The point here is that we need to have a way to define consistent "frames of reference" or "coordinate systems" that give us a starting point for measuring things in space. Critically, to use a coordinate system, we need to define (a) the starting point for which all measurements will begin, we call this the *origin*, (b) the names (and how many) of the dimensions we need to measure to uniquely place an object relative to the origin – we call these the *coordinate axes* (plural) or *axis* (singular), (c) the orientation of the axes (how it is oriented in space relative to another frame). There are two types of coordinate systems that are pertinent: the *GLOBAL* frame defines the origin of the environment relative to which *everything* is defined, and *LOCAL* frames can be defined relative to the GLOBAL frame (i.e., for object locations) or any other frame of reference (i.e., to simplify complex relationships such as character rigs, or scene graphs). An example of a GLOBAL frame is the world coordinate system in a game, whereby you define the origin of the entire virtual world and objects are defined relative to this location. This absolute coordinate system provides a default way to discuss how objects move and the distances between them, and produce consistent rules for animation. An example of a LOCAL frame could be a frame of reference at the base of a particular object; you might find it easier to define the location of the head, hands, and feet of a character relative to a fixed location on their body. We will see how to convert between them once we have more formal definitions.

Aside

Coordinate systems are sometimes interchangeably called axes, coordinate frames, frames of reference, reference frames, or sometimes just frames (see Definition 3.1).

Coordinate frames can be 1D, 2D, 3D, or more! In this book, we will focus specifically on a maximum of three spatial dimensions because we need to be able to visualize our animations on a screen.

1D coordinate frames

A 1D coordinate frame can be defined as a simple number line that can be positive or negative. Let's call this number line $\overrightarrow{x} = (+1)$. Let's denote the origin of measurement $\overrightarrow{o} = 0$, and as such we can measure in two directions on this line: in front of (positive direction) or behind (negative direction) the origin. If we were to think of numbers on this line, we might call them distances from the origin or lengths/displacements. Let's denote the length of the measurement as a scalar value $\| s' \|$, where $\overrightarrow{s}$ is the displacement encoding direction as the sign (positive/negative) and the symbol $\| \cdot \|$ is just notation to say we do not care about direction for that value (length only). Let's say these directions are specifically defined as d_i, where $i = -1$ or $i = +1$. Note that we use vector notation here and that the length of this axis is 1 no matter which direction it is pointing.

We can define any point, $\overrightarrow{v}$, in this space as:

$$\overrightarrow{v} = \overrightarrow{o} + d_i \|s\| \overrightarrow{x}.$$

As an example, we can define a point on this number line that is 5 units behind the origin as:

$$\overrightarrow{v} = \overrightarrow{o} + d_i \|s\| \overrightarrow{x} = 0 + (-1)(5)\overrightarrow{1} = -5.$$

Although this may seem unnecessary for simple 1D numbers on a number line, this concept and notation extends nicely to 2D and 3D and will simplify future concepts in interpolation, locomotion, rotation, and rigid body physics.

2D coordinate frames

Let's define a 2D coordinate frame as a having the following properties:

Origin $\vec{o} = (0, 0)$
Two axes: x-axis, $\vec{x} = (1, 0)$, and y-axis, $\vec{y} = (0, 1)$
The x and y axes are perpendicular (orthonormal)

Similarly to how we defined points in the 1D space, we can define any point as a linear combination as:

$$\vec{v} = \vec{o} + d_{ix}\|s_x\|\vec{x} + d_{iy}\|s_y\|\vec{y}.$$

Thus we can define a point that is 5 units on the positive $\vec{x}$ axis and 3 units below the origin on the $\vec{y}$ axis as:

$$\vec{v} = \vec{o} + d_{ix}\|s_x\|\vec{x} + d_{iy}\|s_y\|\vec{y}$$
$$\vec{v} = (0,0) + (+1)(5)(1,0) + (-1)(3)(0,1)$$
$$\vec{v} = (0,0) + (5,0) + (0,-3) = (0+5+0, 0+0-3) = (5,-3).$$

3D coordinate frames

We can extend this to 3D simply by adding in a third perpendicular axis, the z-axis.

Origin $\vec{o} = (0, 0, 0)$
Three axes: x-axis, $\vec{x} = (1, 0, 0)$, y-axis $\vec{y} = (0, 1, 0)$, and z-axis $\vec{z} = (0, 0, 1)$
The x, y, and z axes are perpendicular (orthonormal) to each other. This means that $\vec{x} \cdot \vec{y} = \vec{x} \cdot \vec{z} = \vec{y} . \vec{z} = 0$ and that they are all unit length.

The same concepts are easily extended in the same manner above, but now we need to specify the distance/length on the z-axis for every point in this space, thus a point $\vec{p} = (x, y, z)$ such as $\vec{p} = (2, 1, -4)$.

Definition 3.1

A *coordinate frame* (or just *frame*, or *reference frame*) contains a position vector plus a set of unit-length vectors that are perpendicular to each other.

$$\textbf{FRAME}\left(\vec{p}, \{\mathbf{E}\}_0^m\right) : \{\mathbf{E}\}_0^m = \left\{\vec{e}_0, \vec{e}_1, \ldots, \vec{e}_m\right\}$$

where

$$\forall (i,j) \in \left\{\vec{e}_i, \vec{e}_j\right\} \rightarrow \vec{e}_i \cdot \vec{e}_j = 0 \qquad \textit{perpendicular}$$
$$\rightarrow \|\vec{e}_i\| = \|\vec{e}_j\| = 1 \qquad \textit{unit length}$$
$$\rightarrow \vec{e}_i = (\mathbf{e}_0, \mathbf{e}_1 \ldots \mathbf{e}_n) \qquad \textit{n-dimensional vectors}$$
$$\rightarrow \vec{p} = (\mathbf{p}_0, \mathbf{p}_1 \ldots \mathbf{p}_n) \qquad \textit{origin}$$

Example

An axis-aligned 3D coordinate frame centered at (1,2,−1)

$$\textbf{FRAME}\left(\vec{p}, \{\mathbf{E}\}_0^3\right):$$
$$\vec{p} = (1, 2, -1)$$
$$\{\mathbf{E}\}_0^3 = \left\{\vec{x}, \vec{y}, \vec{z}\right\} = \{(1,0,0), (0,1,0), (0,0,1)\}$$

3.1.2 Basic primitives: points, lines, planes

Points

Up until now we have been using the notion of a point in space as the basic geometric primitive.

But what is a point in space? A *point* in space is defined generally as an infinitesimally small location in the chosen coordinate system. Its location is defined as an n-tuple that denotes the distance along each axis, such as (2,3) or (3,2,9) (Figure 3.2a). Any point that can be defined in space can be defined in this manner as above. Note that in our definition we need to know the properties of the coordinate system (e.g., origin, directions) as this is the location relative to which these points are measured. If we end up moving or rotating the origin, we can still calculate the values of the points with the above definitions!

Distances between points

Sometimes we need to compute the distance between two points. This is especially useful when determining whether an object is in the vicinity of another object and you want to modify its behavior.

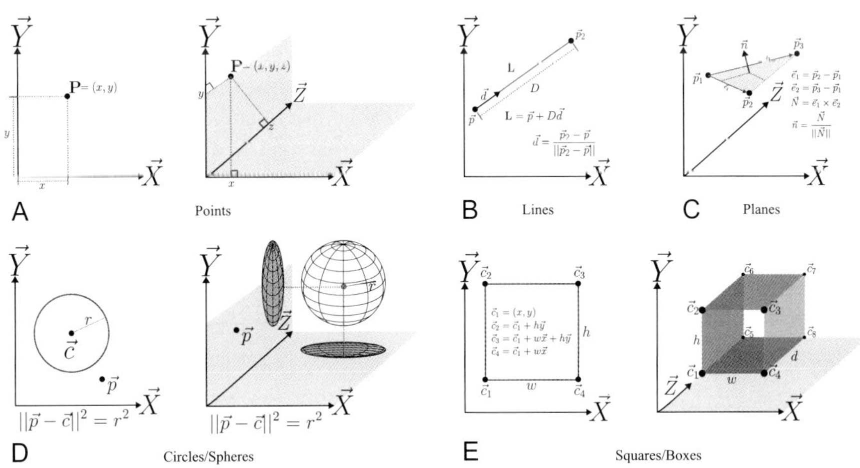

FIGURE 3.2

Basic primitives.

To compute the distance between two points, we rely on the Pythagorean theorem. Good ol' Pythagoras has given us the tool we need to do this. Luckily we have all seen this before in Grade 9 or 10.

The Pythagorean theorem is your friend!

Remember that the squared length of the hypotenuse is related to the sum of the squares of the other sides of the right triangle.

Remember $A^2 = B^2 + C^2$? That's right! A^2 is the distance between two points, namely a point that is B length along one axis and C length along the other axis. If we have a point in space $\vec{p} = (x, y)$, this is always defined relative to the origin, so you can imagine a line passing through the origin directly to the point (A). Thus Pythagoras tells us in 2D and in 3D (and beyond) the distance of the point to the origin! Note that this is EXACTLY the definition of vector length $\|\vec{p}\|$.

If we have two points $\vec{p}_1, \vec{p}_2$, then the distance between them can be easily computed by first computing the vector between them, $\vec{p}_2 - \vec{p}_1$, and then computing the length, (L), of this vector $L = \|\vec{p}_2 - \vec{p}_1\|$.

Lines

A *line* can be defined in a variety of ways. In high school, you probably would have defined a line as having a y-intercept and a slope m. Although these are useful concepts, there is another way that is more functionally useful for computer animation.

The simplest way to think about a line is to define a starting location on the line (the origin), $\vec{o} = (x, y)$, and a unit length direction, $\vec{d}$. We can then easily define any point on the line as $\vec{p} = \vec{o} + D\vec{d}$, where D is just a scalar to denote how far along the direction we want to look. It's like standing at the location defined by $\vec{o}$, looking in the direction $\vec{d}$, then taking D equal steps in that direction ending up in a particular location. You could move in both positive or negative D directions (i.e., stepping forward or backward, respectively). Oh wait! We defined this earlier when we talked about defining points in space! That's right: it is the same equation because a point can also be defined as a line starting from the origin and taking number steps along each axis. See below and Figure 3.2b for the parametric definition of a line.

This relationship holds true in 1D, 2D, 3D, 4D, and beyond. To easily remember the relationship, just remember the phrase: "Lines are *ODD* (*O*rigin, *D*isplacement, *D*irection)" (see Definition 3.2).

Definition 3.2

Parametric Equation of a Line (ODD)

$$\textbf{LINE}\left(\vec{o}, D, \vec{d}\right) \rightarrow \vec{p} = \vec{o} + D\vec{d}$$

where

$$\vec{o} \rightarrow \text{Origin}$$
$$D \rightarrow \text{displacement}$$
$$\vec{d} \rightarrow \text{direction}, \ \|\vec{d}\| = 1 \rightarrow \text{unit length}$$

Planes

For our purposes, you can think of a *plane* as a flat region of space that has both a location (origin) and orientation. We use planes to describe things like the sides of a cube/box, or the ground, or even small planar triangular regions that when stitched together we see a more complex object (e.g., triangular meshes).

Planes can be defined in 2D, 3D, 4D, and so forth. Usually when we think of a plane, we think of a 2D flat plane. In higher dimensions we would usually distinguish them by calling them "hyperplanes," meaning that they are in a higher ("hyper") dimensional space than usual. Do not worry; we will stick to 2D and 3D (see Figure 3.2c and Definition 3.3).

We can define planes by first specifying some important properties of them that let us compute points directly on the planar region. For instance, we have already seen and used a few different planes. A 2D coordinate system itself defines a planar region that can be used to compute any point on that plane using a linear combination of its coordinate axes.

If we define a 2D coordinate system that extends off to infinity along the $\overrightarrow{x}$ and $\overrightarrow{y}$ directions, we would call this the xy-plane. We can compute any point on this plane as

$$\overrightarrow{p} = a\overrightarrow{x} + b\overrightarrow{y}$$

where (a, b) is the two-tuple denoting the distances along each of the axes $\overrightarrow{x} = (1, 0)$ and $\overrightarrow{y} = (1, 0)$. What this means is that we need to define a coordinate system to define the orientation of the plane, and then pin the plane to a particular coordinate by defining a single point that is guaranteed to lie on the plane (to locate it in world coordinates). Note that the axes $\overrightarrow{x}$, $\overrightarrow{y}$ need not be defined always as (1, 0) and (0, 1). They can be any set of axes as long as they are *unit length* and *perpendicular* to each other.

We can also define a plane in 3D in much the same way you have probably seen before in high school, namely that a plane would be equivalent to the equation

$$Ax + By + Cz + D = 0$$

where A, B, C, D are the plane coefficients and $\overrightarrow{p} = (x, y, z)$ defines the point you would substitute in the equation to see if the point lies on the plane or not. When plugging in specific values, we can determine a few things about the relationship between the point and the plane. Specifically, if the result equals zero, then that point lies on the plane. If it is not zero, we note that the sign of the result tells us something useful about the location of that point relative to that plane. If the result is positive, the point is "above" the plane; if the result is negative, the point is "below" the plane. We will use this extensively when talking about collisions later.

The connection between planes and normals

If you are at all interested in 3D modeling or computer graphics for video games, you will have heard the term "normal" or "normal mapping" in the past. A *normal* is simply a term that is used to describe a unit-length vector that denotes the orientation of a plane. In a 3D model we generally represent objects as a list of triangles. Note that each triangle is a small flat region of space that is bounded by the vertices, and thus it is a *plane*! A "normal" vector can be computed as the cross-product of two of the triangles' edges to compute a vector that is perpendicular to the triangle. This "normal" denotes the orientation of the plane itself!

In fact, the plane equation can be specified as:

$$Ax + By + Cz + D = 0 \equiv n_x x + n_y y + n_z z + D = 0$$

where $\vec{n} = \left(n_x, n_y, n_z\right)$ is a unit-length normal vector and D is the offset from the world origin along this vector.

We can rewrite this further using the dot product:

$$\vec{n} \cdot \left(\vec{p} - \vec{o}\right)$$

where $\vec{p}$ is any point $\vec{p} = (x, y, z)$ and $\vec{o} = \left(o_x, o_y, o_z\right)$ is a point guaranteed to be on the plane (i.e., the origin/pin). When this expression evaluates to zero, then we would say that the point $\vec{p}$ lies on the plane.

Note that if for a given point the result is *positive* it is in *front* of the plane, *zero* means the point lies *on* the plane, and *negative* the point lies *behind* the plane.

Definition 3.3

Parametric equation of a plane (NOP)

$$\textbf{PLANE}\left(\vec{n}, \vec{o}, \vec{p}\right) \rightarrow \vec{n} \cdot \left(\vec{p} - \vec{o}\right) = 0$$

where

$\vec{n} \rightarrow$ unit-length normal vector, $\|\vec{n}\| = 1$
$\vec{o} \rightarrow$ origin/point on plane
$\vec{p} \rightarrow$ point to test if on plane

Example

Let's say the normal to our plane is $\vec{n} = (0, 1, 0)$ and we have a point that lies on the plane, $\vec{o} = (10, 5, 2)$, what is the equation of the plane?

Given the plane equation:

$$\textbf{Plane}\left(\vec{n}, \vec{o}, \vec{p}\right) = 0$$

we obtain:

$$\begin{aligned} \textbf{Plane}\left(\vec{n}, \vec{o}, \vec{p}\right) &= 0 \\ \vec{n} \cdot \left(\vec{p} - \vec{o}\right) &= 0 \\ (0, 1, 0) \cdot (x, y, z) - (10, 5, 2) &= 0 \\ (0, 1, 0) \cdot (x - 10, y - 5, 2 - z) &= 0 \\ 0(x - 10) + 1(y - 5) + 0(2 - z) &= 0 \\ y - 5 &= 0 \\ y &= 5 \end{aligned}$$

Intuitively, this means that any point with a y-value of 5 lies on the plane. Anything above 5 will result in a positive value and thus be in front of the plane; similarly anything less than 5 will result in a negative value thus be behind the plane.

3.2 Common primitives for animation

3.2.1 Circles/spheres

Circles! We use circles (see Figure 3.2d) in games to define boundaries of 2D objects for collision purposes. It is easier to check if two circles are colliding than to check if two arbitrary polygonal shapes are colliding. So, we can use this as a first pass to see if the objects are *potentially* colliding. A circle can exist on any 2D plane, so even in 3D we can use them on the ground plane to check if our player is near some object.

Generally, the equation of a circle is

$$r^2 = x^2 + y^2$$

which means that for a circle that lies at the origin, given any point that lies on the surface of the circle (x, y), the sums of the squares of the elements are equal to the square of the radius.

We can rearrange this as $x^2 + y^2 - r^2 = 0$, which makes it clear that given any point and radius, if this relationship holds, then the point lies on the surface of the circle.

This also has the added benefit that if the point does NOT lie on the circle then it will not hold, that is,

$$\begin{aligned}
&\text{if } x^2 + y^2 - r^2 = 0 \rightarrow \text{point is on surface of circle} \\
&\text{if } x^2 + y^2 - r^2 > 0 \rightarrow \text{point is outside circle} \\
&\text{if } x^2 + y^2 - r^2 < 0 \rightarrow \text{point is inside circle}
\end{aligned}$$

Also, we can more succinctly pull these concepts together to note that this equation actually computes the distance of the point to the circle.

Essentially, noting that the following relationship holds for a distance D:

$$D^2 = x^2 + y^2 - r^2$$

$$\text{Thus, } D = \sqrt{x^2 + y^2 - r^2}.$$

Let's define a circle as a function:

$$\textbf{Circle}\left(r, \vec{c}, \vec{p}\right) : \left(\vec{p} - \vec{c}\right) - r^2 = 0$$

where r is the circle radius, $\vec{c} = \left(c_x, c_y\right)$ is the centroid of the circle, and $\vec{p} = (x, y)$ is any point in space we wish to test to see if it lies in, on, or outside of the circle. The result here is the squared distance to the surface of the circle from the point. Thus if it outputs zero, then the point is on the circle; if it is positive, the point is outside the circle; and if it is negative, the point is inside the circle.

Spheres

Spheres are used in 3D games in much the same way circles are in 2D. It is an easy way to represent a volume of space to see if multiple objects are colliding. Because we have defined circles parametrically with vectors, we already know the parametric form of a sphere in 3D (see Figure 3.2d and Definition 3.4).

Definition 3.4

Parametric equation of a circle/sphere (ROP)

$$\textbf{CIRCLE/SPHERE}\left(\mathbf{r}, \vec{o}, \vec{p}\right) \rightarrow \vec{d} \cdot \vec{d} - \mathbf{r}^2 = 0$$

where

$$\begin{aligned} \mathbf{r} &\rightarrow \text{radius of circle/sphere} \\ \vec{o} &\rightarrow \text{origin/center} \\ \vec{p} &\rightarrow \text{point to test} \\ \vec{d} = \vec{p} - \vec{o} &\rightarrow \text{direction vector from center to point} \end{aligned}$$

3.2.2 Squares/boxes

We can define a square as a collection of its corner points (Figure 3.2e):

$$Square(A, B, C, D) = \left((x_1, y_1), (x_2, y_2), (x_3, y_3), (x_4, y_4)\right)$$

or we can define it using a single corner (origin) point and the width/height of the square as offsets as:

$$Square(Sz, C) \quad \text{where} \quad Sz = (w, h),\ C = \left(c_x, c_y\right).$$

This is often used to parameterize squares/boxes with an optional angle θ to denote the orientation of the square/box (if not axis aligned).

If axis aligned, we can then compute the corner locations of a $Square(Sz, C)$ as

$$\begin{aligned} (x_1, y_1) &= \left(c_x, c_y\right) \leftarrow \text{Bottom-Left} \\ (x_2, y_2) &= \left(c_x, c_y + h\right) \leftarrow \text{Top-Left} \\ (x_3, y_3) &= \left(c_x + w, c_y + h\right) \leftarrow \text{Top-Right} \\ (x_4, y_4) &= \left(c_x + w, c_y\right) \leftarrow \text{Bottom-Right} \end{aligned}$$

If not axis aligned, we can then compute the corner locations of a $Square(Sz, C, \theta)$ where θ is a counterclockwise rotation as:

$$\begin{aligned} (x_1, y_1) &= \left(c_x, c_y\right) \leftarrow \text{Bottom-Left} \\ (x_2, y_2) &= \left(c_x - h \sin\theta, c_y + h \cos\theta\right) \leftarrow \text{Top-Left} \\ (x_3, y_3) &= \left(c_x + w \cos\theta - h \sin\theta, c_y + w \sin\theta + h \cos\theta\right) \leftarrow \text{Top-Right} \\ (x_4, y_4) &= \left(c_x + w \cos\theta, c_y + w \sin\theta\right) \leftarrow \text{Bottom-Right} \end{aligned}$$

$$(x_1, y_1) = \vec{c} = (c_x, c_y)$$
$$(x_2, y_2) = \vec{c} + \mathbf{R}[0, h]^T$$
$$(x_3, y_3) = \vec{c} + \mathbf{R}[w, h]^T$$
$$(x_3, y_3) = \vec{c} + \mathbf{R}[w, 0]^T$$

where $\mathbf{R} = \begin{bmatrix} \cos\theta & -\sin\theta \\ \sin\theta & \cos\theta \end{bmatrix}$ is a rotation matrix denoting the orientation of the box.

Boxes

A box is the 3D equivalent of a square (i.e., a cube; see also Figure 3.2e). So we need to parameterize it in a similar fashion. $\mathbf{Box}\left(\vec{c}, \vec{s}, [\widehat{q}|\mathbf{R}]\right)$, where $\vec{c} = (c_x, c_y, c_z)$ is the bottom corner of the box, $\vec{s} = (w, h, d)$, provides the sizes/dimensions of each side of the box and optionally $\widehat{q}|\mathbf{R}$ is a rotation as either a quaternion or a rotation matrix (or other) representation denoting the orientation of the box. We can also define a square as a collection of its corner points

$$Box(A, B, C, D, E, F, G, H)$$
$$= Box\Big((x_1, y_1), (x_2, y_2), (x_3, y_3), (x_4, y_4), (x_5, y_5), (x_6, y_6), (x_7, y_7), (x_8, y_8)\Big),$$

and the points can be defined similarly as above to compute them from the parameterization.

3.2.3 Other primitives

The capsule primitive (Figure 3.3a) is very commonly used to denote the boundaries of a humanoid character as it can fit such a character shape more snugly than a single sphere. It can be thought of as the union of two spheres and a cylinder and is typically treated as such.

Other geometric primitives that are used in computer graphics but to a lesser extent in computer animation are the torus, cone, ellipsoid, and pyramid.

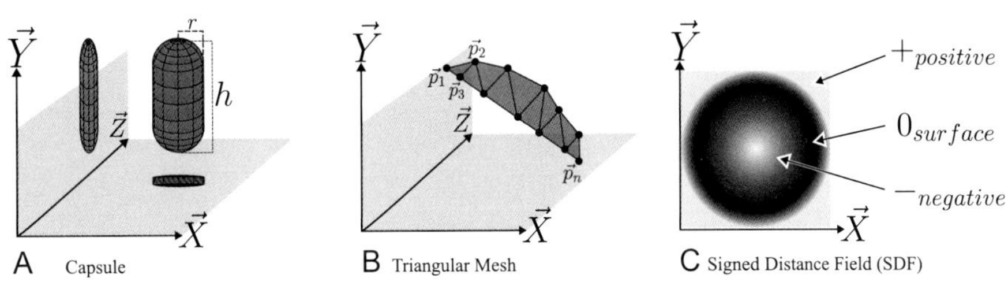

FIGURE 3.3

Other common primitives.

3.2.4 Triangular meshes

GPU hardware has evolved over the years to optimize the rendering of lists of triangles as a fundamental primitive for games and animation. This means that in order to draw our objects fast to the screen, we need to represent them as a set of connected triangles. All modern rendering systems either require that all objects in the scene be represented as triangles or are converted to triangles before rendering generally. This is not necessarily always the case when using ray tracing or ray marching. Ray tracing or ray marching algorithms can handle implicit surface representations (see section 3.2.5).

A triangle can be defined by three points and a normal vector denoting its face orientation, thus it can be considered a plane bounded by three points. A triangular mesh is simply a series of triangles with shared vertices and edges (Figure 3.3b).

3.2.5 Signed distance fields

Signed distance fields, or SDFs, are a common form of an implicit surface representation for 2D and 3D objects. SDFs are an implicit representation of an object where a function $f\left(\vec{p}\right)$ is defined over the entire coordinate space whereby the function returns the distance to the surface of the primitive and the sign of this distance represents whether the point is contained inside (negative value) or outside (positive value) of the object. We have already seen such a function when we defined the parametric form of a circle/sphere. The equation of a sphere centered at the origin can be represented in this way as:

$$f(p(x,y,z),r) = x^2 + y^2 + z^2 - r^2.$$

For a given radius, this function will return the signed distance of an input point to the sphere surface where a value of 0 indicates on the surface of the sphere, positive in front of the sphere, and negative inside of the sphere (see Figure 3.3c).

SDFs are extremely powerful for 3D modeling and animation as they can be combined with Boolean operations (e.g., union, intersection) parametrically. A great set of examples and SDF primitives can be found at [1] and visualized with ShaderToy [2].

3.3 Chapter summary

In this chapter we began our path toward modern computer animation by easing ourselves into defining coordinate systems and a few useful geometric primitives. These will be used and expanded upon throughout the book in future chapters as the basis of defining locomotion and deformation of objects.

3.4 Exercises

Beginner

B1. Take a screenshot of a film/game that you like. Using Photoshop or other image editing software, draw a series of primitives on top of each object that you think should be defined separately. For example, you may think of any moving object as needing a separate primitive definition. Think about the size of the environment in the scene and draw a top-down view of the scene. With an approximate and appropriate scale, add the primitives for each object into the top-down view of the scene. For each primitive, define its parameters (e.g., origin, orientation, size, radius). Define a common coordinate system in one of the corners of the world and define the origin of each primitive in GLOBAL coordinates.

B2. Write the parametric definition of the following primitives with the specified parameters and plot them on a graph:

a. A line between points $\vec{a} = (0, 5)$, $\vec{b} = (2, 3)$

b. A line between points $\vec{a} = (2, -5)$, $\vec{b} = (-2, 2)$

c. A line between points $\vec{a} = (-1, 1)$, $\vec{b} = (1, -2)$

d. A plane with normal $\vec{n} = \left(\frac{1}{\sqrt{2}}, 0, \frac{1}{\sqrt{2}}\right)$ passing through the point $\vec{p} = (2, 2, 3)$

e. A plane with normal $\vec{n} = (1, 0, 0)$ passing through the point $\vec{p} = (10, 2, -2)$

f. A plane with normal $\vec{n} = (0, 0, 1)$ passing through the point $\vec{p} = (0, -1, 6)$

g. A circle with radius $r = 2$ and center $\vec{c} = (2, -3)$

h. A circle with radius $r = 1$ and center $\vec{c} = (10, 8)$

i. A sphere with radius $r = 9$ and center $\vec{c} = (-5, 2, -6)$

j. A square (SQ1) with bottom left corner $\vec{c} = (0, 0)$, and dimensions $\vec{s} = (2, 3)$. Also compute the corners.

k. A square with bottom left corner $\vec{c} = (-5, 2)$, and dimensions $\vec{s} = (3, 2)$. Also compute the corners.

l. SQ1 (above) with orientation $\theta_1 = 45°, \theta_2 = 270°$

Intermediate

I1. Draw two circles with different radii and different center locations on the same graph. Using the parametric definitions of these circles, determine a method/algorithm that checks to see if they are intersecting or not. Think about what the parametric equation gives you (i.e., distance) and how to use that with the parameters (Hint: radii, centers) to determine if they are touching or not. Show with examples various situations where they intersect, overlap, or are separated.

I2. In a game engine or animation package of your choice, create a scene with a number of simple objects in the scene, or they can be complex objects but define a simple collision volume for each of them as one of the primitives above. Find, compute, and write down all of the primitive parameters of these objects.

Advanced

A1. Using these primitive object definitions, write some code in a game engine of choice to apply basic PV and PVA rigid body physics to move their centers in the world.

A2. Write some code that applies trigonometric functions (i.e., sin, cos) to the vertices in a triangular mesh to deform the object over time.

References

[1] https://iquilezles.org/articles/distfunctions/
[2] https://www.shadertoy.com/

CHAPTER

Interpolation: computing "in-between" values

4

Imagine a typical living room: the door is located to one side and the television on the opposite wall. Now, what if you wanted to move an object (the Character), from the door to the television over a fixed period of time (the Duration). The simplest way to think of this is to move the Character at a constant rate in a straight line one step at a time (the Interpolating Interval). What if there were obstacles, like a couch or a pet dog? You would have to define a set of rules for the Character to deviate from their trajectory to move along a different path. How we define these rules/constraints and how we treat the notion of a "path" is the concern of this chapter. Interpolation gives us the language and tools to choose the intermediate locations along these paths no matter if they are straight lines or curves enabling us to position virtual objects smoothly and controllably. This chapter presents the mathematical foundation upon which much of computer animation is built—that of interpolating values. Changing values over time in a deterministic and controllable manner to somehow affect the visuals produced *is essentially* animation (in a strict sense of the word). Interpolation implies that the boundary values and constraints have been specified and all that remains is to fill in the intermediate details. But even filling in the values requires skill and knowledge. Let's begin with the simplest idea, controlling the motion of a single point in space along a line. Once we establish the mechanics for this, we can move to more interesting concepts like controlling that point along a curve, determining intermediate orientations, and working with paths.

4.1 Animation, sampling, and time

Before we begin, we need to first have a quick discussion of how time and animation are connected by what we call "sampling." Consider a video you recorded recently on your phone/camera. Generally, cameras will record at a constant rate we call the "framerate," defined as FPS or frames per second. The higher the value, the more frames are recorded and when played back. Similarly, for our purposes, let's standardize a framerate for animation of 30 FPS (of course if you are playing a game you may want a much higher framerate, such as 60 fps or 100+ fps). This means that for every second of animation, we have 30 individual frames that need to be generated/rendered. Because 1 second contains 1000 milliseconds, each frame would represent an interval of time of $\frac{1000ms}{30fps} = 33.33ms$. During this interval, we

Computer Animation. https://doi.org/10.1016/B978-0-443-13512-5.00004-5

must assume that nothing is changing and that we can compute all of the necessary motion given the results of the previous frame calculation and the initial conditions at the start of the frame. If we are working in a real-time system, this also provides us with a constraint on the computational time we have to perform all of our calculations for each frame. How many frames are in a 3-second animation at 30 fps? In total, we can see that we would have

$$3\ sec \times 30\frac{frames}{sec} = 90\ frames.$$

Often we use timestamps in the form $HH : MM : SS : FF$ to be concise and specific (especially in video editing systems). We can easily convert to a common unit (i.e., milliseconds) by noting the framerate.

Definition 4.1

A timestamp is a particular moment in the animation defined relative to the start of the animation.

$$\begin{aligned}
&\textbf{TIMESTAMP}(t):\\
&\qquad\qquad t \in [t_{start}, t_{end}] \rightarrow \text{ time in global timescale}\\
&\qquad \text{units:}\\
&\qquad\qquad ms \rightarrow \text{milliseconds since start of animation}\\
&\qquad\qquad s \rightarrow \text{seconds since start of animation}\\
&\qquad\qquad HH :: MM :: SS :: FF \rightarrow \text{Hours, Minutes, Seconds, Frames}\\
&\qquad \text{where}\\
&\qquad\qquad HH \in [0, 23], MM, SS \in [0, 59]\\
&\qquad\qquad FF \in [0, FPS] \text{ playback framerate}
\end{aligned}$$

For example, a timestamp of 1 hour, 23 minutes, 11 seconds, and 10 frames recorded at 30 fps can be written concisely 01:23:11:10 and converted as:

$$\left\{\begin{array}{ll}
1\cancel{hr}\frac{60\cancel{min}}{\cancel{hr}}\frac{60\cancel{sec}}{\cancel{min}}\frac{1000ms}{\cancel{sec}} & = 3600000ms\\
+23\cancel{min}\frac{60\cancel{sec}}{\cancel{min}}\frac{1000ms}{\cancel{sec}} & +1380000ms\\
+11\cancel{sec}\frac{1000ms}{\cancel{sec}} & +11000ms\\
+10\cancel{frame}\frac{1000ms}{30\cancel{frame}} & +333.33ms
\end{array}\right\} = 4991333.33ms.$$

To more easily discuss *when* a frame occurs, we will use the language of *global animation time* or *local animation time*. Global animation time refers to the time elapsed since the beginning of the animation. Generally, we would consider this to be the value zero and then every frame afterward is computed relative to the starting point. Local animation time refers to a moment in time that is relative to a particular event or the start of an interval. For example, imagine you have a 3-second animation with a ball moving along a curve for the first 2 seconds, but the last second has the ball moving along a straight line. Now if we wanted to compute the end position of the ball, then we would have to first determine where the ball was at 2 seconds (frame 60), then we can use a different equation from here on out for the last second. The time relative to frame 60 would locally reset to zero; this lets us ask questions about where the ball is relative to this event. *Normalized animation time* is used often when we are discussing an interval of time and need to compute the motion between these boundaries where the value of zero refers to the start of the interval and the value of one refers to the end of the interval. Another way to think of "normalized" time is that of a percentage, 0% defines the beginning, and 100% defines the end. See Figure 4.0 for an example demonstrating the relationships between these various ways of defining time in our animation. Defining time this way lets us more easily create functions that we can "sample" with time as the parameter. Sampling a function just means that we want to compute the value of the function at a particular time (or with specific conditions). For example, if we have a function that defines the movement of an object over time, we could say that we have a function **POSITION**$(t) \rightarrow \vec{p}_t = (x_t, y_t, z_t)$. Given the current state of the object and environment, our function takes in a

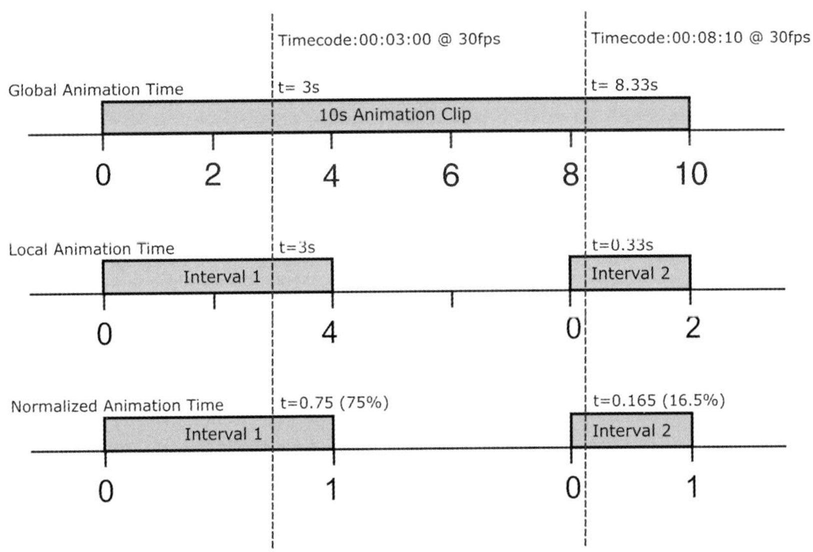

FIGURE 4.0

Examples of various ways to represent animation timing.

parameter of time. By specifying a particular given value for time, we evaluate the particular model representing the objects' motion at a particular moment in time, t, thus computing the position at that moment, $\vec{p_t}$.

4.2 Interpolation

One of the simplest examples of animation is the interpolation of the position of a point in space. But even to do this correctly is nontrivial and requires some discussion of several issues: choosing the appropriate interpolating function to sample, the parameterization of this function based on distance traveled, and maintaining the desired control of the interpolated position over time.

NOTE: Most of this discussion will be in terms of interpolating *spatial* values (to move objects). The reader should keep in mind that ***any*** changeable value involved in the animation (and display) process such as an object's transparency, the camera's focal length, or the color/intensity of a light source could (and probably will) be subjected to interpolation over time.

Often, an animator specifies (usually with a 3D animation tool such as Autodesk Maya/Blender) a list of values associated with a given dynamic parameter at specific "*key*" frames (often called "*keys*"). These keys constrain how this parameter needs to be modified over time as they need to be satisfied at specific moments in the resulting animation. Thus, the keys specify the data at given points in time and all we need to do is generate the data in between (*interpolate*) these keyframes for each parameter stored. Parameters may represent the 2D/3D position of an object, a single joint angle of an appendage of a robot, a quaternion representing its orientation, the transparency attribute of an object, or pretty much any other parameter used in the manipulation and display of computer graphics elements. Whatever the case, values for the parameter of interest must be generated for *all* of the frames in between the specified keys.

Definition 4.2

Keyframes in 3D contain a position and orientation (necessary to place an object at the given time) but may also contain other information relevant to the object behavior/appearance.

KEYFRAME(t) :

$t \in [t_{start}, t_{end}]$ → is the relevant timestamp in a global timescale

$\vec{p_t} = (x, y, z)$ →position at time t

$\hat{q}_t = [w, x, y, z]$ →a unit-quaternion representing orientation at time t

optionally:

$\vec{color} = (r, g, b) \in [0, 1]$ →normalized color at time t

...

For example, if the animator wants the position of an object to be $(-5, 0, 0)$ at frame 22 and $(5, 0, 0)$ at frame 67, then values for the position need to be generated for each frame in between, namely 23 to 66. A simple way would be to assume the object is moving on a line and thus we will see that we could use linear interpolation. But what if the object exhibits other behaviors (e.g., appears to be stopped at frame 22 and needs to accelerate from that position, reach a maximum speed by frame 34, start to decelerate at frame 50, and come to a full stop by frame 67)? Or perhaps instead of stopping at frame 67, the object should continue to position $(5, 10, 0)$ and arrive there at frame 80 by following a nice curved path. The next several sections address these issues of generating points along a path defined by control points and distributing the points along the path according to timing considerations.

Animation is complex. Objects can take circuitous paths throughout an environment, following curves/lines, and a multitude of other parameters can change throughout an animated sequence/scene. To simplify and reduce this complexity, we can focus on developing tools for smaller (simpler) problems and build up the complexity of the system using these smaller tools. Let's define a set of intervals between keyframes or constraints/points that we can then apply an appropriate interpolating function to determine values within this interval.

Definition 4.3

An interval is a continuous section of time bounded by two timestamps in the animation global timescale.

INTERVAL(t_s, t_e):

t_s →global timestamp where interval starts

t_e →global timestamp where interval ends

We will always have one more keyframe/constraint than we do intervals in an animation. For example, even if we are working on a single interval, you can see that this automatically defines time constraints for *two* keyframes (one at the start of the interval and the other at the end). Generally, if we have N key-frames, we have $N - 1$ intervals. This will be important when choosing the appropriate interpolating function.

4.2.1 The appropriate interpolating function

In this section, the discussion covers general issues that determine how to choose the most appropriate interpolation technique and, once it is chosen, how to apply it in the production of an animated sequence. The following issues should be considered when choosing an interpolation function: the need to interpolate versus approximate, algorithm complexity, curve smoothness/continuity, and ability to control the parameter globally versus locally. We first discuss three basic models of interpolation functions followed by discussion of the other considerations.

For this chapter, we wish to define an interpolating function $\mathbf{P}(u)$ that, for a given value of $u \in [0, 1]$, will produce a value that is a point in space, that is, $\vec{p} = \mathbf{P}(u)$.

Definition 4.4: Interpolating Function

Let's more formally define an interpolating function as:

$$\text{INTERPOLATION FUNCTION}: \quad \mathbf{P}(\vec{p_1}, \vec{p_2}, \ldots, \vec{p_m}, u) \rightarrow \vec{p_r}$$

where

$$\begin{aligned} \mathbf{P}(\ldots) &\rightarrow \text{interpolation function of model} \\ \vec{p_i}, i \in [1, m] &\rightarrow \text{n-dimensional constraint vectors} \\ u \in [0, 1] &\rightarrow \text{interpolating parameter} \\ \vec{p_r} &\rightarrow \text{n-dimensional intermediate result given u} \end{aligned}$$

Let's discuss the formal definition of our interpolating functions. First, consider the interpolating parameter, u.

Interpolation versus approximation

Given a set of points to describe a curve, one of the first decisions an animator must make is whether the given values represent actual positions that the curve should pass through (*interpolation*) or whether they are meant merely to control the shape of the curve and do not represent actual positions that the curve will intersect (*approximation*) (Figure 4.1). This distinction is usually dependent on whether the data points are sample points of a desired curve or whether they are being used to design a new curve. In the former case, the desired curve is assumed to be constrained to travel through the sample points, which is, of course, the definition of

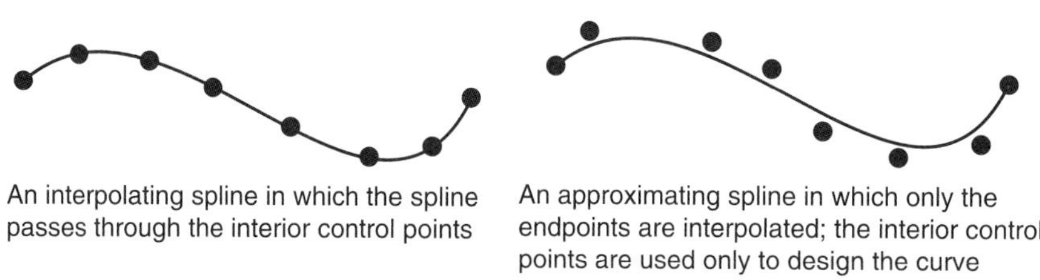

FIGURE 4.1

Comparing interpolation and approximating splines.

an *interpolating spline*.[1] In the latter case, an approximating spline can be used as the animator quickly gets a feel for how repositioning the control points influences the shape of the curve. Commonly used interpolating functions are the Hermite formulation and the Catmull-Rom spline. The Hermite formulation requires tangent information at the endpoints, whereas Catmull-Rom uses only positions the curve should pass through. Parabolic blending, similar to Catmull-Rom, is another useful interpolating function that requires only positional information. Functions that approximate some or all of the control information include Bezier and B-spline curves. See the Appendix for a more detailed discussion of these functions.

In the rest of this discussion, we will consider the case of "interpolating values" and rather than fitting a model to a set of data to approximate and predict, we assume that the chosen model already fits the data as per the animators' wishes.

Complexity

The complexity of the underlying interpolation equation is of concern because this translates into computational efficiency. The simpler the underlying equations of the interpolating function, the faster its evaluation. In practice, polynomials are easy to compute, and we will see that piecewise cubic polynomials $\left(ax^3 + bx^2 + cx + d\right)$ are the lowest-degree polynomials that provide sufficient smoothness while still allowing enough flexibility to satisfy other constraints such as beginning and ending positions and tangents. Polynomials with degree lower than cubic (i.e., parabolas $ax^2 + bx + c$ or straight lines $ax + b$) do not provide for a point of inflection between two endpoints; therefore, it might not fit smoothly to certain data points. Using a polynomial whose degree is higher than cubic typically does not provide any significant advantages and is more costly to evaluate.

Continuity

The smoothness in the resulting curve is a primary consideration. Mathematically, smoothness is determined by how many of the derivatives of the curve equation are continuous. *Zero-order continuity* refers to the continuity of values of the curve itself. Does the curve make any discontinuous jumps in its values? If a small change in the value of the parameter always results in a small change in the value of the function, then the curve has zero-order, or positional, continuity. If the same can be said of the first derivative of the function (the instantaneous change in values of the curve), then the function has *first-order*, or *tangential, continuity*. *Second-order continuity* refers to continuous curvature or instantaneous change of the tangent vector (Figure 4.2). In some geometric design environments, second-order continuity of curves and surfaces may be needed, but often in animation applications, first-order continuity suffices for spatial curves. As explained later in this

---

[1] The term *spline* comes from flexible strips used by shipbuilders and draftsmen to draw smooth curves. In computer graphics, it generally refers to a wide class of interpolating or smoothing functions.

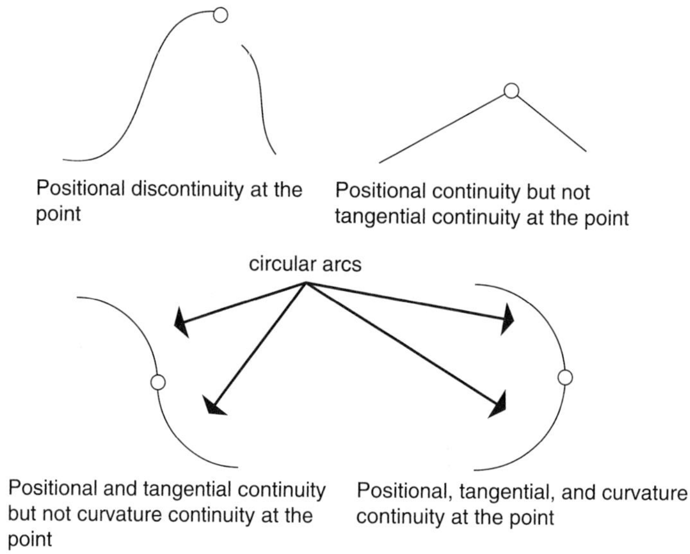

FIGURE 4.2

Continuity (at the point indicated by the small circle).

chapter, when dealing with time-distance curves, second-order continuity can be important.

In most applications, a curve interpolating or approximating more than a few points is defined piecewise; the curve is defined by a sequence of segments where each segment is defined by a single, vector-valued parametric function and shares its endpoints with the functions of adjacent segments. For the many types of curve segments considered here, the segment functions are cubic polynomials. The issue then becomes not the continuity within a segment (which in the case of polynomial functions is of infinite order) but the continuity enforced at the junction between adjacent segments. Hermite, Catmull-Rom, parabolic blending, and cubic Bezier curves can all produce first-order continuity between curve segments. There is a form of compound Hermite curve that produces second-order continuity between segments at the expense of local control (see the next section). A cubic B-spline is second-order continuous everywhere. All of these curves provide sufficient continuity for many animation applications. The Appendix discusses continuity in more mathematical terms, with topics including the difference between *parametric continuity* and *geometric continuity.*

Global versus local control

When designing a curve, a user often repositions one or just a few of the points that control the shape of the curve to tweak just part of the curve. It is usually considered an advantage if a change in a single control point has an effect on a limited region of

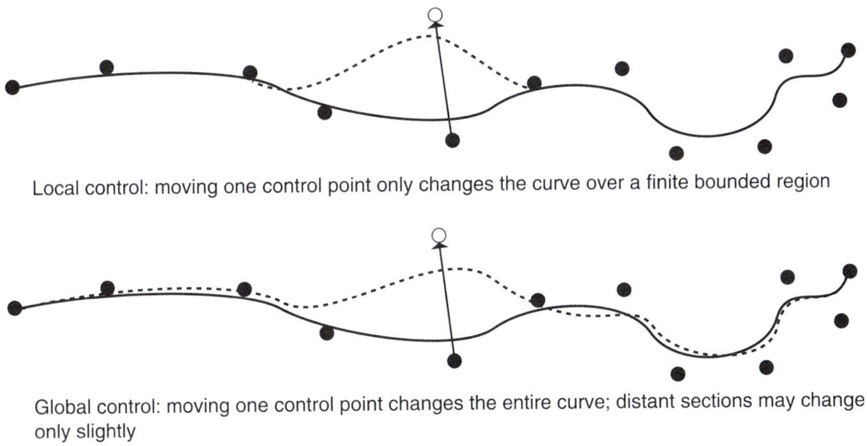

FIGURE 4.3

Comparing local and global effect of moving a control point.

the curve as opposed to affecting the entire curve. A formulation in which control points have a limited effect on the curve is referred to as providing *local control*. If repositioning one control point redefines the entire curve, however slightly, then the formulation provides only *global control*. The well-known Lagrange interpolation [5] is an example of an interpolating polynomial with global control. Figure 4.3 illustrates the difference between local control and global control. Local control is almost always viewed as being the more desirable of the two. Almost all of the composite curves provide local control: parabolic blending, Catmull-Rom splines, composite cubic Bezier, and cubic B-spline. The form of Hermite curves that enforces second-order continuity at the segment junctions does so at the expense of local control. Higher-order continuity Bezier and B-spline curves have less localized control than their cubic forms.

4.2.2 Summary

There are many formulations that can be used to interpolate values. The specific formulation chosen depends on the desired continuity, whether local control is needed, the degree of computational complexity involved, and the information required from the user. The Catmull-Rom spline is often used in creating a path through space because it is an interpolating spline and requires no additional information from the user other than the points that the path is to pass through. Bezier curves that are constrained to pass through given points are also often used. Parabolic blending is an often overlooked technique that also affords local control and is interpolating. Formulations for these curves appear in the Appendix. See Mortenson [5] and Rogers and Adams [6] for more in-depth discussions.

Common interpolation functions

There are a number of common interpolation functions used heavily in computer animation (especially in video game development), namely Linear Interpolation (LERP), Quadratic Interpolation, and forms of Cubic Interpolation. Each of these formulations represent a polynomial function of increasing degree, respectively.

Model 1: LERP—linear interpolation

Let's start with the simplest model. If we have only 2 data points, then this is the best we can do! Essentially linear interpolation (or LERP) assumes that the two data points both lie on the line and completely constrain the interpolation function, thus the data points define a bounded line segment starting from one point and ending at the other. Starting with the equation of a line from Chapter 3, we can rewrite it using the two endpoints resulting in a form that is parameterized by a single scalar, u. In this form, $u = 0$ simplifies to $f(0) = \vec{p_1}$ and $u = 1$ simplifies to $\vec{p_2}$. Simply by smoothly incrementing our parameter u between zero and one results in a new point that travels linearly between the two constraints.

$$\begin{aligned}
\textbf{LINE}(\vec{o}, D, \vec{d}) &\rightarrow \vec{p} = \vec{o} + D\vec{d} \\
\text{where } \vec{d} &= \frac{\vec{p_2} - \vec{p_1}}{||\vec{p_2} - \vec{p_1}||} \quad \text{is a unit vector} \\
\text{and } D &= u(||\vec{p_2} - \vec{p_1}||) \quad \text{proportional to distance} \\
\text{and } u &\in [0, 1] \quad \text{normalized interpolating parameter} \\
f(u) \rightarrow \vec{p} &= \vec{p_1} + u(\cancel{||\vec{p_2} - \vec{p_1}||})\frac{\vec{p_2} - \vec{p_1}}{\cancel{||\vec{p_2} - \vec{p_1}||}} \\
&= \vec{p_1} + u(\vec{p_2} - \vec{p_1}) \quad \leftarrow \text{simplified} \\
&= \vec{p_1} + u\vec{p_2} - u\vec{p_1} \quad \leftarrow \text{expand} \\
&= \vec{p_1} - u\vec{p_1} + u\vec{p_2} \quad \leftarrow \text{re-arrange} \\
&= (1 - u)\vec{p_1} + u\vec{p_2} \quad \leftarrow \text{collect like terms}
\end{aligned}$$

Thus we can succinctly define LERP as follows.

Definition 4.5

Linear interpolation (LERP) is the simplest interpolating function with two constraints.

$$\begin{aligned}
\textbf{LERP}(\vec{p_1}, \vec{p_2}, u) &\rightarrow \vec{r} = (1 - u)\vec{p_1} + u\vec{p_2} \\
\vec{p_1} &\rightarrow \text{n-dimensional vector at start of interval} \\
\vec{p_2} &\rightarrow \text{n-dimensional vector at end of interval} \\
u \in [0, 1] &\rightarrow \text{interpolating parameter} \\
\vec{r} &\rightarrow \text{n-dimensional vector result} \\
\mathbf{P}(u) = au + b &\rightarrow \text{Polynomial Degree}(1)
\end{aligned}$$

NOTE that this is also a polynomial function of degree 1. Consider the 1D version of this along the x-axis: $f(x) = x_0 + Dx$ looks awfully close to $y = mx + b$; we can rewrite our function as $f(x) = Ax + B$ where $A = D$ and $B = x_0$. To completely specify the coefficients we need two equations or two constraints (our endpoints).

Model 2: Quadratic

With LERP, we were able to define our interpolating function to be a function over a single parameter given a set of constraints (endpoints). Because we only had two constraints ($n = 2$), we could only compute a linear polynomial (degree-1) ($n - 1$). Thus if we have three points/constraints we can model a quadratic polynomial $f(x) = ax^2 + bx + c$ and completely determine the coefficients, (a, b, c). One approach to this is to consider the following set of equations:

$$y_0 = ax_0^2 + bx_0 + c$$
$$y_1 = ax_1^2 + bx_1 + c$$
$$y_2 = ax_2^2 + bx_2 + c$$

that can be expressed as matrices as

$$\begin{bmatrix} y_0 \\ y_1 \\ y_2 \end{bmatrix} = \begin{bmatrix} x_0^2 & x_0 & 1 \\ x_1^2 & x_1 & 1 \\ x_2^2 & x_2 & 1 \end{bmatrix} \begin{bmatrix} a \\ b \\ c \end{bmatrix}.$$

Solving for the coefficients can be done by with matrix inversion:

$$\begin{bmatrix} a \\ b \\ c \end{bmatrix} = \begin{bmatrix} x_0^2 & x_0 & 1 \\ x_1^2 & x_1 & 1 \\ x_2^2 & x_2 & 1 \end{bmatrix}^{-1} \begin{bmatrix} y_0 \\ y_1 \\ y_2 \end{bmatrix}$$

However, matrix inversion is computationally costly and only possible if the determinant of the matrix is suitable. Another way to think of this problem is by using the Lagrange form of a quadratic polynomial.

$$\begin{aligned} P(x) &= y_0 L_0(x) + y_1 L_1(x) + y_2 L_2(x) \\ &= y_0 \frac{(x - x_1)(x - x_2)}{(x_0 - x_1)(x_0 - x_2)} + y_1 \frac{(x - x_0)(x - x_2)}{(x_1 - x_0)(x_1 - x_2)} + y_2 \frac{(x - x_0)(x - x_1)}{(x_2 - x_0)(x_2 - x_1)} \end{aligned}$$

$$\{P\}(u) = a\,u^2 + b\,u + c \rightarrow \text{Polynomial Degree}(2)$$

Model 3: Cubic

Probably one of the most utilized polynomial interpolation functions is the cubic polynomial. Thus we have a polynomial that looks like $f(x) = ax^3 + bx^2 + c^x + d$ and as such we require four constraints to define the function completely. Also called "cubic splines," these curves can be constructed in such a way that they either guarantee that the constraint points lie on the curve directly (Catmull-Rom), or in a way where two of the points lie on the curve and the other two specify a constraint on the tangents to the curve at these endpoints (Bezier). Catmull-Rom curves are used widely in video games for interpolating path locations, whereas Bezier curves are generally used in offline modeling/animation tools as they provide the designer a large amount of control.

We can express a cubic spline generally in Hermite form:

$$f(u) = \mathrm{UMP} = \begin{bmatrix} u^3 & u^2 & u & 1 \end{bmatrix} \mathrm{M}_{4\times4} \begin{bmatrix} p_0 \\ p_1 \\ p_2 \\ p_3 \end{bmatrix}$$

where $U = \begin{bmatrix} u^3 & u^2 & u & 1 \end{bmatrix}$ includes the interpolating parameter $u \in [0, 1]$, $\mathbf{P} = [p_0\, p_1\, p_2\, p_3]^T$ is a matrix of points specifying the constraints for the curve, and $\mathbf{M}_{4\times4}$ encodes the relationships between the constraints ultimately specifying our polynomial coefficients. There are two types of cubic polynomials we are interested in, namely the Catmull-Rom and Bezier curves.

Model 4.1: Catmull-Rom

The Catmull-Rom formulation has a few properties that are important to animators. (1) All four constraint points specified are guaranteed to lie on the curve. This property makes it desirable for specifying movement along a curved path specified by a list of waypoints. (2) They are C^1 continuous enabling us to connect multiple segments smoothly and easily. (3) The tangents are computed using the previous point and next point on the curve ensuring smoothness.

Given any four sequential points that lie on a curved path, $\{p_0, p_1, p_2, p_3\}$, the following Catmull-Rom interpolation formulation allows you to compute any point on the interval with the mapping $u \in [0, 1] \rightarrow [p_1, p_2]$ as:

$$f_{\text{Catmull-Rom}}(u) = \begin{bmatrix} u^3 & u^2 & u & 1 \end{bmatrix} \frac{1}{2} \begin{bmatrix} -1 & 3 & -3 & 1 \\ 2 & -5 & 4 & -1 \\ -1 & 0 & 1 & 0 \\ 0 & 2 & 0 & 0 \end{bmatrix} \begin{bmatrix} p_0 \\ p_1 \\ p_2 \\ p_3 \end{bmatrix}$$

This utilizes p_0 and p_3 as controls that specify the tangents into and out of the intervals respectively, whereas p_1 is the start of the interval and p_2 is the end of the interval. Note that although this is a 1D (scalar) formulation, it is easily converted into a nD (vector) formation by specifying the points as rows in **P**. For example, in 3D we would have

$$f_{\text{Catmull-Rom}}(u) = \begin{bmatrix} x_r \\ y^r \\ z^r \end{bmatrix}^T = \begin{bmatrix} u^3 & u^2 & u & 1 \end{bmatrix} \frac{1}{2} \begin{bmatrix} -1 & 3 & -3 & 1 \\ 2 & -5 & 4 & -1 \\ -1 & 0 & 1 & 0 \\ 0 & 2 & 0 & 0 \end{bmatrix} \begin{bmatrix} x_0 & y_0 & z_0 \\ x_1 & y_1 & z_1 \\ x_2 & y_2 & z_2 \\ x_3 & y_3 & z_3 \end{bmatrix}$$

Definition 4.6: Catmull-Rom (Hermite Form)

$$\textbf{CATMULL-ROM}(u) = \mathbf{UMP}$$

$$\text{where } \mathbf{U} = \begin{bmatrix} u^3 & u^2 & u & 1 \end{bmatrix}, \mathbf{M} = \frac{1}{2} \begin{bmatrix} -1 & 3 & -3 & 1 \\ 2 & -5 & 4 & -1 \\ -1 & 0 & 1 & 0 \\ 0 & 2 & 0 & 0 \end{bmatrix}, \mathbf{P} = \begin{bmatrix} p_0 \\ p_1 \\ p_2 \\ p_3 \end{bmatrix}$$

Model 4.2a: Bezier The Bezier cubic spline interpolation formulation:

$$f_{\text{Bezier}}(u) = \begin{bmatrix} u^3 & u^2 & u & 1 \end{bmatrix} \begin{bmatrix} -1 & 3 & -3 & 1 \\ 3 & -6 & 3 & 0 \\ -3 & 3 & 0 & 0 \\ 1 & 0 & 0 & 0 \end{bmatrix} \begin{bmatrix} p_0 \\ p_1 \\ p_2 \\ p_3 \end{bmatrix}$$

where $u \in [0, 1] \rightarrow [p_0, p_3]$ represent the start and endpoints of the interval that lie on the spline, and the interior points $[p_1, p_2]$ represent the tangent controls that do not lie on the spline. You can think of p_1 as a handle point connected by a line to p_0, whereas p_2 can be thought of as a handle connected by a line to p_3.

Definition 4.7: Bezier (Hermite Form)

$$\textbf{BEZIER}(u) = \mathbf{UMP}$$

$$\text{where } \mathbf{U} = \begin{bmatrix} u^3 & u^2 & u & 1 \end{bmatrix}, \mathbf{M} = \begin{bmatrix} -1 & 3 & -3 & 1 \\ 3 & -6 & 3 & 0 \\ -3 & 3 & 0 & 0 \\ 1 & 0 & 0 & 0 \end{bmatrix}, \mathbf{P} = \begin{bmatrix} p_0 \\ p_1 \\ p_2 \\ p_3 \end{bmatrix}$$

Model 4.2b: Bezier—LERP form Rather than specifying a matrix, we can consider the de Casteljau algorithm for specifying a Bezier curve. This gives us the following simple form using six LERPs to construct the final interpolated value.

Definition 4.8: Bezier (LERP Form)

$$\begin{aligned}
&\mathbf{BEZIER}(u) \rightarrow \vec{p} \\
&\text{where} \\
&\overrightarrow{L_{01}} = \mathbf{LERP}(\vec{p_0}, \vec{p_1}, u) \\
&\overrightarrow{L_{12}} = \mathbf{LERP}(\vec{p_1}, \vec{p_2}, u) \\
&\overrightarrow{L_{23}} = \mathbf{LERP}(\vec{p_2}, \vec{p_3}, u) \\
&\overrightarrow{L_{01\rightarrow12}} = \mathbf{LERP}(\overrightarrow{L_{01}}, \overrightarrow{L_{12}}, u) \\
&\overrightarrow{L_{12\rightarrow23}} = \mathbf{LERP}(\overrightarrow{L_{12}}, \overrightarrow{L_{23}}, u) \\
&\vec{p} = \mathbf{LERP}(\overrightarrow{L_{01\rightarrow12}}, \overrightarrow{L_{12\rightarrow23}}, u)
\end{aligned}$$

4.3 Controlling the motion of a point along a curve

Designing the shape of a curve is only the first step in creating an animation path. The speed at which the curve is traced out as the parametric value is increased has to be under the direct control of the animator to produce predictable results. If the relationship between a change in parametric value and the corresponding distance along the curve is not known, then it becomes much more difficult for the animator to produce desired effects. The first step in giving the animator control is to establish a method for stepping along the curve in equal increments. Once this is done, methods for speeding up and slowing down along the curve can be made available to the animator.

Because a position in three-dimensional space is being interpolated, $\mathbf{P}(u)$ can be considered to represent three functions. The x-, y-, and z-coordinates for the positions at the keyframes are specified by the user. Keyframes are associated with specific values of the time parameter, u. The x-, y-, and z-coordinates are considered independently so that, for example, the x-coordinates of the points are used as control values for the interpolating curve so that $X = P_x(u)$, where P_x denotes an interpolating function; the subscript x is used to denote that this specific curve was formed using the x-coordinates of the key positions. Similarly, $Y = P_y(u)$ and $Z = P_z(u)$ are formed so that for any specified time, u, a position (X, Y, Z) can be produced as $\left(P_x(u), P_y(u), P_z(u)\right) = \mathbf{P}(u)$.

It is very important to note that varying the parameter of interpolation (in this case u) by a constant amount does not mean that the resulting values (in this case Euclidean position) will vary by a constant amount. Thus, if positions are being interpolated by varying u at a constant rate, the positions that are generated will not necessarily, in fact will seldom, represent a constant speed (Figure 4.4).

To ensure a constant speed for the interpolated value, the interpolating function has to be parameterized by *arc length*, that is, distance along the curve of interpolation. Some type of reparameterization by arc length should be performed for most applications. Usually this reparameterization can be approximated without adding undue overhead or complexity to the interpolating function.

Three approaches to establishing the reparameterization by arc length are discussed here. One approach is to analytically compute arc length. Unfortunately, many curve formulations useful in animation do not lend themselves to the analytic method, so numeric methods must be applied. Two numeric methods are presented, both of which create a table of values to establish a relationship between parametric value and approximate arc length. This table can then be used to approximate parametric values at equal-length steps along the curve. The first of these numeric methods constructs the table by supersampling the curve and uses summed linear distances to approximate arc length. The second numeric method uses Gaussian quadrature to numerically estimate the arc length. Both methods can benefit from an adaptive subdivision approach to controlling error.

4.3.1 Computing arc length

To specify how fast the object is to move along the path defined by the curve, an animator may want to specify the time at which positions along the curve should be attained. Referring to Figure 4.5 as an example in two-dimensional space, the animator specifies the following frame number and position pairs: (0, A), (10, B), (35, C), and (60, D).

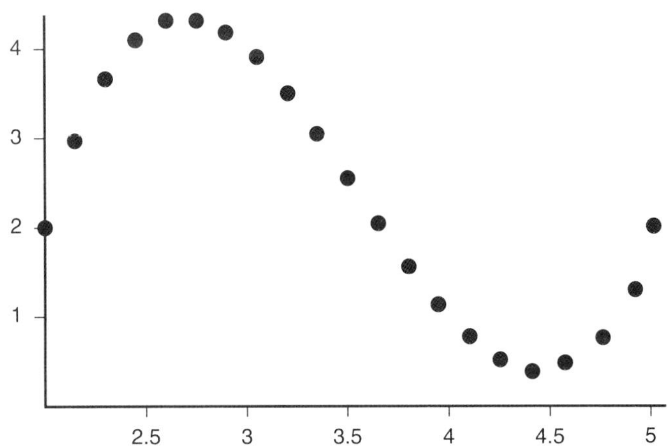

FIGURE 4.4

Example of points produced by equal increments of an interpolating parameter for a typical cubic curve. Notice the variable distance between adjacent points.

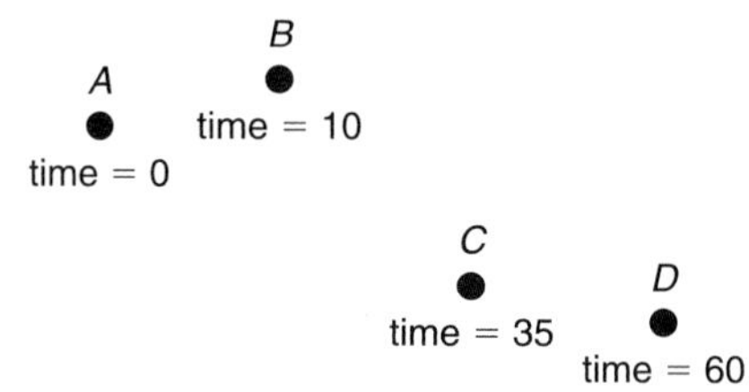

FIGURE 4.5

Position-time pairs constraining the motion.

Alternatively, instead of specifying time constraints, the animator might want to specify the relative velocities that an object should have along the curve. For example, the animator might specify that an object, initially at rest at position A, should smoothly accelerate until frame 20, maintain a constant speed until frame 35, and then smoothly decelerate until frame 60 at the end of the curve at position D. These kinds of constraints can be accommodated in a system that can compute the distance traveled along any span of the curve.

Assume that the position of a 3D object is being interpolated. The objective is to define a parameterized function that evaluates to a point in 3D space as a function of the parametric value; this defines a *space curve*. Assume for now that the function is a cubic polynomial as a function of a single parametric variable (as we will see, this is typically the case), that is, Equation 4.1.

$$\mathbf{P}(u) = \mathbf{a}u^3 + \mathbf{b}u^2 + \mathbf{c}u + \mathbf{d} \tag{4.1}$$

Remember that in 3D this really represents three equations: one for the x-coordinate, one for the y-coordinate, and one for the z-coordinate. Each of the three equations has its own constants a, b, c, and d. The equation can also be written explicitly representing these three equations, as in Equation 4.2.

Interpolating function in parametric form:

$$\begin{aligned}
\mathbf{P}(u) &= (x(u), y(u), z(u)) \\
x(u) &= a_x u^3 + b_x u^2 + c_x u + d_x \\
y(u) &= a_y u^3 + b_y u^2 + c_y u + d_y \\
z(u) &= a_z u^3 + b_z u^2 + c_z u + d_z
\end{aligned}$$

Or equivalently in matrix form:

$$\begin{aligned}
\mathbf{P}(u) &= [x(u)\ y(u)\ z(u)\ 1]^T \\
&= \begin{bmatrix} a_x & b_x & c_x & d_x \\ a_y & b_y & c_y & d_y \\ a_z & b_z & c_z & d_z \\ 0 & 0 & 0 & 1 \end{bmatrix} \begin{bmatrix} u^3 \\ u^2 \\ u \\ 1 \end{bmatrix}
\end{aligned} \tag{4.2}$$

Each of the three equations is a cubic polynomial of the form given in Equation 4.1. The curve itself can be specified using any of the standard ways of generating a spline (see the Appendix or texts on the subject, e.g., [6]). Once the curve has been specified, an object is moved along it by choosing a value of the parametric variable, and then the x-, y-, and z-coordinates of the corresponding point on the curve are calculated.

It is important to remember that in animation, the path swept out by the curve in space is not the only important thing. Equally important is how the path is swept out over time. A very different effect will be evoked by the animation if an object travels over the curve at a strictly constant speed instead of smoothly accelerating at the beginning and smoothly decelerating at the end. As a consequence, it is important to discuss both the curve that defines the path to be followed by the object and the function that relates time to distance traveled. The former is the previously mentioned *space curve* and the term *distance-time function* will be used to refer to the latter. In discussing the distance-time function, the curve that represents the function will be referred to often. As a result, the terms *curve* and *function* will be used interchangeably in some contexts.

Notice that a function is desired that relates time to a position on the space curve. The user supplies, in one way or another (to be discussed in the sections that follow), the distance-time function that relates time to the distance traveled along the curve. The distance along a curve is defined as *arc length* and, in this text, is denoted by s. When the arc length computation is given as a function of a variable u and this dependence is noteworthy, then $s = S(u)$ is used. The arc length at a specific parametric value, such as $S(u_i)$, is often denoted as s_i. If the arc length computation is specified as a function of time, then $S(t)$ is used. Similarly, the function of arc length that computes a parametric value is specified as $u = U(s)$.

The interpolating function relates parametric value to position on the space curve. The relationship between distance along the curve and parametric value needs to be established. This relationship is the *arc length parameterization* of the space curve. It allows movement along the curve at a constant speed by evaluating the curve at equal arc length intervals. Further, it allows acceleration and deceleration along the curve by controlling the distance traveled in a given time interval.

For an arbitrary curve, it is usually not the case that a constant change in the parameter will result in a constant distance traveled. Because the value of the parameterizing variable is not the same as arc length, it is difficult to choose the values of the parameterizing variable so that the object moves along the curve at a desired speed. The relationship between the parameterizing variable and arc length is usually nonlinear. In the special case when a unit change in the parameterizing variable results in a unit change in curve length, the curve is said to be parameterized by arc length. Many seemingly difficult problems in controlling the motion along a path become very simple if the curve can be parameterized by arc length or, if arc length can be numerically computed, given a value for the parameterizing variable.

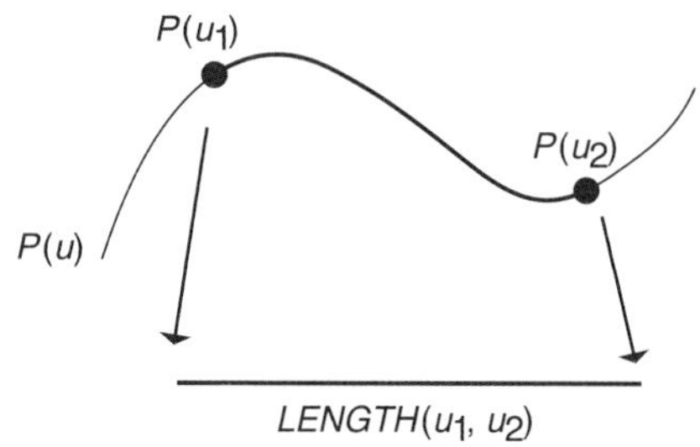

FIGURE 4.6

LENGTH(u_1, u_2).

Let the function *LENGTH*(u_a, u_b) be the length along the space curve from the point $P(u_a)$ to the point $P(u_b)$ (Figure 4.6). Then the two problems to solve are

1. Given parameters u_a and u_b, find *LENGTH*(u_a, u_b).
2. Given an arc length s and a parameter value u_a, find u_b such that $LENGTH(u_a, u_b) = \mathbf{s}$. This is equivalent to finding the solution to the equation $s - LENGTH(u_a, u_b) = 0$.

The first step in controlling the timing along a space curve is to establish the relationship between parametric values and arc length. This can be done by specifying the function $s = S(u)$, which computes, for any given parametric value, the length of the curve from its starting point to the point that corresponds to that parametric value. Then if the inverse, $u = S^{-1}(s) = U(s)$ can be computed (or estimated), the curve can be effectively parameterized by arc length, that is, $P(U(s))$. Once this is done, the second step is for the animator to specify, in one way or another, the distance the object should move along the curve for each time step.

In general, neither of the problems above has an analytic solution, so numerical solution techniques must be used. As stated previously, the first step in controlling the motion of an object along a space curve is to establish the relationship between the parametric value and arc length. If possible, the curve should be explicitly parameterized by arc length by analyzing the space curve equation. Unfortunately, for most types of parametric space curves, it is difficult or impossible to find a closed-form algebraic formula to describe an arc length parameter. For example, it has been shown that B-spline curves cannot, in general, be parameterized this way [3]. As a result, several approximate parameterization techniques have been developed. But first, it is useful to look at the analytic approach.

The analytic approach to computing arc length

The length of the curve from a point $\mathbf{P}(u_a)$ to any other point $\mathbf{P}(u_b)$ can be found by evaluating the arc length integral [4] as in Equation 4.3.

$$s = \int_{u_a}^{u_b} \left| \frac{dP}{du} \right| du \tag{4.3}$$

where the derivative of the space curve with respect to the parameterizing variable is defined to be that shown in Equations 4.4 and 4.5.

$$\frac{d\mathbf{P}}{du} = \left(\frac{dx(u)}{du}, \frac{dy(u)}{du}, \frac{dz(u)}{du} \right) \tag{4.4}$$

$$\left| \frac{d\mathbf{P}}{du} \right| = \sqrt{\left(\frac{dx(u)}{du} \right)^2 + \left(\frac{dy(u)}{du} \right)^2 + \left(\frac{dz(u)}{du} \right)^2} \tag{4.5}$$

For a cubic curve in which $P(u) = au^3 + bu^2 + cu + d$, the derivative of the x-coordinate equation with respect to u is $dx(u)/du = 3a_x u^2 + 2b_x u + c_x$. After squaring this and collecting the terms similarly generated by the y- and z-coordinate equations, the expression inside the radical takes the form of Equation 4.6.

$$Au^4 + Bu^3 + Cu^2 + Du + E \tag{4.6}$$

For the two-dimensional case, the coefficients are given in Equation 4.7; the extension to three-dimensional is straightforward.

$$\begin{aligned} A &= 9\left(a_x^2 + a_y^2\right) \\ B &= 12\left(a_x b_x + a_y b_y\right) \\ C &= 6\left(a_x c_x + a_y b_y\right) + 4\left(b_x^2 + b_y^2\right) \\ D &= 4\left(b_x c_x + b_y c_y\right) \\ E &= c_x^2 + c_y^2 \end{aligned} \tag{4.7}$$

Estimating arc length by forward differencing

As mentioned previously, analytic techniques are not tractable for many curves of interest to animation. The easiest and conceptually simplest strategy for establishing the correspondence between parameter value and arc length is to sample the curve at a multitude of parametric values. Each parametric value produces a point along the curve. These sample points can then be used to approximate the arc length by computing the linear distance between adjacent points. As this is done, a table is built up of arc lengths indexed by parametric values. For example, given a curve $\mathbf{P}(u)$, approximate the positions along the curve for $u = 0.00, 0.05, 0.10, 0.15, \ldots, 1.0$. The table, recording summed distances and indexed by entry number, is represented here as $G[i]$. It would be computed as follows:

$G[0] = 0.0$
$G[1] =$ the distance between $\mathbf{P}(0.00)$ and $\mathbf{P}(0.05)$
$G[2] = G[1]$ plus the distance between $\mathbf{P}(0.05)$ and $\mathbf{P}(0.10)$
$G[3] = G[2]$ plus the distance between $\mathbf{P}(0.10)$ and $\mathbf{P}(0.15)$
...
$G[20] = G[19]$ plus the distance between $\mathbf{P}(0.95)$ and $\mathbf{P}(1.00)$

Table 4.1 Parameter, arc length pairs

Index	Parametric Value (*V*)	Arc Length (*G*)
0	0.00	0.000
1	0.05	0.080
2	0.10	0.150
3	0.15	0.230
4	0.20	0.320
5	0.25	0.400
6	0.30	0.500
7	0.35	0.600
8	0.40	0.720
9	0.45	0.800
10	0.50	0.860
11	0.55	0.900
12	0.60	0.920
13	0.65	0.932
14	0.70	0.944
15	0.75	0.959
16	0.80	0.972
17	0.85	0.984
18	0.90	0.994
19	0.95	0.998
20	1.00	1.000

For example, consider the table of values, V, for u and corresponding values of the function G in Table 4.1.

As a simple example of how such a table could be used, consider the case in which the user wants to know the distance (arc length) from the beginning of the curve to the point on the curve corresponding to a parametric value of 0.73. The parametric entry closest to 0.73 must be located in the table. Because the parametric entries are evenly spaced, the location in the table of the closest entry to the given value can be determined by direct calculation. Using Table 4.1, the index, i, is determined by Equation 4.8 using the distance between parametric entries, $d = 0.05$ in this case, and the given parametric value, $v = 0.73$ in this case.

$$i = \left\lfloor \frac{v}{d} + 0.5 \right\rfloor = \left\lfloor \frac{0.73}{0.05} + 0.5 \right\rfloor = 15 \tag{4.8}$$

A crude approximation to the arc length is obtained by using the arc length entry located in the table at index 15, that is, 0.959. A better approximation can be obtained by interpolating between the arc lengths corresponding to entries on either side of the given parametric value. In this case, the index of the largest parametric entry that is less than the given value is desired (Eq. 4.9).

$$i = \left\lfloor \frac{v}{d} \right\rfloor = \left\lfloor \frac{0.73}{0.05} \right\rfloor = 14 \tag{4.9}$$

An arc length, s, can be linearly interpolated from the approximated arc lengths, G, in the table by using the differences between the given parametric value and the parametric values on either side of it in the table, as in Equation 4.10.

$$\begin{aligned} s &= G[i] + \frac{v - V[i]}{V[i_1] - V[i]}(G[i+1] - G[i]) \\ &= 0.944 + \frac{0.73 - 0.70}{0.75 - 0.70}(0.959 - 0.944) \\ &= 0.953 \end{aligned} \tag{4.10}$$

The solution to the first problem cited above (given two parameters u_a and u_b, find the distance between the corresponding points) can be found by applying this calculation twice and subtracting the respective distances.

The converse situation, that of finding the value of u given the arc length, is dealt with in a similar manner. The table is searched for the closest arc length entry to the given arc length value, and the corresponding parametric entry is used to estimate the parametric value. This situation is a bit more complicated because the arc length entries are not evenly spaced; the table must actually be searched for the closest entry. Because the arc length entries are monotonically increasing, a binary search is an effective method of locating the closest entry. As before, once the closest arc length entry is found the corresponding parametric entry can be used as the approximate parametric value, or the parametric entries corresponding to arc length entries on either side of the given arc length value can be used to linearly interpolate an estimated parametric value.

For example, if the task is to estimate the location of the point on the curve that is 0.75 unit of arc length from the beginning of the curve, the table is searched for the entry whose arc length is closest to that value. In this case, the closest arc length is 0.72 and the corresponding parametric value is 0.40. For a better estimate, the values in the table that are on either side of the given distance are used to linearly interpolate a parametric value. In this case, the value of 0.75 is three-eighths of the way between the table values 0.72 and 0.80. Therefore, an estimate of the parametric value would be calculated as in Equation 4.11.

$$u = 0.40 + \frac{3}{8}(0.45 - 0.40) = 0.41875 \tag{4.11}$$

The solution to the second problem (given an arc length s and a parameter value u_a, find u_b such that $LENGTH(u_a, u_b) = s$) can be found by using the table to estimate the arc length associated with u_a, adding that to the given value of s, and then using the table to estimate the parametric value of the resulting length.

The advantages of this approach are that it is easy to implement, intuitive, and fast to compute. The downside is that both the estimate of the arc length and the interpolation of the parametric value introduce errors into the calculation. These errors can be reduced in a couple of ways.

The curve can be supersampled to help reduce errors in forming the table. For example, 10,000 equally spaced values of the parameter could be used to construct a table consisting of a thousand entries by breaking down each interval into 10 subintervals. This is useful if the curve is given beforehand and the table construction can be performed as a preprocessing step.

Better methods of interpolation can be used to reduce errors in estimating the parametric value. Instead of linear interpolation, higher-degree interpolation procedures can be used in computing the parametric value. Of course, higher-degree interpolation slows down the computation somewhat, so a decision about the speed/accuracy trade-off has to be made.

These techniques reduce the error somewhat blindly. There is no measure for the error in the calculation of the parametric value; these techniques only reduce the error globally instead of investing more computation in the areas of the curve in which the error is highest.

Adaptive approach

To better control error, an *adaptive forward differencing* approach can be used that invests more computation in areas of the curve that are estimated to have large errors. The approach does this by considering a section of the curve and testing to see if the estimate of the segment's length is within some error tolerance of the sum of the estimates for each of the segment's halves. If the difference is greater than can be tolerated, then the segment is split in half and each half is put on the list of segments to be tested. In addition, at each level of subdivision the tolerance is reduced by half to reflect the change in scale. If the difference is within the tolerance, then its estimated length is taken to be a good enough estimate and is used for that segment. Initially, the entire curve is the segment to be tested.

As before, a table is to be constructed that relates arc length to parametric value. Each element of the table records a parametric value and the associated arc length from the start of the curve. It is also useful to record the coordinates of the associated point on the curve. A linked list is an appropriate structure to hold this list because the number of entries that will be generated is not known beforehand; after all points are generated, the linked list can then be copied to a linear list to facilitate a binary search. In addition to the list of entries, a sorted list of segments to be tested is maintained. A segment on the list is defined and sorted according to its range of parametric values.

The adaptive approach begins by initializing the table with an entry for the first point of the curve, $<0.0, \boldsymbol{P}(0)>$, and initializing the list of segments to be tested with the entire curve, $<0.0, 1.0>$. The procedure operates on segments from the list to be tested until the list is empty. The first segment on the list is always the one tested next. The segment's midpoint is computed by evaluating the curve at the middle of the range of its parametric value. The curve is also evaluated at the endpoint of the segment; the position of the start of the segment is already in the table and can be retrieved from there. The length of the segment and the lengths of each of its halves are estimated by the linear distance between the points on the curve. The sum of the estimated lengths of the two halves of the segment is compared with the estimated length of the segment. Equation 4.12 shows the test for the initial entire-curve segment.

$$|\|\mathbf{P}(0.0) - \mathbf{P}(1.0)\| - (\|\mathbf{P}(0.0) - \mathbf{P}(0.5)\| + \|\mathbf{P}(0.5) - \mathbf{P}(1.0)\|)| < \epsilon \tag{4.12}$$

If the difference between these two values is above some user-specified threshold, then both halves, in order, are added to the list of segments to be tested along with their error tolerance ($\epsilon/2^n$ where n is the level of subdivision). If the values are within tolerance, then the parametric value of the midpoint is recorded in the table along with the arc length of the first point of the segment plus the distance from the first point to the midpoint. Also added to the table is the last parametric value of the segment along with the arc length to the midpoint plus the distance from the midpoint to the last point. When the list of segments to be tested becomes empty, a list of $<$ parametric value, arc length $>$ has been generated for the entire curve.

One problem with this approach is that at a premature stage in the procedure two half segments might indicate that the subdivision can be terminated (Figure 4.7). It is usually wise to force the subdivision down to a certain level and then embark on the adaptive subdivision.

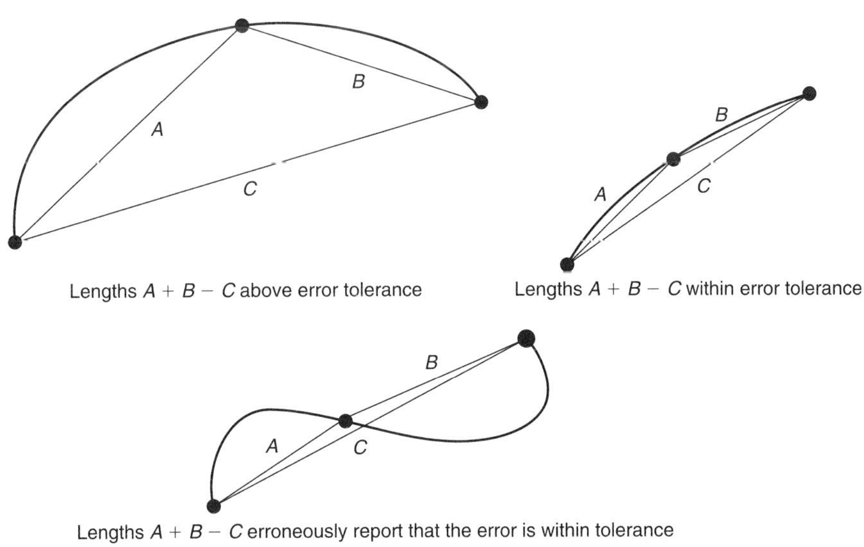

FIGURE 4.7

Tests for adaptive subdivision.

Because the table has been adaptively built, it is not possible to directly compute the index of a given parametric entry as it was with the nonadaptive approach. Depending on the data structure used to hold the final table, a sequential search or, possibly, a binary search must be used. Once the appropriate entries are found, then, as before, a corresponding table entry can be used as an estimate for the value or entries can be interpolated to produce better estimates.

Estimating the arc length integral numerically

For cases in which efficiency of both storage and time are of concern, calculating the arc length function numerically may be desirable. Calculating the length function involves evaluating the arc length integral (refer to Eq. 4.3). Many numerical integration techniques approximate the integral of a function with the weighted sum of values of the function at various points in the interval of integration. Techniques such as Simpson's and trapezoidal integration use evenly spaced sample intervals. Gaussian quadrature [1] uses unevenly spaced intervals in an attempt to get the greatest accuracy using the smallest number of function evaluations. Because evaluation of the derivatives of the space curve accounts for most of the processing time in this algorithm, minimizing the number of evaluations is important for efficiency. Also, because the higher derivatives are not continuous for some piecewise curves, this should be done on a per segment basis.

Gaussian quadrature, as commonly used, is defined over an integration interval from -1 to $+1$. The function to be integrated is evaluated at fixed points in the interval -1 to $+1$, and each function evaluation is multiplied by a precalculated weight (Equation 4.13).

$$\int_{-1}^{1} f(u) = \sum_{i} w_i f(u_i) \tag{4.13}$$

A function, $g(t)$, defined over an arbitrary integration interval $t \in [a, b]$ can be converted to a function, $h(u) = g(f(u))$, defined over the interval $u \in [-1, 1]$ by the linear transformation shown in Equation 4.14. By making this substitution and the corresponding adjustments to the derivative, any range can be handled by the Gaussian integration as shown in Equation 4.15 for arbitrary limits, a and b.

$$t = f(u) = \frac{b-a}{2}u + \frac{b+a}{2} \tag{4.14}$$

$$\begin{aligned} \int_a^b g(t)dt &= \int_{-1}^{+1} g(f(u))f'(u)du \\ &= \left(\frac{b-a}{2}\right)\int_{-1}^{+1} g\left(\frac{b-a}{2}u + \frac{b+a}{2}\right)du \end{aligned} \tag{4.15}$$

The weights and evaluation points for different orders of Gaussian quadrature have been tabulated and can be found in many mathematical handbooks (see the Appendix for additional details).

In using Gaussian quadrature to compute the arc length of a cubic curve, Equations 4.5–4.7 are used to define the arc length function in the form shown in Equation 4.16 after common terms have been collected into the new coefficients. Sample code to implement this is given below in the discussion on adaptive Gaussian integration.

$$\int_{-1}^{1} \sqrt{Au^4 + Bu^3 + Cu^2 + Du + E} \tag{4.16}$$

Adaptive Gaussian integration

Some space curves have derivatives that vary rapidly in some areas and slowly in others. For such curves, Gaussian quadrature will undersample some areas of the curve or oversample some other areas. In the former case, unacceptable error will accumulate in the result. In the latter case, time is wasted by unnecessary evaluations of the function. This is similar to what happens when using nonadaptive forward differencing.

To address this problem, an adaptive approach can be used [2]. Adaptive Gaussian integration is similar to the previously discussed adaptive forward differencing. Each interval is evaluated using Gaussian quadrature. The interval is then divided in half, and each half is evaluated using Gaussian quadrature. The sum of the two halves is compared with the value calculated for the entire interval. If the difference between these two values is less than the desired accuracy, then the procedure returns the sum of the halves; otherwise, as with the forward differencing approach, the two halves are added to the list of intervals to be subdivided along with the reduced error tolerance, $\epsilon/2^n$, where, as before, ϵ is the user-supplied error tolerance and n is the level of subdivision.

Initially the length of the entire space curve is calculated using adaptive Gaussian quadrature. During this process, a table of the subdivision points is created. Each entry in the table is a pair (u, s) where s is the arc length at parameter value u. When calculating $LENGTH(0, u)$, the table is searched to find the values u_i, u_{i+1} such that $u_i < u < u_{i+1}$. The arc length from u_i to u is then calculated using nonadaptive Gaussian quadrature. This can be done because the space curve has been subdivided in such a way that nonadaptive Gaussian quadrature will give the required accuracy over the interval from u_i to u_{i+1}. $LENGTH(0, u)$ is then equal to $s_i + LENGTH(u_i, u)$. $LENGTH(u_a, u_b)$ can be found by calculating $LENGTH(0, u_a)$ and $LENGTH(0, u_b)$ and then subtracting. The code for the adaptive integration and table-building procedure is shown in Figure 4.8.

This solves the first problem posed above; that is, given u_a and u_b find $LENGTH(u_a, u_b)$. To solve the second problem of finding u, which is a given distance, s, away from a given u_a, numerical root-finding techniques must be used as described next.

```
/* ------------------------------------------------------------
 * STRUCTURES
*/

// the structure to hold entries of the table consisting of
// parameter value (u) and estimated length (length)
typedef struct table_entry_structure {
  double u,length;
} table_entry_td;

// the structure to hold an interval of the curve, defined by
// starting and ending parameter values and the estimated
// length (to be filled in by the adaptive integration
// procedure)
typedef struct interval_structure {
  double ua,ub;
  double length;
} interval_td;

// coefficients for a 2D cubic curve
typedef struct cubic_curve_structure {
  double ax,bx,cx,dx;
  double ay,by,cy,dy;
} cubic_curve_td;

// polynomial function structure; a quadric function is generated
// from a cubic curve during the arclength computation
typedef struct polynomial_structure {
  double *coeff;
  int  degree;
} polynomial_td;

/* -------------------------------------------------------------------
 * ADAPTIVE INTEGRATION
 * this is the high-level call used whenever a curve's length is to be computed
*/
void adaptive_integration(cubic_curve_td *curve, double ua, double ub,double
tolerance)
{
   double subdivide();
   polynomial_td func;
   interval_td full_interval;
   double total_length;
   double integrate_func();
   double temp;

   func.degree = 4;
   func.coeff = (double *)malloc(sizeof(double)*5);
func.coeff[4] = 9*(curve->ax*curve->ax + curve->ay*curve->ay);
   func.coeff[3] = 12*(curve->ax*curve->bx + curve->ay*curve->by);
   func.coeff[2] = (6*(curve->ax*curve->cx + curve->ay*curve->cy) +
               4*(curve->bx*curve->bx + curve->by*curve->by)  );
   func.coeff[1] = 4*(curve->bx*curve->cx + curve->by*curve->cy);
```

FIGURE 4.8

Adaptive Gaussian integration of arc length.

```
   func.coeff[0] = curve->cx*curve->cx + curve->cy*curve->cy;
   full_interval.ua = ua; full_interval.ub = ub;
   temp = integrate_func(&func,&full_interval);
   printf("\nInitial guess = %lf; %lf:%lf",temp,ua,ub);
   full_interval.length = temp;
   total_length = subdivide(&full_interval,&func,0.0,tolerance);
   printf("\n total length = %lf\n",total_length);}


/* ---------------------------------------------------------------
 * SUBDIVIDE
 * 'total_length' is the length of the curve up to, but not including,
 *        the 'full interval'
 * if the difference between the interval and the sum of its halves is
 *        less than 'tolerance,' stop the recursive  subdivision
 * 'func' is a polynomial function
 */
double subdivide(interval_td *full_interval, polynomial_td *func, double
total_length, double tolerance){

   interval_td left_interval, right_interval;
   double left_length,right_length;
   double midu;
   double subdivide();
   double integrate_func();
   double temp;
   void add_table_entry();

   midu = (full_interval->u1+full_interval->u2)/2;
   left_interval.ua = full_interval->ua; left_interval.ub = midu;
   right_interval.ua = midu; right_interval.ub = full_interval->ub;
   left_length = integrate_func(func, & left_interval);
   right_length = integrate_func(func, & right_interval);
   temp = fabs(full_interval->length - (left_length+right_length));
   if (temp > tolerance) {
     left_interval.length = left_length;
     right_interval.length = right_length;
     total_length = subdivide(&left_interval, func, total_length, tolerance/2.0);
     total_length = subdivide(&right_interval, func, total_length, tolerance/2.0);
     return(total_length);}

   else {
     total_length = total_length + left_length;
     add table entry(midu,total length);
     total_length = total_length + right_length;
     add_table_entry(full_interval->ub,total_length);
     return(total_length);}}
/* ---------------------------------------------------------------------
 * ADD TABLE ENTRY
 * In an actual implementation, this code would create and add an
 *      entry to a linked list.
 * The code below simply prints out the values.
*/
void add_table_entry(double u, double length)
{
   /* add entry of (u, length) */
   printf("\ntable entry: u: %lf, length: %lf",u,length);
}
```

FIGURE 4.8 cont'd.

```
/* ----------------------------------------------------------------------
 * INTEGRATE FUNCTION
* use Gaussian quadrature to integrate square root of given function
 *          in the given interval
*/
double integrate_func(polynomial_td *func,interval_td *interval)
{
   double x[5] = {.1488743389,.4333953941,.6794095682,.8650633666,
   .9739065285};
   double w[5] =
   {.2955242247,.2692667193,.2190863625,.1494513491,.0666713443};
   double length, midu, dx, diff;
   int  i;
   double evaluate_polynomial();
   double ua,ub;
   ua = interval->ua;
   ub = interval->ub;
   midu = (ua+ub)/2.0;
   diff = (ub-ua)/2.0;
   length = 0.0;
   for (i=0; i<5; i++) {
      dx = diff*x[i];
      length += w[i]*(sqrt(evaluate_polynomial(func,midu+dx)) +
            sqrt(evaluate_polynomial(func,midu-dx)));
   }
   length *= diff;
   return (length);
}


/* -----------------------------------------------------------------
 * EVALUATE POLYNOMIAL
 * evaluate a polynomial using the Horner scheme
*/
double evaluate_polynomial(polynomial_td *poly, double u)
{
   int   i;
   double value;
   value = 0.0;
   for (i=poly->degree; i<=0; i--) {
      value = value*u+poly->coeff[i];
   }
   return value;
}
```

FIGURE 4.8 cont'd.

Find a point that is a given distance along a curve

The solution of the equation $s - LENGTH(u_a, u) = 0$ gives the value of u such that the point $\boldsymbol{P}(u)$ is at arc length s from the point $\boldsymbol{P}(u_a)$ along the curve. Because the arc length is a strictly monotonically increasing function of u, the solution is unique provided that the length of $d\boldsymbol{P}(u)/du$ is not identically 0 over some interval. Newton-Raphson iteration can be used to find the root of the equation because it converges rapidly and requires very little calculation at each iteration. Newton-Raphson iteration consists of generating the sequence of points $\{p_n\}$ as in Equation 4.17.

$$p_n = p_{n-1} - \frac{f(p_{n-1})}{f'(p_{n-1})} \tag{4.17}$$

In this case, f is equal to $s - LENGTH(u_1, U(p_{n-1}))$ where $U(p)$ is a function that computes the parametric value of a point on a parameterized curve. The function $U()$ can be evaluated at p_{n-1} using precomputed tables of parametric value and points on the curve similar to the techniques discussed above for computing arc length; f' is $d\mathbf{P}/du$ evaluated at p_{n-1}.

Two problems may be encountered with Newton-Raphson iteration: some of the p_n may not lie on the space curve at all (or at least within some tolerance) and $d\mathbf{P}/du$ may be 0, or very nearly 0, at some points on the space curve. The first problem will cause all succeeding elements $p_{n+1}, p_{n+2}, \ldots$ to be undefined, whereas the latter problem will cause division by 0 or by a very small number. A zero parametric derivative is most likely to arise when two or more control points are placed in the same position. This can easily be detected by examining the derivative of f in Equation 4.17. If it is small or 0, then binary subdivision is used instead of Newton-Raphson iteration. Binary subdivision can be used in a similar way to handle the case of undefined p_n. When finding u such that $LENGTH(0, u) = s$, the subdivision table is searched to find the values s_i, s_{i+1} such that $s_i < s < s_{i+1}$. The solution, u, lies between u_i and u_{i+1}. Newton-Raphson iteration is then applied to this subinterval.

An initial approximation to the solution is made by linearly interpolating s between the endpoints of the interval and using this as the first iterate. Although Newton-Raphson iteration can diverge under certain conditions, it does not happen often in practice. Because each step of Newton-Raphson iteration requires evaluation of the arc length integral, eliminating the need to do adaptive Gaussian quadrature, the result is a significant increase in speed. At this point it is worth noting that the integration and root-finding procedures are completely independent of the type of space curve used. The only procedure that needs to be modified to accommodate new curve types is the derivative calculation subroutine, which is usually a short program.

4.3.2 Speed control

Once a space curve has been parameterized by arc length, it is possible to control the speed at which the curve is traversed. Stepping along the curve at equally spaced intervals of arc length will result in a constant speed traversal. More interesting traversals can be generated by speed control functions that relate an equally spaced parametric value (e.g., *time*) to arc length in such a way that a controlled traversal of the curve is generated. The most common example of such speed control is *ease-in/ease-out* traversal. This type of speed control produces smooth motion as an object accelerates from a stopped position, reaches a maximum velocity, and then decelerates to a stopped position.

In this discussion, the speed control function's input parameter is referred to as t, for *time*, and its output is *arc length*, referred to as *distance* or simply as s. Constant-velocity motion along the space curve can be generated by evaluating it at equally spaced values of its arc length where arc length is a linear function of t. In practice, it is usually easier if, once the space curve has been reparameterized by arc length, the parameterization is then normalized so that the parametric variable varies between 0 and 1 as it traces out the space curve; the *normalized arc length parameter* is just the arc length parameter divided by the total arc length of the curve. For this discussion, the normalized arc length parameter will still be referred to simply as the arc length.

Speed along the curve can be controlled by varying the arc length values at something other than a linear function of t; the mapping of time to arc length is independent of the form of the space curve itself. For example, the space curve might be linear, whereas the arc length parameter is controlled by a cubic function with respect to time. If t is a parameter that varies between 0 and 1 and if the curve has been parameterized by arc length and normalized, then ease-in/ease-out can be implemented by a function $s = ease(t)$ so that as t varies uniformly between 0 and 1, s will start at 0, slowly increase in value and gain speed until the middle values, and then decelerate as it approaches 1 (Figure 4.9). Variable s is then used as the interpolation parameter in whatever function produces spatial values.

The control of motion along a parametric space curve will be referred to as *speed control*. Speed control can be specified in a variety of ways and at various levels of complexity. But the final result is to produce, explicitly or implicitly, a distance-time function $\mathbf{S}(t)$, which, for any given time t, produces the distance traveled along the space curve (arc length). The space curve defines *where* to go, whereas the distance-time function defines *when*.

Such a function $\mathbf{S}(t)$ would be used as follows. At a given time t, $\mathbf{S}(t)$ is the desired distance to have traveled along the curve at time t. The arc length of the

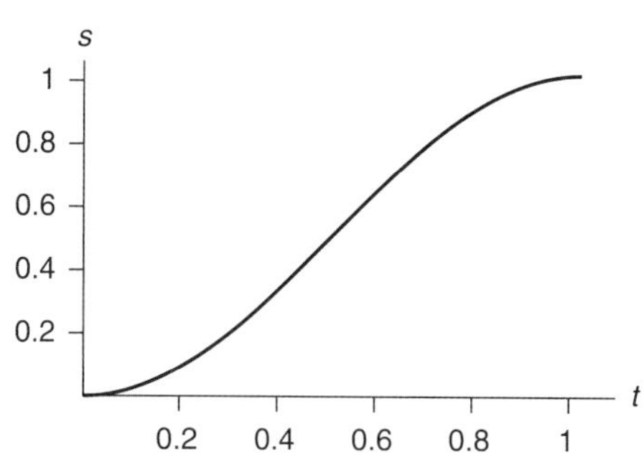

FIGURE 4.9

An example of an *ease*(t) function.

curve segment from the beginning of the curve to the point is $s = S(t)$ (within some tolerance). If, for example, this position is used to translate an object through space at each time step, it translates along the path of the space curve at a speed indicated by $S''(t)$. An arc length table (see Section 4.2.1) can then be used to find the corresponding parametric value $u = U(s)$ that corresponds to that arc length. The space curve is then evaluated at u to produce a point on the space curve, $p = P(u)$. Thus, $p = P(U(S(t)))$.

There are various ways in which the distance-time function can be specified. It can be explicitly defined by giving the user graphical curve-editing tools. It can be specified analytically. It can also be specified by letting the user define the velocity-time curve, or by defining the acceleration-time curve. The user can even work in a combination of these spaces. In the following discussion, the common assumption is that the entire arc length of the curve is to be traversed during the given total time. Two additional optional assumptions (constraints) that are typically used are listed below. In certain situations, it might be desirable to violate one or both of these constraints.

1. The distance-time function should be monotonic in t, that is, the curve should be traversed without backing up along the curve.
2. The distance-time function should be continuous, that is, there should be no instantaneous jumps from one point on the curve to a nonadjacent point on the curve.

Following the assumptions stated above, the entire space curve is to be traversed in the given total time. This means that $0.0 = S(0.0)$ and $total\_distance = S(total\_time)$. As mentioned previously, the distance-time function may also be normalized so that all such functions end at $1.0 = S(1.0)$. Normalizing the distance-time function facilitates its reuse with other space curves. An example of an analytic definition is $S(t) = (2 - t) * t$ (although this does not have the shape characteristic of ease-in/ease-out motion control; Figure 4.10).

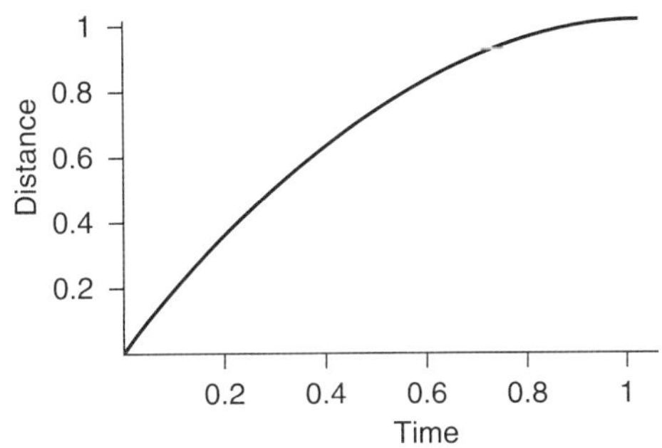

FIGURE 4.10

Graph of sample analytic distance-time function $(2 - t)*t$.

4.3.3 Ease-in/ease-out

Ease-in/ease-out is one of the most useful and most common ways to control motion along a curve. There are several ways to incorporate ease-in/ease-out control. The standard assumption is that the motion starts and ends in a complete stop and that there are no instantaneous jumps in velocity (first-order continuity). There may or may not be an intermediate interval of constant speed, depending on the technique used to generate the speed control. The speed control function will be referred to as $s = ease(t)$, where t is a uniformly varying input parameter meant to represent time and s is the output parameter that is the distance (arc length) traveled as a function of time.

Sine interpolation

One easy way to implement ease-in/ease-out is to use the section of the sine curve from $-\pi/2$ to $+\pi/2$ as the *ease*(t) function. This is done by mapping the parameter values of 0 to +1 into the domain of $-\pi/2$ to $+\pi/2$ and then mapping the corresponding range of the sine functions of -1 to $+1$ in the range 0 to 1. See Equation 4.18 and the corresponding Figure 4.11.

$$s = \mathbf{ease}(t) = \frac{\sin\left(t_{\pi} - \frac{\pi}{2}\right) + 1}{2} \tag{4.18}$$

In this function, t is the input that is to be varied uniformly from 0 to 1 (e.g., 0.0, 0.1, 0.2, 0.3, ...). The output, s, also goes from 0 to 1 but does so by starting off slowly, speeding up, and then slowing down. For example, at $t = 0.25, \boldsymbol{ease}(t) = 0.1465$, and at $t = 0.75, \boldsymbol{ease}(t) = 0.8535$. With the sine/cosine ease-in/ease-out function presented here, the "speed" of s with respect to t is never constant over an interval, rather it is always accelerating or decelerating, as can be seen by the ever-changing slope of the curve. Notice that the derivative of this ease function is 0 at $t = 0$ and at $t = 1$. Zero derivatives at 0 and 1 indicate a smooth acceleration from a stopped position at the beginning of the motion and a smooth deceleration to a stop at the end.

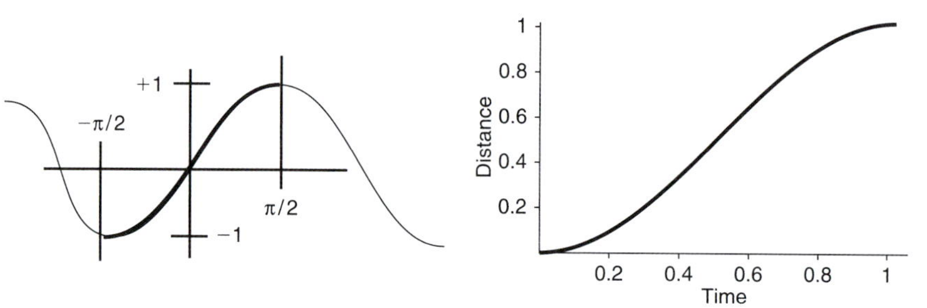

Sine curve segment to use as ease-in/ease-out control

Sine curve segment mapped to useful values

FIGURE 4.11

Using a sine curve segment as the ease-in/ease-out distance-time function.

Using sinusoidal pieces for acceleration and deceleration

To provide an intermediate section of the distance-time function that has constant speed, pieces of the sine curve can be constructed at each end of the function with a linear intermediate segment. Care must be taken so that the tangents of the pieces line up to provide first-order continuity. There are various ways to approach this, but as an example, assume that the user specifies fragments of the unit interval that should be devoted to initial acceleration and final deceleration. For example, the user may specify that acceleration ceases at 0.3 and the deceleration starts at 0.75. That is, acceleration occurs from time 0 to 0.3 and deceleration occurs from time 0.75 to the end of the interval at 1.0. Referring to the user-specified values as k_1 and k_2 respectively, a sinusoidal curve segment is used to implement an acceleration from time 0 to k_1. A sinusoidal curve is also used for velocity to implement deceleration from time k_2 to 1. Between times k_1 and k_2, a constant velocity is used.

The solution is formed by piecing together a sine curve segment from $-\pi/2$ to 0 with a straight line segment (indicating constant speed) inclined at 45 degrees (because the slope of the sine curve at 0 is equal to 1) followed by a sine curve segment from 0 to $\pi/2$. The initial sine curve segment is uniformly scaled by $k_1/(\pi/2)$ so that the length of its domain is k_1. The length of the domain of the line segment is $k_2 - k_1$. And the final sine curve segment is uniformly scaled by $1.0 - k_2/(\pi/2)$ so that the length of its domain is $1.0 - k_2$. The sine curve segments must be uniformly scaled to preserve C^1 (first-order) continuity at the junction of the sine curves with the straight line segment. This means that for the first sine curve segment to have a domain from 0 to k_1, it must have a range of length $k_1/(\pi/2)$; similarly, the ending sine curve segment must have a range of length $1 - k_2/(\pi/2)$. The middle straight line segment, with a slope of 1, will travel a distance of $k_2 - k_1$.

To normalize the distance traveled, the resulting three-segment curve must be scaled down by a factor equal to the total distance traveled as computed by $k_1/(\pi/2) + k_2 - k_1 + 1 - k_2/(\pi/2)$ (Figure 4.12).

The ease function described above and shown in Equation 4.19 is implemented in the code of Figure 4.13.

$$ease(t) = \left(\begin{array}{ll} = \left(k_1 \frac{2}{\pi}\left(\sin\left(\frac{t}{k_1}\frac{\pi}{2} - \frac{\pi}{2}\right)\right) + 1\right)/f & t \le k_1 \\ = \left(\frac{k_1}{\pi/2} + t - k_1\right)/f & k_1 \le t \le k_2 \\ = \left(\frac{k_1}{\pi/2} + k_2 - k_1 + \left((1-k_2)\frac{2}{\pi}\right)\sin\left(\left(\frac{t-k_2}{1-k_2}\right)\frac{\pi}{2}\right)\right)/f & k_2 \le t \end{array} \right) \tag{4.19}$$

where $f = k_1(2/\pi + k_2 - k_1 + (1 - k_2))(2/\pi)$.

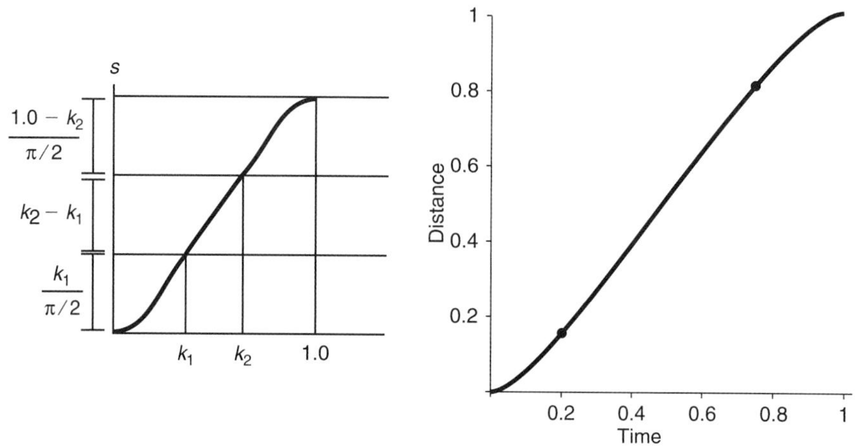

Ease-in/ease-out curve as it is initially pieced together

Curve segments scaled into useful values with points marking segment junctions

FIGURE 4.12

Using sinusoidal segments with constant speed intermediate interval.

```
double ease(float t, float k1, float k2)
{
   double f,s;
   f = k1*2/PI + k2 - k1 + (1.0 - k2)*2/PI;
   if(t < k1)           s = k1*(2/PI)*(sin((t/k1)*PI/2 - PI/2)+1);
   else if (t < k2)     s = (2*k1/PI + t - k1);
         else           s = 2*k1/PI + k2 - k1 + ((1-k2)*(2/PI)) *
                                   sin(((t - k2)/(1.0 - k2))*PI/2);
   return (s/f);
}
```

FIGURE 4.13

Code to implement ease-in/ease-out using sinusoidal ease-in, followed by constant velocity and sinusoidal ease-out.

Single cubic polynomial ease-in/ease-out

A single polynomial can be used to approximate the sinusoidal ease-in/ease-out control (Eq. 4.20). It provides accuracy within a couple of decimal points while avoiding the transcendental function[2] invocations. It passes through the points (0,0) and (1,1) with horizontal beginning and ending tangents of 0. Its drawback is that there is no intermediate segment of constant speed (Figure 4.14).

$$s = -2t^3 + 3t^2 \tag{4.20}$$

[2] A transcendental function is one that cannot be expressed algebraically. That is, it transcends expression in algebra. Transcendental functions include the exponential function, as well as the trigonometric functions such as sine.

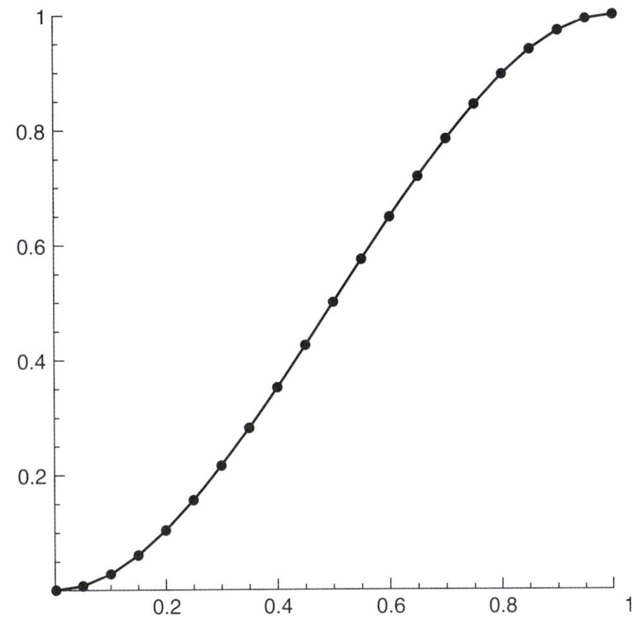

FIGURE 4.14

Ease-in/ease-out polynomial $s = -2t^3 + 3t^2$.

Constant acceleration: parabolic ease-in/ease-out

To avoid the transcendental function evaluation while still providing for a constant speed interval between the ease-in and ease-out intervals, an alternative approach for the ease function is to establish basic assumptions about the acceleration that in turn establish the basic form that the velocity-time curve can assume. The user can then set parameters to specify a particular velocity-time curve that can be integrated to get the resulting distance-time function.

The simple case of no ease-in/ease-out would produce a constant zero acceleration curve and a velocity curve that is a horizontal straight line at some value v_0 over the time interval from 0 to total time, t_{total}. The actual value of v_0 depends on the total distance covered, d_{total}, and is computed using the relationship

$$\mathbf{distance} = speed \cdot time$$

so that

$$v_0 = \frac{d_{\text{total}}}{t_{\text{total}}}.$$

In the case where normalized values of 1 are used for total distance covered and total time, $v_0 = 1$ (Figure 4.15).

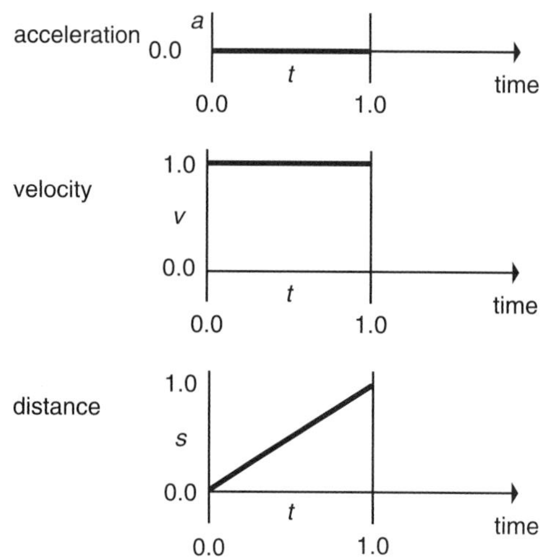

FIGURE 4.15

Acceleration, velocity, and distance curves for constant speed.

The distance-time curve is defined by the integral of the velocity-time curve and relates time and distance along the space curve through a function $S(t)$. Similarly, the velocity-time curve is defined by the integral of the acceleration-time curve and relates time and velocity along the space curve.

To implement an ease-in/ease-out function, constant acceleration and deceleration at the beginning and end of the motion and zero acceleration during the middle of the motion are assumed. The assumptions of beginning and ending with stopped positions mean that the velocity starts out at 0 and ends at 0. In order for this to be reflected in the acceleration/deceleration curve, the area under the curve marked "acc" must be equal to the area above the curve marked "dec," but the actual values of the acceleration and deceleration do not have to be equal to each other. Thus three of the four variables (acc, dec, t_1, t_2) can be specified by the user and the system can solve for the fourth to enforce the constraint of equal areas (Figure 4.16).

This piecewise constant acceleration function can be integrated to obtain the velocity function. The resulting velocity function has a linear ramp for accelerating, followed by a constant velocity interval, and ends with a linear ramp for deceleration (Figure 4.17). The integration introduces a constant into the velocity function, but this constant is 0 under the assumption that the velocity starts out at 0 and ends at 0. The constant velocity attained during the middle interval depends on the total distance that must be covered during the time interval; the velocity is equal to the area below (above) the *acc* (*dec*) segment in Figure 4.16. In the case of normalized time and normalized distance covered, the total time and total distance are equal to 1. The total distance covered will be equal to the area under the velocity curve (see Figure 4.17). The area under the velocity curve can be computed as in Equation 4.21.

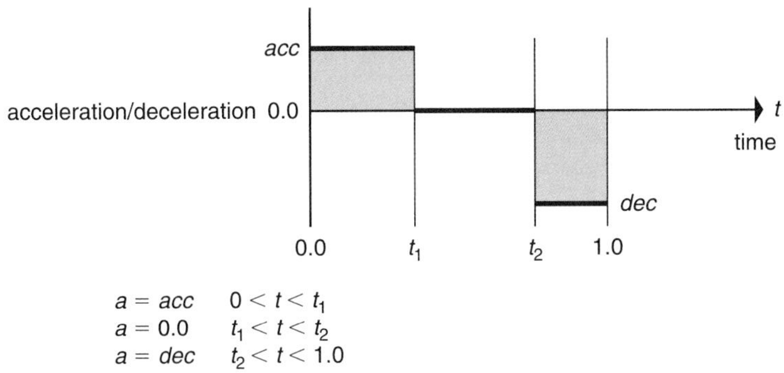

FIGURE 4.16

Constant acceleration/deceleration graph.

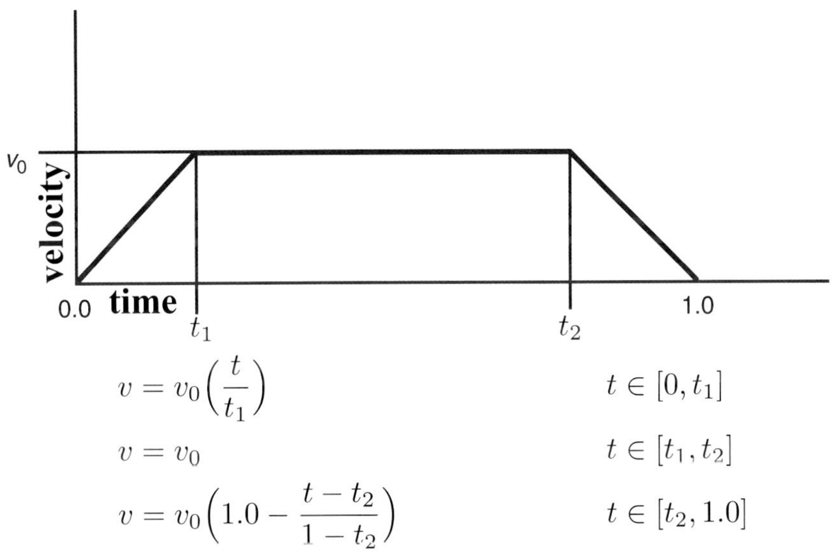

FIGURE 4.17

Velocity-time curve for constant acceleration. Area under the curve equals the distance traveled.

$$
\begin{aligned}
1 &= A_{acc} + A_{constant} + A_{dec} \\
1 &= \frac{1}{2}v_0 t_1 + v_0(t_2 - t_1) + \frac{1}{2}v_0(1 - t_2)
\end{aligned}
\tag{4.21}
$$

Because integration introduces arbitrary constants, the acceleration-time curve does not bear any direct relation to total distance covered. Therefore, it is often more intuitive for the user to specify ease-in/ease-out parameters using the velocity-time curve. In this case, the user can specify two of the three variables, t_1, t_2, and v_0, and the system can solve for the third to enforce the "total distance covered" constraint. For example, if the user specifies the time over which acceleration and deceleration take place, then the maximum velocity can be found by using Equation 4.22.

$$v_0 = \frac{2}{(t_2 - t_1) + 1} \tag{4.22}$$

The velocity-time function can be integrated to obtain the final distance-time function. Once again, the integration introduces an arbitrary constant, but, with the assumption that the motion begins at the start of the curve, the constant is constrained to be 0. The integration produces a parabolic ease-in segment, followed by a linear segment, followed by a parabolic ease-out segment (Figure 4.18).

The methods for ease control based on one or more sine curve segments are easy to implement and use but are less flexible than the acceleration-time and velocity-time functions. These last two functions allow the user to have even more control over the final motion because of the ability to set various parameters.

Common easing functions

The following easing functions are adapted from https://easings.net/. There are many other potential smooth functions with various characteristics (such as bouncing), but these are the most common starting points for fixed easing functions. For more control, we will see later on that a Bezier curve can be used but these are great in a pinch especially for simple transparency fading animations.

Table 4.2

	Ease-In	Ease-Out	EaseInOut
Sinusoidal	$f(u) = 1 - \cos\frac{u\pi}{2}$	$f(u) = \sin\frac{u\pi}{2}$	$f(u) = \frac{1 - \cos u\pi}{2}$
Quadratic	$f(u) = u^2$	$f(u) = 1 - (1 - u)^2$	$f(u) = \begin{cases} u \leq 0.5: & 2u^2 \\ u > 0.5: & 1 - 2(1 - u)^2 \end{cases}$
Cubic	$f(u) = u^3$	$f(u) = 1 - (1 - u)^3$	$f(u) = \begin{cases} u \leq 0.5: & 4u^3 \\ u > 0.5: & 1 - 4(1 - u)^3 \end{cases}$

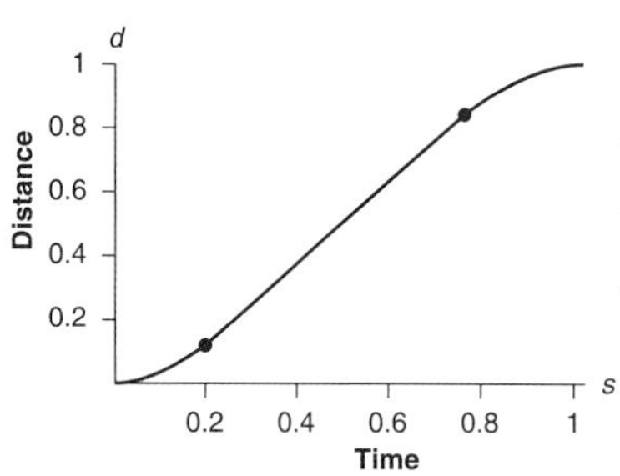

$$d = v_0\left(\frac{t^2}{2t_1}\right) \qquad t \in [0, t_1]$$

$$d = v_0\frac{t_1}{2} + v_0(t - t_1) \qquad t \in [t_1, t_2]$$

$$d = v_0\frac{t_1}{2} + v_0(t_2 - t_1) + \left[v_0 - \frac{v_0\left(\frac{t - t_2}{1 - t_2}\right)}{2}\right](t - t_2) \qquad t \in [t_2, 1.0]$$

FIGURE 4.18

Distance-time function for constant acceleration.

4.3.4 General distance-time functions

When working with velocity-time curves or acceleration-time curves, one finds that the underlying assumption that the total distance is to be traversed during the total time presents some interesting issues. Once the total distance and total time are given, the average velocity is fixed. This average velocity must be maintained as the user modifies, for example, the shape of the velocity-time curve. This can create a problem if the user is working only with the velocity-time curve. One solution is to let the absolute position of the velocity-time curve float along the velocity axis as the user modifies the curve. The curve will be adjusted up or down in absolute velocity to maintain the correct average velocity. However, this means that if the user wants to specify certain velocities, such as starting and ending velocities, or a maximum velocity, then other velocities must change in response to maintain total distance covered.

An alternative way to specify speed control is to fix the absolute velocities at key points and then change the interior shape of the curve to compensate for average velocity. However, this may result in unanticipated (and undesirable) changes in the shape of the velocity-time curve. Some combinations of values may result in unnatural spikes in the velocity-time curve to keep the area under the curve equal to the total distance (equal to 1, in the case of normalized distance). Consequently, undesirable accelerations may be produced, as demonstrated in Figure 4.19.

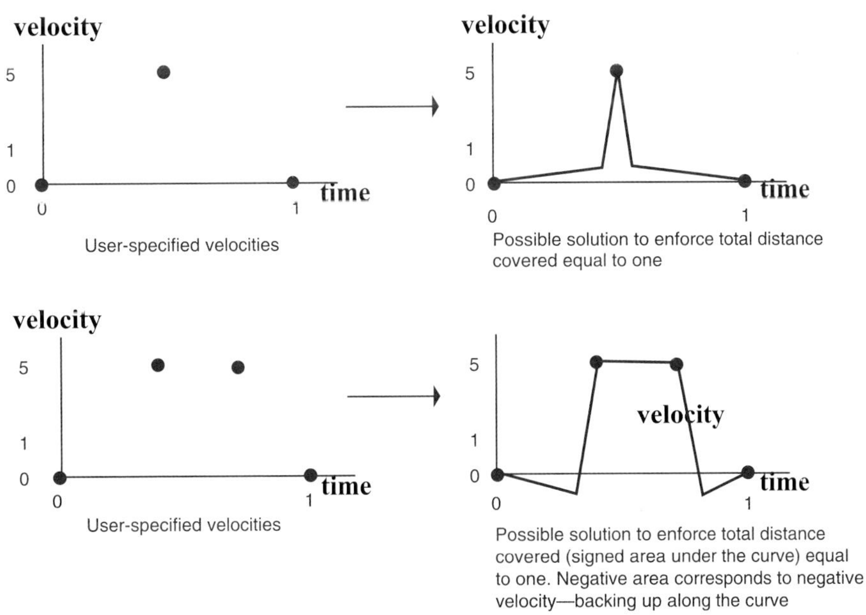

FIGURE 4.19

Some nonintuitive results of user-specified values on the velocity-time curve.

Notice that negative velocities mean that a point traveling along the space curve backs up along the curve until the time is reached when velocity becomes positive again. Usually, this is not desirable behavior.

The user may also work directly with the distance-time curve. For some users, this is the most intuitive approach. Assuming that a point starts at the beginning of the curve at $t = 0$ and traverses the curve to arrive at the end of the curve at $t = 1$, then the distance-time curve is constrained to start at (0, 0) and end at (1, 1). If the objective is to start and stop with zero velocity, then the slope at the start and end should be 0. The restriction that a point traveling along the curve may not back up any time during the traversal means that the distance-time curve must be monotonically increasing (i.e., always have a nonnegative slope). If the point may not stop along the curve during the time interval, then there can be no horizontal sections in the distance-time curve (no internal zero slopes) (Figure 4.20).

As mentioned before, the space curve that defines the path along which the object moves is independent of the speed control curves that define the relative velocity along the path as a function of time. A single space curve could have several velocity-time curves defined along it. A single distance-time curve, such as a standard ease-in/ease-out function, could be applied to several different space curves. Reusing distance-time curves is facilitated if normalized distance and time are used.

Motion control frequently requires specifying positions and speeds along the space curve at specific times. An example might be specifying the motion of a hand as it reaches out to grasp an object; initially the hand accelerates toward the object and then, as it comes close, it slows down to almost zero speed before picking up the object. The motion is specified as a sequence of constraints on time, position (in this case, arc length traveled along a space curve), velocity, and acceleration. Stating the problem more formally, each point to be constrained is an n-tuple, $< t_i, s_i, v_i, a_i, \ldots, >$, where s_i is position, v_i is velocity, a_i is acceleration, and t_i is the time at which all the constraints must be satisfied (the ellipses indicate that higher-order derivatives may be constrained). Define the zero-order constraint problem to be that of satisfying sets of two-tuples, $< t_i, s_i >$, whereas velocity, acceleration, and so on are allowed to take on any values necessary to meet the position constraints at the specified times. Zero-order constrained motion is illustrated at the top of Figure 4.21. Notice that there is continuity of position but not of speed. By extension, the first-order constraint problem requires satisfying sets of three-tuples, $< s_i, v_i, t_i >$, as shown in the bottom illustration in Figure 4.21. Standard interpolation techniques (see the Appendix) can be used to aid the user in generating distance-time curves.

4.3.5 Curve fitting to position-time pairs

If the animator has specific positional constraints that must be met at specific times, then the time-parameterized space curve can be determined directly. Position-time pairs can be specified by the animator, as in Figure 4.22, and the control points of

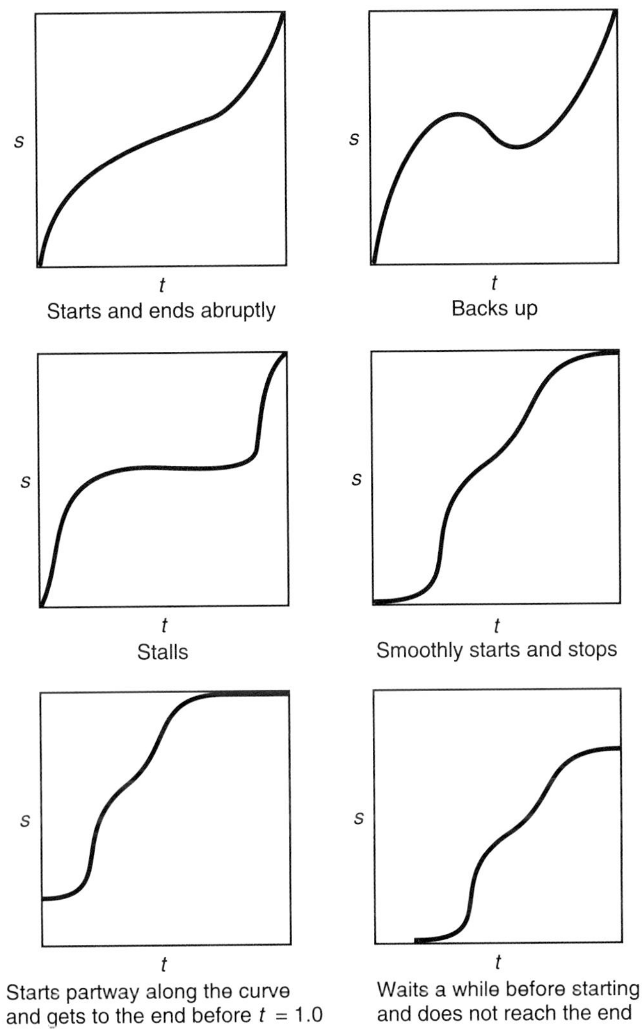

FIGURE 4.20

Sample distance-time functions.

the curve that produce an interpolating curve can be computed from this information [6].

For example, consider the case of fitting a B-spline[3] curve to values of the form $(P_i, t_i), i = 1, \ldots, j$. Given the form of B-spline curves shown in Equation 4.23 of

---

[3] Refer to the Appendix for more information on B-spline curves.

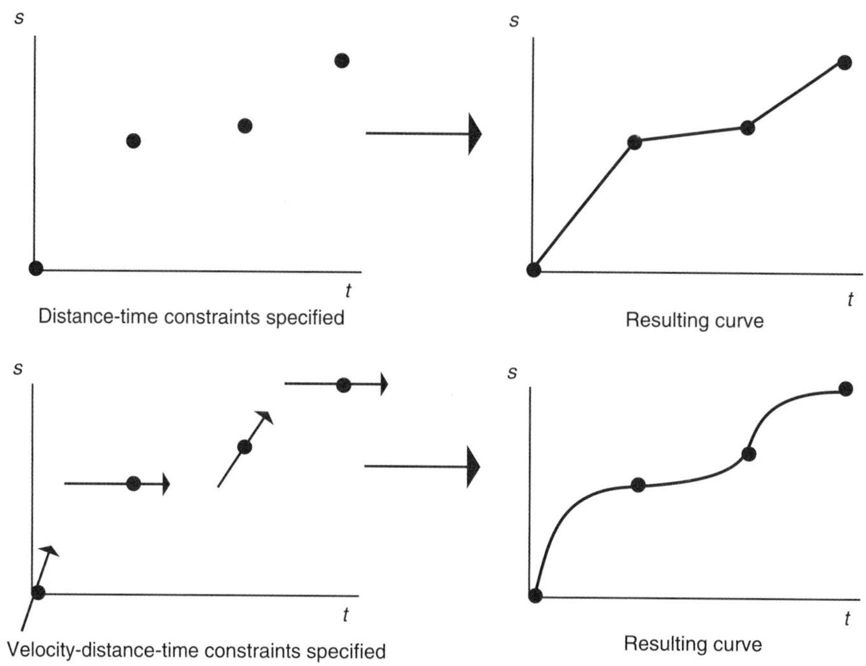

FIGURE 4.21

Specifying motion constraints.

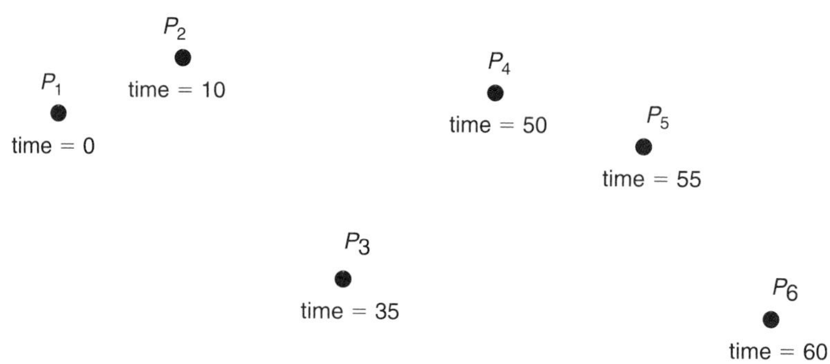

FIGURE 4.22

Position-time constraints.

degree k with $n + 1$ defining control vertices, and expanding in terms of the j given constraints $(2 \leq k \leq n+1 \leq j)$, Equation 4.24 results. Put in matrix form, it becomes Equation 4.25, in which the given points are in the column matrix P, the unknown defining control vertices are in the column matrix B, and N is the matrix of basis functions evaluated at the given times $(t_1, t_2, \ldots, t_j)$.

$$\mathbf{P}(t) = \sum_{i=1}^{n+1} B_i N_{i,k}(t) \tag{4.23}$$

$$\begin{aligned} P_1 &= N_{1,k}(t_1)B_1 + N_{2,k}(t_1)B_2 + \ldots + N_{n+1,k}(t_1)B_{n+1} \\ P_2 &= N_{1,k}(t_2)B_1 + N_{2,k}(t_2)B_2 + \ldots + N_{n+1,k}(t_2)B_{n+1} \\ &\ldots \\ P_j &= N_{1,k}(t_j)B_1 + N_{2,k}(t_j)B_2 + \ldots + N_{n+1,k}(t_j)B_{n+1} \end{aligned} \tag{4.24}$$

$$P = N\,B \tag{4.25}$$

If there are the same number of given data points as there are unknown control points $(2 \le k \le n+1 = j)$, then N is square and the defining control vertices can be solved by inverting the matrix, as in Equation 4.26.

$$B = N^{-1}\,P \tag{4.26}$$

The resulting curve is smooth but can sometimes produce unwanted wiggles. Specifying fewer control points $(2 \le k \le n+1 < j)$ can remove these wiggles but N is no longer square. To solve the matrix equation, the use of the pseudoinverse of N is illustrated in Equation 4.27, but in practice a more numerically stable and robust algorithm for solving linear least-squares problems should be used (e.g., see [1]).

$$\begin{aligned} P &= N\,B \\ N^T P &= N^T\,N\,B \\ \left[N^T\,N\right]^{-1} N^T\,P &= B \end{aligned} \tag{4.27}$$

4.4 Interpolation of orientations

The previous section discussed the interpolation of position through space and time. However, when dealing with objects, animators are concerned not only with the object's position, but also with the object's orientation. An object's orientation can be interpolated just like its position can be interpolated and the same issues apply. Instead of interpolating x, y, z positional values, an object's orientation parameters are interpolated. Just as an object's position is changed over time by applying translation transformations, an object's orientation is changed over time by applying rotational transformations. As discussed in the previous chapter, quaternions are a very useful representation for orientation and they will be the focus here.

4.4.1 Interpolating quaternions

Probably the most important feature of using quaternions is that it avoids the condition known as *gimbal lock* as exhibited when using fixed axis-angle and Euler angles. However, equally important for animation is the ability to interpolate quaternions smoothly and easily.

There are two methods we will discuss in this section to interpolate quaternions commonly referred to as "SLERP" and "**N**-LERP." The preferred method, "SLERP," stands for "**s**pherical **l**inear int**erp**olation" and as we will see it allows us to produce a smoothly changing sequence of intermediate orientations. Although preferred, SLERP comes at a significant computational cost when compared with the alternative "**N**-lerp" (which is computationally faster but has properties that are not always preferable in certain situations).

The Problem Statement

Given two unit-quaternions:

$$\widehat{p} = \left[w_p, x_p, y_p, z_p\right] = \left[\cos\frac{\theta_p}{2}, \sin\frac{\theta_p}{2}\overrightarrow{n_p}\right] \quad \|\widehat{p}\| = 1$$

$$\widehat{q} = \left[w_q, x_q, y_q, z_q\right] = \left[\cos\frac{\theta_q}{2}, \sin\frac{\theta_q}{2}\overrightarrow{n_q}\right] \quad \|\widehat{q}\| = 1$$

and an interpolation parameter $t \in [0, 1]$, we want to produce a function $f(\widehat{p}, \widehat{q}, t) \rightarrow \widehat{r}$ where the result

$$\widehat{r} = [w_r, x_r, y_r, z_r] = \left[cos\frac{\theta_r}{2}, sin\frac{\theta_r}{2}\overrightarrow{n}_r\right] \quad \|\widehat{r}\| = 1$$

is a unit-quaternion representing an intermediate orientation at a particular fraction of the **arc length**, t.

N-Lerp: the fast and easy way

N-Lerp (normalized linear interpolation) is the simplest (and computationally fastest) method to compute an intermediate quaternion between two input quaternions is to just treat them as regular vectors. For example, in 2D if we have 2 vectors $\overrightarrow{v_1} = (1, 1)$, $\overrightarrow{v_2} = (4, 10)$, we can use linear interpolation to find an intermediate point halfway between as:

$$\begin{aligned}\textbf{LERP}(\vec{v}_1, \vec{v}_2, t = 0.5) &= (1 - t)\vec{v}_1 + t\vec{v}_2 \\ \vec{v}_h &= \frac{1}{2}\begin{bmatrix}1\\1\end{bmatrix} + \frac{1}{2}\begin{bmatrix}2\\10\end{bmatrix} \\ &= \frac{1}{2}\begin{bmatrix}5\\11\end{bmatrix} = \begin{bmatrix}2.5\\5.5\end{bmatrix}\end{aligned}$$

Because scalar multiplication and addition is defined for quaternion math in exactly the same manner as with vectors, we can treat a quaternion as simply a four-dimensional vector and perform the same actions to find an intermediate quaternion! Note, however, that this does not guarantee that it preserves the length of the quaternions, which *must* remain at unit length to actually represent an orientation. This can be "fixed" simply by normalizing the quaternion after linearly interpolation hence the "N" for normalized in "N-Lerp." This results in the following operation:

Definition 4.9: N-LERP (normalized LERP)

$$\textbf{N-LERP}(\hat{q}_1, \hat{q}_2, u) \rightarrow \hat{r}_u : \hat{q_{\text{tmp}}} = (1-u)\hat{q}_1 + u\hat{q}_2, \hat{r}_u = \frac{\hat{q_{\text{tmp}}}}{||\hat{q_{\text{tmp}}}||}$$

This is very easy to implement, simple to understand, and does produce an intermediate quaternion. However, the main issue here is that it treats each element $[w, x, y, z]$ of the quaternion as a component that changes linearly throughout the interpolation space. This is easily shown to be false by remembering that for rotations, $w = cos\frac{\theta}{2}$, which is inherently a nonlinear function. To illustrate the main problem with this method, let's consider the geometric interpretation. Imagine two vectors, one pointing on the x-axis (1,0) and one pointing on the y-axis (0,1). If we were to perform a rotation of one of these axes by 90 degrees, they would line up perfectly and if we draw the path of all intermediate rotations we would see that it draws a quarter circle. At any given point on this circle the length from the origin is maintained as the radius of 1 because the vector is unit length. Now, instead of rotating one vector we can draw a line between the two endpoints resulting in a chord of this quarter circle. All linearly interpolated vectors lie on this line. Normalizing the intermediate vectors simply stretches the vector outward to the quarter circle. One can see easily that if you choose your interpolating parameter t to step along this line with a fixed step-size, the arc length between subsequent samples will not be equal. Figure 4.23 shows this effect between points on a two-dimensional circle. From an animation perspective, this means that the object this is applied to will not rotate at a constant rate but rather will speed up and slow down slightly between the keyframes. This may or may not be a deal-breaker for some applications. If the overall distance between orientations is small then this may not be a problem. The solution to this problem is our next method, "SLERP."

SLERP: Spherical linear interpolation

The key insight and difference between N-LERP and SLERP is that rather than linearly interpolating the components of the quaternion we linearly interpolate the angle, θ, itself! Because the angle itself can be incremented linearly, which maintains a constant speed of rotation, we can use this to define a new quaternion that preserves the unit-length and represents an interpolated rotation properly. Intermediate orientations representing constant-speed rotation can be calculated by interpolating directly on the surface of the unit sphere, specifically along the great arc between the two quaternion points. In the previous chapter, it was pointed out that a quaternion, $[\vec{w}, \vec{v}]$, and its negation, $[-\vec{w}, -\vec{v}]$, represent the same orientation. That means that interpolation from one orientation, represented by the

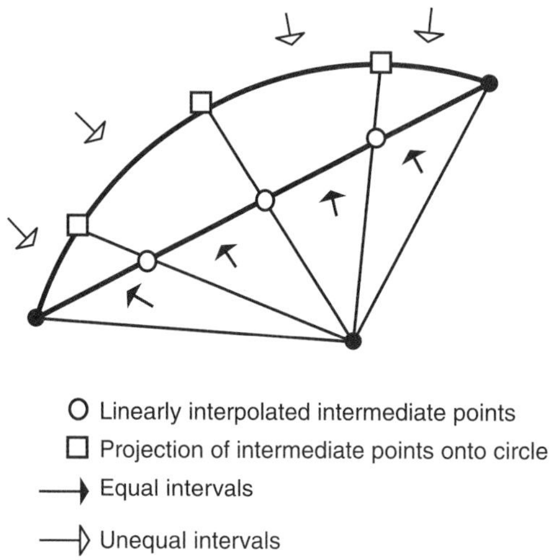

FIGURE 4.23

Equally spaced linear interpolations of straight-line path between two points on a circle generate unequal spacing of points after projecting onto a circle. Interpolating quaternion four-tuples exhibit the same problem.

quaternion $\hat{q}_1$, to another orientation, represented by the quaternion q_2, can also be carried out from $\hat{q}_1$ to $-\hat{q}_2$. The difference is that one interpolation path will be longer than the other. Usually, the shorter path is the more desirable because it represents the more direct way to get from one orientation to the other. The shorter path is the one indicated by the smaller angle between the four-dimensional quaternion vectors. This can be determined by using the four-dimensional dot product of the quaternions to compute the cosine of the angle between $\hat{q}_1$ and $\hat{q}_2$ (Eq. 4.28). If the cosine is positive, then the path from $\hat{q}_1$ to $\hat{q}_2$ is shorter; otherwise the path from $\hat{q}_1$ to $-\hat{q}_2$ is shorter (Figure 4.24).

$$\cos\theta = \hat{q}_1 \cdot \hat{q}_2 = w_1 w_2 + \vec{v}_1 \cdot \vec{v}_2 \tag{4.28}$$

The formula for spherical linear interpolation (***SLERP***) between unit quaternions $\hat{q}_1$ and $\hat{q}_2$ with parameter u varying from 0 to 1 is given in Equation 4.29, where $\hat{q}_1 \cdot \hat{q}_2 = \cos\theta$.

Note that this does not necessarily produce a unit quaternion (due to numerical error/precision), thus it is good practice to normalize the result.

Definition 4.10: Spherical Linear Interpolation (SLERP)

$$\mathbf{SLERP}(\hat{q}_1, \hat{q}_2, u) \rightarrow \hat{r}_u = \frac{\sin((1-u\theta))}{\sin(\theta)}\hat{q}_1 + \frac{\sin(u\theta)}{\sin(\theta)}\hat{q}_2 \tag{4.29}$$

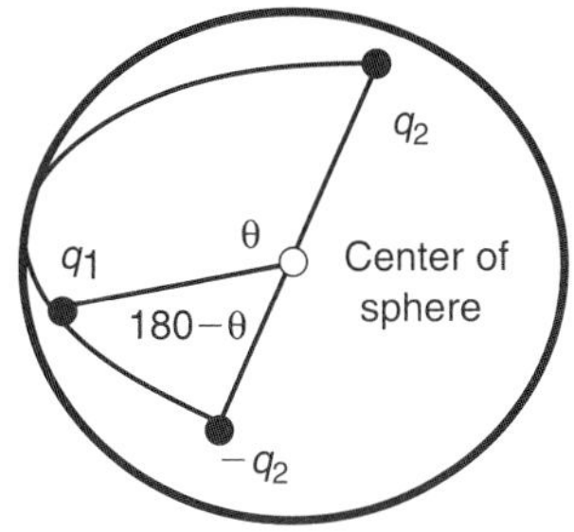

FIGURE 4.24

The closer of the two representations of orientation, q_2, is the better choice to use in interpolation. In this case $-q_2$ is closer to q_1 than q_2. The angle between q_1 and q_2, as measured from the center of the sphere, is computed by taking the dot product of q_1 and q_2. The same is done for $-q_2$.

When interpolating between a series of orientations, SLERP between points on a spherical surface has the same problem as linear interpolation between points in Euclidean space: that of first-order discontinuity (see the Appendix). Shoemake [7] suggests using cubic Bezier interpolation to smooth the interpolation between orientations. Reasonable interior control points are automatically calculated to define cubic segments between each pair of orientations.

To introduce this technique, assume for now that there is a need to interpolate between a sequence of two-dimensional points, $[\ldots, p_{n-1}, p_n, p_{n+1}, \ldots]$; these will be referred to as the *interpolated points*. (How to consider the calculations using quaternion representations is discussed below.) Between each pair of points, two control points will be constructed. For each of the interpolation points, p_n, two control points will be associated with it: the one immediately before it, b_n, and the one immediately after it, a_n.

To calculate the control point following any particular point p_n, take the vector defined by p_{n-1} to p_n and add it to the point p_n. Now, take this point (marked "1" in Figure 4.25) and find the average of it and p_{n+1}. This becomes one of the control points (marked "a_n" in Figure 4.25).

Next, take the vector defined by a_n to p_n and add it to p_n to get b_n (Figure 4.26). Points b_n and a_n are the control points immediately before and after the point p_n. This construction ensures first-order continuity at the junction of adjacent curve segments (in this case, p_n) because the control points on either side of the point are collinear with, and equidistant to, the control point itself.

The end conditions can be handled by a similar construction. For example, the first control point, a_0, is constructed as the vector from the third interpolated point to the second point $(p_1 - p_2)$ and is added to the second point (Figure 4.27).

In forming a control point, the quality of the interpolated curve can be affected by adjusting the distance the control point is from its associated interpolated point while

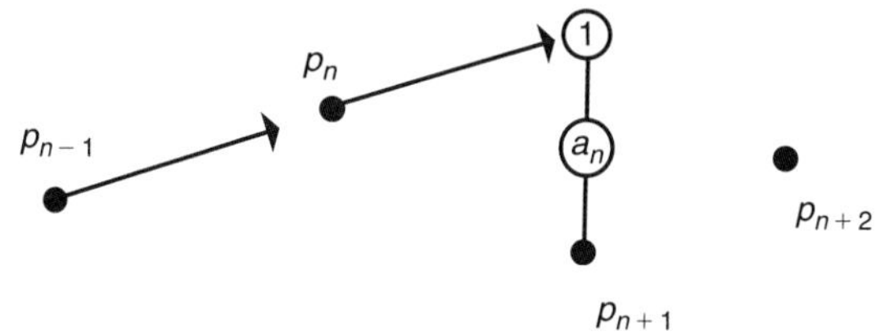

FIGURE 4.25

Finding the control point after p_n: to p_n, add the vector from p_{n-1} to p_n and average that with p_{n+1}.

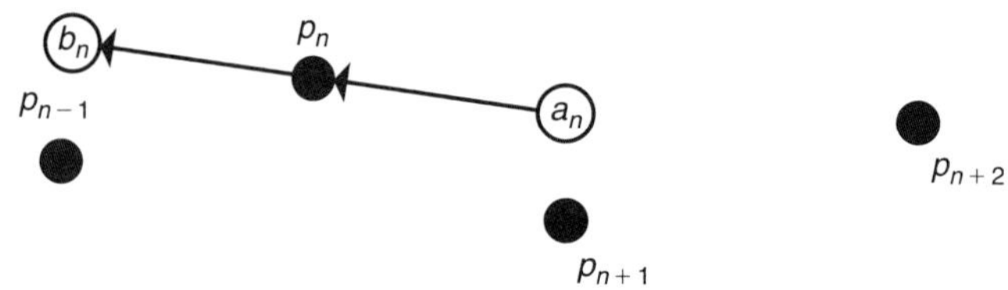

FIGURE 4.26

Finding the control point before p_n: to p_n, add the vector from a_n to p_n.

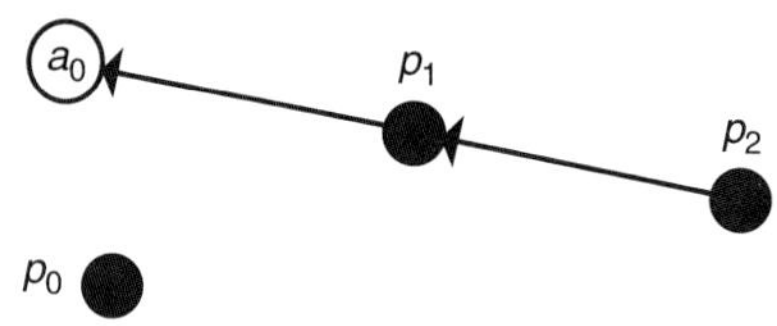

FIGURE 4.27

Constructing the first interior control point.

maintaining its direction from that interpolated point. For example, a new $b_n{}'$ can be computed with a user-specified constant, k, as in Equation 4.30 (and optionally computing a corresponding new $a_n{}'$).

$$b'_n = p_n + k(b_n - p_n) \tag{4.30}$$

Between any two interpolated points, a cubic Bezier curve segment is then defined by the points p_n, a_n, b_{n+1}, and p_{n+1}. The control point b_{n+1} is defined in exactly the same way that b_n is defined except for using p_n, p_{n+1}, and p_{n+2}. The cubic curve segment is then generated between p_n and p_{n+1} (Figure 4.28).

It should be easy to see how this procedure can be converted into the four-dimensional spherical world of quaternions. Instead of adding vectors, rotations are concatenated using quaternion multiplication. Averaging of orientations can easily be done by SLERP-ing to the halfway orientation, which is implemented by adding quaternions (and normalizing). Adding the difference between two

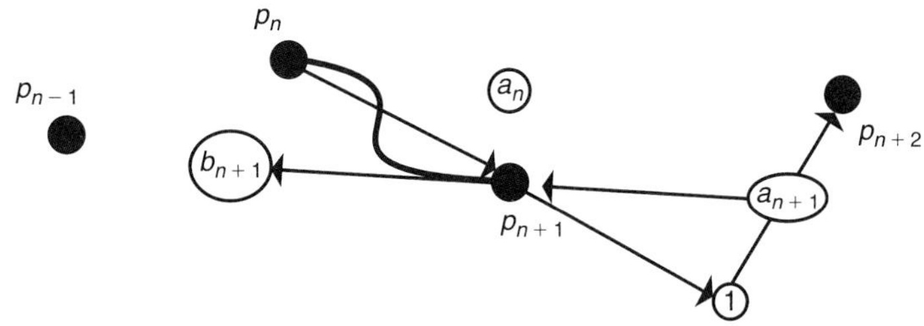

FIGURE 4.28

Construction of b_{n+1} and the resulting curve.

orientations, represented as unit quaternions $\hat{p}$ and $\hat{q}$, to the second orientation, $\hat{q}$, can be affected by constructing the representation of the result, $\hat{r}$, on the four-dimensional unit sphere using Equation 4.31. See the Appendix for further discussion.

$$\hat{r} = 2(\hat{p} \cdot \hat{q})\hat{q} - \hat{p} \tag{4.31}$$

Once the internal control points are computed, the de Casteljau algorithm can be applied to interpolate points along the curve. An example of the de Casteljau construction procedure in the two-dimensional Euclidean case of Bezier curve interpolation is shown in Figure 4.29. See the Appendix for a more complete discussion of the procedure.

The same procedure can be used to construct the Bezier curve in four-dimensional spherical space. For example, to obtain an orientation corresponding to the $u = 1/3$ position along the curve, the following orientations are computed.

```
p1 = slerp (qn,an,1/3)

p2 = slerp (an,bn+1,1/3)

p3 = slerp (bn11,qn11,1/3)

p12 = slerp (p1,p2,1/3)
```

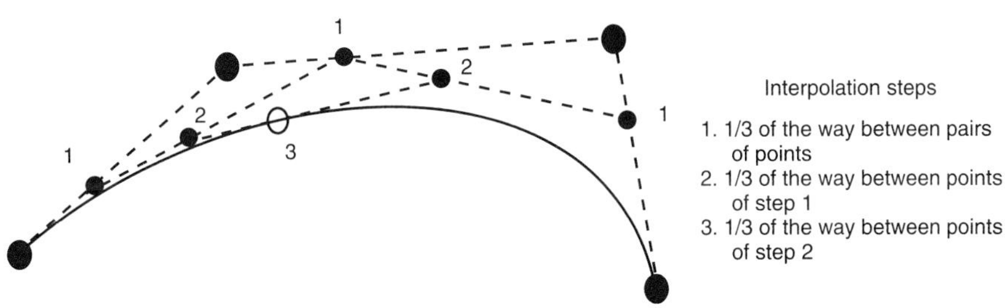

FIGURE 4.29

de Casteljau construction of point on cubic Bezier segment at 1/3 (the point labeled "3").

```
p23 = slerp (p2,p3,1/3)

p = slerp (p12,p23,1/3)
```

where p is the quaternion representing an orientation 1/3 along the spherical cubic spline.

The procedure can be made especially efficient in the case of quaternion representations when calculating points at positions along the curve corresponding to u values that are powers of 1/2. For example, consider calculating a point at $u = 1/4$.

$$
\begin{aligned}
tmp &= \mathbf{SLERP}(\hat{q}_n, \hat{a}_n, 1/2) &&= (\hat{q}_n + \hat{a}_n)/||\hat{q}_n + \hat{a}_n|| \\
\hat{p}_1 &= \mathbf{SLERP}(\hat{q}_n, tmp, 1/2) &&= (\hat{q}_n + tmp)/||\hat{q}_n + tmp|| \\
tmp &= \mathbf{SLERP}(\hat{a}_n, \hat{b}_{n11}, 1/2) &&= (\hat{a}_n + \hat{b}_{n11})/||\hat{a}_n + \hat{b}_{n11}|| \\
\hat{p}_2 &= \mathbf{SLERP}(\hat{a}_n, tmp, 1/2) &&= (\hat{a}_n + tmp)/||\hat{a}_n + tmp|| \\
tmp &= \mathbf{SLERP}(\hat{b}_{n11}, \hat{q}_{n11}, 1/2) &&= (\hat{b}_{n+1} + \hat{q}_{n11})/||\hat{b}_{n+1} + \hat{q}_{n11}|| \\
\hat{p}_3 &= \mathbf{SLERP}(\hat{b}_{n11}, tmp, 1/2) &&= (\hat{b}_{n+1} + tmp)/||\hat{b}_{n+1} + tmp|| \\
tmp &= \mathbf{SLERP}(\hat{p}_1, \hat{p}_2, 1/2) &&= (\hat{p}_1 + \hat{p}_2)/||\hat{p}_1 + \hat{p}_2|| \\
\hat{p}_{12} &= \mathbf{SLERP}(\hat{p}_1, tmp, 1/2) &&= (\hat{p}_1 + tmp)/||\hat{p}_1 + tmp|| \\
temp &= \mathbf{SLERP}(\hat{p}_2, \hat{p}_3, 1/2) &&= (\hat{p}_2 + \hat{p}_3)/||\hat{p}_2 + \hat{p}_3|| \\
\hat{p}_{23} &= \mathbf{SLERP}(\hat{p}_2, tmp, 1/2) &&= (\hat{p}_2 + tmp)/||\hat{p}_2 + tmp|| \\
tmp &= \mathbf{SLERP}(\hat{p}_{12}, \hat{p}_{23}, 1/2) &&= (\hat{p}_{12} + \hat{p}_{23})/||\hat{p}_{12} + \hat{p}_{23}|| \\
\hat{p} &= \mathbf{SLERP}(\hat{p}_{12}, tmp, 1/2) &&= (\hat{p}_{12} + tmp)/||\hat{p}_{12} + tmp||
\end{aligned}
$$

The procedure can be made more efficient if the points are generated in order according to binary subdivision (1/2, 1/4, 3/4, 1/8, 3/8, 5/8, 7/8, 1/16, ...) and temporary values are saved for use in subsequent calculations.

4.5 Working with paths

Definition 4.11

A path is defined as a consecutive set of keyframes with intervals in-between each pair of keys, each interval has a (potentially different) interpolating function:

$$
\mathbf{PATH}(\{K_i\}_0^n, \{T_j, F_j\}_0^{n-1}) \rightarrow
$$

$$
\begin{aligned}
\{K_i\}_0^n &= \{k_1, k_2 \ldots, k_n\} \text{ set of n-keyframes} \\
\{T_j\}_0^{n-1} &= \{t_0^1, t_1^2, \ldots T_{n-1}^n\} \text{ set of time intervals} \\
\{F_j\}_0^{n-1} &= \{f_0^1, f_1^2, \ldots, f_{n-1}^n\} \text{ set of interpolating functions}
\end{aligned}
$$

4.5.1 Path following

Animating an object by moving it along a path is a very common technique and usually one of the simplest to implement. As with most other types of animation, however, issues may arise that make the task more complicated than first envisioned. An object (or camera) following a path requires more than just translating along a space curve, even if the curve is parameterized by arc length and the speed is controlled using ease-in/ease-out. Changing the orientation of the object also has to be taken into consideration. If the path is the result of a digitization process, then often it must be smoothed before it can be used. If the path is constrained to lie on the surface of another object or needs to avoid other objects, then more computation is involved. These issues are discussed below.

4.5.2 Orientation along a path

Typically, a local coordinate system (u, v, w) is defined for an object to be animated. In this discussion, a right-handed coordinate system is assumed, with the origin of the coordinate system determined by a point along the path $\boldsymbol{P}(s)$. As previously discussed, this point is generated based on the frame number, arc length parameterization, and possibly ease-in/ease-out control. This position will be referred to as *POS*. The direction the object is facing is identified with the w-axis, the up vector is identified with the v-axis, and the local u-axis is perpendicular to these two, completing the coordinate system. To form a right-handed coordinate system, for example, the u-axis points to the left of the object as someone at the object's position (*POS*) looks down the w-axis with the head aligned with the v-axis (Figure 4.30).

There are various ways to handle the orientation of the camera as it travels along a path. Of course, which method to use depends on the desired effect of the animation. The orientation is specified by determining the direction it is pointing (the w-axis) and the direction of its up vector (the v-axis); the u-axis is then fully specified by completing the left-handed camera coordinate system (eye space).

Use of the Frenet frame

If an object or camera is following a path, then its orientation can be made directly dependent on the properties of the curve. The Frenet frame[4] can be defined along the curve as a moving coordinate system, $\left[\vec{u}, \vec{v}, \vec{w}\right]$, determined by the curve's tangent and curvature. The Frenet frame changes orientation over the length of the curve. It is defined as normalized orthogonal vectors with w in the direction of the first derivative $(\mathbf{P}(\vec{s}))$, $\vec{v}$ orthogonal to $\vec{w}$ and in the general direction of the second derivative $(\mathbf{P}(\vec{s}))$, and $\vec{u}$ formed to complete, for example, a left-handed coordinate

[4] Note the potential source of confusion between the use of the term frame to mean (1) a frame of animation and (2) the moving coordinate system of the Frenet frame. The context in which the term frame is used should determine its meaning.

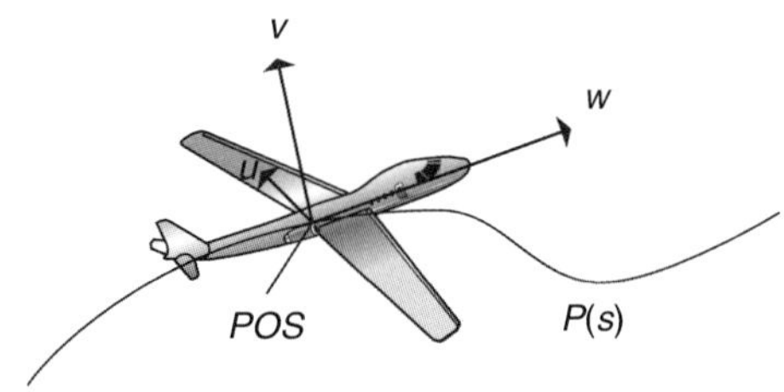

FIGURE 4.30

Object-based, right-handed, local coordinate system.

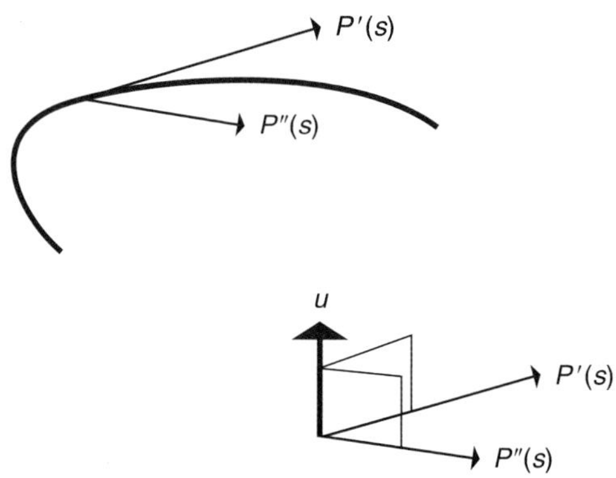

FIGURE 4.31

The derivatives at a point along the curve are used to form the *u* vector.

system as computed in a right-handed space (Figure 4.31). Specifically, at a given parameter value *s*, the left-handed Frenet frame is calculated according to Equation 4.32, as illustrated in Figure 4.32. The vectors are then normalized.

$$\begin{aligned} \widehat{w} &= \mathbf{P}'(\vec{s}) \\ \widehat{u} &= \mathbf{P}'(\vec{s}) \times \mathbf{P}''(\vec{s}) \\ \widehat{v} &= \vec{u} \times \vec{w} \end{aligned} \tag{4.32}$$

Although the Frenet frame provides useful information about the curve, there are a few problems with using it directly to control the orientation of a camera or object as it moves along a curve. First, there is no concept of "up" inherent in the formation of the Frenet frame. The *v* vector merely lines up with the direction of the second derivative. Another problem occurs in segments of the curve that have no curvature $(\mathbf{P}(\vec{u}) = 0)$ because the Frenet frame is undefined. These undefined segments can be dealt with by interpolating a Frenet frame along the segment from the Frenet frames at the boundary of the segment. By definition, there is no curvature along this segment, so the boundary Frenet frames must differ by only a rotation around *w*. Assuming that the vectors have already been normalized, the angular difference

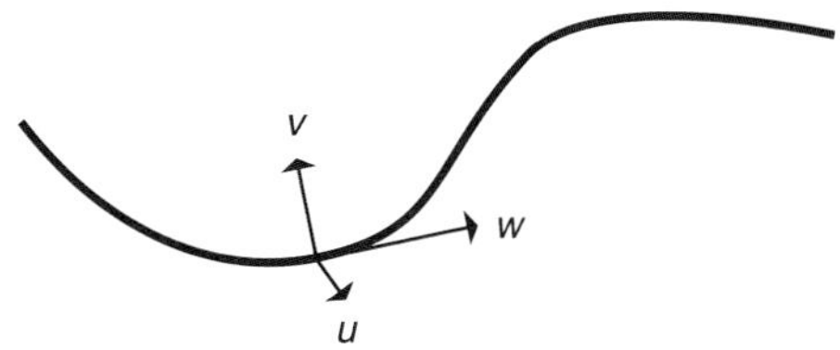

FIGURE 4.32

Left-handed Frenet frame at a point along a curve.

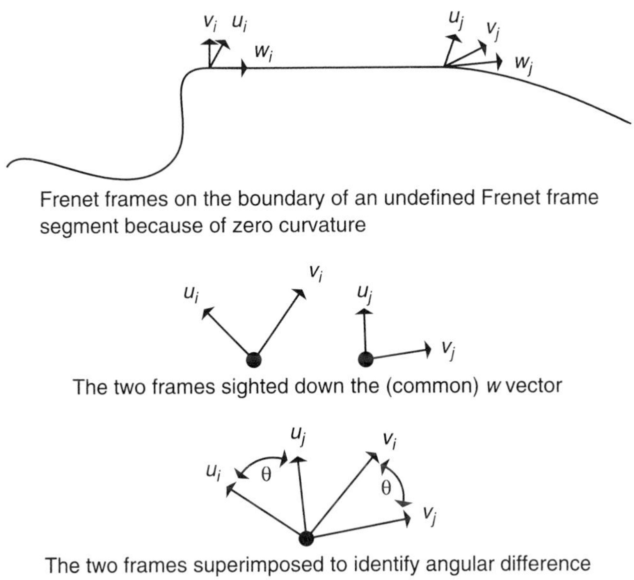

FIGURE 4.33

Interpolating Frenet frames to determine the undefined segment.

between the two can be determined by taking the arccosine of the dot product between the two v vectors so that $\theta = \left(\vec{v}_1 \cdot \vec{v}_2\right)$. This rotation can be linearly interpolated along the no-curvature segment (Figure 4.33).

The problem is more difficult to deal with when there is a discontinuity in the curvature vector as is common with piecewise cubic curves. Consider, for example, a curve composed of two semicircular segments positioned so that they form an **S** (*sigmoidal*) shape. The curvature vector, which for any point along this curve will point to the center of the semicircle that the point is on, will instantaneously switch from pointing to one center point to pointing to the other center point at the junction of the two semicircular segments. In this case, the Frenet frame is defined everywhere but has a discontinuous jump in orientation at the junction (Figure 4.34).

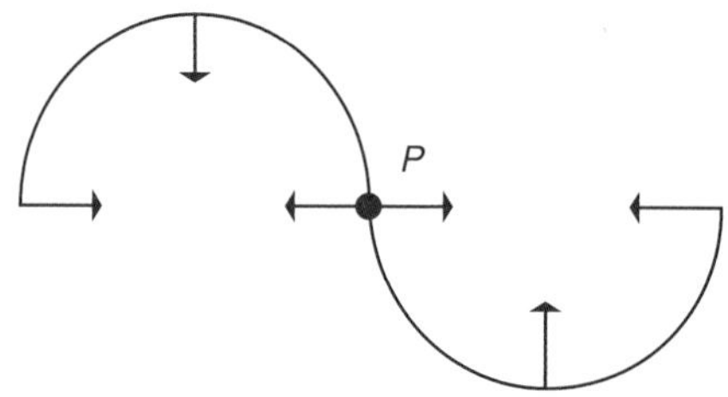

FIGURE 4.34

The curvature vector, defined everywhere but discontinuous, instantaneously switches direction at point *P*.

However, the main problem with using the Frenet frame as the local coordinate frame to define the orientation of the camera or object following the path is that the resulting motions are usually too extreme and not natural looking. Using the *w*-axis (tangent vector) as the view direction of a camera can be undesirable. Often, the tangent vector does not appear to correspond to the direction of "where it's going" even though it is in the instantaneous (analytic) sense. The more natural orientation, for someone riding in a car or riding a bike, for example, would be to look farther ahead along the curve rather than to look tangential to the current location along the curve.

In addition, if the *v*-axis is equated with the up vector of an object, the object will rotate wildly about the path even when the path appears to mildly meander through an environment. With three-dimensional space curves, the problem becomes more obvious as the path bends up and down in space; the camera will flip between being upright and traveling along the path upside down. Although the Frenet frame provides useful information to the animator, its direct use to control object orientation is clearly of limited value. When modeling the motion of banking into a turn, the curvature vector (*u*-axis) does indicate which way to bank and can be used to control the magnitude of the bank. For example, the horizontal component (the component in the *x*-*z* plane) of the *u*-axis can be used as the direction/magnitude indicator for the bank. For a different effect, the animator may want the object to tilt away from the curvature vector to give the impression of the object feeling a force that throws it off the path, such as a person riding a roller coaster.

Camera path following

The simplest method of specifying the orientation of a camera is to set its center of interest (COI) to a fixed point in the environment or, more elegantly, to use the center point of one of the objects in the environment. In either case, the COI is directly determined and is available for calculating the view vector, $\vec{w} = COI - POS$. This is usually a good method when the path that the camera is following is one that circles some arena of action on which the camera's attention must be focused.

This still leaves one degree of freedom to be determined to fully specify the local coordinate system. For now, assume that the up vector, $\vec{v}$, is to be kept "up." *Up* in this case means "generally in the positive y-axis direction," or, for a more mathematical definition, the v-axis is at right angles to the view vector (w-axis) and is to lie in the plane defined by the local w-axis and the global y-axis. The local coordinate system can be computed as shown in Equation 4.33 for a left-handed camera coordinate-system computed in right-handed space. The vectors can then be normalized to produce unit length vectors.

$$\begin{aligned} \vec{w} &= COI - POS \\ \vec{u} &= \vec{w} \times (0,1,0) \\ \vec{v} &= \vec{u} \times \vec{w} \end{aligned} \tag{4.33}$$

For a camera traveling down a path, the view direction can be automatically set in several ways. As previously mentioned, the COI can be set to a specific point in the environment or to the position of a specific object in the environment. This works well as long as there is a single point or single object on which the camera should focus and as long as the camera does not pass too close to the point or object. Passing close to the COI will result in radical changes in view direction (in some cases, the resulting effect may be desirable). Other methods use points along the path itself, a separate path through the environment, or interpolation between positions in the environment. The up vector can also be set in several ways. The default orientation is for the up vector to lie in the plane of the view vector and the global y-axis. Alternatively, a tilt of the up vector can be specified away from the default orientation as a user-specified value (or interpolated set of values). And, finally, the up vector can be explicitly specified by the user.

The simplest method of setting the view vector is to use a delta parametric value to define the COI. If the position of the camera on a curve is defined by $\boldsymbol{P}(s)$, then the COI will be $\boldsymbol{P}(s+\Delta s)$. This, of course, should be after reparameterization by arc length. Otherwise, the actual distance to the COI along the path will vary over time (although if a relatively large Δu is used, the variation may not be noticeable). At the end of the curve, once $s + \Delta s$ is beyond the path parameterization, the view direction can be interpolated to the end tangent vector as s approaches 1 (in the case that distance is normalized).

Often, updating the COI to be a specific point along the curve can result in views that appear jerky. In such cases, averaging some number of positions along the curve to be the COI point can smooth the view. However, if the number of points used is too small or the points are too close together, the view may remain jerky. If n is too large and the points are spaced out too much, the view direction may not change significantly during the traversal of the path and will appear too static. The number of points to use and their spread along the curve are dependent on the path itself and on the effect desired by the animator.

An alternative to using some function of the position path to produce the COI is to use a separate path altogether to define the COI. In this case, the camera's position is specified by $\boldsymbol{P}(s)$, whereas the COI is specified by some $\boldsymbol{C}(s)$. This requires more work by the animator but provides greater control and more flexibility.

Similarly, an up vector path, $U(s)$, might be specified so that the general up direction is defined by $U(s) - P(s)$. This is just the general direction because a valid up vector must be perpendicular to the view vector. Thus, the coordinate frame for the camera could be defined as in Equation 4.34.

$$\begin{aligned} \vec{w} &= \mathbf{C}(s) - \mathbf{P}(s) \\ \vec{u} &= \vec{w} \times (\mathbf{U}(s) - \mathbf{P}(s)) \\ \vec{v} &= \vec{u} \times \vec{w} \end{aligned} \tag{4.34}$$

Instead of using a separate path for the COI, a simple but effective strategy is to fix it at one location for an interval of time and then move it to another location (using linear spatial interpolation and ease-in/ease-out temporal interpolation) and fix it there for a number of frames, and so on. The up vector can be set as before in the default "up" direction.

4.5.3 Smoothing a path

For cases in which the points making up a path are generated by a digitizing process, the resulting curve can be too jerky because of noise or imprecision. To remove the jerkiness, the coordinate values of the data can be smoothed by one of several approaches. For this discussion, the following set of data will be used: {(1, 1.6), (2, 1.65), (3, 1.6), (4, 1.8), (5, 2.1), (6, 2.2), (7, 2.0), (8, 1.5), (9, 1.3), (10, 1.4)}. This is plotted in Figure 4.35.

Smoothing with linear interpolation of adjacent values

An ordered set of points in two-space can be smoothed by averaging adjacent points. In the simplest case, the two points, one on either side of an original point, P_i, are averaged. This point is averaged with the original data point (Eq. 4.35). Figure 4.36 shows the sample data plotted with the original data. Notice how linear interpolation tends to draw the data points in the direction of local concavities. Repeated applications of the linear interpolation to further smooth the data would continue to draw the reduced concave sections and flatten out the curve.

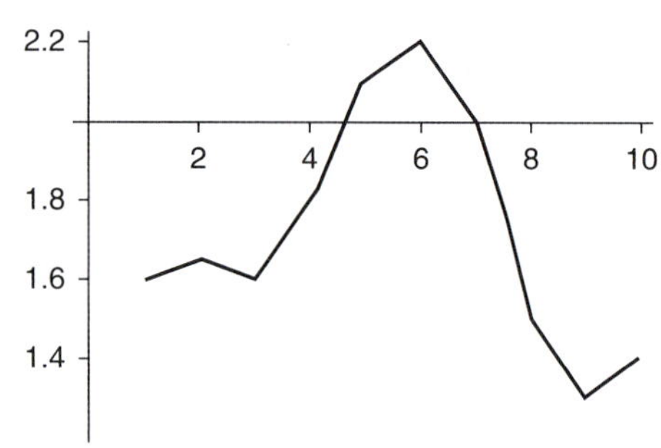

FIGURE 4.35

Sample data for path smoothing.

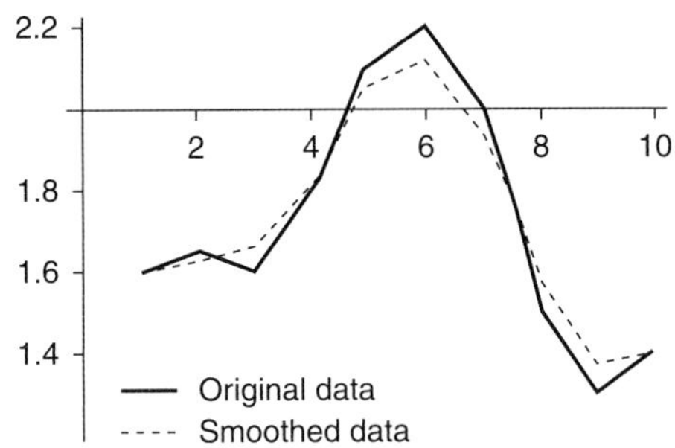

FIGURE 4.36

Sample data smoothed by linear interpolation.

$$P'_i = \frac{P_i + \dfrac{P_{i-1} + P_{i+1}}{2}}{2} = \frac{1}{4}P_{i-1} + \frac{1}{2}P_i + \frac{1}{4}P_{i+1} \tag{4.35}$$

Smoothing with cubic interpolation of adjacent values

To preserve the curvature but still smooth the data, the adjacent points on either side of a data point can be used to fit a cubic curve that is then evaluated at its midpoint. This midpoint is then averaged with the original point, as in the linear case. A cubic curve has the form shown in Equation 4.36. The two data points on either side of an original point, P_i, are used as constraints, as shown in Equation 4.37. These equations can be used to solve for the constants of the cubic curve (a, b, c, d). Equation 4.36 is then evaluated at $u = 1/2$; and the result is averaged with the original data point (Figure 4.37). Solving for the coefficients and evaluating the resulting cubic curve is a bit tedious, but the solution needs to be performed only once and can be put in terms of the original data points, $P_{i-2}, P_{i-1}, P_{i+1}$, and P_{i+2}. This is illustrated in Figure 4.38.

$$P(u) = au^3 + bu^2 + cu + d \tag{4.36}$$

$$\begin{aligned}
P_{i-2} &= \mathbf{P}(0) = d \\
P_{i-1} &= \mathbf{P}\left(\frac{1}{4}\right) = a\frac{1}{64} + b\frac{1}{16} + c\frac{1}{4} + d \\
P_{i+1} &= \mathbf{P}\left(\frac{3}{4}\right) = a\frac{27}{64} + b\frac{9}{16} + c\frac{3}{4} + d \\
P_{i+2} &= a + b + c + d
\end{aligned} \tag{4.37}$$

For the end conditions, a parabolic arc can be fit through the first, third, and fourth points, and an estimate for the second point from the start of the dataset can be computed (Figure 4.39). The coefficients of the parabolic equation, $\boldsymbol{P}(u) = au^2 + bu + c$, can be computed from the constraints in Equation 4.38, and the equation can be used to solve for the position $P_1 = \boldsymbol{P}(1/3)$.

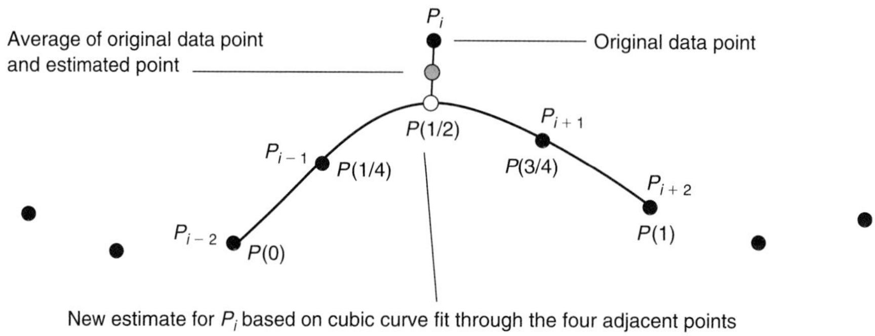

FIGURE 4.37

Smoothing data by cubic interpolation.

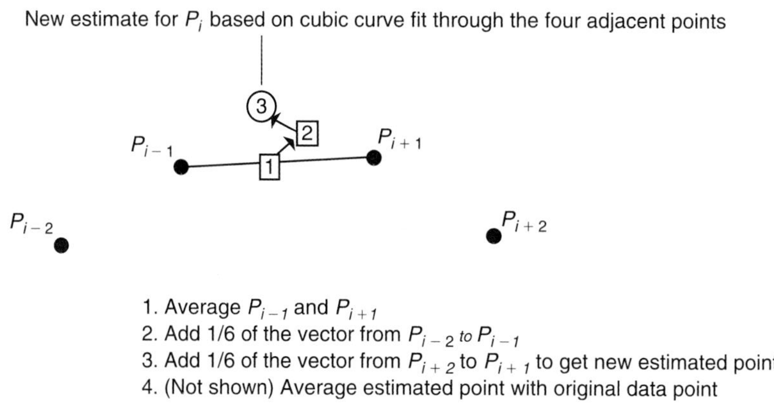

FIGURE 4.38

Geometric construction of a cubic estimate for smoothing a data point.

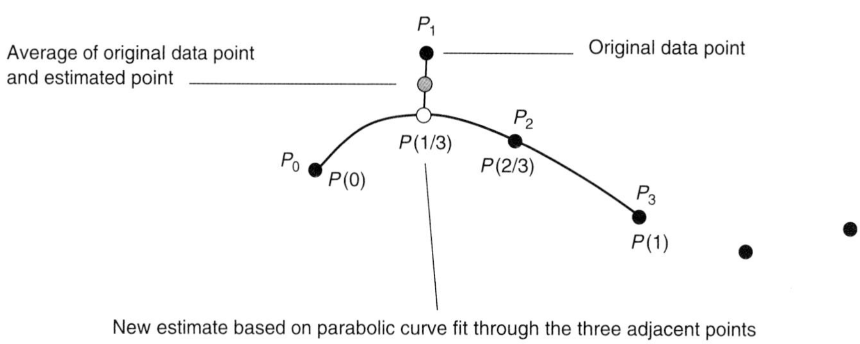

FIGURE 4.39

Smoothing data by parabolic interpolation.

$$P_0 = \mathbf{P}(\mathbf{0}), P_2 = \mathbf{P}\left(\frac{2}{3}\right), P_3 = \mathbf{P}(1) \tag{4.38}$$

This can be rewritten in geometric form and the point can be constructed geometrically from the three points $P'_1 = P_2 + (1/3)(P_0 - P_3)$ (Figure 4.40). A similar procedure can be used to estimate the data point second from the end. The very first and very last data points can be left alone if they represent hard constraints, or parabolic interpolation can be used to generate estimates for them as well, for example, $P'_0 = P_3 + 3(P_1 - P_2)$. Figure 4.41 shows cubic interpolation to smooth the data with and without parabolic interpolation for the endpoints.

Smoothing with convolution kernels

When the data to be smoothed can be viewed as a value of a function, $y_i = f(x_i)$, the data can be smoothed by convolution. Figure 4.42 shows such a function where the x_i

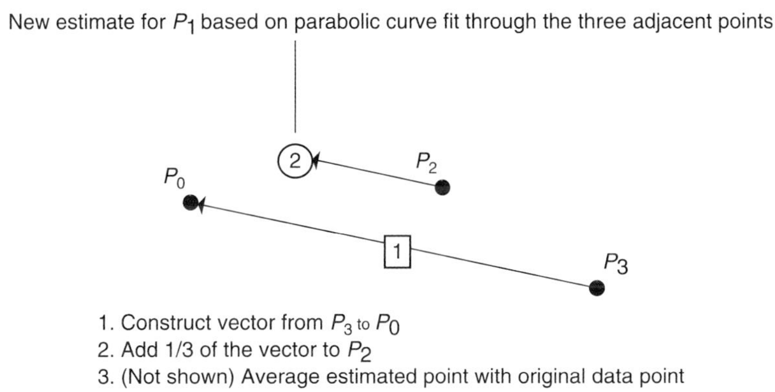

FIGURE 4.40

Geometric construction of a parabolic estimate for smoothing a data point.

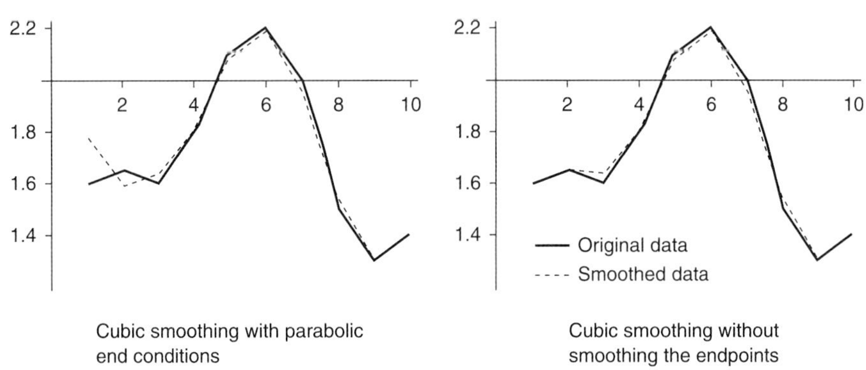

FIGURE 4.41

Sample data smoothed with cubic interpolation.

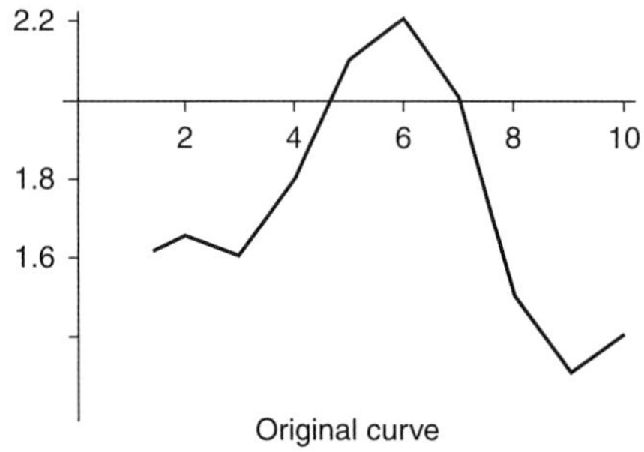

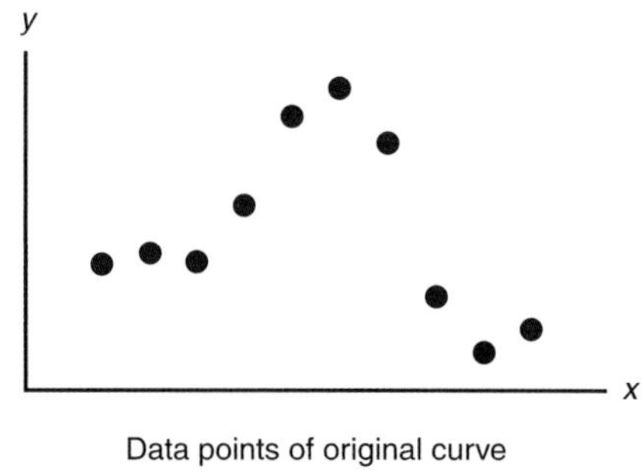

FIGURE 4.42

Sample function to be smoothed.

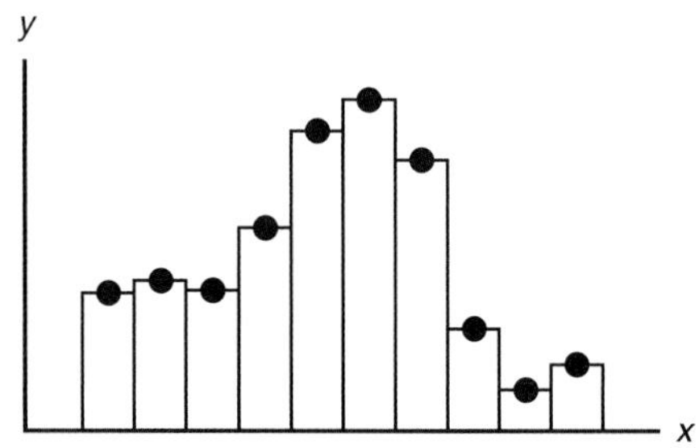

FIGURE 4.43

Step function defined by data points of the original curve.

are equally spaced. A smoothing kernel can be applied to the data points by viewing them as a step function (Figure 4.43). Desirable attributes of a smoothing kernel include the following: it is centered around 0, it is symmetric, it has finite support, and the area under the kernel curve equals 1. Figure 4.44 shows examples of some possibilities. A new point is calculated by centering the kernel function at the position where the new point is to be computed. The new point is calculated by summing the area under the curve that results from multiplying the kernel function, $g(u)$, by the corresponding segment of the step function, $f(x)$, beneath it (i.e., *convolution*). Figure 4.45 shows a simple tent-shaped kernel applied to a step function. In the continuous case, this becomes the integral, as shown in Equation 4.39, where $[-s, \ldots, s]$ is the extent of the support of the kernel function.

$$\mathbf{P}(x) = \int_{-s}^{s} f(x+u)g(u)du \tag{4.39}$$

The integral can be analytically computed or approximated by discrete means. This can be done either with or without averaging down the number of points making up the path. Additional points can also be interpolated. At the endpoints, the step

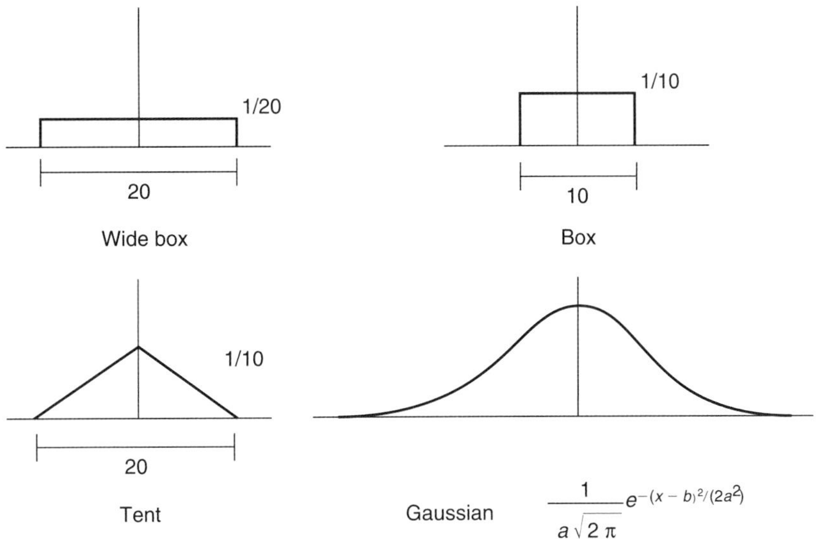

$$\frac{1}{a\sqrt{2\pi}}e^{-(x-b)^2/(2a^2)}$$

FIGURE 4.44

Sample smoothing kernels.

function can be arbitrarily extended so as to cover the kernel function when centered over the endpoints. Often the first and last points must be fixed because of animation constraints, so care must be taken in processing these. Figure 4.45 shows how a tent kernel is used to average the step function data; Figure 4.46 shows the sample data smoothed with the tent kernel.

Smoothing by B-spline approximation

Finally, if an approximation to the curve is sufficient, then points can be selected from the curve, and, for example, B-spline control points can be generated based on the selected points. The curve can then be regenerated using the B-spline control points, which ensures that the regenerated curve is smooth even though it no longer passes through the original points.

4.5.4 Determining a path along a surface

If one object is to move across the surface of another object, then a path across the surface must be determined. If start and destination points are known, it can be computationally expensive to find the shortest path between the points. However, it is not often necessary to find the absolute shortest path. Various alternatives exist for determining suboptimal yet reasonably direct paths.

An easy way to determine a path along a polygonal surface mesh is to determine a plane that contains the two points and is generally perpendicular to the surface. *Generally perpendicular* can be defined, for example, as the plane containing the

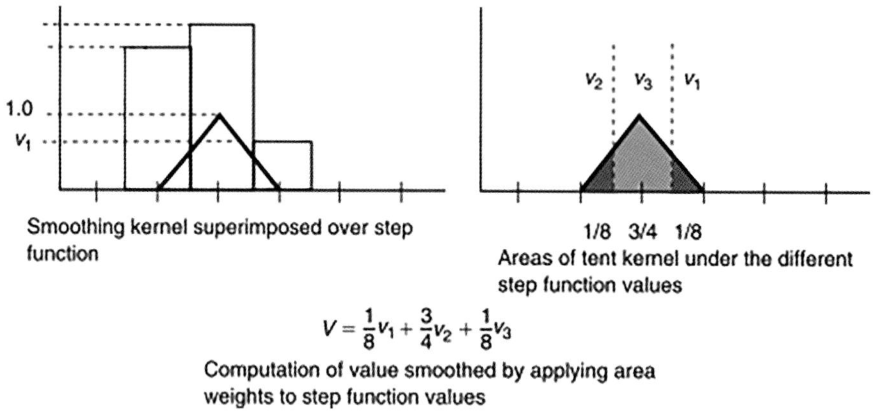

FIGURE 4.45

Example of a tent-shaped smoothing filter.

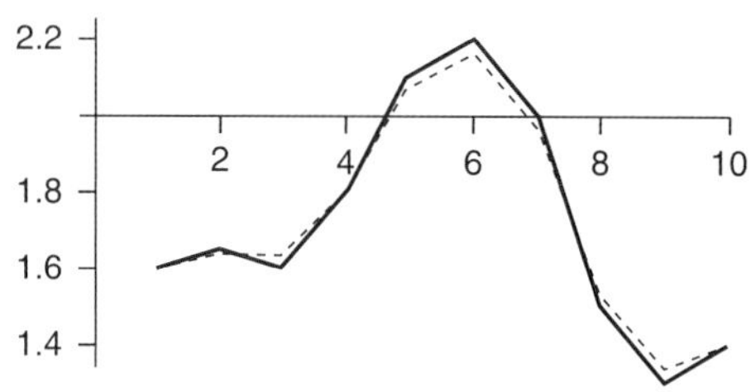

FIGURE 4.46

Sample data smoothed with convolution using a tent kernel.

two vertices and the average of the two vertex normals that the path is being formed between. The intersection of the plane with the faces making up the surface mesh will define a path between the two points (Figure 4.47).

If the surface is a higher-order surface and the known points are defined in the u, v coordinates of the surface definition, then a straight line (or curve) can be defined in the parametric space and transferred to the surface. A linear interpolation of u, v coordinates does not guarantee the most direct route, but it should produce a reasonably short path.

Over a complex surface mesh, a greedy-type algorithm can be used to construct a path of edges along a surface from a given start vertex to a given destination vertex. For each edge emanating from the current vertex (initially the start vertex), calculate the projection of the edge onto the unit vector from the current vertex to the destination vertex. Divide this distance by the length of the edge to get the cosine of the angle between the edge and the straight line. The edge with the largest cosine is the

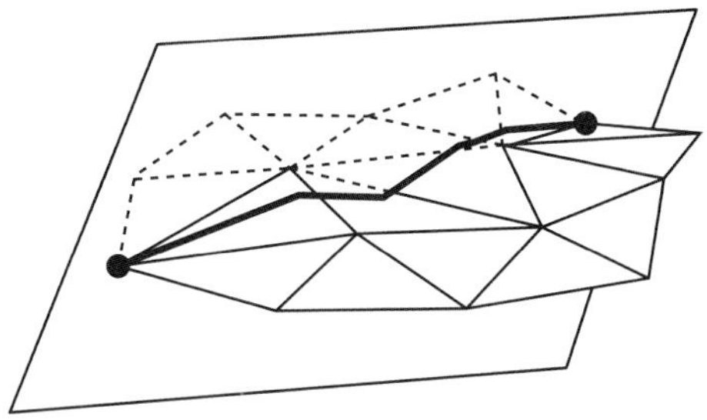

FIGURE 4.47

Determining a path along a polygonal surface mesh by using plane intersection.

edge most in the direction of the straight line; choose this edge to add to the path. Keep applying this until the destination edge is reached. Improvements to this approach can be made by allowing the path to cut across polygons to arrive at points along edges rather than by going vertex to vertex. For example, using the current path point and the line from the start and end vertices to form a plane, intersect the plane with the plane of the current triangle. If the line of intersection falls inside of the current triangle, use the segment inside of the triangle as part of the path. If the line of intersection leaving the current vertex is outside of the triangle, find the adjacent triangle and use it as the current triangle, and repeat. For the initial plane, the start and end vertex can be used along with some point on the surface that is judged to lie in the general direction of the path that is yet to be determined.

If a path downhill from an initial point on the surface is desired, then the surface normal and global "up" vector can be used to determine the downhill vector. The cross-product of the normal and global up vector defines a vector that lies on the surface perpendicular to the downhill direction. So the cross-product of this vector and the normal vector define the downhill (and uphill) vector on a plane (Figure 4.48). This same approach works with curved surfaces to produce the instantaneous downhill vector.

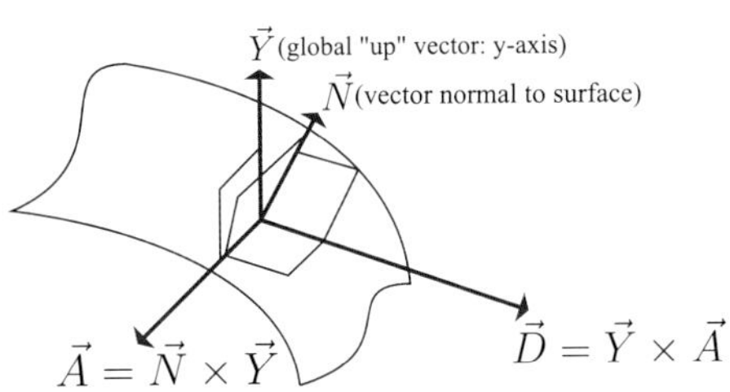

FIGURE 4.48

Calculating the downhill vector, *D*.

4.6 Chapter summary

Interpolation is fundamental to animation, and the ability to understand and control the interpolation process is extremely important in programming computer animation systems. As we have seen, interpolation can be performed using various forms and models for the interpolation functions. All forms of data can be interpolated including pixel color/opacity, position, orientation, and shape parameters. Controlling this process can be done using keyframes, reparameterizing using arc length and numerical methods, or analytically determined. In any case, interpolation forms the foundation for all computer animation techniques/algorithms, animation software, and video game engines.

4.7 Exercises

Beginner

B1. Convert the following times to the indicated format:

a. $1.5s \rightarrow ms$
b. $190288ms \rightarrow s$
c. $6.54s \rightarrow frames$ @ $30fps$
d. $973467\, frame \rightarrow ms$ @ $60fps$

B2. Suppose you have a 10 minute animation clip (@ 30fps) with 3 important intervals defined as:

$$\textbf{Interval}_1 = [2.5s, 3\ min], \textbf{Interval}_2 = [4\ min, 00::06::50::23], \textbf{Interval}_1 = [00::06::51::23, 00::09::45::14].$$

a. Determine the duration of each interval.
b. Express each interval in
  i. timecode format
  ii. seconds
  iii. frames
c. For the following times, determine the interval in which they sample, compute which frame it refers to, and express the normalized time code of the frame relative to the clip.
  i. 12s, 13s, 175s, 321s, 244s
  ii. 00::00:11::11, 00::02:27::08, 00::05:54::25, 00::07:02::19, 00::09:43::05

B3. Given the following sets of endpoints, $\vec{p}_1, \vec{p}_2$, and interpolating parameter, $t \in [0, 1]$, use LERP to compute the interpolated point.

a. $\vec{p}_1 = (1, 4, -1), \vec{p}_2 = (10, -4, 9), t = 0.2$
b. $\vec{p}_1 = (5, 4, -6), \vec{p}_2 = (-10, 9, 50), t = 0.2$
c. $\vec{p}_1 = (2, -12, 8), \vec{p}_2 = (21, 4, 5), t = 0.16$

d. $\vec{p}_1 = (8,7,2), \vec{p}_2 = (53,5,3), t = 0.57$
e. $\vec{p}_1 = (6, -40, 7), \vec{p}_2 = (-78,7,2), t = 0.89$
f. $\vec{p}_1 = (100, -4, 5), \vec{p}_2 = (73,9,1), t = 0.76$

B4. Given the following sets of four points, $\vec{p}_1, \vec{p}_2, \vec{p}_3, \vec{p}_4$, and interpolating parameter, $t \in [0, 1]$, draw the spline on a graph and use Catmull-Rom interpolation to compute the interpolated point on the cubic spline.
a. $\vec{p}_1 = (-1,4), \vec{p}_2 = (-4,9), \vec{p}_3 = (5,4), \vec{p}_4 = (9,5), t = 0.2$
b. $\vec{p}_1 = (1,4), \vec{p}_2 = (2,5), \vec{p}_3 = (7,2), \vec{p}_4 = (9,3), t = 0.57$
c. $\vec{p}_1 = (-6, -7), \vec{p}_2 = (-7,2), \vec{p}_3 = (-4,5), \vec{p}_4 = (9,1), t = 0.76$

B5. Given the following sets of four points, $\vec{p}_1, \vec{p}_2, \vec{p}_3, \vec{p}_4$, and interpolating parameter, $t \in [0, 1]$, draw the spline on a graph and use Bezier interpolation (Hermite form) to compute the interpolated point on the cubic spline. For this use $\vec{p}_2, \vec{p}_3$ as the tangents connected to the endpoints.
a. $\vec{p}_1 = (0,4), \vec{p}_2 = (-4,9), \vec{p}_3 = (5,4), \vec{p}_4 = (5,9), t = 0.2$
b. $\vec{p}_1 = (1,0), \vec{p}_2 = (5,3), \vec{p}_3 = (7, -2), \vec{p}_4 = (3,8), t = 0.57$
c. $\vec{p}_1 = (-6, -7), \vec{p}_2 = (-2,0), \vec{p}_3 = (4, -5), \vec{p}_4 = (1,7), t = 0.76$
d. Do a, b, and c again using the LERP form of Bezier interpolation.

Intermediate

I1. For the following axis-angle rotations, $(\vec{a}_1, \theta_1), (\vec{a}_2, \theta_2)$, compute their quaternion representations $(\hat{q}_1, \hat{q}_2)$ and compare the results of N-LERP and SLERP of each pair given the list of interpolating parameters $u \in [0, 1]$.
a. $\vec{a}_1 = (1,0,0), \theta_1 = 25°, \vec{a}_2 = (0,1,0), \theta_2 = 90°, u = \{0.5, 0.75\}$
b. $\vec{a}_1 = (0,0,1), \theta_1 = 25°, \vec{a}_2 = (0,1,0), \theta_2 = 90°, u = \{0.5, 0.6\}$
c. $\vec{a}_1 = (0,0,1), \theta_1 = 25°, \vec{a}_2 = (1,0,0), \theta_2 = 90°, u = \{0.8, 0.1\}$

I2. Given the Bezier spline: $\vec{p}_1 = (-6, -7, 1), \vec{p}_2 = (-2,0,0), \vec{p}_3 = (4, -5, 2), \vec{p}_4 = (1,7, -1)$:
a. Compute the Frenet frame at $t = \{0.3, 0.4, 0.7\}$.
b. Compute the arc length by sampling the spline with a step of 0.1, compute the straight line distance between subsequent samples, and compute the total cumulative distance.

Advanced

A1. Given the Bezier spline from the previous question, compute the arc length using an adaptive Gaussian scheme. Write a function in your engine/language of choice that takes a Bezier curve and which sampling scheme (adaptive, nonadaptive), and returns the arc length at a specified sampling time. Write unit-tests to evaluate your results.

A2. In a game engine/language of your choice, compute a path-following system that has the following features:

  a. You can specify a path as a set of points.

  b. You can select each interval and specify the interpolation scheme as either LERP, Catmull-Rom, or Bezier. When Bezier is selected, allow the user to specify the tangents for the interval.

  c. Place an object at the start of the path and use your system to update the location of the object over time.

  d. Compute the arc length of each interval and ensure that your movement maintains a constant/controllable speed.

  e. Add functionality to compute the Frenet frame and apply the resulting orientation to your object at each step.

References

[1] Burden R, Faires J. Numerical analysis. 8th ed. Brooks-Cole; 2005.

[2] Guenter B, Parent R. Computing the arc length of parametric curves. IEEE Comput Graph Appl 1990;10(3):72−8.

[3] Judd C, Hartley P. Parametrization and shape of B-spline curves for CAD. Comput Aided Des 1980;12(5):235−8.

[4] Litwinowicz P, Williams L. Animating images with drawings. In: Glassner A, editor. Proceedings of SIGGRAPH 94, Computer graphics proceedings, annual conference series. Orlando, Florida: ACM Press; 1994. p. 409−12. ISBN 0-89791-667-0.

[5] Mortenson M. Geometric modeling. New York: John Wiley & Sons; 1985.

[6] Rogers D, Adams J. Mathematical elements for computer graphics. New York: McGraw-Hill; 1976.

[7] Shoemake K. Animating rotation with quaternion curves. In: Barsky BA, editor. Computer graphics (proceedings of SIGGRAPH 85), 19. San Francisco, Calif; 1985. p. 143−52.

CHAPTER

Physics-based movement

5

5.1 Why physics?

Physics is the language of *motion*. Thus it is fundamental to defining locomotion systems that simulate moving objects. It provides us with the rules for describing how objects move over time, giving us ways to determine/compute their locations given a set of initial conditions and constraints. When trying to achieve realism in motion, physics provides us with the ability to animate characters and objects believably as they move in the real world. This requires us to define rules not only for movement of a single object but for the movement of many objects and their interactions and responses to external forces or constraints.

Many areas of animation are solely reliant on physics to define the movement of objects or media; for example, visual effects for film that simulate natural phenomena must adhere to physical principles to appear believable. Other forms of animation will use physics as a piece of the puzzle and augment with traditional animation principles (e.g., squash and stretch/timing) to create visual appeal or be unique. Either way, physics simulation in software allows us to define the types of movement and accuracy we require, apply appropriate constraints for movement, and also create visual appeal by realistically simulating nonrealistic constraints (e.g., imagine deforming an object by attaching invisible springs to portions of the object and physically simulating the masses attached to the spring to create a wobbly/deformable body). We want to be able to move many objects that speed up and slow down, that bounce off of other objects simultaneously. We want to have objects that are connected to others as if they were connected by rubber bands or springs, and we want to have objects that are connected to each other rigidly but move together in unison. Animators are often more concerned with the general quality of motion than with precisely controlling the position and orientation of each object in each frame. Such is the case with physically based animation.

5.2 Physically based animation

In *physically based animation,* forces are typically used to maintain relationships among geometric elements. Note that these forces may or may not be physically

Computer Animation. https://doi.org/10.1016/B978-0-443-13512-5.00005-7

accurate. Animation is not necessarily concerned with accuracy, but it is concerned with believability, which is sometimes referred to as being *physically realistic*. Some forces may not relate to physics at all—they may model constraints that an animator may wish to enforce on the motion, such as directing a ball to go toward contacting a bat. For the purposes of this chapter, the use of forces to control motion will be referred to as physically based animation whether or not the forces are actually trying to model some aspect of physics. When modeling motion that is produced by an underlying mechanism, such as the principles of physics, a decision has to be made concerning the level of fidelity at which to model the process. For example, wrinkles in a cloth can be modeled by trying to characterize common types of wrinkles and where they typically occur on a piece of cloth. On the other hand, the physics (stresses and strains) of the individual threads of cloth could be modeled in sufficient detail to give rise to naturally occurring wrinkles. Modeling the surface characteristics of the process, as in the former case, is usually computationally less expensive and easier to program, but it lacks flexibility. The only effects produced are the ones explicitly modeled. Modeling the physics of the underlying process usually incurs a higher computational expense but is more flexible—the inputs to the underlying process can usually produce a greater range of surface characteristics under a wider range of conditions. There are often several different levels at which a process can be modeled. In the case of the cloth example, a triangular mesh can be used to model the cloth as a sheet of material (which is what is usually done). The quest for the animation programmer is to provide a procedure that does as little computation as possible while still providing the desired effects and controls for the animator. The advantage to the animator, when physical models are used, is that they are relieved of low-level specifications of motions and only need to be concerned with specifying high-level relationships or qualities of the motion. For our example of cloth, instead of specifying where wrinkles might go and the movement of individual vertices, the animator would merely be able to set parameters that indicate the type and thickness of the cloth material. For this, the animator trades off having specific control of the animation—wrinkles will occur wherever the process model produces them.

For the most part, we are concerned with *dynamic control*—specifying the underlying forces that are then used to produce movement. First, let's review basic physics as it pertains to locomotion, followed by two common examples of physical simulation used in animation: spring meshes and particle systems. Rigid body dynamics and the use of constraints are then discussed.

5.3 Simulating rigid bodies

First things first. When (and how) do we simulate physics?

Let's consider a single object moving over a set of frames, let's say 30 frames. If our framerate is 30 frames per second, then we have 30 frames in which we need to know the pose of this object so we can draw it. We need to keep track of the time elapsed because our previous frame of the simulation, compute the next pose for each object in the scene, and finally update the state of the scene with the new objects. The scene state will contain all constraints and relationships we need to consider when moving our objects through the virtual world (e.g., some areas are not traversable or make an object move more slowly/faster as they traverse through, collision volumes). It is important to keep track of the time between updates for a few reasons: it is good practice to do so and connects nicely to physics and math formalisms; in real-time simulations and games, our framerate (and thus time it takes between updates) may change due to other processes or systems on the computer running the simulation; computer hardware specifications vary widely, and you want your simulation to run consistently for all users; to obtain higher accuracy in some situations, it is necessary to update our physics more often than our framerate, so we cannot rely on a particular elapsed time for all calculations.

5.4 Physics engines

There has been much effort placed into developing highly accurate and computationally efficient algorithms to simulate physics over the years, which has resulted in a number of amazing pieces of software and software development libraries enabling both animators and developers to create amazing animations. Industry standard software packages such as Maya, 3DS Max, Blender, and Houdini all incorporate efficient physics simulation systems capable of real-time (or near real-time) computation depending on how many bodies they are simulating. In video games, Unity, Unreal, and Godot provide built-in physics simulation that enables simulation on the central processing unit (CPU) and graphics processing unit (GPU) (for millions of particles) to enable real-time realistic movement and collision response. They all have limitations due to their real-time needs (i.e., games need to run faster, at 30–60 fps minimum), and as such they tend to approximate solutions to fluid dynamics or other volumetric vector field simulation problems (as they are data and computationally heavy). Other third-party physics simulation packages exist, such as EmberGen (which enables real-time fire/fluids/smoke and explosions efficiently), Havok (a 3D physics engine for games), Bullet (an open-source 3D physics engine), and Box2D (a popular open-source 2D physics engine for games). Throughout this chapter, we will use examples from Box2D to highlight connections between math and software design for various concepts.

5.4.1 What needs to be updated?

Ultimately, we want to update the position and orientation of each object in each frame. What happens when the objects collide with each other? What if they are connected in some fashion (imagine pulling a rope tied to an object)? What if a number of objects are connected by rubber bands of different stiffness, or if some objects are connected rigidly together? To take these types of situations into account, the animation system must not only update the position/orientation of each object but also perform Collision Detection (to check if any objects are colliding) and Collision Response (to apply forces to the object based on any collisions), Solve for other constraints that apply to the objects, and finally Resolve these constraints by applying appropriate forces.

5.4.2 Object and system state

To keep things organized, let's write all of the information we need to calculate or keep track of for a particular object in one spot. We call this the "state" of the object, and we keep it in a data structure called the *state vector* (the state vector is also a function of time, $S(t)$). The state vector consists of the object's position ($\mathbf{p}(t)$), orientation ($\mathbf{R}(t)$), linear momentum ($\mathbf{P}(t)$), and angular momentum ($\mathbf{L}(t)$) (Equation 5.1) at a particular moment in time. Static (unchanging) object attributes may also be included to organize everything such as the object's mass, M, and its object-space inertia tensor, I_{object}. At any time, an object's time-varying inertia tensor ($\mathbf{I}(t)$), angular velocity ($\omega(t)$), and linear velocity ($\mathbf{v}(t)$) can be computed (Equations 5.2–5.4). The time derivative of the object's state vector can now also be expressed as in Equation 5.5.

$$\mathbf{S}(t) = \begin{bmatrix} \mathbf{p}(t) \\ \mathbf{R}(t) \\ \mathbf{P}(t) \\ \mathbf{L}(t) \end{bmatrix} = \begin{bmatrix} \mathbf{Pose}_t\{\mathbf{p}(t), \mathbf{R}(t)\} \\ \mathbf{LinearMomentum}_t \\ \mathbf{AngularMomentum}_t \end{bmatrix} \tag{5.1}$$

$$\mathbf{I}(t) = \mathbf{R}(t)\mathbf{I}_{\text{object}}\mathbf{R}(t)^T \tag{5.2}$$

$$\omega(t) = \mathbf{I}(t)^{-1}\mathbf{L}(t) \tag{5.3}$$

$$\mathbf{v}(t) = \frac{\mathbf{P}(t)}{\mathbf{M}} \tag{5.4}$$

$$\frac{d}{dt}\mathbf{S}(t) = \frac{d}{dt}\begin{bmatrix} \mathbf{p}(t) \\ \mathbf{R}(t) \\ \mathbf{P}(t) \\ \mathbf{L}(t) \end{bmatrix} = \begin{bmatrix} \mathbf{v}(t) \\ \omega(t)\mathbf{R}(t) \\ \mathbf{F}(t) \\ \tau(t) \end{bmatrix} \tag{5.5}$$

5.4.3 Simplest simulation update

The above is enough information to run a **basic** simulation. Once the derivative information is available, a differential equation solver can be used to update the state vector. In the simplest implementation, **Euler's method** can be used to update the values of the state array; that is, the values of the state vector are updated by multiplying their time derivatives by the length of the time step (Equation 5.6).

$$\int_t^{t+\delta t} \mathbf{S}(t)dt \approx \mathbf{S}(t+\delta t) = \mathbf{S}(t) + \frac{d}{dt}\mathbf{S}(t)\delta t \tag{5.6}$$

Euler's method is the simplest to implement but is known to accumulate a large amount of error with large time steps; thus care must be taken to ensure δt is small. In practice, **Runge-Kutta methods** (especially fourth-order) have found popularity because of their trade-off in speed, accuracy, and ease of implementation (see note on integration methods below).

Care must be taken in updating the orientation of an object. Because the derivative information from earlier is only valid instantaneously, if it is used to update the orientation rotation matrix, then the columns of this matrix can quickly become non-orthogonal and not unit length. At the very least, the column lengths should be renormalized after being updated. A better method is to update the orientation matrix by applying to its columns the axis-angle rotation implied by the angular velocity vector, $\omega(t)$. The magnitude of the angular velocity vector represents the angle of rotation about the axis along the angular velocity vector. Alternatively, quaternions can be used to represent both the object's orientation and the orientation derivative, and its use here is functionally equivalent to the axis-angle approach.

5.5 Simulation software, game engines, and time updates

Unity engine

In Unity, the function **FixedUpdate( )** is called at a constant rate every 0.02 seconds by default. This provides standardized performance and reliability. If your framerate is 100 frames per second for visuals, the **FixedUpdate** function will be called 50 times per second no matter how your framerate changes. Obviously, if your computations in this function exceed 0.02 seconds, there will be a performance impact. The time elapsed can be accessed as $\delta t =$ Time.fixedDeltaTime.

Additionally, the function **Update( )** is called every frame. If your framerate is 100 frames per second, then **Update** is called 100 times every second. It is important to note that your calculations in this function will affect performance; thus you need to ensure you use the time elapsed for any calculation as $\delta t =$ Time.fixedDeltaTime.

Unreal engine

Unreal provides time functionality and tracking with the idea of a clock "ticking." All actors in the scene are ticked once per frame. There is a bit of complexity to ensure that the ticks for various components in the scene are synchronized, and the engine manages this with a set of "Tick Groups" that tick in a specific order: **PrePhysics, DuringPhysics, PostPhysics,** and **PostUpdateWork**. In Unreal blueprints, the "Event Tick" provides the delta seconds since previous tick for the actor.

Godot

In the Godot game engine, the ***_process(delta)*** function is called each frame and acts similarly to Unity's **Update()** function. The delta variable passed into the function is the time elapsed in seconds since the last update. Another way to accomplish timing in Godot is using a **Timer** Node that acts as a countdown timer that fires when it reaches zero [1]. This can be used to define callbacks and coroutines that need to emit at a particular time.

Blender and animation packages

Animation software works differently than game engines as they require higher accuracy at the expense of computational time. For Blender, Maya, 3DS Max and so on, the goal here is not to provide real-time calculations but rather accurate calculations, which could take more time depending on the complexity of the scene and algorithms used. This enables the simulation of a much broader set of physical simulation algorithms and processes such as fluid simulations, highly complex volumetric simulations (e.g., clouds), and destruction or fracturing of objects. Thus the timing in these software packages can be set accurately per frame and computed based upon the algorithm required to provide results within a specified error.

5.6 Modeling rigid body dynamics

Building on the notation defined in previous chapters, we can quickly combine these ideas to define simple rigid body mechanics that will enable us to animate and move objects. Here we define only the absolutely necessary concepts most commonly used to animate objects; this is by no means a thorough examination of a complete view of physics, but it will be good enough for the beginner to get things started. As we progress, more complex concepts that build on these will be introduced as needed. A rigid body is simply a body that can be described by a geometric primitive (or set of primitives) that do not deform based on the mechanical operations applied to them. For instance, a wooden crate is rigid as you can move it, slide it, rotate it, and its dimensions remain the same as its original conditions. Let's assume that our characters and all objects can be defined in this way, which makes it easier to position them in space. We can relax this later, but for now this notion will make the basic locomotion strategies very straightforward. Also, as we go forward we will be using Δt to define discrete time steps (i.e., those that are measured by a computer), and δt is the continuous time step equivalent. Similarly, we will use subscripts to denote discrete vectors at particular times. For example, $\mathbf{p}(t)$ is a way to represent the position of an object as a continuous function of time, whereas we use $\vec{p}_t$ to denote a discrete sample of that function (which is a vector in a coordinate system) at time t.

We can denote the position of a rigid body by a set of parameters where some are static/unchanging (e.g., width, height, length, material properties) and others that are dynamic (e.g., position, velocity, acceleration, forces applied). The static properties define the initial state of the object, and the dynamic properties must be computed for each frame of animation and depend upon both internal (behavior driven) and external (physics driven, i.e., gravity) forces.

5.6.1 Position, pose, velocity, acceleration, forces

Position: The position of a rigid body at time t is defined as a vector, $\mathbf{p}(t) = \overrightarrow{p_t}$.
Orientation: The orientation of a rigid body is defined as a rotational representation. For simplicity, let's use a rotation matrix $\mathbf{R}(t) = \mathbf{R}_t$ to denote its orientation at time t.
Pose: In Chapter 2, we defined the pose of a rigid body as the set of a body's position and orientation at a given time t, $\mathbf{Pose}(t) = \mathbf{Pose}_t = \left\{\overrightarrow{p_t}, \mathbf{R}(t)\right\}$.

To incorporate dynamics, we need to define simple relationships that enable us to compute the complete pose of the object given its previous pose (i.e., the pose at time $t-1$) and any other info in the scene acting upon the object.

Let's consider linear movement only. This means the object is not rotating, just moving. We have a few different models we can employ depending on how the object should be moving.

Model 1: Position-velocity (PV)

The simplest motion model we can employ is to move an object in a straight line at a constant speed. Let's say the object is moving at 12 units/second (S) along the x-axis ($\vec{d}$). We can encode both the speed and direction of movement in the velocity vector:

$$\vec{v} = S\frac{\vec{d}}{\left\|\vec{d}\right\|}$$

Note that we've explicitly added a normalization to the direction vector as this needs to be a unit direction (hence a length of 1) to ensure that the length of the velocity vector is exactly the speed, S. For most characters, we can think of the velocity vector as the direction of movement or "facing" direction as you typically would have objects looking where they are going (but not always, of course).

As we move forward, we will use the notation of Δt to denote the change in time between the previous and current calculation frames (time interval).

Putting this together, we have our simplest physics model:

$$\vec{p}_{\text{current}} = \vec{p}_{\text{prev}} + \vec{v}\Delta t$$

This assumes that the velocity is constant for the entire duration of the interval, Δt, between the previous and current update times.

Note for the more math minded: This is the simplest solution to a partial differential equation for position (Euler's method) as shown above.

$$\int_t^{t+\delta t} \mathbf{p}(t)dt \approx \mathbf{p}(t+\delta t) = \mathbf{p}(t) + \frac{d}{dt}\mathbf{p}(t)\delta t \approx \overrightarrow{p_t} + \overrightarrow{v_t}\Delta t$$

Given $\overrightarrow{v_t} \approx \mathbf{v}(t) = \frac{d}{dt}\mathbf{p}(t)$, we can see the connection here between our vector form above and the standard calculus form.

Model 2: PV + acceleration (PVA)

In the PV model, our body is moving in a straight line constantly because the direction encoded in the velocity vector is unchanging. We can define a similar relationship as above but in two steps where we first consider updating the velocity, and then use this to update the position.

To do this, we need to specify the acceleration vector, which encodes how the velocity should change over the time interval.

One way to do this is to first update the velocity and then use this new velocity to update the position. Think of this like (1) determining which way to move or aiming (update velocity) and then (2) taking a step along this direction (update position).

$$\begin{aligned}\vec{v}_{\text{new}} &= \vec{v}_{\text{prev}} + \vec{a}\Delta t \\ \vec{p}_{\text{current}} &= \vec{p}_{\text{prev}} + \vec{v}_{\text{new}}\Delta t.\end{aligned}$$

This "works" but is not the most accurate in terms of simulation, as large errors can accumulate.

Alternatively, a slightly better approach would be to consider that the velocity is changing throughout the interval (because you have a different speed/direction from when you began moving than when you finish moving), so using the average velocity over the interval will provide a slightly better approximation to the movement.

Consider the following. Let's say we have this equation for velocity:

$$\vec{v}_{\text{new}} = \vec{v}_{\text{prev}} + \vec{a}\Delta t.$$

By adding $\vec{v}_{\text{prev}}$ to both sides, we get

$$\vec{v}_{\text{new}} + \vec{v}_{\text{prev}} = \vec{v}_{\text{prev}} + \vec{v}_{\text{prev}} + \vec{a}\Delta t$$

and simplifying

$$\vec{v}_{\text{new}} + \vec{v}_{\text{prev}} = 2\vec{v}_{\text{prev}} + \vec{a}\Delta t$$

... followed by dividing both sides by 2 to get the average velocity, we get

$$\begin{aligned}\frac{\vec{v}_{\text{new}} + \vec{v}_{\text{prev}}}{2} &= \vec{v}_{\text{prev}} + \frac{1}{2}\vec{a}\Delta t \\ \vec{v} &= \vec{v}_{\text{prev}} + \frac{1}{2}\vec{a}\Delta t\end{aligned}.$$

This gives us an expression for the *average* velocity $\vec{v}$ of the body over the time interval.

Substituting this back into the original expression for position updates, we get

$$\begin{aligned}\vec{p}_{\text{current}} &= \vec{p}_{\text{prev}} + \vec{v}\Delta t \\ &= \vec{p}_{\text{prev}} + \left(\vec{v}_{\text{prev}} + \frac{1}{2}\vec{a}\Delta t\right)\Delta t. \\ &= \vec{p}_{\text{prev}} + \vec{v}_{\text{prev}} + \frac{1}{2}\vec{a}(\Delta t)^2\end{aligned}$$

This is a slightly better representation for accuracy purposes. Because the error is bounded by the size of the interval, using smaller intervals will mitigate this problem.

Note for the more calculus minded:

$$\begin{aligned}\int_t^{t+\delta t} \mathbf{p}(t)dt &\approx \mathbf{p}(t+\delta t) = \mathbf{p}(t) + \frac{d}{dt}\mathbf{p}(t)\delta t + \frac{d^2}{dt^2}\mathbf{p}(t)\delta t^2 \\ &\approx \vec{p}_t + \vec{v}_t\Delta t + \frac{1}{2}\vec{a}_t(\Delta t)^2\end{aligned}.$$

Given $\vec{v}_t \approx v(t) = \frac{d}{dt}\mathbf{p}(t)$ and $\vec{a}_t \approx a(t) = \frac{d}{dt}\mathbf{v}(t) = \frac{d^2}{dt^2}\mathbf{p}(t)$

Model 3: PVA + force (PVAF)

But what if the acceleration needs to be calculated differently each frame due to actions of objects in the scene? Enter the use of Force.

Isaac Newton gave us a simple tool to use, $\vec{F} = m\vec{a}$, which says that the total force applied to the rigid body is directly proportional to both the mass and acceleration of the body. Also note that the total force is actually a vector quantity. Thus the total force can be computed as the "sum of all forces" currently applied to the object for the duration of the interval.

Thus, $\vec{F} = \sum_i \vec{f}_i$ for all forces, $\vec{f}_i$ applied.

Given a number of forces applied to the object, we can now use the following update methodology:

$$\begin{aligned}\vec{F} &= \sum_i \vec{f}_i \\ \vec{a} &= \frac{\vec{F}}{m} \\ \vec{v}_{current} &= \vec{v}_{prev} + \vec{a}\Delta t \\ \vec{p}_{\text{current}} &= \vec{p}_{\text{prev}} + \vec{v}_{\text{prev}}\Delta t + \frac{1}{2}\vec{a}(\Delta t^2)\end{aligned}$$

and then reset for the next calculation frame:

$$\begin{aligned}\vec{v}_{prev} &= \vec{v}_{current} \\ \vec{p}_{\text{prev}} &= \vec{p}_{\text{current}}\end{aligned}.$$

Performing these operations for each frame of animation provides a set of basic rigid-body calculations.

But … what about orientation?

The models discussed above are simple models that work well for updating our positions, but what about the rotation/orientation of the object? There are a few ways to handle orientation. One way to handle orientation is simply to ignore rotational/angular physics and use the linear velocity vector as the facing direction and update our orientation as needed using the Frenet frame algorithm. This is not the most elegant solution, but it works well for some situations; for example, if we are using steering algorithms for a non-player-character in a game. Sometimes it is "good enough" just to update the direction the object is facing with linear physics and subsequently play an appropriate animation clip.

The other way to handle orientation is to model the angular physics of the object. Let's encode the orientation of a rigid body as a quaternion, $\widehat{q}t$. The goal is to compute a new quaternion, $\widehat{q}t + \Delta t$, that accurately reflects the physical angular motion. We can define our angular velocity as a quaternion as follows. The angular speed (ω) represents how fast the object is rotating and as such is $\omega = \frac{\theta}{dt}$. If we have a normalized axis of rotation $\overrightarrow{a}$, $\|\overrightarrow{a}\| = 1$ that the object is rotating around, then our angular velocity vector is expressed as $\overrightarrow{\omega} = \omega\overrightarrow{a}$ and as a pure quaternion as $\widehat{\omega} = \left(0, \overrightarrow{\omega}\right)$.

Using a first-order Taylor series expansion, we would get the PV equivalent approximation as $\widehat{q}t + \delta t = \widehat{q}t + \frac{d\widehat{q}t}{dt}dt$. The derivative of $\frac{d\overrightarrow{q}_t}{dt} = \frac{1}{2}\widehat{\omega}\widehat{q}t$ the quaternion can be defined as $\frac{d\widehat{q}t}{dt} = \frac{1}{2}\widehat{\omega}\widehat{q}\text{t}$, and thus we can integrate using Euler integration for small time steps as $\widehat{q}_t + \Delta t = \widehat{q}_t + \frac{\Delta t}{2}\widehat{\omega}\widehat{q}_t$. [2]. In practice, although this is a linear approximation, it does work well for small time steps, especially when objects are rotating smoothly and reasonably slow. Obviously, this can be expanded to second order and beyond for more accurate simulation. For animation purposes, it is generally combined or blended with solutions from an interpolation scheme for more control as needed.

A note on integration methods

For the calculus-minded reader, you will have noticed that the above calculations are an implementation of a simple integration scheme to compute the position (and velocity) over time. Note that our velocity is simply the change of position over time (or rather the derivative of the position over time), thus $\overrightarrow{p}_t = \overrightarrow{p}_{t-1} + \overrightarrow{p}\delta t$ where $\overrightarrow{p} = d\overrightarrow{p}/dt = \overrightarrow{v}_t$. Similarly, the second derivative, $\overrightarrow{p} = d\overrightarrow{v}/dt = \overrightarrow{a}_t$, is our acceleration vector at time t.

We can define $h = \delta t$ as our integration range (or step size). The above equations demonstrate basic rigid-body simulation using an integration method called **Euler** integration, which is suitable for basic calculations and simple simulations; however, there is some error that creeps into the result. Euler integration assumes that the derivative is constant for the entire integration step (and as such accumulates quite a bit of error). As seen above, Euler integration is used here to update both the velocity and the position; thus the error is compounded, which could lead to a fast unbounded error. Luckily, this doesn't occur in practice generally because our integration step size is quite small. For the most part, this is fine, but it is important to consider for your application whether this is a concern. There are other numerical integration methods that improve the error, such as Verlet integration and Runge-Kutta integration methods. Probably one of the most widely used integration methods due to its simplicity, accuracy, and ease of implementation is the Runge-Kutta method. This fourth-order method evaluates the derivative four times (start, end, and twice in the middle at different points), so there is an additional fixed computational cost.

Runge-Kutta Method (RK4): Given a function that computes the derivative (velocity) of the body position (y) at a given time, t, and the integration step size (length of the interval), the fourth-order RK4 method can be defined as:

$$\begin{aligned}\text{Given}: f(t,y) &= \frac{dy}{dt}, y(t_0) = y_0 \\ y_{n+1} &= y_n + \frac{h}{6}(k_1 + 2k_2 + 2k_3 + k_4) \\ t_{n+1} &= t_n + h\end{aligned}$$

where

$$\begin{aligned}k_1 &= f(t_n, y_n) \\ k_2 &= f\left(t_n + \frac{h}{2}, y_n + h\frac{k_1}{2}\right) \\ k_3 &= f\left(t_n + \frac{h}{2}, y_n + h\frac{k_2}{2}\right) \\ k_4 &= f(t_n + h, y_n + hk_3)\end{aligned}$$

5.6.2 More physics concepts

Center of mass

The center of mass of an object is defined by the integration of the differential mass times its position in the object. In computer graphics, the mass distribution of an object is typically modeled by individual points, which is usually implemented by assigning a mass value to each of the object's vertices. If the individual masses are given by m_i, then the total scalar mass, **M**, of the object is represented by Equation 5.7. Using an object coordinate system that is located at the center of mass is often useful when modeling the dynamics of a rigid object. For the current discussion, it is assumed that $\mathbf{p}(t)$ is the center of mass of an object. If the location of each mass point in world space is given by $\mathbf{q}_i(t)$, then the center of mass is just the weighted average by Equation 5.8.

$$\mathrm{M} = \sum_i m_i \tag{5.7}$$

$$\mathrm{p}(t) = \frac{\sum_i (m_i \mathbf{q}_i(t))}{\mathbf{M}} \tag{5.8}$$

Viscosity

Viscosity resists movement through a medium (e.g., air, water, syrup). A force due to viscosity (f_v) is negatively proportional to the velocity of the object (v) (Equation 5.9).

$$f_v = -k_v v \tag{5.9}$$

Momentum

The linear momentum of an object is simply its velocity scaled by its mass. In a closed system (i.e., a system in which energy is not changing), total momentum is conserved. This can be used to solve for unknowns in the system. For a system consisting of multiple objects in which there are no externally applied forces, the total momentum is constant (c) (Equation 5.10).

$$\mathbf{c} = \sum_i m_i \vec{v}_i \tag{5.10}$$

The object's local coordinate system is assumed to be located at its center of mass. The linear component acts on this center of mass, and the angular component is with respect to this center. Linear momentum and angular momentum need to be updated for interacting objects because these values are conserved in a closed system. Saying that the linear momentum is conserved in a closed system, for example, means that the sum of the linear momentum does not change if there are no outside influences on the system. The case is similar for angular momentum. That they are conserved means they can be used to solve for unknown values in the system, such as linear velocity and angular velocity.

Linear momentum

Linear momentum is equal to velocity times mass (Equation 5.11). The total linear momentum, $\mathbf{P}(t)$, of a rigid body is the sum of the linear momentum of each particle (Equation 5.12). For a coordinate system whose origin coincides with the center of mass, Equation 5.12 simplifies to the mass of the object times its velocity (Equation 5.13). Further, because the mass of the object remains constant, taking the derivative of momentum with respect to time establishes a relationship between linear momentum and linear force (Equation 5.14). This states that the force acting on a body is equal to the change in momentum. Interactions composed of equal but opposite forces result in no change in momentum (i.e., momentum is conserved).

$$\vec{\mathbf{P}} = m\vec{v} \tag{5.11}$$

$$\mathbf{P}(t) = \sum_i m_i \frac{d}{dt} q_i(t) \tag{5.12}$$

$$\mathbf{P}(t) = \mathbf{M}\mathbf{v}(t) \tag{5.13}$$

$$\frac{d}{dt}\mathbf{P}(t) = \mathbf{M}\frac{d}{dt}\mathbf{v}(t) = \mathbf{F}(t) \tag{5.14}$$

Angular momentum

Angular momentum, **L**, is a measure of the *rotating* mass weighted by the distance of the mass from the axis of rotation. Imagine you have a wheel that's rotating but you stick something heavy on one side of it. What do you expect to happen? The wheel should feel lopsided and rotate at different speeds as it moves. This happens because the mass is affecting the speed of rotation (angular velocity), which is basically what angular momentum describes. In computer animation, we typically will have objects made up of n vertices, $\mathbf{Q} = \left\{\overrightarrow{q}_i\right\}_i^n$. Let's consider each vertex, $\overrightarrow{q}_i$, to have a mass m_i. We need to define the momentum relative to the object's center of mass, $\overrightarrow{p}$, so we first define the vector from the center of mass toward each vertex in the object, $\overrightarrow{r}_i = \overrightarrow{q}_i - \overrightarrow{p}$. To incorporate a rotation, we note this vector is rotating relative to its center of mass; thus we have $\mathbf{R}(t)\overrightarrow{r}_i$. We can express the velocity of that point given the angular velocity as $\overrightarrow{\omega} \times \mathbf{R}(t)\overrightarrow{r}_i$ and weight it by its mass, $m_i\left(\overrightarrow{\omega} \times \mathbf{R}(t)\overrightarrow{r}_i\right)$. You can think of this as kind of defining the linear momentum at the point (so it is a vector that says how fast that point is moving at this moment given how fast the object is spinning and how heavy the point is). If we take the cross product of this vector with $R(t)\overrightarrow{r}_i$, we get the angular momentum of that point, $L_i = R(t)\overrightarrow{r}_i \times m_i\left(\overrightarrow{\omega} \times \mathbf{R}(t)\overrightarrow{r}_i\right)$. Finally, we do this for all points in the objects and add them up to get the *total* angular momentum of the object, $\mathbf{L}(t) \approx \sum L_i$ (Equation 5.15).

$$
\begin{aligned}
\overrightarrow{r}_i &= \left(\overrightarrow{q}_i - \overrightarrow{p}\right) \\
\overrightarrow{r}_i' &= \mathbf{R}(t)\overrightarrow{r}_i \\
L_i &= \overrightarrow{r}_i' \times m_i\left(\overrightarrow{\omega} \times \overrightarrow{r}_i'\right) \\
&= m_i\left(\overrightarrow{r}_i' \times \left(\overrightarrow{\omega} \times \overrightarrow{r}_i'\right)\right) \\
\mathbf{L} &= \sum_i^n L_i = \sum_i^n m_i\left(\overrightarrow{r}_i' \times \left(\overrightarrow{\omega} \times \overrightarrow{r}_i'\right)\right)
\end{aligned}
\tag{5.15}
$$

Inertia tensor

Angular momentum is related to angular velocity in much the same way that linear momentum is related to linear velocity, $\mathbf{P}(t) = \mathbf{M}\mathbf{v}(t)$ (Equation 5.16). However, in the case of angular momentum, a matrix is needed to describe the distribution of mass of the object we call the inertia tensor ($\mathbf{I}(t)$). The inertia tensor is a symmetric 3×3 matrix with 6 unique terms and is defined for the untransformed object as $\mathbf{I}_{\text{object}}$ (Equation 5.17). Essentially, each term describes the density of mass within the object's coordinate system and is used to define how angular momentum affects each axis as the body rotates. Terms of the matrix are calculated by integrating over the object (e.g., Equation 5.18). In Equation 5.18 the density of an object point, $\overrightarrow{q}_i$, is $\rho\overrightarrow{q}_i$. For the discrete case, Equation 5.19 is used. In a center-of-mass—centered object space, the inertia tensor for a transformed object depends on the orientation,

$\mathbf{R}(t)$, of the object but not on its position in space. Thus it is dependent on time. It can be transformed according to the transformation of the object by Equation 5.20. Its inverse, which we will need later, is transformed in the same way.

$$\mathbf{L}(t) = \mathbf{I}(t)\omega(t) \tag{5.16}$$

$$\mathbf{I}_{\text{object}} = \begin{bmatrix} I_{xx} & I_{xy} & I_{xz} \\ I_{xy} & I_{yy} & I_{xz} \\ I_{xz} & I_{yz} & I_{zz} \end{bmatrix} \tag{5.17}$$

$$\mathbf{I}_{xx} = \iiint \left(\rho(q)\left(q_y^2 + q_z^2\right)\right) dxdydz \tag{5.18}$$

$$\begin{aligned} \mathbf{I}_{xx} &= \sum_i m_i\left(y_i^2 + z_i^2\right) & \mathbf{I}_{xy} &= \sum_i m_i x_i y_i \\ \mathbf{I}_{yy} &= \sum_i m_i\left(x_i^2 + z_i^2\right) & \mathbf{I}_{xz} &= \sum_i m_i x_i z_i \\ \mathbf{I}_{zz} &= \sum_i m_i\left(x_i^2 + y_i^2\right) & \mathbf{I}_{yz} &= \sum_i m_i y_i z_i \end{aligned} \tag{5.19}$$

$$\mathbf{I}(t) = \mathbf{R}(t)\mathbf{I}_{\text{object}}\mathbf{R}(t)^T \tag{5.20}$$

Torque

Think of torque (τ) as rotational force. Analogous to linear velocity and linear acceleration are angular velocity (ω) and angular acceleration (α). The mass of an object is essentially a measure of its resistance to movement. Analogously, the moment of inertia matrix is a measure of an object's resistance to change in orientation. The relationship to torque, moment of inertia, and angular acceleration is similar to the familiar $f = ma$ (Equation 5.21).

$$\tau = \mathbf{I}\alpha \tag{5.21}$$

The torque that arises from the application of forces acting on a point of an object $\vec{q}_i$ is given by Equation 5.23.

$$\mathbf{F} = \sum_i f_i(t) \rightarrow \widetilde{\mathbf{F}}_t = \sum_i \vec{f}^{\,i}_t \tag{5.22}$$

$$\begin{aligned} \vec{\tau}(t) &= \left(\vec{q}^{\,i}_t - \vec{p}_t\right) \times \vec{f}^{\,i}_t \\ \tau &= \sum \vec{\tau}_i(t) \end{aligned} \tag{5.23}$$

In a manner similar to the relation between linear force and the change in linear momentum, torque equals the change in angular momentum (Equation 5.24). If no torque is acting on an object, then angular momentum is constant. However, the angular velocity of an object does not necessarily remain constant even in the case of no torque. The angular velocity can change if the distribution of mass of an object changes, such as when a spinning ice skater pulls their arms in toward their body to spin faster. This action brings the mass of the skater closer to the center of mass. Angular momentum is a function of angular velocity, mass, and the distance the mass is from the center of mass. To maintain a constant angular momentum, the angular velocity must increase if the distance of the mass decreases.

$$\dot{\mathbf{L}}(t) = \tau(t) \tag{5.24}$$

5.7 Particle systems

Animations and video games these days use an immense amount of visual effects to achieve visual appeal, such as magical effects, sparks, fire, and smoke (see Figure 5.1). Much of these effects can be achieved using **Particle Systems** and a combination of physics simulation, keyframe animations, layering, and blending. A particle system is simply a collection of a large number of "particles" that have physical (for movement and interaction) and visual (for rendering) properties.

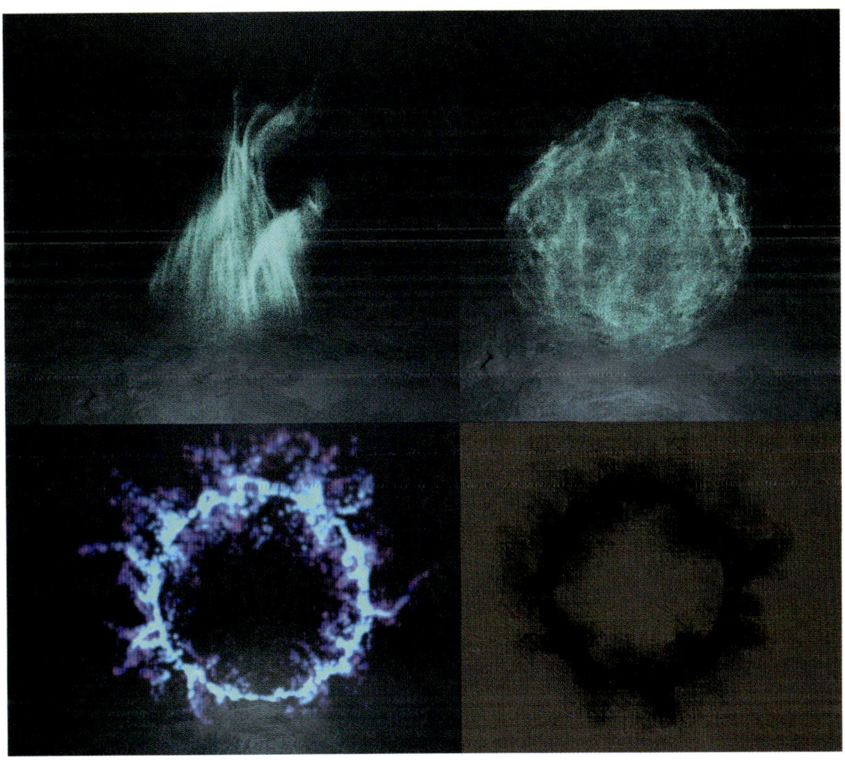

FIGURE 5.1

Examples of particle systems. (Screen capture of "Cool Visual Effects" (Unity 2022, URP) using free asset [27].)

Each of these properties is typically animated in some fashion using either physics simulation (to move each particle) and keyframing/interpolation (to fade them in/out, change color/opacity, and so on). Let's think of a particle as a small, point-like rigid body and a particle system containing hundreds, thousands, even millions of these particles. Because of the large number of elements typically found in a particle system, simplifying assumptions are used in both the rendering and the calculation of their motions. Various implementations make different simplifying assumptions.

Some of the common assumptions made are the following:

- Particles do not collide with other particles.
- Particles do not cast shadows, except in an aggregate sense.
- Particles only cast shadows on the rest of the environment, not on each other.
- Particles do not reflect light; they are each modeled as point light sources.

These are common assumptions, yet by no means are they required. In nonreal-time simulations, you may want each particle to emit light, cast shadows, or collide with each other, which can be accomplished at computational cost. For real-time applications in game engines, these restrictions are slowly being alleviated by increased GPU speeds.

Particles are often modeled as having a finite lifespan, so that during an animation there may be hundreds of thousands of particles used but only thousands actually active at any one time. Randomness and noise functions (e.g., Perlin noise) are commonly introduced into most of the modeling and processing of particles to avoid repetition and patterns unless desired.

In computing a frame of motion for a particle system, the following steps are taken (see Figure 5.2):

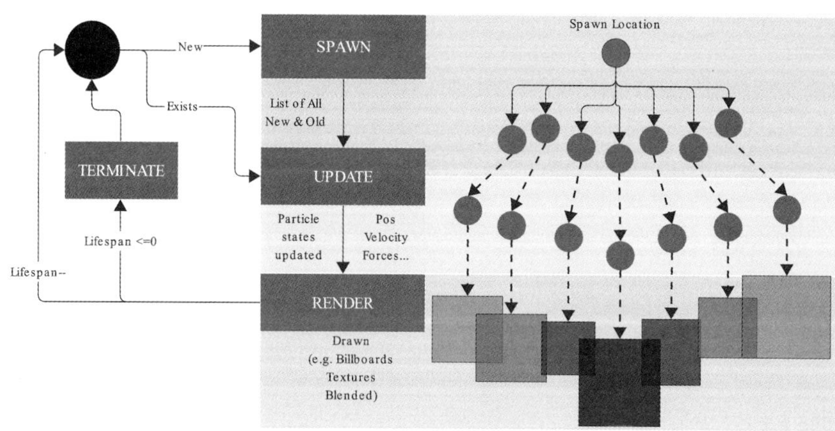

FIGURE 5.2

The life of a particle.

- **Spawn:** Any new particles that are born during this frame are generated, and each new particle is assigned initial attributes.
- **Terminate:** Any particles that have exceeded their allocated lifespan are terminated.
- **Update:** The remaining particles are simulated, and their parameters are interpolated/updated.
- **Render:** The particles are rendered using the desired primitive/mesh.

The steps are then repeated for each frame of the animation. If the user can enforce the constraint that there is a maximum number of particles active at any one time, then the data structure can be static and particle data structures can be reused as one dies and another is created in its place.

5.7.1 Particle generation

Particles are typically generated according to a controlled stochastic process. For each frame, a random number of particles are generated using some user-specified distribution centered at the desired average number of particles per frame (Equation 5.25). The distribution could be uniform or Gaussian or anything else the animator wants. In Equation 5.25, *Rand(_)* returns a random number from -1.0 to $+1.0$ in the desired distribution, and r scales it into the desired range. If the particles are used to model a fuzzy object, then it is best to make the number of particles a function of the area, A, of the screen covered by the object to control the number of particles generated (Equation 5.26). The features of the random number generator, such as average value and variance, can be a function of time to enable the animator to have more control over the particle system.

$$\#\text{ of particles} = n + \mathbf{Rand}() * r \tag{5.25}$$

$$\#\text{ of particles} = n(\mathbf{A}) + \mathbf{Rand}() * r \tag{5.26}$$

5.7.2 Particle attributes

The attributes of a particle determine its motion status, its appearance, and its life in the particle system. Typical attributes include the following but can include any dynamic parameter that needs to be controlled to a achieve the intended visual effect (see Figure 5.3):

- Position
- Velocity
- Shape parameters
- Color
- Transparency
- Lifetime

Each of the attributes is initialized when the particle is created. Again, to avoid uniformity, the user typically randomizes values in some controlled way. The

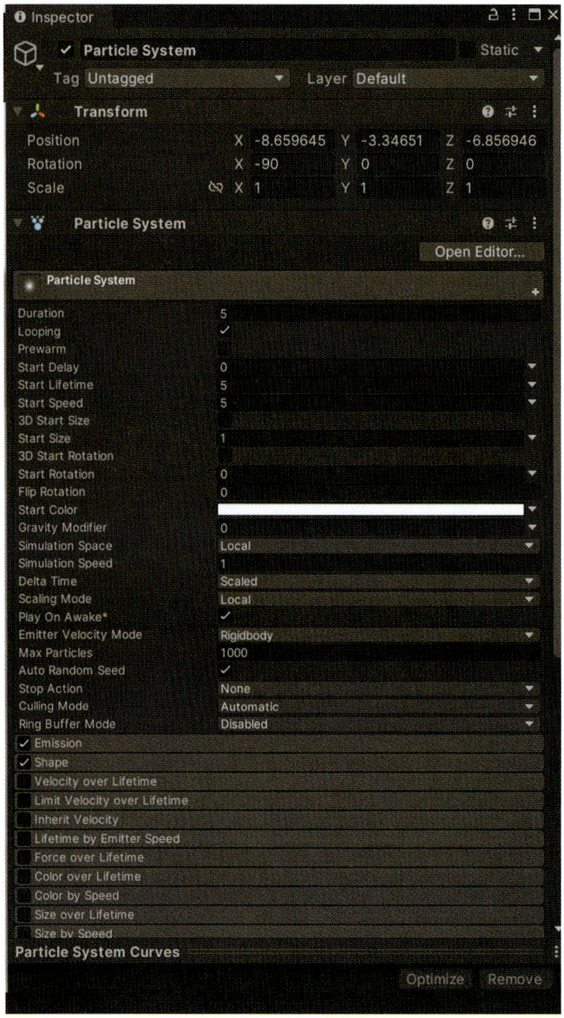

FIGURE 5.3

Particle attributes in Unity 2023.

position and velocity are updated according to the particle's motion. The shape parameters, color, and transparency control the particle's appearance.

5.7.3 Particle termination

At each new frame, each particle's lifetime attribute is decremented by 1. When the attribute reaches zero, the particle is removed from the system. This completes the particle's life cycle and can be used to keep the number of particles active at any one time within some desired range of values.

5.7.4 Particle animation

Typically, each active particle in a particle system is animated throughout its life. This activation includes not only its position and velocity but also its display attributes: shape, color, and transparency. To animate the particle's position in space, the user considers forces and computes the resultant particle acceleration. The velocity of the particle is updated from its acceleration, and then the average of its old velocity and newly updated velocity is computed and used to update the particle's position. Gravity, other global force fields (e.g., wind), local force fields (vortices), and collisions with objects in the environment are typical forces modeled in the environment.

The particle's color and transparency can be a function of global time, its own lifespan remaining, its height, and so on. The particle's shape can be a function of its velocity. For example, an ellipsoid can be used to represent a moving particle where the major axis of the ellipsoid is aligned with the direction of travel and the ratio of the ellipsoid's length to the radius of its circular cross section is related to its speed.

5.7.5 Particle rendering

To simplify rendering, model each particle as a point light source so that it adds color to the pixel(s) it covers but is not involved in the display pipeline (except to be hidden) or shadowing. In some applications, shadowing effects have been determined to be an important visual cue. The density of particles between a position in space and a light source can be used to estimate the amount of shadowing. See Blinn [3], Ebert et al. [4], and Reeves [5] for some of these considerations. For more information on particle systems, see Reeves and Blau [6] and Sims [7].

5.7.6 Particle system representation

A particle is represented by a tuple $[x, v, f, m]$, which holds its position, velocity, force accumulator, and mass. It can also be used to hold any other attributes of the particle such as its age and color.

```
typedef struct particle_struct {
        vector3D    p;
        vector3D    v;
        vector3D    f;
        float    mass;
} particle;
```

The state of a particle, $[x, v]$, will be updated by $[v, f/m]$ by the ordinary differential equation solver. The solver can be considered to be a black box to the extent that the actual method used by the solver does not have to be known.

A particle system is an array of particles with a time variable [$*p$, n, t].

```
typedef struct particleSystem_struct {
     particle   *p;    // array particle information
     int         n;    // number of particles
     float       t;    // current time (age) of the particle system
} particleSystem;
```

Updating particle system status

For each time step, the particle system is updated by the following steps:

1. For each particle, zero out the force vector.
2. For each particle, sum all forces affecting the particle.
3. Form the state array of all particles.
4. Form the update array of all particles.
5. Add the update array to the state array.
6. Save the new state array.
7. Update the time variable.

5.7.7 Forces on particles

Forces can be unary or binary and typically arise from the particle's relationship to the environment. Additional forces might be imposed by the animator to better control the animation. Unary forces include gravity and viscous drag. Particle pair forces, if desired, can be represented by springs and dampers. However, implementing particle pair forces for each possible pair of particles can be prohibitively expensive in terms of computational requirements. Auxiliary processing, such as the use of a spatial bucket sort, can be employed to consider only n nearest neighbor pairs and reduce the computation required, but typically particle-particle interaction is ignored. Environmental forces arise from a particle's relationship to the rest of the environment such as gravity, wind, air viscosity, and responding to collisions; most of these may be modeled using simple physics.

5.7.8 Particle lifespan

Typically, each particle will have a lifespan. The particle data structure itself can be reused in the system, so that a particle system might have tens of thousands of particles over the life of the simulation but only, for example, 1000 in existence at any one time. Initial values are set pseudorandomly so that particles are spawned in a controlled manner but with some variability.

5.8 Nonrigid bodies (flexible)

Not all objects in reality, however, are rigid; rather most are nonrigid and flexible in some manner. This means that the objects will bend, break, stretch, or otherwise deform throughout their lifespans. Simulating nonrigid bodies is challenging computationally as it requires us to consider material properties during simulation, which can become quite unwieldy due to the number of parameters involved. Common techniques for animation are to rely upon concepts such as springs, particles, and volumetric fluid simulation in small volumes to add visual interest to our animations. Imagine you had a cube and you wanted it to physically wiggle like jelly. One way would be to add virtual springs from each vertex to every other vertex and set the tension relatively high. If these rigid bodies were used to drive connected joints in a 3D model mesh, then the object could deform appropriately.

5.8.1 Springs

One of the most useful tools to incorporate some use of forces into an animation is the use of a spring-damper pair as in Figure 5.4. A spring is a common tool for modeling flexible objects, to keep two objects at a prescribed distance, or to insert temporary control forces into an environment. Notice that a spring may correspond to a geometric element, such as a thread of a cloth, or it may be defined simply to maintain a desired relationship between two points (sometimes called a *virtual spring*), such as a distance between the centers of two spheres. When attached to an object, a spring imparts a force on that object depending on the object's location relative to the other end of the spring. The magnitude of the spring force (f_s) is proportional to the difference between the spring's rest length (L_r) and its current length (L_c) and is in the direction of the spring. The constant of proportionality (k_s), also called the *spring constant,* determines how much the spring reacts to a change in length—its *stiffness*. The force is applied to both ends of the spring in opposite directions.

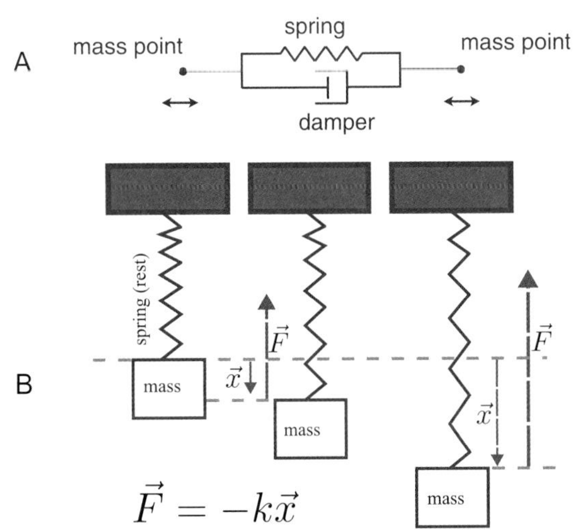

FIGURE 5.4

Spring-damper configuration.

Keeping it simple, Hooke's law says that the spring force can be modeled as $\vec{F} = -k\vec{x}$, where k is the spring constant describing the strength of the spring (higher values mean stronger spring) and $\vec{x}$ is the displacement of the end of the spring from its rest position. Damping is required to enable the simulation to come back to a steady state, otherwise it will continue on forever, so we can model it simply as $\vec{F} = -k\vec{x} - b\vec{v}$, where b is the damping coefficient and $\vec{v}$ is the relative velocity between the endpoints connected by the spring. This assumes only linear force and no angular forces will be modeled, but it is a good start. The total force would be modeled as $\vec{F}_{total} = \vec{f}_{gravity} + \vec{f}_{\text{spring}} + \vec{f}_{\text{damping}}$.

In physical simulations, the challenge in using a spring-damper system is in selecting an appropriate time step, setting the spring and damper constants, and setting the mass of the object so that the resulting motion is desirable. Some combinations of a small time step, large mass, a high damping constant, and a low spring constant might result in a system that is not very lively, where the object slowly moves toward the fixed point going slower and slower. On the other hand, a larger time step, a smaller mass, a lower damping constant, and a higher spring constant might result in a system that moves too much, resulting in a mass that oscillates around the fixed point, getting further and further away from it with each time step. Balancing these parameters to get the desired effect can be tricky.

Various physically based approaches have been proposed that model elastic and inelastic behavior, viscoelasticity, plasticity, and fracture (e.g.,[8], [9], [10], [11], [12], [13]). Here the simplest approach is presented. Flexibility is modeled by a mass-spring-damper system simulating the reaction of the body to external forces.

5.8.2 Mass-spring-damper modeling of flexible objects

Probably the most common approach to modeling flexible shapes is the mass-spring-damper model. The most straightforward strategy is to model each vertex of an object as a point mass and each edge of the object as a spring. Each spring's rest length is set equal to the original length of the edge. A mass can be arbitrarily assigned to an object by the animator and the mass evenly distributed among the object's vertices. If there is an uneven distribution of vertices throughout the object definition, then masses can be assigned to vertices in an attempt to more evenly distribute the mass. Spring constants are similarly arbitrary and are usually assigned uniformly throughout the object to some user-specified value. It is most common to pair a damper with each spring to better control the resulting motion at the expense of dealing with an extra set of constants for the dampers. To simplify the following discussion and diagrams, the spring-damper pairs will be referred to simply as springs with the understanding that there is usually an associated damper.

As external forces are applied to specific vertices of the object, either because of collisions, gravity, wind, or explicitly scripted forces, vertices will be displaced relative to other vertices of the object. This displacement will induce spring forces, which will impart forces to the adjacent vertices and reactive forces back to the initial vertex. These forces will result in further displacements, which will induce more spring forces throughout the object resulting in more displacements and so on. The result will be an object that is wriggling and jiggling as a result of the forces propagating along the edge springs and producing constant relative displacements of the vertices.

One of the drawbacks with using springs to model the effects of external forces on objects is that the effect has to propagate through the object, one time step at a time. This means that the number of vertices used to model an object and the length of edges used have an effect on the object's reaction to forces. Because the vertices carry the mass of the object, using a different distribution of vertices to describe the same object will result in a difference in the way the object reacts to external forces.

5.8.3 A simple example

In a simple two-dimensional example, an equilateral triangle composed of three vertices and three edges with uniform mass distribution and uniform spring constants will react to an initial external force applied to one of the vertices (Figure 5.5). Here an external force, $\vec{F}$, is applied to vertex $\mathbf{V}_2$, pushing it generally toward the other two vertices. Assume that the force is momentary and is applied only for one time step during the animation. At the application of the force, an acceleration, $\vec{a}_2 = \vec{F}/m_2$, is imparted to vertex $\mathbf{V}_2$ by the force. The acceleration gives rise to a velocity at point $\mathbf{V}_2$, which in turn creates a change in its position. At the next time step, the external force has already been removed, but because vertex $\mathbf{V}_2$ has been displaced, the lengths of edges $\mathbf{E}_{12}$ and $\mathbf{E}_{23}$ have been changed. As a result of this, a spring force is created along the two edges. The spring that models edge $\mathbf{E}_{12}$ imparts a restoring force to vertices $\mathbf{V}_1$ and $\mathbf{V}_2$ while the spring that models edge $\mathbf{E}_{23}$ imparts a restoring force to vertices $\mathbf{V}_2$ and $\mathbf{V}_3$. Notice that the springs push back against the movement of $\mathbf{V}_2$, trying to restore its position, while at the same time they are pushing the other two vertices away from $\mathbf{V}_2$. In a polygonal mesh, the springs associated with mesh edges propagate the effect of the force throughout the object.

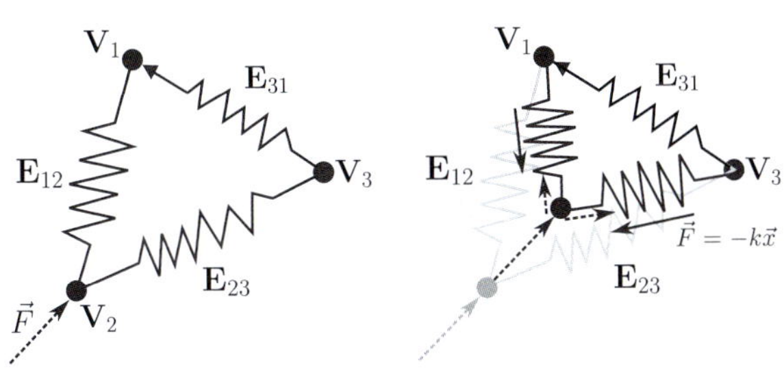

FIGURE 5.5

A simple spring-mass model of a flexible object.

If the only springs (or spring-dampers) used to model an object are ones associated with the object edges, the model can have more than one stable configuration. For example, if a cube's edges are modeled with springs, during applications of extreme external forces, the cube can turn inside out. Additional spring dampers can help to stabilize the shape of an object. Springs can be added across the object's faces and across its volume. To help prevent such undesirable, but stable, configurations in a cube, one or more springs that stretch diagonally from one vertex across the interior of the cube to the opposite vertex can be included in the model. These springs will help to model the internal material of a solid object (Figure 5.6).

If specific angles between adjacent faces (dihedral angles) are desired, then angular springs (and dampers) can be applied. The spring resists deviation to the rest angle between faces and imparts a torque along the edge that attempts to restore the rest angle (Equation 5.27 and Figure 5.7). The damper works to limit the resulting motion. The torque is applied to the vertex from which the dihedral angle is measured; a torque of equal magnitude but opposite direction is applied to the other vertex.

$$\hat{\tau} = k_S(\theta(t) - \theta_r) - k_d\dot{\theta}(t) \tag{5.27}$$

Alternatively, a linear spring could be defined between points A and B in Figure 5.7 to maintain the appropriate angle at the shared edge.

Depending on the size of forces applied to the spring's mass points, the size of the spring constant (and damper constant), and the size of the time step used to sample the system, a spring simulation may numerically explode, resulting in computed

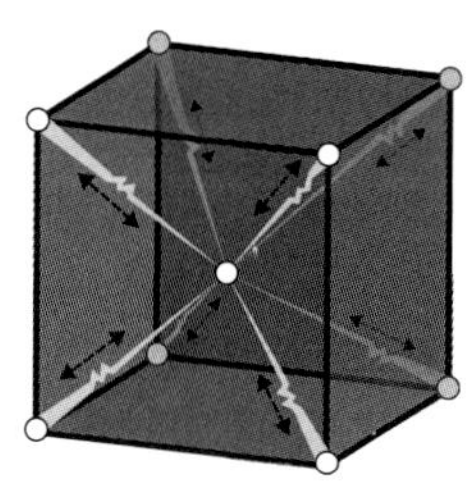

FIGURE 5.6

Interior springs to help stabilize the object's configuration.

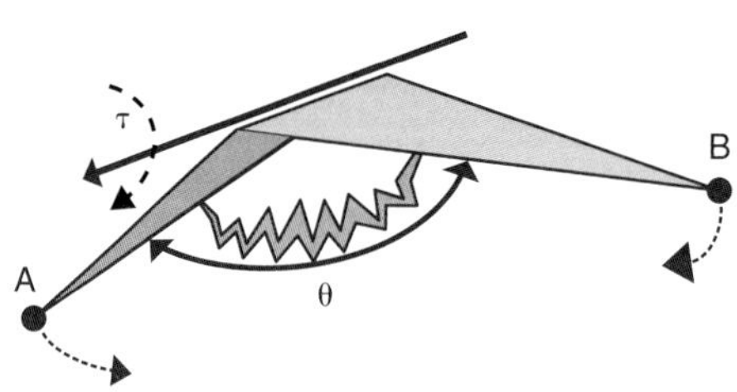

FIGURE 5.7

An angular spring imparting restoring torques.

behavior in which the motions get larger and larger over the course of time. This is because the force is (wrongly) assumed to be constant throughout the time step while, in fact, it is constantly changing as the spring length changes as it progresses from one time sample to the next. As mentioned before, modifying spring, damper, mass, and time step values can be adjusted to help control the simulation, but finding appropriate values can be tricky. Alternatively (or additionally) various simulation magnitudes, such as forces, accelerations, or velocities, can be clamped at maximum values to help control the motion.

5.8.4 Virtual springs

Virtual springs introduce forces into the system that do not directly model physical elements. These can be used to control the motion of objects in a variety of circumstances. In the previous section, it was suggested that virtual springs can be used to help maintain the shape of an object. Virtual springs with zero rest lengths can be used to constrain one object to lie on the surface of another, for example, or with nonzero rest lengths, to maintain separation between moving objects.

Proportional derivative controllers (PDCs) are another type of virtual spring used to keep a control variable and its derivative within the neighborhood of desired values. For example, to maintain a joint angle and joint velocity close to desired values, the user can introduce a torque into a system. If the desired values are functions of time, PDCs are useful for biasing a model toward a given motion while still allowing it to react to system forces, as in Equation 5.28.

$$\hat{\tau} = k_S(\theta(t) - \theta_d(t)) - k_d\left(\dot{\theta}(t) - \dot{\theta}_d(t)\right) \tag{5.28}$$

Springs, dampers, and PDCs are an easy and handy way to control the motion of objects by incorporating forces into a physically based modeling system. The springs can model physical elements in the system and represent arbitrary control forces. Dampers and PDCs are commonly used to keep system parameters close to desired values. They are not without problems, however. One drawback to using springs, dampers, and PDCs is that the user-supplied constants in the equations can be difficult to choose to obtain a desired effect. A drawback to using a spring mesh is that the effect of the forces must ripple through the mesh as the force propagates from one spring to the next. Still, they are often a useful and effective tool for the animator.

5.9 Enforcing soft and hard constraints

One of the main problems with using physically based animation is for the animator to get the object to do what they want while having it react to the forces modeled in the environment. One way to solve this is to place constraints on the object that restrict some subset of the degrees of freedom (DOF) of the object's motion. The remaining DOF are subject to the physically based animation system. Constraints are simply requirements placed on the object. For animation, constraints can take the form of colocating points, maintaining a minimum distance between objects, or requiring an object to have a certain orientation in space. The problem for the animation system is in enforcing the constraints while the object's motion is controlled by some other method.

If the constraints are to be strictly enforced, then they are referred to as *hard constraints*. If the constraints are relations the system should only attempt to satisfy, then they are referred to as *soft constraints*. Satisfying hard constraints requires more sophisticated numerical approaches than satisfying soft constraints. To satisfy hard constraints, computations are made that search for a motion that reacts to forces in the system while satisfying all of the constraints. As more constraints are added to the system, this becomes an increasingly difficult problem. Soft constraints are typically incorporated into a system as additional forces that influence the final motion. One way to model flexible objects is to create soft distance constraints between the vertices of an object. These constraints, modeled by a mesh of interconnected springs and dampers, react to other forces in the system such as gravity and collisions to create a dynamic structure. Soft constraint satisfaction can also be phrased as an energy minimization problem in which deviation from the constraints increases the system's energy. Forces are introduced into the system that decrease the system's energy.

Another way to gain animator control is to use *kinematic constraints* where the object is completely controlled by the animator but still retains any attachments to other physical objects. For example, in the jelly cube example, the animator may wish to have a point in the center that operates under kinematic constraints but is connected with virtual springs to other parts of the cube. This would allow the animator to control a single point using keyframes, interactivity, or interpolation to drive the movement of the object while it still retains the physical jelly-like properties.

Aside

Hard constraints are strictly enforced and *must* be satisfied completely (e.g., collision resolution constraints).

Soft constraints are not strictly enforced but influence movement and may be partially satisfied (e.g., flexible models).

Kinematic constraints are not simulated, but they retain connections to hard/soft constraints (e.g., keyframing/interpolating the position of a rigid body connected to simulated objects with springs).

5.9.1 Energy minimization

The concept of a system's energy can be used in a variety of ways to control the motion of objects. Used in this sense, energy is not defined solely as physically realizable, but it is free to be defined in whatever form serves the animator. Energy functions can be used to pin objects together, to restore the shape of objects, or to minimize the curvature in a spline as it interpolates points in space.

As presented by Witkin, Fleischer, and Barr [14], energy constraints induce restoring forces based on arbitrary functions of a model's parameters. The current state of a model can be expressed as a set of parameter values. These are external parameters such as position and orientation, as well as internal parameters such as joint angles, the radius of a cylinder, or the threshold of an implicit function. They are any value of the object model subject to change. The set of state parameters will be referred to as ψ.

A constraint is phrased in terms of a nonnegative smooth function, $E(\psi)$, of these parameters, and a local minimum of the constraint function is searched for in the space of all parametric values. The local minimum can be searched for by evaluating the gradient of the energy function and stepping in the direction of the negative of the gradient, $-\nabla E$. The gradient of a function is the parameter space vector in the direction of greatest increase of that function. Usually, the parametric state set will have quite a few elements, but for illustrative purposes, suppose there are only two state parameters. Taking the energy function as the surface of a height function of those two parameters, one can consider the gradient as pointing uphill from any point on that surface (Figure 5.8). Given an initial set of parameters, ψ_0, the parameter function at time zero is defined as $F(0) = \psi_0$. From this it follows that $F(t) = -\nabla E$. The force vector in parameter space is the negative of the gradient of the energy function, $-\nabla E$. Any of a number of numerical techniques can be used to solve the equation, but a particularly simple one is Euler's method, as shown in Equation 5.29.

$$F(t_{i+1}) = F(t_i) - h\nabla E \tag{5.29}$$

Determining the gradient, ∇E, is usually done numerically by stepping along each dimension in parameter space, evaluating the energy function, and taking differences between the new evaluations and the original value.

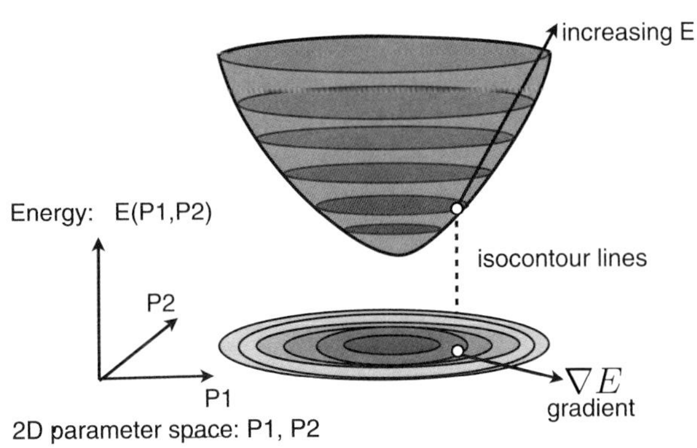

FIGURE 5.8

Sample simple energy function.

Three useful functions

As presented by Witkin, Fleischer, and Barr [14], three useful functions in defining an energy function are as follows:

- The parametric position function, $P(u, v)$
- The surface normal function, $N(u, v)$
- The implicit function, $I(x)$

The parametric position function and surface normal function are expressed as functions of surface parameters u and v (although for a given model, the surface parameters may be more complex, incorporating identifiers of object parts, for example). Given a value for u and v, the position of that point in space and the normal to the surface at that point are given by the functions. The implicit function takes as its parameter a position in space and evaluates to an approximation of the signed distance to the surface where a point on the surface returns a zero, a point outside the object returns a positive distance to the closest point on the surface, and a point inside the object returns a negative distance to the closest point on the surface. These functions will, of course, also be functions of the current state of the model, ψ.

Useful constraints

The functions above can be used to define several useful constraint functions. The methods of Witkin, Fleischer, and Barr [14] can also lead to several intuitive constraint functions. The functions typically are associated with one or more user-specified weights; these are not shown.

Point to fixed point

The point Q in space is fixed and is given in terms of absolute coordinate values. The point P is a specific point on the surface of the model and is specified by the u, v parameters. The energy function will be zero when these two points coincide.

$$E = |P(u, v) - Q|^2 \tag{5.30}$$

Point to point

A point on the surface of one object is given, and a point on the surface of a second object is given. The energy function will be zero when they coincide. Notice that within a constant, this is a zero-length spring. Also notice that the orientations of the objects are left unspecified. If this is the only constraint given, then the objects could completely overlap or partially penetrate each other to satisfy this constraint.

$$E = \left|P^a(u_a, v_a) - P^b(u_b, v_b)\right|^2 \tag{5.31}$$

Point-to-point locally abutting

The energy function is zero when the points coincide, and the dot product of the normals at those points is equal to -1 (i.e., they are pointing away from each other).

$$E = \left|P^a(u_a, v_a) - P^b(u_b, v_b)\right|^2 + N^a(u_a, v_a) \cdot N^b(u_b, v_b) + 1 \tag{5.32}$$

Floating attachment

With the use of the implicit function of object b, a specific point on object a is made to lie on the surface of object b.

$$E = \left(I^b\left(P^a(u_a, v_a)\right)\right)^2 \tag{5.33}$$

Floating attachment locally abutting

A point of object a is constrained to lie on the surface of b, using the implicit function of object b as previously mentioned. In addition, the normal of object a and the point must be collinear to and in the opposite direction of the normal of object b at the point of contact. The normal of object b is computed as the gradient of its implicit function.

Other constraints are possible. Witkin, Fleischer, and Barr [14] present several others, as well as some examples of animations using this technique.

$$E = \left(I^b\left(P^a(u_a, v_a)\right)\right)^2 + N^a(u_a, v_a) \cdot \frac{\nabla I^b\left(P^a(u_a, v_a)\right)}{\left|\nabla I^b\left(P^a(u_a, v_a)\right)\right|} + 1 \tag{5.34}$$

Energy constraints are not hard constraints

Although such energy functions can be implemented quite easily and can be effectively used to assemble a structure defined by relationships such as the ones discussed previously, a drawback to this approach is that the constraints used are not *hard constraints* in the sense that the constraint imposed on the model is not always met. For example, if a point-to-point constraint is specified and one of the points is moved rapidly away, the other point, as moved by the constraint satisfaction system, will chase around the moving point. If the moving point comes to a halt, then the second point will, after a time, come to rest on top of the first point, thus satisfying the point-to-point constraint.

5.9.2 Space-time constraints

Space-time constraints view motion as a solution to a constrained optimization problem that takes place over time in space. Hard constraints, which include equations of motion and nonpenetration constraints and locating the object at certain points in time and space, are placed on the object. An objective function that is to be optimized is stated, for example, to minimize the amount of force required to produce the motion over some time interval.

The material here is taken from Witkin and Kass [15]. Their introductory example will be used to illustrate the basic points of the method. Interested readers are urged to refer to that article, as well as follow-up articles on space-time constraints (e.g., [16], [17]).

Space-time particle

Consider a particle's position to be a function of time, $p(t)$. A time-varying force function, $f(t)$, is responsible for moving the particle. Its equation of motion is given in Equation 5.35.

$$m\ddot{p}(t) - f(t) - mg = 0 \tag{5.35}$$

Given the function $f(t)$ and values for the particle's position and velocity, (t_0) and $p(t_0)$, at some initial time, the position function, $p(t)$, can be obtained by integrating Equation 5.35 to solve the initial value problem.

However, the objective here is to determine the force function, $f(t)$. Initial and final positions for the particle are given, as well as the times the particle must be at these positions (Equation 5.36). These equations along with Equation 5.35 are the constraints on the motion.

$$x(t_0) = a \quad x(t_1) = b \tag{5.36}$$

The function to be minimized is the fuel consumption, which here, for simplicity, is given as $|f|^2$. For a given time period $t_0 < t < t_1$, this results in Equation 5.37 as the function to be minimized subject to the time-space constraints and the motion equation constraint.

$$R = \int_{t0}^{t1} |f|^2 dt \tag{5.37}$$

In solving this, discrete representations of the functions $p(t)$ and $f(t)$ are considered. Time derivatives of x are approximated by finite differences (Equations 5.38 and 5.39) and substituted into Equation 5.35 to form n physics constraints (Equation 5.40) and the two boundary constraints (Equation 5.41).

$$\dot{p}_i = \frac{p_i - p_{i-1}}{h} \tag{5.38}$$

$$\ddot{p}_i = \frac{p_{i+1} - 2p_i + p_{i-1}}{h^2}. \tag{5.39}$$

$$p_i = m\frac{p_{i+1} - 2p_i + p_{i-1}}{h^2} - f - mg = 0 \tag{5.40}$$

$$c_a = |p_1 - a| = 0 \quad c_b = |p_n - b| = 0 \tag{5.41}$$

If one assumes that the force function is constant between samples, the object function, R, becomes a sum of the discrete values of f. The discrete function R is to be minimized subject to the discrete constraint functions, which are expressed in terms of the sample values, p_i and f_i, that are to be solved for.

Numerical solution

The problem as stated fits into the generic form of constrained optimization problems, which is to "find the S_j values that minimize R subject to $C_i(S_j) = 0$." The S_j values are the p_i and f_i. Solution methods can be considered black boxes that request current values for the S_j values, R, and the C_i values, as well as the derivatives of R and the C_i with respect to the S_j as the solver iterates toward a solution.

The solution method used by Witkin and Kass [15] is a variant of sequential quadratic programming [18]. This method computes a second-order Newton-Raphson step in R, which is taken irrespective of any constraints on the system. A first-order Newton-Raphson step is computed in the C_i to reduce the constraint functions. The step to minimize the objective function, R, is projected onto the null space of the constraint step, that subspace in which the constraints are constant to a first-order approximation. Therefore as steps are taken to minimize the constraints, a particular direction for the step is chosen that does not affect the constraint minimization and that reduces the objective function.

Because it is first-order in the constraint functions, the first derivative matrix (the Jacobian) of the constraint function must be computed (Equation 5.42). Because it is second-order in the objective function, the second derivative matrix (the Hessian) of the objective function must be computed (Equation 5.43). The first derivative vector of the objective function must also be computed, $\frac{\partial R}{\partial S_j}$.

$$\mathbf{J}_{ij} = \frac{\partial C_i}{\partial S_j} \tag{5.42}$$

$$\mathbf{H}_{ij} = \frac{\partial^2 R_i}{\partial S_i \partial S_j} \tag{5.43}$$

The second-order step to minimize R, irrespective of the constraints, is taken by solving the linear system of equations shown in Equation 5.44. A first-order step to drive the C_{js} to zero is taken by solving the linear system of equations shown in Equation 5.45.

The final update is $\Delta S_j = \widehat{S}_j + \widetilde{S}_j$. The algorithm reaches a fixed point when the constraints are satisfied, and any further step that minimizes R would violate one or more of the constraints.

$$-\frac{\partial}{\partial S_j}(R) = \sum_j \mathbf{H}_{ij}\widehat{S}_j \tag{5.44}$$

$$-C_i - \sum_j \mathbf{J}_{ij}(\widehat{S}_j + \widetilde{S}_j) \tag{5.45}$$

Although one of the more complex methods presented here, space-time constraints are a powerful and useful tool for producing realistic motion while maintaining given constraints. They are particularly effective for creating the illusion of self-propelled objects whose movement is subject to user-supplied time constraints.

5.9.3 Bodies in collision

When an object starts to move in any kind of environment, chances are that sooner or later it will bump into something. If nothing is done about this in a computer animation, the object will penetrate and then pass through other objects. Other types of contact include objects sliding against and resting on each other. All of these types of contact require the calculation of forces to accurately simulate the reaction of one object to another. This is performed during the Collision system and generally consists of two stages: (1) Collision detection, where algorithms are employed to determine whether or not a collision has occurred between two or more objects, and (2) Collision resolution, in which the reactions of colliding objects must be considered based on the intended interactions—that is, should they bounce, or stop, or trigger another action?

Detection is strictly a kinematic issue in that it has to do with the positions and orientations of objects and how they change over time. Resolution is usually a dynamic issue in that forces that are a result of the collision are computed and used to produce new motions for the objects involved.

Collision detection considers the movement of one object relative to another. In its most basic form, testing for a collision amounts to determining whether there is intersection in the static position of two objects at a specific instance in time. In a more sophisticated form, the movement of one object relative to the other object during a finite time interval is tested for overlap. These computations can become quite involved when dealing with complex geometries.

Collision response is a consideration in physically based simulation. The geometric extent of the object is not of concern but rather the distribution of its mass. Localized forces at specific points on the object impart linear and rotational forces onto the other objects involved.

In dealing with the time of collision, there are two options. The first is to proceed as best as one can from this point in time by calculating an appropriate reaction to the current situation by the particle involved in the collision (the penalty method). This option allows penetration of the particle before the collision reaction takes place. Of course, if the particle is moving rapidly, this penetration might be visually significant. If multiple collisions occur in a time interval, they are treated as occurring simultaneously even though handling them in their correct sequential order may have produced different results. Although more inaccurate than the second option, this is simpler to implement and often gives acceptable results.

The second option is to back up time t_i to the first instant that a collision occurred and determine the appropriate response at the time of collision. If multiple collisions occur in a time interval, then time is backed up to the point at which the first collision took place. In complex environments in which collisions happen at a high rate, this constant backing up of time and recomputing the motion of objects can become quite time-consuming.

There are three common options for collision response: a strictly kinematic response, the penalty method, and the calculation of an impulse force. The kinematic response is quick and easy. It produces good visual results for particles and spherically shaped objects. The penalty method introduces a temporary, nonphysically based force to restore nonpenetration. It is typically used when response to the collision occurs at the time step when penetration is detected (as opposed to backing up time). The advantage of this technique is that it is easy to compute and the force is easily incorporated into the computational mechanism that simulates rigid-body movement. Calculating the impulse force is a more precise way of introducing a force into the system and is typically used when time is backed up to the point of first contact. Detecting collisions and reacting to them are discussed next.

Particle-plane collision and kinematic response

One of the simplest illustrative situations to consider for collision detection and response is that of a particle traveling at some velocity toward a stationary plane at an arbitrary angle (Figure 5.9). The task is to detect when the particle collides with the plane and have it bounce off the plane. Because a simple plane is involved, its planar equation can be used (Equation 5.46). $E(p)$ is the planar function; a, b, c, and d are coefficients of the planar equation; and p is, for example, a particle's position in space that has no physical extent of its own. Points on the plane satisfy the planar equation, that is, $E(p) = 0$. Assuming for now that the plane represents the ground, the planar equation can be formed so that for points above the plane, the planar equation evaluates to a positive value, $E(p) > 0$; for points below the plane, $E(p) < 0$.

$$E(p) = ap_x + bp_y + cp_2 + d = 0 = \vec{N} \cdot \vec{p} \text{ where } \vec{N} = (a, b, c, d) \text{ is the homogeneous plane normal and } \vec{p} = \left(p_x, p_y, p_z, 1\right) \text{ is the homogeneous point to test.} \tag{5.46}$$

The particle travels toward the plane as its position is updated according to its average velocity over the time interval, as in Equation 5.47. At each time step t_i, the particle is tested to see if it is still above the plane, $E(p(t_i))\rangle 0$. As long as this evaluates to a positive value, there is no collision. The first time t at which $E(p(t_i))\langle 0$ indicates that the particle has collided with the plane at some time before now. What to do with that information? The collision has already occurred, and something has to be done about it.

$$\vec{p}_{t+1} - \vec{p}_t + \underbrace{\vec{v}_t}_{\text{avg}} \Delta t \tag{5.47}$$

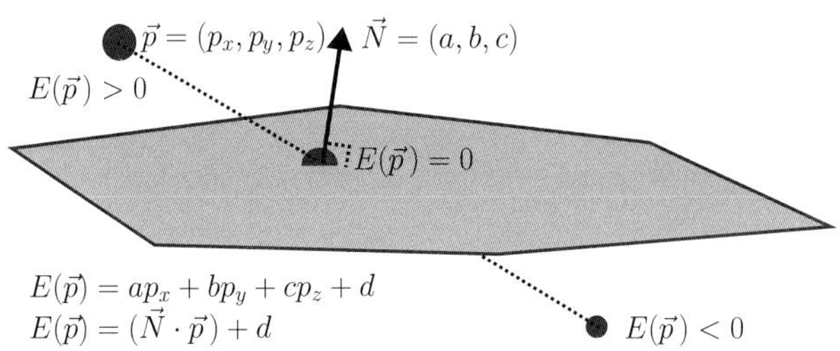

FIGURE 5.9

Point-plane collision.

In simple kinematic response, when penetration is detected, the velocity of the particle is decomposed, using the normal to the plane ($\vec{N}$), into the normal component and the perpendicular-to-the-normal component (Figure 5.10). The normal component of the velocity vector is negated by subtracting it out of the original velocity vector and then subtracting it out again. To reduce the height of each successive bounce, a damping factor, $0 < k < 1$, can be applied when subtracting it out the second time (Equation 5.48). This bounces the particle off a surface at a reduced velocity. This approach is not physically based, but it produces reasonable visuals, especially for particles and spherically shaped objects. Incorporating kinematic response to collisions with the ground produces Figure 5.11.

$$\begin{aligned}\vec{v}_{t+1} &= \vec{v}_t - (\vec{v}_t \cdot \vec{N})\vec{N} - k(\vec{v}_t \cdot \vec{N})\vec{N} \\ &= \vec{v}_t - (1+k)(\vec{v}_t \cdot \vec{N})\vec{N}\end{aligned} \tag{5.48}$$

The penalty method

When objects penetrate due to temporal sampling, a simple method of constructing a reaction to the implied collision is the *penalty method*. As the name suggests, a point is penalized for penetrating another object. In this case, a spring, with a zero rest length, is momentarily attached from the offending point to the surface it penetrated in such a way that it imparts a restoring force on the offending point. For now, it is

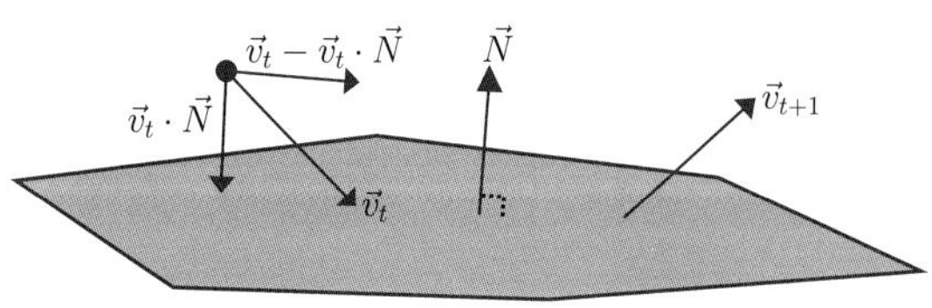

FIGURE 5.10

Kinematic solution for collision reaction.

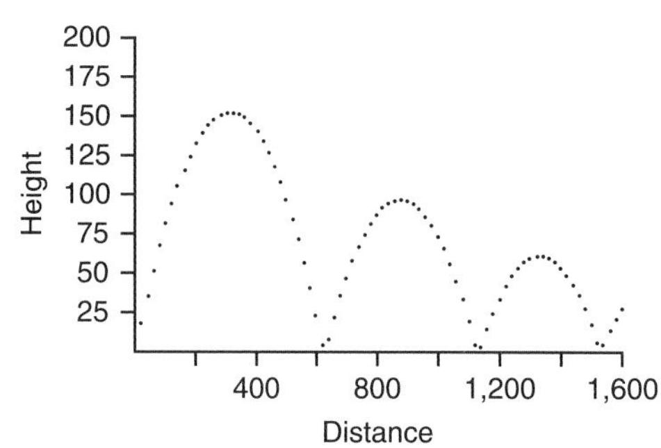

FIGURE 5.11

Kinematic response to collisions with ground using 0.8 as the damping.

assumed that the surface it penetrates is immovable and thus does not have to be considered as far as collision response is concerned. The closest point on the penetrated surface to the penetrating point is used as the point of attachment (Figure 5.12). The spring, therefore, imparts a force on the point in the direction of the penetrated surface normal and with a magnitude according to Hooke's law ($F = -kd$). A mass assigned to the point is used to compute a resultant acceleration ($a = F/m$), which contributes an upward velocity to the point. When this upward velocity is combined with the point's original motion, the point's downward motion will be stopped and reversed by the spring, whereas any component of its motion tangent to the surface will be unaffected. Although easy to implement, this approach is not ideal. An arbitrary mass (m) must be assigned to the point, and an arbitrary constant (k) must be determined for the spring. It is difficult to control because if the spring constant is too weak or if the mass is too large, then the collision will not be corrected immediately. If the spring constant is too strong or the mass is too small, then the colliding surfaces will be thrown apart in an unrealistic manner. If the point is moving fast relative to the surface it penetrated, then it may take a few time steps for the spring to take effect and restore a state of nonpenetration. If the desired velocity after the next time step is known, then this can be used to help determine the spring constants.

Using the previous example and implementing the penalty method produces the motion traced in Figure 5.13. In this implementation, a temporary spring is

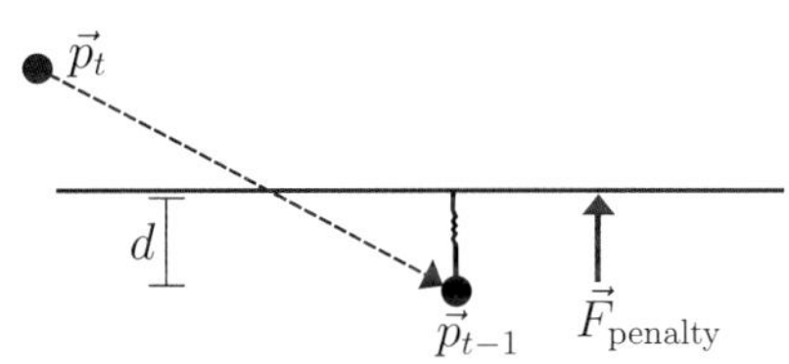

FIGURE 5.12

Penalty spring.

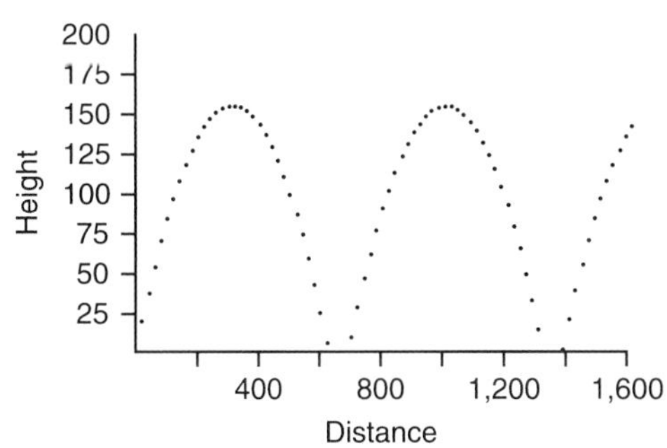

FIGURE 5.13

Penalty method with a spring constant of 250 and a point mass of 10, for example, from section 5.9.3.

introduced into the system whenever both the y component of the position and the y component of the velocity vector are negative; a spring constant of 250 and a point mass of 10 are used. Although the spring force is easy to incorporate with other system forces such as gravity, the penalty method requires the user to specify control parameters that typically require a trial-and-error process to determine appropriate values because of other forces that may be present in the system.

When used with polyhedra objects, the penalty force can give rise to torque when not acting in line with the center of mass of an object. When two polyhedra collide, the spring is attached to both objects and imparts an equal but opposite force on the two to restore nonpenetration.

Testing polyhedra

In environments in which objects are modeled as polyhedra, at each time step each polyhedron is tested for possible penetration against every other polyhedron. A collision is implied whenever the environment transitions from a nonpenetration state to a state in which a penetration is detected. A test for penetration at each time step can miss some collisions because of the discrete temporal sampling, but it is sufficient for many applications.

Various tests can be used to determine whether an overlap condition exists between polyhedra, and the tests should be chosen according to computational efficiency and generality. Bounding box tests, also known as min-max tests, can be used to quickly determine if there is any chance for an intersection. A bounding box can easily be constructed by searching for the minimum and maximum values in x, y, z. Bounding boxes can be tested for overlap. If there is no overlap of the bounding boxes, then there can be no overlap of the objects. If the object's shape does not match a rectangle well, then a bounding sphere or bounding slabs (pairs of parallel planes at various orientations that bound the object) can be used. A hierarchy of bounding shapes can be used on object groups, individual objects, and individual faces. If these bounding tests fail to conclusively establish that a nonoverlap situation exists, then more elaborate tests must be conducted.

Most collisions can be detected by testing each of the vertices of one object to see if any are inside another polyhedron and then testing each of the vertices of the other object to see if any are inside the first. To test whether a point is inside a convex polyhedron, each of the planar equations for the faces of the object is evaluated using the point's coordinates. If the planes are oriented so that a point to the outside of the object evaluates to a positive value and a point to the inside of the object evaluates to a negative value, then the point under consideration has to evaluate to a negative value in all of the planar equations to be declared inside the polyhedron.

Testing a point to determine if it is inside a concave polyhedron is more difficult. One way to do it is to construct a semi-infinite ray emanating from the point under consideration in any particular direction. For example, $y = \mathrm{P}_y$, $z = P_z$, $x > P_x$ defines a line parallel to the x-axis going in the positive direction from the point P. This semi-infinite ray is used to test for intersection with all of the faces of the object, and the intersections are counted; an odd number of intersections means that the point is inside the object, and an even number means that the point is outside. To intersect a ray with a face, the ray is intersected with the planar equation of the face, and then the point of intersection is tested to see if it is inside the polygonal face.

Care must be taken in correctly counting intersections if this semi-infinite ray intersects the object exactly at an edge or vertex or if the ray is collinear with an edge of the object. (These cases are similar to the situations that occur when scan converting concave polygons.) Although this does not occur very often, it should be dealt with robustly. Because the number of intersections can be difficult to resolve in such situations, it can be computationally more efficient to simply choose a semi-infinite ray in a different direction and start over with the test.

One can miss some intersection situations if performing only these tests. The edges of each object must be tested for intersection with the faces of the other object and vice versa to capture other overlap situations. The edge-face intersection test consists of two steps. In the first step, the edge is tested for intersection with the plane of the face (i.e., the edge vertices are on opposite sides of the plane of the face), and the point of intersection is computed if it exists. In the second step, the point of intersection is tested for two-dimensional containment inside the face. The edge-face intersection tests capture almost all of the penetration situations,[1] but because it is the more expensive of the two tests, it is usually better to perform the vertex tests first (Figure 5.14).

In any of these tests, vertices of one object that lie exactly in the plane of a face from the other object are a special case that must be handled carefully. Usually, it is sufficient to logically and consistently push such a vertex to one side of the plane.

Often, a normal that defines the plane of intersection is used in the collision response calculations. For collisions that are detected by the penetration tests, one of two collision situations can usually be established by looking at the relative

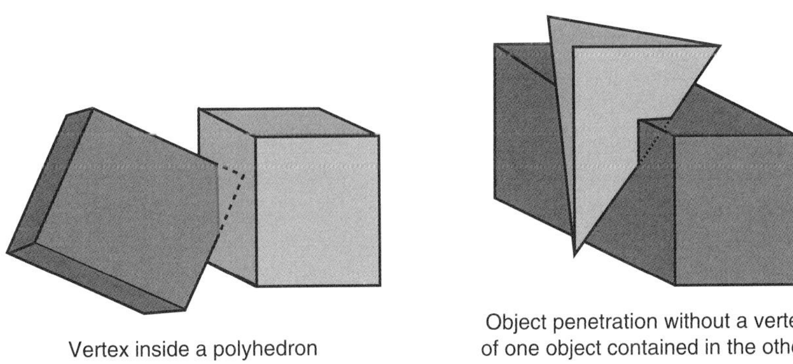

FIGURE 5.14

Detecting polyhedra intersections.

[1] The edge-face intersection test will miss the case when one object is entirely inside of the other; this case is handled by testing a single vertex from each object to see if it is inside the other object..

motion of the objects. Either a vertex has just penetrated a face, or an edge from one object has just intersected an edge from the other object. In either case, the plane of intersection can be established. When a vertex has penetrated a face, a normal to the face is used. When there is an edge-edge intersection, the normal is defined as the cross-product of the two edges.

In certain limited cases, a more precise determination of collision can be performed. For example, if the movement of one object with respect to another is a linear path, then the volume swept by one object can be determined and intersected with the other object whose position is assumed to be static relative to the moving object. If the direction of travel is indicated by a vector, *V*, then front faces and back faces with respect to the direction of travel can be determined. The *boundary edges* that share a front face and a back face can be identified; *boundary vertices* are the vertices of boundary edges. The volume swept by the object is defined by the original back faces, the translated positions of the front faces, and new faces and edges that are extruded in the direction of travel from boundary edges and boundary vertices (Figure 5.15). This volume is intersected with the static object.

Impulse force of collision

To allow for more accurate handling of the moment of collision, time can be "backed up" to the point of impact, the reaction can be computed, and the time can be moved forward again. Although more accurate in its reconstruction of events, this approach can become very computationally intense in complex environments if many closely spaced collisions occur. However, for a point-plane collision, the impulse can be simplified because the angular velocity can be ignored.

The actual time of collision within a time interval can be searched for by using a binary search strategy. If it is known that a collision occurred between t_{i-1} and t_i, these times are used to initialize the lower ($L = t_{i-1}$) and upper ($U = t_i$) bounds on the time interval to be tested. At each iteration of the search, the point's position is tested at the middle of the bounded interval. If the test indicates that the point has not collided yet, then the lower bound is replaced with the middle of the time interval.

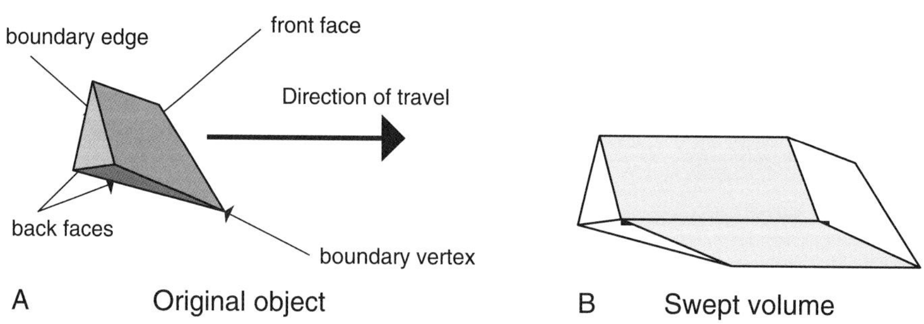

FIGURE 5.15

Sweep volume by translating front-facing faces and extruding new edges from original boundary vertices and extruding new faces from original boundary edges.

Otherwise, the upper bound is replaced with the middle of the time interval. This test repeats with the middle of the new time interval and continues until some desired tolerance is attained. The tolerance can be based either on the length of the time interval or on the range of distances the point could be on either side of the surface.

Alternatively, a linear-path constant-velocity approximation can be used over the time interval to simplify the calculations. The position of the point before penetration and the position after penetration can be used to define a linear path. The point of intersection along the line with a planar surface can be calculated analytically. The relative position of the intersection point along this line can be used to estimate the precise moment of impact (Figure 5.16).

As previously discussed, at the time of impact, the normal component of the point's velocity can be modified as the response to the collision. A scalar, the coefficient of restitution, between zero and 1 can be applied to the resulting velocity to model the degree of elasticity of the collision (Figure 5.17).

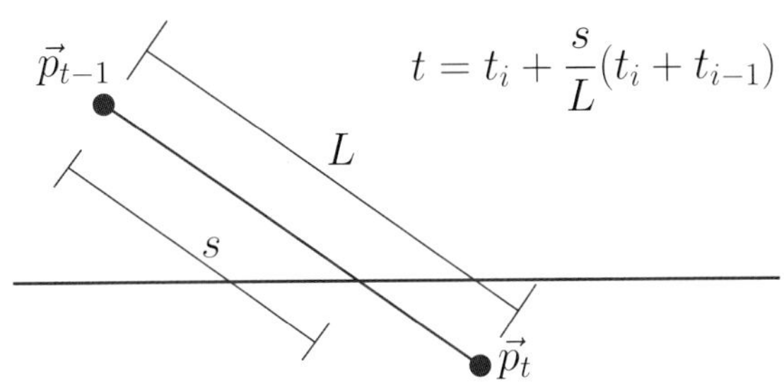

FIGURE 5.16

Linearly estimating time of impact, t.

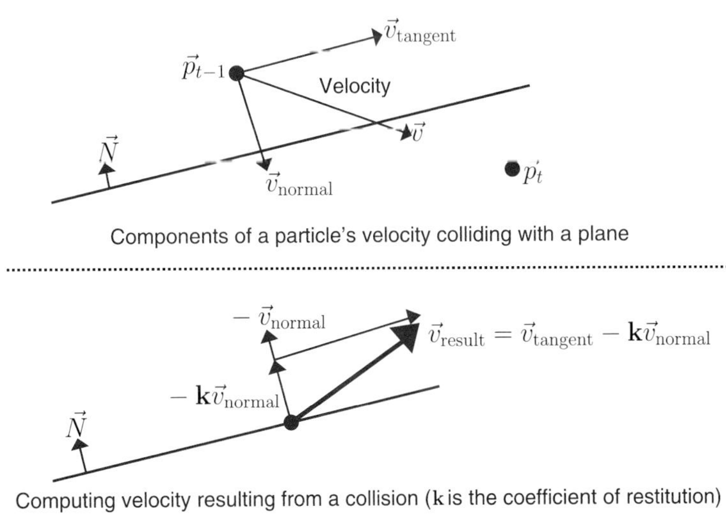

FIGURE 5.17

Impact response of a point with a plane.

Computing impulse forces

Once a collision is detected and the simulation has been backed up to the point of intersection, the reaction to the collision can be calculated. By working back from the desired change in velocity due to a collision, an equation that computes the required change in momentum can be formed. This equation uses a new term, called *impulse*, expressed in units of momentum. The impulse, **J**, can be viewed as a large force acting over a short time interval (Equation 5.49). The change in momentum **P**, and therefore the change in velocity, can be computed once the impulse is known (Equation 5.50).

$$\mathbf{J} = \mathbf{F}\Delta t \tag{5.49}$$

$$\mathbf{J} = \mathbf{F}\Delta t = M\vec{a}\Delta t = M\Delta\vec{a} = \Delta\left(M\vec{a}\right) = \Delta\mathbf{P} \tag{5.50}$$

To characterize the elasticity of the collision response, the user selects the coefficient of restitution, in the range $0 \le k \le 1$, which relates the relative velocity before the collision, $\vec{v}^{\,+}_{rel}$ to the relative velocity after the collision in the direction normal to the surface of contact, $\vec{N}$ (Equation 5.51). Impulse is a vector quantity in the direction of the normal to the surface of contact, $\mathbf{J} = j\vec{N}$. To compute **J**, the equations of how the velocities must change based on the equations of motion before and after the collision are used. These equations use the magnitude of the impulse, j, and they are used to solve for its value.

$$\vec{v}^{\,+}_{rel}(t) = -k\vec{v}^{\,-}_{\mathrm{rel}}(t) \tag{5.51}$$

Assume that the collision of two objects, A and B, has been detected at time t. Each object has a position for its center of mass $\left(\vec{c}_A(t), \vec{c}_B(t)\right)$, linear velocity $\left(\vec{v}_A(t), \vec{v}_B(t)\right)$, and angular velocity $\left(\vec{\omega}_A(t), \vec{\omega}_B(t)\right)$. The points of collision $\left(\vec{p}_A(t), \vec{p}_B(t)\right)$ have been identified on each object (Figure 5.18).

At the point of intersection, the normal to the surface of contact, $\vec{N}$, is determined depending on whether it is a vertex-face contact or an edge-edge contact. The relative positions of the contact points with respect to the center of masses

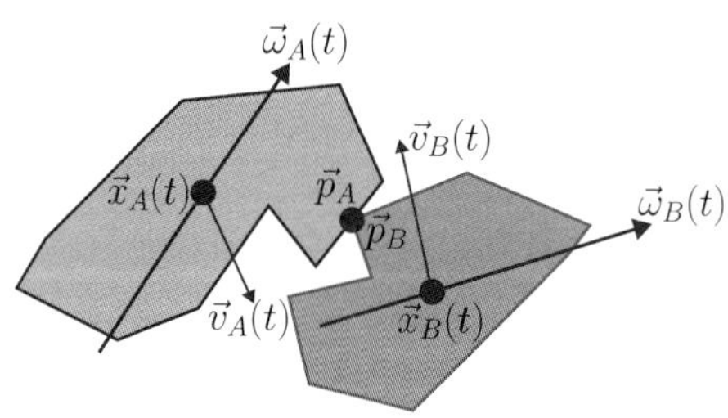

FIGURE 5.18

Configuration of colliding objects.

are $\vec{r}_A$ and $\vec{r}_B$, respectively (Equation 5.52). The relative velocity of the contact points of the two objects in the direction of the normal to the surface is computed by Equation 5.53. The velocities of the points of contact are computed as in Equation 5.54.

$$\begin{aligned}\vec{r}_A(t) &= \vec{p}_A(t) - \vec{c}_A(t)\\ \vec{r}_B(t) &= \vec{p}_B(t) - \vec{c}_B(t)\end{aligned} \tag{5.52}$$

$$\vec{v}_{\text{rel}}(t) = \left(\left(\dot{\vec{p}}_A(t) - \dot{\vec{p}}_B(t)\right) \cdot \vec{N}\right)\vec{N} \tag{5.53}$$

$$\begin{aligned}\dot{\vec{p}}_A(t) &= \vec{v}_A(t) + \vec{\omega}_A(t) \times \vec{r}_A(t)\\ \dot{\vec{p}}_B(t) &= \vec{v}_B(t) + \vec{\omega}_B(t)\times\vec{r}_B(t)\end{aligned}$$

The linear and angular velocities of the objects before the collision $\left(\vec{v}_A^-, \vec{\omega}_B^-\right)$ are updated by the impulse to form the linear and angular velocities after the collision, $\left(\vec{v}_A^+, \vec{\omega}_B^+\right)$. The linear velocities are updated by adding in the effect of the impulse scaled by one over the masses $(\mathbf{M}_A, \mathbf{M}_B)$ (Equation 5.55). The angular velocities are updated by computing the effect of the impulse on the angular velocity of the objects (Equation 5.56).

$$\begin{aligned}\vec{v}_A^+(t) &= \vec{v}_A^-(t) + \frac{j\vec{N}}{\mathbf{M}_A}\\ \vec{v}_B^+(t) &= \vec{v}_B^-(t) + \frac{j\vec{N}}{\mathbf{M}_B}\end{aligned} \tag{5.55}$$

$$\begin{aligned}\vec{\omega}_A^+(t) &= \vec{\omega}_A^-(t) + \mathbf{I}_A^-\left(\vec{r}_A(t) \times j\vec{N}\right)\\ \vec{\omega}_B^+(t) &= \vec{\omega}_B^-(t) + \mathbf{I}_B^-\left(\vec{r}_B(t) \times j\vec{N}\right)\end{aligned} \tag{5.56}$$

To solve for the impulse, form the difference between the velocities of the contact points after collision in the direction of the normal to the surface of contact (Equation 5.57). The version of Equation 5.54 for velocities after collision is substituted into Equation 5.57. Equations 5.55 and 5.56 are then substituted into that to produce Equation 5.58. Finally, substituting into Equation 5.51 and solving for j produces Equation 5.59.

$$\vec{v}_A^+(t) = \left(\left(\dot{\vec{p}}_A^+(t) - \dot{\vec{p}}_B^+(t)\right) \cdot \vec{N}\right)\vec{N} \tag{5.57}$$

$$\vec{v}_{\text{rel}}(t) = \vec{N}\left(\left(\vec{v}_A^+(t) + \vec{\omega}_A^+(t) \times \vec{r}_A(t)\right) - \left(\vec{v}_B^+(t) + \vec{\omega}_B^+(t)\times\vec{r}_B(t)\right)\right) \tag{5.58}$$

$$j = \frac{-(1+k)\vec{v}_{\text{rel}}^-}{\mathbf{M}_A^{-1} + \mathbf{M}_B^{-1} + \vec{N}\left(\mathbf{I}_A^{-1}(t)\left(\vec{r}_A(t) \times \vec{N}\right) \times \vec{r}_A(t) - \mathbf{I}_B^{-1}(t)\left(\vec{r}_B(t) \times \vec{N}\right) \times \vec{r}_B(t)\right)} \tag{5.59}$$

Contact between two objects is defined by the point on each object involved in the contact and the normal to the surface of contact. A point of contact is tested to see if an actual collision is taking place. When collision is tested for, the velocity of the contact point on each object is calculated. A collision is detected if the component of the relative velocity of the two points in the direction of the normal indicates the contact points are approaching each other.

If there is a collision, then Equation 5.59 is used to compute the magnitude of the impulse (Figure 5.19). The impulse is used to scale the contact normal, which can then be used to update the linear and angular momenta of each object.

If there is more than one point of contact between two objects, then each must be tested for collision. Each time a collision point is identified, it is processed for updating the momentum as above. If any collision is processed in the list of contact points, then after the momenta have been updated, the contact list must be traversed again to see if there exist any collision points with the new object momenta. Each time one or more collisions are detected and processed in the list, the list must be traversed again; this is repeated until it can be traversed and no collisions are detected.

Friction

An object resting on the surface of another object (the *supporting object*) is referred to as being in a state of *resting contact* with respect to that supporting object. In such a case, any force acting on the first object is decomposed into a component parallel to the contact surface and a component in the direction of the normal of the contact surface, called the *normal force*, $\boldsymbol{F_N}$ (Figure 5.20). If the normal force is toward the supporting object, and if the supporting object is considered immovable, such as the ground or a table, the normal force is immediately and completely canceled by a

Compute $\overrightarrow{\Delta p_A}, \overrightarrow{\Delta p_B}$
$V_{\text{relative}} = \vec{N} \cdot (\overrightarrow{\Delta p_A} - \overrightarrow{\Delta p_B})$
if $V_{\text{relative}} >$ threshold
  compute j ; magnitude of impulse to apply
  $\vec{J} = j * \vec{N}$
  $\vec{P}_A = \vec{P}_A + \vec{J}$; update object A linear momentum
  $\vec{P}_B = \vec{P}_B - \vec{J}$; update object B linear momentum
  $\vec{L}_A = \vec{L}_A + \vec{r}_A \times \vec{J}$; update object A angular momentum
  $\vec{L}_B = \vec{L}_B - \vec{r}_B \times \vec{J}$; update object B angular momentum
else if $V_{\text{relative}} > -$threshold
  update as resting contact
else
  objects are moving away from each other

FIGURE 5.19

Computing the impulse force of collision.

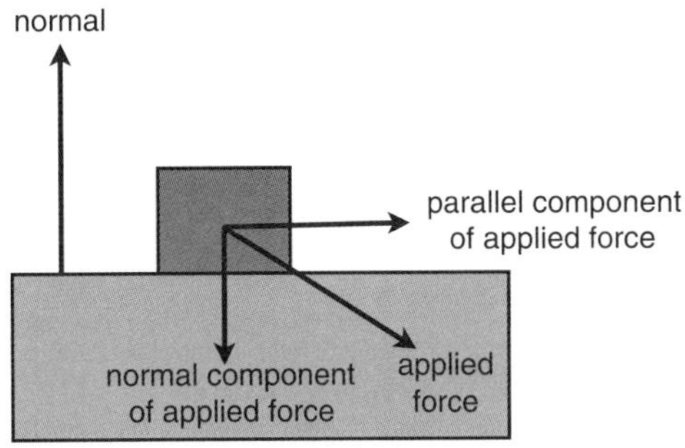

FIGURE 5.20

Normal and parallel components of applied force.

force equal and opposite in direction that is supplied by the supporting object. If the supporting object is movable, then the normal force is applied transitively to the supporting object and added to the forces being applied to the supporting object. If the normal force is directed away from the supporting object, then it is simply used to move the object up and away from the supporting object.

The component of the force applied to the object that is parallel to the surface is responsible for sliding (or rolling) the object along the surface of the supporting object. If the object is initially stationary with respect to the supporting object, then there is typically some threshold force, due to *static friction*, that must be exceeded before the object will start to move. This static friction force, F_s, is a function of the normal force, F_N (Equation 5.60). The constant μ_s is the coefficient of static friction and is a function of the two surfaces in contact.

$$\mathbf{F}_s = \mu_s \mathbf{F}_{\overrightarrow{N}} \tag{5.60}$$

Once the object is moving along the surface of the supporting object, there is a *kinetic friction* that works opposite to the direction of travel. This friction creates a force, opposite to the direction of travel, which is a linear function of the normal force, $\boldsymbol{F}_k$, on the object (Equation 5.61). The constant μ_k is the coefficient of kinetic friction and is a function of the two surfaces in contact.

$$\mathbf{F}_k = \mu_k \mathbf{F}_{\overrightarrow{N}} \tag{5.61}$$

Resting contact

Computing the forces involved in resting contact is one of the more difficult dynamics problems for computer animation. The exposition here follows that found in Baraff's work [19]. The solution requires access to quadratic programming, the implementation of which is beyond the scope of this book. An example situation in which several objects are resting on one another is shown in Figure 5.21.

For each contact point, there is a force normal to the surface of contact, just as in colliding contact. The objective is to find the magnitude of that force for a given

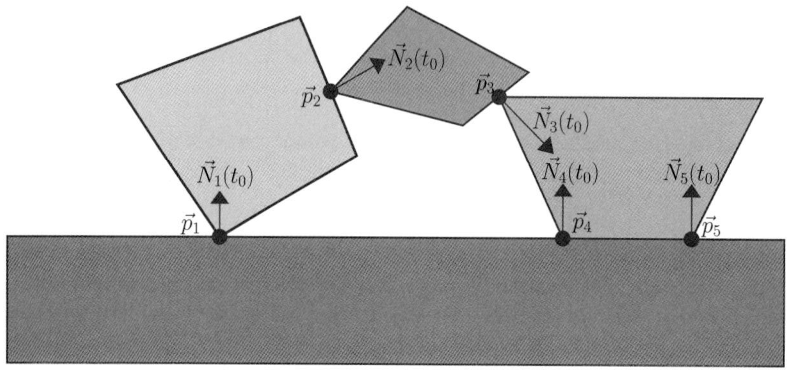

FIGURE 5.21

Multiple-object resting contacts.

configuration of objects. These forces (1) have to be strong enough to prevent interpenetration; (2) must only push objects apart, not together; and (3) have to go to zero at the point of contact at the moment that objects begin to separate.

To analyze what is happening at a point of contact, use a distance function, d_i, which evaluates the distance between the objects at the ith point of contact. Assuming objects A and B are involved in the ith contact and the points involved in the ith contact are $\overrightarrow{p}_A$ and $\overrightarrow{p}_B$ from the respective objects, then the distance function is given by Equation 5.62.

$$d_i = \left(\overrightarrow{p}_A - \overrightarrow{p}_B\right) \cdot \overrightarrow{N}_i \tag{5.62}$$

If d_i is zero, then the objects involved are still in contact. Whenever $d_i > 0$, the objects are separated. One of the objectives is to avoid $d_i < 0$, which would indicate penetration.

Assume at some time t_0, the distance between objects is zero. To prevent object penetration from time t_0 onward, the relative velocity of the two objects must be greater than or equal to zero, $\dot{d}_i \geq 0$ when $t > t_0$. The equation for relative velocity is produced by differentiating Equation 5.62 and is shown in Equation 5.63. At t_0, the objects are touching, so $t_0 : \overrightarrow{p}_A = \overrightarrow{p}_B$. This results in Equation 5.64. In addition, for resting contact, $t_0 : \dot{d}_i = 0$.

$$\forall t\colon \dot{d}_i = \dot{\overrightarrow{N}}_i \cdot \left(\overrightarrow{p}_A - \overrightarrow{p}_B\right) + \overrightarrow{N}_i \cdot \left(\dot{\overrightarrow{p}}_A - \dot{\overrightarrow{p}}_B\right) \tag{5.63}$$

Because $t_0 : d_i = \dot{d}_i = 0$, penetration will be avoided if the second derivative is greater than or equal to zero, $\forall t : \ddot{d}_i \geq 0$. The second derivative is produced by differentiating Equation 5.63 as shown in Equation 5.64. Remembering $t_0 : \overrightarrow{p}_A = \overrightarrow{p}_B$, one finds that the second derivative simplifies as shown in Equation

5.65. Notice that Equation 5.65 further simplifies if the normal to the surface of contact does not change ($t_0 : \dot{\vec{n}}_i = 0$).

$$\forall t: \ddot{d}_i = \left(\ddot{\vec{p}}_A - \ddot{\vec{p}}_B\right) \cdot \vec{N}_i + \left(\dot{\vec{p}}_A - \dot{\vec{p}}_B\right) \cdot \dot{\vec{N}}_i + \left(\dot{\vec{p}}_A - \dot{\vec{p}}_B\right) \cdot \ddot{\vec{N}}_i \tag{5.64}$$

$$t_0: \ddot{d}_i = 2\left(\dot{\vec{p}}_A - \dot{\vec{p}}_B\right) \cdot \dot{\vec{N}}_i + \left(\ddot{\vec{p}}_A - \ddot{\vec{p}}_B\right) \cdot \vec{N}_i \tag{5.65}$$

The constraints on the forces as itemized at the beginning of this section can now be written as equations: the forces must prevent penetration (Equation 5.66); the forces must push objects apart, not together (Equation 5.67); and either the objects are not separating or, if the objects are separating, then the contact force is zero (Equation 5.68).

$$d_i \geq 0 \tag{5.66}$$

$$f_i \geq 0 \tag{5.67}$$

$$\ddot{d}_i f_i = 0 \tag{5.68}$$

The relative acceleration of the two objects at the ith contact point, $t_0 : \ddot{d}_i$, is written as a linear combination of all of the unknown f_{ij} terms (Equation 5.69). For a given contact, j, its effect on the relative acceleration of the bodies involved in the ith contact point needs to be determined. Referring to Equation 5.65, the component of the relative acceleration that is dependent on the velocities of the points, $\dot{\vec{n}}_i\left(\dot{\vec{p}}_A - \dot{\vec{p}}_B\right)$, is not dependent on the force f_j and is therefore part of the b_i term. The component of the relative acceleration dependent on the accelerations of the points involved in the contact, $t_0 : \vec{n}_i\left(\ddot{\vec{p}}_A - \ddot{\vec{p}}_B\right)$, is dependent on f_j if object A or object B is involved in the jth contact. The acceleration at a point on an object arising from a force can be determined by differentiating Equation 5.54, producing Equation 5.70 where $\vec{r}_A = \vec{p}_A - \vec{c}_A$

$$\ddot{\vec{d}}_i(t) = \vec{b}_i + \sum_{j=1}^{n} (a_{ij} f_i) \tag{5.69}$$

$$\ddot{\vec{p}}_A = \dot{\vec{v}}_A + \left(\dot{\vec{\omega}}_A \times \vec{r}_A\right) + \vec{\omega}_A \times \left(\vec{\omega}_A \times \vec{r}_A\right) \tag{5.70}$$

In Equation 5.70, $\dot{\vec{v}}_A(t)$ is the linear acceleration as a result of the total force acting on object A divided by its mass. A force f_j acting in direction $\vec{N}_j(t_0)$ produces $f_j\left(\mathbf{M}_A \cdot \vec{N}_j(t_0)\right)^{-1}$. Angular acceleration, $\dot{\vec{\omega}}_A(t)$, is formed by differentiating Equation 5.3 and produces Equation 5.71, in which the first term contains torque and therefore relates the force f_j to $\ddot{\vec{p}}_A(t)$, whereas the second term is independent of the force f_j and so is incorporated into a constant term, b_i.

$$\ddot{\vec{\omega}}_A = \mathbf{I}_A^{-1}\vec{\tau}_A + \mathbf{I}_A^{-1}(\vec{L}_A \times \vec{\omega}_A) \tag{5.71}$$

The torque from force f_j is $(\vec{p}_j - \vec{c}_A) \times f_j\vec{N}_j$. The total dependence of $\ddot{\vec{p}}_A(t)$ on f_j is shown in Equation 5.72. Similarly, the dependence of $\ddot{\vec{p}}_B(t)$ on f_j can be computed. The results are combined as indicated by Equation 5.65 to form the term a_{ij} as it appears in Equation 5.69.

$$f_j(\vec{N}_j\mathbf{M}_A^{-1} + (\vec{p}_j - \vec{c}_A \times \vec{N}_j) \times \vec{r}_A) \tag{5.72}$$

Collecting the terms not dependent on an f_i and incorporating a term based on the net external force, $t_0 : \vec{F}_A$, and net external torque, $t_0 : \vec{\tau}_A$ acting on A, the part of $\ddot{\vec{p}}_A(t)$ independent of the f_i is shown in Equation 5.73. A similar expression is generated for $\ddot{\vec{p}}_B(t)$. To compute b_i in Equation 5.69, the constant parts of $\ddot{\vec{p}}_A(t)$ and $\ddot{\vec{p}}_B(t)$ are combined and dotted with $\vec{N}_i$. To this, the term $\dot{\vec{n}}_i(\dot{\vec{p}}_A - \dot{\vec{p}}_B)$ is added.

$$\frac{\vec{F}_A}{\mathbf{M}_A} + \left(\mathbf{I}_A^{-1}\vec{\tau}_A + \vec{\omega}_A \times \left(\vec{\omega}_A \times \vec{r}_A\right)\right) + \left(\mathbf{I}_A^{-1}\left(\vec{L}_A \times \vec{\omega}_A\right) \times \vec{r}_A\right) \tag{5.73}$$

Equation 5.69 must be solved subject to the constraints in Equations 5.67 and 5.68. These systems of equations are solved by *quadratic programming*. It is nontrivial to implement. Baraff [19] uses a package from Stanford [20–23]. Baraff notes that the quadratic programming code can easily handle $\ddot{\vec{d}}_i(t) = 0$ instead of $\ddot{\vec{d}}_i(t) \geq 0$ to constrain two bodies to never separate. This enables the modeling of hinges and pin-joints.

5.9.4 Dynamics of linked hierarchies

Applying forces to a linked figure, such as when falling under the force of gravity or taking a blow to the chest from a heavy object, results in complex reactions as the various links pull and push on each other. There are various ways to deal with the resulting motion depending on the quality of motion desired and the amount of computation tolerated. We consider two approaches here: constrained dynamics and the Featherstone equations.

Constrained dynamics

Geometric point constraints can be used as an alternative to rigid body dynamics [23]. In a simple case, particles are connected together with distance constraints. A mass particle (e.g., representing the torso of a figure) reacts to an applied force resulting in a spatial displacement. The hierarchy is traversed starting at the initially displaced particle. During traversal, each particle is repositioned to reestablish the distance constraint with respect to a particle already processed. Figure 5.22 shows frames from a simple example.

When an impulse force is applied to the torso of a figure, the torso reacts to the force as an independent rigid body. The appendages react to the force by enforcing distance constraints one link at a time traversing the hierarchy from the root outwards as shown in Figure 5.23.

In reality, however, as the torso reacts to the applied force, the appendages exert forces and torques on the torso as it tries to move away from them. The full equations of motion must account for the dynamic interactions among all the links. The Featherstone equations do this.

The Featherstone equations

The actual forces of one link acting on adjacent links can be explicitly calculated using basic principles of physics. The effect of one link on any attached links must be computed. The equations presented here are referred to as the *Featherstone equations* of motion [24–26]. In a nutshell, the algorithm uses four hierarchy-traversal loops: initializing link velocities (from root outward), initializing link values (from root outward), updating values (from end effector inward), and computing accelerations (from root outward).

The notation to relate one link to the next is shown in Figure 5.24.

A *spatial notation*, which combines the angular and linear components, has been developed to make the computations more concise [24]. The spatial velocity vector is a six-element vector of angular velocity and the linear velocity (Equation 5.74).

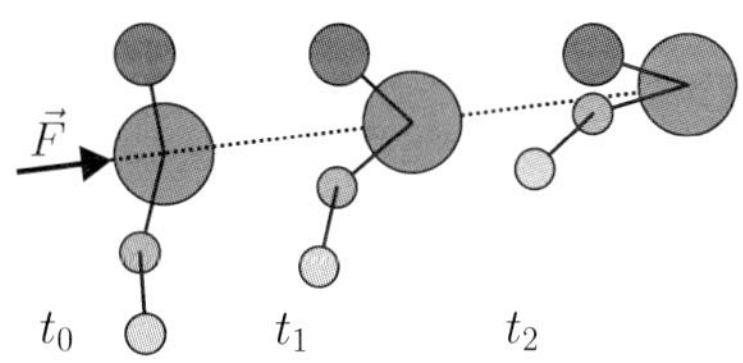

FIGURE 5.22

Frames from a sequence of constrained dynamics. The large sphere's motion is driven by outside forces; the small spheres are repositioned to satisfy distance constraints.

FIGURE 5.23

Sequence of impulse force applied to linked figure. Motion is generated by constrained dynamics with Unity 6's ragdoll.

(Image courtesy Domin Lee.)

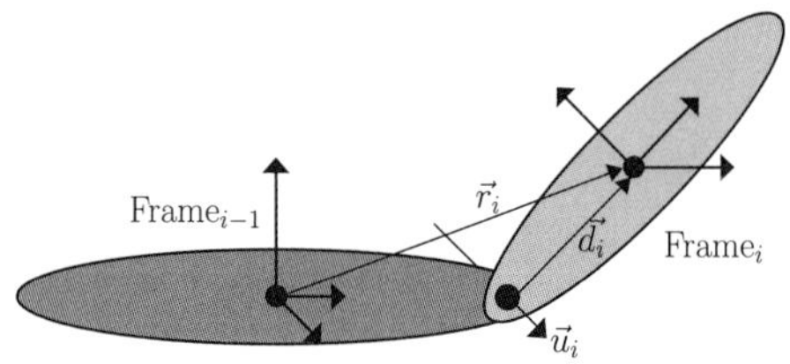

FIGURE 5.24

Vectors relating one coordinate frame to the next: u_i is the axis of revolution associated with *Frame$_i$*; r_i is the displacement vector from the center of *Frame$_{i-1}$* to the center of *Frame$_i$*; d_i is the displacement vector from the axis of revolution to the center of *Frame$_i$*.

$$\hat{v} = \begin{bmatrix} \vec{\omega} \\ \vec{v} \end{bmatrix} \tag{5.74}$$

Similarly, the spatial acceleration vector is made of angular and linear acceleration terms (Equation 5.75).

$$\hat{a} = \begin{bmatrix} \vec{\alpha} \\ \vec{a} \end{bmatrix} \tag{5.75}$$

The force vector (Equation 5.76) and mass matrix (Equation 5.77) are defined so that $f = \widehat{M}\hat{a}$ holds in the spatial notation.

$$\hat{f} = \begin{bmatrix} \vec{f} \\ \vec{\tau} \end{bmatrix} \tag{5.76}$$

$$\widehat{M} = \begin{bmatrix} 0 & \mathbf{M} \\ \mathbf{I} & 0 \end{bmatrix} \tag{5.77}$$

The spatial axis is given by combining the axis of rotation of a revolute joint and the cross-product of that axis with the displacement vector from the axis to the center of the frame (Equation 5.78).

$$\widehat{S}_i = \begin{bmatrix} \vec{u}_i \\ \vec{u}_i \times \vec{d}_i \end{bmatrix} \tag{5.78}$$

Using Equation 5.79 to represent the matrix cross-product operator, if $\vec{r} = (r_x, r_y, r_z)$ is the translation vector and R is the rotation matrix between coordinate frames, then Eq. 5.80 transforms a value from frame F to frame G.

$$\vec{r} = (r_x, r_y, r_z) \rightarrow \mathbf{r}_\times = r* = \begin{bmatrix} 0 & -r_z & r_y \\ r_z & 0 & -r_x \\ -r_y & r_x & 0 \end{bmatrix} \tag{5.79}$$

$$\mathbf{G}\hat{\times}\mathbf{F} = \begin{bmatrix} \mathbf{R} & 0 \\ \mathbf{r}_{\times}\mathbf{R} & \mathbf{R} \end{bmatrix} \tag{5.80}$$

Armed with this notation, a procedure that implements the Featherstone equations can be written succinctly [24,26]. The interested reader is encouraged to refer to Mirtich's PhD dissertation [26] for a more complete discussion.

Computing accurate dynamics is a nontrivial thing to do. However, because of the developed literature from the robotics community and the interest from the computer animation community, understandable presentations of the techniques necessary are available to the mathematically inclined. For real-time applications, approximate methods that produce visually reasonable results are very accessible.

5.10 More advanced concepts

5.10.1 Cloth

Cloth is a type of object that is commonly encountered in everyday living in a variety of forms, most notably in the form of clothes, but also as curtains, tablecloths, flags, and bags. Because of its ubiquity, it is a type of object worth devoting special attention to modeling and animating. Cloth is any human-made material made out of fibers. It can be woven, knotted, or pressed (e.g., felt). The distinguishing attributes of cloth are that it is thin, flexible, and has some limited ability to be stretched. In addition, there are other cloth-like objects, such as paper and plastic bags, that have similar attributes that can be modeled with similar techniques. However, for purposes of this discussion, woven cloth, a frequently encountered type of cloth-like object, will be considered.

Woven cloth, as well as some knotted cloth, is formed by a rectilinear pattern of threads. The two directions of the threads are typically referred to as *warp*, in the longitudinal direction, and *weft*, in the side-to-side direction and orthogonal to the warp direction. The thread patterns of cloth vary by the over-under structure of the threads. For example, in a simple weave, each thread of the warp goes over one weft thread and then under the next. The over-under of adjacent warp rows are offset by one thread. This same over-under pattern holds for the weft threads relative to the warp threads. Other patterns can be used, such as over-over-under and over-over-under-under. For more variety, different over-under patterns can be used in the weft and warp directions. Such differences in the weave pattern make the material more or less subject to shear and bend.

Because cloth is thin, it is usually modeled as a single sheet of geometric elements, that is, it is not modeled as having an interior or having any depth. Because it is flexible and distorts easily, cloth of any significant size is usually modeled by a large number of geometric elements typically on the order of hundreds, thousands, or even tens of thousands of elements. The number of elements depends on the desired quality of the resulting imagery and the amount of computation that can be tolerated. Because of the large number of elements, it is difficult for the animator to realistically animate cloth using simple positioning tools, so more automatic, and computationally intensive, approaches are employed. Major cloth features, such as simple draping, can be modeled directly or the underlying processes that give rise to those features can be modeled using physically based methods.

The main visual feature of cloth is simple draping behavior. This draping behavior can be modeled kinematically just by modeling the fold that is generated between fixed points of the cloth (see the next section). This is possible in simple static cases where the cloth is supported at a few specific points. However, in environments where the cloth is subject to external forces, a more physically based approach is more appropriate. Because cloth can be stretched to some limited degree, a common approach to modeling cloth is the use of a mass-spring-damper system. Modifying the mass-spring-damper parameters provides for some degree of modeling various types of cloth material and various types of cloth weave. The spring model, being physically based, also allows the cloth mesh to react to external forces from the environment, such as gravity, wind, and collisions. Real-time systems, such as computer games or interactive garment systems, place a heavy demand on computational efficiency not required of offline applications, and techniques have to be selected with an appropriate quality-cost trade-off. At the other extreme, the approach of using finite element methods for modeling can provide very accurate simulation results, but it will not be discussed here.

5.11 Chapter summary

If complex realistic motion is needed, the models used to control the motion can become complex and mathematically expensive. However, the resulting motion is oftentimes more natural looking and believable than that produced using kinematic (e.g., interpolation) techniques. Although modeling physics is a nontrivial task, oftentimes it is worth the investment. It should be noted that there has been much work in this area that has not been included in this chapter. Some other physically based techniques are covered in later chapters that address specific animation tasks.

5.12 Exercises

Beginner

B1. An object starts at position $\vec{a}$ and is moving in the direction $\frac{\vec{C}}{\|\vec{C}\|}$ at speed $S = 2m/s$.

a. What is the position of the object at $t = 0s, t = 1s,\ t = 2s, t = 10s,$ $t = 100s$?

b. If, at $t = 5s$, it changes its direction instantaneously to $\frac{\vec{d}}{\|\vec{d}\|}$ but maintains its speed, where is the object at $t = 5s, t = 10s, t = 100s$?

B2. An object starts at position $\vec{a}$ with no speed. It accelerates along the direction of $\frac{\vec{C}}{\|\vec{C}\|}$ with a constant acceleration of $0.5m/s^2$.

a. Use the PVA model to determine the position and velocity of the object at $t = 0s, t = 1s, t = 2s, t = 3s, t = 4s, t = 10s$

b. Create a spreadsheet (e.g., in Excel or Google Sheets) that uses the PVA model to plot all positions from $t = 0 \ldots t = 1000$ with a constant $\Delta t = 0.5s$. What do you notice about the result?

c. Incorporate gravity using $\vec{g} = \vec{a} = (0, -G_{\text{strength}}, 0)$. Show the results using $G_{\text{strength}} = 1, G_{\text{strength}} = 2, G_{\text{strength}} = 9.81$.

Intermediate

I1. Imagine two objects with respective positions $\vec{p}_1 = (0, 0, 0)$, $\vec{p}_1 = (100, 100, 100)$. Object 1 moves at constant velocity with direction toward the point $\vec{d} = (1, 1, 1)$ and speed $S_1 = 10m/s$. Object 2 is moving at constant acceleration, starting with no velocity but a force constantly pushing it toward the origin with a strength of $0.1m/s^2$. Determine, through both simulation and analytically, the location and timing of the impact of these two objects.

I2. Develop a particle system in a game engine/API of choice with the following capabilities:

a. Specify the spawn location (or method, i.e., spawn from a point or other primitive).

b. Track the lifespan of each particle and terminate when ≤ 0.

c. Update using PVA + F and clamp the particle speed/acceleration within specified ranges.

d. Specify random range for each parameter when initialized.

e. Draw as a point or a textured billboard (e.g., quad-facing camera).

f. Incorporate ability to create attraction forces to given locations.

g. Try to achieve stylized fire movement, an explosion.

Advanced

A1. Develop a physics simulation class that lets you simulate PV, PVA, and incorporate forces into the movement of an object. Create a series of unit tests to demonstrate the correctness and compare it with results from a spreadsheet implementation.

A2. In your basic physics simulation class, add the ability to use springs and demonstrate a simple mass-spring with dampers.

A3. In your game engine of choice, implement a simple simulation of flexible, nonrigid objects using springs. Hint: use a number of springs to connect vertices (or multiple objects) together and demonstrate them moving like jelly when you apply movement/forces to the object.

References

[1] Godot. "Timer." Godot engine documentation, docs.godotengine.org/en/stable/classes/class_timer.html. Accessed 19 June 2024.

[2] Dam EB, Koch M, Lillholm M. Quaternions, interpolation and animation. 2000. https://web.mit.edu/2.998/www/QuaternionReport1.pdf. [Accessed 19 June 2024].

[3] Blinn J. Light reflection functions for simulation of clouds and dusty surfaces. In: Computer graphics. Proceedings of SIGGRAPH 82, 16(3). Boston, Mass; 1982. p. 21–9.

[4] Ebert D, Carlson W, Parent R. Solid spaces and inverse particle systems for controlling the animation of gases and fluids. Vis Comput 1994;10(4):179–90.

[5] Reeves W. Particle systems: a technique for modeling a class of fuzzy objects. In: Computer graphics. Proceedings of SIGGRAPH 83, 17(3). Detroit, Mich; 1983. p. 359–76.

[6] Reeves W, Blau R. Approximate and probabilistic algorithms for shading and rendering structured particle systems. In: Barsky BA, editor. Computer graphics. Proceedings of SIGGRAPH 85, 19(3). San Francisco, Calif; 1985. p. 31–40.

[7] Sims K. Particle animation and rendering using data parallel computation. In: Baskett F, editor. Computer graphics. Proceedings of SIGGRAPH 90, 24(4). Dallas, Tex; 1990. p. 405–14. ISBN 0-201-50933-4.

[8] Gourret J, Magnenat-Thalmann N, Thalmann D. Simulation of object and human skin deformations in a grasping task. In: Lane J, editor. Computer graphics. Proceedings of SIGGRAPH 89, 23(3). Boston, Mass; 1989. p. 21–30.

[9] Haumann D. Modeling the physical behavior of flexible objects. In: SIGGRAPH 87 course notes: topics in physically based modeling. Anaheim, Calif; 1987.

[10] O'Brien J, Hodges J. Graphical modeling and animation of brittle fracture. In: Rockwood A, editor. Computer graphics. Proceedings of SIGGRAPH 99, annual conference series. Los Angeles, Calif: Addison-Wesley Longman; 1999. p. 137–46. ISBN 0-20148-560-5.

[11] Terzopoulos D, Fleischer K. Modeling inelastic deformation: viscoelasticity, plasticity, fracture. In: Dill J, editor. Computer graphics. Proceedings of SIGGRAPH 88, 22(4). Atlanta, Ga; 1988. p. 269–78.

[12] Terzopoulos D, Platt J, Barr A, Fleischer K. Elastically deformable models. In: Stone MC, editor. Computer graphics. Proceedings of SIGGRAPH 87, 21(4). Anaheim, Calif; 1987. p. 205–14.

[13] Terzopoulos D, Witkin A. Physically based models with rigid and deformable components. IEEE Comput Graph Appl 1988:41–51.

[14] Witkin A, Fleischer K, Barr A. Energy constraints on parameterized models. In: Stone MC, editor. Computer graphics. Proceedings of SIGGRAPH 87, 21(4). Anaheim, Calif; 1987. p. 225–32.

[15] Witkin A, Kass M. Spacetime constraints. In: Dill J, editor. Computer graphics. Proceedings of SIGGRAPH 88, 22(4). Atlanta, Ga; 1988. p. 159−68.
[16] Cohen M. Interactive spacetime control for animation. In: Catmull EE, editor. Computer graphics. Proceedings of SIGGRAPH 92, 26(2). Chicago, Ill; 1992. p. 293−302. ISBN 0-201-51585-7.
[17] Ngo J, Marks J. Spacetime constraints revisited. In: Kajiya JT, editor. Computer graphics. Proceedings of SIGGRAPH 93, annual conference series. Anaheim, Calif; 1993. p. 343−50. ISBN 0-201-58889-7.
[18] Gill P, Murray W, Wright M. Practical optimization. New York: Academic Press; 1981.
[19] Baraff D. Rigid body simulation. In: Course notes, SIGGRAPH 92. Chicago, Ill; 1992.
[20] Gill P, Hammarling S, Murray W, Saunders M, Wright M. User's guide for LSSOL: a fortran package for constrained linear least-squares and convex quadratic programming, technical report sol 84-2. Systems optimization laboratory, department of operations research. Stanford University; 1986.
[21] Gill P, Murray W, Saunders M, Wright M. User's guide for NPSOL: a fortran package for nonlinear programming, technical report sol 84-2. Systems optimization laboratory. Department of Operations Research, Stanford University; 1986.
[22] Gill P, Murray W, Saunders M, Wright M. User's guide for QPSOL: a fortran package for quadratic programming, technical report sol 84-6. Systems optimization laboratory, department of operations research. Stanford University; 1984.
[23] van Overveld C, Barenburg B. All you need is force: a constraint-based approach for rigid body dynamics in computer animation. In: Terzopoulos D, Thalmann D, editors. Proceedings of computer animation and simulation '95. Springer Computer Science; 1995. p. 80−94.
[24] Featherstone R, Orin D. Robot dynamics: equations and algorithms.
[25] Kokkevis E. Practical physics for articulated characters. In: Game developers conference; 2004.
[26] Mirtich B. Impulse-based dynamic simulation of rigid body systems. Ph.D. dissertation. Fall: University of California at Berkeley; 1996.
[27] The Developer. Cool visual effects - part 1 - URP support: VFX particles. Unity Asset Store, assetstore.unity.com/packages/vfx/particles/cool-visual-effects-part-1-urp-support-176571. Accessed 19 June 2024.

CHAPTER

Controlling objects "intelligently"

6

This chapter presents methods for precisely specifying the motion of objects. Whereas the previous chapters presented basics of interpolating values, this chapter addresses how to use those basics to facilitate the production of computer animation. With these techniques, there is little uncertainty about the positions, orientations, and shapes to be produced. The computer is used only to calculate the actual values. Procedures and algorithms are used in a very direct manner in which the animator has very specific expectations about the motion produced on a frame-by-frame basis. These techniques are typified by the user setting precise conditions, such as beginning and ending values for position and orientation, and having the intermediate values filled in by some interpolative procedure. Later chapters cover "higher-level" algorithms in which the animator gives up some precision to produce motion with certain desired qualities. The techniques of this chapter deal with low-level, more precise control of motion that is highly constrained by the animator.

6.1 Keyframe systems

We begin with a discussion of keyframe animation systems (the computer animation version of the original hand-drawn animation technique). Many of the early computer animation systems were key-frame systems (e.g., [1,2,3,4]). Most of these were two-dimensional systems based on the standard procedure used for hand-drawn animation, in which master animators define and draw the keyframes of the sequence to be animated. In hand-drawn animation, assistant animators have the task of drawing the intermediate frames by mentally inferring the action between the keys. The keyframes occur often enough in the sequence so that the intermediate action is reasonably well defined, or the keys are accompanied by additional information to indicate placement of the intermediate frames. In computer animation, the term *keyframe* has been generalized to apply to any variable whose value is set at specific keyframes and from which values for the intermediate frames are interpolated according to some prescribed procedure. These variables have been referred to in the literature as *articulation variables* (*avars*) [5], and the systems are sometimes referred to as *track based*. It is common for such systems to provide an interactive interface with which the animator can specify the key values and can control the interpolation curve by manipulating tangents or interior

Computer Animation. https://doi.org/10.1016/B978-0-443-13512-5.00006-9

control points. For example, see Figure 6.1. Early three-dimensional keyframe systems include TWIXT [6] and BBOP [7].

Because these animation systems keep the hand-drawn strategy of interpolating two-dimensional shapes, the basic operation is that of interpolating one (possibly closed) curve into another (possibly closed) curve. The interpolation is straightforward if the correspondence between lines in the frames is known in enough detail so that each pair of lines can be interpolated on a point-by-point basis to produce lines in the intermediate frames. This interpolation requires that for each pair of curves in the keyframes, the curves have the same number of points and that for each curve, whether open or closed, the correspondence between the points can be established.

Of course, the simplest way to interpolate the points is using linear interpolation (LERP) between each pair of keys. For example, see Figure 6.2. Moving in arcs and allowing for ease-in/ease-out can be accommodated by applying any interpolation technique, provided that a point can be identified over several keyframes.

Point-by-point correspondence information is usually not known, and even if it is, the resulting interpolation is not necessarily what the user wants. The best one can expect is for the curve-to-curve correspondence to be given. The problem is, given two arbitrary curves in keyframes, to interpolate a curve as it "should" appear in intermediate frames. For example, observe the egg splatting against the wall in Figure 6.3.

For illustrative purposes, consider the simple case in which the keyframes *f*1 and *f*2 consist of a single curve (Figure 6.4). The curve in frame *f*1 is referred to as $\boldsymbol{P}(u)$, and the curve in frame *f*2 is referred to as $\boldsymbol{Q}(v)$. This single curve must be interpolated for each frame between the keyframes in which it is defined. To simplify the discussion, but without loss of generality, it is assumed that the curve, although it may wiggle some, is a generally vertical line in both keyframes.

Some basic assumptions are used about what constitutes reasonable interpolation, such as the fact that if the curve is a single continuous open segment in frames *f*1 and *f*2, then it should remain a single continuous open segment in all the intermediate frames. Also assumed is that the top point of *P*, $\boldsymbol{P}(0)$, should interpolate to the top point in *Q*, $\boldsymbol{Q}(0)$, and, similarly, the bottom points should interpolate. However,

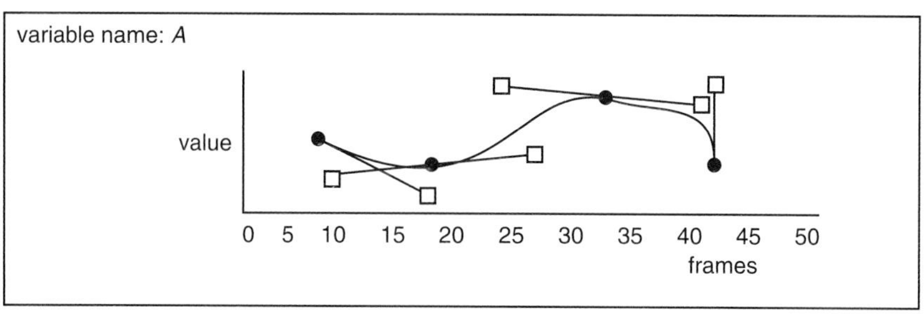

FIGURE 6.1

Sample interface for specifying interpolation of key values and tangents at segment boundaries.

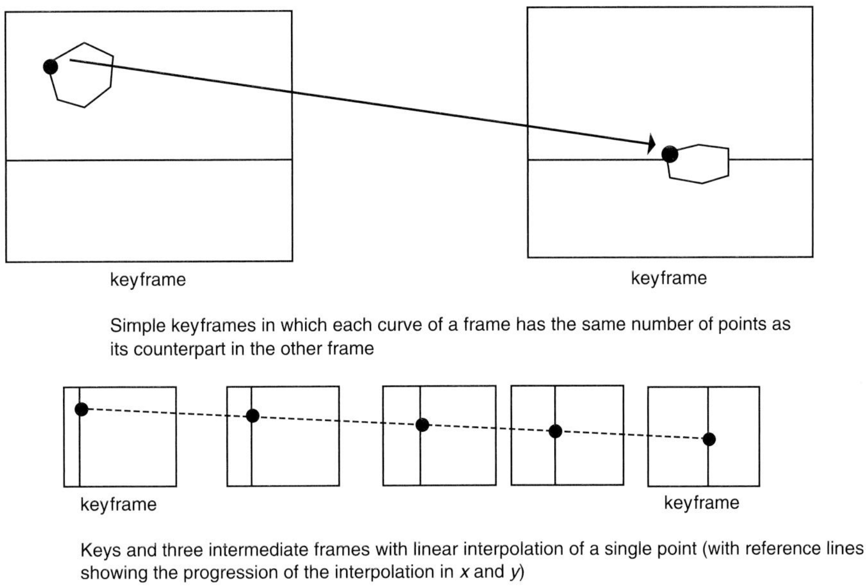

FIGURE 6.2

Simple key and intermediate frames. A specific point is identified in both keyframes; the interpolation of the point over intermediate frames is shown with auxiliary lines showing its relative placement in the frames.

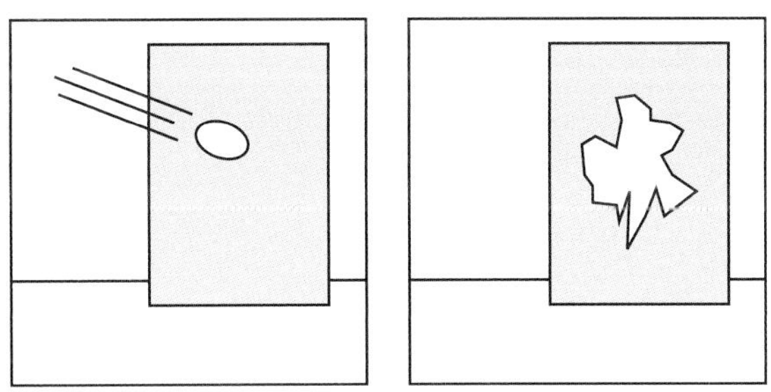

FIGURE 6.3

Object splatting against a wall. The shape must be interpolated from the initial egg shape to the splattered shape.

what happens at intermediate points along the curve is so far left undefined (other than for the obvious assumption that the entire curve P should interpolate to the entire curve Q; that is, the mapping should be one-to-one and onto, also known as a *bijection*).

If both curves were generated with the same type of interpolation information, for example, each is a single, cubic Bezier curve, then intermediate curves could

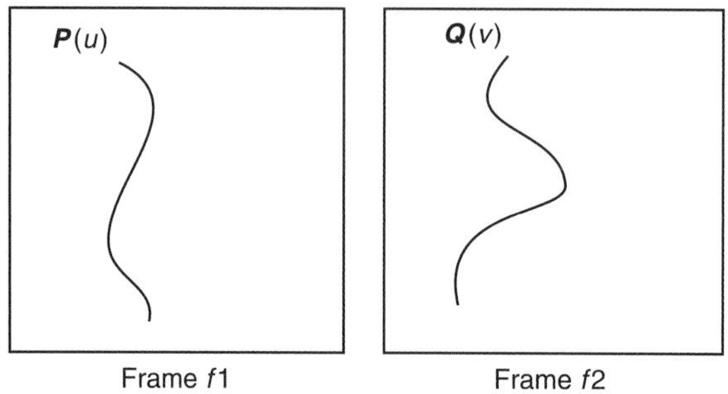

FIGURE 6.4

Two keyframes showing a curve to be interpolated.

be generated by interpolating the control points and reapplying the Bezier interpolation. Another alternative would be to use interpolating functions to generate the same number of points on both curves. These points could then be interpolated on a point-by-point basis. Although these interpolations get the job done, they might not provide sufficient control to a user who has specific ideas about how the intermediate curves should look.

Reeves [8] proposes a method of computing intermediate curves using *moving point constraints,* which allow the user to specify more information concerning the correspondence of points along the curve and the speed of interpolation of those points. The basic approach is to use surface patch technology (two spatial dimensions) to solve the problem of interpolating a line in time (one spatial dimension, one temporal dimension).

The curve to be interpolated is defined in several keyframes. Interpolation information, such as the path and speed of interpolation defined over two or more of the keys for one or more points, is also given (Figure 6.5).

The first step is to define a segment of the curve to interpolate, bounded on top and bottom by interpolation constraints. LERP of the very top and very bottom of the curve, if not specified by a moving point constraint, is used to bind the top and bottom segments. Once a bounded segment has been formed, the task is to define an intermediate curve based on the constraints (Figure 6.6). Various strategies can be used to define the intermediate curve segment, $C_t(u)$ in Figure 6.6, and are typically applications of surface patch techniques. For example, tangent information along the curves can be extracted from the curve definitions. The endpoint and tangent information can then be interpolated along the top and bottom interpolation boundaries. These can then be used to define an intermediate curve, $\boldsymbol{C}_t(u)$, using Hermite interpolation.

6.1.1 Keyframe data

What types of things are usually stored in a keyframe? The simplest answer to this question is "anything." A "keyframe" contains all pertinent information related to a

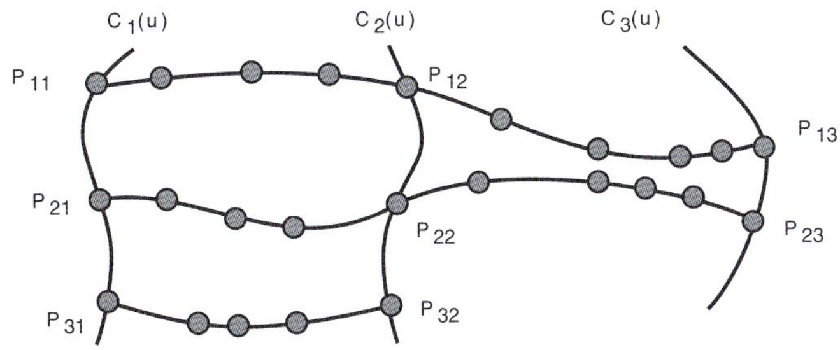

FIGURE 6.5

Moving point constraints showing the key points specified on the key curves, as well as the intermediate points.

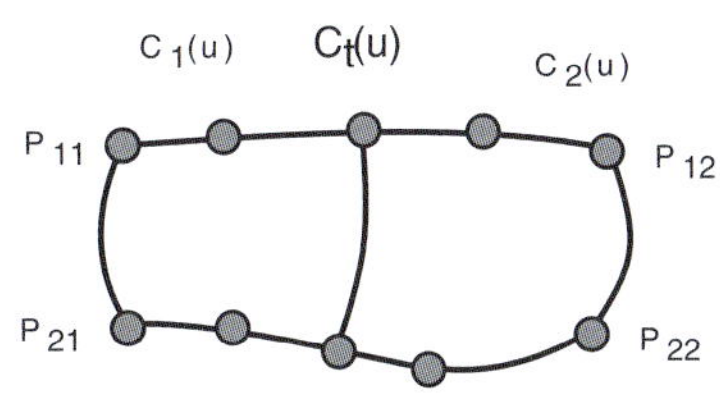

FIGURE 6.6

Patch defined by interpolation constraints made up of the boundary curve segments C_1 and C_{2u}.

changing parameter in the animation. In the Blender 4.1 manual [9], a "keyframe is simply a marker of time which stores the value of a property." For example, if we want to animate the color of an object ($\vec{c} = (r, g, b)$ where $r, g, b \in [0, 1]$) from red to blue (over the course of 30 frames) to green (over the next 30 frames), then we would need to specify 3 keyframe (one for each color, namely $\mathbf{K}_0 = \left\{\vec{c_0} = (1, 0, 0)\right\}, \mathbf{K}_{30} = \left\{\vec{c_{30}} = (0, 1, 0)\right\}, \mathbf{K}_{60} = \left\{\vec{c_{60}} = (0, 0, 1)\right\}$). Common basic data stored for moving objects are its position (to control movement), orientation (as Euler angles or quaternion, to control direction), scale (to control size), alpha (to control transparency/opacity), and color (to control its appearance). However, in modern animation packages and game engines, the animator has the ability to control almost every parameter in the scene including individual object vertices/normals (for deformations), bones/rigs (to more easily control character movement), material properties, cameras, and even system properties (i.e., Booleans/conditions) that affect the rendering process itself.

6.1.2 Sampling between keyframes

Consider the timeline of the animation with a set of keyframe specified (as above in the color example). To render each frame of the animation, the system MUST determine how to generate the values of all dynamic parameters before rendering. The animator is required to specify *how* these values are generated by choosing an interpolation scheme and/or mapping the range to a parameter curve. In most animation systems, each keyframed parameter can be controlled by an animation curve that can be completely specified/modified by the animator, whereas the typical default scheme is the simplest LERP between successive keyframe. In Blender, these curves are called "F-Curves," and the animator can set a different interpolation scheme for each interval. The sampling/interpolation function can typically be either "Constant" (keep the keyframed value until the next key), "Linear" (use LERP to sample a line segment with the interval keyframes as the endpoints), "Quadratic" (use the interval keys plus an animator specified control point/handle to sample a quadratic polynomial), or "Bezier" (use the interval keys plus two animator specified control points/tangents to sample a Bezier cubic polynomial). A number of other strategies can be used to specify the constraints on the curve at the interval junctions, but generally these systems allow for complete control.

6.1.3 Animation languages

An *animation language* is made up of structured commands that can be used to encode the information necessary to produce animations. If well designed, an animation language can have enough expressive power to describe a wide variety of motions. Most languages are *script based*, which means they are composed of text instructions; the instructions are recorded for later evaluation. Script-based languages can also be *interpreted* in which the animation is modified as new instructions are input by the user. Some languages are graphical in which, for example, flowchart-like diagrams encode relationships between objects and procedures. Nadia Magnenat-Thalmann and Daniel Thalmann present an excellent survey that includes many early script-based animation systems [10], and Steve May presents an excellent overview of animation languages from the perspective of his interest in procedural representations and encapsulated models [5]. Much of the discussion here is taken from these sources.

The first animation systems used general-purpose programming languages (e.g., Fortran) to produce the motion sequences. The language was used to compute whatever input values were needed by the rendering system to produce a frame of the animation. In these early systems, there were no special facilities in the language itself that were designed to support animation. Therefore each time an animation was to be produced, there was overhead in defining graphical primitives, object data structures, transformations, and renderer output.

A language that does provide special facilities to support animation can use special libraries developed to augment a general purpose programming language (e.g., an implementation of an applied programming interface), or it can be a specialized language designed from the ground up specifically for animation. In either case, typical features of an animation language include built-in input/output operations for graphical objects, data structures to represent objects and to support the hierarchical composition of objects, a time variable, interpolation functions, functions to animate object hierarchies, affine transformations, rendering-specific parameters, parameters for specifying camera attributes and defining the view frustum, and the ability to direct the rendering, viewing, and storing of one or more frames of animation. The program written in an animation language is often referred to as a *script*.

The advantage of using an animation language is twofold. First, the specification of an animation written in the language, the script, is a hard-coded record of the animation that can be used at any time to regenerate it. The script also allows the animation to be iteratively refined because it can be incrementally changed and a new animation generated. Second, the use of programming constructs enables an algorithmic and deterministic approach to motion control. The animation language, if sufficiently powerful, can interpolate values, compute arbitrarily complex numerical quantities, implement behavioral rules, and so on. The disadvantage of using an animation language is that it is, fundamentally, a programming language and thus requires the user (animator) to be a programmer. The animator must be trained not only in the arts but also in the art of programming.

Artist-oriented animation languages

To accommodate animators not trained in the art of computer programming, several simple animation languages were designed from the ground up with the intention of keeping the syntax simple and the semantics easy to understand (e.g., [11,12,13]). In the early days of computer graphics, almost all animation systems were based on such languages because there were few artists with technical backgrounds who were able to effectively program in a full-fledged programming language. These systems, as well as some of those with graphical user interfaces (e.g., [14,15,16]), were more accessible to artists but also had limited capabilities.

In these simple animation languages, typical statements referred to named objects, a transformation, and a time at which (or a span of time over which) to apply the transformation to the object. They also tended to have a syntax that was easy to parse (for the interpreter/compiler) and easy to read (for the animator). The following examples are from ANIMA II [13].

```
set position <name> <x> <y> <z> at frame <number>
set rotation <name> [X,Y,Z] to <angle> at frame <number>
change position <name> to <x> <y> <z>
        from frame <number> to frame <number>
change rotation <name> [X,Y,Z] by <angle>
        from frame <number> to frame <number>
```

Specific values or variable names could be placed in the statements, which included an indicator as to whether the transformation was relative to the object's current position or absolute in global coordinates. The instructions operated in parallel; the script was not a traditional programming language in that sense.

As animators became more adept at writing animation scripts in such languages, they tended to demand that more capability be incorporated into the language. As Steve May [5] points out, "By eliminating the language constructs that make learning animation languages difficult, command [artist-oriented] languages give up the mechanisms that make animation languages powerful." The developers found themselves adding looping constructs, conditional control statements, random variables, procedural calls, and data structure support. An alternative to developing a full featured animation programming language from scratch was to add support for graphical objects and operations to an existing language such as C/C++, Python, Java, or LISP. For example, Steve May developed a scheme-based animation language called AL [17].

Full-featured programming languages for animation

Languages have been developed with simplified programming constructs, but such simplification usually reduces the algorithmic power of the language. As users become more familiar with a language, the tendency is to want more of the algorithmic power of a general purpose programming language put back into the animation language. More recently, animation systems have been developed that are essentially user interfaces implemented by a scripting language processor. Users can use the system strictly from the interface provided, or they can write their own scripts using the scripting language.

One example of such a system is AutoDesk's Maya. The scripting language is called MEL, and there is an associated animation language whose scripts are referred to as expressions [18]. Maya's interface is written in MEL, so anything that can be done using the interface can be done in a MEL script (with a few exceptions). MEL scripts are typically used for scene setup. The scene is represented as a network of nodes that is traversed each time the frame is advanced in a timeline.

Expressions create nodes in the network that are therefore executed each frame. The input to, and output from, an expression node link to the attributes of other nodes in the scene. Object nodes have attributes such as geometric parameters and normals. Transformation nodes have attributes such as translation, rotation, and scale. A transformation node is typically linked to an object node to transform the object data into the world coordinate system. Using expression nodes, the translation of one object could, for example, affect the rotation of other objects in the scene. The following sample script creates an expression that controls the z-rotation of the object named "slab" based on the z-translation of a sphere named "sphere1." During the first frame, translation values for the objects are initialized. For each subsequent frame, two of the sphere's translation values are set as a function of the frame number, and the z-rotation of slab is set as a function of the sphere's z-translation value.

```
if (frame == 1) {
  slab.translateY = 0;
  sphere1.translateX = -25;
  sphere1.translateY = 15;    }else{
  sphere1.translateX = 25*sin(frame/100);
  sphere1.translateZ = 25*cos(frame/100) - 25;
  slab.rotateZ = 10*sphere1.translateZ + 90;
}
```

Articulation variables

A feature used by several languages is associating the value of a variable with a function, most notably of time. The function is specified procedurally or designed interactively using interpolating functions. Then a script, or other type of animation system, when it needs a value of the variable in its computation, passes the time variable to the function, which returns its value for that time to the computation. This technique goes by a variety of names, such as *track, channel,* or *articulation variable*. The term *articulation variable*, often shortened to *avar,* stems from its common use in some systems to control the articulation of linked appendages.

The use of avars, when an interactive system is provided to the user for inputting values or designing the functions, allows a script-based animation language to incorporate some interaction during the development of the animation. It also allows digitized data and arbitrarily complex functions to be easily incorporated into an animation by associating these with a particular avar.

Graphical languages

Graphical representations, such as those used in the commercial Houdini system [19], represent an animation by a dataflow network (Figure 6.7). An acyclic graph is used to represent objects, operations, and the relationships among them. Nodes of the graph have inputs and outputs that connect to other nodes, and data are passed from node to node by arcs of the graphics that are interactively specified by the user. A node represents an operation to perform on the data being passed into the node, such as an object description. A transformation node will operate on an object description passed into the node and will produce a transformed object representation as output. Inputs to a node can also be used to parameterize a transformation or a data generation technique and can be set interactively, set according to an articulation variable, or set according to an arbitrary user-supplied procedure. This is a very effective way to visually design and represent the dependencies among various computations, functions, and values.

Actor-based animation languages

Actor-based languages are an object-oriented approach to animation in which an actor (encapsulated model [5]) is a graphical object with its associated data and procedures, including geometric description, display attributes, and motion control. Reynolds [20] popularized the use of the term *actor* in reference to the encapsulated models he uses in his ASAS (the American Society of Animal Science and the Assessment of SpondyloArthritis International Society) system.

The basic idea is that the data associated with a graphical object should not only specify its geometry and display characteristics but also describe its motion. Thus the encapsulated model of a car includes how the doors open, how the windows roll down, and, possibly, the internal workings of the engine. Communication with the actor takes place by way of message passing; animating the object is carried out by passing requests to the actor for certain motions. The current status of the

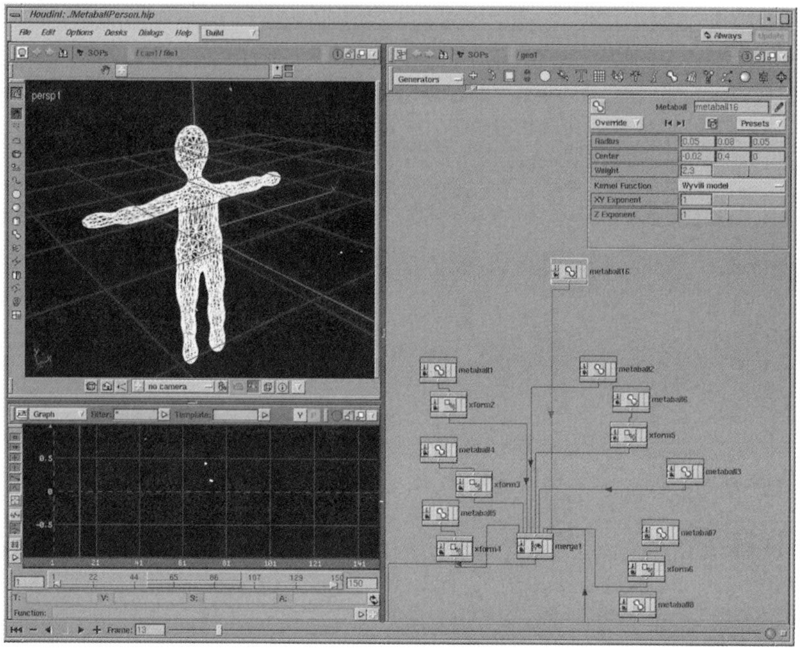

FIGURE 6.7

Sample Houdini dataflow network and the object it generates.

actor can be extracted by sending a request for information to the actor and receiving a message from the actor.

Actor-based systems provide a convenient way of communicating the time-varying information pertaining to a model. However, the encapsulated nature of actors with the associated message passing can result in inefficiencies when they are used with simulation systems in which all objects have the potential to affect all others.

6.1.4 Animation clips

For our purposes, let's consider an animation clip as a short animation with a specified duration. When working with video, we may consider the notion of a video clip—a short snippet of video. We place a number of these clips onto a timeline to create the final video. Similarly, for an animation of any duration, we can consider the entire animation as a sequence of smaller animation clips. Each clip may be tied to particular effects or particular objects to define their animation or locomotion parameters, and some clips can be blended together to create transitions (similar to fading two video clips from one to another). An animation clip can be viewed generally as maintaining a set of controllable parameters with a list of keyframes and associated interpolating functions that sits on a timeline at a particular moment in the animation and can be activated/deactivated. Most importantly, an animation clip can be "sampled" at any given time to provide the values of the animated parameters at that particular time.

6.2 Paths for locomotion

In section 4.5, we discussed how to mathematically represent paths as a set of keyframes, intervals, and interpolating functions. That perspective enables us to effectively define the data that is relevant to an objects' appearance or motion at significant locations. The set of interpolating functions enables us to sample our keyframes at any location. But how do we pull all of this together appropriately and efficiently to create systems that allow us to easily control objects? In Chapter 4, we defined a path as a consecutive set of keyframes with intervals in-between each pair of keys where each interval has a (potentially different) interpolating function. When it comes to locomotion we are concerned mainly with the position (or Pose) of an object. We can use paths in a variety of ways depending on the use case. In the context of pure animation, a path can be defined as the set of keyframes in which we interpolate our object position. From an artificial intelligence (AI) for games perspective, a path does not necessarily have a one-to-one relationship with the position of the object as it could be used to guide objects rather than setting their positions directly. When used as a guide, rather than keyframes we call the locations of interest "waypoints" and store any parameters in the waypoint that need to be matched/aligned by nearby objects. The simplest example is an enemy patrolling back and forth between two doorways. We would define a path as two waypoints (the locations of the doors) and an interpolation function (LERP). Thus if the object is "following" this path, we can sample a point on the path to use as a target for moving the enemy. When the enemy reaches the destination, you then select the next target based on a policy for wrapping back to the start of the path or not. We can then rely on our knowledge of interpolation from Chapter 4 to be able to sample points along these paths parameterized on time and/or arc length. Generally, we would use these sampled points as targets in which we want objects to move toward using steering behaviors, as we discuss later in this chapter.

When developing your own system, some important base features of a waypoint path system are the following:

- Easily specify multiple paths (add/remove waypoints to a path, create new paths/ path segments)
- Sample the path parameterized on time (see Chapter 4)
- Sample the path parameterized on arc length (see Chapter 4)
- Compute the "closest" point on the path to a given point
  - This can be implemented as either returning the closest waypoint (i.e., keyframe position) or as finding the closest interval and computing the perpendicular distance to a line segment (approximation) or sampling using cubic spline interpolation functions for higher accuracy

- Detect when an object has reached a waypoint
  - Ensure you specify a reasonable radius around each waypoint that determines how close is "close enough"
- Easily transition between paths/path segments smoothly
  - This can be done by using a reasonable look-ahead to sample the target path (to transition toward) and defining a new path segment from the transition start location to this new location
- Find the shortest path between two locations
  - This requires the use of a reasonable method for representing the traversable environment coupled with a shortest-path search algorithm such as A* (see later sections)

6.2.1 But what about the "intelligence" for control?

Although keyframe interpolation and physically based motion control are significant methods for controlling motion, *behavioral animation* attempts to model the reasoning process of a self-directed synthetic character. Such characters are commonly referred to as agents, as actors, or as being autonomous. As discussed previously, there are a variety of ways to specify motion. In *keyframe animation,* for example, the animator precisely specifies values for animation parameters as specific frames and selects an interpolation procedure to fill in the remaining values for the in-between frames. There is not much mystery as to what the parametric values will be or what the motion will look like. In *physically based animation,* such as rigid body dynamics, the animator might specify starting values for some of the physical simulation parameters (e.g., initial position and velocity). The animator generally knows what the animation will look like but does not have a good idea of the intermediate parametric values as an object falls, collides, and bounces. This is an example of model-based animation where there is an underlying model controlling the motion. In this case the model is physics—or at least some approximation to it.

Behavioral animation is another type of model-based animation in which it is the cognitive processes that are being modeled. The term *cognitive process* refers to any behavior that can be attributed to mental activity, voluntary or involuntary, that is reacting to the environment—essentially, nonphysically based procedural motion. The cognitive processes can be as simple as moving toward a light or as complex as balancing self-preservation, mood swings, and personality disorders.

Whereas modeling complex cognitive processes might be necessary for creating a believable autonomous character in a game, simple cognitive processes are often sufficient for modeling crowd behavior. Development of behavioral animation has been motivated by applications of virtual reality (VR), computer games, military simulations, and the film industry. Behavioral animation can be used to evaluate environmental design such as escape facilities in a burning building. It also can be used to create massive crowds for films, to supply background animation, or to provide stimulus for virtual environments.

Modeling behavior can be useful for several reasons:

- To relieve the animator from dealing with details when background animation is not of primary importance
- To generate animation on the fly, as in a game or virtual reality application
- To inspect the results of a simulation (i.e., to evaluate the environment relative to a certain behavior)
- To populate virtual environments

Synthetic characters with built-in rules of behavior are often referred to as *actors* or *intelligence agents*. When a figure is meant to be the embodiment of a user in a virtual environment, the term *avatar*[1] is often used. At the highest levels of abstraction, the animator takes on the role of a director. At the animator's command are intelligent characters who know how to get the job done: they only need to be told what to do. It is the character's job to find a way to do it. The animator ceases to animate and only directs the action in a very general way. The implied objective is that the behavior be realistic, or at least believable, so that character *appears* to be autonomous.

There are two general aspects of behavioral animation: cognitive modeling and aggregate behavior. Cognitive modeling can range from a simple cause-and-effect—based system to an attempt to model psychological changes in an agent's mental makeup under environmental influences. This aspect of computer animation is in the realm of agent-based AI. Aggregate behavior refers to how the individuals making up a group are modeled and how their behavior contributes to the quality of the group's motion as a whole.

6.2.2 Cognitive modeling

The task of modeling intelligence and cognition is the problem domain of AI. Aspects of behavior modeling are addressed in computer animation because of the spatial aspects and the imagery produced, and not by focusing on the accuracy of the mental processes being modeled. At all levels of cognitive modeling, the character *senses* the environment, *processes* the sensory information possibly with respect to their internal state and traits, and then *responds* with actions that interact with the synthetic environment and possibly with changes to the internal state. At the basic level, a simple reasoning mechanism suffices, such as use of a decision tree or case-based reasoning. More sophisticated approaches might model personality and mood of the character. For example, a rule-based approach is often used and can prove effective, although there are problems of scale. A common approach is to use a database of simple actions (e.g., simple SIMS games) as a library of behaviors and have appropriate behavior kick in when conditions are satisfied. Simple rules of

[1] In Hindu mythology, an *avatar* is an incarnation of a deity (especially Vishnu) in human or animal form.

the form (<cond>, <behavior>) can determine activity with the implication of executing the activity when the condition is met: *if* (<cond_i> is TRUE) *then* do activity_i. Of course, the condition can be arbitrarily complex, as can the activity.

When more than one precondition is met, some arbitration strategy must be in place. A simple method is to say that the first condition satisfied is activated, so order of rules sets the priority of rules. For a simple example, consider the behaviors of walking, running, standing, and turning. One of the major issues with this approach is transitioning from one activity to another. The simple solution is to have a neutral behavior to start and end each behavior, for example, standing.

STAND → WALK → TURN → RUN→STAND

A more sophisticated approach is to blend from one activity to another with either precomputed transitions or transitions computed on the fly. Adding more activities requires that more rules are added and more transitions are needed. Meta-rules can be added to reason about the rules, such as when to apply, which are compatible, and so forth. Higher levels of cognitive modeling often refer to themselves as modeling intelligence and individuality. Instead of directly reacting to environmental conditions, a cognitive structure is created that can more realistically sense the environment, alter the mental state, and reason about conditions using internal representations while filtering everything through mental states.

6.2.3 Aggregate behavior

Managing complexity is one of the most important uses of the computer in animation, and nothing exemplifies that better than particle systems. A *particle system* is a large collection of individual elements, which, taken together, represent a conglomerate fuzzy object. Both the behavior and the appearance of each individual particle are very simple. The individual particles typically behave according to simple physical principles with respect to their environment but not with respect to other particles of the system. When viewed together, the particles create the impression of a single, dynamic complex object. This illusion of a greater whole is referred to as *emergent behavior* and is an identifying characteristic of particle systems, flocking, and, to a lesser extent, crowds. Often behavioral animation is concerned with a large number of characters. The primitive behaviors of flocking and prey-predator activity, as well as crowd modeling, are common examples. One of the problems when dealing with a large group of behavioral characters is that knowledge about nearby characters is often required. Particle systems do not exhibit this complexity because there is (typically) no particle-particle interaction. There is only simple physical interaction with the environment. But when knowledge of nearby characters is required, the processing complexity is n-squared, where n is the number of characters. Even when interactions are limited to some k nearest neighbors, it is still necessary to find those k nearest neighbors out of the total population of n.

One way to find the nearest neighbors efficiently is to perform a 3D bucket sort and then check adjacent buckets for neighbors. Such a bucket sort can be updated incrementally by adjusting bucket positions of any members that deviate too much from the bucket center as the buckets are transformed along with the flock. There is, of course, a time-space trade-off involved in bucket size: the smaller the buckets, the more buckets needed, but the fewer members per bucket on average. This does not completely eliminate the *n*-squared problem because of worst-case distributions, but it is effective in practice.

The members of a flock, typically fewer in number than particles in a particle system, usually behave according to more sophisticated physics (e.g., flight) and a bit of intelligence (e.g., collision avoidance). Simple cognitive processes that control the movement of a member are modeled and might include such behavior as goal-directed motion and the steering to maintain separation from neighbors. Adding more intelligence to the members in a group results in more interesting individual behaviors, which is sometimes referred to as *autonomous behavior*. Modeling autonomous behavior tends to involve fewer participants, less physics, and more intelligence. Particle systems, flocking, and crowd behavior are examples of independently behaving members of groups with varying levels of autonomy, physical characteristics, and simulated motions (Table 6.1). If a larger number of autonomous agents is modeled, crowds are created that share some of the same emergent qualities as flocks and particle systems.

6.3 Finite state machines

Finite state machines (FSMs) are the simplest pattern we can use to add some intelligence into our animations as they allow objects to respond to environmental stimuli and change behaviors based on a combination of internal and external factors. Ranging from simple to highly complex, FSMs are used to guide our objects through decision-making processes. The simplest way to think about FSMs is that each object is assigned a "state of mind" (or simply "state") that determines what actions are currently *possible* and how the object must move. Only when something triggers a change in this state does the object change its behavior by performing a transition to a new state subsequently entering the new state of mind enabling a potentially

Table 6.1 Aggregate Behavior

Type	Number of Elements	Incorporated Physics	Intelligence
Particles	10^2–10^4	Much—with environment	None
Flocks	10^1–10^3	Some—with environment and other elements	Limited
Crowds	10^1–10^2	Usually little physics, but depends on interaction with environment	Varies from little to much

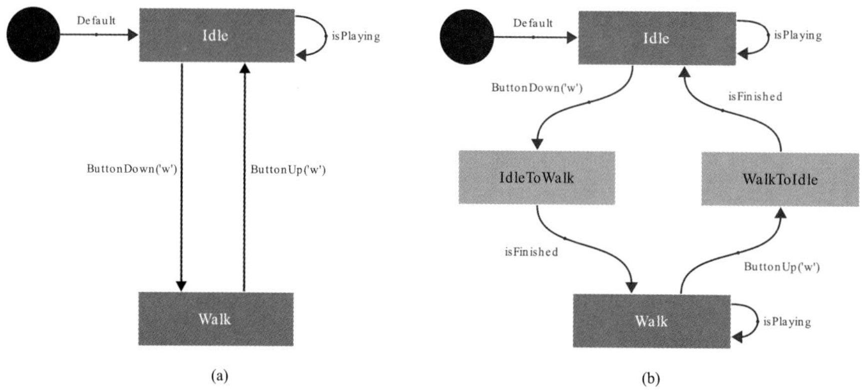

FIGURE 6.8

Simple finite state machine (FSM) Example. (a) A 2-state FSM (Idle, Walk) that changes when the "w" key is pressed, (b) incorporating intermediate transition animation states to play either predefined or blended animations to ensure smoothness between clips.

different set of actions to be performed. See Figure 6.8 for an example of a simple finite state diagram.

6.3.1 What is a state?

A state is a placeholder for data that represents a particular state of mind or action state of the character. For example, imagine we have a character that we wish to be able to walk, run, jump, and so forth. We would have to enumerate all of the potential actions that the character can perform at any given time and create an animation that can be played at that time. Let's say our character has the following states: Idle, Walk, Jump, and Fall. We can define each of these states as simply playing a particular animation clip and moving with an appropriate locomotion strategy. Now think about what happens if you want the character to walk (i.e., in a game you push the joystick forward). The state would have to transition to a new state (Walk), which can then play a new animation and employ a different locomotion strategy until another event occurs, such as hitting an object, pressing a button, or letting go of the joystick.

Generally speaking, a state requires all data needed to perform the actions of the represented cognitive behavior and access to the environment or context data required to make decisions. The decisions that need to be made may be as simple as which state or transition needs to be triggered given the current state of play.

From an implementation perspective, the "State" design pattern [21] can be used to define and manage state transitions and communication.

6.3.2 The state manager/machine: how to transition between states

For each *FSM*, we need a manager or *MachineContext* that manages the communication between the main animation system and the object itself. This manager retains the current state of the machine and any other information it requires to make decisions regarding routing messages between the relevant objects. In the simplest form, the *MachineContext* will keep a *currentState*, a function to *Set* the current state, and an *Update* function. The job of the *Update* function is simply to relay the call to the object *Update()* function (which occurs on regular intervals) to the current state itself. The state handles its own internal update and determines if a transition to a new state must occur. One easy way to handle this is to create a *Transition()* object that inherits from State and takes in the state it is transitioning *from*, the state it is transitioning *to*, and the *time* duration (if any) required to perform the transition.

If the transition condition is met, then the *MachineContext* can be set to this Transition state, which can handle the appropriate blending based on its internal model. This abstraction enables the creation of a variety of transition types (e.g., linear blend, parabolic blend, cubic blend, immediate, custom blend, blend-trees) with very little additional complexity in the software design itself.

```
class MachineContext {
      void SetState(State theNewState) theCurrentState = theNewState;
      void Update() theCurrentState.Update(this);
      // member variables
      State theCurrentState;
}
abstract class State {
        public abstract void SetData(...);
        public abstract void HandleState(MachineContext fsm);
}
class StateRun: public State {
        override void Update(Context fsm){...}
}
class StateIdle : public State {
        override void Update(Context fsm) {
          if(<condition is met>){
            if(<transition> )
                 transition.StartTransition(this, new StateRun()),
                     duration);
                 fsm.SetState(transition)
              else fsm.SetState(new StateRun());
          }
      }
}
class TransitionLinearBlend : public State{
```

```
    override void StartTransition(State FROM, State TO, float
DURATION) {...}
    override void Update(Context fsm){// ... update transition}
        // member variables
    State fromState, toState;
    float duration;
}
```

6.3.3 FSM example 1: Animation transitions

A transitional animation can be either authored by an artist/animator or performed automatically depending on the desired level of control. If complete control is required, then the animation team may author each transition as a concrete animation clip that plays the appropriate animation frames. For example, imagine we have a character that starts in an Idle state and can transition into a walking state, then we would have to author the Idle, Walk, IdleToWalk, and WalkToIdle animation clips and trigger the IdleToWalk/WalkToIdle appropriately (Figure 6.8). This quickly becomes unwieldy in systems with multiple objects as you now are required to author every possible transition between all possible animation states. As the complexity of the system grows, more and more work is placed at the feet of the animation team.

More automatic ways to handle transitions are to define the transitions as a set of blending/interpolation functions that blend between two or more animation clips. For example, you may have the Idle and Walk animation clips and a transition that blends the two clips together with a linear blend (LERP) for positions, or a spherical LERP (SLERP) for rotations. A custom blend function (e.g., a Bezier curve) can be used to define the weights of the clips throughout the transition duration. Then only a few parameters (e.g., speed/duration) and blending function needs to be authored for each transition. We will delve into this in more detail in later chapters.

6.3.4 FSM example 2: boss battle

Imagine a simple boss battle in a game like *Super Mario Odyssey* (Nintendo Switch). Usually these bosses may have a number of different strategies to choose from for attacking the player depending on a variety of factors such as their health, the player location, what items (if any) the player may be holding, and so forth. In Figure 6.9, we see an example of an FSM that might implement a simple battle with three different attack strategies. You can see that the enemy stays in the default Idle state until the player is visible/within range. Depending on the current health of the enemy, the appropriate attack strategy is initiated. Subsequently, within each attack pattern, the enemy performs the appropriate actions as stated in the subgraph, and ultimately, if a condition is met, a transition is triggered back to the Idle state or to the next Attack pattern. Finally, if the health remaining is zero or less, the FSM transitions to the Death state.

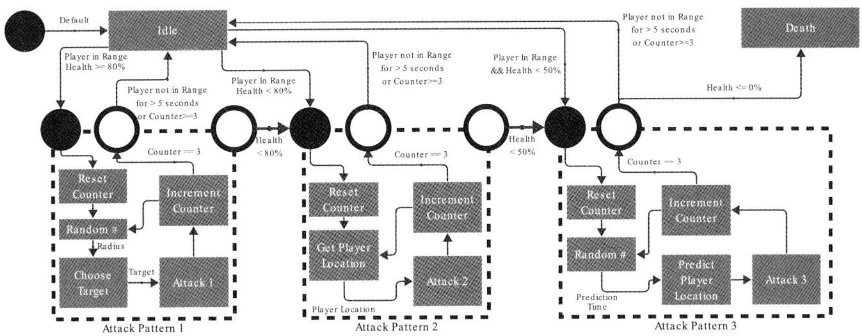

FIGURE 6.9

Boss battle. A finite state machine that defines the behavior of a boss enemy that has three distinct attack pattern/strategies that are triggered based on whether the player is in range and the health of the enemy.

6.4 Steering behaviors

The goal of steering behaviors [22] is to provide a way to move objects in a controllable manner at a higher level of abstraction. We want to have a way that moves objects in a "natural" way but we can direct them with a language that makes a bit of sense. For example, in English, we might describe objects as "wandering around," "pursuing" their prey, or "fleeing" a predator. But how might we define simple rules to perform these actions? To do so, we can define a number of simple fundamental behaviors that can be (1) easily specified at a high level, (2) easily implemented in a rigid body simulation, or (3) can be combined to create more complex behavior.

6.4.1 Basic behaviors

In the following, we will first define our basic framework for movement given a target using the standard rigid body update we have seen previously. We will then turn to discuss how this framework can be easily leveraged to create more interesting behaviors such as turning toward and aligning our object toward a target (Facing/Alignment), moving toward or away from a target (Seek/Flee), randomly moving in a smooth manner to give the inanimate object some degree of "life" (Wander), the ability to try and move toward an anticipated location (Pursue/Evade), slow down when approaching the target (Arrival/Departure), and finally how to include Obstacle avoidance into the locomotion framework.

Basic movement and targets

For simplicity, we assume that our object is defined as a rigid body. Thus we have access to its position, velocity, acceleration, and some notion of its orientation. We assume our pose is defined as having a position vector $\left(\vec{p}(t)\right)$ and an orientation

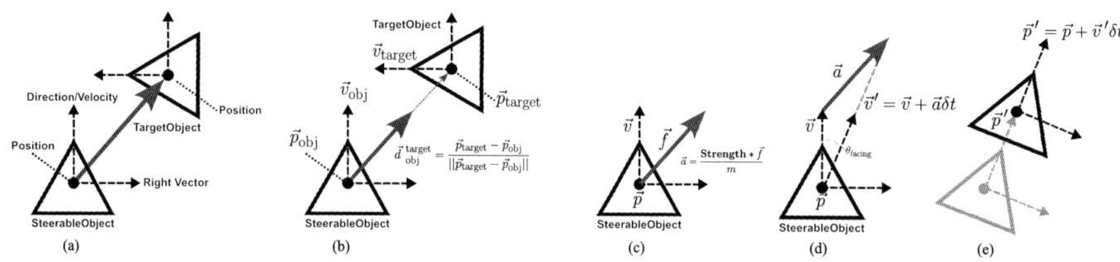

FIGURE 6.10

Steering basics. Steerable and target objects and appropriate required data labeled by (a) function and (b) vector notation. (c) Steering is performed by defining "Forces" that push the object based on desired behavior. (d) Object to rotate toward the alignment direction and update its velocity. (e) Position update step.

(Rot(t)), which can be converted between a quaternion ($\widehat{q}$) and a rotation matrix ($\mathbf{R}_{3\times3}$). We further note that it is sometimes simpler to think of the rotation matrix as a coordinate frame (as in the Frenet frame), where we specify the three columns in terms of the direction and up vectors (see Method 6.1). Figure 6.10 demonstrates the general geometry we are referring to here.

Method 6.1

The Frenet frame method

$$\begin{aligned}
\text{Pose}(t) &= \overrightarrow{p}(t), \text{Rot}(t) \\
\text{Rot}(t) &= \widehat{q} \Leftrightarrow \mathbf{R}_{3\times3} \\
\mathbf{R}_{3\times3} &= \left[\overrightarrow{dir} \;\; \overrightarrow{up} \;\; \left(\overrightarrow{dir} \times \overrightarrow{up} \right) \right]
\end{aligned}$$

We will use Euler integration for our movement update equations (and leave it up to the reader to modify for other integration schemes). If we use the PVA + F model as our foundation, we formulate steering for linear locomotion, as shown in Method 6.2.

Method 6.2

Steering update (general)

$$\textbf{SteeringUpdate}_{\text{Linear}}(\Delta t) \longleftarrow \begin{cases}
\overrightarrow{p}_{\text{new}} = \overrightarrow{p}_{\text{old}} + \overrightarrow{v}_{\text{old}} \Delta t & \\
\overrightarrow{v}_{\text{new}} = \overrightarrow{v}_{\text{old}} + \overrightarrow{a}_{\text{old}} \Delta t & \overrightarrow{v}_{\text{new}} \in [v_{min}, v_{max}] \\
\overrightarrow{a}_{\text{new}} = \dfrac{\overrightarrow{F}_{\text{total}}}{m_{\text{object}}} & \overrightarrow{a}_{\text{new}} \in [a_{min}, a_{max}] \\
\overrightarrow{F}_{\text{total}} = \sum_i \overrightarrow{f}_{\text{steer}_i} &
\end{cases}$$

From this set of equations, you can see how the velocity and acceleration are clamped between a range that can be set by the animator and that to "steer" the object, we simply need to define the set of steering forces based on the desired behavior.

$$\vec{f}_{\text{steer}_i} = \text{ForceStrength}_i * \overrightarrow{\text{SteeringDirection}_i} \quad \left\|\vec{f}\right\| \le F_{\max}$$

Note that the steering direction vector *must* be a unit vector to ensure that its magnitude is equal to the specified force strength. This essentially is stating in each update, the object accelerates in the steering direction. To change *where* the object is moving, we need to create rules on how to compute the direction and strength of the steering force for our desired behavior.

We can also define our angular update; however, there are a number of ways to perform angular steering that may be advantageous depending on the desired behavior. For instance, if you are able to estimate the angular velocity vector, then you can update the quaternion using Euler integration; or if you have a target orientation (i.e., keyframe), you can interpolate toward that direction; or you could directly set the orientation to be aligned with the computed velocity (or acceleration). Also, we will need to define a way to shift our timestamp from our global animation time into a value between zero and 1. We can do this by specifying the time interval and perform the following:

$$\textbf{NormalizeTime}(t) = \frac{t - t_{\text{start}}}{t_{\text{end}} - t_{\text{start}}}, \quad t \in [t_{\text{start}}, t_{\text{end}}].$$

For each of the following behaviors, we assume the pose is defined for our current object and a target object and we have access to the current pose and velocities of all potential targets:

$$\text{Pose}_{\text{object}} = \left\{\vec{p}_{\text{object}}, \text{Rot}_{\text{object}}\right\} \text{ and } \text{Pose}_{\text{target}} = \left\{\vec{p}_{\text{target}}, \text{Rot}_{\text{target}}\right\}.$$

The unit direction vector from object to target is:

$$\vec{d}_{\text{object}}^{\,\text{target}} = \frac{\vec{p}_{\text{target}} - \vec{p}_{\text{object}}}{\left\|\vec{p}_{\text{target}} - \vec{p}_{\text{object}}\right\|}.$$

Now, we need to create a set of rules for updating the steering forces and choice of target. How these are chosen will determine the behavior that emerges.

Facing/alignment

My mother always said "make sure you look where you are going" when I was a child. This is the job of *Facing* or *Alignment*. Given a target object, we want to smoothly update our steerable object to face toward the direction of the target. This can be accomplished in a number of ways.

- **Physics:** Given the direction vectors of both our object and the target, we note that the angular velocity is simply the cross-product between them. This can be scaled by the desired speed and the normalized time to obtain an "angular step" we can use in our quaternion integration scheme using the Euler method as shown in Method 6.3.

- **Interpolation:** We can alternatively leverage spherical linear interpolation (SLERP) from previous chapters to create a new orientation quaternion from both our object and the target orientations as shown in Method 6.4.
- **Vector alignment:** Another method for alignment is to align our direction vector with another vector directly using the Frenet frame algorithm (see Method 6.5).

Method 6.3

Physics (angular update for steering)

$$\mathbf{Physics}_{\text{ang}}(\vec{d}_{\text{object}}, \vec{d}_{\text{target}}, \Delta t) \leftarrow \begin{cases} \vec{\omega} = \vec{d}_{\text{object}} \times \vec{d}_{\text{target}} \\ s = ||\vec{\omega}|| \in [s_{\text{min}}, s_{\text{max}}] \\ \mathrm{S}_t = s * \mathbf{NormalizeTime}(t + \Delta t) \\ \hat{\omega} = [0, \mathrm{S}_t * \mathbf{Normalize}(\vec{\omega})] \\ \hat{q}_{t+\Delta t} = \mathbf{Normalize}(\hat{q}_t + \frac{1}{2}\hat{\omega}\hat{q}_t\Delta t) \end{cases}$$

Method 6.4

Angular interpolation alternative (angular update for steering)

$$\mathbf{Interpolate}_{\text{ang}}(\hat{q}_t, \hat{q}_{\text{target}}, \Delta t) \leftarrow \begin{cases} u = \mathbf{NormalizeTime}(t + \Delta t) \\ \hat{q}_{t+\Delta t} = \mathbf{SLERP}(\hat{q}_t, \hat{q}_{\text{target}}, u) \end{cases}$$

Method 6.5

Alignment

$$\mathbf{AlignWith}_{\text{ang}}(\vec{d}) \leftarrow \begin{cases} \vec{d}_t = \mathbf{Normalize}(\vec{d}) \\ \vec{L}_{tmp} = \vec{d}_t \times \overrightarrow{\mathrm{Up}}_{\text{world}} \\ \vec{u}_t = \vec{d}_t \times \vec{L}_{tmp} \end{cases}$$

Seek and flee

The base of all steering behaviors is the *Seek* behavior. Given a target object position, $\vec{p}_{target}$, SEEK aims to move smoothly toward the target. Thus, we can compute a force vector that "pushes" our object in the *direction* of the target with a desired strength each frame. The update function returns this force vector, $\vec{f}_{seek}$, toward the target thus accelerating toward the target (see Method 6.6 and Figure 6.11a). FLEE is the opposite of Seek, that is, accelerate in the opposite direction (see Method 6.7 and Figure 6.11b).

Method 6.6

Steering behavior (Seek)

SEEK$(\vec{p}_{\text{target}}, \text{ForceStrength}_{\text{seek}})$:

1. **Direction:**Compute direction to target:

   $$\vec{d}^{\,\text{target}}_{\text{object}} = \vec{p}_{\text{target}} - \vec{p}_{\text{object}}$$

2. **Normalize:**

   $$\vec{d} = \frac{\vec{d}^{\,\text{target}}_{\text{object}}}{||\vec{d}^{\,\text{target}}_{\text{object}}||}$$

3. **Facing:** Step orientation towards target

   $$\text{Interpolate}_{\text{ang}}(\hat{q}_{\text{object}}, \hat{q}_{\text{target}}, \Delta t_{\text{step}})$$

4. **Compute:** Seek Force

   $$\vec{f}_{\text{seek}} = \text{ForceStrength}_{\text{seek}} * \vec{d}^{\,\text{target}}_{\text{object}}$$

5. **Remaining Rigid-Body update**

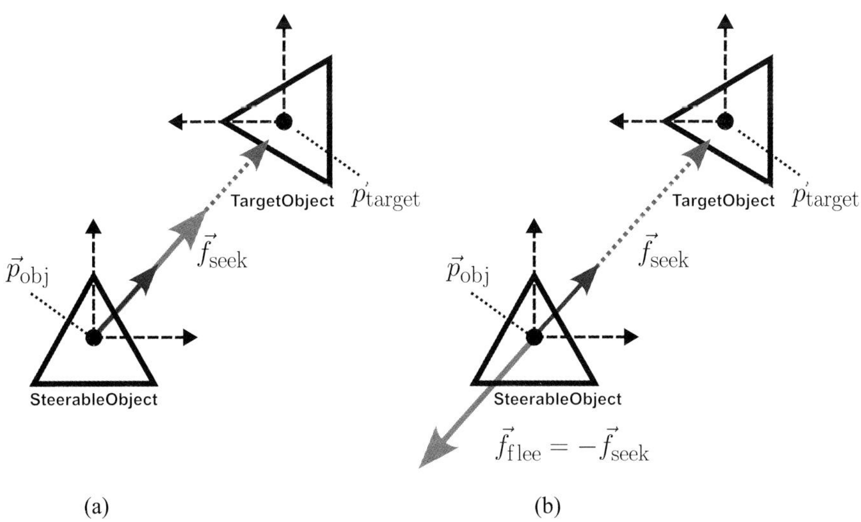

FIGURE 6.11

Steering: (a) Seek and (b) Flee. Seek accelerates in the direction of the target, and Flee accelerates away from the target.

Method 6.7

Steering behavior (Flee)

$$\textbf{FLEE}(\vec{p}_{\text{target}}, \text{ForceStrength}_{\text{flee}}):$$

1. **Compute:** Seek Force

   $\vec{f}_{\text{seek}} = \textbf{SEEK}(\vec{p}_{\text{target}}, \text{ForceStrength}_{\text{flee}})$

3. **Facing:** Step orientation away from target

   $\text{Interpolate}_{\text{ang}}(\hat{q}_{\text{object}}, \hat{q}^{c}_{\text{target}}, \Delta t_{\text{step}})$

4. **Compute:** Flee Force

   $\vec{f}_{\text{flee}} = -\vec{f}_{\text{seek}}$

5. **Remaining Rigid-Body update**

Wander

The goal of wander is to have the object meander along "randomly." To do so, we can randomly pick a target point that is in front of our object chosen such that our object does not have to turn too far to the left or right as we want our object to meander smoothly and not make any sudden changes to its orientation. We can do this by choosing an aiming location at a specified distance, D, along the objects' direction vector and imagining a circle around this aiming location of a fixed radius, r (see Method 6.8 and Figure 6.12). If we constrain any random offset from the aiming location to the circle, we will have a point that is within a given angle constraint from our original direction. We then simply Seek to this new point in our update. These two parameters (D, r) enable us to control the angle and range at which the target location is chosen, influencing the intended behavior.

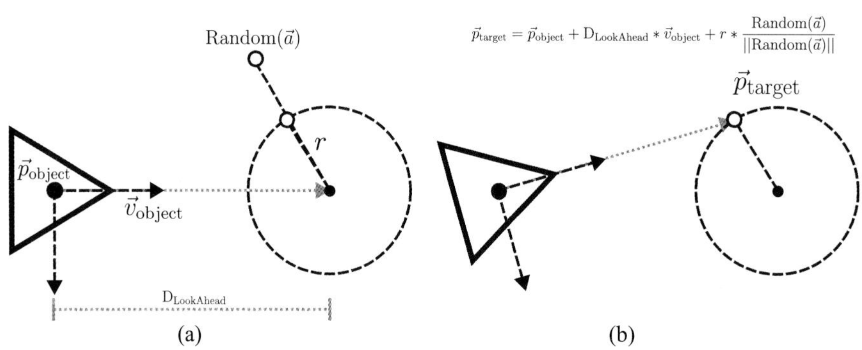

FIGURE 6.12

Steering: Wander (a) defines a look-ahead location at a predefined distance in the direction of movement and randomly selects a point relative to the look-ahead, and (b) the random point is normalized to a given radius that defines a target to seek toward.

Method 6.8

Steering behavior (Wander)

WANDER$(D, r, \text{ForceStrength}_{\text{wander}})$:

1.**Compute:** Aiming target

$$\vec{p}_{\text{aim}} = \vec{p}_{\text{object}} + D\frac{\vec{d}_{\text{object}}}{||\vec{d}_{\text{object}}||}$$

2.**Compute:** randomized location

$$\vec{R} = \textbf{rand}(x, y, z)$$

3.**Compute:** Constrained offset

$$\vec{o}_{\text{offset}} = r\frac{\vec{R}}{||\vec{R}||}$$

3.**Compute:** target location

$$\vec{p}_{\text{target}} = \vec{p}_{\text{aim}} + \vec{o}_{\text{offset}}$$

2.**Seek:** towards Target

$$\vec{f}_{\text{wander}} = \textbf{SEEK}(\vec{p}_{\text{target}}, \text{ForceStrength}_{\text{wander}})$$

5. **Remaining Rigid-Body update**

Pursue and evade

Related to Seek/Flee, *Pursue* (see Method 6.9 and Figure 6.13a) and *Evade* (see Method 6.10 and Figure 6.13b) try to "cut the object off at the pass," or rather run toward the future location of the target. This essentially allows the object to anticipate the location of the target in a given period of time. To achieve this, we extrapolate the location of the target using its current location and its velocity/direction and then seek to or away from the prediction.

Method 6.9

Steering behavior (Pursue)

PURSUE$(\vec{p}_{\text{target}}, \vec{v}_{\text{target}}, \Delta t_{\text{predict}}, \text{ForceStrength}_{\text{pursue}})$:

1.**Predict:** future location of target

$$\vec{p}_{\text{predicted}} = \vec{p}_{\text{target}} + \vec{v}_{\text{target}}\Delta t_{\text{predict}}$$

2.**Seek:** towards prediction

$$\vec{f}_{\text{pursue}} = \textbf{SEEK}(\vec{p}_{\text{predicted}}, \text{ForceStrength}_{\text{pursue}})$$

5. **Remaining Rigid-Body update**

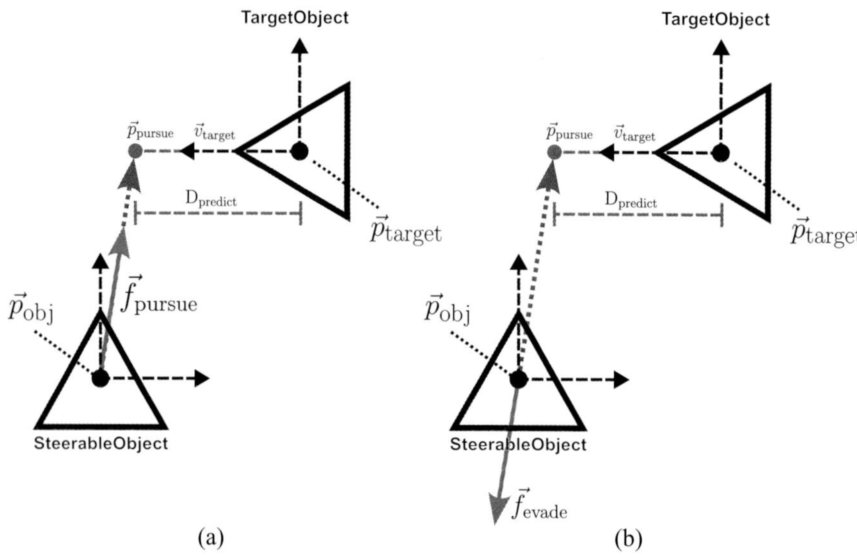

FIGURE 6.13

Steering: (a) Pursue and (b) Evade. Similar to Seek/Flee but using a prediction as the target location. The prediction is extrapolated using the target objects' position and facing direction/velocity.

Method 6.10

Steering behavior (Evade)

$$\textbf{EVADE}(\vec{p}_{\text{target}}, \vec{v}_{\text{target}}, \Delta t_{\text{predict}}, \text{ForceStrength}_{\text{evade}}):$$

1.**Compute:** Pursue force

$$\vec{f}_{\text{pursue}} = \textbf{PURSUE}(\vec{p}_{\text{target}}, \vec{v}_{\text{target}}, \ldots)$$

2.**Seek:** away from prediction

$$\vec{f}_{\text{evade}} = -\vec{f}_{\text{pursue}}$$

5. **Remaining Rigid-Body update**

Arrival

Sometimes, you may wish an object to arrive at a given location and stop. If you continually use the Seek/Pursue behaviors, the object may never actually stop at a given location; in fact it may overshoot the object, causing the appearance of instability and noise. The arrival behavior simply slows down an object if they are within a given distance from the target (see Method 6.11 and Figure 6.14). We do this by attenuating the force such that it is proportional to the distance from the final target location. In the following, we assume that the steering force $\vec{f}$ has already been computed and that $s_{slowdown} \leq 1$, in practice 0.99 or 0.98 are reasonable values.

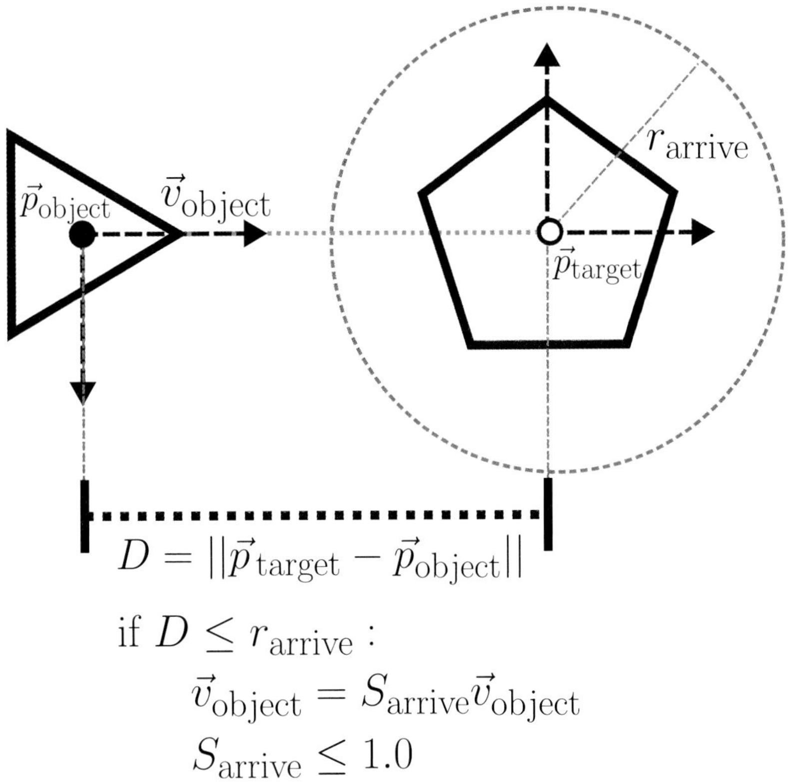

FIGURE 6.14

Steering: Arrival behavior. If the object is within an "arrival" distance, the velocity magnitude is scaled in each frame and clamped when it falls below a threshold to stop the object.

Method 6.11

Steering behavior (Arrival)

ARRIVAL$(\vec{p}_{\text{target}}, r, \vec{f}, s_{slowdown}, \text{ForceStrength}_{\text{arrival}})$:

1. **Compute:** Distance to target

   $d = ||\vec{p}_{\text{target}} - \vec{p}_{\text{object}}||$

2. **Attenuate:** by distance if within radius

   if $(d \leq r)$

   $s = s_{slowdown} * d$

   else $s = d$

3. **Compute:** arrival force

   $$\vec{f}_{\text{arrival}} = s * \text{ForceStrength}_{\text{arrival}} * \frac{\vec{f}}{||\vec{f}||}$$

5. **Remaining Rigid-Body update**

Path follow

To follow a path using this steering framework, we simply have to choose a target along a given path and seek toward it! Here it is assumed that you have the ability to sample the path using an arc length parameterization (as discussed in Chapter 4), and that you can query the path for the closest point on the path, which can be done quickly by computing the distance of the object to each key location in the path (waypoint method) or by computing the perpendicular distance to the closest interval and sampling the path at that location (see Method 6.12 and Figure 6.15).

Method 6.12

Steering behavior (Path following)

$\textbf{FOLLOW}(\textbf{PATH}, D_{\text{lookAhead}}, \text{ForceStrength}_{\text{FOLLOW}}):$

1.**Get:** Closest Waypoint on path

$\vec{p}_{\text{waypoint}} = \textbf{PATH}.\text{closestTo}(\vec{p}_{\text{object}})$

2.**Sample:** point on path using look ahead (arc length)

$\vec{p}_{\text{target}} = \textbf{PATH}.\text{sample}(\vec{p}_{\text{waypoint}}, D_{\text{lookAhead}})$

3.**Seek:** towards target

$\vec{f}_{\text{follow}} = \textbf{SEEK}(\vec{p}_{\text{target}}, \text{ForceStrength}_{\text{FOLLOW}})$

4. **Remaining Rigid-Body update**

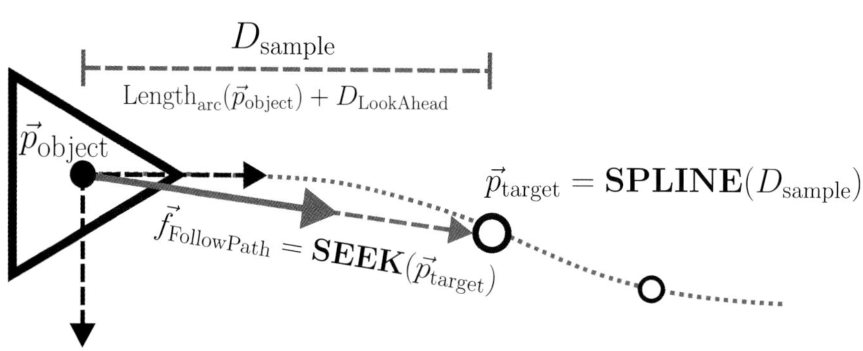

FIGURE 6.15

Steering: Path following. A target location is determined by sampling the path/spline parameterized by arc length at a distance in front of the object to seek toward.

Avoidance

Avoidance behaviors are a modification of the steering force that moves it away from an object within a collision zone. This is done by extrapolating a query location in front of our object, querying the collision system and determining an offset force (in the direction perpendicular to the direction we are facing, i.e., our coordinate-frame "right" vector) to adjust our steering such that we avoid the object (see Method 6.13 and Figure 6.16).

Method 6.13

Steering behavior (Avoidance)

$\textbf{AVOID}(\vec{f}_{\text{steering}}, \vec{p}_{\text{avoid}}, r_{\text{avoid}}, D_{\text{lookAhead}}):$

1. **Extrapolate:**

$$\vec{p}_{\text{query}} = \vec{p}_{\text{object}} + \vec{v}_{\text{object}} * D_{\text{lookAhead}}$$

2. **Query:** Collision System

$$q_{\text{result}} = \textbf{COLLISION\_QUERY}(\vec{p}_{\text{avoid}}, \vec{p}_{\text{query}})$$

$$q_{\text{result}} \in \textbf{Boolean}(\text{True}, \text{False})$$

$$\vec{f}_{\text{offset}} = \vec{p}_{\text{avoid}} \pm r_{\text{avoid}} * \vec{e}_{\text{right}}$$

$$\vec{e}_{\text{right}} \leftarrow R_{\text{object}} = \begin{bmatrix} \vec{e}_{\text{dir}} & \vec{e}_{\text{up}} & \vec{e}_{\text{right}} \end{bmatrix}$$

3. **Adjust:** steering force

$$\vec{f}_{\text{avoid}} = \vec{f}_{\text{steering}} + q_{\text{result}} * \vec{f}_{\text{offset}}$$

4. **Remaining Rigid-Body update**

6.4.2 Combining behaviors

Given the simple behaviors as described previously, we can now think about how we may combine them to create new types of behaviors. Because each provides a force vector that is used to "push" the object during its locomotion update, we can combine the results of multiple behaviors through a weighted sum. For example, if we had two objects, one that we wish to seek toward and the other that we wish to flee, we could compute the steering forces from both of these behaviors ($\vec{f}_{flee}, \vec{f}_{\text{seek}}$). Assigning a weight to each of them such that the weights are normalized enable us to combine the effects of both $\vec{f}_{\text{result}} = w_{seek}\vec{f}_{\text{seek}} + w_{flee}\vec{f}_{\text{flee}}$, where $w_{seek} + w_{\text{flee}} = 1$. Making one of these weights larger than the other would influence the behavior of the object more.

In general, we would combine *all* behavior steering forces that are active as:

$$\vec{F}_{\text{totalSteering}} = \sum_i w_i \vec{f}_{\text{i}}, \quad \sum_i w_i = 1.$$

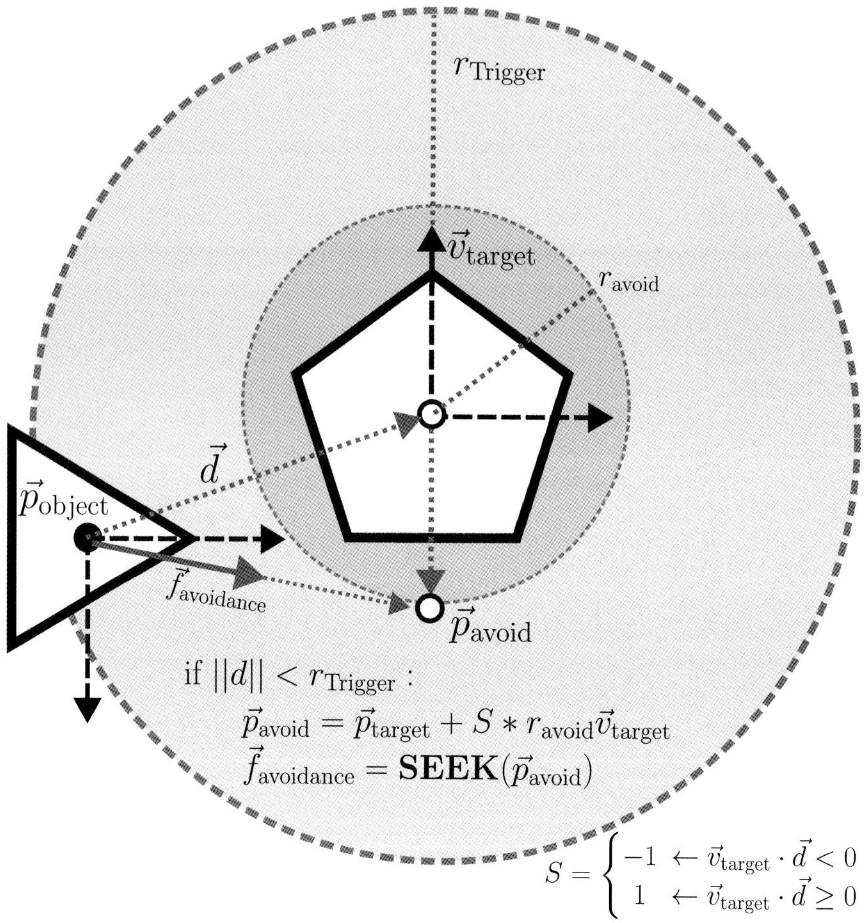

FIGURE 6.16

Steering: Avoidance. If either a predicted collision query or if the object is within a collision distance of an object to avoid, a new target is selected using either the surface normal or the object's velocity to extrapolate a point that is at a safe distance from the object. By seeking toward this new location, the object will have a better chance to avoid the collision.

At this point, you should be able to see how a system could leverage FSMs to activate behaviors on an object based on the intended interaction with the scene and how control of such behaviors can be maintained through interpolation and normalization of the weights.

Combining steering forces like this can result in interesting emergent behaviors for crowds or other groupings of objects. In Reynolds' original paper, he developed the notion of "boids" to simulate flocking behaviors observed in groups of birds. To do this, a set of steering forces needs to be computed for each boid that (1) aligns the boid to the average direction of the group, (2) pulls the boid toward the center of the group, and (3) pushes the boid away from the center of the group. By managing the weights of these steering forces and enabling boids to enter/leave a group with some heuristic, relatively complex looking movement can emerge (see Figure 6.17 for an example).

6.5 Crowds

A crowd is a large group of people physically grouped (crowded) together. But the term "crowd" has been applied to a wide variety of scenarios, such as a collection of individuals reacting to the environment, a mass of hundreds of thousands of armed warriors in a feature-length film where individual identification is practically impossible, and dots on a screen showing movement from room to room during a fire simulation. For this discussion, a crowd is considered to be the animation of representations of a large number of individuals where the individuals are not the primary focus of the animation and detailed inspection of individuals by the viewer is not expected. This distinguishes a crowd from an environment containing multiple agents in which the individual activity of the agents is important. The use of multiple agents is just that: some number of behaviorally animated characters where the actions of individuals are discernible and important and the viewer would be inspecting the activity of individuals in the environment. The emphasis here is on animation of multiple figures where the global nature of the activity is the primary consideration.

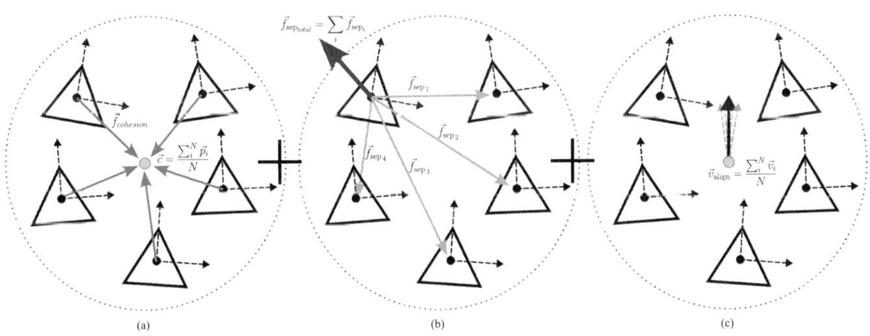

FIGURE 6.17

Steering: Flocking. Combining multiple behaviors through a weighted sum enables new emergent behaviors. Here, three forces are defined based on nearby (within a given radius) objects: (a) Cohesion, in which each object is "pulled" toward the center (average location) of the neighboring objects; (b) Separation, in which each object is "pushed" away from nearby objects (scaled by distance); and (c) Alignment, in which the direction of movement is aligned toward the average velocity of the nearby objects.

There are two main applications of graphical crowd modeling. The first is as a visual effect. Perhaps the obvious one is the use in a feature-length film to fill in the movement or activity of a mass of people in battle scenes or populating an environment with activity or creating an audience in the bleachers of a stadium. In battle scenes, for example, it is common to have the first row or two of characters to be live actors, whereas all the background activity is synthetic characters. Managing the complexity of such crowds has become an important issue in the visual effects industry and is being addressed by software products such as Massive [12,20]. Computer games are another obvious example of this application. In this type of crowd, the appearance and motion of the individuals must be organized to be believable, not distracting, and computationally efficient.

The second application of graphical crowd modeling is as a simulation of activity in a space to better understand that activity. Here the visuals are not the focus. The distribution and spatial relationship of crowd members with respect to each other and with respect to the environment are the main concerns. For example, crowd animation might be used to model the translocation of a mass of people, such as a crowd entering an amusement park or exiting a stadium, to evaluate the various pathways through an environment for traffic flow. A related use that has received a fair amount of attention recently is evacuation simulation. In these cases, the appearance of the individuals has no value; it is only the location of the members and how they traverse the environment while trying to escape some threat, such as fire, usually in a building. Here, cognitive modeling and subsequent data gathering are the important tasks. The visuals are either not important at all or are of secondary importance. Often the crowd members are represented merely as dots in a bird's-eye view of a building floor plan.

6.5.1 Crowd behaviors

There are certain behaviors that individuals of a crowd assume because they are members of the crowd. These behaviors are similar to that found in members of a flock: collision avoidance and maintaining crowd membership. Simulating crowd behavior is both an interesting and challenging research area. Using Reynolds' flock of boids as a reference, crowd members engage in collision avoidance, match the velocity of neighbors, and stay close to other crowd members. For example, in finding seats in a theater or evacuating a building, the flow of the crowd can be studied.13 However, as opposed to typical models of flocking behavior, crowd flow can be multidirectional. Using psychology literature as a source for how people behave in crowds (e.g., [18]), one of the main activities found in crowds is the avoidance of oncoming people when traversing an environment. Various rules can be derived by looking at actual behavioral studies, as seen in the following:

- In high density, start avoiding at 5 feet or nearer; in low density, avoidance can start at 100 feet

- In low density, change paths; in high density, rotate body and side step (*step and slide*)
- Open (front to other person, men) versus closed (back to other person, women)
- In changing path, move to open side, else tend to move to right
- Avoid people moving in the same direction by slowing down or overtaking them and resuming the original course after the pass has been completed

6.5.2 Internal structure

There are higher cognitive behaviors that create substructures within the group. Although a crowd can exhibit an aggregate behavior (e.g., *mob mentality*) that is similar to the flocking behavior of birds and emerges from localized motion of the flock members, it is usually made up of smaller groups of people in which the group members interact closely. Group membership is dynamic, and group interaction often occurs [10].

Groups are formed by common urges (e.g., going for lunch), belief systems (e.g., political allies), and emotional state (e.g., soccer fans), as well as by spatial proximity. Individuals of a crowd may or may not have a group membership. Qualities of an individual relevant to group membership include the following:

- A changeable belief system: From experiences, senses (e.g., vision) understanding the nature of things as a result of learning, and causes and effects (from seeing or experiencing a sequence of events)
- Time-varying biases, propensities, disposition, inclination, tendency, and emotional state: Things that will be satisfied if possible and if there are enough extra degrees of freedom in attaining a goal or desire to satisfy secondary desires
- Goals, desires: Definite objectives that the agent is trying to satisfy

6.5.3 Crowd control

Similar to flocking behavior, individual crowd members are typically represented as being aware of nearby crowd members and must be managed to avoid collisions. As opposed to flocking behavior, there is less concern about the effect of physics on the crowd members because crowds are often land-based animals (e.g., humans) where collisions are avoided rather than detected and movement occurs in two-dimensional space. However, because of the large number of members typically found in a crowd, strategies for controlling the motion of each member must be very efficient for many applications. Three main strategies have been used to control crowds: rules, forces, and flows. Rules have been discussed under the topic of intelligent behavior. For crowds, usually simple rules are used to keep the computation cost low. Forces can be used that are similar to those found in particle systems but must be organized so as to prevent collisions. The work by Helbing (e.g., [19]) concerning what he calls *social forces* is basically an extension of Reynolds' work on flocking behavior that is applied to social interactions in crowds. In the third approach to crowd control, the movement of crowd members has been compared to flow fields. This is usually effective for crowds that are massive in the number of members, and only positional information of an individual is needed.

6.6 Motion planning

What if we wanted objects to get to a particular location in the environment but avoid obstacles? What if we wanted them to get there using the shortest possible path? We do this by employing simple motion planning and search algorithms with an appropriate representation of the world. Imagine a world defined as a grid of cells where each cell is either traversable or not. We can pick a starting location to place our object and another cell to denote the goal/target. The question of how to get there in the shortest possible number of steps can be computed using graph theory from computer science. Here each cell is connected to its traversable neighborhood cells by an edge. We then can employ standard graph search algorithms to find the path through this graph that minimizes a Distance function. The most common solution to this problem is the A* algorithm. The goal of A* is to find a path that minimizes a function comprising two functions: (1) the "distance so far" metric, or the cost of getting to this cell given the path taken; and (2) a "heuristic" that estimates the distance to the final target. The heuristic can encode a variety of factors in the environment and is domain specific. The goal of the A* algorithm is to minimize the sum of these two functions such that the total distance traveled along the path toward the destination is "optimal." The details of the implementation of A* is beyond the scope of this book; however, the interested reader should explore [20] to learn more about A* and alternatives.

6.6.1 But what if my scene is not a 2D grid?

Representing the world as a 2D grid is not necessary for A*. All that needs to exist is a notion of connectedness. A common approach in 3D environments is called a Navigation Mesh, or NavMesh, that approximates the geometry of the scene at an abstracted level. NavMeshes contain vertices and edges (and thus it is a graph) and invisible edges can be defined for specific behaviors, such as jumping onto platforms or performing parkour-style jumps between two walls to climb them. Each edge would encode the difficulty of performing the appropriate/necessary action in its heuristic function to enable the A* algorithm to choose it appropriately depending on the situation.

6.7 Chapter summary

In this chapter, we discussed keyframe systems from a high-level perspective followed by how we can use these notions to define paths that can be interpolated appropriately. We then discussed how we can use these paths in a locomotion system for non-player-characters or objects that need to be controlled by the system. This led us naturally into FSMs to define a structure for making decisions based on a simple cognitive modeling approach. We then discussed how we could encode and combine steering behaviors to create emergent behaviors and how FSMs could connect with these ideas for control. This gives you a good starting point to be able to pull together a fairly complex behavior-driven locomotion system. There are many optimizations and alternative ways to solve these locomotion problems to increase performance and manage complexity. This is definitely not the end but rather the beginning of a journey into the realm of agent-based artificial intelligence. The next few chapters will transition away from *locomotion* into *animation*-specific algorithms and how we can connect locomotion with animation to create systems that are aesthetically pleasing.

6.8 Exercises

Beginner

B1. In terms of "keyframe"—based animation systems, what does "sampling" refer to?
B2. What are the basic elements of an FSM?
B3. What problem does an FSM solve?
B4. How can we use FSMs for locomotion?
B5. List all of the steering behaviors we defined in section 6.4 and describe succinctly how each of them works.

Intermediate

I1. Modify Figure 6.9 to include a new more difficult stage with a different attack strategy. What are the values and variables that need to be considered to transition to/from the new stage?
I2. Create an FSM for a simple Tic-Tac-Toe game. How would you encode the board locations? How would you make decisions about these locations? Can you come up with a way to use as few states as possible?
I3. Imagine an animation of an underwater school of fish just happily swimming in the ocean. Imagine that each fish can either swim along a predefined path or move with a group of friends in the same direction. Also imagine a shark enters the area and the fish must try to swim away from the shark. Show how FSMs and Steering behaviors can be linked in this situation to encode and simulate such behaviors.

Advanced

A1. Develop a general FSM system that can be configured to demonstrate the FSM in Figure 6.9.

A2. Go beyond and investigate hierarchical FSMs and provide a simple implementation of one that demonstrates why this concept is useful.

A3. Implement each of the steering behaviors and demonstrate how to combine their behaviors with a weighted sum. Control each of the weights with an FSM that is triggered by either global scene conditions or local conditions relative to the agent itself (e.g., current actions/beliefs/input).

A4. Go beyond and research the flocking behavior of boids and implement these steering behaviors in a game engine to control a crowd walking around an environment. Use A* and NavMeshes to define the environment and group goals/targets for movement.

References

[1] Burtnyk N, Wein M. Computer generated key frame animation. J Soc Motion Pict Telev Eng 1971;8(3):149–53.

[2] Burtnyk N, Wein M. Interactive skeleton techniques for enhancing motion dynamics in key frame animation. Commun ACM 1976;19(10):564–9.

[3] Catmull E. The problems of computer-assisted animation. In: Computer graphics. Proceedings of SIGGRAPH 78, 12(3). Atlanta, Ga; 1978. p. 348–53.

[4] Litwinowicz P. Inkwell: a $2^1/_2$-D animation system. In: Sederberg TW, editor. Computer graphics. Proceedings of SIGGRAPH 91, 25(4). Las Vegas, Nev; 1991. p. 113–22.

[5] May S. Encapsulated models: procedural representations for computer animation. Ph.D. Dissertation. Ohio State University; 1998.

[6] Gomez J. Twixt: a 3D animation system. Comput Graph 1985;9(3):291–8.

[7] Stern G. BBOP—a program for 3-dimensional Animation. In: Nicograph 83 proceedings. Tokyo, Dec '83. p. 403–404.

[8] Reeves W. In-betweening for computer animation utilizing moving point constraints. In: Computer graphics. Proceedings of SIGGRAPH 81, 15(3). Dallas, Tex; 1981. p. 263–70.

[9] Keyframes. Keyframes - Blender 4.1 Manual. 2024. docs.blender.org/manual/en/latest/animation/keyframes/index.html.

[10] Magnenat-Thalmann N, Thalmann D. Computer animation: theory and practice. New York: Springer-Verlag; 1985.

[11] Hackathorn R, Parent R, Marshall B, Howard M. An interactive Micro-computer based 3D animation system. In: Proceedings of Canadian Man-computer communications society conference 81. Ontario: Waterloo; 1981. p. 181–91.

[12] Magnenat-Thalmann N, Thalmann D, Fortin M. Miranim: an extensible Director-oriented system for the animation of realistic images. IEEE Comput Graph Appl 1985;5(3):61–73.

[13] Hackathorn R, Anima II. A 3D color animation system. In: George J, editor. Computer graphics. Proceedings of SIGGRAPH 77, 11(2). San Jose, Calif; 1977. p. 54–64.

[14] Defanti T. The digital component of the circle graphics habitat. In: Proceedings of the national computer conference 76, vol. 45. New York; June 7–10. Montvale, New Jersey: AFIPS Press; 1976. p. 195–203.

[15] Mezei L, Zivian A. ARTA: an interactive animation system. In: Proceedings of information processing 71. Amsterdam: North-Holland; 1971. p. 429–34.
[16] Talbot P, Carr IIIJ, Coulter JR, Hwang R. Animator: an on-line two-dimensional film animation system. Commun ACM 1971;14(4):251–9.
[17] May SAL. The animation language. 2005. http://accad.osu.edu/smay/AL/scheme.html.
[18] Wilkins M, Kazmier C. MEL scripting for maya animators. San Francisco, California: Morgan Kaufmann; 2003.
[19] Houdini 2.0: user guide. Toronto: Side Effects Software; 1997.
[20] Reynolds C. Computer animation with scripts and actors. In: Computer graphics. Proceedings of SIGGRAPH 82, 16(3). Boston, Mass.; 1982. p. 289–96.
[21] Freeman E, Robson E. Head first design patterns: building extensible and maintainable object-oriented software. 2nd ed. O'Reilly Media; 2021.
[22] Reynolds CW. Steering behaviors for autonomous characters. Game developers conference; 1999.

CHAPTER

Basic animation techniques

7

7.1 Flipbooks

A common metaphor for 2D computer animation is the "sprite sheet" or "flipbook." The digital flipbook emerges from traditional and historical cel animation techniques as discussed in Chapter 1. Older (and new) 2D video games make use of the concept of a flipbook to create interesting animations. They can also be used as the *primary* animation technique for characters or as a *secondary* technique for visual effects (e.g., fire, magic).

A "flipbook" is a set of images that when shown successively (and at a reasonable framerate) provide the illusion of motion. Consider Figure 7.1, where a flipbook is shown that contains four animation clips/states (Slide, Walk, Idle, Jump). Each clip contains an ordered list of frames and different clips that need not have the same number of frames (in general). In the Unity game engine, each frame of a sprite animation is stored as a separate animation clip and the *dopesheet* view displays each frame at its corresponding time on the timeline (Figure 7.2). Similarly, the Unreal engine has a "Paper 2D Flipbook" component. Common data structures used to internally store a flipbook can be as simple as an array per animation clip containing the sprite image sequence and an array/list/dictionary of clips to store multiple animations. Transitions between flipbook clips can only be done by switching between clips and as such can be visually jarring if not performed on an appropriate frame. Thus care must be taken to ensure that state transitions can only occur at specific frames to mitigate these issues. Other than characters, flipbooks can also be used to fake complex simulations such as fire, fog/smoke, blood gushing, waterfalls and more; for example, EmberGen is a tool dedicated to simulating realistic fluids, fire, and smoke, resulting in flipbook animations of these simulations (see Figure 7.3 and [1]).

7.1.1 Flipbooks in 3D

The concept of the flipbook can also be extended to 3D models quite easily. Rather than storing a list of images and flipping between them for each frame of the animation, one can store a separate 3D model per animation frame. There are two primary issues when considering 3D flipbooks: memory consumption and authoring. This

Computer Animation. https://doi.org/10.1016/B978-0-443-13512-5.00007-0

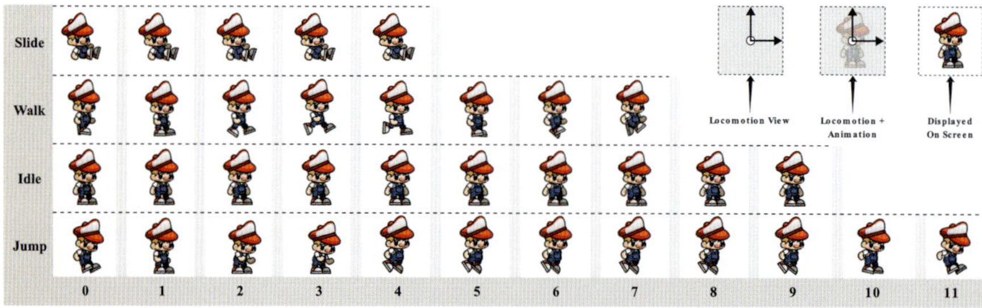

FIGURE 7.1

Example of a sprite sheet/flipbook showing four animation clips (Slide, Walk, Idle, Jump), each with varying numbers of frames. (Sprites from [https://www.gameart2d.com/red-hat-boy-free-sprites.html] under Creative Common Zero (CC0) license.) *Top right* shows the data view from the perspectives of locomotion (box with coordinate frame), locomotion + animation (box + coordinate frame + image), and displayed on screen (image only).

approach can consume a lot of memory because each frame stores the entire 3D geometry (vertices/edges). Imagine a scenario where you had a 3D character with 10K vertices and 20K triangles. If each vertex contains a 3D coordinate (x,y,z) and a 2D texture coordinate (u,v) and each triangle contains 3 indices to vertices, the memory consumption for a single model in this scenario could be 10K × (3 × 4 bytes) + 20K × (3 indices × 4 bytes), or approximately 360 KB per frame. Not bad! But if a single animation clip has 30 frames, then that clip is approximately 10.8 MB (30 × 360 KB) of memory. Considering that in a video game you will require many animation clips per character (and many characters) this adds up quickly (and never mind if you want to store more data per vertex such as normals, colors, etc.).

7.2 Morphing

The word *morph* is derived from morphology or rather the study of structure or form [2], and in the context of computer animation we use the term *metamorphosis*, meaning to undergo transformation [3]. In essence, *morphing* is a technique used to smoothly transform one object into another object over time. This computer animation technique was used in movies and television in the late 1980s, for example in *Flight of the Navigator* (1986), *Willow* (1988), and *Indiana Jones and the Last Crusade* (1989). Morphing became popular in the 1990s with its appearance in many blockbuster films. In *Terminator 2: Judgment Day* (1991) [4], the main antagonist (the T-1000) used morphing as its defining characteristic allowing it to transform into other characters and objects. On television, *Star Trek: Deep Space Nine* (1993) introduced Odo (played by René Auberjonois), a shapeshifter who could morph into various objects/animals. More recently, the morphing technique has been leveraged in new generative AI

FIGURE 7.2
Dopesheet view in Unity animator view showing timecode for each flipbook frame.

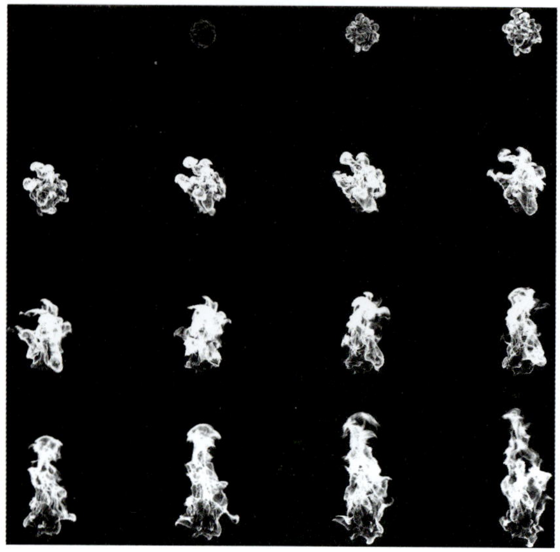

FIGURE 7.3

Flipbook sprite sheet created by EmberGen.

Table 7.1 Flipbook

Animation Technique: The Flipbook		
Advantages	**Disadvantages**	**Use Cases**
• Easy to implement • Can add visual complexity without additional computation (e.g., fluids, smoke, fire) • Art teams are well versed in traditional animation techniques	• Visually inflexible • Changes to animations must be performed at the image level • Cannot easily be interpolated (exception of fade-in/fade-out) • Memory (especially for 3D)	• 2D sprite animations • User interface elements • Particle effects • Visual effects such as fire, magic • Billboards • Environmental effects

techniques to enable temporal consistency and to transform images using diffusion-style methods such as in DiffMorpher (2024) [5].

7.2.1 Morphing versus deformation

Whereas morphing is a form of deformation, not all deformation is morphing. We will see later that we can deform objects to attain different shapes used in conjunction with a skeletal rig to skin characters. The underlying goals of these two techniques are similar; however, when we are discussing morphing, we really mean that we have two instances of the same input data and want to generate new intermediate versions combined to create a new instance that contains characteristics of both of the inputs.

7.2.2 Morphing: the technique

In general, the morphing technique can be characterized as a function of two aligned datasets (source, target) and an interpolating function. The function interpolates the data resulting in a new instance where each component of the datasets are interpolated with the given interpolating function (see Definition 7.1).

Definition 7.1

$$D_u \leftarrow \mathbf{MORPH}(D_{\text{source}}, D_{\text{target}}, f_{\text{interp}}, u)$$

$$\text{where } D_{\text{source}} = \left\{{}^{S}d_i\right\}_{i=0}^{N}, D_{\text{target}} = \left\{{}^{T}d_i\right\}_{i=0}^{N}, D_{\text{u}} = \left\{{}^{T}d_i\right\}_{i=0}^{N}$$

$$\forall i \in [0, N] : {}^{T}d_i = f_{\text{interp}}({}^{S}d_i, {}^{T}d_i, u)$$

This assumes that there are three datasets composed of the same number of components and that they are aligned. The actual type of data does not matter to the algorithm; however, the data should exist in a coordinate system that can be smoothly interpolated by the function to achieve continuous, smooth, and plausible results. Generally, the algorithm can be seen in Algorithm 7.1; note that the optional reparameterization step can be used to apply a spline to control the morph speed (i.e., for easing).

```
Algorithm 7.1: Morph (General)

    MORPH (D_source, D_target, u) :
        [optional] u = Re-parameterize (u)
        for each i ∈ [0, N] do
            D_u[i] = Interpolate (D_source[i], D_target[i], u)
        return D_u
```

7.2.3 Morphing images

There are several techniques in the literature for morphing one image into another. Here we briefly overview three popular approaches: (1) simple but naive, (2) mesh-based warping, and (3) feature-based warping.

Simple but naive

The simplest way to morph two images is to simply interpolate each pixel as if the two images were perfectly aligned (see Algorithm 7.2). Although naive, it has its uses for fading the images in/out or controlling transparency of the imagery. The main disadvantage of this approach is that the geometry of the image subject is not considered and thus is not preserved (Figure 7.4).

Algorithm 7.2: Morph (Naïve)

> **MORPH** ($I_{\text{source}}, I_{\text{target}}, u_{\text{interp}}$) **:**
>
> > **[optional]** $u_{\text{interp}} =$ **Re-parameterize** (u_{interp})
> >
> > **for each pixel** (u, v) **do**
> >
> > > $I_u[u, v] =$ InterpolateRGBA ($I_{\text{source}}[u, v], I_{\text{target}}[u, v], u_{\text{interp}}$)
> >
> > **return** I_u

In an attempt to preserve the shape of the objects represented in the images more precisely, we need an intermediate representation that lets us define which pixels need to be interpolated. Rather than assuming that each pixel is aligned with the 1D array pixel index (i) or even the 2D image coordinate (u,v), we can specify a mapping function $f_{map}(u, v) \mapsto (u', v')$ that maps input image coordinates, (u,v), in the source image into pixel coordinates in the destination image, (u', v') (see Algorithm 7.3). How we specify this mapping function is the key to preserving shape.

Algorithm 7.3: Morph (Naïve-2)

> **MORPH** ($I_{\text{source}}, I_{\text{target}}, u$) **:**
>
> > **[optional]** $u =$ **Re-parameterize** (u)
> >
> > **for each pixel** (u, v) **do**
> >
> > > $(u', v') = f_{\text{map}}(u, v)$
> > >
> > > $I_u[u, v] =$ InterpolateRGBA ($I_{\text{source}}[u', v'], I_{\text{target}}[u', v'], u$)
> >
> > **return** I_u

A note on image warping: Generally, it is usually better to specify the "inverse" mapping $f_{map}^{-1}(u', v') \mapsto (u, v)$, as the mapping function will most likely map source

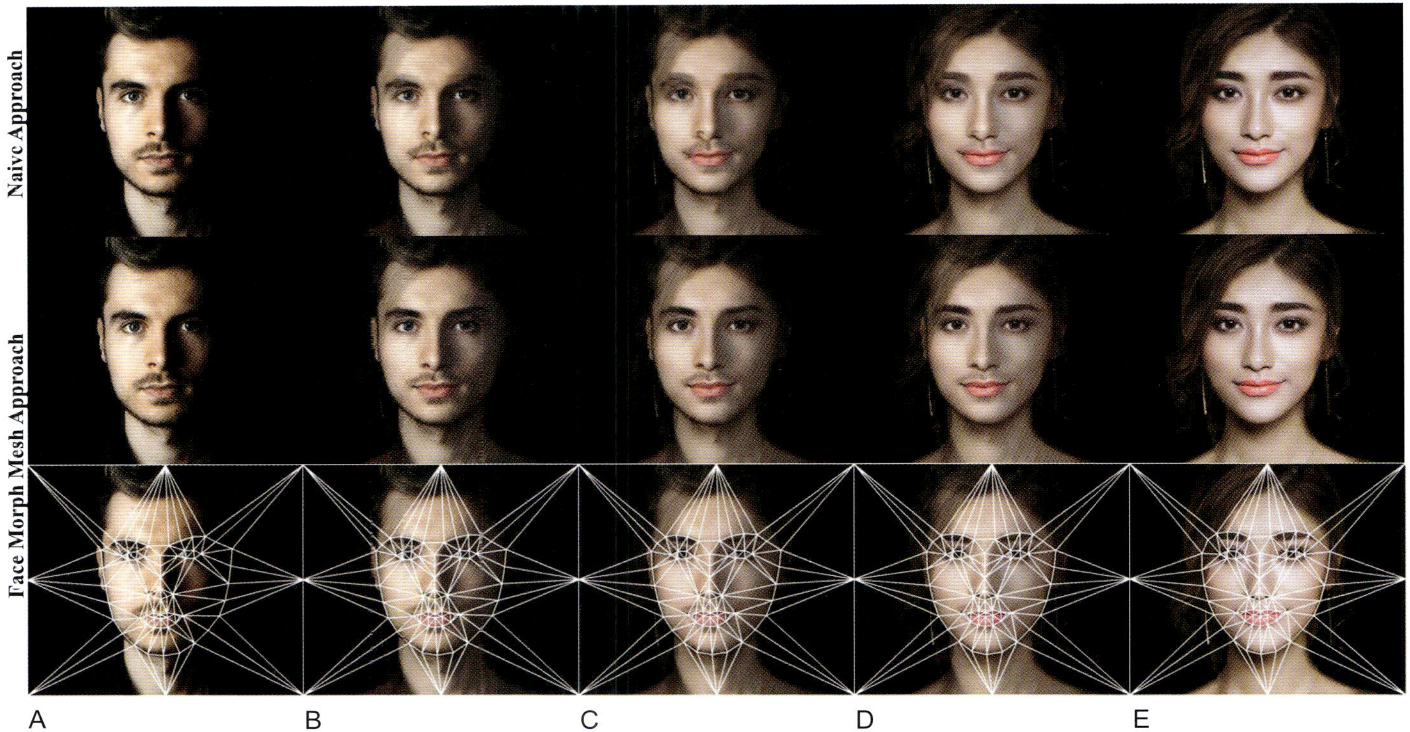

FIGURE 7.4

Morphing faces using naive image blending approach *(top)* versus using a face detector + mesh warping approach (*middle:* results, *bottom:* mesh used to warp images between source and target): (a) 0% (source), (b) 25%, (c) 50%, (d) 75%, and (e) 100% (target).

(Photo of woman (morph target) from [https://www.pexels.com/photo/woman-wearing-black-spaghetti-strap-top-415829/] under Creative Common Zero (CC0) license. Photo of man (morph source) from [https://www.pexels.com/photo/man-in-brown-polo-shirt-614810/] under Creative Common (CC) license.)

pixels to the same output pixel at times causing holes in the resulting image. To alleviate this problem, you iterate through each destination pixel mapping it to the source image using this inverse mapping function. Because the result will most likely not be an exact pixel value, a bilinear (or similar) interpolation function should be used to sample from the source image [6].

Mesh-/grid-based approaches

One technique is to specify the mapping function as a set of 2D meshes (or grids) superimposed on each image [7]. These meshes impose a coordinate space to map one image to the other. Consider the image in Figure 7.5 where a mesh with 9 vertices (b–c) are arranged by the user on a grid (note that the grid is further subdivided, but these vertices are not controlled directly by the user). Each vertex is connected along the linear axes to the other vertices on the edge of the image, and Bezier control points can be manipulated at each vertex of the mesh to deform the grid. We call this a *curvilinear grid* because the vertices are curves but connected in a linear fashion along rows/columns. To achieve morphing between the images, the grid locations in one image must correspond to the final intended location in the target image; the same grid must be used for both images (as they must have a one-to-one mapping; Figure 7.6). A curved mesh is then generated using the grid intersection points as control points for an interpolation scheme such as Catmull-Rom or Bezier splines.

To generate an intermediate image at some $u \in [0, 1]$ along the way from the source image to the target image, the vertices (points of intersection of the curves) of the source and destination are interpolated to form an intermediate grid. This interpolation can be done linearly, or grids from adjacent keyframes can be used to perform higher-order interpolation. Pixels from the source and destination images are stretched and compressed according to the intermediate grid so that warped versions of both the source image and the destination grid are generated. A two-pass procedure can be used to accomplish this (described in the next section), and finally a cross-dissolve is performed on a pixel-by-pixel basis between the two warped images to generate the final image (Figure 7.7).

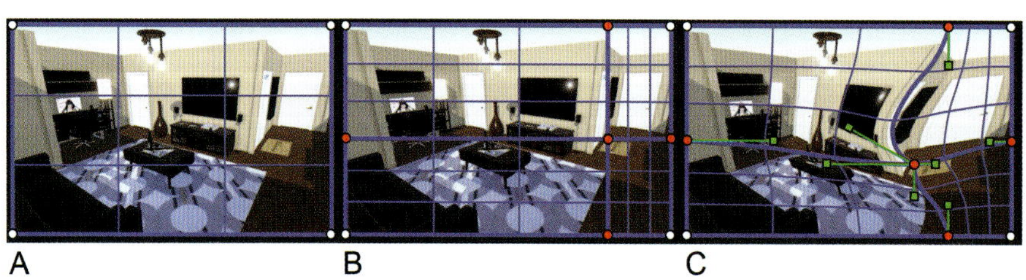

FIGURE 7.5

Grid approach for image deformation/warping. A curvilinear grid defines warping function and inverse warping from target to source ensures no holes appear in the result. (a) Source image with initial grid, (b) control points in red subdivide grid at higher density, (c) warped image using green tangent control points to define warp function as bezier surface.

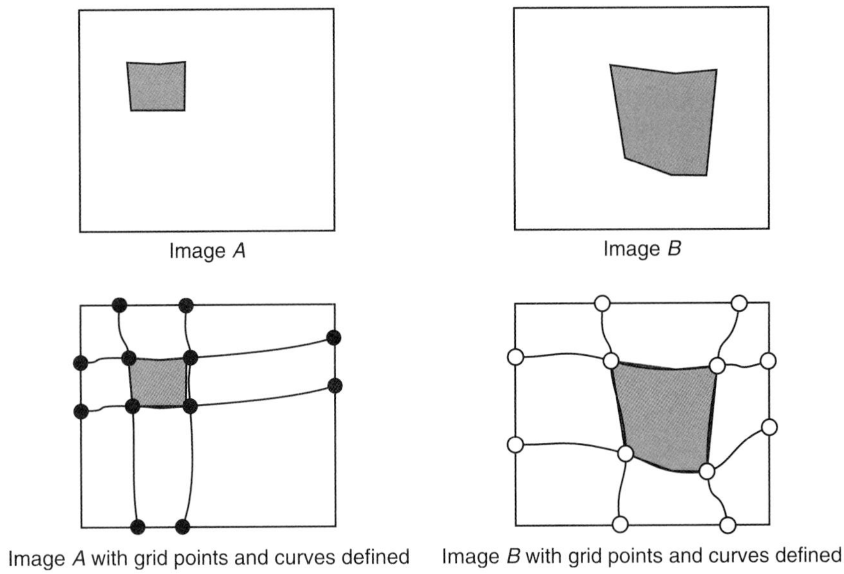

FIGURE 7.6

Sample grid definitions.

For purposes of explaining the two-pass procedure, it will be assumed that it is the source image to be warped to the intermediate grid, but the same procedure is used to warp the destination image to the intermediate grid. First, the pixels from the source image are stretched and compressed in the x direction to fit the interpolated grid. These pixels are then stretched and compressed in the y direction to fit the intermediate grid. To carry this out, an auxiliary grid is computed that, for each grid point, uses the y-coordinate from the corresponding grid point of the source image grid and the x-coordinate from the corresponding point of the intermediate grid. The source image is stretched/compressed in x by mapping it to the auxiliary grid, and then the auxiliary grid is used to stretch/compress pixels in y to map them to the intermediate grid. In the next discussion, it is assumed the curves are numbered left to right and bottom to top; a curve's number is referred to as its *index*.

Figure 7.8 illustrates the formation of the auxiliary grid from the source image grid and the intermediate grid. Once the auxiliary grid is defined, the first pass uses the source image and auxiliary grids to distort the source pixels in the x direction. For each row of grid points in both the source and the auxiliary grid, a cubic Catmull-Rom spline is defined in pixel coordinates. The leftmost and rightmost columns define straight lines down the sides of the images; this is necessary to include the entire image in the warping process. See the top of Figure 7.9. For each scanline, the x-intercepts of the curves with the scanline are computed. These define a grid coordinate system on the scanline. The position of each pixel on the scanline in

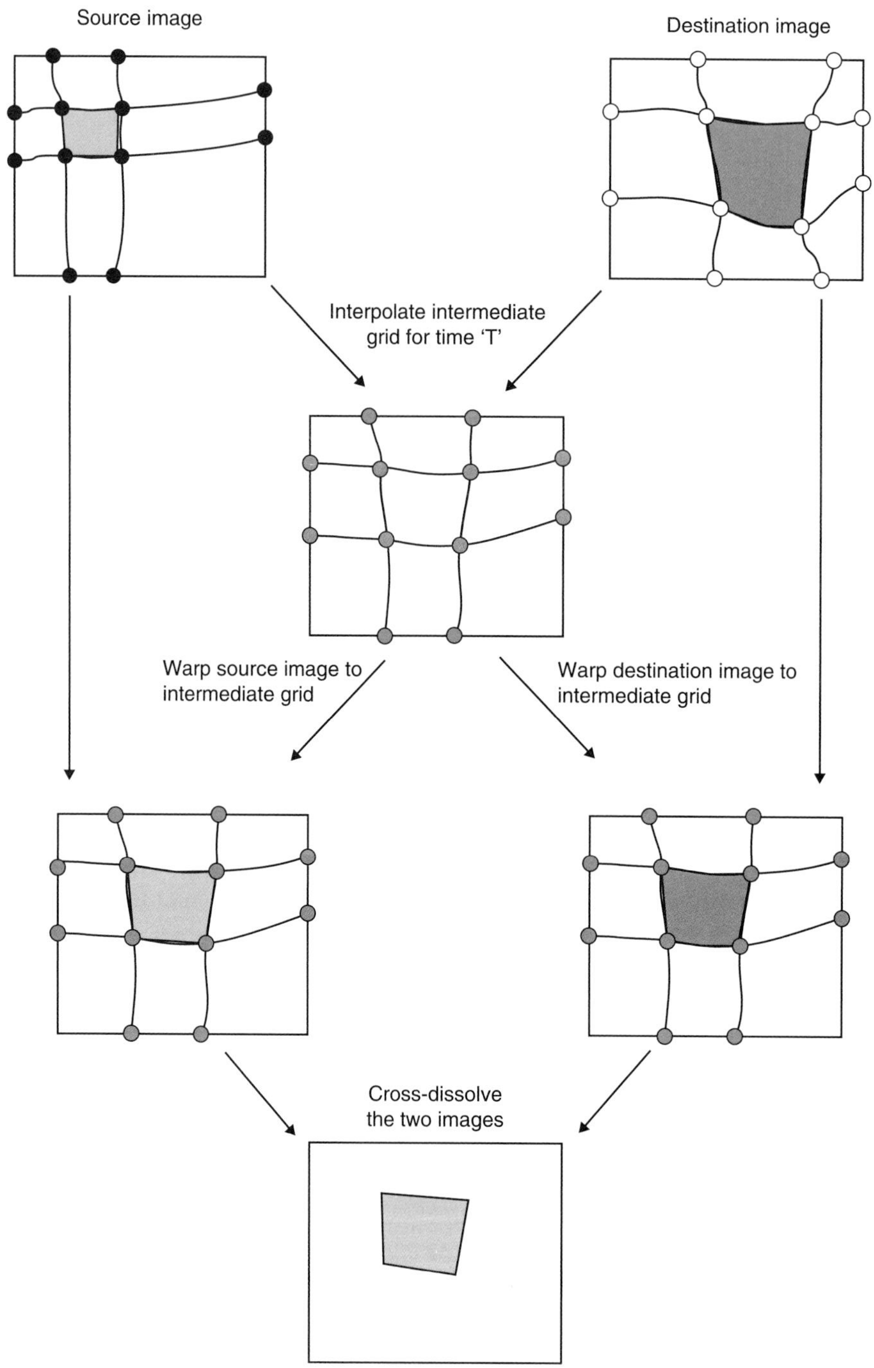

FIGURE 7.7

Interpolating to intermediate grid and cross-dissolve.

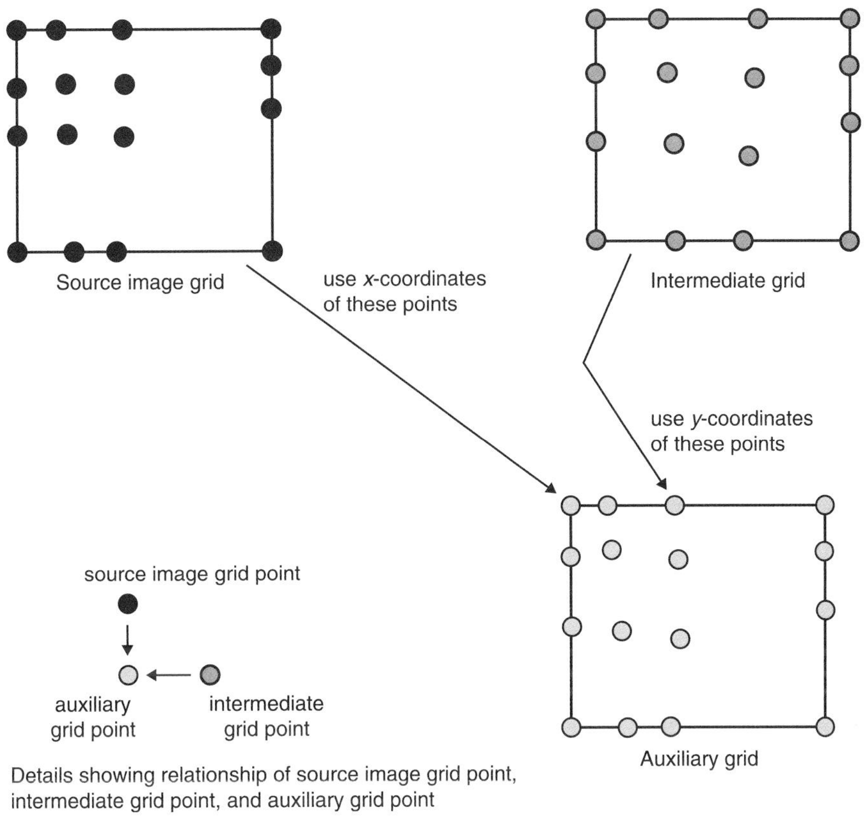

FIGURE 7.8

Formation of auxiliary grid for two-pass warping of source image to intermediate grid.

the source image is determined relative to the x-intercepts by computing the Catmull-Rom spline passing through the two-dimensional space of the (grid index, x-intercept) pairs. See the middle of Figure 7.9. The integer values of $x \pm 1/2$, representing the pixel boundaries, can then be located in this space and the fractional index value recorded. In the auxiliary image, the x-intercepts of the curves with the scanline are also computed, and for the corresponding scanline, the source image pixel boundaries can be mapped into the intermediate image by using their fractional indices and locating their x positions in the auxiliary scanline. See the bottom of Figure 7.9. Once this is complete, the color of the source image pixel can be used to color in auxiliary pixels by using fractional coverage to affect antialiasing.

The result of the first phase generates colored pixels of an auxiliary image by averaging source image pixel colors on a scanline-by-scanline basis. The second phase repeats the same process on a column-by-column basis by averaging auxiliary image pixel colors to form the intermediate image. The columns are processed by

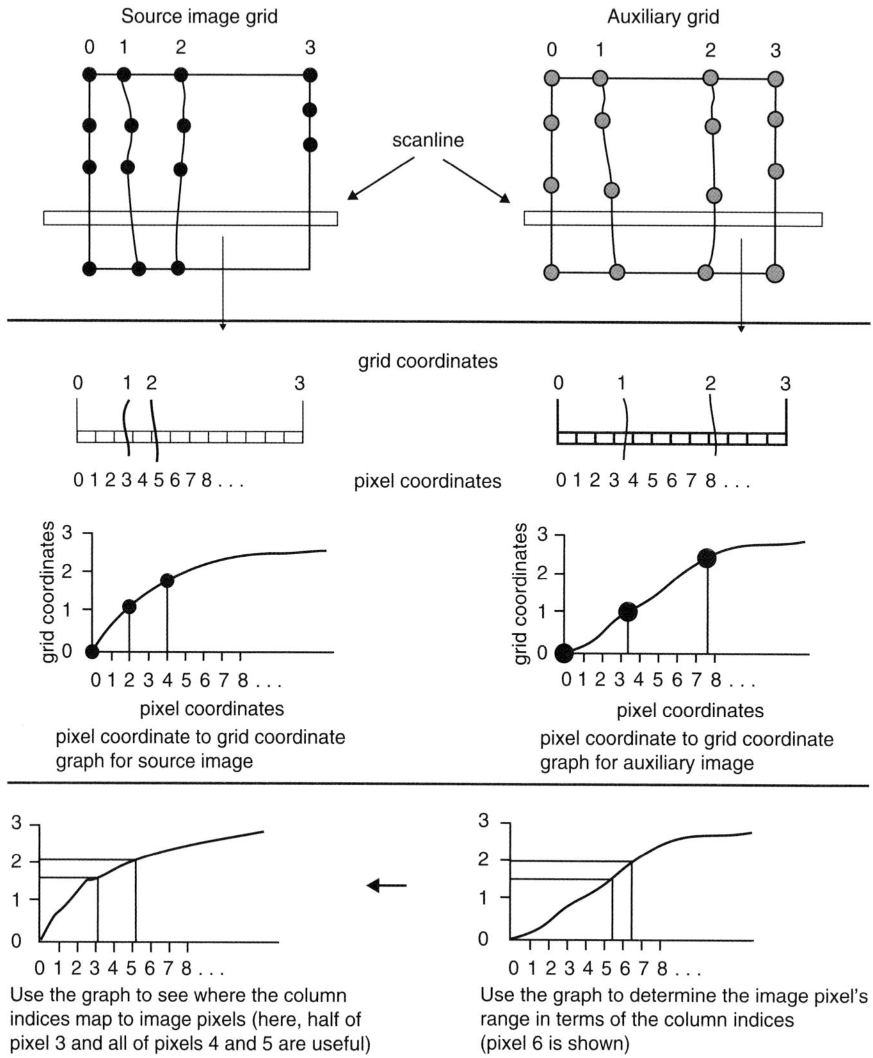

FIGURE 7.9

For a given pixel in the auxiliary image, determine the range of pixel coordinates in the source image (e.g., pixel 6 of auxiliary grid maps to pixel coordinates 3.5 to 5 of the source image).

using the horizontal grid curves to establish a common coordinate system between the two images (Figure 7.10).

This two-pass procedure is applied to both the source and the destination images with respect to the intermediate grid. Once both images have been warped to the same intermediate grid, the important features are presumably (if the user has done a good

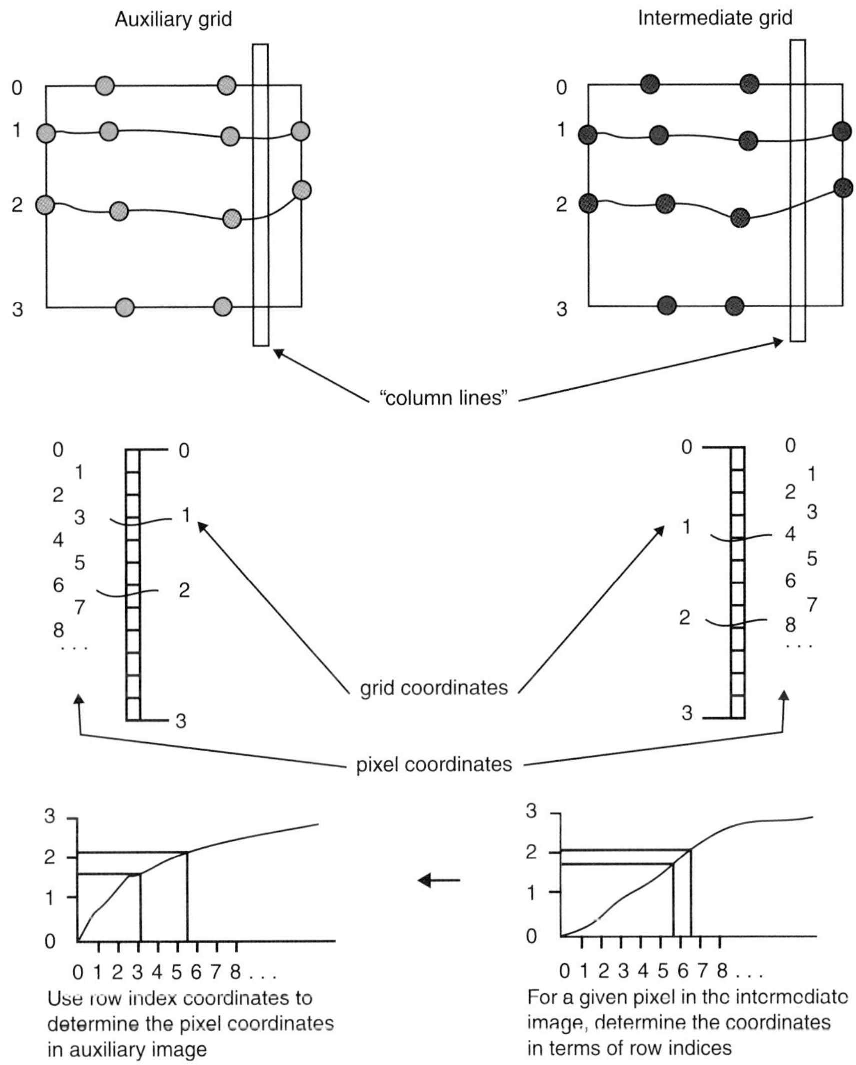

FIGURE 7.10

Establishing the auxiliary pixel range for a pixel of the intermediate image (e.g., pixel 6 of the intermediate grid maps to pixel coordinates 3.5 to 5 of the auxiliary image).

job of establishing the grids on the two images) in similar positions. At this point, the images can be cross-dissolved on a pixel-by-pixel basis. The cross-dissolve is merely a blend of the two colors from corresponding pixels (see Equation 7.1).

$$I[u,v] = \alpha I_1[u,v] + (1-\alpha)I_2[u,v] \tag{7.1}$$

where (u, v) are pixel coordinates and $\alpha \in [0, 1]$ is the linear blend factor.

In the simplest case, a linear function (LERP) can be used to blend the image pixel values. However, as Wolberg [7] points out, a nonlinear blend is often more visually appealing. It is also useful to be able to locally control the cross-dissolve rates based on aesthetic concerns. For example, in one of the first popular commercials to use morphing, in which a car morphs into a tiger, the front of the car is morphed into the head of the tiger at a faster rate than the tail to add to the dynamic quality of the animated morph. This is apparent also in Michael Jackson's *Black or White* music video, where you can find actors' faces morphing with various features (e.g., ears, eyes, hair) interpolating at different rates throughout the video [8,9].

Animated images/video can be morphed using the user-defined coordinate grids for various key images in each of two animation sequences. The coordinate grids for a sequence are then interpolated over time so that at any one frame in the sequence a coordinate grid can be produced for that frame. The interpolation is carried out on the x and y positions of the grid intersection points; cubic interpolation such as Catmull-Rom is typically used. Once a coordinate grid has been produced for corresponding images in the animated sequences, the morphing procedure reduces to the static image case and proceeds according to the previous description (Figure 7.11).

Feature-based approach

Instead of using a coordinate grid, the user can establish the correspondence between images by using feature lines/curves [10]. Lines are drawn on the two images to identify features that correspond to one another, and these feature lines are interpolated to form an intermediate feature line set. The interpolation can be based on interpolating endpoints or on interpolating center points and orientation. In either case, a mapping for each pixel in the intermediate image is established to each interpolated feature line, and a relative weight is computed that indicates the amount of influence that feature lines should have on the pixel. The mapping is used in the source image to locate the source image pixel that corresponds to the intermediate image pixel. The relative weight is used to average the source image locations generated by multiple feature lines into a final source image location. This location is used to determine the color of the intermediate image pixel. This same procedure is used on the destination image to form its intermediate image. These intermediate images are then cross-dissolved to form the final intermediate image.

Consider the mapping established by a single feature line, defined by two endpoints and oriented from P_1 to P_2. In effect, the feature line establishes a local two-dimensional coordinate system (U, V) over the image. For example, the first point of the line can be considered the origin. The second point of the line establishes the unit distance in the positive V-axis direction and scale. A line perpendicular to this line and of unit length extending to its right (as one stands on the first point and looks toward the second point) establishes the U-axis direction and scale. The coordinates (u, v) of a pixel relative to this feature line can be found by simply computing the pixel's position relative to the U- and V-axes of a local coordinate system defined by that feature line. Variable v is the projection of $(P - P_1)$ onto the

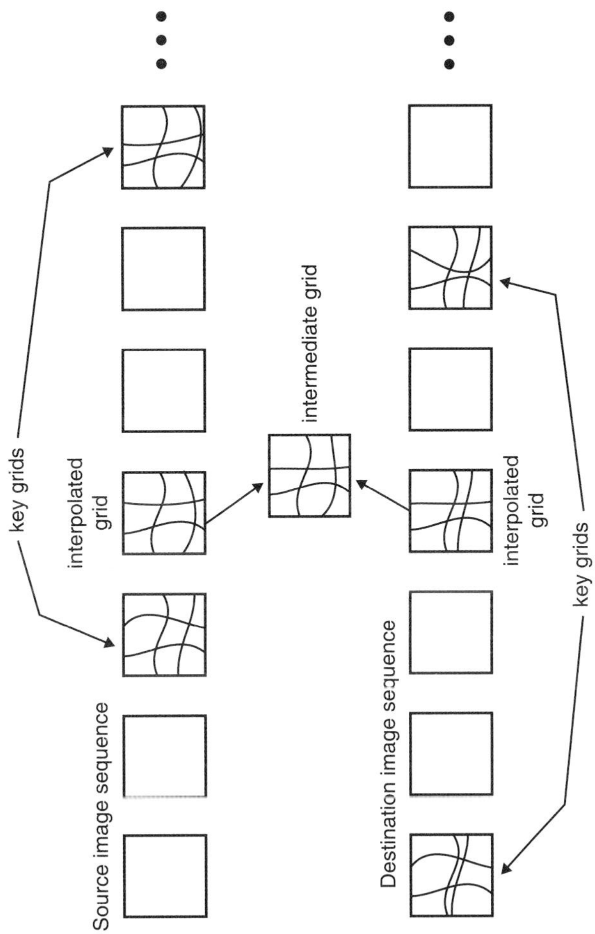

FIGURE 7.11

Morphing of animated sequences.

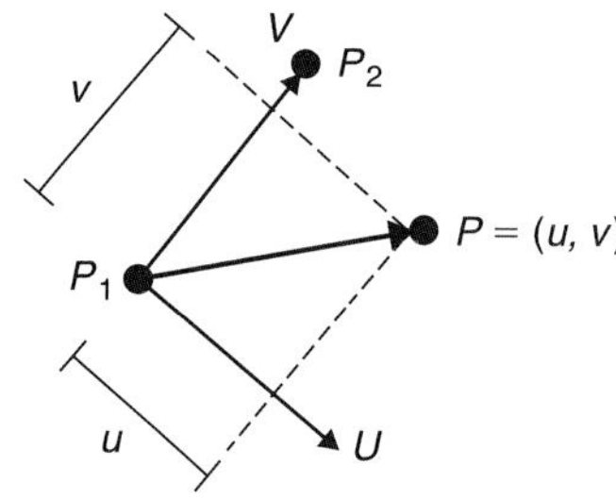

$$v = (P - P_1)\cdot\frac{(P_2 - P_1)}{|P_2 - P_1|^2}$$

$$u = \left|(P - P_1) \times \frac{(P_2 - P_1)}{|P_2 - P_1|^2}\right|$$

FIGURE 7.12

Local coordinate system of a feature in the intermediate image.

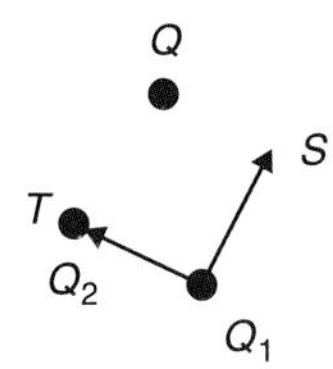

$$T = Q_2 - Q_1$$
$$S = (T_y - T_x)$$
$$Q = Q_1 + uS + vT$$

FIGURE 7.13

Relocating a point's position using local coordinates in the source image.

direction of $(P_2 - P_1)$, normalized to the length of $(P_2 - P_1)$. u is calculated similarly (Figure 7.12).

Assume that the points P_1 and P_2 are selected in the intermediate image and used to determine the (u, v) coordinates of a pixel. Given the corresponding feature line in the source image defined by the points Q_1 and Q_2, a similar two-dimensional coordinate system, (S, T), is established. Using the intermediate pixel's u- and v-coordinates relative to the feature line, one can compute its corresponding location in the source image (Figure 7.13).

To transform an image by a single feature line, each pixel of the intermediate image is mapped back to a source image position according to the equations above. The colors of the source image pixels in the neighborhood of that position are then used to color in the pixel of the intermediate image (Figure 7.14).

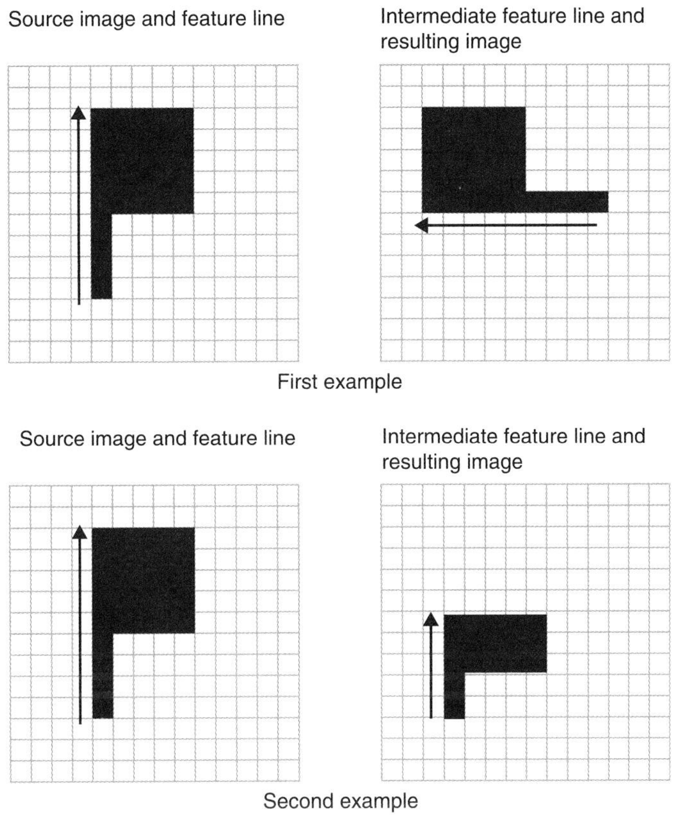

FIGURE 7.14

Two examples of single-feature line morphing.

Of course, the mapping does not typically transform an intermediate image pixel back to the center of a source image pixel. The floating point coordinates of the source image location could be rounded to the nearest pixel coordinates, which would introduce aliasing artifacts. To avoid such artifacts in the intermediate image, the corner points of the intermediate pixel could be mapped back to the source image, which would produce a quadrilateral area in the source image; the pixels, wholly or partially contained in this quadrilateral area, would contribute to the color of the destination pixel.

The mapping described so far is an affine transformation. For image pairs to be really interesting and useful, multiple line pairs must be used to establish correspondences between multiple features in the images. For a pair of images with multiple feature lines, each feature line pair produces a displacement vector from an intermediate image pixel to its source image position. Associated with this displacement is a weight based on the pixel's position relative to the feature line in the intermediate image. The weight presented by Beier and Neely [10] is shown in Equation 7.2.

$$W = \left(\frac{|Q_2 - Q_1|^p}{a + \text{dist}} \right)^b \tag{7.2}$$

The line is defined by points Q_1 and Q_2, and *dist* is the distance that the pixel is from the line. The distance is measured from the finite line segment defined by Q_1 and Q_2 so that if the perpendicular projection of P onto the infinite line defined by Q_1 and Q_2 falls beyond the finite line segment, then the distance is taken to be the distance to the closer of the two endpoints. Otherwise, the distance is the perpendicular distance to the finite line segment. User-supplied parameters (a, b, and p in Eq. 7.2) control the overall character of the mapping. As *dist* increases, w decreases but never goes to zero; as a practical matter, a lower limit could be set below which w is clamped to zero and the feature line's effect on the point is ignored above a certain distance. If a is nearly zero, then pixels on the line are rigidly transformed with the line. Increasing a makes the effect of lines over the image smoother. Increasing p increases the effect of longer lines. Increasing b makes the effect of a line fall off more rapidly. As presented here, these parameters are global; for more precise control these parameters could be set on a feature line-by-feature line basis. For a given pixel in the intermediate image, the displacement indicated by each feature line pair is scaled by its weight. The weights and the weighted displacements are accumulated. The final accumulated displacement is then divided by the accumulated weights. This gives the displacement from the intermediate pixel to its corresponding position in the source image. See the code segment in Figure 7.15.

When morphing between two images, the feature lines are interpolated over some number of frames. For any one of the intermediate frames, the feature line induces a mapping back to the source image and forward to the destination image. The corresponding pixels from both images are identified and their colors blended to produce a pixel of the intermediate frame. In this way, feature-based morphing produces a sequence of images that transform from the source image to the destination image.

The transformations implied by the feature lines are fairly intuitive, but some care must be taken in defining transformations with multiple line pairs. Pixels that lie on a feature line are mapped onto that feature line in another image. If feature lines cross in one image, pixels at the intersection of the feature lines are mapped to both feature lines in the other image. This situation essentially tries to pull apart the image and can produce unwanted results. Also, some configurations of feature lines can produce non-intuitive results. Other techniques in the literature (e.g., [11]) have suggested algorithms to alleviate these shortcomings.

Face detector approach

Faces are common targets to morph due to the prevalence of easy to use face detectors (e.g., dlib [12], OpenCV [13]). One approach (see Algorithm 7.4) is to find the faces in both images and perform a triangulation of the detected face features to get a triangular mesh. For each triangle in the mesh, you can now compute an affine/planar transformation to transform one triangle into the other. Finally, by sampling

```
//=====================================================================

//XY structure
typedef struct xy_struct {
   float x,y;
}xy_td;


//FEATURE
// line in image1: p1,p2;
// line in image2: q1,q2
// weights used in mapping: a,b,p
// length of line in image2
typedef struct feature_struct {
   xy_td p1,p2,q1,q2;
   float a,b,p;
   float plength,qlength;
}feature_td;


//FEATURE LIST
typedef struct featureList_struct {
   int num;
   feature_td *features;
}featureList_td;

// ---------------------------------------------------------------
//    MORPH
// ---------------------------------------------------------------
void morph(featureList_td *featureList)
{
   Float a,b,p,plength,qlength;
   xy_td p1,p2,q1,q2;
   xy_td vp,wp,vq,wq,v,qq;
   int   ii,jj,indexI,indexD;
   float idisp,jdisp;
   float t,s,vx,vy;
   float weight;
   char  background[3];

   background[0] = background[1] = background[2] = 120;
   for (int i=0; i<HEIGHT; i++) {
      for (int j=0; j<WIDTH; j++) {
         weight = 0;
         idsp = jdsp = 0.0;
         for (int k=0; k<featureList->num; k++) {
            // get info about kth feature line
            a = featureList->features[k].a;
            b = featureList->features[k].b;
            p = featureList->features[k].p;
            p1 = featureList->features[k].p1;
            p2 = featureList->features[k].p2;
            q1 = featureList->features[k].q1;
            q2 = featureList->features[k].q2;
            plength = featureList->features[k].plength;
            qlength = featureList->features[k].qlength;
```

FIGURE 7.15

Code using feature lines to morph from source to destination image

```
                // get local feature coordinate system in image1
                vp.x = p2.x-p1.x;
                vp.y = p2.y-p1.y;
                wp.x = vp.y;
                wp.y = -vp.x;
                // compute local coordinates of pixel (i,j)
                v.x = j-q1.x;
                v.y = i-q1.y;
                s = (v.x*vp.x + v.y*vp.y)/plength;
                t = (v.x*wp.y - v.y*wp.x)/plength;
                // map the pixel to the source image
                jj = (int)(q1.x + s*v1.x + t*wp.x);
                ii = (int)(q1.y + s*v1.y + t*wp.y);
                // compute distance of pixel (Iii,jj) from line segment q1q2
                If (s<0.0) {
                      v.x = jj - q2.x;
                      v.y = ii - w2.y;
                      t = sqrt(v.x*v.x + v.y*v.y);
                }
                else t = fabs(t*qlength);
                t = pow(pow(qlength,p)/(a+t,b);
                jdisp + = (jj-j)*t;
                idisp + = (ii-i)*t;
                weight + = t;
            }
            jdisp /= weight;
            idisp /= weight;
            ii = (int)(i+idisp);
            jj = (int)(j+jdisp);
            indexI = (WIDTH*i+j)*3;
            if ((ii<0) || (ii>=HEIGHT) || (jj<0) || (jj>=WIDTH) ) {
                image2[indexD] = background[0];
                image2[indexD+1] = background[1];
                image2[indexD+2] = background[2];
            }
            else {
                indexS = (WIDTH*ii+jj)*3;
                imageI[indexI] = image1[indexS];
                imageI[indexI+1] = image1[indexS+1];
                imageI[indexI+2] = image1[indexS+2];
            }
        }
    }
}
```

FIGURE 7.15 cont'd.

one image by this affine transform you can blend the images together. Another way is to split the triangle into a small number of rectangular patches and compute the affine transform this way, but care must be taken when incorporating the blended pixels into the result to mask the result by the affected triangular region. Results of this approach can be seen in Figure 7.4.

Algorithm 7.4: Morph (Face Detection)

```
Face1,Face2 = Detect Faces in both images
Mesh1,Mesh2 = Delaunay Triangulation of face features
alpha = Get BlendFactor from Animation curve
for each TriIndex do
    {Tri1,Tri2} = GetTriangles(TriIndex, Mesh1,Mesh2)
    {P1,P2} = (u,v)'s from Images(Tri1,Tri2)
    patches= Split Tri1,Tri2 into small rectangular patches
    for each {patchI1,patchI2} in patches do
        T = computeAffineTransform(patchI1→patchI2)
        WarpedPatch_1 = apply(T) to warp patchI1
        BlendedPatch = LERP(WarpedPatch_1, patchI2, alpha)
        Incorporate BlendedPatch into ResultImage
    end
    return ResultImage
end
```

7.2.4 Morphing shapes

Until now we have discussed morphing on an image basis. However, the same techniques can be applied to general shapes and polygons in 2D and 3D. Let's consider a mesh in 2D or 3D as a collection of vertices with edges. We can safely assume that both meshes have the same topology (required), and thus we only need to take care of the vertices. This means that we have two meshes with the same topology specifying a source and target. The only differences between these meshes are that their vertices have moved to a different location. To generate an "in-between" morphed intermediate mesh, we simply need to interpolate each vertex between the two targets. This works perfectly well with both 2D and 3D shapes. This technique is sometimes called the use of blend-shapes or shape-interpolation.

Algorithm 7.5: Morph (Target Mesh)

Mesh (M):

$$\mathrm{M}^{\text{name}} = \begin{cases} \{\vec{v}_i\}_0^N & \text{set of vertices} \\ \{\vec{e}_{ij}\} & \text{set of edges:} \quad \vec{e}_{ij} = \mathrm{EDGE}(\vec{i}, \vec{j}) \end{cases}$$

MORPH ($\mathrm{M}_{\text{source}}, \mathrm{M}_{\text{target}}, u$) **:**

[optional] u = **Re-parameterize** (u)

for each $i \in [0, N]$ **do**

$\vec{v}_i^{\text{result}}$ = Interpolate ($\vec{v}_i^{\text{source}}, \vec{v}_i^{\text{target}}, u$)

return D_u

7.2.5 Morphing characters

We can easily apply the `Algorithm 7.5` to characters stored as 3D flipbooks as long as their topology does not change between targets. Video games in the mid-1990s used this as their primary form of character animation. For example, id Software's *Quake* series stored a base mesh for the character in memory, and each animation was simply a definition of the location of each vertex for every frame of animation. Thus the topology only needed to be specified once and the animation simply had to replace the vertex locations for the current animation. The same morphing technique is used between frames to increase smoothness. Thus at any given animation time, the source and target are the closest previous (source) and next (target) frames' mesh vertices. The interpolation parameter is simply the normalized time as a percentage between these two frames. To reduce memory consumption, we can store a static base mesh containing all of the per-vertex information and topology, and each animation frame would then store only offsets from this base mesh.

Blending multiple morph targets

A simple extension of the basic morph target concept is to consider how to use multiple linearly blended morph targets to generate the resulting mesh. For example, consider the following example for faces as shown in Figure 7.16. There we have a base mesh in a neutral pose and a target mesh that has the same topology as the base. Performing weighted sum over all vertices between these two meshes, we can smoothly control the result using a single parameter (the weight).

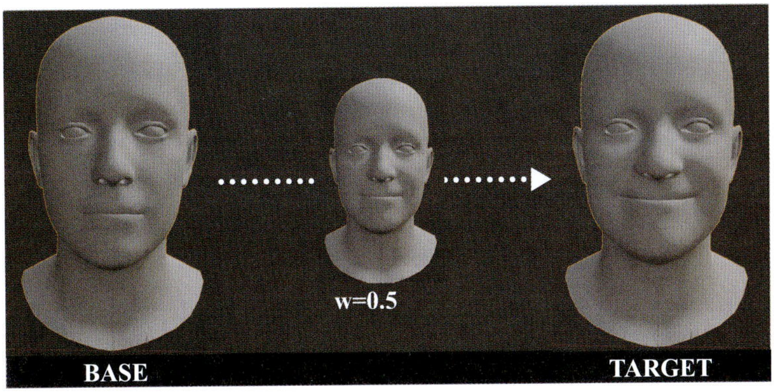

FIGURE 7.16

3DMM (3D Morphable Models). A 3DMM of a face (FLAME) demonstrating the use of a single weight mapped to one principle component axis of the 3DMM smoothly transitions between Base (neutral) and Target (smile) pose. The weights for each axis are then controlled for higher degree of control and different emotions/phonemes.

Let's express this as a simple LERP:

$$\begin{aligned} M_{\text{res}} = \; & w_{\text{Neutral}}\mathbf{M}_{\text{Neutral}} + w_{\text{Emotion}}\mathbf{M}_{\text{Emotion}} \\ & \text{where } w_{\text{Neutral}} + w_{\text{Emotion}} = 1 \end{aligned}$$

You can start to see how this can be expanded to more than two targets; for example, if you have three targets (Happy, Sad, Angry), then you have the following relationship:

$$\begin{aligned} M_{\text{res}} = \; & w_{\text{Happy}}\mathbf{M}_{\text{Happy}} + w_{\text{Sad}}\mathbf{M}_{\text{Sad}} + w_{\text{Angry}}\mathbf{M}_{\text{Angry}} \\ & \text{where } w_{\text{Happy}} + w_{\text{Sad}} + w_{\text{Angry}} = 1 \end{aligned}$$

and more generally, we have N morph targets and N weights expressed as a linear weighted sum:

$$M_{\text{res}} = \sum_{i}^{N} w_i \mathbf{M}_i \quad \text{where} \quad \sum_{i}^{N} w_i = 1$$

This technique is also sometimes referred to as linear blend skinning when we have a skeletal rig controlling the deformation, as we will see later.

3D Morphable Models (3DMM)

Probably one of the most successful use-cases of the above technique is its extension and generalization to what are now known as 3D Morphable Models (3DMMs). Introduced by Blanz and Vetter [14], the 3DMM has become a foundational concept for creating animated faces from video/images [15], and the concept has been extended to represent a wide range of human body forms [16].

The goal of a 3DMM is to represent a large quantity of data with a small number of parameters such that specifying a combination of these parameters can reconstruct the input data well. The 3DMM specifies a base mesh and a large parameter space of shapes and expressions. Each single dimensional parameter encodes and represents a complete set of vertices in the mesh (or offsets to vertices that are modified by this parameter).

For faces, consider the 3DMM in Figure 7.17 that shows how a 3DMM (data from [17]) can be used to achieve complex expressions by varying only two

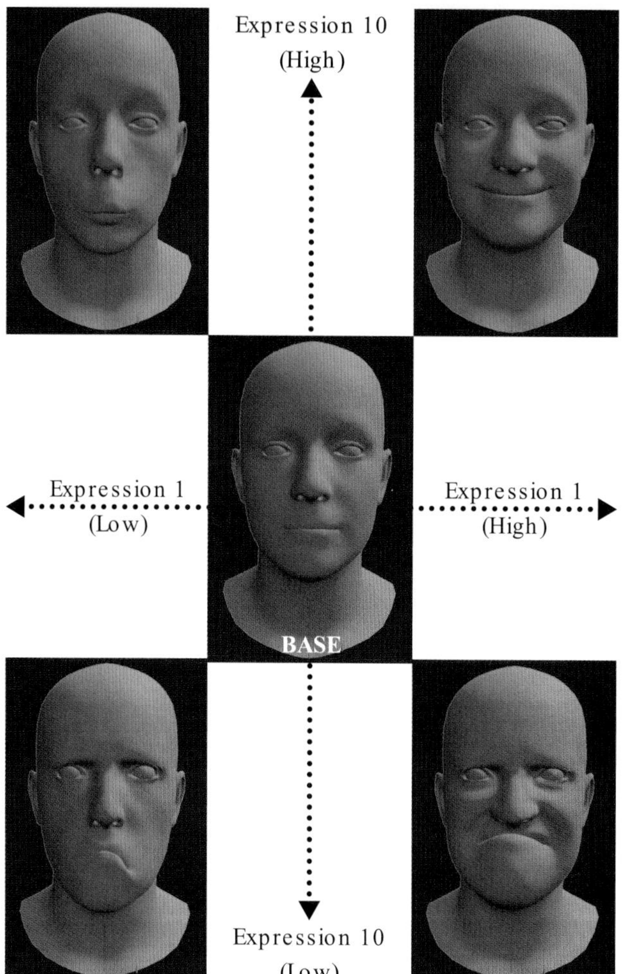

FIGURE 7.17

3DMM (3D Morphable Models). Demonstrating use of a 3DMM (FLAME) to controlling blending between multiple expressions.

parameters. Here the base mesh is deformed along two orthogonal parameters (expression 1 and expression 10). In [17], the final resulting mesh is defined as

$$\begin{aligned} B_s\left(\vec{\beta}; \mathbf{S}\right) &= \sum_{n=1}^{|\vec{\beta}|} \beta_n \mathbf{S}_n \\ \text{Shape Coefficients}: \vec{\beta} &= \left[\beta_1, \ldots, \beta_{|\vec{\beta}|}\right] \\ \text{Shape Basis}: \mathbf{S} &= \left[\mathbf{S}_1, \ldots, \mathbf{S}_{|\vec{\beta}|}\right] \in \Re^{3N \times |\vec{\beta}|} \end{aligned}$$

where the Shape Coefficients are the controllable parameters (the weights) and the Shape Basis vectors are an orthogonal basis set derived using principal components analysis of a large number of 4D face scans registered to a common coordinate system. With this model, one can quite effectively represent a large variety of face types and expressions. To animate a 3DMM, you simply need to keyframe the Shape Coefficient weights and interpolate them over time. Because this particular 3DMM is derived from actual data, the paper provides a method to optimize the shape coefficients to closely match an input image, enabling a method for authoring these keyframes using a video performance as input. There are a number of 3DMMs currently available, such as the FLAME [17] and the ICT-FaceKit [18]. More than just faces, this technique has been applied to complete bodies as well, such as the popular SMPL model [16]; its extension to include hands and expressive faces SMPL-X [18]; SMPLIFY-X [19], STAR [20], which is an optimized version of SMPL with fewer blend-shapes adding local control to the blend-shapes; and SUPR [21], which is a unified representation (head, hands, feet, body) that captures more expressive nuance than SMPL-X. These 3DMMs have also been extended and applied to infants (SMIL [22]) and animals (SMAL [23]).

7.3 Character animation

In the previous sections, we discussed how we can combine the use of morph targets and interpolation to create character animations. Those techniques have their uses, but the most common form of character animation is the use of a skeletal rig coupled with authored animation clips or motion capture performances. In this section, we form the basis of how we represent skeletal rigs with hierarchical joints, how to manipulate these joints to animate them with authored animation clips (forward kinematics [FK]), and ways to compute solutions to the inverse kinematics [IK] problem to constrain and place specific joints at given locations.

Human bodies are made of bone, skin, muscle, blood, and other types of specialized tissues. Luckily, we only need to consider the metaphors of bone and skin for most of our purposes. Bones are the underlying frame upon which everything in our body is supported (without bones, we would just be a pile of goo!), and our skin folds over our bones and tissue to define our outward aesthetic appearance. We can think of our skin as "influenced" by the movement of our underlying bone structure. For example, if we move our arm, we want our skin to come with it! Thus there is a connection between the bone structure of our characters and their outward appearances. First, we will discuss how to define, move, and control the underlying skeletal structure to pose and animate our characters. Second, we will discuss ways to connect the "skin" to these skeletons so our characters can appropriately portray their appearance.

7.3.1 Skeletons, armatures, and rigs

The foot bone's connected to the leg bone.

The leg bone's connected to the knee bone.

The knee bone's connected to the thigh bone.

Doin' the skeleton dance.

—**The Skeleton Dance [24]**

We have all seen simple drawings/representations of the human skeleton (especially around Halloween!). But, how might you precisely describe a skeleton to someone who cannot see? You might describe it as a set of bones connected together at a set of joints in a particular order. You would have to describe the length of each bone and which end is connected to which joint. You would then have to describe how each joint can move, how far can it rotate, and along which directions. The important characteristics are that we need to (1) define a set of bones, (2) define a set of joints to connect them, (3) define rules for rotating our joints (transformations), and (4) propagate these transforms to move any further connected bones.

Types of rigs

We call the set of bones and joints *animation rigs,* or just *rigs*. In manufacturing, a rig is a piece of specialized equipment (e.g., drilling rig, oil rig). For our purposes, a rig is an organized data structure defining spatial relationships. We will define some tools we need to manipulate parts of the rig (e.g., rotate joints), measure distances (e.g., from one joint to another), express the world joint locations, and express joint-joint relationships. Rigs for animation can come in a few different forms depending on the use case. Here we will refer to the *Animation Rig* as the underlying structure formed by the set of bones and joints and the *Control Rig* as a set of user-defined controls that can help in the authoring process. As you can see in Figure 7.18, the character mesh (a) is defined separately from the bone structure (b) and the joint locations (c). The rig is aligned with the mesh (d–e), and a control rig (f) can be formed to constrain the motion along specific axes and coupled with FK and IK solvers to more easily specify the desired pose of the character.

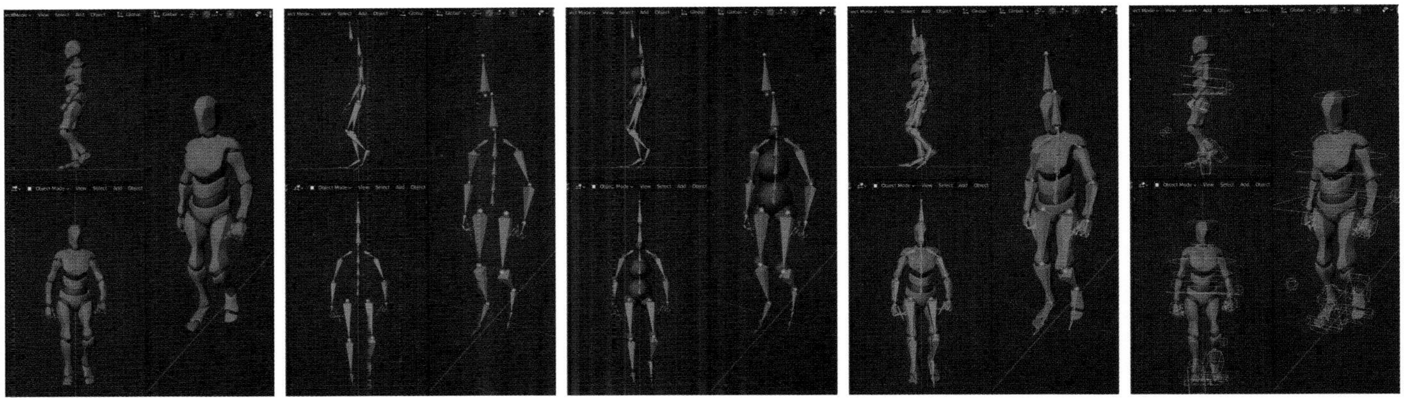

FIGURE 7.18

Skeletal rig types (using example from Adobe Mixamo in Blender): (a) character mesh, (b) skeletal rig (bones), (c) bones showing joints, (d) mesh with rig overlaid, and (e) control rig for animator (created using Mixamo Control Rig Addon).

Definition 7.2: Skeletal Rig 1

A skeleton is a graph defined by a set of Joints and Bones:

$$\textbf{Skeleton} \leftarrow \textbf{Graph}(\mathcal{J}, \mathcal{B}) = \begin{cases} \mathcal{J} = [J_1, \ldots, J_M] & \text{set of Joints} \\ \mathcal{B} = [\mathbf{B}_1, \ldots, \mathbf{B}_N] & \text{set of Bones} \end{cases}$$

Bones and joints

Bones are rigid (i.e., they don't bend) and they have a fixed length (they don't stretch). Bones are connected by a joint at a fixed location. It is at this joint location where movement occurs (if the joint rotates, the bone connected to it rotates)—we will see later that there are actually many different types of joints enabling different types of movement.

Essentially, we need a way to isolate and control various parts of the model. If we want to be able to have the character walk, we need to be able to easily control and move the spine, hips, legs, feet, arms, head, and hands separately and distinctly. This requires us to define a solid invisible frame that exists alongside the aesthetic appearance of the character.

In the Unity game engine, the minimum number of bones in a "humanoid" is 15 bones. This is enough to provide good control and decent quality. Obviously, there are instances in which we may need more control than this. For example, if we want articulated fingers or control of facial features (eyes, mouth, ears), then we will require more bones. In the classic video game *Uncharted 2* for the Sony PlayStation 3, the main character, Drake, has 97 bones dedicated just to his face, 30 to 40 bones just for his fingers, and 30 to 40 bones for the rest of his body [25]. In Adobe's Mixamo, the standard rig has 65 bones with articulated fingers. In Figure 7.19, a closeup

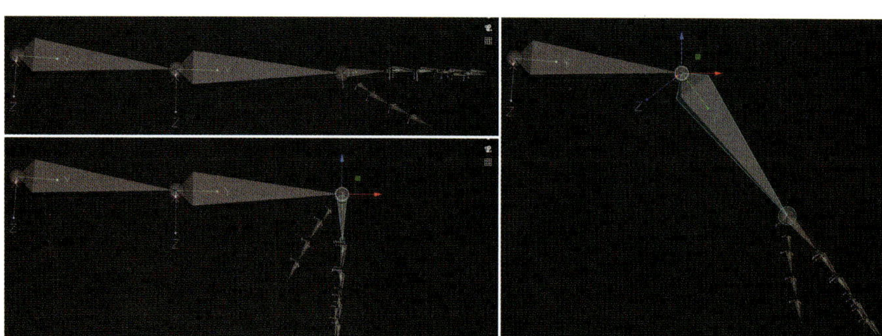

A B

FIGURE 7.19

Example arm rig: (a) applying local rotation at wrist joint and (b) applying local rotation at elbow joint.

of the arm rig in Mixamo demonstrates how the local rotation of one joint affects all subsequent connected bones/joints.

Definition 7.3: Bones and Joints

A bone contains its length (scalar) and a reference to the associated joint(s). Each joint provides a transformation between two coordinate frames (A and B). We use this notation to define a joint FROM frame A to frame B. This transform can be encoded in any manner but typically in either a {quaternion, translation vector, and scale} set or a homogeneous transformation matrix.

$$
\begin{aligned}
B_i &= \{L_i, {}^B\mathbf{Joint}_A \leftarrow {}^C\mathbf{Joint}_B \\
{}^B\mathbf{Joint}_A &\leftarrow \{\mathbf{T}_{\text{local}}, {}^B\mathbf{T}_A\} \\
&\text{where } \mathbf{T}_{\text{local}} \leftarrow \text{ local transform} \\
&{}^B\mathbf{T}_A \mapsto [{}^B\mathbf{Rot}_A(\cdot)\vec{t}_B] \\
&{}^B\mathbf{T}_A = \begin{bmatrix} {}^B\mathbf{R}_A & \vec{t}_B \\ \vec{0} & 1 \end{bmatrix}_{4\times4} \text{ and } \vec{v}_B = {}^B\mathbf{T}_A\vec{v}_A
\end{aligned}
$$

Example 1

Consider the placement of a single bone in Figure 7.20a–b. The bone B_1 connects two joints: $\mathbf{J}_1$ is aligned with the world frame and $\mathbf{J}_2$ is the end effector joint. Rather than just using subscripts for naming, we can use the following subscript/superscript notation to define the connections between frames. For instance, for $\mathbf{J}_1$ we can state that ${}^W\mathbf{J}_1$ is a joint that connects frame 1 to the world frame. This notation also indicates direction; for instance ${}^W\mathbf{J}_1$ indicates that the transform stored here encodes the transformation "*from*" frame 1 "*to*" the world frame, whereas ${}^1\mathbf{J}_W$ would be the opposite (inverse) transformation. Similarly ${}^1\mathbf{J}_2$ is a joint "*from*" frame 2 "*to*" frame 1. We can express the example in our notation as $B_1 = \{L_1, {}^W\mathbf{J}_1 \leftarrow {}^1\mathbf{J}_2\}$ and our joint from the frame 1 to the world is thus ${}^W\mathbf{J}_1 = \{{}^W\mathbf{Rot}_1(\cdot), {}^W\vec{t}_1\}$.

Example 2

Consider the placement of bones in Figure 7.20c–d. Expressing this with our notation, we have:

$B_1 = \{L_1, {}^W\mathbf{J}_1 \leftarrow {}^1\mathbf{J}_2\}$ and $B_2 = \{L_2, {}^1\mathbf{J}_2 \leftarrow {}^2\mathbf{J}_3\}$. We thus have the following transformations stored in our joints: ${}^W\mathbf{T}_1$, ${}^1\mathbf{T}_2$, and ${}^2\mathbf{T}_3$.

Imagine if we have a point expressed in our joint frame 2 ($\overrightarrow{p}_{2(\text{local})}$) and we want to express it relative to the world frame ($\overrightarrow{p}_{2(\text{world})}$). We first have to transform the

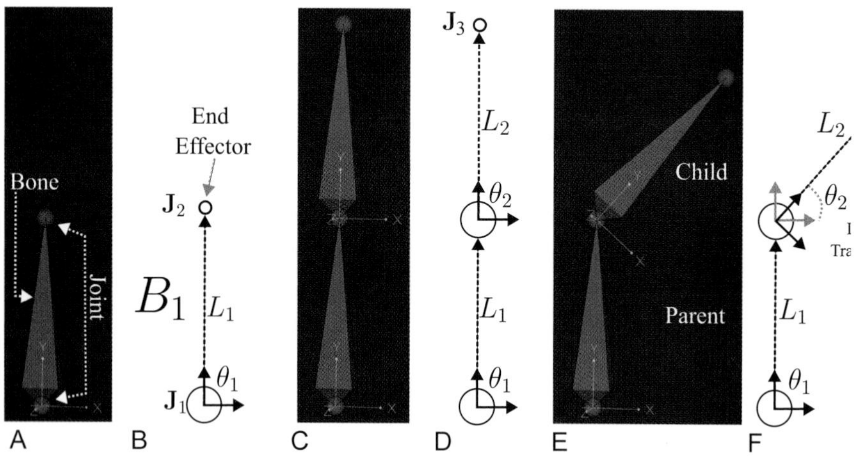

FIGURE 7.20

Bones: definitions and relationships: (a–b) single bone, (c–d) two bones, and (e–f) parent-child relationship. Joint transforms are propagated throughout the kinematic chain using parent-child connections and local transforms at joints. Note here the *y*-axis at each joint frame points along bone toward the end-effector.

point "*from*" frame 2 "*to*" frame 1 and then subsequently transform the resulting point "*from*" frame 1 "*to*" the world frame. Thus we need to apply ${}^{1}\mathbf{T}_2$ and subsequently ${}^{W}\mathbf{T}_1$.

First, we transform our point from frame 2 to frame 1:

$$\vec{p}_{1(\text{local})} = {}^{1}\mathbf{T}_2\,\vec{p}_{2(\text{local})} = {}^{1}\mathbf{Rot}_2\left(\vec{p}_{2(\text{local})}\right) + {}^{1}\vec{t}_2$$

Next, we transform the result into the world frame as:

$$\vec{p}_{1(\text{world})} = {}^{W}\mathbf{T}_1\,\vec{p}_{1(\text{local})} = {}^{W}\mathbf{Rot}_1\left(\vec{p}_{1(\text{local})}\right) + {}^{W}\vec{t}_1$$

We can express this in one step by concatenating our transformations into one matrix as:

$$\begin{aligned}\vec{p}_{(\text{world})} &= {}^{W}\mathbf{T}_1\,{}^{1}\mathbf{T}_2\vec{p}_{2(\text{local})}\\ &= ({}^{W}\mathbf{T}_{\not{1}}\,{}^{\not{1}}\mathbf{T}_2)\vec{p}_{2(\text{local})}\\ &= ({}^{W}\mathbf{T}_2)\vec{p}_{2(\text{local})}\end{aligned}$$

Example 3

Using the results from Example 2, what if we have the point expressed relative to the world frame and want to express it relative to the joint frame? More specifically, what if we had the same bone configuration but only had point $\vec{p}_{1(\text{world})}$ and we wanted it to express this point relative to joint 2 ($\vec{p}_{2(\text{local})}$)?

Working backward, we can see the following relationship:

$$\begin{aligned}\vec{p}_{2(\text{local})} &= ({}^{2}\mathbf{T}_{\text{world}})\vec{p}_{(\text{world})}\\ &= ({}^{2}\mathbf{T}_{\not{1}}{}^{\not{1}}\mathbf{T}_{\text{world}})\vec{p}_{(\text{world})}\\ &= {}^{2}\mathbf{T}_{1}{}^{1}\mathbf{T}_{\text{world}}\,\vec{p}_{(\text{world})}\end{aligned}$$

Clearly, we need two matrices: ${}^{2}\mathbf{T}_{1}{}^{1}\mathbf{T}_{\text{world}}$. But we don't have those! We have ${}^{1}\mathbf{T}_{2}{}^{\text{world}}\mathbf{T}_{1}$. Luckily, we can convert them because ${}^{2}\mathbf{T}_{1} = \left({}^{1}\mathbf{T}_{2}\right)^{-1}$ and ${}^{1}\mathbf{T}_{\text{world}} = \left({}^{\text{world}}\mathbf{T}_{1}^{-1}\right)$.

In general, transformation matrices are related to their inverses as seen in Equations 7.3 and 7.4:

$$\begin{aligned}{}^{B}\mathbf{T}_{A} &= \left({}^{A}\mathbf{T}_{B}\right)^{-1}\\ \begin{bmatrix}\mathbf{R} & \vec{t}\\ \vec{0} & 1\end{bmatrix} &= \begin{bmatrix}\mathbf{R}^{T} & -\mathbf{R}^{T}\vec{t}\\ \vec{0} & 1\end{bmatrix}.\end{aligned} \tag{7.3}$$

$$\begin{aligned}\vec{\mathbf{v}}' - \mathbf{T}\vec{\mathbf{v}} &\mapsto \mathbf{R}\vec{v} + \vec{t} && \left(\vec{\mathbf{v}} = \left[\vec{v} + 1\right]^{T}\right)\\ \vec{v}' &= \mathbf{R}\vec{v} + \vec{t} && (\text{transform equation})\\ \vec{v}' - \vec{t} &= \mathbf{R}\vec{v}\\ \mathbf{R}^{T}\left(\vec{v}' - \vec{t}\right) &= \mathbf{R}^{T}\mathbf{R}\vec{v}\\ \mathbf{R}^{T}\vec{v}' - \mathbf{R}^{T}\vec{t}' &= \mathbf{I}\vec{v} && \left(\text{identity}: R^{T}R = 1\right)\\ \vec{v} &= \mathbf{R}^{T}\vec{v}' - \mathbf{R}^{T}\vec{t}' && (\text{solving for v})\\ \vec{\mathbf{v}} &= \mathbf{T}'\vec{\mathbf{v}}'\\ \mathbf{T}' &= \begin{bmatrix}\mathbf{R}^{T} & -\mathbf{R}^{T}\vec{t}\\ \vec{0} & 1\end{bmatrix}\\ \therefore \text{if } \mathbf{T} &\mapsto {}^{B}\mathbf{T}_{A} \quad \text{then } {}^{A}\mathbf{T}_{B} = \mathbf{T}'\end{aligned} \tag{7.4}$$

7.3.2 Hierarchical animation and scene graphs

By coupling the above definitions to an appropriate data structure, a method emerges to animate skeletons by specifying the local joint rotations in a complex hierarchical manner. We will see in this section that this is highly related to the notion of a "scene graph" and is often called *hierarchical modeling* or *hierarchical animation*. Hierarchical modeling is the enforcement of relative location constraints among objects organized in a tree-like structure. Planetary systems are one type of hierarchical model. In planetary systems, moons rotate around planets, which rotate around a sun, which moves in a galaxy. A common type of hierarchical model used in graphics has objects that are connected end to end to form multibody jointed chains. Such hierarchies are useful for modeling animals and humans so that the joints of the limbs are manipulated to produce a figure with moving appendages. Such a figure is often referred to as *articulated* and the movement of an appendage by changing the configuration of a joint is referred to as *articulation*. Because the connectivity of the figure is built into the structure of the model, the animator does not need to make sure that the objects making up the limbs stay attached to one another.

Much of the material concerning the animation of hierarchies in computer graphics comes directly from the field of robotics (e.g., [26]). The robotics literature discusses the modeling of *manipulators*, a sequence of objects connected in a chain by *joints*. The rigid objects forming the connections between the joints are called *links,* and the free end of the chain of alternating joints and links is called the *end effector*. The local coordinate system associated with each joint is referred to as the *frame*.

Robotics is concerned with all types of joints in which two links move relative to one another. Graphics, on the other hand, is concerned primarily with *revolute* joints, in which one link rotates about a fixed point of the other link. The links are usually considered to be pinned together at this point, and the link farther down the chain rotates while the other one remains fixed—at least as far as this joint is concerned. The other type of joint is the *prismatic* joint, in which one link translates relative to another (Figure 7.21).

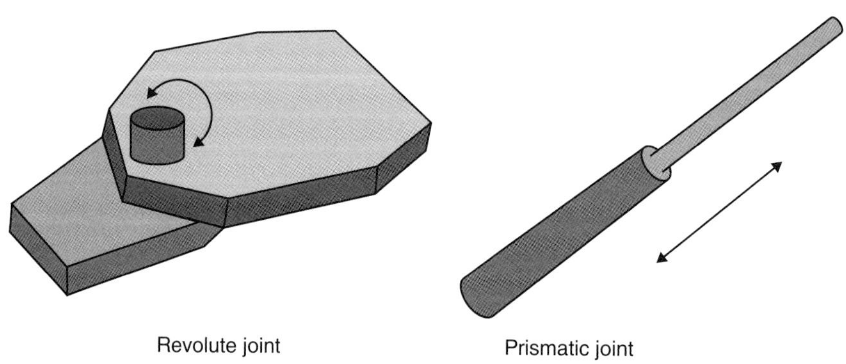

FIGURE 7.21

The two basic single degree of freedom joints.

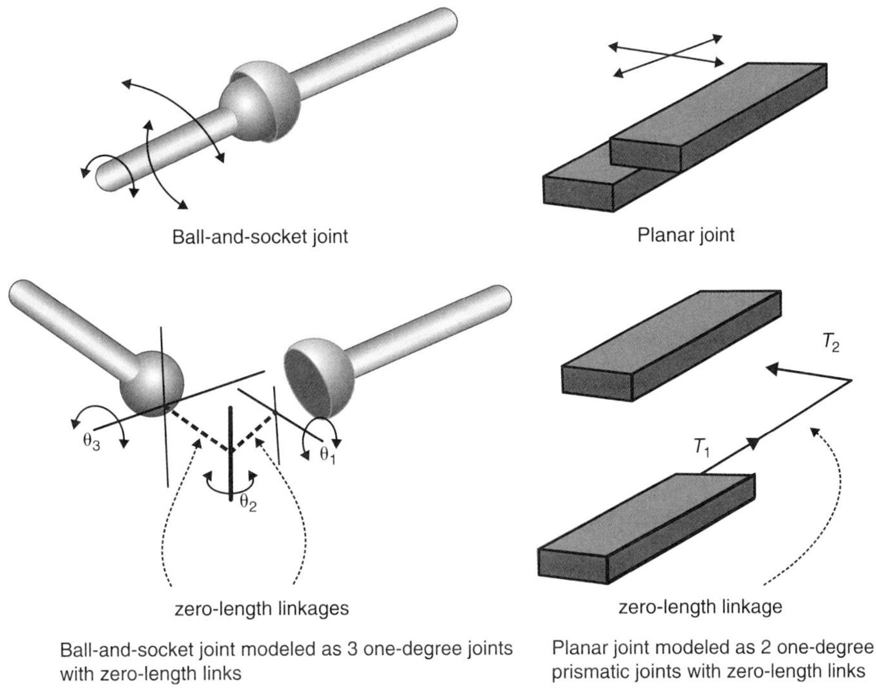

FIGURE 7.22

Modeling complex joints.

The joints of Figure 7.21 allow motion in one direction and are said to have one *degree of freedom* (DOF). Structures in which more than one DOF are coincident are called *complex joints*. Complex joints include the planar joint and the ball-and-socket joint. Planar joints are those in which one link slides on the planar surface of another. Sometimes when a joint has more than one ($n > 1$) DOF, such as a ball-and-socket joint, it is modeled as a set of n one-DOF joints connected by $n - 1$ links of zero length (Figure 7.22). Alternatively, multiple DOF joints can be modeled by using a multiple-valued parameter such as Euler angles or quaternions.

Data structure for hierarchical modeling

Human figures and animals are conveniently modeled as hierarchical linkages. Such linkages can be represented by a tree structure of *nodes* connected by *arcs*.[1] The highest node of the tree is the *root node*, which corresponds to the root object of the hierarchy whose position is known in the global coordinate system. The position

[1] The connections between nodes of a tree structure are sometimes referred to as links; however, the robotics literature refers to the objects between the joints as links. To avoid overloading the term *links*, *arcs* is used here to refer to the connections between nodes in a tree.

of all other nodes of the hierarchy will be located relative to the root node. A node from which no arcs extend downward is referred to as a *leaf node*. "Higher up in the hierarchy" refers to a node that is closer to the root node. When discussing two nodes of the tree connected by an arc, the one higher up the hierarchy is referred to as the *parent node*, and the one farther down the hierarchy is referred to as the *child node*.

The mapping between the hierarchy and tree structure relates a node of the tree to information about the object part (the link) and relates an arc of the tree (the joint) to the transformation to apply to all of the nodes below it in the hierarchy. Relating a tree arc to a figure joint may seem counterintuitive, but it is convenient because a node of the tree can have several arcs emanating from it, just as an object part may have several joints attached to it. In a discussion of a hierarchical model presented by a specific tree structure, the terms *node, object part,* and *link* are used interchangeably because all refer to the geometry to be articulated. Similarly, the terms *joint* and *arc* are used interchangeably.

In the tree structure, there is a root arc that represents a global transformation to apply to the root node (and, therefore, indirectly to all of the nodes of the tree). Changing this transformation will rigidly reposition the entire structure in the global coordinate system (Figure 7.23).

A node of the tree structure contains the information necessary to define the object part in a position ready to be articulated. In the case of rotational joints, this means that the point of rotation on the object part is made to coincide with the origin. The object data may be defined in such a position, or there may be a transformation matrix contained in the node that, when applied to the object data, positions it so. In

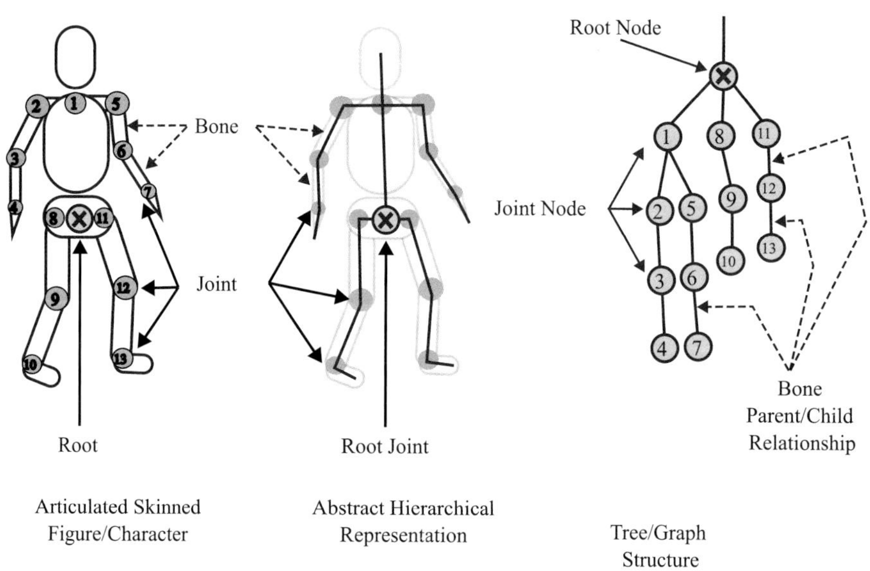

FIGURE 7.23

Example of a tree structure representing a hierarchical structure.

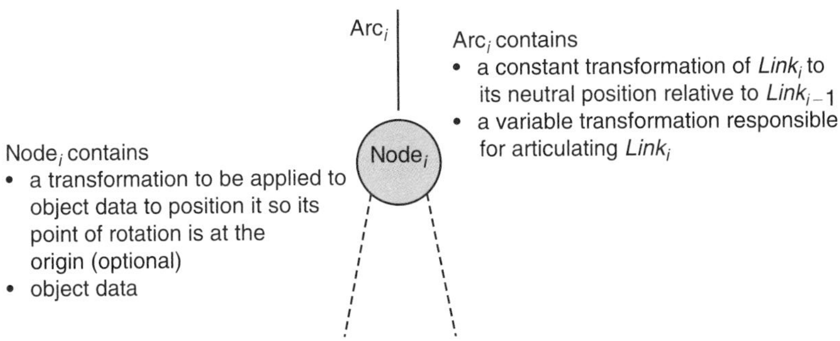

FIGURE 7.24

Arc and node definition.

either case, all of the information necessary to prepare the object data for articulation is contained at the node. The node represents the transformation of the object data into a link of the hierarchical model.

Two types of transformations are associated with an arc leading to a node. One transformation rotates and translates the object into its position of attachment relative to the link one position up in the hierarchy. This defines the link's neutral position relative to its parent. The other transformation is the variable information responsible for the actual joint articulation (Figure 7.24).

A simple example

Consider the simple, two-dimensional three-link example of Figure 7.25. In this example, there is assumed to be no transformation at any of the nodes; the data are defined in a position ready for articulation. $Link_0$, the root object, is transformed to its orientation and position in global space by T_0. Because all of the other parts of the hierarchy will be defined relative to this part, this transformation affects the entire assemblage of parts and thus will transform the position and orientation of the entire structure. This transformation can be changed over time to animate the position and orientation of the rigid structure. $Link_1$ is defined relative to the untransformed root object by transformation T_1. Similarly, $Link_{1.1}$ is defined relative to the untransformed $Link_1$ by transformation $T_{1.1}$. These relationships can be represented in a tree structure by associating the links with nodes and the transformations with arcs. In the example shown in Figure 7.26, the articulation transformations are not yet included in the model.

An arc in the tree representation contains a transformation that applies to the object represented by the node to which the arc immediately connects. This transformation is also applied to the rest of the linkage farther down the hierarchy. The vertices of a particular object can be transformed to their final positions by concatenating the transformations higher up the tree and applying the composite transformation matrix to the vertices. A vertex, V_0, of the root object, $Link_0$, is located in the

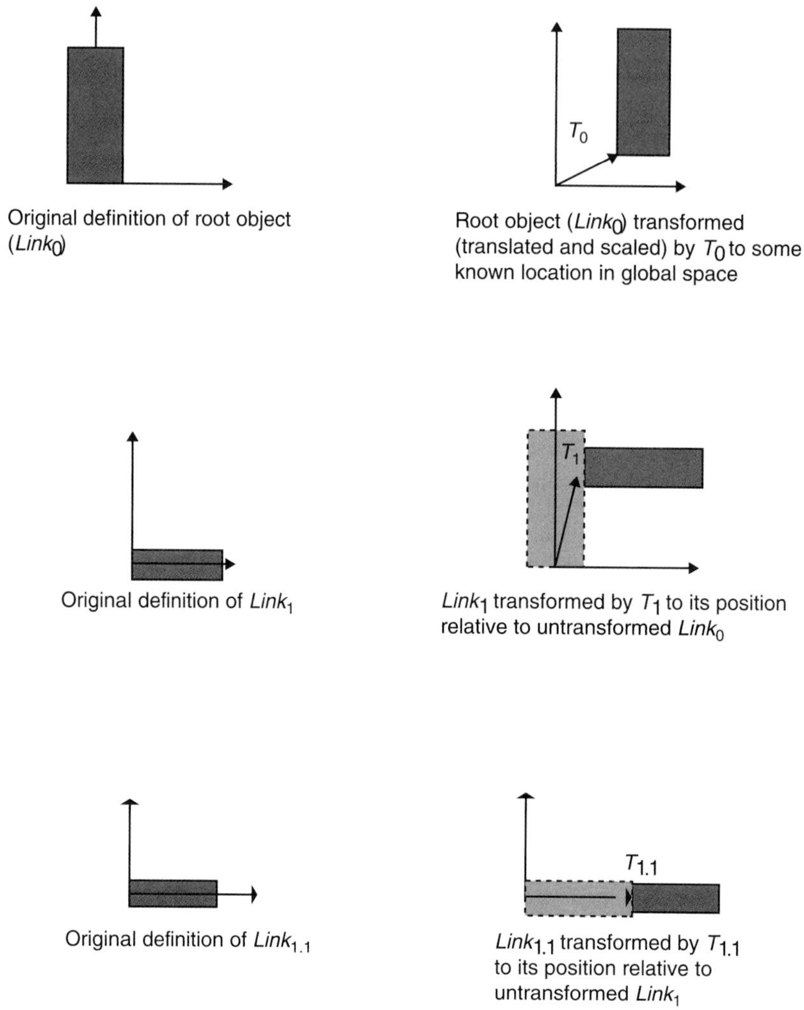

FIGURE 7.25

Example of a hierarchical model.

world coordinate system, V'_0, by applying the rigid transformation that affects the entire structure; see Equation 7.5.

$$V'_0 = T_0 V_0 \tag{7.5}$$

A vertex of the $Link_1$ object is located in the world coordinate system by transforming it first to its location relative to $Link_0$ and then relocating it (conceptually along with $Link_0$) to world space by Equation 7.6.

$$V'_1 = T_0 V_1 V_1. \tag{7.6}$$

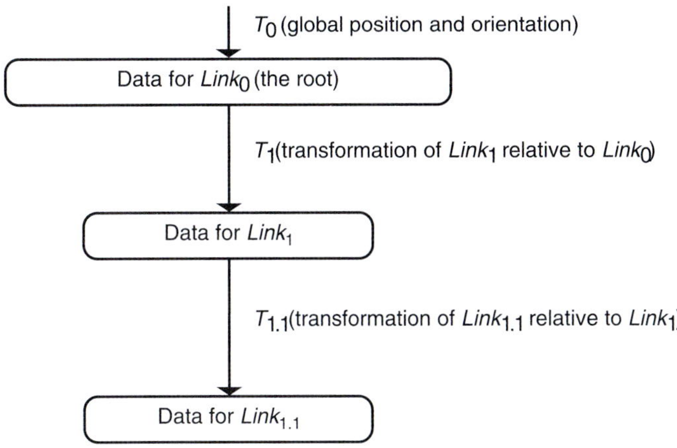

FIGURE 7.26

Example of a tree structure.

Similarly, a vertex of the $Link_{1.1}$ object is located in world space by Equation 7.7.

$$V'_{1.1} = T_0 T_1 T_{1.1} V_{1.1} \tag{7.7}$$

Notice that as the tree is traversed farther down one of its branches, a newly encountered arc transformation is concatenated with the transformations previously encountered.

As previously discussed, when one constructs the static position of the assembly, each arc of the tree has an associated transformation that rotates and translates the link associated with the child node relative to the link associated with the parent node. To easily animate a revolute joint, also associated with the arc is a parameterized (variable) transformation, $R_i(\theta_i)$, which controls the rotation at the specified joint (Figure 7.27). In the tree representation that implements a revolute joint, the rotation transformation is associated with the arc that precedes the node representing the link to be rotated (Figure 7.28). The rotational transformation is applied to the link before the arc's constant transformation. If a transformation is present at the node (for preparing the data for articulation), then the rotational transformation is applied after the node transformation and before the arc's constant transformation.

To locate a vertex of $Link_1$ in world space, one must first transform it via the joint rotation matrix. Once that is complete, then the rest of the transformations up the hierarchy are applied (Equation 7.8).

$$V'_1 = T_0 T_1 R_1(\theta_1) V_1 \tag{7.8}$$

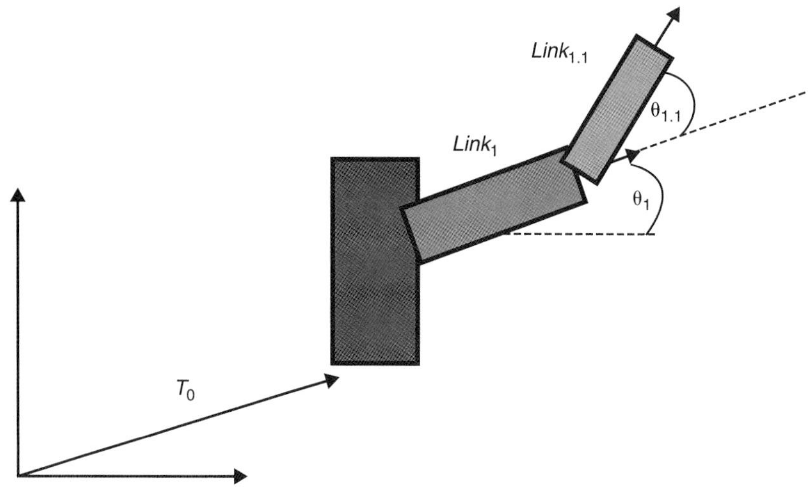

FIGURE 7.27

Variable rotations at the joints.

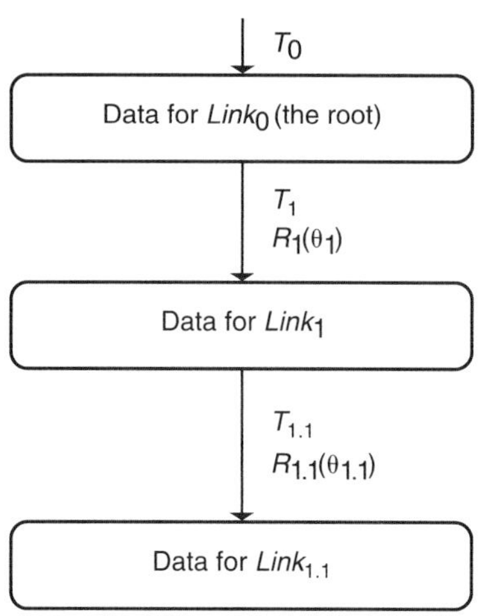

FIGURE 7.28

Hierarchy showing joint rotations.

A vertex of $Link_{1.1}$ is transformed similarly by compositing all of the transformations up the hierarchy to the root, as in Equation 7.9.

$$V'_{1.1} = T_0 T_1 R_1(\theta_1) T_{1.1} R_{1.1}(\theta_{1.1}) V_1 \tag{7.9}$$

In the case of a second appendage, the tree structure would reflect the bifurcations (or multiple branches if more than two). Adding another arm to our simple example results in Figure 7.29.

The corresponding tree structure would have two arcs emanating from the root node, as in Figure 7.30. Branching in the tree occurs whenever multiple appendages emanate from the same object. For example, in a simplified human figure, the root

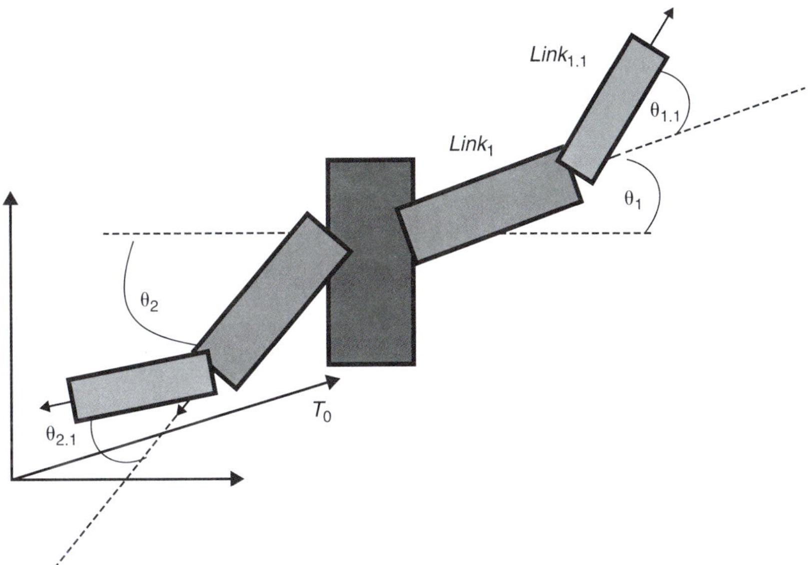

FIGURE 7.29

Hierarchy with two appendages.

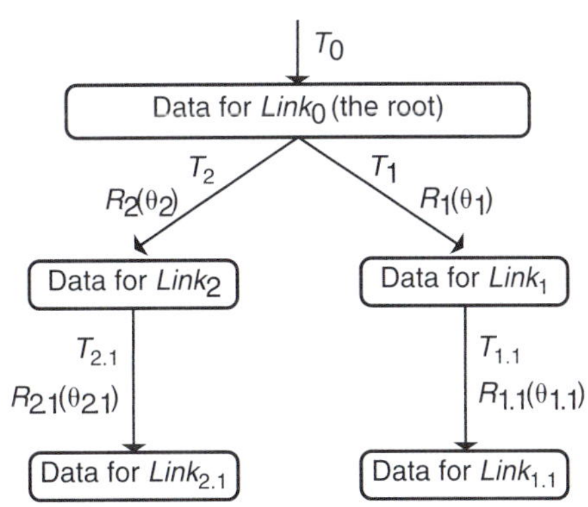

FIGURE 7.30

Tree structure corresponding to hierarchy with two appendages.

hip area (Figure 7.23) might branch into the torso and two legs. If prismatic joints are used, the strategy is the same; the only difference is that the rotation transformation of the joint (arc) is replaced by a translation.

7.3.3 Local coordinate frames and transforms

In setting up complex hierarchies and in applying complex constraints (such as with IK), it is convenient to be able to define points in the local coordinate system (frame) associated with a joint and to have a well-defined method for converting the coordinates of a point from one frame to another. A common use for this method is to convert points defined in the frame of a joint to the global coordinate system for display purposes. In the example above, a transformation matrix is associated with each arc to represent the transformation of a point from the local coordinate space of a child node to the local coordinate space of the parent node. Successively applying matrices farther up the hierarchy can transform a point from any position in the tree into world coordinates. The inverse of the transformation matrix can be used to transform a point from the parent's frame to the child's frame. In the three-dimensional case, 4×4 transformation matrices can be used to describe the relation of one coordinate frame to the next. Robotics has adopted a more concise and more appropriate parameterization for physical devices called the *Denavit-Hartenberg notation*. Although this notation is not used much in graphics anymore because it lacks flexibility appropriate for synthetic linkages, it remains an effective way to describe the physical configurations used in robotics. As seen before, we will use a similar technique here to specify the directionality of our joint transformations for animation. In particular, we can boil it down to the simple form

$$ {}^{\mathrm{TO}}\mathbf{T}_{\mathbf{FROM}} $$

where T is a transformation that takes points in the coordinate system **FROM** and expresses them relative to the coordinate frame **TO**. For example, we can take points that relative to our **HAND** and express them relative to our **ELBOW** with the transformation ${}^{\mathrm{ELBOW}}\mathbf{T}_{\mathbf{HAND}}$.

We could take this further and combine this with the transformation from our elbow to our shoulder (${}^{\mathrm{SHOULDER}}\mathbf{T}_{\mathbf{ELBOW}}$) by concatenating (multiplying matrices) these transformations in the appropriate order we can see that as long as the inner FROM/TO frames align then the labels will cancel out leaving a transformation that results from the original frame to the intended frame:

$$ \begin{aligned} {}^{\mathbf{SHOULDER}}\mathbf{T}_{\mathbf{HAND}} &= {}^{\mathbf{SHOULDER}}\mathbf{T}_{\mathbf{ELBOW}}\,{}^{\mathbf{ELBOW}}\mathbf{T}_{\mathbf{HAND}} \\ &= {}^{\mathbf{SHOULDER}}\mathbf{T}_{\cancel{\mathbf{ELBOW}}}\,{}^{\cancel{\mathbf{ELBOW}}}\mathbf{T}_{\mathbf{HAND}} \end{aligned} $$

If you write them in the wrong order, you will see that they don't align, and thus you've arranged or defined them incorrectly:

$$^{\mathbf{SHOULDER}}\mathbf{T}_{\mathbf{HAND}} \neq {}^{\mathbf{ELBOW}}\mathbf{T}_{\mathbf{HAND}}\,{}^{\mathbf{SHOULDER}}\mathbf{T}_{\mathbf{ELBOW}}$$

Aside

Transformation ordering in a chain/sequence is important.

Generally, in a kinematic chain/sequence between 3 joints A, B, C connected by 2 bones, AB, BC, in the sequence $A \rightarrow B \rightarrow C$, we can define the transformations between joints as: $A \rightarrow B : {}^{B}\mathbf{T}_{A}$, $B \rightarrow C : {}^{C}\mathbf{T}_{B}$. Thus, we can compute the transformation from $A \rightarrow C$ by concatenating these transformations in the appropriate order:

$$^{\mathbf{C}}\mathbf{T}_{\mathbf{A}} = {}^{\mathbf{C}}\mathbf{T}_{\mathbf{B}}\,{}^{\mathbf{B}}\mathbf{T}_{\mathbf{A}}$$

When implementing a kinematic linkage, especially when the linkage contains joints with multiple DOF, there are options to consider when choosing the method to implement rotational parameterization of a local coordinate frame. Part of the issue involves the user interface. What kind of information is required from the user to specify the rotational values at the joint? Users are often already comfortable with specifications such as *x-y-z* Euler angles. The other part of the issue involves the method used to implement the rotations to produce the required transformations. If the user specifies the rotation(s) interactively, then the operations are mapped directly to this internal representation. Quaternions are often used to actually implement the transformations to avoid the gimbal lock problem with Euler and fixed-angle representations.

Where are the animation parameters?

Each joint has a local transformation that describes how the joint is transforming its points relative to its current state. This is what we need to specify in our "animation." For instance, if we want our elbow to rotate by +45 degrees, thus rotating our forearm upward, then we need to rotate the angle in our local elbow transformation. Each transformation can thus be controlled using the quaternion specified (or Euler angles) at each time step in the animation. By smoothly interpolating or setting these angles, we can achieve smooth animation and control of the skeleton's bones/joints. Thus a local transformation for our elbow would be defined as $T_{local} = T_{elbow} = \begin{bmatrix} R_\theta & \vec{0}_{3\times1} \\ \vec{0}_{1\times3} & 1 \end{bmatrix}$, where θ is our controllable local parameter.

7.4 Poseable rigs: forward kinematics

So far, we have seen how skeletons are defined, as a graph of bones and joints, and we defined the language of how to discuss transformations between different bones/joints. But what now? Ultimately, our goal in computer animation is to have our character rendered to the screen. To do this, we need all joint locations to be defined in the common world coordinate system. This means that ultimately we need to define the transformation between for each joint to transform points defined relative to the joint and express them in the world coordinate system: **world→joint** : $^{world}\mathbf{T}_{\mathbf{joint}}$. This is the job of FK.

The FK algorithm answers the question "where are my joints in the world?" given the animated parameters (joint angles) and the rig structure (parent/child relationships).

7.4.1 Parent-child relationships

To do this, we need to define the notion of a parent-child relationship in the hierarchy.

Given joints *A, B, C* and bones *AB, BC*, where *A* is the root node, then we would say that A is the parent of B (and B is the child of A). Similarly, B is the parent of C (and C is the child of B). Each node can be the parent of any number of children, but ultimately there is a single root node in the hierarchy that all nodes stem from. For character rigs, the hip or groin joint is generally the "root" of the kinematic structure. For each node/joint, we can specify (1) local transformations of the node $\mathbf{T}_{local}$ (the animated parameter) and (2) the joint transformations as $^{parent}\mathbf{T}_{child}$ that defines how to transform points in this node to its parent based on the kinematic structure.

7.4.2 Forward kinematics

Given the relationships defined in the rig and the resulting joint angles provided by interpolating or setting the animation parameters in the transformations for each joint, we can define the FK algorithm to compute the joinT→world transformations of each joint/node in the rig/graph. This is done using a depth-first traversal of the rig starting from the root node to the leaf nodes as seen in `Algorithm 7.6` in the UpdateTransform() function.

ALGORITHM 7.6: FK (Forward Kinematics)

```
class Node{
    ------------------------------------
    // local animated transformations
    T_joint
    // joint to parent transform
    parentT_joint
    // joint to world transform (to be computed)
    worldT_joint
    // list of children connected
    List<Node> Children;
    ------------------------------------
    void UpdateTransform(Node parent, Time t){
        // update local transformations (Animation)
        T_joint = AnimateJoint(t)

        if(parent != null)
            worldT_joint = parentT_joint T_joint
        else
            worldT_joint = T_joint

        // compute node to world transform
        foreach child in Children
            child->Update(this)
    }
    Transform AnimateJoint(Time t){
        // sample motion capture or animation data
    }
}
...
// each frame (or after any modification of rig/parameters)
Node root=Rig->GetRoot();
root->UpdateTransform(null, Time::GetAnimTime())
```

A completely specified set of linkage parameters results in the positioning of the hierarchical figure is called a *pose*. A pose is specified by a vector (the *pose vector*) consisting of one parameter for each DOF. Unfortunately, getting an end effector to a specific desired position by specifying joint values can be tedious for the user. Often, it is a process of trial and error. To avoid the difficulties in having to specify all of the joint values, IK is sometimes used, in which the desired position and orientation of the end effector are given and the internal joint values are calculated automatically. Specifying the pose and performing FK lets us define complete character rigs that can easily be keyframed and animated (see Figure 7.19).

Definition 7.4: Pose

Given a skeletal rig:

$$\textbf{Skeleton} \leftarrow \textbf{Graph}(J, B) = \begin{cases} J = [J_1, \ldots, J_M] \text{ set of Joints} \\ B = [\mathbf{B_1}, \ldots, \mathbf{B}_N] \text{ set of Bones} \end{cases}$$

with joints

$$\Theta_t = \left\{ \vec{\theta}_1(t), \ldots, \vec{\theta}_M(t) \right\}$$

then the set of local joint rotation parameters, Θ_t, at time t is called a *pose*. These local rotation parameters are thus transformed into world space with *forward kinematics*.

7.4.3 Inverse kinematics

If the FK algorithm answers the question "where are my joints in the world?" given a particular rig and pose, then the IK algorithm answers the question "what are my joint angles?" given a target location for the end effector.

In IK, the desired position and possibly orientation of the end effector are given by the user along with the initial pose vector. From this, the joint values required to attain that configuration are calculated, giving the final pose vector. For example, imagine we want to ensure our character's foot is actually on the ground or if we want their hand to look as if they are grasping a ladder rung, then we know where the hand or foot needs to end up so we have to compute the rest of their angles to ensure that their hand or foot actually lands at this location.

The IK problem can have zero, one, or more solutions (possibly infinite). If there are so many constraints on the configuration that *no* solution exists, the system is called *overconstrained*. If there are relatively few constraints on the system and there are *many* solutions to the problem posed, then it is *underconstrained*. The *reachable workspace* is the volume that the end effector can reach. The *dexterous workspace* is the volume that the end effector can reach in any orientation.

Once the joint values are calculated, the figure can be animated by interpolating from the initial pose vector values to the final pose vector values calculated by IK. However, for large differences between initial and final pose vectors, this does not provide precise control over the path that the end effector follows. Alternatively, a series of intermediate end effector positions (and possibly orientations) can first be calculated, and each one of these then used as input to an IK problem. In this way, the path the end effector takes is prescribed by the animator.

If the mechanism is simple enough, then the joint values (the pose vector) required to produce the final desired configuration can be calculated analytically. Given an initial pose vector and the final pose vector, intermediate configurations can be formed by interpolation of the values in the pose vectors, thus animating the mechanism from its initial configuration to the final one. However, if the mechanism is too complicated for analytic solutions, then an incremental approach can be used that employs a matrix of values (the *Jacobian*) that relates changes in the values of the joint parameters to changes in the end effector position and orientation. The end effector is iteratively nudged until the final configuration is attained within a given tolerance. In addition to the Jacobian, there are other incremental formulations that can be used to effect IK solutions.

Solving a simple system by analysis

For sufficiently simple mechanisms, the joint values of a final desired position can be determined analytically by inspecting the geometry of the linkage. Consider a simple two-link arm in two-dimensional space with two rotational DOFs. Link lengths are L_1 and L_2 for the first and second link, respectively. If a position is fixed for the base of the arm at the first joint, any position beyond $|L_1 - L_2|$ units from the base of the link and within $L_1 + L_2$ of the base can be reached (Figure 7.31).

Assume for now (without loss of generality) that the base is at the origin. In a simple IK problem, the user gives the (X, Y) coordinate of the desired position for the end effector. The joint angles, θ_1 and θ_2, can be determined by computing the distance from the base to the goal and using the law of cosines to compute the interior angles. Once the interior angles are computed, the rotation angles for the two

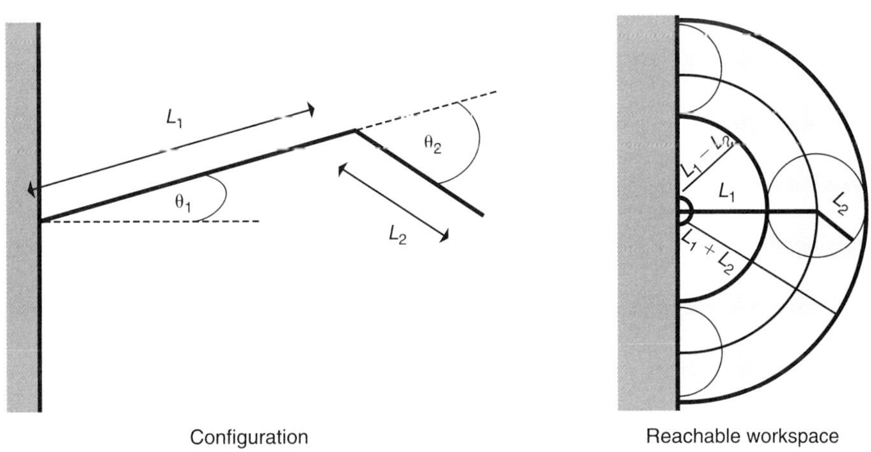

FIGURE 7.31

Simple linkage.

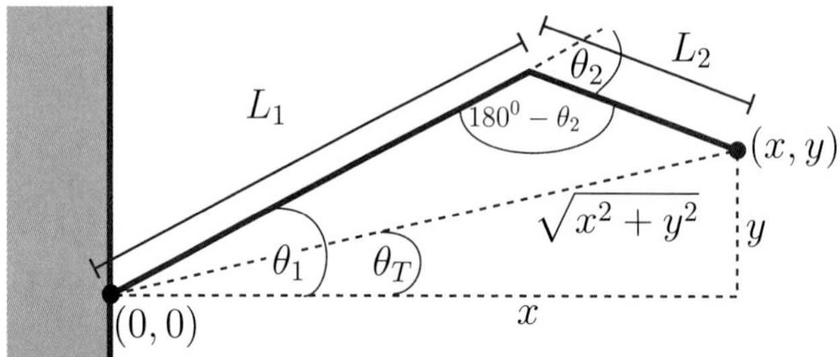

$$\cos(\theta_T) = \frac{x}{\sqrt{x^2 + y^2}} \qquad \text{(SOH}\mathbf{CAH}\text{TOA)}$$

$$\therefore \theta_T = \cos^{-1}\left(\frac{x}{\sqrt{x^2 + y^2}}\right) \qquad \text{(solve for } \theta_T\text{)}$$

$$\cos(\theta_1 - \theta_T) = \frac{L_1^2 + x^2 + y^2 - L_2^2}{2L_1\sqrt{x^2 + y^2}} \qquad \text{(cosine rule)}$$

$$\therefore \theta_1 = \cos^{-1}\left(\frac{L_1^2 + x^2 + y^2 - L_2^2}{2L_1\sqrt{x^2 + y^2}}\right) + \theta_T \qquad \text{(solve for } \theta_1\text{)}$$

$$\cos(180^o - \theta_2) = -\cos(\theta_2) = \frac{L_1^2 + L_2^2 - (x^2 + y^2)}{2L_1L_2} \qquad \text{(cosine rule)}$$

$$\theta_2 = \cos^{-1}\left(\frac{L_1^2 + L_2^2 - x^2 - y^2}{2L_1L_2}\right) \qquad \text{(solve for } \theta_2\text{)}$$

FIGURE 7.32

Analytic solution to a simple inverse kinematics problem.

links can be computed (Figure 7.32). Of course, the first step is to make sure that the position of the goal is within the reach of the end effector; that is, $|L_1 - L_2| \leq \sqrt{X^2 + Y^2} \leq L_1 + L_2$.

In this simple scenario, there are only two solutions that will give the correct answer; the configurations are symmetric with respect to the line from (0, 0) to (*X*, *Y*). This is reflected in the equation in Figure 7.32; the inverse cosine is two-valued in both plus and minus theta ($\pm\theta$). However, for more complicated cases, there may be infinitely many solutions that will give the desired end effector location.

The joint values for relatively simple linkages can be solved by algebraic manipulation of the equations that describe the relationship of the end effector to the base frame. Most linkages used in robotic applications are designed to be simple enough for this analysis. However, for many cases that arise in computer animation, analytic solutions are not tractable. In such cases, iterative numeric solutions must be relied on.

The Jacobian

Many mechanisms of interest to computer animation are too complex to allow an analytic solution. For these, the motion can be incrementally constructed. At each time step, a computation is performed that determines a way to change each joint angle to direct the current position and orientation of the end effector toward the desired configuration. There are several methods used to compute the change in joint angle, but most involve forming the matrix of partial derivatives called the *Jacobian*.

To explain the Jacobian from a strictly mathematical point of view, consider the six arbitrary functions of Equation 7.10, each of which is a function of six independent variables. Given specific values for the input variables, x_i, each of the output variables, y_i, can be computed by its respective function.

$$\begin{aligned} y_1 &= f_1(x_1, x_2, x_3, x_4, x_5, x_6) \\ y_2 &= f_1(x_1, x_2, x_3, x_4, x_5, x_6) \\ y_3 &= f_1(x_1, x_2, x_3, x_4, x_5, x_6) \\ y_4 &= f_1(x_1, x_2, x_3, x_4, x_5, x_6) \\ y_5 &= f_1(x_1, x_2, x_3, x_4, x_5, x_6) \\ y_6 &= f_1(x_1, x_2, x_3, x_4, x_5, x_6) \end{aligned} \tag{7.10}$$

These equations can also be used to describe the change in the output variables relative to the change in the input variables. The differentials of y_i can be written in terms of the differentials of x_i using the chain rule. This generates Equation 7.11.

$$dy_i = \frac{\partial f_i}{\partial x_1} dx_1 + \frac{\partial f_i}{\partial x_2} dx_2 + \frac{\partial f_i}{\partial x_3} dx_3 + \frac{\partial f_i}{\partial x_4} dx_4 + \frac{\partial f_i}{\partial x_5} dx_5 + \frac{\partial f_i}{\partial x_6} dx_6 \tag{7.11}$$

Equations 7.10 and 7.11 can be put in vector notation, producing Equation 7.12.

$$Y = FX, \quad dY = \frac{\partial F}{\partial X} dX \tag{7.12}$$

A matrix of partial derivatives, $\overline{\partial X}$, is called the *Jacobian* and is a function of the current values of x_i. The Jacobian can be thought of as mapping the velocities of X to the velocities of Y (Equation 7.13).

$$\dot{Y} = J(X)\dot{X} \tag{7.13}$$

At any point in time, the Jacobian is a function of the x_i. At the next instant of time, X has changed and so has the transformation represented by the Jacobian.

When one applies the Jacobian to a linked appendage, the input variables, x_i, become the joint values and the output variables, y_i, become the end effector position and orientation (in some suitable representation such as *x-y-z* fixed angles).

$$Y = \begin{bmatrix} p_x & p_y & p_z & \alpha_x & \alpha_y & \alpha_z \end{bmatrix}^T \tag{7.14}$$

In this case, the Jacobian relates the velocities of the joint angles, $\dot{\theta}$, to the velocities of the end effector position and orientation, $\dot{Y}$ (Equation 7.15).

$$V = \dot{Y} = J(\theta)\dot{\theta} \tag{7.15}$$

V is the vector of linear and rotational velocities and represents the desired change in the end effector. The desired change will be based on the difference between its current position/orientation to that specified by the goal configuration. These velocities are vectors in three-space, so each has an x, y, and z component (Equation 7.16).

$$V = \begin{bmatrix} v_x & v_y & v_z & \omega_x & \omega_y & \omega_z \end{bmatrix}^T \tag{7.16}$$

$\dot{\theta}$ is a vector of joint value velocities, or the changes to the joint parameters, which are the unknowns of the equation (Equation 7.17).

$$\dot{\theta} = \begin{bmatrix} \dot{\theta}_1 \ldots \dot{\theta}_n \end{bmatrix}^T \tag{7.17}$$

J, the Jacobian, is a matrix that relates the two and is a function of the current pose (Equation 7.18).

$$J = \begin{bmatrix} \frac{\partial p_x}{\partial \theta_1} & \frac{\partial p_x}{\partial \theta_2} & \cdots & \frac{\partial p_x}{\partial \theta_n} \\ \frac{\partial p_y}{\partial \theta_1} & \frac{\partial p_y}{\partial \theta_2} & \cdots & \frac{\partial p_y}{\partial \theta_n} \\ \cdots & \cdots & \cdots & \cdots \\ \frac{\partial p_z}{\partial \theta_1} & \frac{\partial p_z}{\partial \theta_2} & \cdots & \frac{\partial p_z}{\partial \theta_n} \end{bmatrix} \tag{7.18}$$

Each term of the Jacobian relates the change of a specific joint to a specific change in the end effector. For a revolute joint, the rotational change in the end effector, ω, is merely the velocity of the joint angle about the axis of revolution at the joint under consideration. For a prismatic joint, the end effector orientation is unaffected by the joint articulation. For a rotational joint, the linear change in the end effector is the cross-product of the axis of revolution and a vector from the joint to the end effector. The rotation at a rotational joint induces an instantaneous linear direction of travel at the end effector. For a prismatic joint, the linear change is identical to the change at the joint (Figure 7.33).

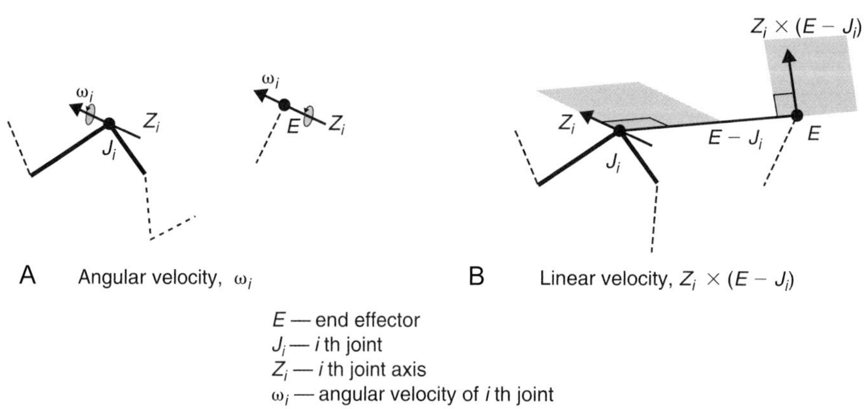

FIGURE 7.33

Angular and linear velocities induced by joint axis rotation.

The desired angular and linear velocities are computed by finding the difference between the current configuration of the end effector and the desired configuration. The angular and linear velocities of the end effector induced by the rotation at a specific joint are determined by the computations shown in Figure 7.33. The problem is to determine the best linear combination of velocities induced by the various joints that would result in the desired velocities of the end effector. The Jacobian is formed by posing the problem in matrix form.

In assembling the Jacobian, it is important to make sure that all of the coordinate values are in the same coordinate system. It is often the case that joint-specific information is given in the coordinate system local to that joint. In forming the Jacobian matrix, this information must be converted into some common coordinate system such as the global inertial (world) coordinate system or the end effector coordinate system. Various methods have been developed for computing the Jacobian based on attaining maximum computational efficiency given the required information in local coordinate systems, but all methods produce the derivative matrix in a common coordinate system.

A simple example

Consider the simple three-revolute-joint, planar manipulator of Figure 7.34. In this example, the objective is to move the end effector, *E*, to the goal position, *G*. The orientation of the end effector is of no concern in this example. The axis of rotation of each joint is perpendicular to the figure, coming out of the paper. The effect of an incremental rotation, g_i, of each joint can be determined by the cross-product of the joint axis and the vector from the joint to the end effector, V_i (Figure 7.35), and form the columns of the Jacobian. Notice that the magnitude of each g_i is a function of the distance between the locations of the joint and the end effector.

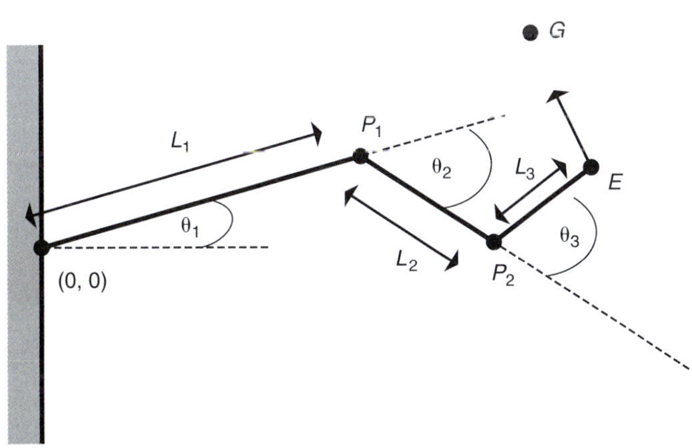

FIGURE 7.34

Planar three-joint manipulator.

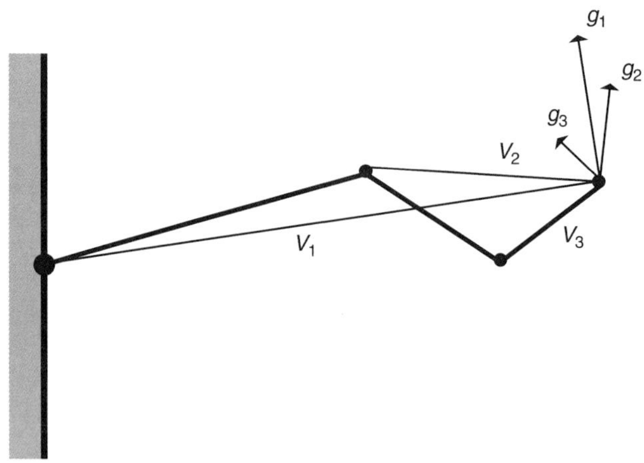

FIGURE 7.35

Instantaneous changes in position induced by joint angle rotations.

The desired change to the end effector is the difference between the current position of the end effector and the goal position (Equation 7.19).

$$V = \begin{bmatrix} (G-E)_x \\ (G-E)_y \\ (G-E)_z \end{bmatrix} \tag{7.19}$$

A vector of the desired change in values is set equal to the Jacobian matrix (Equation 7.20) multiplied by a vector of the unknown values, which are the changes to the joint angles.

$$J = \begin{bmatrix} ((0,0,1)\times E)_x & ((0,0,1)\times (E-P_1))_x & ((0,0,1)\times (E-P_2))_x \\ ((0,0,1)\times E)_y & ((0,0,1)\times (E-P_1))_y & ((0,0,1)\times (E-P_2))_y \\ ((0,0,1)\times E)_z & ((0,0,1)\times (E-P_1))_z & ((0,0,1)\times (E-P_2))_z \end{bmatrix} \tag{7.20}$$

7.4.4 FABRIK: a simpler iterative solution to IK

Although the Jacobian method enables us to compute solutions to complex systems of equations, it is not the simplest to understand, implement, or use in a computer animation system. Sometimes the constraints are not well formed or are ill-conditioned. Ultimately, because there is potentially an infinite number of closed-form solutions, we must seek other iterative solutions to the IK problem that are both efficient to compute and that provide a solution that is "good enough" for aesthetic purposes.

FABRIK, or Forward And Backward Reverse Inverse Kinematics solver [27], is an algorithmic tool that is popular in solving small IK problems suitable for computer animation solutions in real time. The key insight here is that short kinematic chains with a small number of IK constraints can be solved (within adequate error bounds) in only a few iterations through a traversal of the chain from the end effector the root and back again. FABRIK first assumes the IK constraint is satisfied at the end effector (essentially snapping the end to the IK target) and propagating the joint angles backward through the chain to the root. Once the root is reached, the root is snapped back to its original location as an IK constraint and the algorithm traverses back to the end-effector, essentially "fixing" any errors along the way. With even a single iteration, the chain achieves a very good estimate of the final solution and subsequent iterations can refine the accuracy. FABRIK has subsequently been extended to fairly complex human rigs [28] for use with character animations, as well as solving for robot end-effector locations in highly confined spaces [29], which can be difficult to accomplish with traditional Jacobian methods.

7.4.5 Rigging

So far, we have seen how to define a skeletal rig, how to define the relationships between bones, and how to compute the transformations using FK and IK. But how do we take the resulting skeletal rig and actually apply it to a character mesh so we can render it properly? This is the process we call "rigging." Rigging a character defines the relationship between the vertices of a character mesh and each bone/joint that can affect. If the leg joints move, you want the mesh vertices to move accordingly. More importantly, if we move a character's hand, we don't want it to affect the vertices of our foot (generally). So we need to define a way that is localized and efficient.

Given a mesh, $\textbf{Mesh}\rightarrow\left\{\vec{v}_n, \vec{e}_m\right\}$, containing N vertices and M edges, a rig connects mesh vertices to skeletal joints (with J joints) with a set of scalar weights, $W_{nj} = \left\{\ldots, w_{nj}, \ldots\right\}$ where a given weight $w_{nj} \leq 1$ specifies the percentage of influence of joint j on vertex n.

$\textbf{Rig}\rightarrow\left\{\textbf{Skeleton}(J, B), \textbf{Mesh}, W_{nj}\right\}$ where for each vertex, the sum of all weights must equal 1.

One way to specify this is as a matrix where each column corresponds to a vertex in the mesh and each row corresponds to a joint in the rig.

$$\textbf{map}(\mathcal{J}, \textbf{Mesh}) \mapsto \begin{array}{c} \\ \textbf{J}_1 \\ \textbf{J}_2 \\ \vdots \\ \textbf{J}_J \end{array} \begin{array}{c} \begin{array}{cccc} v_1 & v_2 & \cdots & v_N \end{array} \\ \begin{bmatrix} w_{11} & w_{21} & \cdots & w_{N1} \\ \vdots & \vdots & \ddots & \vdots \\ \vdots & \vdots & \ddots & \vdots \\ w_{1J} & w_{2J} & \cdots & w_{NJ} \end{bmatrix} \end{array}$$

Each column must sum to 1 to ensure all weights are normalized properly. For efficiency and to ensure that vertices are affected locally, the majority of this matrix are zeros and only a small number of joints (e.g., 4–8) in local regions affect individual vertices. This matrix is either computed automatically or specified by an artist/animator using weight painting in their modeling package (e.g., Blender, Maya). The weights are performed once while the model is in a "rest" pose (sometimes called a "bind" pose) which is usually a neutral pose such as a "t-pose" (arms extended outward) or "a-pose" (arms extended downward loosely). In such a rest pose, all transformations are set to zero (or recorded and known). The results of weight painting a character in Blender can be seen in Figure 7.36 and Figure 7.37, which shows the vertex color coded corresponding to the influence the selected joint has on the vertex. As you can see, the vertices most impacted by the bone are shown in red and lie along the axis of the bone, and the weights taper off and go beyond the joint to influence the skin around the joint slightly.

7.4.6 Skinning

For each frame of animation, we perform the following actions: (1) animate all local rotations or sample motion capture (or perform procedural animation) for all joints, (2) perform FK, (3) perform IK, and (4) deform the mesh (skinning). The act of deforming the character mesh with a given rig is called "skinning" (Figure 7.38). Given the weight matrix above, the goal of skinning is to deform each vertex in the mesh by the joints that affect it after FK and IK have been performed, given a rig and weight mapping. We can express the skinning equation as:

$$\vec{v}_i' = \sum_i^N w_{ij} \, {}^{\text{world}}\mathbf{T}_j \left({}^{j}\mathbf{T}_{\text{rest}}\right) \vec{v}_{\text{i}} \quad \forall_{j \in J} \tag{7.21}$$

Here we can see that the transformations ${}^{\text{world}}\mathbf{T}_j$ are the result of the FK/IK process and as such take vertices that are expressed relative to the joint and transform them using the joint animation into the world frame. Before applying this to the vertex, however, we note that the vertex actually is in a special "rest" frame where the rig has been defined and weights have been authored (e.g., t-pose). Thus, we first need to transform this vertex from the rest frame into the particular joint frame, ${}^{j}\mathbf{T}_{\text{rest}} \vec{v}_i$. This is sometimes called the inverse bind pose as it is actually the particular joint to world transform of the rig from the rest/bind pose. We can see that ${}^{j}\mathbf{T}_{\text{rest}} = {}^{rest}\mathbf{T}_{\text{j}}^{-1}$, and thus you will sometimes see the skinning equation expressed as:

$$\vec{v}_i' = \sum_i^N w_{ij} \, {}^{\text{world}}\mathbf{T}_j \left({}^{\text{rest}}\mathbf{T}_j\right)^{-1} \vec{v}_i \quad \forall_{j \in J} \tag{7.22}$$

A common simplification is to zero out all of the rotations and scales in the resting bind pose once the rig is defined, leaving only the translation (position) of

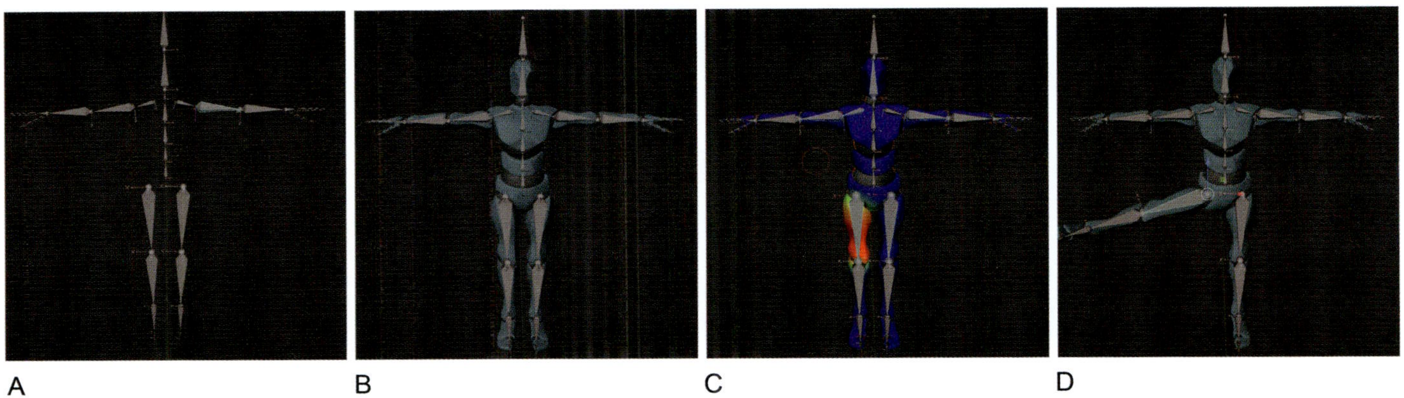

FIGURE 7.36

Forward kinematics and skinning weights: (a) skeletal rig, (b) rig + mesh, and (c) right thigh bone weights for skinning (note the locality and falloff of the weights as it approaches the joints).

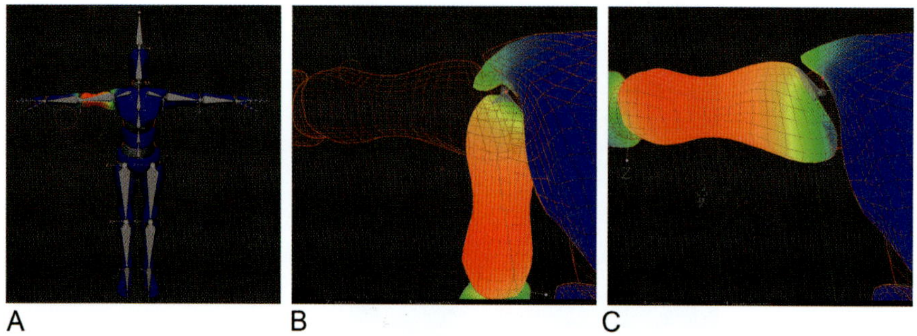

FIGURE 7.37

Weights for skinning: (a) right arm bone selected showing weights, (b) before and after rotating shoulder joint note the subtle deformation of the mesh just above the joint, and (c) no rotation applied.

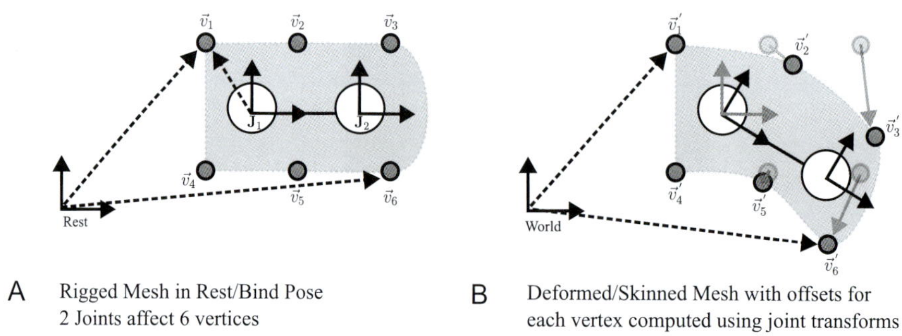

FIGURE 7.38

Deforming mesh vertices by joint rotation.

the joint in the joint to rest pose transformation. If this is the assumption, then the skinning equation can be simplified to

$$\vec{v_i}' = \sum_i^N w_{ij} \, {}^{\text{world}}\mathbf{T}_j\left(\vec{v_i} - \vec{t_j}\right) \quad \forall_{j \in J} \tag{7.23}$$

where $\vec{t_i}$ is the position of the joint j in the resting bind pose. In Figure 7.39, we demonstrate how the skinning equation works to deform a single vertex that is influenced by two joints. In (b), the point is transformed by the local transformation in the first joint causing it to move relative to the joint. The resulting displaced vertex is expressed in world coordinates using the results of the FK equation for this joint resulting in a new vertex that has been deformed by joint 1; let's call this vertex $\vec{v_3}'(\text{world})_1$. Similarly, we can displace the original vertex by the transformation in joint 2 (c) resulting in $\vec{v_3}'(\text{world})_2$. The final vertex needs to incorporate both

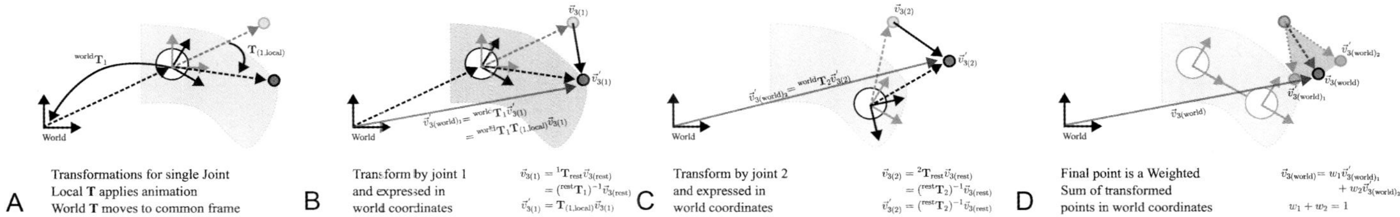

FIGURE 7.39

Skinning effect of two joint rotations on vertex.

of these deformed vertices (d), and thus we simply multiply them by the influence weight of each joint and add them together to get a final vertex $\vec{v}_3(\text{world}) = w_1 \vec{v}_3{}'(\text{world})_1 + w_2 \vec{v}_3{}'(\text{world})_1$. Note that the sum of the weights is normalized to 1. This sum can be performed because both vertices are already expressed relative to the world frame. One can easily see that if the joints are equally weighted, then $w_1 = w_2 = 0.5$, which simplifies to the average of the two vertices. The sum over all joints generalizes this to the skinning equation above.

7.4.7 Ragdolls

Ragdolls are an effective way to engage the physics engine in an animation system or game engine for character animation. By applying forces to the various nodes in our skeletal rig, we can have them fall down and crumple using physics. In this scenario it is important to apply constraints and collision boundaries to each bone/joint to ensure they don't self-intersect. Ragdolls can be switched to at any given moment in an animation, and the results can be blended with the FK/IK solutions before skinning, providing the system/animator with a degree of control. This can allow interesting procedural animations: imagine a scenario where your character is running and jumps off of a building; at some point you may wish to have the physics engine override the animation system, thus a ragdoll is initialized with a given pose, and over a short period of time (a few frames) the physics ragdoll animation can be blended in rather than purely the animation rig. The physics system will then simulate masses at each joints enabling a more "realistic" falling animation given the unique physical characteristics of the environment. After the character hits the ground, you can once again blend the ragdoll animation into a particular animation clip, such as getting up off the ground and returning to a neutral or idle pose.

7.5 Chapter summary

In this chapter, we explored the foundations of character animation from an algorithmic perspective. We discussed how to morph images and characters using interpolation schemes. We followed that up with how we define skeletal rigs and discussed how they can be animated using FK and IK. Finally, we discussed how these rigs are used to deform a mesh using the skinning equation to render our mesh to the frame.

7.6 Exercises

Beginner

B1 Describe the similarities and differences between 2D sprites and 3D morph targets.

B2 What is a skeletal rig?
B3 What is the difference between a bone and a joint?
B4 What types of joints do we need to use for a skeletal rig?
B5 What is the skinning equation?
B6 What is the difference between FK and IK?
B7 What is a 3D morphable model, and what can it be used for?

Intermediate

I1 Draw a rig with the following joints and bones connecting them:

- Joints(A,B,C,D), Bones(AB, AC, CD), Root(A)
- Joints(A,B,C,D), Bones(AD, AB, BC), Root(A)
- Joints(A,B,C,D), Bones(BA, BC, CD), Root(B)

I2 In the following rigs, (1) name all of the transformations required for FK and (2) show the resulting transformation sequence for each joint after FK:

- Joints(A,B,C,D), Bones(AB, AC, CD), Root(A)
- Joints(A,B,C,D), Bones(BA, BC, CD), Root(B)

I3 For the following rig, what is the transformation (1) from C to the root, (2) from A to D, and (3) from C to D.

- Joints(A,B,C,D), Bones(AB, AC, CD), Root(A)

I4 Implement a 3D morph target animation system using simple shapes and demonstrate 3D shape morphing (e.g., a sphere morphing into a cube). Ensure that all targets have the same number of vertices and they are ordered in the same ordering.

Advanced

A1 Implement the FK algorithm for a very simple set of bones/joints and demonstrate how to animate each joint independently.

A2 Read the FABRIK paper and show how it would work for the following IK problem drawing each step of the way:

- Joints(A,B,C,D), Bones(AB, BC, CD), Root(A) = (0,0), initial resting pose is along the *x*-axis.
  (a) Length of each bone =1 unit and IKTarget = (5,5)
  (b) Length of each bone = 1 unit and IKTarget = (1,1)

A3 Implement the basic FABRIK algorithm for IK.

References

[1] "EmberGen." JangaFX, https://jangafx.com/software/embergen/ Accessed 2 Jul. 2024.
[2] "Morphology." Merriam-Webster.com Dictionary, Merriam-Webster, https://www.merriam-webster.com/dictionary/morphology. Accessed 2 Jul. 2024.

[3] "Morph." Merriam-Webster.com Dictionary, Merriam-Webster, https://www.merriam-webster.com/dictionary/morph. Accessed 2 Jul. 2024.
[4] Cameron J. The terminator 2: judgement day. Carolco Pictures; 1991.
[5] Zhang K, Zhou Y, Xu X, Dai B, Pan X. Proceedings of the IEEE/CVF conference on computer vision and pattern recognition (CVPR). 2024. p. 7912–21.
[6] Wu E, Zheng X. Composition of novel views through an efficient image warping. Vis Comput 2003;19:319–28. https://doi.org/10.1007/s00371-002-0183-x.
[7] Wolberg G. Image morphing: a survey. Vis Comput 1998;14(8–9):360–72.
[8] Michael Jackson - Black or White (1991) - First full photorealistic face morphing. Ultimate history of CGI. YouTube Channel; 2018. https://www.youtube.com/watch?v=n5b_nIzdvfI. [Accessed 2 July 2024].
[9] Michael Jackson - Black or White - CGI making of (1991). Ultimate history of CGI. YouTube Channel; 2019. https://www.youtube.com/watch?v=8CU5SVwzSzs&t=6s. [Accessed 2 July 2024].
[10] Beier T, Neely S. Feature-based image metamorphosis. Seminal Graphics Papers: Pushing the Boundaries 2023;2:529–36.
[11] Litwinowicz P, Williams L. Animating Images with Drawings. In: Glassner A, editor. Proceedings of SIG- GRAPH 94, Computer Graphics Proceedings, Annual Conference Series. Orlando, Fla.: ACM Press; July 1994. p. 409–12. ISBN 0-89791-667-0.
[12] Davis E, King. Dlib-ml: a machine learning toolkit. J Mach Learn Res 2009;10:1755–8. http://dlib.net/. [Accessed 2 July 2024].
[13] Bradski G. The OpenCV library. Dr. Dobb's J Softw Tools 2000. https://opencv.org/. [Accessed 2 July 2024].
[14] Blanz V, Vetter T. Face recognition based on fitting a 3D morphable model. In: IEEE transactions on pattern analysis and machine intelligence, 25(9); 2003. p. 1063–74. https://doi.org/10.1109/TPAMI.2003.1227983.
[15] Liao Z, Su Z, Dong L. Animatable 3D facial detail reconstruction from in-the-wild images. In: Proceedings of the 2024 7th international conference on image and graphics processing (ICIGP '24). New York, NY, USA: Association for Computing Machinery; 2024. p. 244–51. https://doi.org/10.1145/3647649.3647689.
[16] Loper M, Mahmood N, Romero J, Pons-Moll G, Black MJ. SMPL: a skinned multi-person linear model. In: Seminal graphics papers: pushing the boundaries. 1st ed., 2. New York, NY, USA: Association for Computing Machinery; 2023. p. 851–66. https://doi.org/10.1145/3596711.3596800. Article 88.
[17] Li T, et al. Learning a model of facial shape and expression from 4D scans. ACM Trans Graph 2017;36(6):194:1–194:17. https://doi.org/10.1145/3130800.3130813.
[18] Li R, et al. Learning formation of physically-based face attributes. arXiv [Cs.CV]. 2020. http://arxiv.org/abs/2004.03458. arXiv, https://github.com/ICT-VGL/ICT-FaceKit. [Accessed 2 July 2024].
[19] Pavlakos G, et al. Expressive body capture: 3D hands, face, and body from a single image. Proc IEEE Conf Comput Vis Pattern Recognit 2019:10975–85.
[20] Osman AAA, et al. STAR: a sparse trained articulated human body regressor. European conference on computer vision (ECCV). 2020. p. 598–613. https://star.is.tue.mpg.de.
[21] Osman AAA, et al. SUPR: a sparse unified part-based human body model. European conference on computer vision (ECCV). 2022. https://supr.is.tue.mpg.de.
[22] Hesse N, et al. Learning and tracking the 3D body shape of freely moving infants from RGB-D sequences. Trans Pattern Anal Mach Intell 2019.

[23] Zuffi S, et al. 3D menagerie: modeling the 3D shape and pose of animals. IEEE conf. On computer vision and pattern recognition (CVPR). 2017. https://smal.is.tue.mpg.de/.

[24] "Skeleton Dance.", Super Simple, Skyship Entertainment, https://supersimple.com/song/skeleton-dance/ Accessed 2 Jul. 2024.

[25] McIntosh T. Animation and player control in uncharted: drake's fortune and uncharted II: among thieves, game developers conference 2010 (GDC). San Francisco, USA; 2010. March 9–13 Available at, https://gdcvault.com/play/1012300/Animation-and-Player-Control-in. [Accessed 2 July 2024].

[26] Craig J. Introduction to Robotics Mechanics and Control. New York: Addison-Wesley; 1989.

[27] Aristidou A, Lasenby J. FABRIK: a fast, iterative solver for the Inverse Kinematics problem. Graph Models 2011;73(5):243–60.

[28] Aristidou A, Chrysanthou Y, Lasenby J. Extending FABRIK with model constraints. Comp Anim Virtual Worlds 2016;27:35–57. https://doi.org/10.1002/cav.1630.

[29] Niu P, Han L, Huang Y, Yan L. Shape-controllable inverse kinematics of hyper-redundant robots based on the improved FABRIK method. Robotica 2024;42(1): 225–41. https://doi.org/10.1017/S0263574723001455.

CHAPTER

Acquiring animation data

8

8.1 Animation authoring tools

A multitude of animation authoring tools exist for 2D and 3D animation that are widely used by professionals and hobbyists (Table 8.1).

8.2 Overview of motion capture technologies

Motion capture (also known as mocap) is a standard technique to capture, or digitize, motion to map it onto a graphical object. Most often, it is used to map human-like motion onto a synthetic figure. The common technology used in mocap is overviewed, focusing on the most common technology, passive optical systems. The

Table 8.1 Animation Authoring Tools

Software	Cost	2D	3D	Rig	Type
Spine [2]	$	X	—	X	Character
Moho Pro [3]	$	X	—	—	X
Cartoon Animator [4]	$	X	—	X	X
After Effects [5]	$	X	—	X	VFX
Toon Boom [6]	$	X	—	—	X
Open Toonz [7]	Free	X	—	—	X
Dragon Bones [8]	Free	X	—	X	X
Blender [9]	Free	X	X	X	X
Maya [10]	$	X	X	X	X
3DS Max [11]	$	X	X	X	X
MotionBuilder [12]	$	—	X	X	Character
Cinema 4D [13]	$	X	X	—	X
LightWave 3D [14]	$	X	X	X	X
Houdini [15]	$	—	X	—	Procedural
EmberGen [16]	$	—	X	—	VFX
iClone [17]	$	—	X	X	Character

Computer Animation. https://doi.org/10.1016/B978-0-443-13512-5.00008-2

processing pipeline of mocap data is reviewed including reconstruction of joint position and dealing with drop-outs. Also presented are some of the postprocessing techniques that can be applied to the mocap data to make it more useful.

The goal of motion capture is to accurately acquire (record) movement data (i.e., joint rotations) of a physical subject such that the data can be transferred easily to another digital character.

The subject whose motion is to be captured (sometimes referred to as the *talent*) is usually instrumented in some way so that positions of key feature points can be easily detected and recorded.

Historically, there have been a number of approaches for motion capture technologies with the most popular being a combination of *electromagnetic sensors, inertial sensors,* and *optical (camera-based)* approaches using visible markers.

8.2.1 Mechanical tracking systems

Mechanical tracking systems are those that place sensors on the subject that measure the relative or absolute rotation of two bones connected at a joint. By placing a sensor at each joint, accurately measuring the bone lengths and offsets, and knowing the kinematic structure of the rig, the joint transformations can be recorded. Using the known rig structure and forward kinematics, the absolute joint transformations can be computed.

How it works: the technology

Digital rotary encoders are used to measure the angle of a shaft as it rotates. These encoders can be either optical (photodiode used to measure black/white transitions of either an LED that is obstructed or not or a black/white known pattern), mechanical (potentiometers change resistance as it rotates, or similar to a brushed motor contact is made with sensors at specific locations as the shaft rotates), or using Hall effect magnetic sensors. Either way, the encoders provide a measurement of how much the shaft has rotated. From a joint-kinematics perspective, this is a direct measurement of a 1D joint rotation angle.

Major players

Puppetworks (1995) created their puppet digital stop-motion armature (1997) and subsequently a full Body Tracker (1998, [18]), which used rotary encoders and fixed bone lengths that had to be meticulously precalibrated and was prone to breakage.

Another notable mechanical motion capture suit comes from Analogus (1994), who released their Gypsy (1997) suit line. Version 2 (1998), Gypsy 2.5 by Meta Motion (2000), incorporating IMUs in the Gypsy Gyro-18 (2004) and Gypsy 4 (2004) [19], and finally their last product Gypsy 7 (2010) (distributed by MotionWerx). These suits were less cumbersome than the Puppetworks system; however, they still limited movement of the performer and ultimately lost out to inexpensive optical systems that didn't have these issues.

Advantages

The kinematic structure provided fast measurements with very low-latency and they mimicked the structure of the tracked skeletal rig. Plus, they looked super cool! :)

Drawbacks/issues

The need to wear a specialized suit with an exoskeleton limited the range of motion, was cumbersome to wear, and required meticulous setup and calibration before use.

8.2.2 Ultrasonic/acoustic tracking systems

Ultrasonic, or acoustic, tracking systems rely on the use of small speakers that emit an ultrasonic "chirp" and a microphone listening for that chirp to track the 6 degrees of freedom (6-DOF) pose of an object.

How it works: the technology

Given a speaker and a receiver (microphone) and a chirp emitted at time t, the receiver will sense this signal at $t + \Delta t$ (a delay of Δt). Because $\text{SPEED} = \frac{\text{DISTANCE}}{\text{TIME}}$ and we know the speed of sound in air, we can compute the distance traveled as $\text{DISTANCE} = \text{SPEED}_{\text{sound}} \times \Delta t$. Thus if we measure the time we emit and receive the chirp accurately, we can estimate the distance between source and receiver. This is called the *time-of-flight* approach to directly estimate the distance. Now, by placing three receivers with known offset from each other, we can estimate three different distances to the same signal, enabling us to triangulate the position by solving for the intersection of three spheres with radii set to the estimated distances.

Major players

Probably the first consumer-level motion controller was the Mattel Power Glove (1989), which used acoustic sensors to measure the distance between the television and the player to trigger button events such as "punching" when the player punched. The Deering prototype (1992) [20] for virtual reality used acoustic sensors to track a person's head and controller in front of a PC.

Probably one of the most successful commercial versions of the acoustic tracking systems were from Intersense (1996) with their Constellation (1998), and IS-900 (IMU + acoustic) products that incorporated IMUs for fast motion and acoustic trackers to correct for error and provide absolute positioning.

Advantages

Acoustic sensors and receivers are very low cost and can provide quite high accuracy. They also work in the presence of dust, fog, and smoke, as well as in the dark, which is difficult for some optical systems.

Drawbacks/issues

Acoustic sensors require filtering in situations where there are high frequencies in the environment (e.g., jingling keys) as they increase the noise in the signal. Also, echoes must be eliminated/reduced and the products can become quite bulky to wear. They have a low update rate (10–25 Hz) and a limited tracking range.

8.2.3 Electromagnetic tracking systems

Electromagnetic (EM) tracking (also called *magnetic tracking*) uses sensors that measure characteristics of the local magnetic field along each axis enabling accurate estimation of the 6-DOF pose of each sensor. By placing a sensor at each joint (and calibrating/measuring bone lengths), the entire forward kinematics can be recorded while the subject is performing [21].

How it works: the technology

Placing a coil of wire into the vicinity of a magnetic field will induce a current in the wire whose strength is determined by the distance from the magnetic field source. By arranging three coils perpendicular to each other (to form a coordinate frame), both the absolute position and orientation of the sensor can be estimated by solving a system of equations.

Major players

Historically, the main players in the EM tracking space were Polhemus (1988) [22] and Ascension (1986) [23]. Polhemus introduced their AC Fastrak (1994) system and more recently their VIPER (2020) system; these require cabling and they did not produce a wireless version but were popular in the virtual reality research space. Ascension (1986) introduced their DC field system, the Flock of Birds (1991), and their full-body MotionStar (1995) system, which provided a wireless option in 1997. NDI (Northern Digital, 1981) [24] spun out of the University of Waterloo and focused on medical tracking applications for training introducing their Polaris (1996) and Aurora (2003) in this space. In the consumer level market, Sixense Entertainment (2007) [25] worked with Razer to produce the Hydra (2011) 6-DOF gaming controller following it up with the STEM system (2013) as a Kickstarter.

Rokoko (2014) [26] has recently begun offering the Coil Pro (2023) as an EM base emitter that works with their IMU motion capture suits to increase accuracy and provide an absolute frame of reference.

Advantages

The 6-DOF pose of each sensor can be recorded and displayed in real time (with predictable latency).

Drawbacks/issues

Magnetic tracking systems require an environment devoid of magnetic field distortions, Ascension's trackers used DC fields, which were sensitive to ferrous materials (but not aluminum), whereas Polhemus used AC fields, which were less sensitive to ferrous materials but had issues with aluminum, copper, and carbon steel. These sensitivities would cause eddy currents and noise in the system limiting the range and accuracy in the presence of these materials.

Performers' movements were restricted due to the need to wear bulky sensors and specialized suits. Sensors required cables (requiring a cabling harness) or very low-latency wireless transmission (requiring a battery pack and bulky transmitter at the time) to send data to the central processor. The former requires that the subject be tethered with some kind of cabling harness.

8.2.4 Inertial systems

Inertial measurement units (IMUs) use a combination of sensors (accelerometers, gyroscopes) that measure physical properties of movement (acceleration and angular velocity) and state estimation algorithms (i.e., Kalman filters) to accurately estimate the 3-DOF/6-DOF pose of the sensor. These are usually coupled with a magnetic sensor to acquire absolute direction to magnetic north. These are commonly included in cell phones for use as video game controls, tilt sensors, and as input to 3D reconstruction and map applications for providing directions.

How it works: the technology

Accelerometers measure linear acceleration. As an object moves, it accelerates; thus we can measure its movement along each axis with an accelerometer because $\vec{p_t} = \vec{p_{t-1}} + \vec{v}\,dt + \frac{1}{2}\vec{a}\,dt^2$, and $\vec{v_t} = \vec{v_{t-1}} + \vec{a}\,dt$. Thus if we measure our linear acceleration, $\vec{a}$, we can compute our position/displacement! Unfortunately, there is error in each integral causing issues in a nonideal system (real systems). The issue is that we cannot disambiguate linear acceleration due to movement from gravity; sensors actually measure $\vec{a} = \vec{a}_{\text{movement}} + \vec{a}_{\text{gravity}}$. Because gravity is constant, we can subtract it in the world frame, but we must first know the orientation.

Gyroscopes measure angular velocity along an axis, if we have three gyros measuring the angular velocity of our frame, we can estimate our orientation accurately. If we measure our orientation with a quaternion, then $\hat{q}' = \hat{q} + \frac{1}{2}\hat{\omega}\hat{q}dt$, where $\hat{\omega}$ is our angular velocity pure quaternion. This can be used to rotate gravity into our accelerometer frame of reference to remove its influence improving our estimate of linear acceleration. Commonly, an extended Kalman filter (or indirect error Kalman filter) is used for sensor fusion and to estimate the 6-DOF pose. Recently, machine learning has been used to estimate the pose from a small subset of active IMU sensors in smartwatches and earbuds [27].

Major players

Intersense (1996) [28] was one of the first companies to create a commercially available IMU system. Their InertiaCube (2000), v2 (2002), v3, and v4 (2016) were geared toward the robotics, military, and medical fields, and more recently their NavChip 3 (2019) incorporates a system-on-chip IMU.

Nintendo [29] introduced the Wii (2006), which included a controller with three accelerometers (for relative motion) and an optical sensor (for absolute position). They subsequently introduced the Wii MotionPlus (2009) and Wii RemotePlus

(2010), which included three gyroscopes to measure angular velocity to increase orientation accuracy.

Rokoko (2014) [26] uses inertial measurement units in their motion capture suits, Smart Suit (2014) and recently Smartsuit 2 Pro (2022). These use only IMUs and clever software solutions to estimate full body pose in real time. Noitom (2012) [30] introduced the Perception Neuron (2012), 2 (2018), and 3 (2021), using IMUs for full-body motion capture.

Advantages

Inexpensive sensors are readily available as system-on-chip integrated circuits with high update rates (100 Hz+) and state estimation is a well-known and well-developed area in the aerospace and robotics industries (well-known solutions and software).

Drawbacks/issues

Relative sensing only, thus one must use external sensors to correct errors in the positional state since these errors accumulate quickly. These systems are usually coupled with magnetic sensors to correct absolute orientation error and gyroscope drift, as well as GPS for absolute positioning and are often coupled with cameras for absolute positioning in studios.

8.2.5 Optical systems

Optical systems use cameras in either "inside-out" (dynamic cameras placed on tracked object) or "outside-in" (static cameras looking at object to track) configurations. For animation, the common approach is the "outside-in" approach and the use of visible markers placed on the performer's joints/body. There is more detail on this in the next section.

How it works: the technology

The commonly known "outside-in" motion capture approach places many retroreflective markers on a subject and records their performance from a number of surrounding synchronized cameras. The cameras have a ring of LEDs surrounding the lens that emit infrared light into the scene, which is reflected back to the cameras due to the retroreflectors. The markers thus show up very brightly and can easily be found in the images. These image points are matched to a known rig configuration and triangulated using previously calibrated camera parameters (intrinsics and extrinsics), creating a set of 3D points. These points are then mapped to a skeletal rig and recorded.

Major players

The original motion-capture solution for the entertainment industry came from Vicon (1984) [31], who is still the leader in that space. They released Vicon 370E (1996), their first full-body camera system for entertainment, and more recently their complete system Valkyrie (2022) can combine cameras and inertial units. NaturalPoint (1997) [32] competes in the video game development motion-capture space with their OptiTrack product line, where you can mix and match cameras. Their software Arena (2007) and Motive v1 (2013), v2 (2017), and v3 (2021) are easy to use and can track multiple human performances simultaneously.

Advantages

The technology is highly accurate, well known, and multiple people can be tracked simultaneously, and large systems can be made to cover large studio areas. Animals, cameras, and lights (not just humans) can be tracked.

Drawbacks/issues

Large systems tend to be expensive, the cameras must be calibrated, and this calibration must be done often. Also, performers must wear special tight-fitting suits (although lightweight) and markers.

8.2.6 Markerless motion capture

Markerless motion capture systems use computer vision techniques to fit a skeletal rig to video without using special markers. The goal is to capture performers in a more natural state of performance in clothes that don't impede their performance and reduce the setup time before capture.

How it works: the technology

Markerless systems range in the actual technology and algorithms used. Some use many synchronized color cameras (Organic Motion, Captury) to estimate 3D locations of the performer and fit a skeleton to the data. Others (iPi Soft) use RGB-D (Kinect) cameras to capture 3D information directly to fit the skeleton, and more recent systems use machine learning (DeepMotion, Move.ai) and 3D morphable models (Meshcapade).

Major players

Organic Motion (2007–2013) [33] pioneered the first commercial markerless motion capture system. Their system was based around isolating a subject (background removal and masking) coupled with 3D volume intersection to reconstruct the subject in 3D, creating a reasonable 3D representation of the subject. They then fit a skeleton and track it at a high update rate to ensure accuracy. Although no longer available, this method spurred research and development into markerless motion capture. Since then, we have seen the Captury [34] partner with DARI (Dynamic Athletic Research Institute) [35] providing a markerless solution and iPi Soft [36] provide a solution using Microsoft Azure Kinect cameras or Sony PlayStation Eye Cameras. Recently, Qualisys released their Miqus Hybrid (2019) camera solution partnered with Theia for their tracking software, as did Vicon to provide a markerless option in their Vicon Nexus ecosystem (2023). Deep learning AI-based solutions that have emerged from Move.ai [37], Deep Motion [38], Plask.ai [39], and Rokoko Vision [40] are among the leaders in this space. Also, recently, the researchers who developed the SMPL 3D morphable human model have spun off a company Meshcapade [41] that uses SMPL-based models to accurately estimate both the body-type and capture motion from a single video. This is the first of its kind and is an exciting development. Much of the research on using deep learning for motion capture is based upon the open-source OpenPose [42] library that fits a human skeleton to video and works quite well in practice. Finally, EasyMocap [43] is an open source project aimed at providing tools for creating your own markerless motion capture system.

Advantages

Performers are not required to wear markers or a tight-fitting suit or any equipment that may restrict movement.

Drawbacks/issues

The accuracy of these systems is not as good as marker-based systems but good enough for animation purposes. The use of deep learning approaches are also limited by the range of available training data.

8.3 Traditional motion capture (optical) systems

When you think of motion capture, you think of actors in front of green screens wearing funny suits with dots or foam balls all over them (Figure 8.1). This is the hallmark of the traditional motion capture optical system. These systems rely on multiple calibrated cameras and tracked optical markers that are tracked,

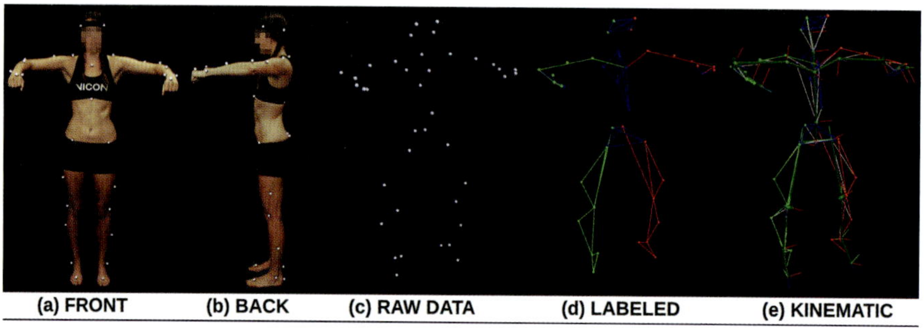

FIGURE 8.1

Images showing progression of optical motion capture session: (a) and (b) optical marker placement, (c) three-dimensional reconstruction positions of marker, (d) identified markers, (e) applied to skeleton.

(Images used courtesy of Vicon Motion systems (© Vicon Motion Systems Ltd UK registered no. 1801446, www.vicon.com).)

triangulated, and fit to a skeletal rig in real time, producing accurate joint rotations of the performer as they move. The optical approach is quite scalable as you can have as many cameras as you desire, which can help to increase the capture volume and/or improve accuracy. The infrastructure costs range from low cost (US $5000 to US $10,000) to extremely expensive (US $100k+) but result in turnkey solutions that are guaranteed to provide high-quality animation data.

Special markers are used to ensure that the cameras viewing the scene can easily (and quickly) estimate the subpixel location of a known location on the performer and can also be used to identify which location it corresponds to (e.g., whether this a shoulder marker or a head marker). Synchronized images are captured and processed to extract the centers of the marker locations, resulting in a set of 2D pixel locations of each visible marker in each camera. Using the camera calibration data, these 2D locations can be filtered (to get rid of noise and erroneous pixels) and matched (correspondence), and the 3D point is estimated using a linear least squares solver.

Because orientation information is not directly generated, more markers are required than with other tracking systems (EM or IMU based); luckily, the markers required for optical systems are made of lightweight foam! A combination (or clusters) of joint and midsegment markers and their ratios help disambiguate the matching process.

8.3.1 Motion capture infrastructure

Traditional motion capture systems require a sophisticated combination of hardware and software. In terms of hardware, systems generally require:

- Cameras and lenses that have a wide variety of resolutions, framerates, and fields of view
- Camera mounts (swivel-ball heads for accurate positioning)
- Tripods (or a truss) to mount the cameras
- A high-end PC
- Cables to connect and power the cameras
- Synchronization equipment to ensure all cameras capture the same moment in time
- Power-over-ethernet switches to power the cameras
- Calibration tools such as a known wand or coordinate frame
- A number of suits of different sizes for various performers
- Sets of markers, which are considered consumables as they break or can be lost easily

8.3.2 Markers

Passive markers do not emit light or require a power source as they are not controlled electronically. Examples of passive markers are retroreflective foam balls and fiducial markers.

Active markers emit some form of signal or light into the scene to aid in finding and identifying them. These are not very popular in the animation space as they increase cost and require cabling but are popular in the medical field for super high-resolution tracking at very high framerates. An example of an active marker system is NDI's Optotrack Certus, which used strobed LEDs as markers allowing them to both find and identify the marker at a high spatial and temporal resolution.

Commonly, markers are in the form of small foam balls coated with a retroreflective paint attached to the performers' joints and limbs. Cameras containing an infrared blaster ring around the sensor emits infrared light into the scene. Due to the nature of the retroreflective paint, the light is bounced directly back to the camera that emitted it, increasing the brightness of the marker pixels. This makes it easier to find all of the markers in the images as the sensor exposure can be controlled to reduce interference and a simple threshold can be applied to each pixel resulting in a black image with only the markers present. This requires specialized camera equipment and the emission of extra energy (infrared light) into the scene. Sometimes this is not desirable; for instance, if you are filming a movie on location, it would be expensive and challenging to set up a complete motion capture system in the field. In these situations, the actor can wear a suit with markers that can be found using a combination of color, contrast, and shape. For example, high-contrast circles (black circle on white square, white circle on black square) can be easily found with simple well-known computer vision techniques in color video. These are typically called fiducial markers [44] and can encode marker IDs using binary coding schemes.

8.3.3 Processing the images

The objective of motion capture is to reconstruct the 3D motion of a physical subject and apply it to a digital model. With optical systems, three major tasks need to be undertaken. First, the 2D images must be processed to locate, identify, and correlate the markers in multiple synchronized video streams. Second, the 3D locations of the markers need to be reconstructed from their two-dimensional locations. Third, the 3D marker locations must be constrained to a model of the physical system whose motion is being captured (e.g., a triangulated surface model of the performer). The first requires some basic image-processing techniques, simple logic, usually some user input, and sometimes a bit of luck. The second requires camera calibration and enough care to overcome numerical inaccuracies. The third requires satisfying constraints between relative marker positions.

Optical markers are attached to the performer using Velcro strips or some other suitable method. The markers are usually positioned close to joints because these are the structures of interest in animating a figure. The difference between the position of the marker and that of the joint is one source of error in motion capture systems. This is further complicated if the marker moves relative to the joint during the motion of the figure. The background can be removed to simplify the processing. Finding the position of a single marker in a video frame in which the marker is visible is the easy part, as you can preset the exposure of the camera to a high value to ensure only the markers are visible (as they are bright due to the infrared reflections) and any pixels below some threshold can be safely discarded. Modern cameras used can perform this onboard with specialized integrated circuits (ICs) at the high framerates needed to capture fast movements. Once all of the visible markers have been extracted, each individual marker must be tracked over the video sequence. Sometimes this can be done with simple domain knowledge. For example, if the motion is constrained to be normal walking, then the ankle markers (or foot markers, if present) can be assumed to always be the lowest markers, and they can be assumed to always be within some small distance from the bottom of the image. Frame-to-frame coherence can be employed to track markers by making use of the position of a marker in a previous frame and knowing something about the limits of its velocity and acceleration. For example, knowing that the markers are on a walking figure and knowing something about the camera position relative to the figure, one can estimate the maximum number of pixels that a marker might travel from one frame to the next and thus help track it over time.

Unfortunately, one of the realities of optical motion capture systems is that periodically one or more of the markers are occluded or misidentified. In situations in which several markers are used, this can cause problems in successfully tracking a marker throughout the sequence. Some simple heuristics can be used to track markers that drop from view for a few frames and that do not change their velocity much over that time. But these heuristics are not foolproof (and this is, of course, why they are called heuristics). The result of failed heuristics can be markers swapping paths in midsequence or the introduction of a new marker when, in fact, a marker is simply reappearing again. Marker swapping can happen even when markers are not occluded. If markers pass within a small distance of each other, they may swap paths because of numerical inaccuracies of the system. Sometimes these problems can be resolved when the three-dimensional positions of markers are constructed. At other times, user intervention is required to resolve ambiguous cases. See Figure 8.1 for an example of mocap data processing.

A constant problem with motion capture systems is noise. Noise can arise from the physical system; for example, metallic objects can reflect the infrared light causing spurious pixels, or markers can move on the performer's body during the performance. Noise also arises from the sampling process; the markers are sampled in time and space, and errors can be introduced in all dimensions. A typical error might result in inaccurate positioning of a feature point by half a centimeter. For some animations, this can be a significant error.

To deal with the noise, the user can condition the data before they are used in the reconstruction process. Data points that are radically inconsistent with typical values can be thrown out, and the rest can be filtered. The objective is to smooth the data without removing any useful features. A simple weighted average of adjacent values can be used to smooth the curve. The number of adjacent values to use and their weights are functions of the desired smoothness. Generally, this must be selected by the user.

8.3.4 Camera calibration

Before the three-dimensional position of a marker can be reconstructed, it is necessary to know the locations and orientations of cameras in world space and the intrinsic properties of the cameras such as focal length, image center, and aspect ratio [45].

A simple pinhole camera model is used for the calibration. This is an idealized model that does not accurately represent certain optical effects often present in real cameras, but it is usually sufficient for computer graphics and image-processing applications. The pinhole model defines the basic projective geometry used to describe the imaging of a point in three-space. For example, the camera's coordinate system is defined with the origin at the center of projection and the plane of projection at a focal-length distance along the positive z-axis, which is pointed toward the camera's center of interest (Figure 8.2). Equivalently, the projection plane could be a focal length along the negative z-axis on the other side of the center of projection from the center of interest; this would produce an inverted image, but the mathematics would be the same.

The image of a point is formed by projecting a ray from the point to the center of projection (Figure 8.3). The image of the point is formed on the image (projection) plane where this ray intersects the plane. The equations for this point, as should be familiar to the reader, are formed by similar triangles. Camera calibration is performed by recording a number of image space points whose world space locations are known. These pairs can be used to create an overdetermined set of linear equations that can be solved using a least-squares solution method. This is only the most basic computation needed to fully calibrate a camera with respect to its intrinsic

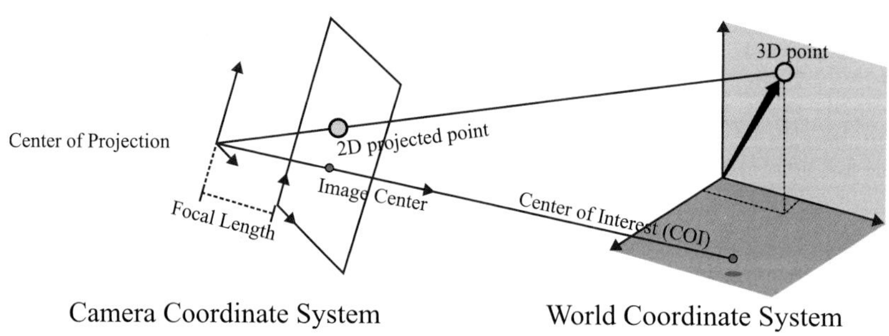

FIGURE 8.2

Camera model.

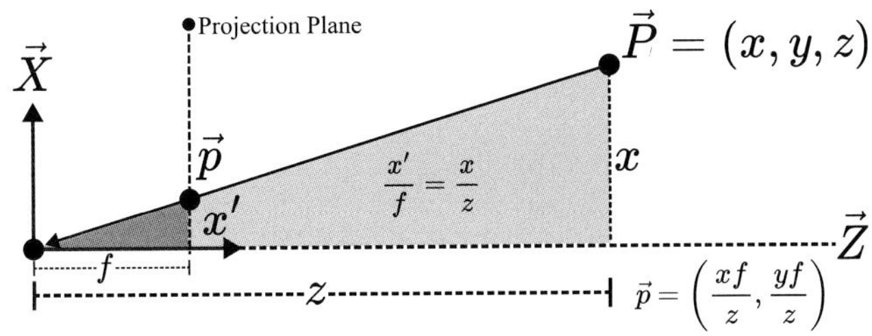

FIGURE 8.3

Y-Z projection of a world space point onto the image plane in the camera coordinate system.

properties and its environment. In the most general case, there are nonlinearities in the lens, focal length, camera tilt, and other parameters that need to be determined.

8.3.5 Three-dimensional position reconstruction

To reconstruct the three-dimensional coordinates of a marker, the user must locate its position in at least two views relative to known camera positions, $\vec{\mathbf{C}}_1$ and $\vec{\mathbf{C}}_2$. In the simplest case, this requires two cameras to be set up to record marker positions (Figure 8.4). The greater the orthogonality of the two views, the better the chance for an accurate reconstruction.

If the position and orientation of each camera are known with respect to the global coordinate system, along with the position of the image plane relative to the camera, then the images of the point to be reconstructed ($\vec{\mathbf{I}}_1$ and $\vec{\mathbf{I}}_2$) can be used to locate the point, $\vec{P}$, in three-space (Figure 8.4). Using the location of a

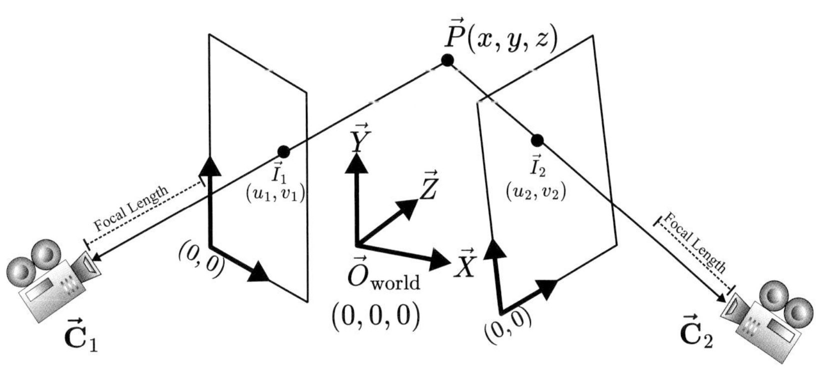

FIGURE 8.4

Two-camera view of a point.

camera, the relative location of the image plane, and a given pixel location on the image plane, the user can compute the position of that pixel in world coordinates. Once that is known, a vector from the camera through the pixel can be constructed in world space for each camera (Equations 8.1 and 8.2).

$$\vec{\mathbf{C}}_1 + k_1\left(\vec{\mathbf{I}}_1 - \vec{\mathbf{C}}_1\right) = P \tag{8.1}$$

$$\vec{\mathbf{C}}_2 + k_2\left(\vec{\mathbf{I}}_2 - \vec{\mathbf{C}}_2\right) = P \tag{8.2}$$

By setting these equations equal to each other:

$$\vec{\mathbf{C}}_1 + k_1\left(\vec{\mathbf{I}}_1 - \vec{\mathbf{C}}_1\right) = \vec{\mathbf{C}}_2 + k_2\left(\vec{\mathbf{I}}_2 - \vec{\mathbf{C}}_2\right)$$

we can see this represents three equations with two unknowns, k_1 and k_2, which can be easily solved—in an ideal world. Noise tends to complicate the ideal world. In practice, these two equations will not exactly intersect, although if the noise in the system is not excessive, they will come close. So, in practice, the points of closest encounter must be found on each line. This requires that a $\overrightarrow{P_1}$ and a $\overrightarrow{P_2}$ be found such that $\vec{P_r}$ is on the line from Camera 1, $\overrightarrow{P_1}$ is on the line from Camera 2, and $\vec{P_2}\vec{P_1}$ is perpendicular to each of the two lines (Equations 8.3 and 8.4).

$$\left(\vec{P}_2 - \vec{P}_1\right) \cdot \left(\vec{\mathbf{I}}_1 - \vec{\mathbf{C}}_1\right) = 0 \tag{8.3}$$

$$\left(\vec{P}_2 - \vec{P}_1\right) \cdot \left(\vec{\mathbf{I}}_2 - \vec{\mathbf{C}}_2\right) = 0 \tag{8.4}$$

Solving for $\vec{P_1}$ and a $\vec{P_2}$ can be done using a least squares approach. Once the points $\vec{P_1}$ and a $\vec{P_2}$ have been calculated, the midpoint of the chord between the two points can be used as the location of the reconstructed point. In the case of multiple markers in which marker identification and tracking have not been fully established for all of the markers in all of the images, the distance between $\vec{P_1}$ and a $\vec{P_2}$ can be used as a test for correlation between $\vec{\mathbf{I}}_1$ and $\vec{\mathbf{I}}_2$. If the distance between $\vec{P_1}$ and a $\vec{P_2}$ is too great, then this indicates that $\vec{\mathbf{I}}_1$ and $\vec{\mathbf{I}}_2$ are probably not images of the same marker and a different pairing needs to be tried. Smoothing can also be performed on the reconstructed three-dimensional paths of the markers to further reduce the effects of noise on the system.

Multiple markers

The number and positioning of markers on a human figure depend on the intended use of the captured motion and the software system required. In the OptiTrack system, their standard base skeleton rig required 41 markers. Some of these are "joint" markers placed along the joint rotational axis of each joint and others are "segment"

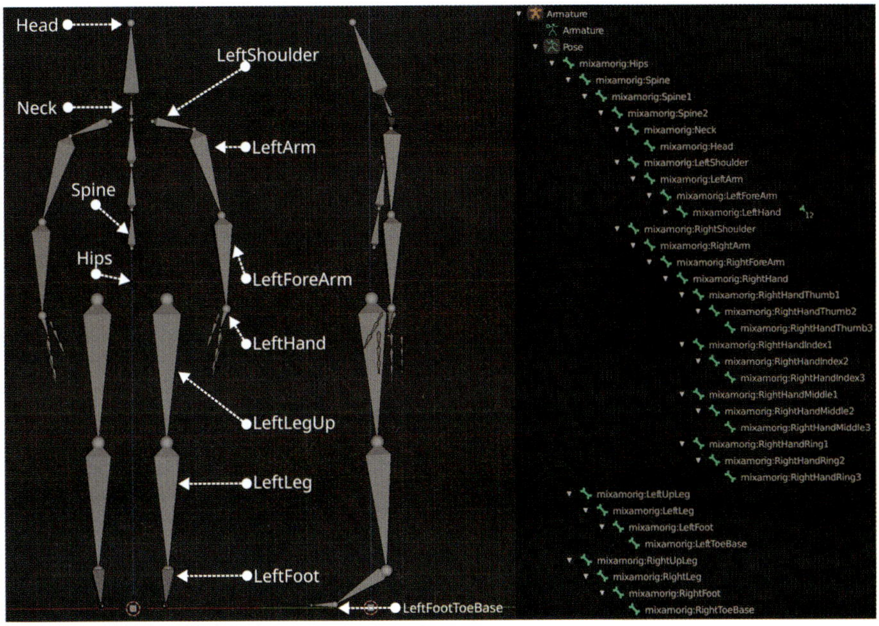

FIGURE 8.5

Complete optical marker set [6].

markers placed on the bone segments between joints. To reduce symmetry, some segment markers are placed closer to one joint than the other to disambiguate between left and right limbs. Three markers in a triangle formation are used for each joint to form either a coordinate system or planar patch. More markers can be used to increase accuracy and enable higher detail (e.g., fingers/face) with specialized processing (Figure 8.5). Menache [1] suggests an addition of three per foot for some applications. Also refer back to Figure 8.1, which shows a sample marker set on mocap talent.

Multiple cameras

As the number of markers increases and the complexity of the motion becomes more involved, there is greater chance for marker occlusion. To reconstruct the three-dimensional position of a marker, the system must detect and identify the marker in at least two images. As a result, a typical system may have eight cameras simultaneously taking images.

8.3.6 Fitting to the skeleton

Once the motion of the individual markers looks smooth and reasonable, they are attached to the underlying skeletal rig structure. The position of each marker in each frame is used to absolutely position a specific joint of the skeleton. As a first approximation to controlling the motion of the skeleton, this works fine. However, on closer inspection, problems often exist. The problem with using the markers to directly specify position is that, due to noise, smoothing, and other inaccuracies, distances between joints of the skeleton will not be precisely maintained over time. This change in bone length can be significant. Length changes of 10% to 20% are common. In many cases, this is not acceptable. For example, this can cause *foot-sliding* of the skeleton (also known as *skating*). Inverse kinematics used to lock the foot to the ground can counteract this skating.

One source of the problem is that the markers are located not at the joints of the performers but outside the joints at the surface. This means that the point being digitized is displaced from the joint itself. Although a constant distance is maintained on the performer, for example between the knee joint and the hip joint, it is not the case that a constant distance is maintained between a point to the side of the knee joint and a point to the side of the hip joint.

The one obvious correction that can be made is logically relocating the digitized positions so that they correspond more accurately to the positions of the joints. This can be done by using marker information to calculate the joint position. The distance from the marker to the actual joint can be determined easily by visual inspection. However, the problem with locating the joint relative to a marker is that there is no orientation information directly associated with the marker. This means that, given a marker location and the relative distance from the marker to the joint, the user does not know in which direction to apply the displacement to locate the joint.

One solution is to put markers on both sides of the joint. With two marker locations, the joint can be interpolated as the midpoint of the chord between the two markers. Although effective for joints that lend themselves to this approach, the approach does not work for joints that are complex or more inaccessible (e.g., hip, shoulder, spine), and it doubles the number of markers that must be processed.

A little geometry can be used to calculate the displacement of the joint from the marker. A plane formed by three markers can be used to calculate a normal to a plane of three consecutive joints, and this normal can be used to displace the joint location. Consider the elbow. If there are two markers at the wrist (commonly used to digitize the forearm rotation), the position of the true wrist can be interpolated between them. Then the wrist-elbow-shoulder markers can be used to calculate a normal to the plane formed by those markers. Then the true elbow position is calculated by offsetting from the elbow marker in the direction of the normal by the amount measured from the performer. By recalculating the normal every frame, the user can easily maintain an accurate elbow position throughout the performance. In most cases, this technique is very effective. A problem with the technique is that when the arm straightens out, the wrist-elbow-shoulder becomes (nearly) collinear. Usually, the normal can be interpolated during these periods of congruence from accurately computed normals on either side of the interval. This approach keeps limb lengths much closer to being constant.

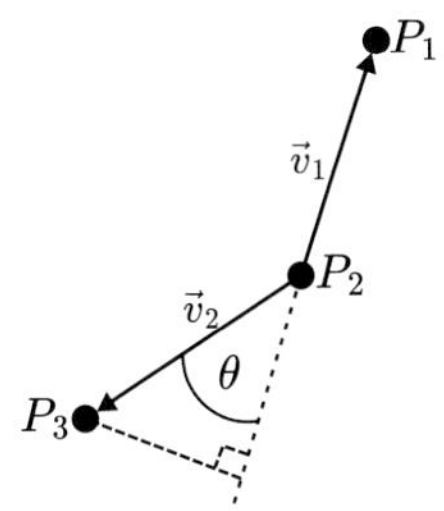

$$\vec{v}_1 = P_1 - P_2$$
$$\vec{v}_2 = P_3 - P_2$$
$$\vec{v}_1 \cdot \vec{v}_2 = ||\vec{v}_1||||\vec{v}_2|| \cos(\theta)$$
$$\cos(\theta) = \frac{\vec{v}_1 \cdot \vec{v}_2}{||\vec{v}_1||||\vec{v}_2||}$$
$$\theta = \cos^{-1}\left(\frac{\vec{v}_1 \cdot \vec{v}_2}{||\vec{v}_1||||\vec{v}_2||}\right)$$

FIGURE 8.6

One-degree-of-freedom rotational joint.

Now that the joint positions are more consistent with the skeleton to be articulated, they can be used to control the skeleton. To avoid absolute positioning in space and further limb-length changes, one typically uses the digitized positions to calculate joint rotations. For example, in a skeletal hierarchy, if the positions of three consecutive joints have been recorded for a specific frame, then a third of the points in the hierarchy is used to calculate the rotation of that limb relative to the limb represented by the first two points (Figure 8.6).

After posing the model using the calculated joint angles, it might still be the case that, because of inaccuracies, feature points of the model violate certain constraints such as avoiding floor penetration. The potential for problems is particularly high for end effectors, such as the hands or feet, which must be precisely positioned. Often, these must be independently positioned, and then the joints higher up the hierarchy (e.g., knee, hip) must be adjusted to compensate for any change to the end effector position.

8.3.7 Output from motion capture systems

As the previous discussion has outlined, there is a lot of processing that must be done to convert the raw video data from the cameras to joint angles for a figure. Fortunately, motion capture software is available to enable the user to set up the marker set hierarchy, calibrate cameras, and automate as much of the marker processing as possible, as well as provide interactive tools when user input is required to resolve ambiguities. The result can be used to animate a figure or be saved to a file for later use.

Various de facto standard file formats exist for motion capture data. Among the commonly used formats are simple CSV (comma-separated values), FBX (Autodesk format), and BVH (Biovision Hierarchy). Although the various formats differ in their specifics, they all have the same basic information: the static information describing the joint hierarchy and the time-varying information containing the values for each DOF for each joint.

The joint hierarchy is described by (1) defining the joints including the number and type of each DOF, the order that DOF parameters are given, optional joint limits, and (2) defining the hierarchical connectivity including the location of the joint relative to the previous joint.

```
Example BVH File:

HIERARCHY

ROOT J-NAME0

{

 OFFSET 0.000000 0.000000 0.000000

 CHANNELS 6 Xposition Yposition Zposition Zrotation Xrotation Yrotation

 JOINT J-NAME1

 {

      OFFSET 0.000000 8.000000 0.000000

      CHANNELS 3 Zrotation Xrotation Yrotation

      JOINT J-NAME2

      {

       ...

      }

MOTION

Frames: 31

Frame Time: 0.033333

22.126386 9.974766 -1.473736 ...
```

In this simplified example, joint names are just for user identification, the indentation indicates child-parent relationships, the offset is the location of the current joint relative to its parent, and the DOF line indicates the number of DOFs for that joint and the order they appear in the data. Optionally, joint limits can be specified.

The time-varying data records the reconstructed joint angles over some number of frames. In the preceding example, there are 31 frames in the file, the length of each frame in seconds and the actual motion data. Each line of motion data is a single sample in time of the entire hierarchy specified. The number of values on a line corresponds to the total DOFs of the figure, and they are given in the order they appear in the hierarchy information; for example, it would be specified as the values of each joint as it is read in order as:

J0.x J0.y J0.z J0.xR J0.yR J0.zR J1.xR J1.yR J1.zR J2....

Processing the signals

The values of an individual parameter of the captured motion (e.g., a joint angle) can be thought of, and dealt with, as a time-varying signal. The signal can be decomposed into frequencies, time-warped, interpolated with other signals, and so forth. The challenge for the animator in using these techniques is in understanding that, although the original signal represents physically correct motion, there is nothing to guarantee physical correctness once the signal has been modified.

Motion signal processing considers how frequency components capture various qualities of the motion [46]. The lower frequencies of the signal are considered to represent the base activity (e.g., walking) while the higher frequencies are the idiosyncratic movements of the specific individual (e.g., walking with a limp). Frequency bands can be extracted, manipulated, and reassembled to allow the user to modify certain qualities of the signal while leaving others undisturbed. To do this, the signal is successively convolved with expanded versions of a filter kernel (e.g., 1/16, 1/4, 3/8, 1/4, 1/16). The frequency bands are generated by differencing the convolutions. Gains of each band are adjusted by the user and can be summed to reconstruct a motion signal.

Motion warping warps the signal to satisfy user-supplied keyframe—like constraints [47]. The original signal is $\theta(t)$ and the keyframes are given as a set of (θ_i, t_i) pairs. In addition, there is a set of time warp constraints $\left(t_j, t_j'\right)$. The warping procedure first creates a time warp mapping $t = g(t')$ by interpolating through the time warp constraints and then creates a motion curve warping, $\theta(t) = f(\theta, t)$. This function is created by scaling and/or translating the original curve to satisfy the keyframe constraints, $\theta'(t) = a(t)\theta(t) + b(t)$; whether to scale or translate can be user-specified. Once the functions $a(t)$ and $b(t)$ for the keyframes are set, the functions $a(t)$ and $b(t)$ can be interpolated throughout the time span of interest. Combined, these functions establish a function $\theta(t')$ that satisfies the keyframe and time warp constraints by warping the original function.

Retargeting the motion

What happens if the synthetic character doesn't match the dimensions (e.g., limb length) of the captured subject? Does the motion have to be recaptured with a new subject that does match the synthetic figure better? Or does the synthetic figure have to be redesigned to match the dimensions of the captured subject? One solution is to map the motion onto the mismatched synthetic character and then modify it to satisfy important constraints.

This is referred to as *motion retargeting* [48]. Important constraints include such things as avoiding foot penetration of the floor, avoiding self-penetration, not letting feet slide on the floor when walking, and so forth. A new motion is constructed, as close to the original motion as possible, while enforcing the constraints. Finding the new motion is formulated as a space-time, nonlinear constrained optimization problem. This technique is beyond the scope of this book, and the interested reader is encouraged to consult the work by Michael Gleicher (e.g., [48]).

8.3.8 Animation clips and blending

The result from the motion capture process is a series of animation clips. Each clip is composed of a duration (time), the number of frames recorded, a sequence of transformations per joint per frame, and some metadata determining its name and looping parameters. For film, this may be the endpoint where we can take these clips into our animation software, apply the clip to our rigged character, and render out our scene. Video games use motion capture differently to animate their characters. Game characters are controlled by either the system or the user, and there are many potential actions and animations that can occur in an interactive environment.

Consider the main player character in a 3D game such as Naughty Dog's *Uncharted* game series. The playable character must behave in a way that they look "alive" when not being interacted with but also transition to a given action when the player presses a button. Imagine that each clip represents a particular action such as "Jump," "Run," or "Idle." We could easily assign a unique motion capture clip to each of these states and design a finite state machine (FSM) to control the character.

Clip transitions

The main issue with the naive FSM approach is that there are potential sharp jumps, irregularities, or artifacts when a player presses a button before an animation clip has completed. In Figure 8.7(a), the Walk clip completes before entering the Run animation state. If these frames are close enough (which can be authored by the animator), the jump between them may not be noticed. However, in Figure 8.7(b) the player presses the button that changes to the Run state immediately. Rather than switching

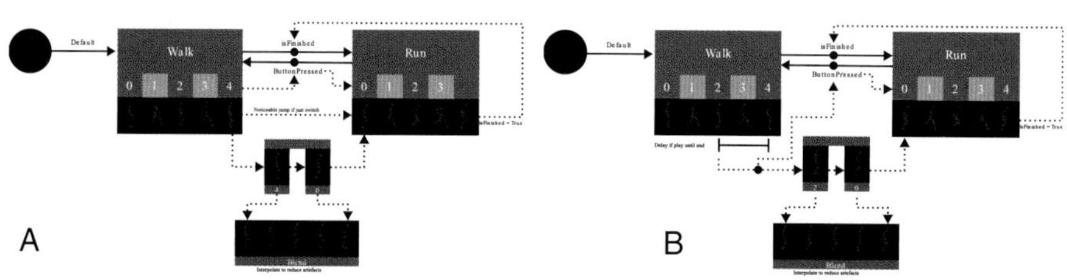

FIGURE 8.7

Animation clip transitions and blending. (a) Walk to Run, a visual jump appears if animation frames are suddenly switched between Walk frame 4 (end) and Run frame 0 (start). Can be alleviated by careful authoring or Blending *(bottom)*. (b) Walk to Run interrupted by button press. If you continue to play to the end, you incur a delay, causing latency; it is better to blend directly from Walk frame 2 to Run frame 0 (start).

from the preauthored frame to the start frame of the new clip, there is a noticeable difference between the poses in frame 2 (Walk) and frame 0 (Run). To remedy this, one could imagine just running the Walk animation until frame 4 (Walk) before changing states, however this incurs a multiframe penalty causing potentially noticeable latency. One could also blend between source and target frames over a transition period, which can be authored and tested to balance responsiveness versus smoothness.

Layers, masks, and blend-trees

Most animation packages enable you to combine multiple animation clips through a combination of layering, blending, and joint masking. This allows you to reuse animation clips to create completely new animations that are not explicitly authored. For example, imagine you have a character where you have authored an Idle animation clip, a Walk animation clip, and an "Aiming" clip relative to the idle pose; you can combine these three existing animations to create a new animation on the fly that incorporates the Aiming and Walk clips.

For our purposes, a single pose is simply a list of joint transformations to be applied during forward kinematics. Combining two poses requires that we interpolate each joint (Figure 8.8), $\mathbf{J}_j$, appropriately by an interpolation parameter (weight, w_j), which can easily be performed with quaternions using spherical linear interpolation (SLERP).

Each animation clip contains a series of poses (keyframes, Figure 8.9). For any time t, we can sample a clip on the global timeline by interpolating between each keyframe for the given normalized time between samples (t_n).

For each frame, we can query the animation system to provide us with a complete pose for our character. The final pose can be computed using a single animation clip (sampled as above) or by sampling multiple clips and interpolating based on a set of blend weights (Figure 8.10).

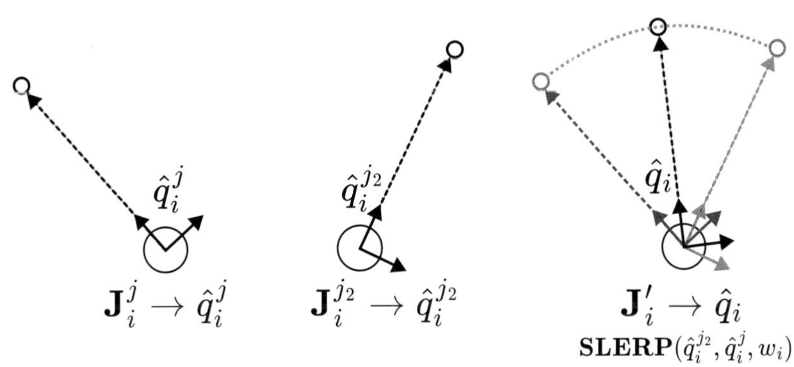

FIGURE 8.8

Example of two joints with different pose quaternions *(left, middle)*. The *right* image shows spherical linear interpolation (SLERP) of these joints with parameter *w*.

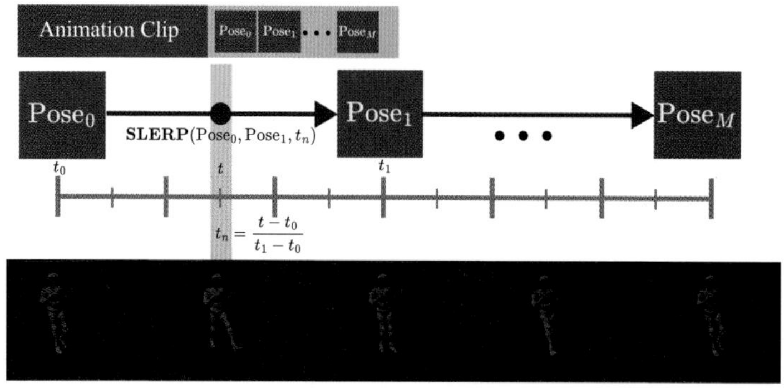

FIGURE 8.9

Animation clips contain a list of poses, and each pose is a list of joint transformations of a rig. Poses can occur at any animation time frame and should be "sampled" with interpolation between poses for smoothness.

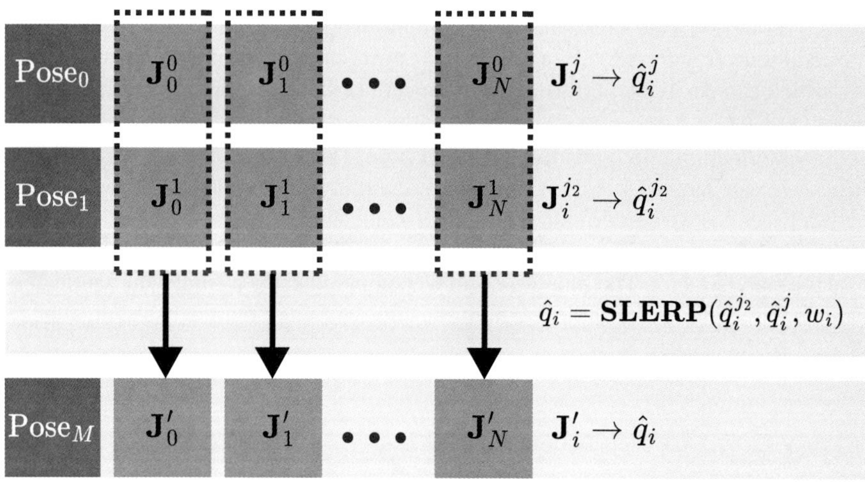

FIGURE 8.10

Combining two poses (Pose_0 and Pose_1). Joint transforms must be sampled from each pose, and each joint quaternion is interpolated with SLERP.

In Unity (and Unreal), you can create a set of animation layers containing the logic for how to combine (and transition between) multiple animation clips. In Figure 8.11, there are three layers defined: (1) a base neutral Idle pose, (2) a layer for just lower body movements, and (3) a layer just for upper body movements. In every frame, each layer is sampled resulting in a complete pose for the character. Each layer may be weighted (i.e., used to blend the pose into the base layer each frame), and layers blend together using either an "override" operation or an "additive" operation. The override operation replaces the joint transforms of the previous

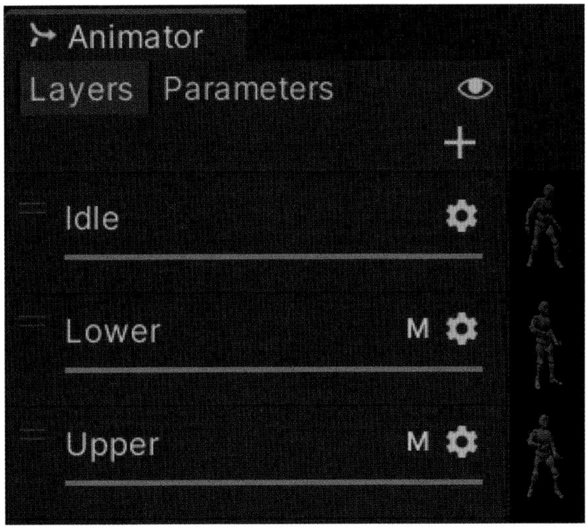

FIGURE 8.11

Example animation layers in Unity. Idle is a neutral base pose, and Upper and Lower apply masks to affect only specific joints. Each layer is sampled every frame and blended into the final result using the layer weight.

layer using the layer weight to blend, and the additive operation performs *additive blending*. Additive blending is used when the animation layer produces a pose "offset" from the previous layer and is useful for adding randomness, breathing, or other fine details where you want to retain the first animation characteristics but modify them slightly.

Layer masks can be used to isolate and limit the final layer pose to particular joints. For example, in Figure 8.12 a mask limits the animation blend between the source and target to only the lower limbs, which could be useful for applying a walk animation to the legs only. Similarly, in Figure 8.13 the upper body is isolated showing the effect of modifying the layer blend weight between the two input poses.

Each animation layer also can contain logic (FSM) to handle transitions between states (e.g., jump, run, walk), and each state can contain either an animation clip or a blend-tree to combine multiple clips.

A blend-tree is a simple and effective way to combine more than one clip into a single pose in a controlled manner. In Figure 8.14, a blend-tree combines two animation clips for the lower body layer masked layer. As the weight parameter changes, the two clips are interpolated and blended resulting in an output pose. Each blend-tree can have as many inputs as desired, but care must be taken to ensure the blend parameter is mapped to each clip with either a linear or spline curve or a directional map (i.e., to map joystick directions to specific clip directions).

Blend-trees can occur as inputs to other blend-trees. In Figure 8.15, three clips are blended by using two blend-trees with different controllable parameters. If the

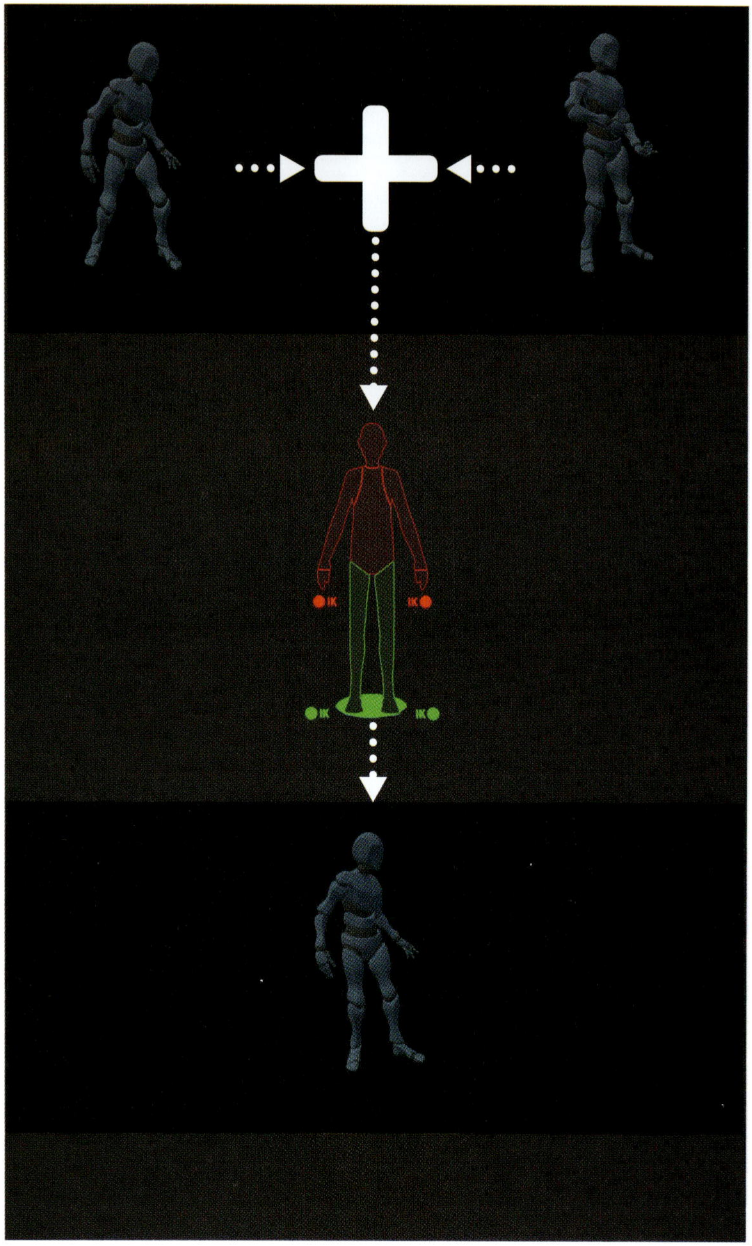

FIGURE 8.12

Layer mask lower. Two poses combined with a layer mask to isolate the legs.

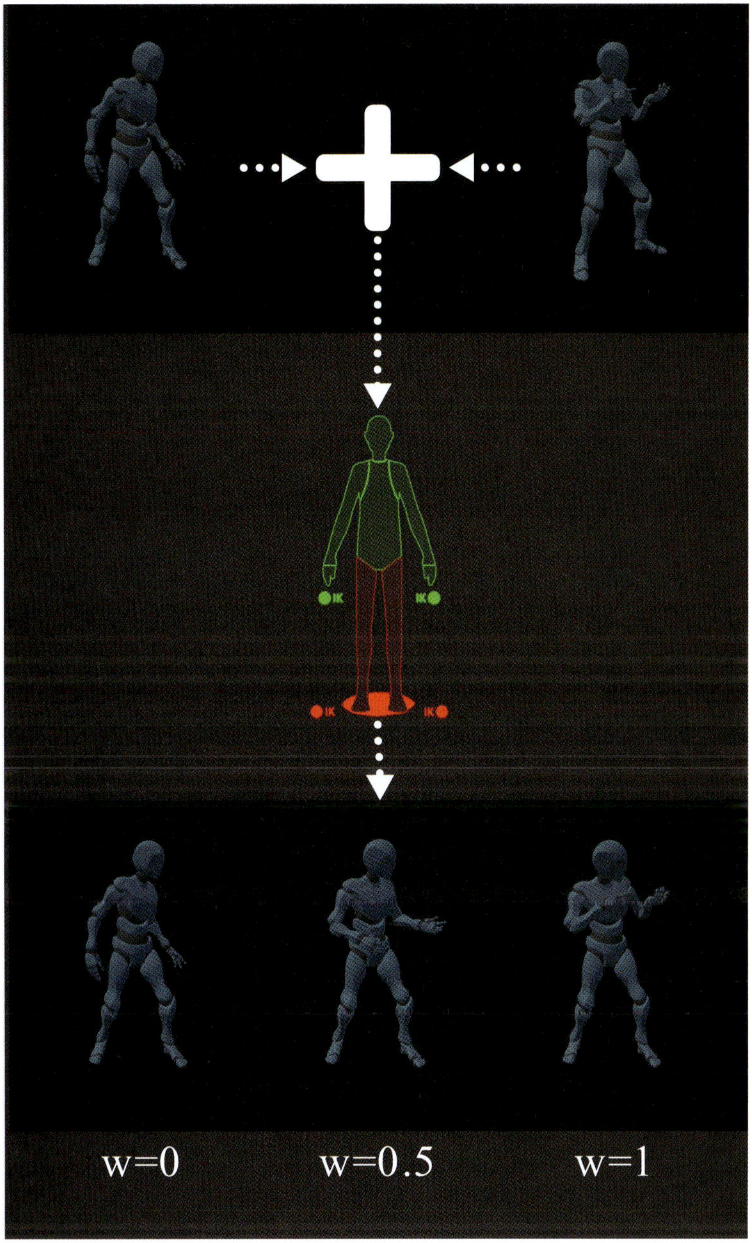

FIGURE 8.13

Layer mask. Controlling weight parameter to blend smoothly between two poses affecting only the upper body.

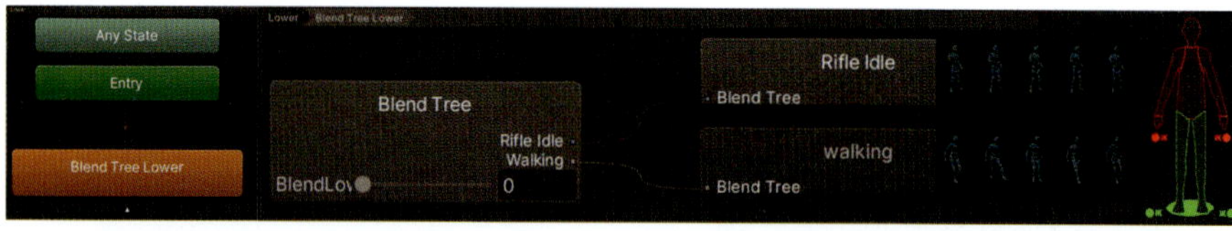

FIGURE 8.14

Example blend-tree for lower body blending between idle and walking clips.

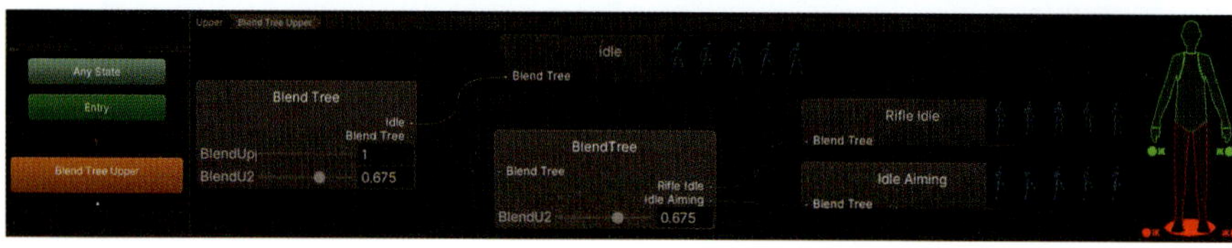

FIGURE 8.15

Example blend-tree for upper body showing nested blend-tree.

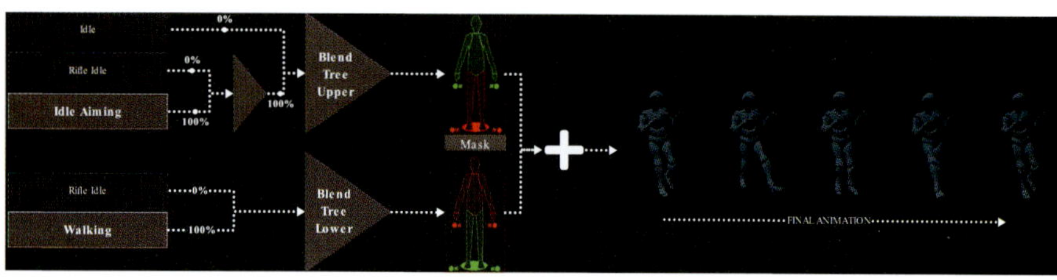

FIGURE 8.16

Diagram of complete blend-tree example. Single parameter controls blend between rifle aiming and idle animations for arms only.

first blend parameter controls the blend between an idle pose and the result from a secondary blend-tree, this sub-tree controls the blending between a different idle pose for holding a rifle and a second clip for aiming. By controlling these two parameters, the system can easily transition smoothly between idle with no weapon, idle with a weapon, and aiming this weapon.

Putting it all together (see Figures 8.16 and 8.17), we can combine multiple layers (lower and upper) containing different logic and blend-trees to combine different animation clips. In every frame, (1) each layer is sampled to generate a pose from the internal state machine and blend-trees, (2) the appropriate joints are masked out (based on the specified avatar mask), and (3) the result is blended into the final pose to be applied during skinning and rendering. Figure 8.16 shows the resulting frames while walking (lower body) and using the RifleIdle pose so the character can hold a weapon. By smoothly interpolating the BlendTree parameter weight between this clip and the IdleAiming clip, the character incorporates

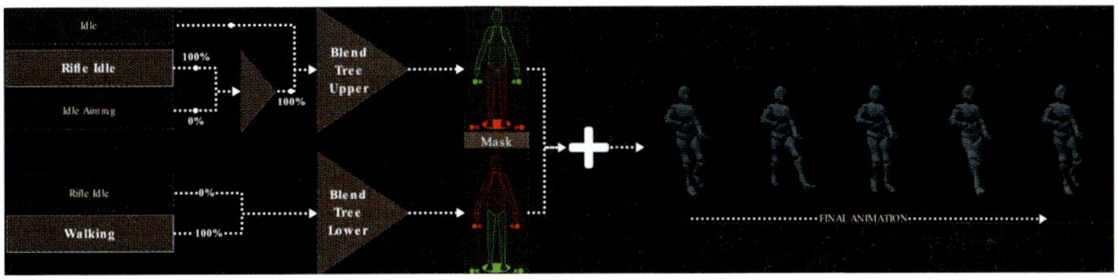

FIGURE 8.17

Diagram of complete blend-tree example. Aiming clip for arms weighted to 100%.

the aiming animations smoothly while retaining the walking animations on the lower body due to the masks. Many animations can be combined in this way enabling the ability to create new animations from a set of existing clips. The sky's the limit!

From blend-trees to motion matching

Even with useful tools such as blend-trees, it is still challenging and time-consuming to author motion capture animations for characters as many clips still need to be captured, cleaned up, labeled, integrated, and tested, and yet still transitions between clips can be choppy or sudden.

More natural transitions between segments can be created by blending the end of one segment into the beginning of the next one. Such transitions may look awkward unless the portions to be blended are similar. Similarity can be defined as the sum of the differences over all DOFs over the time interval of the blend. Both motion signal processing and motion warping can be used to isolate, overlap, and then blend two motion segments together automatically with motion graphs [49].

To animate a longer activity, motion segments can be strung together to form a longer activity. Techniques such as motion graphs identify good transitions between segments in a motion database [50] [51] [52]. When the system is confronted with a request for a motion task, the sequence of motions that satisfies the task is constructed from the segments in the motion capture database. Preprocessing can identify good points of transition among the motion segments and can cluster similar motion segments to reduce search time. Allowing minor modifications to the motion segments, such as small changes in duration and distance traveled, can help improve the usefulness of specific segments. Finally, selecting among alternative solutions usually means evaluating a motion sequence based on obstacle avoidance, distance traveled, time to completion, and so forth.

In [53], Ubisoft introduced a technique called Motion Matching that attempts to simplify the authoring and clip identification process. The technique requires only a single motion capture file that contains all possible motions you want the character to perform (care must be taken to design the capture appropriately). They then define a similarity metric that lets you query the database with any pose to find the closest pose within specific constraints. The playhead is then moved to the new location and pose sampling continues. This was improved upon using neural networks with a

Learned Motion Matching approach [54], which improves performance, accuracy, and latency.

The Motion Matching technique has recently been incorporated into Unreal Engine (5.4) [55], unlocking the next generation of animation tools for all developers.

8.4 Performance capture versus motion capture

There is a difference between capturing a "performance" and capturing "motion." Capturing motion implies that only the motion is important, and thus we need to ensure that we estimate the joint rotations of the individual so we can apply this motion to various other characters in our animations.

Performance capture can be more than just capturing motion. In particular, there can be subtle nuances to a performance that cannot easily be captured with joints. These nuances can be the movement of the performers' clothes, hair movement, eye movement, or even subtle muscles and changes in skin color (e.g., blushing) that may make a performance more natural or impactful. Obviously, this is the realm of art. There are a number of technologies that have been developed that aim to capture these nuances more effectively in recent years.

How it works: the technology

Various technologies go beyond motion capture to acquire more subtle performance nuances. In particular, we will discuss techniques based on volumetric video and Gaussian splatting.

Volumetric video technologies are those that use cameras to capture the visual appearance and movement of a complete 3D volume of space akin to a hologram. Volumetric video is essentially a 4D video where each frame is a textured 3D model rather than an image. Studio systems use upwards of 50 to 100 calibrated and synchronized cameras in a multiview stereo setup that captures a scene from multiple angles. The data is processed to extract 3D point clouds, further processing extracts textured meshes (if desired) per frame and encoded to remove redundancies (i.e., through nonrigid mesh tracking and deformation) and fit a skeletal rig to the results. Indie-level technologies use multiple color + depth (RGB-D) cameras such as the Microsoft Azure Kinect (now Orbbec Femto series), Intel Realsense, or other stereo cameras to capture 3D information directly. These systems fuse the 3D points into a single calibrated volume using filtering techniques resulting in point clouds and/or textured meshes to be input into a similar processing pipeline.

Gaussian Splatting [56] is a technique related to photogrammetry [57] but where the output is not just a set of 3D points but "splats" that when projected and blended onto an image provides a photorealistic rendering of the input sequence with fewer holes than standard photogrammetry. Moreover, as the splats encode viewing parameters, nuances of color, texture, and lighting are also captured automatically enabling high-quality rendering from novel viewpoints. Hair can be rendered accurately without actual hair geometry. Although this technique works with static scenes, there has been work to extend it to dynamic performances [58] by connecting the splat parameters with a 3D morphable model mesh that can be animated.

Major players

Studio-level volumetric capture systems have historically been produced by 4Dviews (2007–present) [59], 8i (2014–present) [60], Yoom (2016–present) [61], Metastage (2018–present) [62], Intel Studios (2018–2020) [63], and Microsoft Mixed Reality Studios (2017–2023) [64]. Although these systems generally have high-quality output, they also have the highest infrastructure cost of all volumetric capture systems, which creates a significant barrier for artists, indie-game developers, and researchers interested in experimenting in this space.

Indie-level volumetric capture systems rely on either the Microsoft Azure Kinect or Intel Depthsense cameras. Scatter (2010–present) [65] developed Depthkit (single camera) and Depthkit Studio (up to 10) which was purchased by Evercoast (2017–present) [66] in 2024. Soar (2017–2022) [67] developed their real-time multicamera RGB-D solution. Although the final output quality is lower than studio-level systems, the hardware infrastructure costs for these systems are much lower generally. However, due to the scarcity of freely available software solutions, commercial multiview RGB-D software comes at a premium cost.

Machine learning methods have emerged that show extreme promise in directing the next phase of algorithms in the performance capture space. Volograms (2018–present) [68] developed an AI-based solution (Volu) using deep learning to fit a human morphable model to single images from a smartphone. Meta introduced their Pixel Codec Avatars (2021) [69], which was extended to be drivable by a skeletal rig [70].

Gaussian splatting is still in research and development, but the leaders in this space are currently Luma AI (2021–present) [71] with their web-based Gaussian splatting solutions and Toolbox AI (2020, purchased by Niantic 2021) with their iOS App (Scaniverse [72]) that creates Gaussian splats locally on your phone. These require static scenes at time of writing.

Connecting the ideas from Meta's drivable volumetric models, 3DMMs, and Gaussian splatting shows extreme promise. For example, in [73] and [74], high-quality photorealistic and drivable full-body avatars are created from video inputs. Also in [75] and [58], similar ideas are focused on faces learning the parameters of a rigged avatar that is controllable by animators and face tracking.

Advantages

Volumetric video captures performance and appearance rather than purely joint movements. A rig can still be extracted from the data (with some effort) to manipulate captured performances. Gaussian splatting techniques can capture high quality, retaining small intricate details, and meshes can be used to inform the splat rendering during novel animations.

Disadvantages

Volumetric video systems are expensive and require significant infrastructure. The lack of open-source software has historically limited its development. Gaussian splatting is still in its infancy but shows significant promise; however, it requires significant amounts of data to train a 4D animatable model.

8.5 Chapter summary

Motion capture is a very powerful and useful tool that has become popular in recent years in the film and gaming industries. Its role in animation will continue to expand and increase as tools and techniques used to modify, combine, and adapt motion capture data become more sophisticated. Markerless motion capture systems and techniques have made it easier to capture motions, and machine learning techniques will continue to evolve this space, making it ever easier to capture high-quality animations from video sources. Current research into performance capture techniques involving Gaussian splatting, and 3DMMs are at the forefront of this space enabling unparalleled photorealism and performance fidelity.

References

[1] Menache A. Understanding motion capture for computer animation and video games. New York: Morgan Kaufmann; 2000.
[2] Esoteric Software. Spine esotericsoftware.com/ Accessed July, 2024.
[3] Lost Marble, Moho Pro, moho.lostmarble.com, Accessed July, 2024.
[4] Reallusion, Cartoon animator, reallusion.com/cartoon-animator, Accessed July, 2024.
[5] Adobe, After effects, adobe.com/ca/products/aftereffects.html, Accessed July, 2024.
[6] Toon Boom Animation Inc., toonboom.com, Accessed July, 2024.
[7] Digital Video S.p.A., Open toonz, opentoonz.github.io, Accessed July, 2024.
[8] Egret, Dragon bones, dragonbones.github.io, Accessed July, 2024.
[9] Blender Foundation, Blender, blender.org, Accessed July, 2024.
[10] Autodesk, Maya, autodesk.com/ca-en/products/maya, Accessed July, 2024.
[11] Autodesk, 3DSMax, autodesk.com/ca-en/products/3ds-max, Accessed July, 2024.
[12] Autodesk, Motionbuilder, autodesk.com/products/motionbuilder, Accessed July, 2024.
[13] Maxon, Cinema4D, maxon.net/en/cinema-4d, Accessed July, 2024.
[14] Lightwave 3D, lightwave3d.com, Accessed July, 2024.
[15] SideFX, Houdini, sidefx.com, Accessed July, 2024.
[16] JangaFX, EmberGen, jangafx.com/software/embergen, Accessed July, 2024.
[17] Reallusion, iClone, reallusion.com/iclone, Accessed July, 2024.
[18] Archive.org, Puppetworks news Gemini, https://web.archive.org/web/19990507163604/http://www.puppetworks.com/Gemini.htm, Accessed July, 2024.
[19] METAmotion, Metamotion gypsy explained, metamotion.com/gypsy/gypsy-motion-capture-system-mocap.htm, Accessed July, 2024.
[20] Michael Deering. High resolution virtual reality. In: SIGGRAPH 26, 2; 1992. p. 195–202. https://doi.org/10.1145/142920.134039.

[21] Santoni F, De Angelis A, Moschitta A, Carbone P. MagIK: a hand-tracking magnetic positioning system based on a kinematic model of the hand. In: IEEE Trans on Inst and Meas, 70; 2021. p. 1–13. https://doi.org/10.1109/TIM.2021.3065761. Art no. 9507313.

[22] Polhemus, polhemus.com, Accessed July, 2024.

[23] Archive.org. Ascension technology corporation. 2005. https://web.archive.org/web/20050303005317/http://www.ascension-tech.com. Accessed July, 2024.

[24] Northern Digital Inc., ndigital.com, Accessed July, 2024.

[25] Archive.org. Sixense entertainment. 2019. web.archive.org/web/20191101042106/www.sixense.com. Accessed July, 2024.

[26] Rokoko; rokoko.com, Accessed July, 2024.

[27] Mollyn V, et al. IMUPoser: full-body pose estimation using IMUs in phones, watches, and earbuds. Proc of the ACM CHI '23 Conference 2023. https://doi.org/10.1145/3544548.3581392.

[28] Thales Defense & Security, Inc., Intersense, intersense.com Accessed July, 2024.

[29] Nintendo, nintendo.com, Accessed July, 2024.

[30] Noitom, noitom.com, Accessed July, 2024.

[31] Vicon Motion Systems Ltd, vicon.com, Accessed July, 2024.

[32] Natural Point, Optitrack, optitrack.com, Accessed July, 2024.

[33] Archive.org, Organic Motion markerless motion capture, web.archive.org/web/20160522032229/http://www.organicmotion.com, Accessed July, 2024.

[34] Captury, captury.com Accessed July, 2024.

[35] DARI Motion, darimotion.com Accessed July, 2024.

[36] iPiSoft LLC, ipisoft.com Accessed July, 2024.

[37] Move AI, move.ai Accessed July, 2024.

[38] DeepMotion, Animate3D, deepmotion.com/animate-3d, Accessed July, 2024.

[39] Plask, plask.ai Accessed July, 2024.

[40] Rokoko, Rokoko vision, rokoko.com/products/vision, Accessed July, 2024.

[41] Meshcapade GmbH, meshcapade.com Accessed July, 2024.

[42] Cao Z, et al. OpenPose: realtime multi-person 2D pose estimation using Part Affinity fields. IEEE Trans Pattern Anal Mach Intell 2019.

[43] EasyMoCap - make human motion capture easier. 2021. http://github.com/zju3dv/EasyMocap.

[44] Kalaitzakis M, Cain B, Carroll S, et al. Fiducial markers for pose estimation. J Intell Robot Syst 2021;101:71. https://doi.org/10.1007/s10846-020-01307-9.

[45] Tuceryan M, Greer D, Whitaker R, Breen D, Crampton C, Rose E, et al. Calibration requirements and procedures for a monitor-based augmented reality system. IEEE Trans Vis Comput Graph 1995;1(3):255–73. ISSN 1077-2626.

[46] Bruderlin A, Williams L. Motion signal processing. In: Cook R, editor. Proceedings of SIGGRAPH 95, computer graphics, annual conference series. Los Angeles, Calif: Addison-Wesley; 1995. p. 97–104. Reading, Massachusetts. ISBN 0-201-84776-0.

[47] Witkin A, Popovic Z. Motion warping. In: Cook R, editor. Computer graphics, proceedings of SIGGRAPH 95, annual conference series. Los Angeles, Calif: Addison–Wesley; 1995. p. 105–8. Reading, Massachusetts. ISBN 0-201-84776-0.

[48] Gleicher M. Retargeting motion to new characters. In: Cohen M, editor. Proceedings of SIGGRAPH 98, computer graphics, annual conference series. Orlando, Fla: Addison-Wesley; 1998. p. 33–42. ISBN 0-89791-999-8.

[49] Kovar L, Gleicher M. Flexible automatic motion blending with registration curves. In: Breen D, Lin M, editors. Symposium on computer animation. San Diego, Ca: Eurographics Assoc; 2002. p. 214–24.

[50] Kovar L, Gleicher M, Pighin F. Motion graphs. In: Proceedings of SIGGRAPH 2002, computer graphics, annual conference series. San antonio, tex; 2002. p. 473–82.

[51] Lee J, Chai J, Reitsma P, Hodgins J, Pollard N. Interactive control of avatars animated with human motion data. In: Computer graphics, proceedings SIGGRAPH 2002. USA; 2002. p. 491–500.

[52] Reitsma P, Pollard N. Evaluating motion graphs for character navigation. In: Symposium on computer animation. Grenoble, France. p. 89–98.

[53] Clavet S. Motion matching and the road to next-gen animation. GDC 2016.

[54] Holden D, Kanoun O, Perepichka M, Popa T. Learned motion matching. ACM Trans Graph 2020;39(4):13. https://doi.org/10.1145/3386569.3392440. Article 53.

[55] Motion Matching in Unreal Engine | Unreal Engine 5.4 Documentation | Epic Developer Community, Epic Games, dev.epicgames.com/documentation/en-us/unreal-engine/motion-matching-in-unreal-engine. Accessed July 2024.

[56] Kerbl B, et al. 3D Gaussian splatting for real-time radiance field rendering. ACM Trans Graph 2023;42(4). repo-sam.inria.fr/fungraph/3d-gaussian-splatting/.

[57] Hartley R, Zisserman A. Multiple view geometry in computer vision. Cambridge university press; 2003.

[58] Qian S, et al. GaussianAvatars: photorealistic head avatars with rigged 3D Gaussians. IEEE/CVF Conf CVPR 2024:20299–309.

[59] 4DViews, 4dviews.com Accessed July, 2024.

[60] 8i, 8i.com Accessed July, 2024.

[61] YOOM, Accessed July, 2024.

[62] Metastage, metastage.com Accessed July, 2024.

[63] Intel studios showcases volumetric production at 77th venice international film festival. Intel Newsroom 2020. Press Release.

[64] Microsoft mixed reality capture studios create holograms to educate and entertain. Microsoft News Source 2019. Press Release.

[65] Scatter, scatter.nyc Accessed July, 2024.

[66] Evercoast, evercoast.com Accessed July, 2024.

[67] Archive.org. Soar. 2022. Accessed July, 2024, web.archive.org/web/20220701191117/streamsoar.com.

[68] Volograms, volograms.com Accessed July, 2024

[69] Ma S, Simon T, Saragih J, Wang D, Li Y, De La Torre F, et al. Pixel codec avatars. IEEE/CVF Conf CVPR 2021:64–73.

[70] Remelli E, Bagautdinov T, Saito S, Wu C, Simon T, Wei SE, et al. Drivable volumetric avatars using texel-aligned features. In: ACM SIGGRAPH; 2022. p. 1–9.

[71] Luma AI, Interactive scenes, lumalabs.ai/interactive-scenes, Accessed July, 2024.

[72] Niantic Inc.; Scaniverse, scaniverse.com Accessed July, 2024.

[73] Zielonka W, et al. Drivable 3D Gaussian avatars. arXiv [Cs.CV] 2023. http://arxiv.org/abs/2311.08581. arXiv.

[74] Hu L, et al. GaussianAvatar: towards realistic human avatar modeling from a single video via animatable 3D Gaussians. IEEE/CVF Conf CVPR 2024.

[75] Xu Y, et al. Gaussian head avatar: ultra high-fidelity head avatar via dynamic Gaussians. Proceedings of the IEEE/CVF Conf CVPR 2024.

CHAPTER

Modeling and animating human figures

9

Modeling and animating an articulated figure is one of the most formidable tasks that an animator can be faced with. It is especially challenging when the figure is meant to realistically represent a human. There are several major reasons for this. First, the human figure is a very familiar form. This familiarity makes each person a critical observer. When confronted with an animated figure, a person readily recognizes when its movement does not "feel" or "look" right. Second, the human form is very complex, with more than 200 bones and 600 muscles. When fully modeled with linked rigid segments, the human form is endowed with approximately 200 degrees of freedom (DOFs). The deformable nature of the body's surface and underlying structures further complicates the modeling and animating task. Third, human-like motion is not computationally well defined. Some studies have tried to accurately describe human-like motion, but typically these descriptions apply only to certain constrained situations. Fourth, there is no one definitive motion that is human-like. Differences resulting from genetics, culture, personality, and emotional state all can affect how a particular motion is carried out. General strategies for motion production have not been described, nor have the nuances of motion that make each of us unique and uniquely recognizable. Although the discussion in this chapter focuses primarily on the human form, many of the techniques apply to any type of articulated figure.

Table 9.1 provides the definitions of the anatomical terms used here. Particularly noteworthy for this discussion are the terms that name planes relative to the human figure: *sagittal, coronal,* and *transverse*.

Table 9.1 Selected Terms From Anatomy

Sagittal plane	Perpendicular to the ground and divides the body into right and left halves
Coronal plane	Perpendicular to the ground and divides the body into front and back halves
Transverse plane	Parallel to the ground and divides the body into top and bottom halves
Distal	Away from the attachment of the limb
Proximal	Toward the attachment of the limb
Flexion	Movement of the joint that decreases the angle between two bones
Extension	Movement of the joint that increases the angle between two bones

Computer Animation. https://doi.org/10.1016/B978-0-443-13512-5.00009-4

9.1 The body: structure

One of the most difficult challenges in computer graphics is the creation of virtual humans. Representing human figures successfully requires solutions to several very different problems. The visible geometry of the skin can be created by a variety of techniques, differing primarily in the skin detail and the degree of representation of underlying internal structures such as bone, muscle, and fatty tissue. Geometry for hair and clothing can be simulated with a clear trade-off between accuracy and computational complexity. The way in which light interacts with skin, clothing, and hair can also be calculated with varying degrees of correctness, depending on visual requirements and available resources.

Techniques for simulating virtual humans have been created that allow for modest visual results that can be computed quickly. Other approaches may give extremely realistic results by simulating individual hairs, muscles, wrinkles, or clothing threads. These methods may consequently also require excessive amounts of computation time to generate a single frame of animation. The discussion in this section focuses solely on the representation of virtual humans. It addresses animation issues where necessary to discuss how the animation techniques affect the figure's creation.

9.1.1 Anatomy (basics for reference)

It helps to have a high-level rudimentary understanding of basic human anatomy as it pertains to animation as reference. Human bodies are composed of a rigid skeleton (bones) with a layer of muscles connected to bones at specific locations, followed by layers of fatty tissue and elastic skin that conforms to the shape of these layers. Figure 9.1 shows a turnaround of the basic musculoskeletal system and structure.

To model the basic body human shape, Figure 9.2 shows the basic proportions and the major shapes to consider for the "average male." Although there is a large variation of heights and shapes, the major proportions are generally applicable to most humanoid characters. It is important to note that females tend to have higher and slightly broader hips than males. Figure 9.3 provides details on the anatomical naming of the relevant shapes, bones, and muscles. When modeling a humanoid it is helpful to begin and practice these basic shapes before worrying about visual details. The details can always be added afterward when sculpting the final character. Finally, adding bones and an animation rig to various models that mimic this basic skeletal anatomy allows for the animation system to deform any mesh that is properly attached to it, whether it has very few or very high numbers of polygons (Figure 9.4).

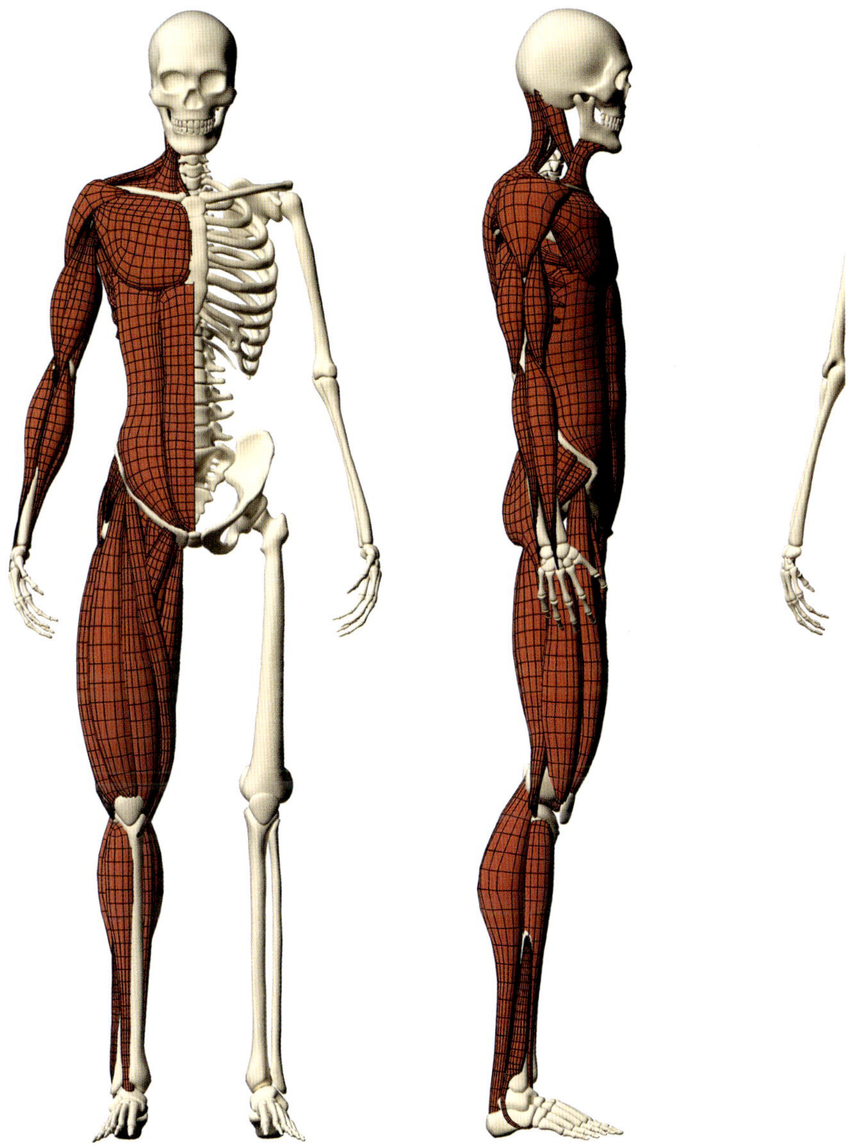

FIGURE 9.1

Turnaround of the male human musculoskeletal structure. *Left:* Skeletal and simple muscle shapes (see "Ecorche—WIP" [https://skfb.ly/T6Xt] by VeryCrunchyTaco is licensed under Creative Commons Attribution [http://creativecommons.org/licenses/by/4.0/]). *Right:* Refined muscle detail shown as an Ecorche model (see "Ecorche practice. Downloadable" [https://skfb.ly/LpRX] by martinjario is licensed under Creative Commons Attribution [http://creativecommons.org/licenses/by/4.0/]).

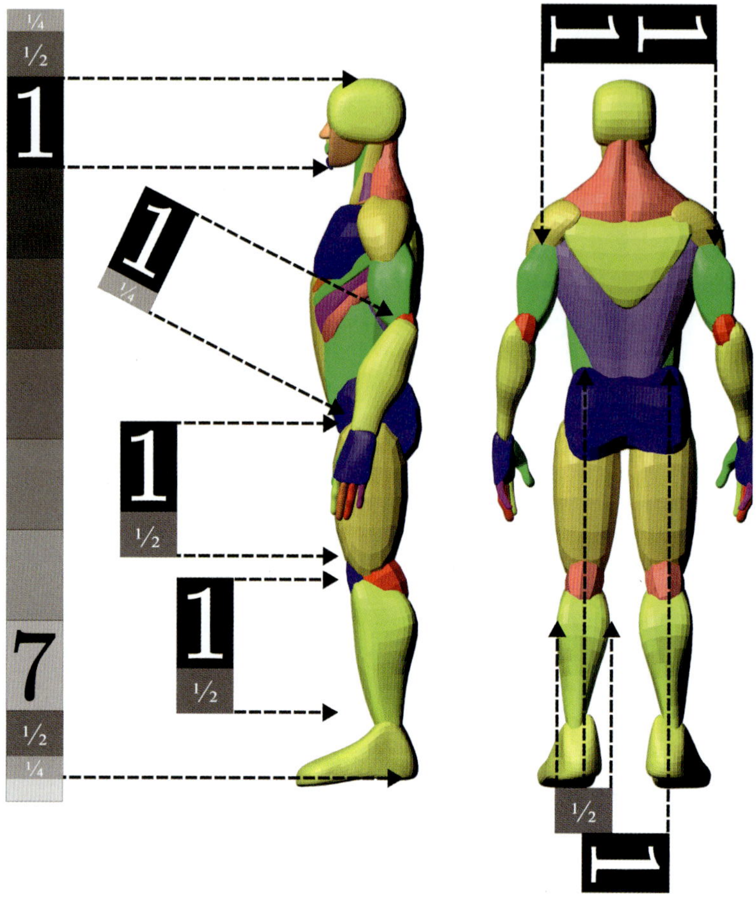

FIGURE 9.2

Basic proportions and shapes of the average humanoid male.

9.1.2 Representation

Many methods have been developed for creating and representing the geometry of a virtual human's body. They vary primarily in visual quality and computational complexity. Usually these two measures are inversely proportional.

The vast majority of human figures are modeled using a boundary representation constructed from either polygons (often quads/triangles) or patches (usually nonuniform rational B-splines [NURBS]). These boundary shell models are usually modeled manually in one of the common off-the-shelf modeling packages (e.g.,[1]). The purpose of the model being produced dictates the technique used to create it. If the figure is constructed for real-time display in a game on a low-end PC or gaming console, usually it will be assembled from a relatively low number

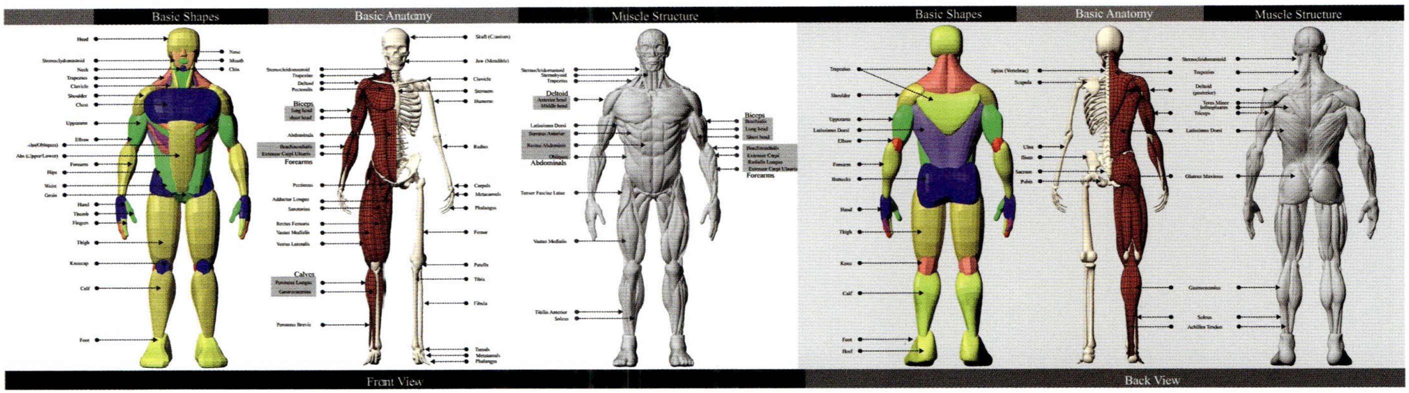

FIGURE 9.3

Human anatomy labeled with anatomical names showing basic shapes, skeleton, and basic muscle shapes (see "Ecorche—WIP" [https://skfb.ly/T6Xt] by VeryCrunchyTaco is licensed under Creative Commons Attribution [http://creativecommons.org/licenses/by/4.0/]) and muscle details (see "Ecorche practice. Downloadable" [https://skfb.ly/LpRX] by martinjario is licensed under Creative Commons Attribution [http://creativecommons.org/licenses/by/4.0/]). *Left:* Front view. *Right:* Back view.

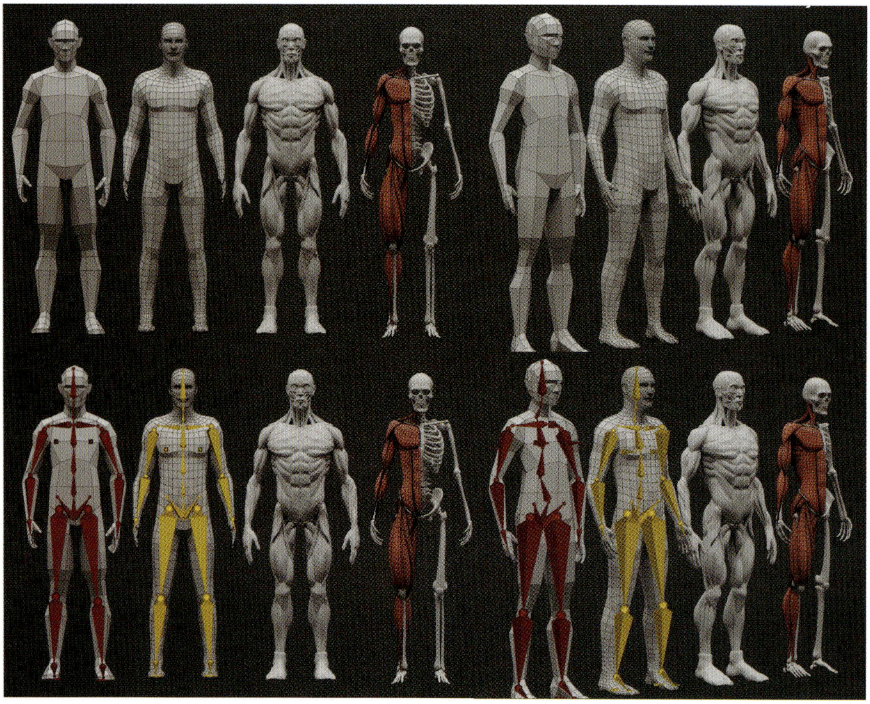

FIGURE 9.4

Set of human models with varying levels of topological detail and humanoid animation rig. Low-poly mesh (see "Low-poly Male Base Mesh" [https://skfb.ly/SESK] by decodigo is licensed under Creative Commons Attribution [http://creativecommons.org/licenses/by/4.0/]), male base-mesh (see "Male Base-mesh" [https://skfb.ly/oqG8M] by Miles0707 is licensed under Creative Commons Attribution [http://creativecommons.org/licenses/by/4.0/]) with good topology, muscle details (see "Ecorche—WIP" [https://skfb.ly/T6Xt] by VeryCrunchyTaco is licensed under Creative Commons Attribution [http://creativecommons.org/licenses/by/4.0/]), skeletal structure and muscle shapes (see "Ecorche—WIP" [https://skfb.ly/T6Xt] by VeryCrunchyTaco is licensed under Creative Commons Attribution [http://creativecommons.org/licenses/by/4.0/]).

of triangles that can be rendered efficiently. Rendering techniques such as normal mapping creates the illusion of high amounts of detail in such models. If the figure will be used in an animation that will be rendered off-line by a high-end rendering package, it might be modeled with NURBS patch data to obtain smooth curved contours. Factors such as viewing distance and the importance of the figure to the scene can be used to select from various levels of detail at which to model the figure for a particular sequence of frames.

Polygonal representations

Polygonal models (see Figure 9.4) typically consist of a set of vertices and a set of faces. Polygonal human figures can be constructed out of multiple objects (frequently referred to as *segments*), or they can consist of a single polygonal mesh. When multiple objects are used, they are generally arranged in a hierarchy of joints and rigid segments. Rotating a joint rotates all of that joint's children (e.g., rotating a hip joint rotates all of the child leg segments and joints around the hip). If a single mesh is used, then rotating a joint must deform the vertices surrounding that joint, as well as rotate the vertices in the affected limb.

Various constraints may be placed on the polygonal mesh's topology depending on the software that will be displaying the human. Many real-time rendering engines require polygonal figures to be constructed from triangles. Some modeling programs require that the object remain closed.

Polygonal representations are primarily used either when rendering speed is of the essence, as is the case in real-time systems such as games, or when topological flexibility is required. The primary problem with using polygons as a modeling primitive is that it takes far too many of them to represent a smoothly curving surface. It might require hundreds or thousands of polygons to achieve the same visual quality as could be obtained with a single NURBS patch.

Spline/patch representations

Virtual humans constructed with an emphasis on visual quality are frequently built from a network of cubic patches, for example NURBS[2,3] or by using subdivision surfaces with recursive algorithms such as the Catmull-Clark technique[4,5,6,7] resulting in a bicubic uniform B-spline.

NURBS control points defining these patches are manipulated to sculpt the surfaces of the figure. Smooth continuity must be maintained at the edges of the patches, which often proves challenging. Complex topologies also can cause difficulties, given the rectangular nature of the patches. Although patches can easily provide much smoother surfaces than polygons in general, it is more challenging to add localized detail to a figure without adding a great deal of more global data. Hierarchical splines provide a partial solution to this problem[8].

Several other methods have been used for representing virtual human figures. However, they are used more infrequently because of a lack of modeling tools or because of their computational complexity.

Implicit surfaces[9] can be employed as sculpting material for building virtual humans. Frequently the term "metaballs" is used for spherical implicit surfaces. Metaballs resemble clay in their ability to blend with other nearby primitives. Although computationally expensive to render, they provide an excellent organic look that is perfect for representing skin stretched over underlying tissue, which can be retopologized into a smooth manifold mesh.

Subdivision surfaces combine the topological flexibility of polygonal objects with the resultant smoothness of patch data. They transform a low-resolution polygonal model into a smooth form by recursively subdividing the polygons as necessary.[10]

Probably the most computationally demanding representation method is volumetric modeling. Whereas all of the previously mentioned techniques merely store information about the surface qualities of a virtual human, volumetric models store information about the entire interior space as well. Because of its extreme computational requirements, this technique is limited almost exclusively to the medical research domain, where knowledge of the interior of a virtual human is crucial.

As computers continue to become more powerful, more attempts are being made to more accurately model the interior of humans to get more realistic results on the visible surfaces. There have been several "layered" approaches, where some attempt has been made to model underlying bone and/or muscle and its effect on the skin.

Chen and Zeltzer[11] use a finite element approach to accurately model a human knee, representing each underlying muscle precisely, based on medical data. Several authors have attempted to create visually reasonable muscles attached to bones and then generate skin over the top of the muscle (e.g., [12], [13]). Thalmann's lab takes a hybrid approach of modeling muscles with implicit surfaces (metaballs), producing cross sections of these metaballs along the body's segments, and then lofting polygons between the cross sections to produce the final surface geometry.[10,14] Chadwick et al.[15] use free form deformations (FFDs) to produce artist-driven muscle bulging and skin folding.

With the advent of morphable models,[16] parameterized approaches have become popular to modeling humans such as in Unreal's Metahuman,[17] Reallusion's Character Creator,[18] and full-body parametric models such as SMPL,[19] SMPL-X,[20] and SUPR[21].

9.2 The body: modeling

Geometric data can be acquired by a number of means. By far the most common method is to have an artist create the figure using interactive software tools. The quality of the data obtained by these means is of course completely dependent on the artist's skills and experience. Another method of obtaining data, digitizing real humans, is becoming more prevalent as the necessary hardware becomes more affordable. Data representing a specific individual are often captured using photogrammetry,[22,23] depth sensors,[24,25] or deep learning approaches.[26,27,28]

9.2.1 Surface detail

After the geometry for a virtual figure has been constructed, its surface properties must also be specified. As with the figure's geometry, surface properties can be produced by an artist, scanned from real life, or procedurally generated. Color, as well as specular, diffuse, bump, normal, and displacement maps may be generated.

Accurately positioning the resulting textures requires the generation of texture coordinates.

9.2.2 Layered approach to human figure modeling

A common approach to animating the human figure is to construct the figure in layers consisting of skeleton, muscles, and skin. The skeletal layer is responsible for the articulation of the form. The muscle layer is responsible for deforming the shape as a result of skeletal articulation. The skin is responsible for carrying the appearance of the figure.

Chadwick et al.[15] introduced the layered approach to figure animation by incorporating an articulated skeleton, surface geometry representing the skin, and an intermediate muscle layer that ties the two together. The muscle layer is not anatomically based, and its only function is to deform the surface geometry as a function of joint articulation. The muscle layer implements a system of FFD lattices in which the surface geometry is embedded. The lattice is organized with two planes on each end that are responsible for maintaining continuity with adjoining lattices, and the interior planes are responsible for deforming the skin to simulate muscle bulging (Figure 9.5). As the joint flexes, the interior planes elongate perpendicular to the axis of the link. The elongation is usually not symmetrical about the axis and is designed by the animator. For example, the upper-arm FFD lattice elongates as the elbow flexes. Typically, the FFD for the upper arm is designed to produce the majority of the skin deformation in the region of the biceps. A pair of FFD lattices is used on either side of each joint to isolate the FFDs responsible for muscle bulging from the more rigid area around the joint. In addition, the joint FFDs are designed to maintain continuity on the outside of the joint and create the skin crease on the inside of the joint.

Blender contains the notion of a "bendy-bone" or "B-bone" that can be used to deform your mesh as if there were a lattice between the head and tail of the bone. These can be used to provide a decent simulation of muscle deformation. To do so, you create a bone placed at the main insertion point of the muscle (i.e., the shoulder joint) and a bendy-bone that stretches from this insertion point to the end of the muscle (i.e., the elbow joint). A "stretch-to" bone-constraint is then applied to stretch to an object (or nonparented bone) at the end location. As long as the middle bendy-bone has many segments it will bend smoothly and retain the volume of the middle bone within specified limits. This bendy bone can then be skinned to a mesh and weight-painted appropriately to achieve a muscle deformation that is quite convincing (Figure 9.6).

Artistic anatomy can be used to guide analysis of the human form.[29,30,31] Bones, muscles, tendons, and fatty tissue are modeled to occupy the appropriate volumes. Scheepers[29] identifies the types of muscles sufficient for modeling the upper torso of the human figure: linear muscles, sheet muscles, and bendable sheet muscles. Tendons are modeled as part of the muscles and attach to the skeleton. Muscles deform according to the articulation of the skeleton. See Figure 9.7 for an example.

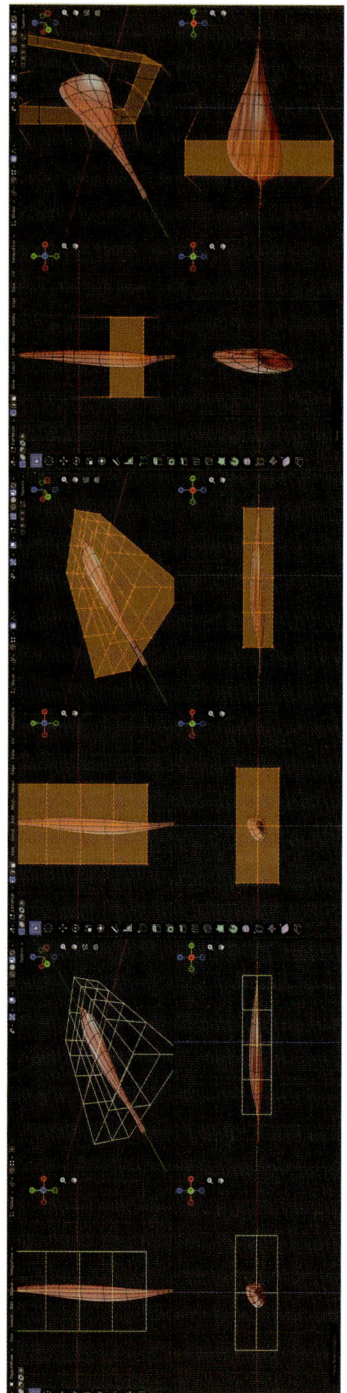

FIGURE 9.5

A free form deformation lattice in Blender to deform a single of muscle mesh (see “Simple arm anatomy” [https://skfb.ly/6vFQW] by Krogor is licensed under Creative Commons Attribution-ShareAlike [http://creativecommons.org/licenses/by-sa/4.0/]). *Left:* Lattice wire frame with model shown (note how the endpoints of the mesh are not within the lattice because they should not deform). *Middle:* Lattice faces highlighted. *Right:* Internal lattice faces scaled on the vertical axis demonstrating how the lattice deforms the mesh to bulge the muscle.

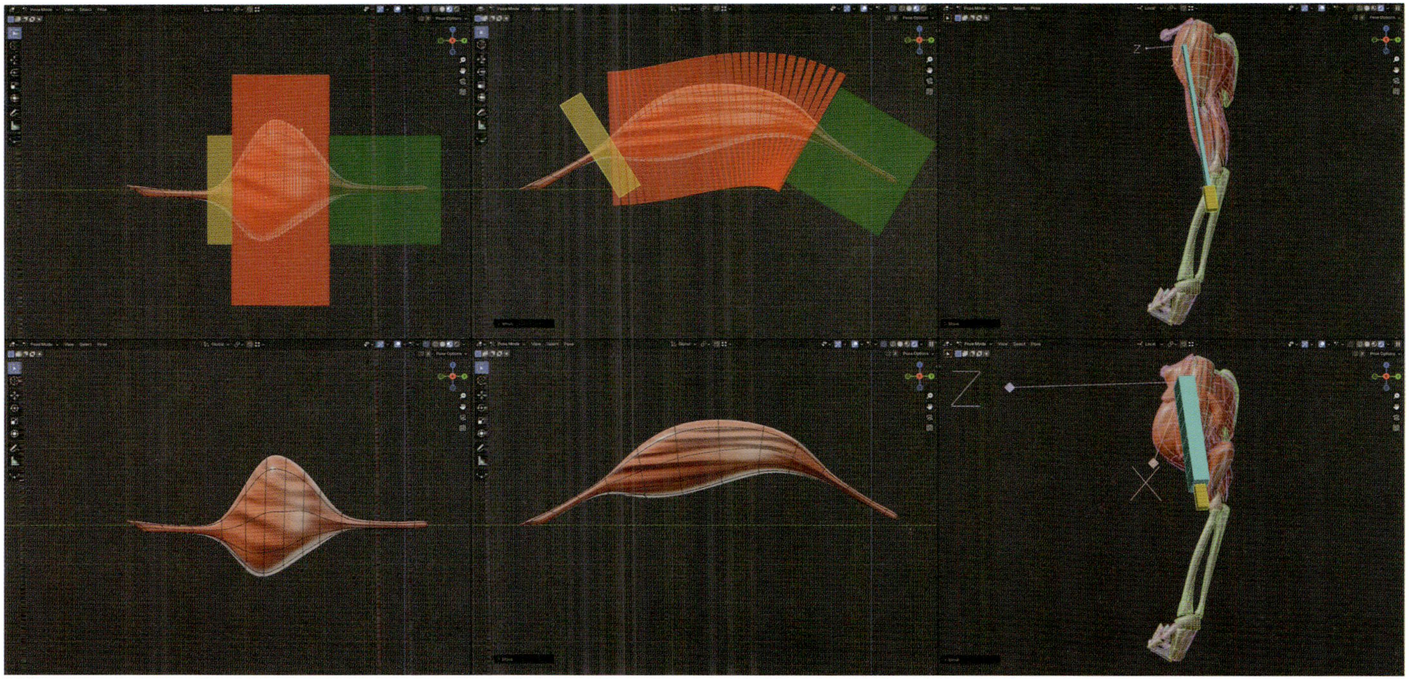

FIGURE 9.6

Bendy-bone deformation demonstration in Blender of muscle mesh (see "Simple arm anatomy" [https://skfb.ly/6vFQW] by Krogor is licensed under Creative Commons Attribution-ShareAlike [http://creativecommons.org/licenses/by-sa/4.0/]). *Left:* Side view of muscle *(bottom)* and bendy bone *(top)* when squished. *Middle:* Showing how rotation of endpoints and movement of target results in stretching/bulging. *Right:* Applied to an arm model with rest pose *(top)* and squished to bulge the bicep *(bottom)*. Note this is exaggerated for demonstration purposes.

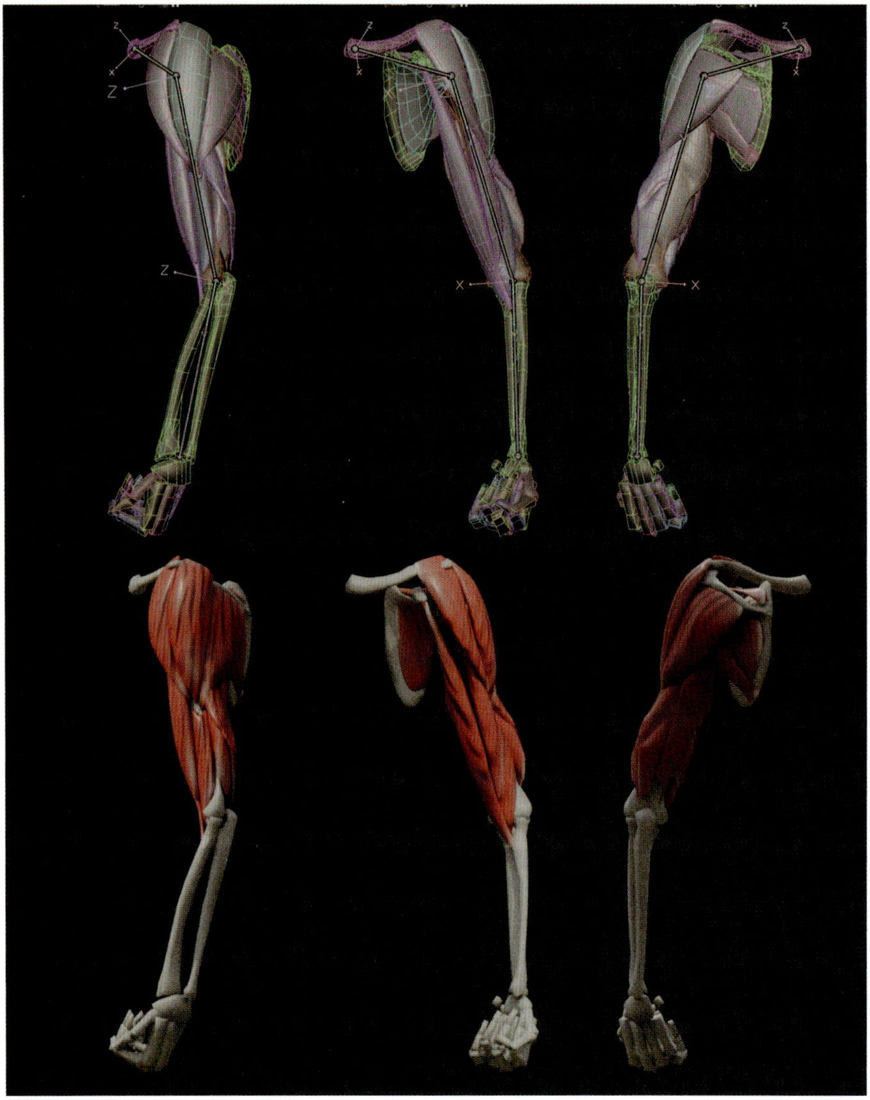

FIGURE 9.7

Articulated arm with muscles based on anatomical structure (see “Simple arm anatomy” [https://skfb.ly/6vFQW] by Krogor is licensed under Creative Commons Attribution-ShareAlike [http://creativecommons.org/licenses/by-sa/4.0/]). *Top:* Wire frame to show basic shapes and rigid skeletal inspired armature. *Bottom:* Rendered with materials.

These muscles populate the skeletal figure in the same manner that actual muscles are arranged in the human body (see Figures 9.3 and 9.8). To deform the skin according to the underlying structure (muscles, tendons, and fatty tissue), the user defines implicit functions so that the densities occupy the volume of the corresponding anatomy. Ellipsoids are used for muscles, cylinders for tendons, and flattened ellipsoids for fat pads. The implicit primitives are summed to smooth the surface and further model underlying tissue. The skin, modeled as a B-spline surface, is defined by floating the control points of the B-spline patches to the isosurface of the summed implicit primitives. This allows the skin to distort as the underlying skeletal structure articulates and muscles deform. Applying the technique described previously with bendy-bones can mimic this quite easily (Figure 9.9).

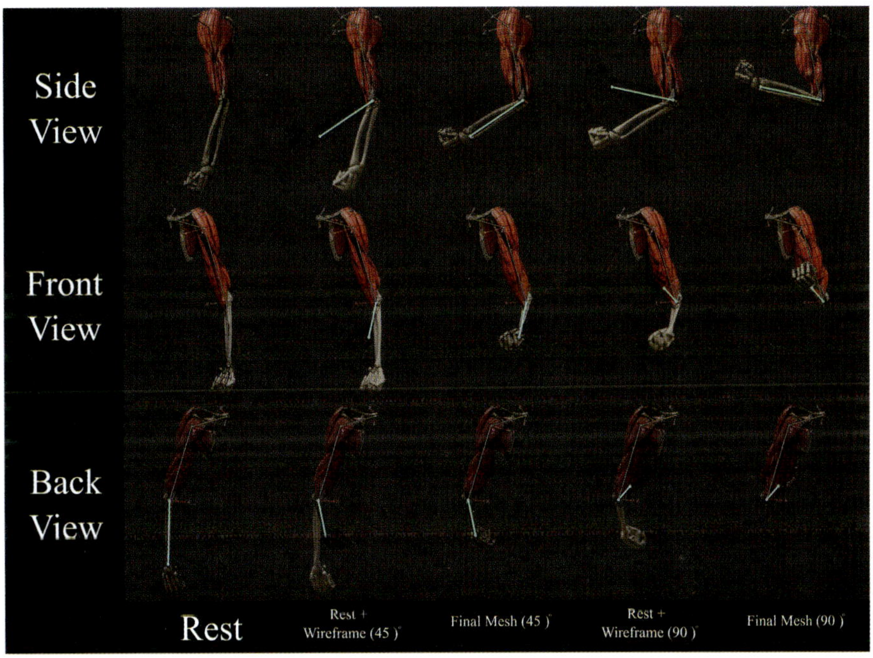

FIGURE 9.8

Demonstration of elbow rotation and impact on muscle movement using bendy-bone armature in Blender. Wire frames are shown before rendering skinned results to highlight differences in muscles from previous iteration.

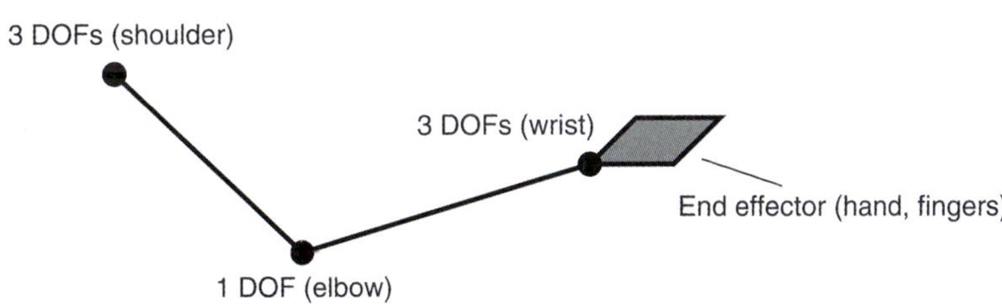

FIGURE 9.9

Basic conceptual model of the human arm.

9.2.3 Modeling the arm

The basic model of the human arm, ignoring the joints of the hand for now, can be most simply represented as a 7-DOF manipulator (Figure 9.9): 3 DOFs are at the shoulder joint, 1 at the elbow, and 3 at the wrist. A *configuration* or *pose* for the arm is a set of 7 joint angles, 1 for each of the 7 DOFs of the model.

Forearm rotation presents a problem. In Figure 9.9, the forearm rotation is associated with the wrist. However, in reality, the forearm rotation is not associated with a localized joint like most of the other DOFs of the human figure; rather, it is distributed along the forearm itself as the two forearm bones (radius and ulna) rotate around each other. Sometimes this rotation is associated with the elbow instead; other implementations create a "virtual" joint midway along the forearm to handle forearm rotation.

Of course, the joints of the human arm have limits. For example, the elbow can flex to approximately 20 degrees and extend to typically around 180 degrees. Allowing a figure's limbs to exceed the joint limits would certainly contribute to an unnatural look. Most joints are positioned with least strain somewhere in the middle of their range and rarely attain the boundaries of joint rotation unless forced. More subtly, joint limits may vary with the position of other joints, and further limits are imposed on joints to avoid intersection of appendages with other parts of the body. For example, if the arm is moved in a large circle parallel to and to the side of the torso, the muscle strain causes the arm to distort the circle at the back. As another example, in some individuals tendons make it more difficult to fully extend the knee when one is bending at the hip (the motion used to touch one's toes).

If joint limits are enforced, some general motions can be successfully obtained by using forward kinematics. Even if an object is to be carried by the hand, forward kinematics in conjunction with attaching the object to the end effector creates a fairly convincing motion. But if the arm/hand must operate relative to a fixed object, such as a knob, inverse kinematics is necessary. Unfortunately, the normal methods of inverse kinematics, using the pseudoinverse of the Jacobian, are not guaranteed to give human-like motion. As explained in previous chapters, in some orientations a singularity may exist in which a DOF is "lost" in Cartesian space. For example, the motion can be hard to control in cases in which the arm is fully extended.

According to the model shown in Figure 9.9, if only the desired end effector position is given, then the solution space is underconstrained. In this case, multiple solutions exist, and inverse kinematic methods may result in configurations that do not look natural. As noted, there are methods for biasing the solution toward desired joint angles. This helps to avoid violating joint limits and produces more human-like motion but still lacks any anatomical basis for producing human-like configurations.

It is often useful to specify the goal position of the wrist instead of the fingers to better control the configurations produced. But even if the wrist is fixed (i.e., treated as the end effector) at a desired location, and the shoulder is similarly fixed, there are still a large number of positions that might be adopted that satisfy both the constraints and the joint limits. Biasing the joint angles to orientations preferable for certain tasks can reduce or eliminate multiple solutions.

To more precisely control the movement, the user can specify intermediate positions and orientations for the end effector as well as for intermediate joints. Essentially, this establishes key poses for the linkage. Inverse kinematics can then be used to step from one pose to the next so that the arm is still guided along the path. This affords some of the savings of using inverse kinematics while giving the animator more control over the final motion.

The formal inverse Jacobian approach can be replaced with a more procedural approach based on the same principles to produce more human-like motion. In human motion, the joints farther away from the end effector (the hand) have the most effect on it. The joints closer to the hand change angles to perform the fine orientation changes necessary for final alignment. This can be implemented procedurally by computing the effect of each DOF on the end effector by taking the cross-product of the axis of rotation, ω_1, with the vector from the joint to the end effector, V_1 (Figure 9.10). In addition, because the arm contains a 1-DOF angle (elbow), a plane between the shoulder, the elbow, and the wrist is formed, and the arm's preferred positions dictate a relatively limited rotation range for that plane. Once the plane is fixed, the shoulder and elbow angles are easy to calculate and can be easily adjusted on that plane (Figure 9.11). Some animation packages (e.g., Blender,

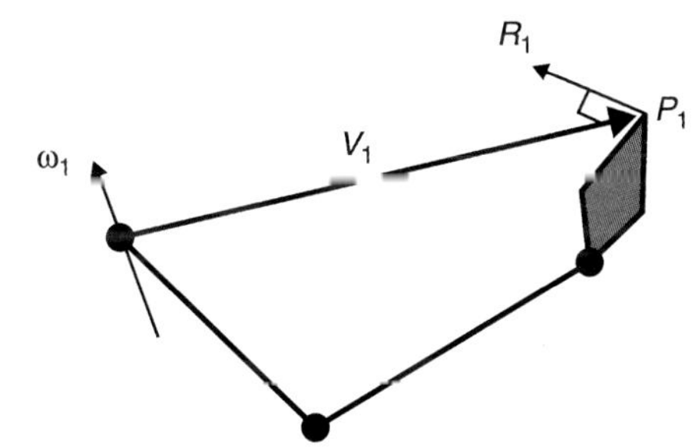

FIGURE 9.10

Effect of the first degrees of freedom (DOF) on the end effector: $R_1 = \omega_1 \times V_1$.

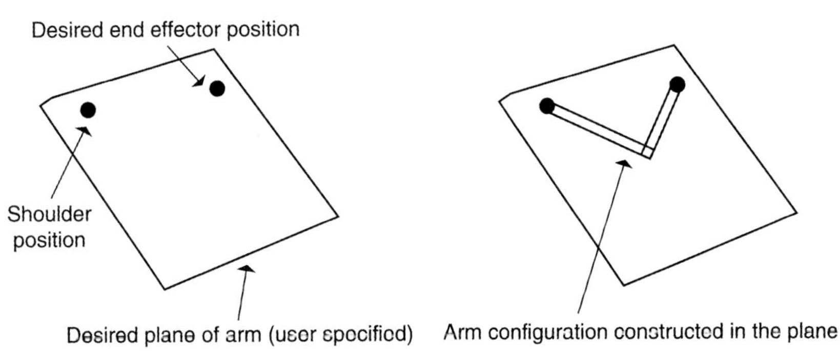

FIGURE 9.11

Constructing the arm in a user-specified plane.

Maya) allow the animator to specify an inverse kinematic solution based on such a plane and to rotate the plane as desired.

Some neurological studies, notably those by Lacquaniti and Soechting[32] and Soechting and Flanders[33], suggest that the arm's posture is determined from the desired location of the end effector (roughly "fixing the wrist's orientation"), and then the final wrist orientation is tweaked for the nature of the object and the task. The model developed by Kondo[34] for this computation makes use of a spherical coordinate system. A set of angles for the shoulder and elbow is calculated from the desired hand and shoulder position and then adjusted if joint limitations are violated. Finally, a wrist orientation is calculated separately. The method is described, along with a manipulation planner for trajectories of cooperating arms, by Koga et al.[35].

9.2.4 The shoulder joint

The shoulder joint requires special consideration. It is commonly modeled as a ball joint with 3 coincident DOFs. The human shoulder system is actually more complex. Scheepers[29] described a more realistic model of the clavicle and scapula along with a shoulder joint, in which three separate joints with limited range provide very realistic-looking arm and shoulder motion. Scheepers also provided an approach to the forearm rotation problem using a radioulnar (midforearm) joint (Figure 9.12).

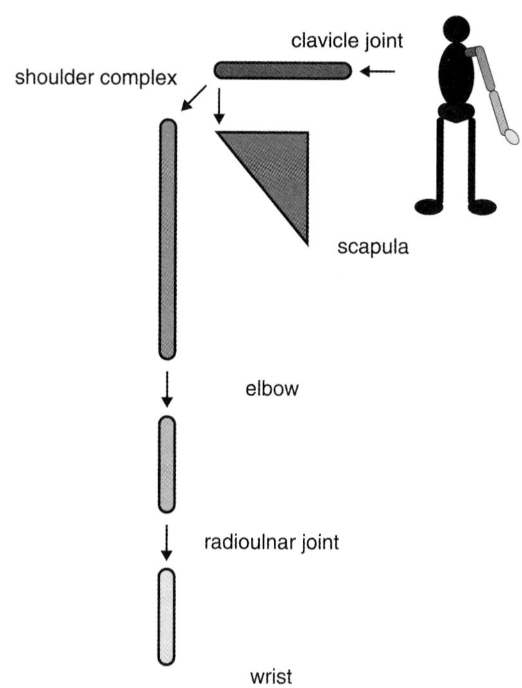

FIGURE 9.12

Conceptual model of the upper limb.

9.2.5 The hand

To include a fully articulated hand in the arm model, one must introduce many more joints (and thus DOFs). A simple hand configuration may consist of a palm, four fingers, and a thumb, with joints and DOFs as shown in Figure 9.13.

A model similar to Figure 9.13 is used by Rijpkema and Girard[36] in their work on grasping. Scheepers[29] uses 27 bones, but only 16 joints are movable. Others use models with subtler joints inside the palm area to get human-like action.

If the hand is to be animated in detail, the designer must pay attention to types of grasp and how the grasps are to be used. The opposable thumb provides humans with great manual dexterity: the ability to point, grasp objects of many shapes, and exert force such as that needed to open a large jar of pickles or a small jewelry clasp. This requires carefully designed skeletal systems. Studies of grasping show at least 16 different categories of grasp, most involving the thumb and one or more

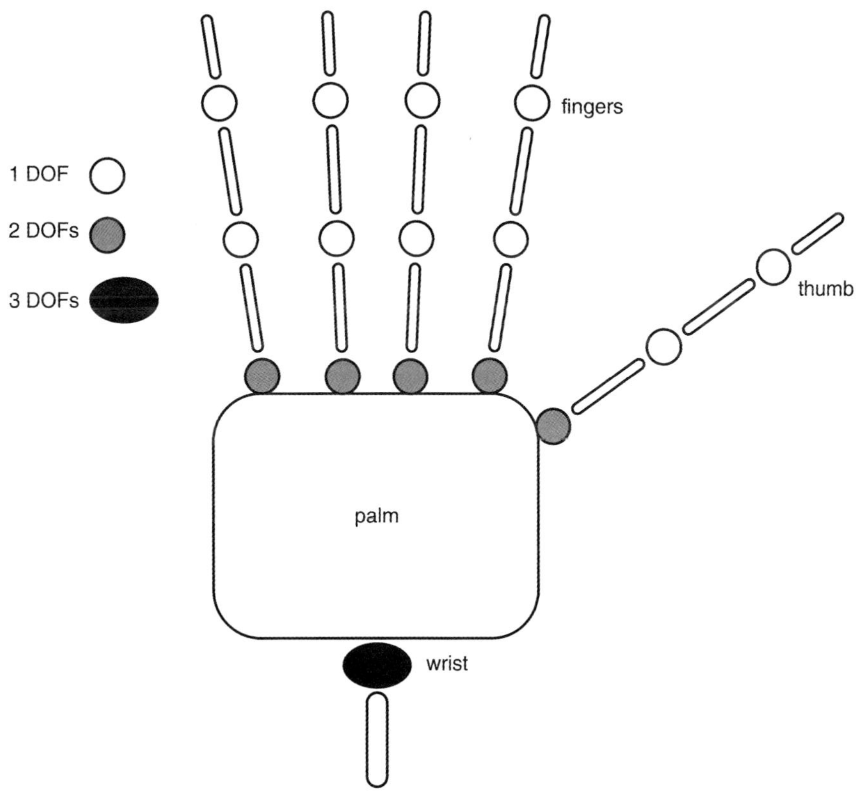

FIGURE 9.13

Simple model of hands and fingers. *DOF*, Degrees of freedom.

fingers. For a given task, the problem of choosing which grasp is best (most efficient and/or most credible) adds much more complexity to the mere ability to form the grasp. Approaches to grasping are either procedural (e.g., [36], [37], [38], [39]) or data driven (e.g., [40], [41]).

Simpler models combine the four fingers into one surface and may eliminate the thumb (Figure 9.14). This reduces both the display complexity and the motion control complexity. Display complexity, and therefore image quality, can be maintained by using the full-detail hand model but coordinating the movement of all the joints of the four fingers with one "grasping" parameter (Figure 9.15), even though this only approximates real grasping action.

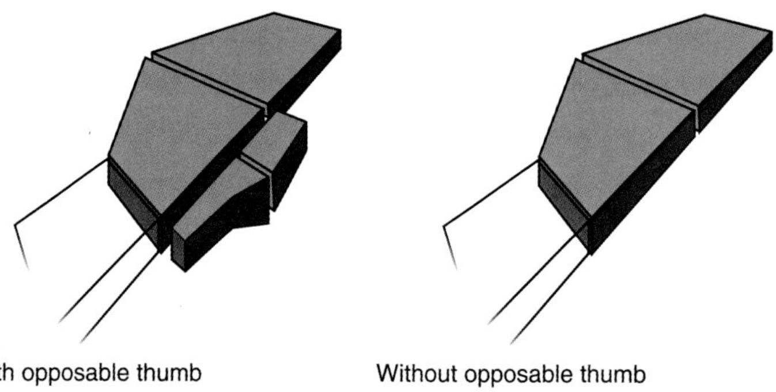

FIGURE 9.14

Simplified hands.

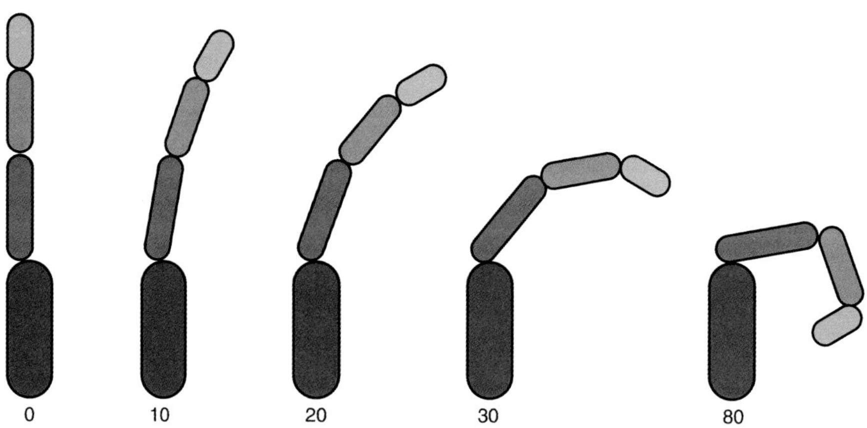

FIGURE 9.15

Finger flexion controlled by single parameter; the increase in joint angle (degrees) per joint is shown.

9.3 The body: animation

9.3.1 Rigging

Rigging, as used here, refers to setting up interactive controls to facilitate animation of a character or other object. In the case of a character, a rig might be set up to control taking a step or waving a hand. Typically, a character rig facilitates the animation of a character by providing a high-level control that manipulates multiple DOFs in a coordinated manner. This not only makes animating the character easier, but it also provides consistency for the character's movements.

9.3.2 Geometry deformation

For a user to animate a virtual human figure, the figure's limbs and other parts must be able to be moved and/or deformed. The method of manipulation used is largely determined by the way the figure is being represented. Very simple figures, usually used for real-time display, are often broken into multiple rigid subparts, such as a forearm, a thigh, or a head. These parts are arranged in a hierarchy of joints and segments such that rotating a joint rotates all of the child segments and joints beneath it in the hierarchy.[42] Although this method is quick, it yields suboptimal visual results at the joints, particularly if the body is textured, because the rigid parts merely overlap and occlude each other at the joint.

A single skin is commonly used for polygonal figures. When a joint is rotated, the appropriate vertices are deformed to simulate rotation around the joint. Several different methods can be used for this, and, as with most of these techniques, they involve trade-offs of realism and speed.

The simplest and fastest method is to bind each vertex to exactly one bone. When a bone rotates, the vertices move along with it. This works well with rigid and mechanical structures such as robots where components are rigid (do not deform) and must move with the skeletal structure.

Better results can be obtained, at the cost of additional computation, if the vertices surrounding a joint are weighted so that their position is affected by multiple bones.

Although weighting the effects of bone rotations on vertices results in smoother skin around joints, severe problems can still occur with extreme joint bends. FFDs have been used in this case to simulate the skin-on-skin collision and the accompanying squashing and bulging that occur when a joint such as the elbow is fully bent.[15] The precise placement of joints within the body greatly affects the realism of the surrounding deformations. Joints must be placed strictly according to anthropometric data, or unrealistic bulges will result. Some joints require more complicated methods for realistic deformation. Using only a simple, single 3-DOF rotation for a shoulder or vertebra can yield very poor results.

A few systems have attempted to construct more complex, anatomically based joints.[8,43] The hands in particular can require significantly more advanced deformation techniques to animate realistically.[44]

Surface deformations that would be caused by changes in underlying material, such as muscle and fat in a real human, can be produced in a virtual human by a number of means. Methods range from those that simply allow an animator to specify muscular deformations to those that require complex dynamics simulations of the various tissue layers and densities.[29,45]

9.3.3 Reaching and grasping

One of the most common human figure animation tasks involves movement of the upper limbs. A synthetic figure may be required to reach and operate a control, raise a coffee cup from a table up to their mouth to drink, or turn a complex object over and over to examine it. It is computationally simpler to consider the arm as an appendage that moves independently of the rest of the body. In some cases, this can result in unnatural-looking motion. To produce more realistic motion, the user often involves additional joints of the body in executing the motion. In this section, the arm is considered in isolation. It is assumed that additional joints, if needed, can be added to the reaching motion in a preprocessing step that positions the figure and readies it for independently considered arm motion.

9.3.4 Coordinated movement

Adding to the difficulties of modeling and controlling the various parts of the upper limb is the difficulty of inter-joint cooperation in a movement and assigning a specific motion to a particular joint. It is easy to demonstrate this difficulty. Stretch out your arm to the side and turn the palm of the hand so it is first facing up; then rotate the hand so it is facing down and try to continue rotating it all the way around so that the palm faces up again. Try to do this motion by involving first only the hand/wrist/forearm and then the upper arm/shoulder. Adding motion of the torso including the clavicle and spine, which involves more DOFs, makes this task simpler to accomplish, but also makes the specification of realistic joint angles more complex. It is difficult to determine exactly what rotation should be assigned to which joints at what time to realistically model this motion.

Interaction between body parts is a concern beyond the determination of which joints to use in a particular motion. Although viewing the arm and hand as a separate independent system simplifies the control strategy, its relation to the rest of the body must be taken into account for a more robust treatment of reaching. Repositioning, twisting, and bending of the torso, reactive motions by the other arm, and even counterbalancing by the legs are often part of movements that only appear to belong to a single arm. It is nearly impossible for a person reaching for an object to keep the rest of the body in a fixed position. Rather than extend joints to the edges of their limits and induce stress, other body parts may cooperate to relieve muscle strain or maintain equilibrium.

Arm manipulation is used in many different full-body movements. Even walking, which is often modeled as an activity of the legs only, involves the torso, the arms, and even the head. The arm often seems like a simple and rewarding place to begin modeling human figure animation, but it is difficult to keep even this task at a simple level.

9.3.5 Reaching around obstacles

To further complicate the specification and control of reaching motion, there may be obstacles in the environment that must be avoided. Of course, it is not enough to merely plan a collision-free path for the end effector. The entire limb sweeps out a volume of space during reach that must be completely devoid of other objects to avoid collisions. For sparse environments, simple reasoning strategies can be used to determine the best way to avoid obstacles.

As more obstacles populate the environment, more complex search strategies might be employed to determine the path. Various path-planning strategies have been proposed. For example, given an environment with obstacles, an artificial potential field can be constructed as a function of the local geometry. Obstacles impart a high potential field that attenuates based on distance. Similarly, the goal position imparts a low potential into the field. The gradient of the field suggests a direction of travel for the end effector and directs the entire linkage away from collisions (Figure 9.16). Such approaches are susceptible to local minima traps that need to

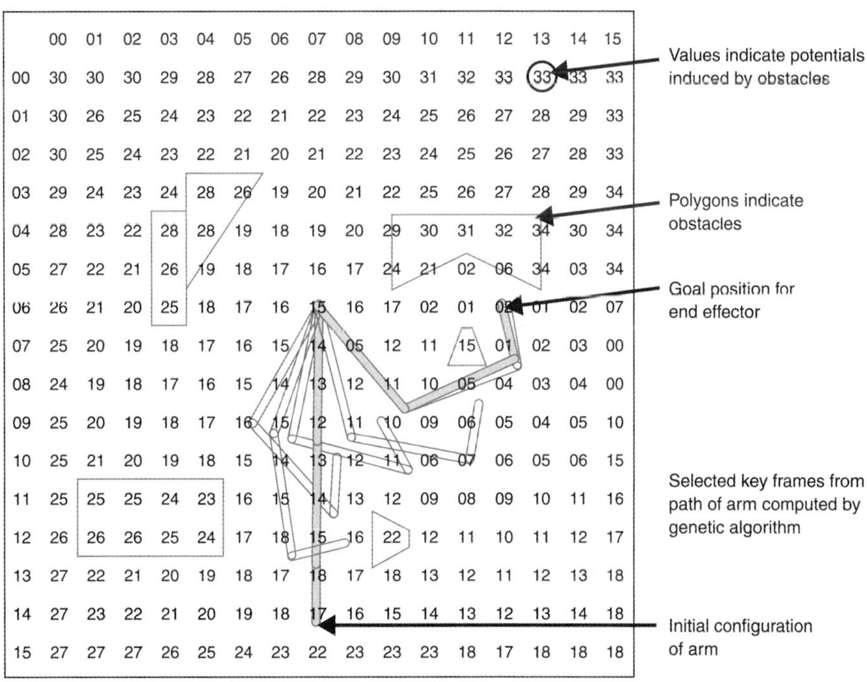

FIGURE 9.16

Path planning result.[48]

be dealt with. Genetic algorithms, for example, have been used to search the space for a global minimum.[46] The genetic fitness function can be tailored to find an optimal path in terms of one of several criteria such as shortest end-effector distance traveled, minimum torque, and minimum angular acceleration.

Such optimizations, however, produce paths that would not necessarily be considered human-like. Optimized paths will typically come as close as possible to critical objects in the path to minimize the fitness function. Humans seldom generate such paths in their reaching motions. The complexity of human motion is further complicated by the effect of vision on obstacle avoidance. If the figure "knows" there is an object to avoid but is not looking directly at it, then the reaching motion will incorporate more leeway in the path than it would if the obstacle were directly in the field of view. Furthermore, the cost of collision can influence the resulting path: it costs more to collide with a barbed-wire fence than a towel, and the path around these obstacles should probably be quite different.

9.3.6 Strength

As anyone who has ever changed a spark plug in a car knows, avoiding all the obstacles and getting a tool in the correct position is only half the battle. Once in position, the arm and hand must be in a configuration in which there is enough strength available to actually dislodge the plug. To simulate more realistic motions, strength criteria can be incorporated into the task planning.[42] As previously noted, typical reaching motion problems are usually underconstrained, allowing for multiple solutions. The solution space can be searched for a specific motion that is acceptable in terms of the amount of strain it places on the figure.

When a specific motion is proposed by a kinematic planner, it can be evaluated according to the strain it places on the body. The strain is determined by computing the torque necessary at each joint to carry out the motion and rating the torque requirements according to desirability. Given the current pose for the figure, the required joint accelerations, and any external forces, the torque required at each joint can be calculated. For each joint, the maximum possible torque for both flexion and extension is given as a function of the joint's angle as well as that of neighboring joints. A *comfort* metric can be formed as the ratio of currently requested torque and maximum possible torque. The *comfort level* for the figure is computed by finding the maximum torque ratio for the entire body. The most desirable motions are those that minimize the maximum torque ratio over the duration of the motion.

Once a motion has been determined to be unacceptable, it must be modified to bring its comfort level back to within acceptable ranges. This can be done by initiating one or more strategies that reduce the strain. Assume that a particular joint has been identified that exceeds the accepted comfort range. If other joints in the linkage can be identified that produce a motion in the end effector similar to that of the problem joint and that have excess torque available, then increasing the torques at these joints can compensate for reduced torque at the problem joint. It may also be possible to include more joints in the linkage, such as the spine in a reaching motion, to reformulate the inverse kinematic problem in the hope of reducing the torque at the problem joint.

9.3.7 Walking

Walking, along with reaching, is one of the most common activities in which the human form engages. It is a complex activity that, for humans, is learned only after an extended trial-and-error process. An aspect that differentiates walking from typical reaching motions, besides the fact that it uses the legs instead of the arms, is that it is basically cyclic. Whereas its cyclic nature provides some uniformity, acyclic components such as turning and tripping occur periodically. In addition, walking is responsible for transporting the figure from one place to another and is simultaneously responsible for maintaining balance. Thus dynamics plays a much more integral role in the formation of the walking motion than it does in reaching.

An aspect of walking that complicates its analysis and generation is that it is dynamically stable but not statically stable. This means that if a figure engaged in walking suddenly freezes, the figure is not necessarily in a balanced state and would probably fall to the ground. For animation purposes, this means that the walking motion cannot be frozen in time and statically analyzed to determine the correct forces and torques that produce the motion. As a result, knowledge of the walking motion, in the form of either empirically gathered data[47] or a set of parameters adjustable by the animator, is typically used as the global control mechanism for walking behavior. Attributes such as stride length, hip rotation, and foot placement can be used to specify what a particular walk should look like. A state transition diagram, or its equivalent, is typically used to transition from phase to phase of the gait.[48,49,50,51] Calculation of forces and torques can then be added, if desired, to make the nuances of the motion more physically accurate and more visually satisfying. Kinematics can be used to entirely control the legs, whereas the forces implied by the movement of the legs are used to affect the motion of the upper body.[44,52] Alternatively, kinematics can be used to establish constraints on leg motion such as leg swing duration and foot placement. Then the forces and torques necessary to satisfy the constraints can be used to resolve the remaining DOF of the legs.[49,50,51] In some cases, forward dynamic control can be used after determining the forces and torques necessary to drive the legs from state to state.[46]

Understanding the interaction of the various joints involved in locomotion is the first step in understanding and modeling locomotion. The walking and running cycles are presented first. Then the walk cycle is broken down in more detail, showing the complex movements involved. For this discussion, walking is considered to be locomotion characterized by one or both feet touching the ground at any point in time as opposed to running, where at most only one foot is on the ground at any point in time.

Walk cycle

The walk cycle can be broken down into various phases[49] based on the relation of the feet to their points of contact with the ground (Figure 9.17). The *stride* is defined by the sequence of motions between two consecutive repetitions of a body configuration.[47] The *left stance* phase of a stride is initiated with the right foot on the ground and the left heel just starting to strike the ground. During this phase, the body is supported by both feet until the right foot pivots up and the right toe leaves the ground. The left stance phase continues as the right foot leaves the ground and starts swinging forward and as the right heel strikes the ground and both feet are once again on the ground. The left toe leaving the ground terminates the left stance phase. The *right swing phase* is the period in which the right toe leaves the ground, the right leg swings forward, and the right heel strikes the ground. Notice that the right swing phase is a subinterval of the left stance phase. The end of the right swing phase initiates the right stance phase, and analogous phases now proceed with the roles of the left leg and the right leg switched. The walking cycle is characterized by alternating periods of single and double support.

Run cycle

The run cycle can also be described as a sequence of phases. It differs from the walk cycle in that both feet are off the ground at one time and at no time are both feet on

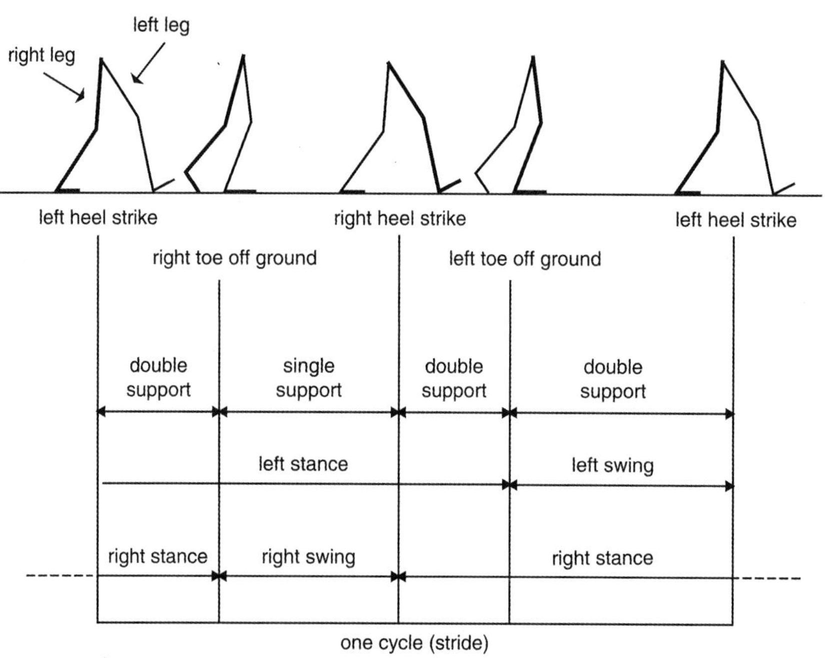

FIGURE 9.17

Walk cycle.[32]

the ground. As in the walk cycle, the *stance* is the duration that a foot is on the ground. Thus the *left stance*, defined by the left heel strike and left toe lift, has the right foot off the ground. This is followed by a period of *flight*, during which both feet are off the ground, with the right foot swinging forward. The flight is terminated by the right heel strike, which starts the *right stance* (Figure 9.18). Notice that the left and right stances do not overlap and are separated by periods of flight.

Pelvic transport

For this discussion, let the pelvis represent the mass of the upper body being transported by the legs. Using a simplified representation for the legs, Figure 9.19 shows

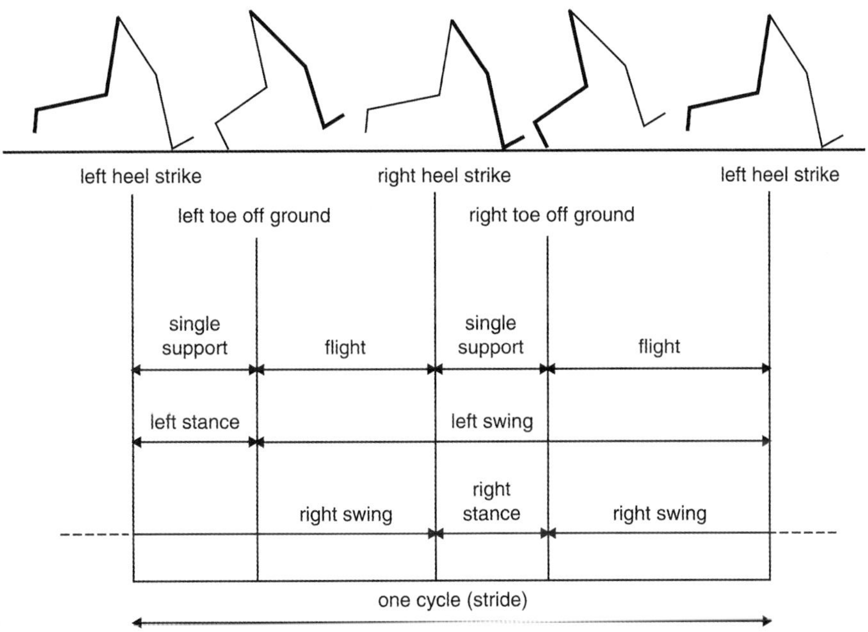

FIGURE 9.18

Run cycle.[12]

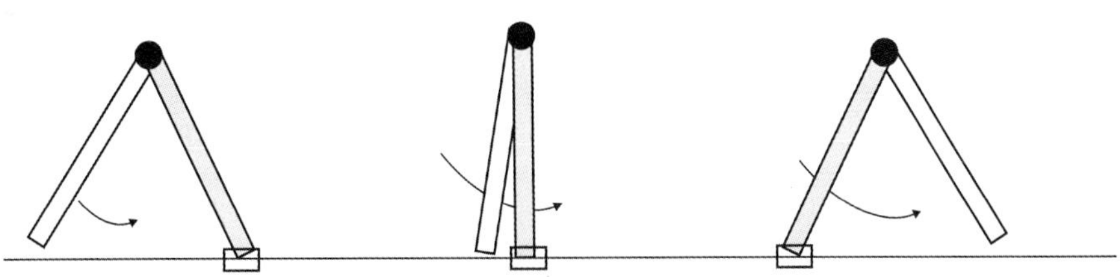

A Start of stance B Midstance C End of stance

FIGURE 9.19

Position of pelvis during stance phase (sagittal plane). (a) Start of stance, (b) midstance, and (c) end of stance. Box indicates supporting contact with floor.

how the pelvis is supported by the stance leg at various points during the stance phase of the walk cycle. Figure 9.20 shows these positions superposed during a full stride and illustrates the abutting of two-dimensional circular arcs describing the basic path of the pelvis as it is transported by the legs.

Pelvic rotation

The pelvis represents the connection between the legs and the structure that separates the legs in the third dimension. Figure 9.21 shows the position of the pelvis during various points in the walking cycle, as viewed from above. The pelvis rotates about a vertical axis centered at the stance leg, helping to lengthen the stride as the swing leg stretches out for its new foot placement. This rotation of the pelvis above the stance leg means that the center of the pelvis follows a circular arc relative to the top of that leg. The top of the stance leg is rotating above the point of contact with the floor (Figure 9.21), so the path of the center of the pelvis resembles a sinusoidal curve (Figure 9.22).

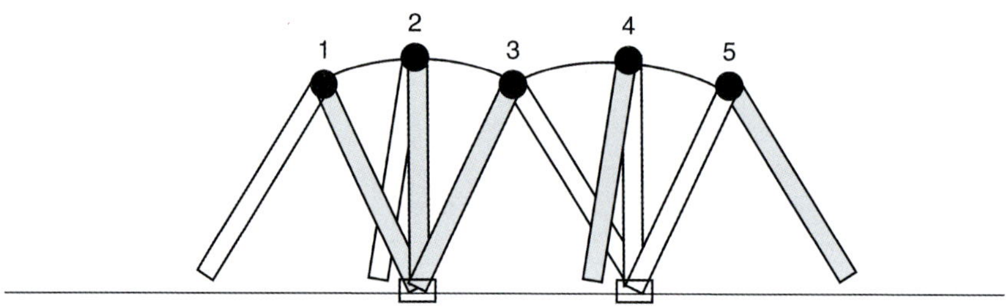

FIGURE 9.20

Transport of pelvis by intersecting circular arcs (sagittal plane).

FIGURE 9.21

Pelvic orientation during stance phase (transverse plane).

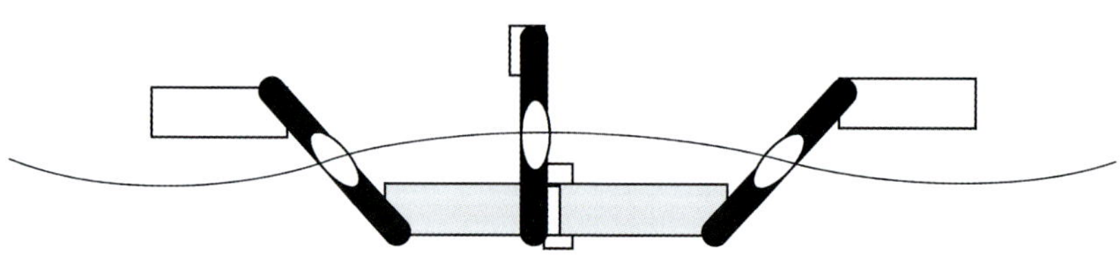

FIGURE 9.22

Path of the pelvic center from above (transverse plane), exaggerated for illustrative purposes.

Pelvic list

The transport of the pelvis requires the legs to lift the weight of the body as the pelvis rotates above the point of contact with the floor (Figure 9.23). To reduce the amount of lift, the pelvis lists by rotating in the coronal plane.

Knee flexion

As shown in Figure 9.23, in a pelvic list with one-piece legs, the swing leg would penetrate the floor. Bending at the knee joint (flexion) allows the swing leg to safely pass over the floor and avoid contact (Figure 9.24). Flexion at the knee of the stance leg also produces some leveling out of the pelvic arcs produced by the rotation of the pelvis over the point of contact with the floor. In addition, extension just before contact with the floor followed by flexion of the new stance leg at impact provides a degree of shock absorption.

Ankle and toe joints

The final part of the puzzle to the walking motion is the foot complex, consisting of the ankle, the toes, and the foot itself. This complex comprises several bones and many DOFs and can be simply modeled as two hinge joints per foot (Figure 9.25). The ankle and toe joints serve to further flatten out the rotation of the pelvis above the foot as well as to absorb some shock.

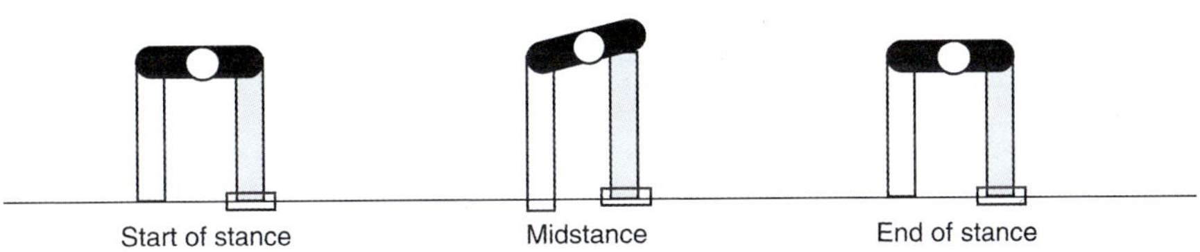

FIGURE 9.23

Pelvic list to reduce the amount of lift (coronal plane).

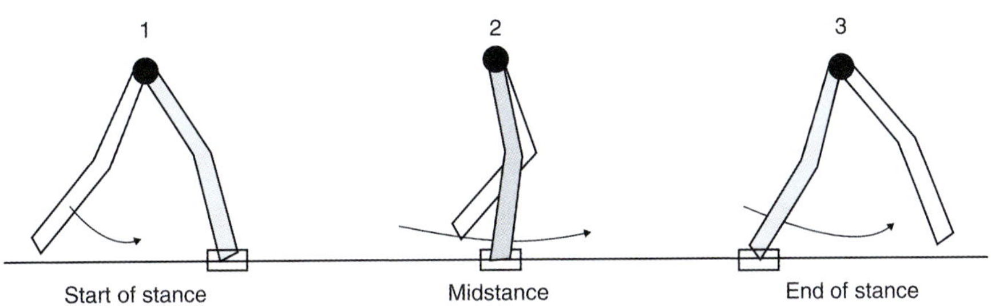

FIGURE 9.24

Knee flexion allowing for the swing leg to avoid penetrating the floor, leveling the path of the pelvis over the point of contact, and providing some shock absorption (sagittal plane).

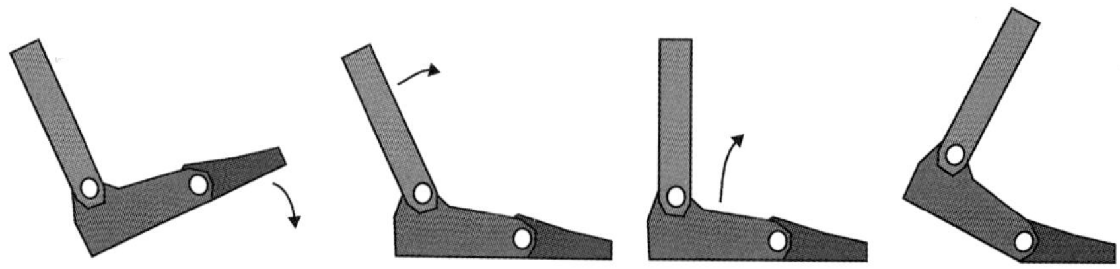

FIGURE 9.25

Rotation due to ankle-toe joints.

9.3.8 The kinematics of the walk

Animation of the leg can be performed by appropriate control of the joint angles. As previously mentioned, a leg's walk cycle is composed of a stance phase and a swing phase. The stance phase duration is the time from heel strike to toe lift. The swing phase duration is the time between contact with the ground—from toe lift to heel strike. The most basic approach to generating the walking motion is for the animator to specify a list of joint angle values for each DOF involved in the walk. There are various sources for empirical data describing the kinematics of various walks at various speeds. Figures 9.26 through 9.30, from Inman, Ralston,

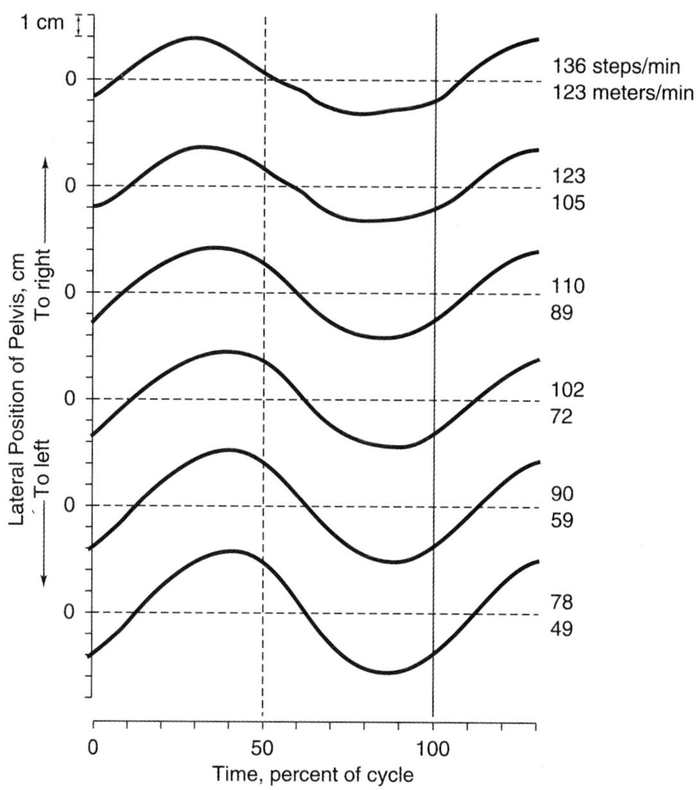

FIGURE 9.26

Lateral displacement of pelvis.[32]

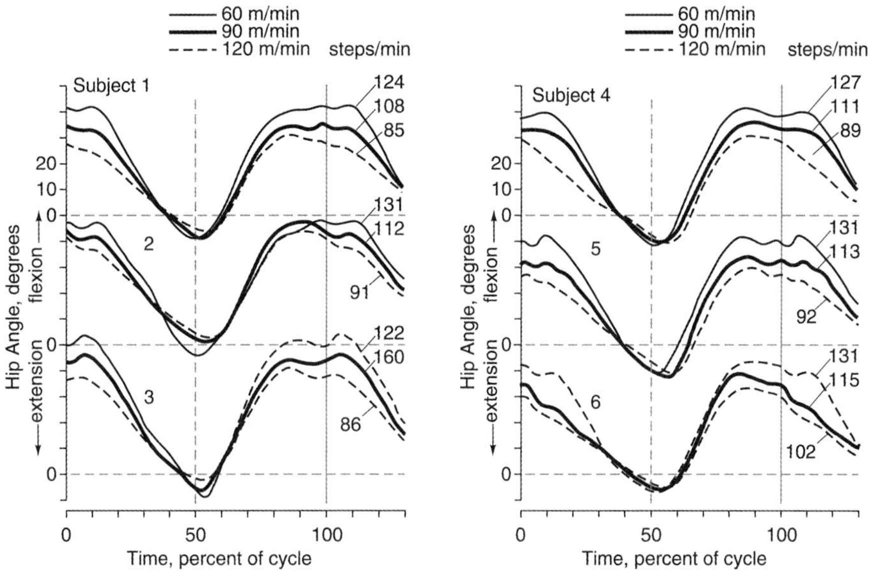

FIGURE 9.27

Hip angles.[32]

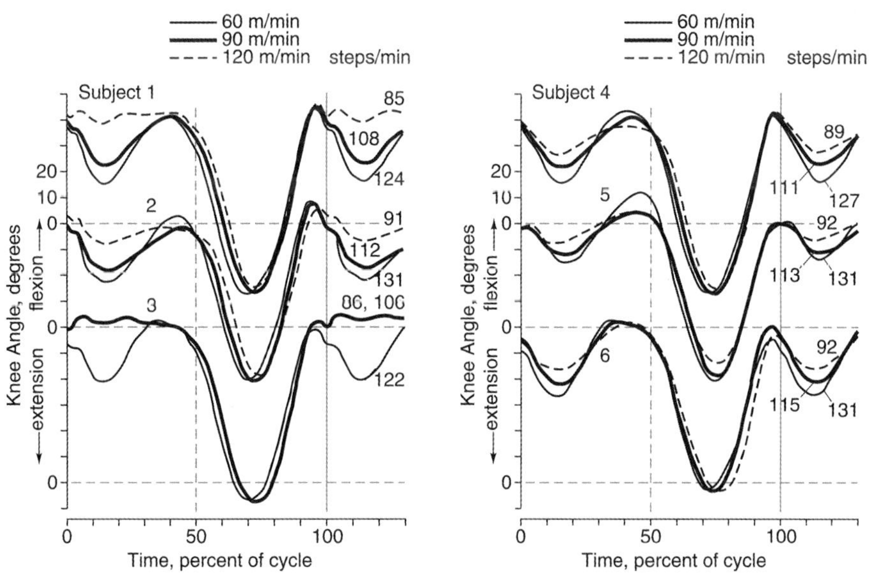

FIGURE 9.28

Knee angles.[32]

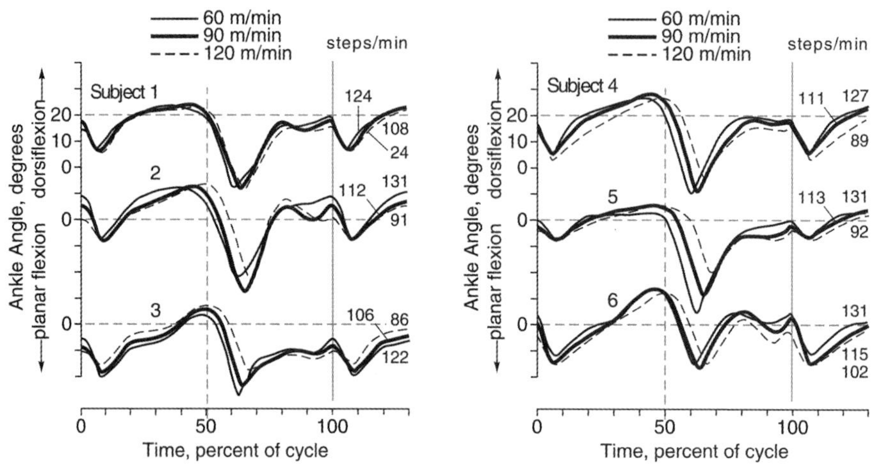

FIGURE 9.29

Ankle angles.[32]

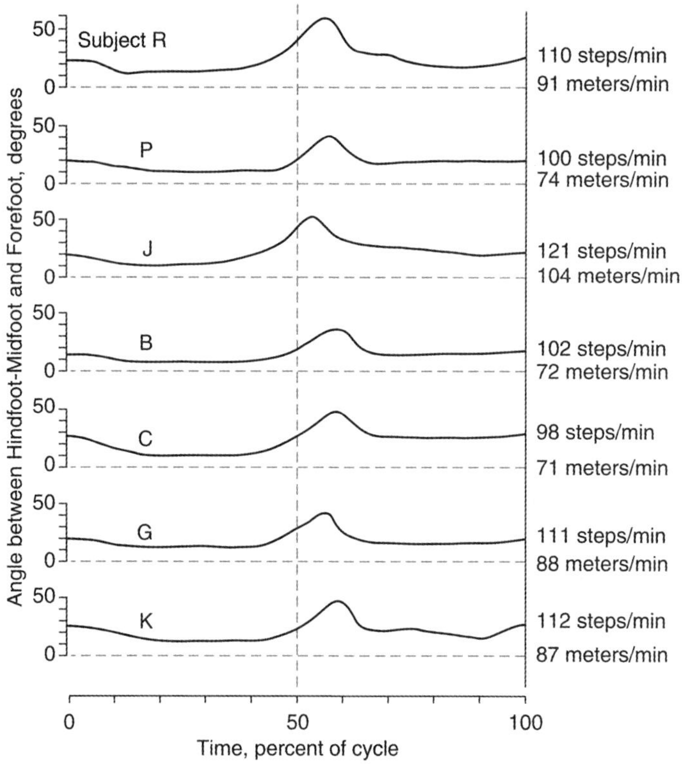

FIGURE 9.30

Toe angles.[32]

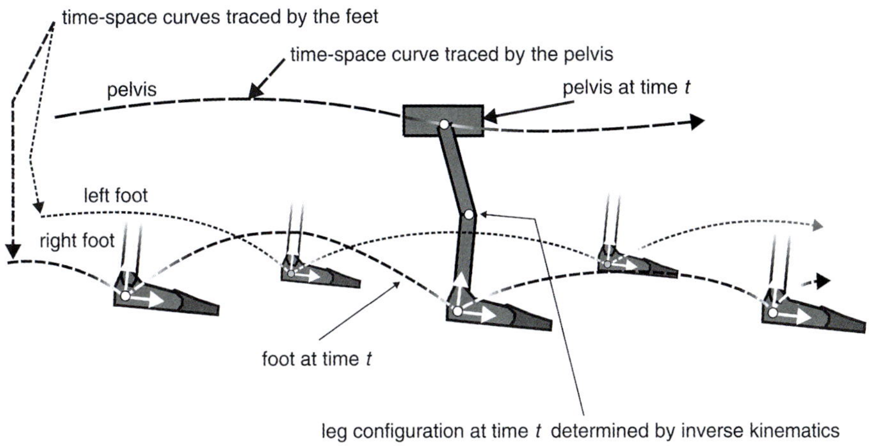

FIGURE 9.31

Pelvis and feet constraints satisfied by inverse kinematics.

and Todd,[47] graph the angles over time for the various joints involved in the walk cycle, as well as giving values for the lateral displacement of the pelvis.

Specifying all the joint angles, either on a frame-by-frame basis or by interpolation of values between key frames, is an onerous task for the animator. In addition, it takes a skilled artist to design values that create unique walks that deviate in any way from precisely collected clinical data. When creating new walks, the animator can specify kinematic values such as pelvic movement, foot placement, and foot trajectories. Inverse kinematics can be used to determine the angles of the intermediate joints.[48] By constructing the time-space curves traced by the pelvis and each foot, the user can determine the position of each for a given frame of the animation. Each leg can then be positioned by considering the pelvis fixed and the leg a linked appendage whose desired end-effector position is the corresponding position on the foot trajectory curve (Figure 9.31). Sensitivity to segment lengths can cause even clinical data to produce configurations that fail to keep the feet in solid contact with the floor during walking. Inverse kinematics is also useful for forcing clinical data to maintain proper foot placement.

9.3.9 Using dynamics to help produce realistic motion

Dynamic simulation can be used to map specified actions and constraints to make the movement more accurate physically. However, as Girard and Maciejewski[53] point out, an animator who wants a particular look for a behavior often wants more control over the motion than a total physical simulation provides (Girard and Maciejewski discussed this in relation to walking, but it obviously applies in many situations where physically reasonable, yet artistically controlled motion is desired). Dynamics must be intelligently applied so that it aids the animator and does not become an obstacle that the animator must work around. In addition, to make the computations tractable, the animator almost always simplifies the dynamics. There are several common types of simplifications: (1) some dynamic effects are ignored, such as the effect of the swing leg on balance; (2) relatively small temporal variations are ignored and a force is considered constant over some time interval, such as the upward push of the stance leg; (3) a complex structure, such as the 7-DOF leg, is replaced for purposes of the dynamic computations by a simplified but somewhat dynamically equivalent structure, such as a 1-DOF telescoping leg; and (4) computing arbitrarily complex dynamic effects is replaced by computing decoupled dynamic components, such as separate horizontal and vertical components, which are computed independently of each other and then summed.

In achieving the proper motion of the upper body, the legs are used to impart forces to the mass of the upper body as carried by the pelvis. An upward force can be imparted by the stance leg on the mass of the upper body at the point of connection between the legs and the torso, that is, the hips.[52,53] To achieve support of the upper body, the total upward acceleration due to the support of the legs has to cancel to total downward acceleration due to gravity. As simplifying assumptions, the effect of each leg can be considered independent of the other(s), and the upward force of a leg on the upper body during the leg's stance phase can be considered constant. As additional assumptions, horizontal acceleration can be computed independently for each leg and can be considered constant during the leg's stance phase (Figure 9.32). The horizontal force of the legs can be adjusted automatically to produce the average velocity for the body as specified by the animator, but the fluctuations in instantaneous velocity over time help to create visually more appealing motion than constant velocity alone would. The temporal variations in upward and forward acceleration at each hip due to the alternating stance phases can be used to compute pelvic rotation and pelvic list to produce even more realistic motion.

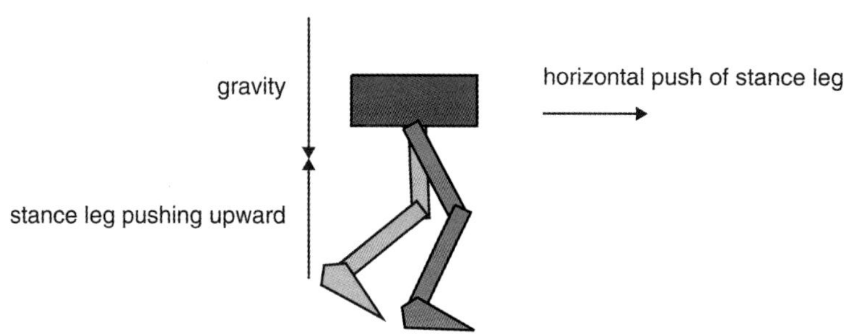

FIGURE 9.32

Horizontal and vertical dynamics of stance leg: gravity and the vertical component must cancel over the duration of the cycle. The horizontal push must account for the average forward motion of the figure over the duration of the cycle.

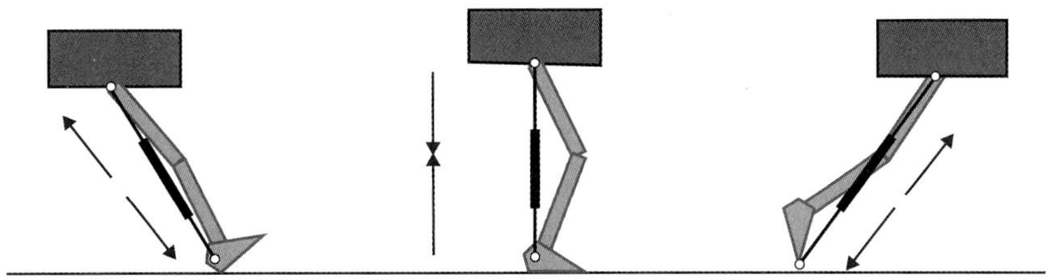

FIGURE 9.33

Telescoping joint with kinematically fit leg complex.

More physics can be introduced into the lower body by modeling the leg dynamics with a telescoping joint (implemented as a parallel spring-damper system) during the stance phase. The upward force of the leg during the stance phase becomes time varying as the telescoping joint compresses under the weight of the upper body and expands under the restoring forces of the leg complex (upper leg, lower leg, foot, and associated joints). The telescoping mechanism simulates the shock-absorbing effect of the knee-ankle-toe joints. The leg complex is then fit to the length of the telescoping joint by inverse kinematics (Figure 9.33). During the swing phase, the leg is typically controlled kinematically and does not enter into any dynamic considerations.

Incorporating more physics into the model, the kinematic control information for the figure can be used to guide the motion (as opposed to constraining it). A simple inverse dynamics computation is then used to try to match the behavior of the system with the kinematic control values. Desired joint angles are computed based on high-level animator-supplied parameters such as speed and the number of steps per unit distance. Joint torques are computed based on proportional-derivative servos (Eq. 9.1). The difference between the desired angle, denoted by the underbar, and the current angle at each joint is used to compute the torque to be applied at the next time step. The angular velocities are treated similarly. These torque values are smoothed to prevent abrupt changes in the computed motion. However, choosing good values for the gains (k_s, k_v) can be difficult and usually requires a trial-and-error approach.

$$\tau = k_s\left(\widehat{\theta}_i - \theta_i\right) + k_v\left(\dot{\widehat{\theta}}_i - \dot{\theta}_i\right) \tag{9.1}$$

9.3.10 Forward dynamic control

In some cases, forward dynamic control instead of kinematic control can be effectively used. Kinematics still plays a role. Certain kinematic states, such as maximum forward extension of a leg, trigger activation of forces and torques. These forces and torques move the legs to a new kinematic state, such as maximum backward extension of a leg, which triggers a different sequence of forces and torques.[46] The difficulty with this approach is in designing the forces and torques necessary to produce a reasonable walk cycle (or other movement, for that matter). In some cases it may be possible to use empirical data found in the biomechanics literature as the appropriate force and torque sequence.

9.4 Chapter summary

The human figure is an interesting and complex form. It has a uniform structure but contains infinite variety. As an articulated rigid structure, it contains many DOFs, but its surface is deformable. Modeling and animating hair in any detail is also enormously complex. Moreover, the constant collision and sliding of cloth on the surface of the body represents significant computational complexity.

One of the things that makes human motion so challenging is that no single motion can be identified as correct human motion. Human motion varies from individual to individual for a number of reasons, but it is still recognizable as reasonable human motion, and slight variations can seem odd or awkward. There are a variety of motion nuances between people, but at the same time, are very consistent for a particular person, for a particular ethnic group, for a particular age group, for a particular weight group, or for a particular emotional state.

9.5 Exercises

Beginner

B1. Experiment with lattice deformation modifiers and mesh deformation modifiers as shown in Figure 9.5.

B2. Create a single bendy-bone and demonstrate its deformation on a basic model of a bicep muscle as shown in Figure 9.6.

Intermediate

I1. Using your single bendy-bone muscle from above, create two sets of bones for an arm, one that is completely rigid and one that contains bendy-bones for the muscles that follow the anatomical structure of the arm. Note that your rigid model should have a single bone for the forearm, but you should have at least two bendy-bones in each forearm. Think about how the bones move when you rotate your wrist.

Advanced

A1. Recreate the basic shapes of the human form as shown in Figure 9.2. Work on just these shapes and keep them as separate objects. Once you are happy with the result, rig this model using the basic human rig and only use parenting to the bone (without weights) to animate these components rigidly.

A2. Fuse your basic shapes into a single object and use voxel remeshing to keep only the surface. Remesh the result using quadriflow or similar retopology methods (or practice your own retopology skills). When you are happy with the result, apply your human rig to this new model using automatic weighting (or use automatic rigging tools like Mixamo or AccuRig) to obtain a rig that deforms smoothly. Using this rig, animate a walk cycle and a run cycle by finding references (or creating your own references). Ensure you consider the weight of the movement, the trajectory of the pelvis, and the moments in which each foot makes contact and leaves the ground. To help your animation, ensure you have created a set of inverse kinematics constraints and tweak as necessary to obtain a natural result.

References

[1] B. Foundation, "blender.org - Home of the Blender project - Free and Open 3D Creation Software," blender.org. [Online]. Available: https://www.blender.org/. Accessed: Jul. 26, 2024.

[2] Piegl L. On NURBS: a survey. IEEE Comput. Graph. Appl. 1991;11(01):55–71. https://doi.org/10.1109/38.67702.

[3] Dimas E, Briassoulis D. 3D geometric modelling based on NURBS: a review. Adv. Eng. Softw. 1999;30(9):741–51. https://doi.org/10.1016/S0965-9978(98)00110-0.

[4] Kazakov M. Catmull-Clark subdivision for geometry shaders. In: Proceedings of the 5th international conference on Computer graphics, virtual reality, visualisation and interaction in Africa. AFRIGRAPH '07. New York, NY, USA: Association for Computing Machinery; 2007. p. 77–84. https://doi.org/10.1145/1294685.1294699.

[5] Lai S, Cheng FF. Adaptive rendering of Catmull-Clark subdivision surfaces. In: Ninth international conference on computer aided design and computer graphics (CAD-CG'05); 2005. p. 6. https://doi.org/10.1109/CAD-CG.2005.18.

[6] Bolz J, Schröder P. Rapid evaluation of Catmull-Clark subdivision surfaces. In: Proceedings of the seventh international conference on 3D Web technology. Web3D '02. New York, NY, USA: Association for Computing Machinery; 2002. p. 11–7. https://doi.org/10.1145/504502.504505.

[7] Qin H, Mandal C, Vemuri BC. Dynamic Catmull-Clark subdivision surfaces. IEEE Trans. Vis. Comput. Graph. 1998;4(3):215–29. https://doi.org/10.1109/2945.722296.

[8] Hierarchical B-spline refinement | ACM SIGGRAPH Computer Graphics." [Online]. Available: https://dl.acm.org/doi/10.1145/378456.378512. Accessed: Jul. 26, 2024.

[9] Museth K, Breen DE, Whitaker RT, Barr AH. Level set surface editing operators. In: Proceedings of the 29th annual conference on Computer graphics and interactive techniques. San Antonio, Texas: ACM; 2002. p. 330–8. https://doi.org/10.1145/566570.566585.

[10] DeRose T, Kass M, Truong T. Subdivision surfaces in character animation. In: Proceedings of the 25th annual conference on Computer graphics and interactive techniques. SIGGRAPH '98. New York, NY, USA: Association for Computing Machinery; 1998. p. 85–94. https://doi.org/10.1145/280814.280826.

[11] Pump it up: computer animation of a biomechanically based model of muscle using the finite element method: ACM SIGGRAPH Computer Graphics: Vol 26, No 2." [Online]. Available: https://dl.acm.org/doi/10.1145/142920.134016. Accessed: Aug. 14, 2024.

[12] Sannier G, Magnenat-Thalmann N. A user-friendly texture-fitting methodology for virtual humans. In: International CG, editor. Hasselt/Diepenbeek. Belgium: IEEE Computer Society; 1997.

[13] Ward K, Lin M, Lee J, Fisher S, Macri D. Modeling hair using level-of-detail representations. In: International conference on computer animation and social agents; 2003. p. 41−7.

[14] Boulic R, et al. The HUMANOID environment for interactive animation of multiple deformable human characters. In: Post F, Göbel M, editors. Computer graphics forum, 14(3). Blackwell; 1995. p. 337−48.

[15] Chadwick J, Haumann D, Parent R. Layered construction for deformable animated characters. In: Lane J, editor. Computer graphics. Proceedings of SIGGRAPH 89, 23(3). Boston; 1989. p. 243−52.

[16] Blanz V, Vetter T. A morphable model for the synthesis of 3D faces. In: Rockwood A, editor. Computer graphics. Proceedings of SIGGRAPH '99. Los Angeles, Calif: Addison-Wesley Longman; 1999. p. 187−94.

[17] MetaHuman | Realistic Person Creator," Unreal Engine.[Online]. Available: https://www.unrealengine.com/en-US/metahuman. Accessed: Jul. 26, 2024.

[18] "AI 3D Head Generator | Headshot 2 | Character Creator," AI 3D Head Generator | Headshot 2 | Character Creator. [Online]. Available: https://www.reallusion.com/character-creator/headshot/. Accessed: Jul. 26, 2024.

[19] Loper M, Mahmood N, Romero J, Pons-Moll G, Black MJ. SMPL: a skinned multi-person linear model. ACM Trans. Graph. 2015;34:248:1−248:16. https://doi.org/10.1145/2816795.2818013.

[20] Pavlakos G, et al. Expressive body capture: 3D hands, face, and body from a single image. 2019. p. 10975−85. https://doi.org/10.1109/cvpr.2019.01123.

[21] Osman AAA, Bolkart T, Tzionas D, Black MJ. SUPR: a sparse unified part-based human representation. 2022. p. arXiv. https://doi.org/10.48550/arXiv.2210.13861. arXiv:2210.13861.

[22] Gesslein T, Scherer D, Grubert J. BodyDigitizer: an open source photogrammetry-based 3D body scanner. 2017. https://doi.org/10.48550/arXiv.1710.01370. arXiv:1710.01370.

[23] Yang Y, Xu J, Elkhuizen WS, Song Y. The development of a low-cost photogrammetry-based 3D hand scanner. HardwareX 2021;10:e00212. https://doi.org/10.1016/j.ohx.2021.e00212.

[24] Scaniverse - 3D Scanner - Gaussian Splatting - LiDAR." [Online]. Available: https://scaniverse.com/. Accessed: Jul. 26, 2024.

[25] Newcombe RA, et al. KinectFusion: real-time dense surface mapping and tracking. 2011 10th IEEE Int. Symp. Mix. Augment. Real. 2011;null:127−36. https://doi.org/10.1109/ISMAR.2011.6092378.

[26] Loper M, Mahmood N, Romero J, Pons-Moll G, Black MJ. In: SMPL: a skinned multi-person linear model, 34(3); 2015. p. 248. https://doi.org/10.1145/2816795.2818013.

[27] Bogo F, Kanazawa A, Lassner C, Gehler PV, Romero J, Black MJ. Keep it SMPL: automatic estimation of 3D human pose and shape from a single image. 2016. p. 561−78. https://doi.org/10.1007/978-3-319-46454-1_34.

[28] Shao Z, et al. SplattingAvatar: realistic real-time human avatars with mesh-embedded Gaussian splatting. In: Proceedings of the IEEE/CVF conference on computer vision and pattern recognition (CVPR); 2024. p. 1606–16.
[29] Scheepers F. Anatomy-based surface generation for articulated models of human figures. Ohio State University; 1996. PhD Thesis.
[30] F. Scheepers, R. Parent, W. Carlson, and S. May, "Anatomy-based modeling of the human musculature," in Whitted T, editor. Computer Graphics. Proceedings of SIGGRAPH 97, Annual Conference Series, pp. 163–172.
[31] Wilhelms J, van Gelder A. Anatomically based modeling. In: Whitted T, editor. Computer graphics. Proceedings of SIGGRAPH 97, annual conference series. Los Angeles, Calif: Addison-Wesley; 1997. p. 173–80.
[32] Lacquaniti F, Soechting JF. Coordination of arm and wrist motion during a reaching task. J. Neurosci. 1982;2(2):399–408.
[33] Soechting J, Flanders M. Errors in pointing are due to approximations in sensorimotor transformations. J. Neurophysiol. 1989;62(2):595–608.
[34] Kondo K. Inverse kinematics of a human arm. Stanford University; 1994. Technical Report STAN-CS-TR-94-1508.
[35] Koga Y, Kondo K, Kuffner J, Latombe J-C. Planning motions with intentions. In: Glassner A, editor. Computer graphics. Proceedings of SIGGRAPH 94, annual conference series. Orlando, Fla: ACM Press; 1994. p. 395–408.
[36] Rijpkema H, Girard M. Computer animation of knowledge-based human grasping. In: Sederberg TW, editor. Computer graphics, Proceedings of SIGGRAPH 91, 25(4). Las Vegas: Nev; 1991. p. 339–48.
[37] Aydin Y, Kakajiima M. Database guided computer animation of human grasping using forward and inverse kinematics. Comput. Graph. 1999;23:145–54.
[38] Huang Z, Boulic R, Magnenat-Thalmann N, Thalmann D. A multi-sensor approach for grasping and 3D interaction. Comput. Graph. Int. 1995.
[39] Mas Sanso R, Thalmann D. A hand control and automatic grasping system for synthetic actors. Eurographics 1994;94.
[40] Kry P, Pai D. Interaction capture and synthesis. Trans. Graph. 2006;25(3).
[41] Pollard NS, Zordan VB. Physically based grasping control from example. In: Symposium on computer animation; 2005. p. 2005.
[42] H. A. W. Group, "Specification for a Standard Humanoid." [Online]. Available: http://ece.uwaterloo.ca/h-anim/spec1.1/
[43] Pandzic I, Capin T, Magnenat-Thalmann N, Thalmann D. Developing simulation techniques for an interactive clothing system. In: Proceedings of VSMM '97. Geneva, Switzerland; 1997. p. 109–18.
[44] Gourret J-P, Magnenat-Thalmann N, Thalmann D. Simulation of object and human skin deformations in a grasping task. In: Lane J, editor. Computer graphics. Proceedings of SIGGRAPH 89, 23(3). Boston; 1989. p. 21–30.
[45] Nedel L, Thalmann D. Modeling and deformation of the human body using an anatomically-based approach. In: Animation C, editor. 98. Philadelphia, Pa: IEEE Computer Society; 1998.
[46] McKenna M, Zeltzer D. Dynamic simulation of autonomous legged locomotion. In: Baskett F, editor. Computer graphics. Proceedings of SIGGRAPH 90, 24(4). Dallas: Tex; 1990. p. 29–38.
[47] Inman V, Ralston H, Todd F. Human walking. Baltimore, Maryland: Williams & Wilkins; 1981.

[48] Bruderlin A, Calvert T. Knowledge-driven, interactive animation of human running. In: Davis WA, Bartels R, editors. Graphics interface '96. Canadian human-computer communications society; 1996. p. 213–21.

[49] Bruderlin A, Calvert T. Goal-directed, dynamic animation of human walking. In: Lane J, editor. Computer graphics. Proceedings of SIGGRAPH 89, 23(3). .: Boston, Mass; 1989. p. 233–42.

[50] Hodgins J, Wooten W, Brogan D, O'Brien J. Animating human athletics. In: Cook R, editor. Computer graphics. Proceedings of SIGGRAPH 95. Los Angeles, Calif: Addison-Wesley; 1995. p. 71–8.

[51] Raibert M, Hodgins J. Animation of dynamic legged locomotion. In: Sederberg TW, editor. Computer graphics. Proceedings of SIGGRAPH 91, 25(4). Las Vegas: Nev; 1991. p. 349–58.

[52] Torkos N, van de Panne M. Footprint-based quadruped motion synthesis. In: Booth K, Fournier A, editors. Graphics. Interface '98; 1998. p. 151–60.

[53] Girard M, Maciejewski A. A. Computational modeling for the computer animation of legged figures. In: Computer graphics. Proceedings of SIGGRAPH 85. San Francisco; 1985. p. 263–70.

CHAPTER

Facial animation

10

Realistic facial animation is one of the most difficult tasks that a computer animator can be asked to do. Human faces are familiar to us all. Facial motion adheres to an underlying, well-defined structure but is idiosyncratic. A face has a single mechanical articulator but has a flexible covering capable of subtle expression and rapid, complex lip movements during speech.

The face is an important component in modeling a figure, because it is the main instrument for communication and for defining a figure's mood and personality. Animation of speech is especially demanding because of the requirement for audio synchronization (and therefore is often referred to as *lip-sync animation*). In addition, a good facial model should be capable of geometrically representing a specific person (called *conformation* by Parke [1] and *static* by others, e.g., [2]).

Facial models can be used for cartooning, for realistic character animation, for telecommunications to reduce bandwidth, and for human-computer interaction (HCI). In cartooning, facial animation has to be able to convey expression and personality that is often exaggerated. In realistic character animation, the geometry and movement of the face must adhere to the constraints of realistic human anatomy.

With the adoption of conferencing technology (i.e., Zoom, Google Meet, Microsoft Teams) into our society and through the emergence of "VTubers," we have seen a desire to use digital avatars in place of live humans in these contexts for entertainment purposes. This requires the use of realtime algorithms that can track and map video of our face movements to digital avatars in an effective and efficient manner. In addition to the issues addressed by other animation tasks, facial animation often has the constraint of precise timing with respect to an audio track during lip-syncing and some expressions. Despite its name, lip-syncing involves more than just the lips; the rigid articulation of the jaw and the muscle deformation of the tongue must also be considered.

10.1 The uncanny valley

The uncanny valley is a phenomenon posited originally by Japanese roboticist and researcher Mori [3], who suggested that there is a dip in "affinity" (the extent to which an individual likes something) as robots approach realistic human appearance

Computer Animation. https://doi.org/10.1016/B978-0-443-13512-5.00010-0

and movements. This phenomenon is apparent not only in human-like robots but also in our reactions to digital avatars in general. Figure 10.1 shows a high level "effect" of the phenomenon, which has been studied extensively quantitatively and qualitatively by psychologists [4–6] and computer scientists [7–9]. The reason for this dip in affinity is thought to occur due to how our brains have evolved to discern human faces very effectively and thus any deviation from what our brain thinks is "human" evokes negative emotions. When confronted with images depicting large deviations from the human form (i.e., depictions of animals/aliens/stylized animations), our mind can easily label discern that they are nonhuman (or rather depictions that are not human); however, when confronted with depictions of increasing subtle deviations from what we consider is "human," people express increasing levels of dissatisfaction with language like "weird," "strange," "odd," and "unpleasant."

Figure 10.1 also shows the potential effect that moving or animated/dynamic depictions exacerbate the problem, amplifying the strangeness if nonhuman depictions do not move quite as expected. From an animation perspective, this phenomenon has had significant implications for techniques used to create computer-generated characters for film/movies [9–11]; if the lip-sync, lighting, resolution, or movement isn't quite right it removes the viewer from the experience, hence the ever-increasing desire for high-quality motion and facial animation capture technology. With the increased computational power of modern PCs and graphics cards, we are now seeing significant efforts in the video game industry to create realistic and interactive characters that cross the uncanny valley. Tools such as Metahuman Creator/Animator [12] and Reallusion's Character Creator [13] use a large number of blend-shapes allowing animators to model subtle facial movements; however, anecdotally they are not quite at the point of complete believability and fall directly into the uncanny valley. The gap of believability is rapidly closing however with the advent of more sophisticated deep learning techniques to create avatars. Questions

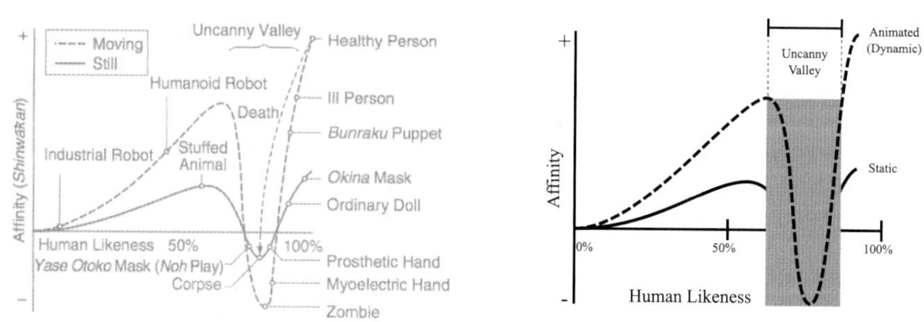

FIGURE 10.1

Depiction of the uncanny valley [3], static and animated avatars exhibit different levels of "uncanniness."

remain regarding the ethics and trust of using digital avatars especially in applications in which they are being used to influence behavior [14–16].

10.2 Faces: structure

10.2.1 Anatomy

The anatomical structure of the human face [17–19] consists of (1) an underlying skeletal bone structure (skull) containing a single rigid articulatory component, the jaw; (2) eyes that can rotate and fixate; (3) veins/arteries to move blood; (4) muscles to allow for movement; (5) layers of skin; and (6) hair. The surface of the skull is covered with muscles, most of which (at least indirectly) connect areas of the skin to positions on the skull. These muscles tug on the skin to create movement, often recognizable as expressions. Features of the skin include eyelids, mouth, and eyebrows. The skin has various expressive wrinkles such as on the forehead and around the mouth.

As with the rest of the body, muscles provide the driving force for the face (Figure 10.2 and Table 10.1). However, unlike the rest of the body, the muscles mainly move the skin into interesting positions, producing recognizable lip and skin configurations and, in speech, modify the sounds emanating from the labial opening. In particular, the muscles around the mouth are extremely flexible and

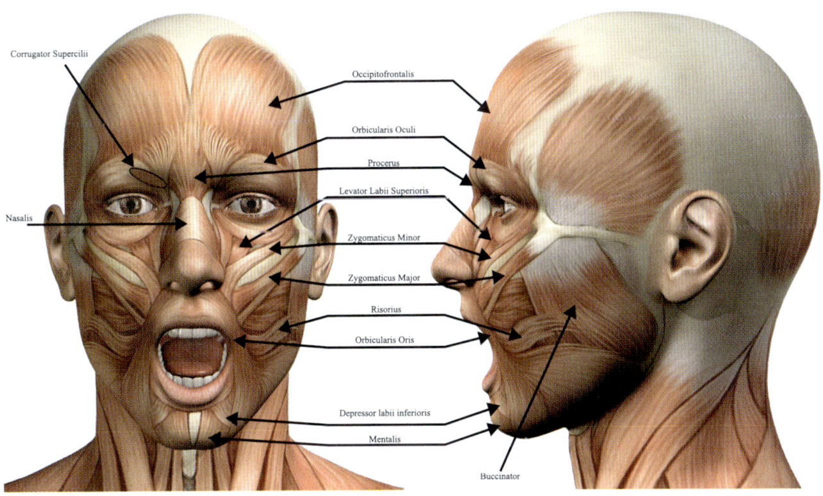

FIGURE 10.2

Facial anatomical structure depicting the muscles in the face. Image from kjpargeter on Freepik.com.

capable of producing a variety of shapes and subtle movements. A muscle of particular importance is the *orbicularis oris* (Figure 10.2), which wraps around the mouth and is connected to several muscles attached to the skull and is integral in lip movement.

10.2.2 Action units for animation

The facial action coding system (FACS) is the result of research conducted by the psychologists Ekman and Friesen [20] with the objective of deconstructing all facial expressions into a set of basic facial movements. These movements, called action units (AUs) when considered in combination, can be used to describe all facial expressions. First published in 1978, FACS is widely used to this day for reference and as a basis for blend-shape–based algorithms [21–27].

Forty-six AUs are identified in the study, and they provide a clinical basis from which to build a facial animation system. Examples of AUs are brow lowerer, inner brow raiser, wink, cheek raiser, upper lip raiser, and jaw drop. See Figure 10.3 for an example of diagrammed AUs and [28] for a visual FACS reference. Given the AUs, an animator can build a facial model that is parameterized according to the motions of the AUs. A facial animation system can be built by giving a user access to a set of variables that are in one-to-one correspondence with the AUs. A parametric value controls the amount of the facial motion that results from the associated AU. By setting a variable for each AU, the user can generate all of the facial expressions analyzed by Ekman and Friesen [20]. By using the value of the variables to

Table 10.1 Facial Muscles and Their Functions for Driving Expressions (see Figure 10.2)

Muscle	Main Function	Expressions
Orbicularis oris	closing lips	anger, sadness
Occipitofrontalis	pull scalp back, raise brow, wrinkle forehead	surprise, concern
Orbicularis oculi	closing eyelids, draws skin toward nose	anger, sadness
Procerus	pulls skin between eyebrows downward	anger
Levator labii superioris	moves upper lip	smiling, smugness
Depressor labii inferioris	exposes teeth, moves lower lip	smiling
Mentalis	moves lower lip, wrinkles chin	pouting
Zygomaticus major	curls upper lip	smiling, disdain
Zygomaticus minor	moves upper lip	smiling
Buccinator	flattens cheek, pulls corners of mouth	whistling, smiling
Risorius	pulls corner of mouth outward and upward	smiling, grinning
Corrugator supercilii	moves eyebrows downward	frowning
Nasalis	moves nasal skin, nostril flaring	exertion

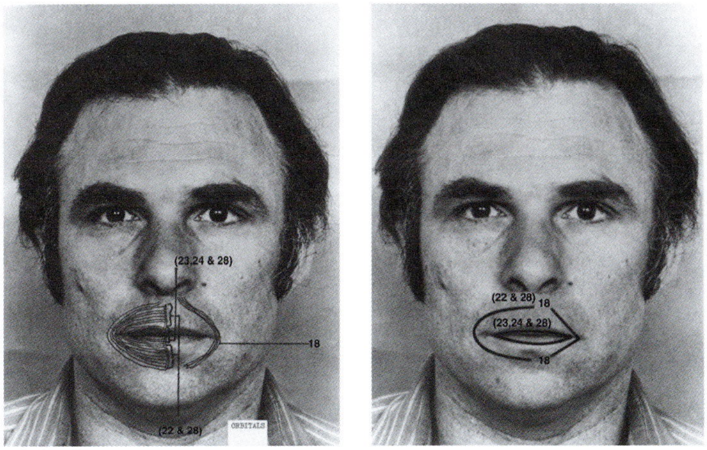

FIGURE 10.3

Three action units (AUs) of the lower face [13].

interpolate the degree to which the motion is realized and by interpolating their value over time, the user can then animate the facial model. By combining the AUs in nonstandard ways, the user can also generate many truly strange expressions.

Although this work is impressive and is certainly relevant to facial animation, two of its characteristics should be noted before it is used as a basis for a facial animation system. First, the FACS is meant to be *descriptive* of a static expression, not generative. Second, FACS is not time based, and facial movements are analyzed only relative to a neutral pose. This means that the AUs were not designed to *animate* a facial model in all the ways that an animator may want to control a face. In addition, the FACS describes facial expressions, not speech. The movements for forming individual phonemes, the basic units of speech, were not specifically incorporated into the system. However, the AUs still provide a great starting point for describing the basic movements and structure for facial animation systems even if they were never intended for this purpose.

10.3 Faces: modeling

Depending on the objective of the animation, there are various ways to model the human face.

As with all animation, trade-offs include realism and computational complexity. Facial structure is different depending on whether you are modeling a realistic character or a stylized character (see Figure 10.4).

Although the structure of modeling a 3D face does not need to be 100% accurate to human physiology, following the general muscular structure allows for smooth

FIGURE 10.4

Example of continuum between realistic and stylized faces, image created with Krea.ai (model: CGI, prompt: male face, [Pixar style], big eyes) by varying AI strength.

deformation when transferring motion to the model from a face-animation motion capture rig.

For example, Figure 10.5 shows a stylized head with the general flow of the polygonal structure. Figure 10.6 shows how such anatomically inspired topology is modeled in two different base meshes; the FLAME morphable model *(left)* and a very clean base mesh from 3DScanstore.com. In both of these meshes, note the topology flow around the mouth/eyes and nose that approximates anatomical structure. Figure 10.7 demonstrates how the FLAME topology accurately enables various expressions.

For more realistic facial animation, more complex facial models are used whose surface geometry more closely corresponds to that of a real face, and the animation of these models is correspondingly more complex. For an excellent in-depth presentation of facial animation, see the book by Parke and Waters [29]. An overview is given here.

The first problem confronting an animator in facial animation is creating the geometry of the facial model to make it suitable for animation. This in itself can be very difficult. Facial animation models vary widely from simple geometry to anatomy based. Generally, the complexity is dictated by the intended use. When deciding on the construction of the model, important factors are geometry data acquisition method, motion control and corresponding data acquisition method, rendering quality, and motion quality. The first factor concerns the method by which the actual geometry of the head of the subject or character is obtained. The second factor concerns the method by which the data describing changes to the geometry are obtained. The quality of the rendered image with respect to smoothness and surface attributes is the third concern. The final concern is the corresponding quality of the computed motion.

The model can be discussed in terms of its static properties and its dynamic properties. The statics deal with the geometry of the model in its neutral form, whereas the dynamics deal with the deformation of the geometry of the model during animation. Facial models are either polygonal or higher order. Polygonal models are used most often for their simplicity (e.g., [1], [29–31]); splines are chosen when a smooth surface is desired.

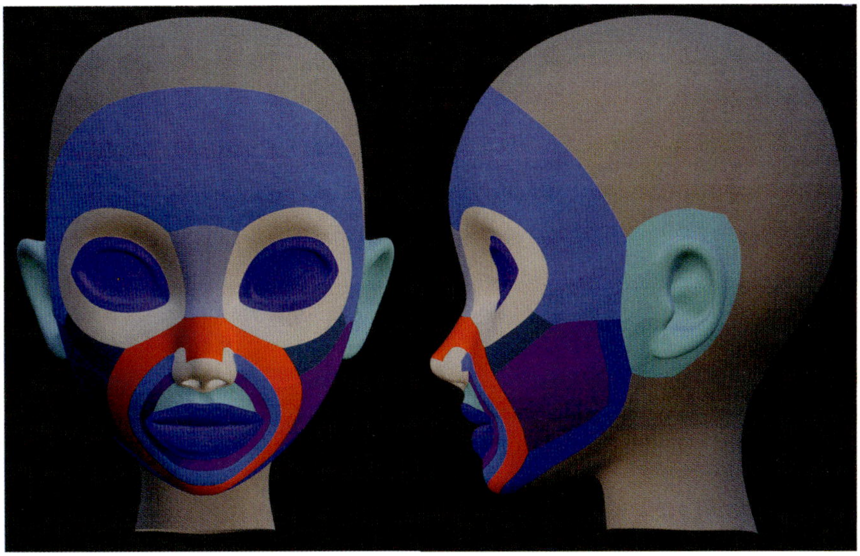

FIGURE 10.5

Simple topology. Stylized face mesh with texture showing areas to flow quads/triangles that follow anatomical structure. ("Face topology" [https://skfb.ly/6AJt6] by masterFELLA is licensed under Creative Commons Attribution [http://creativecommons.org/licenses/by/4.0/].)

Polygonal models are relatively easy to create and can be deformed easily. However, the smoothness of the surface is directly related to the complexity of the model, and polygonal models are visually inferior to other methods of modeling the facial surface. Data acquisition methods only sample the surface, producing discrete data, and surface fitting techniques are subsequently applied.

Spline models typically use bicubic, quadrilateral surface patches, such as Bezier or B-spline nonuniform rational B-splines (NURBS), to represent the face. Although surface patches offer the advantage of low data complexity in comparison to polygonal techniques when generating smooth surfaces, they have several disadvantages when it comes to modeling an object such as the human face. With standard surface patch technology, a rectangular grid of control points is used to model the entire object. As a result it is difficult to maintain low data complexity while incorporating small details and sharp localized features, because entire rows and/or entire columns of control information must be added. Thus a small addition to one local area of the surface to better represent a facial feature means that information has to be added across the entire surface.

Hierarchical B-splines, introduced by Forsey and Bartels [32], are a mechanism by which local detail can be added to a B-spline surface while avoiding the global modifications required by standard B-splines. Finer resolution control points are

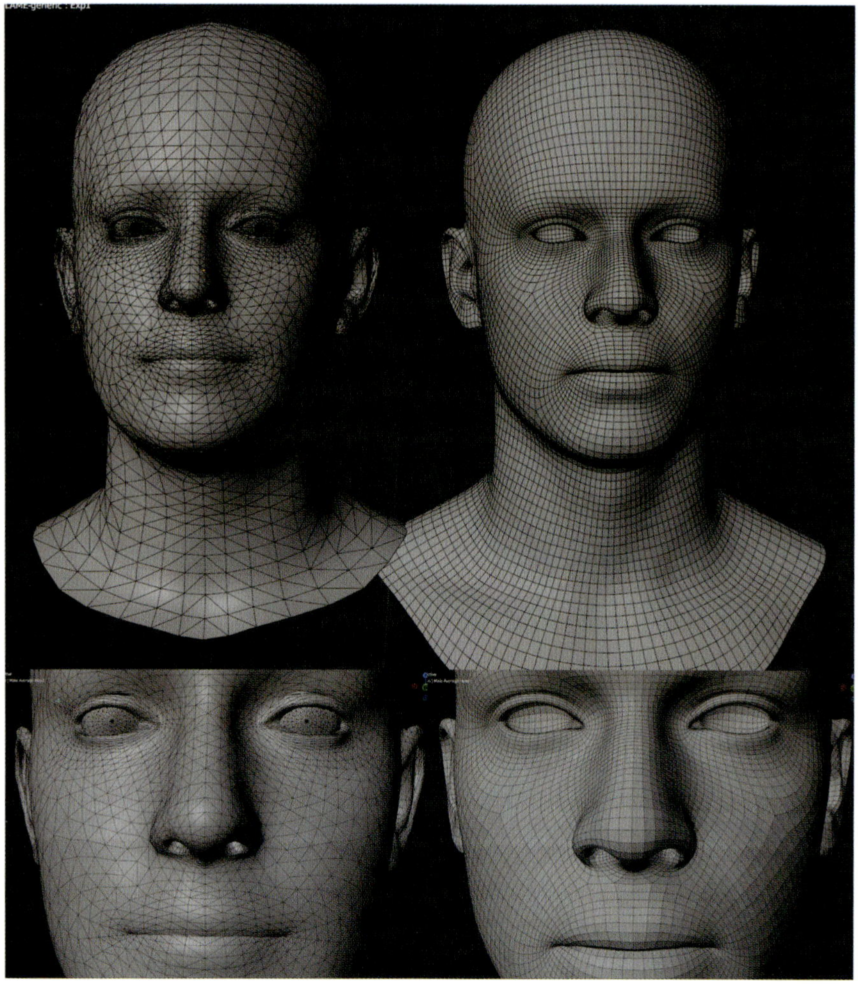

FIGURE 10.6

Face mesh topology. *Left:* FLAME base mesh (triangular mesh); *Right:* 3DScanStore base mesh (quad mesh). Note that both follow anatomical structure around the mouth, nose, and eyes to ensure smooth deformation. (The FLAME 3DMM Model by Max Planck Institute for Intelligent Systems [https://flame.is.tue.mpg.de/modellicense.html] is licensed under Creative Commons Attribution. *Right:* Base Mesh provided as free asset Copyright 3DScanStore [https://www.3dscanstore.com/blog/Free-Base-Mesh].)

carefully laid over the coarser surface while continuity is carefully maintained. In this way, local detail can be added to a surface. The organization is hierarchical, so finer and finer detail can be added. The detail is defined relative to the coarser surface so that editing can take place at any level.

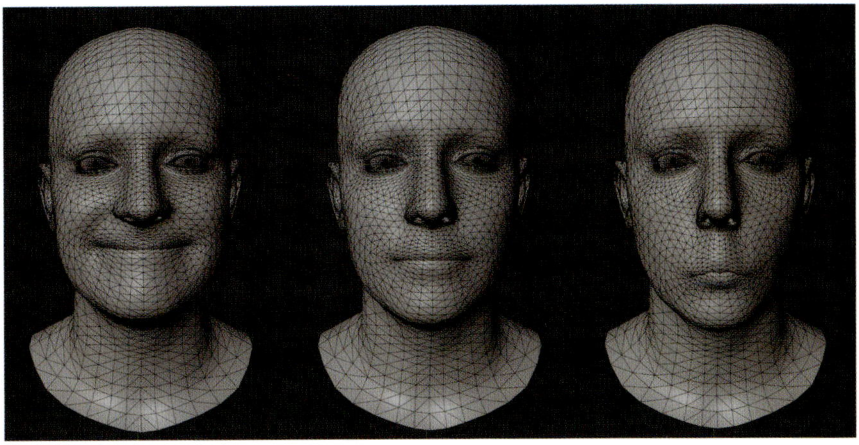

FIGURE 10.7

FLAME 3DMM example expressions.

10.3.1 Creating a continuous surface model

Creating a model of a human head from scratch is not easy. Not only must the correct shape be generated, but when facial animation is the objective, the geometric elements (vertices, edges) must be placed appropriately so that the motion of the surface can be controlled precisely. If the model is dense in the number of geometric elements used, then the placement becomes less of a concern, but in relatively low resolution models it can be an issue. Of course, one approach is to use an interactive system and let the user construct the model. This is useful when the model to be constructed is a fanciful creature or a caricature or must meet some aesthetic design criteria. Although this approach gives an artist the most freedom in creating a model, it requires the most skill. There are three approaches used to construct a model: refining from a low-resolution model, modifying a high-resolution simple shape, and designing the surface out from high-resolution areas.

Subdivision surfaces (e.g., [33]) use a polygonal control mesh that is refined, in the limit, to a smooth surface. The refinement can be terminated at an intermediate resolution, rendered as a polygonal mesh, vertices adjusted, and then refined again. In this manner, the designer can make changes to the general shape of the head at relatively low resolution.

Subdivision surfaces have the advantage of being able to create local complexity without global complexity. They provide an easy-to-use, intuitive interface for developing new models, and provisions for discontinuity of arbitrary order can be accommodated [33]. However, they are difficult to interpolate to a specific dataset, which makes modeling a specific face problematic.

Alternatively, the designer may start with a relatively high-resolution simple shape such as a sphere. The designer pushes and pulls on the surface to form the general features of the face and refines areas as necessary to form the face. Another alternative is to build the surface out from the expressive regions of the face: the mouth and eyes. This approach can be used to ensure that these regions are flexible enough to support the intended animation.

Besides the interactive design approach, there are two main methods for creating facial models: digitization using some physical reference and modification of an existing model. The former is useful when the model of a particular person is desired; the latter is useful when animation control is already built into a generic model. For example, 3D scanning technology or photogrammetry can be used to capture very high-quality 3D digital representations of an individual (Figure 10.8); however, the topology is generally a polygon soup and must be retopologized for animation purposes. One method to retopologize is to start with a model with good topology, align it as close as possible to the 3D scan, scale it so the features match up, and subsequently apply a shrink-wrap modifier (see Figure 10.8) or use a tool such as FaceForm's Wrap software.

As with any model, a physical sculpture of the desired object can be generated with clay, wood, or plaster and then digitized, most often using a mechanical or magnetic digitizing device. A two-dimensional, surface-based coordinate grid can be drawn on the physical model, and the polygons can be digitized on a polygon-by-

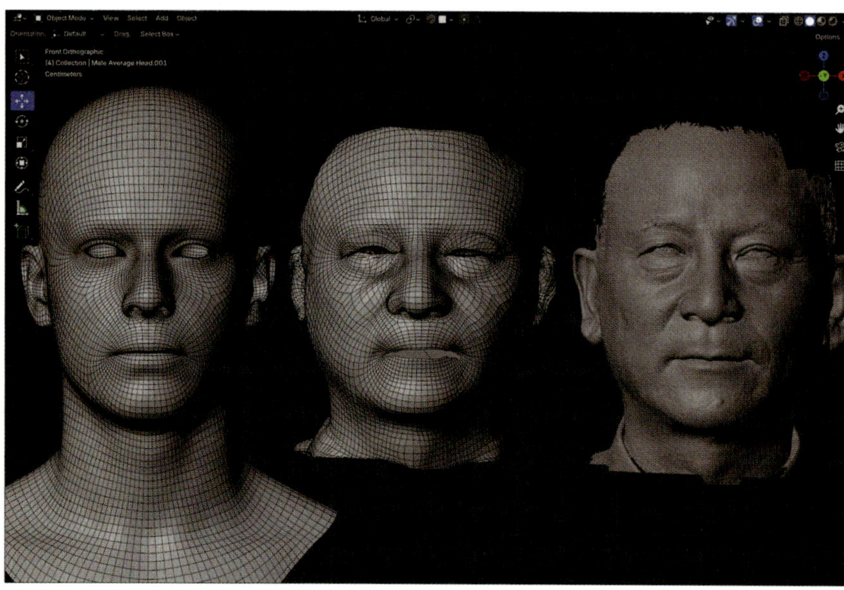

FIGURE 10.8

Shrink wrapping model onto 3D Scan in Blender. *Left:* Base mesh from 3DScanstore.com; *Right:* 3D face scan. *Middle:* Base mesh shrink wrapped onto scan, normals can be baked from the 3D scan onto the new mesh to preserve visual details. (*Middle:* "Human Face" [https://skfb.ly/6VKnY] by thunk3d.scanner is licensed under Creative Commons Attribution [http://creativecommons.org/licenses/by/4.0/.])

polygon basis. Postprocessing can identify unique vertices, and a polygonal mesh can be easily generated. The digitization process can be fairly labor-intensive when large numbers of polygons are involved, which makes using an actual person's face a bit problematic.

Muraki [34] presents a method for fitting a blobby model (implicitly defined surface formed by summed, spherical density functions) to range data by minimizing an energy function that measures the difference between the isosurface and the range data. By splitting primitives and modifying parameters, the user can refine the isosurface to improve the fit.

Models can also be generated from photographs. This has the advantage of not requiring the presence of the physical model once the photograph has been taken, and it has applications for video conferencing and compression. Although most of the photographic approaches modify an existing model by locating feature points, a common method of generating a model from scratch is to take front and side images of a face on which grid lines have been drawn (Figure 10.9). Point correspondences can be established between the two images either interactively or by locating common features automatically, and the grid in three-space can be reconstructed. Symmetry is usually assumed for the face, so only one side view is needed and only half of the front view is considered.

Modifying an existing model is a popular technique for generating a face model. Of course, someone had to first generate a generic model. But once this is done, if it is created as a parameterized model and the parameters were well designed, the model can be used to try to match a particular face, to design a face, or to generate a family of faces. In addition, the animation controls can be built into the model so that they require little or no modification of the generic model for particular instances.

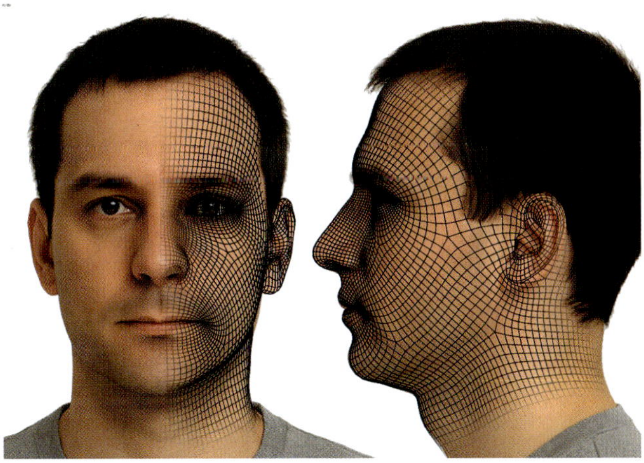

FIGURE 10.9

Image of Head with topology overlaid. This topology is helpful as a guide for digitizing a face from images.

One of the most often used approaches to facial animation employs a parameterized model originally created by Parke [1,35]. The parameters for his model of the human face are divided into two categories: *conformational* and *expressive*. The conformational parameters are those that distinguish one individual's head and face from another's. The expressive parameters are those concerned with animation of an individual's face; these are discussed later. Symmetry between the sides of the face is assumed. Conformal parameters control the shape of the forehead, cheekbone, cheek hollow, chin, and neck. There are several scale distances between facial features:[1] head x, y, and z; chin to mouth and chin to eye; eye to forehead; eye x and y; and widths of the jaw, cheeks, nose bridge, and nostril. Other conformal parameters translate features of the face: chin in x and z; end of nose x and z; and eyebrow z. Even these are not enough to generate all possible faces, although they can be used to generate a wide variety.

Parke's model was not developed based on any anatomical principles but from the intuitions from artistic renderings of the human face. Facial anthropometric statistics and proportions can be used to constrain the facial surface to generate realistic geometries of a human head [36]. Variational techniques can then be used to create realistic facial geometry from a deformed prototype that fits the constraints. This approach is useful for generating heads for a crowd scene or a background character. It may also be useful as a possible starting point for some other character; however, the result will be influenced heavily by the prototype used.

The MPEG-4 standard proposes tools for efficient encoding of multimedia scenes. It includes a set of *facial definition parameters* (FDPs) [37,38] that are devoted mainly to facial animation for purposes of video teleconferencing. Figure 10.10 shows the feature points defined by the standard. Once the model is defined in this way, it can be animated by an associated set of *facial animation parameters* (FAPs) [37,38], also defined in the MPEG-4 standard. MPEG-4 defines 68 FAPs. The FAPs control rigid rotation of the head, eyeballs, eyelids, and mandible. Other low-level parameters indicate the translation of a corresponding feature point, with respect to its position in the neutral face, along one of the coordinate axes [39].

One other interesting approach to generating a model of a face from a generic model is fitting it to images in a video sequence [36]. Although not a technique developed for animation applications, it is useful for generating a model of a face of a specific individual. A parameterized model of a face is set up in a three-dimensional viewing configuration closely matching that of the camera that produced the video images. Feature points are located on the image of the face in the video and are also located on the three-dimensional synthetic model. Camera parameters and face model parameters are then modified to more closely match the video by using the pseudoinverse of the Jacobian. (The Jacobian is the matrix of partial derivatives that relates changes in parameters to changes in measurements.) By

[1] In Parke's model, the z-axis is up, the x-axis is oriented from the back of the head toward the front, and the y-axis is from the middle of the head out to the left side.

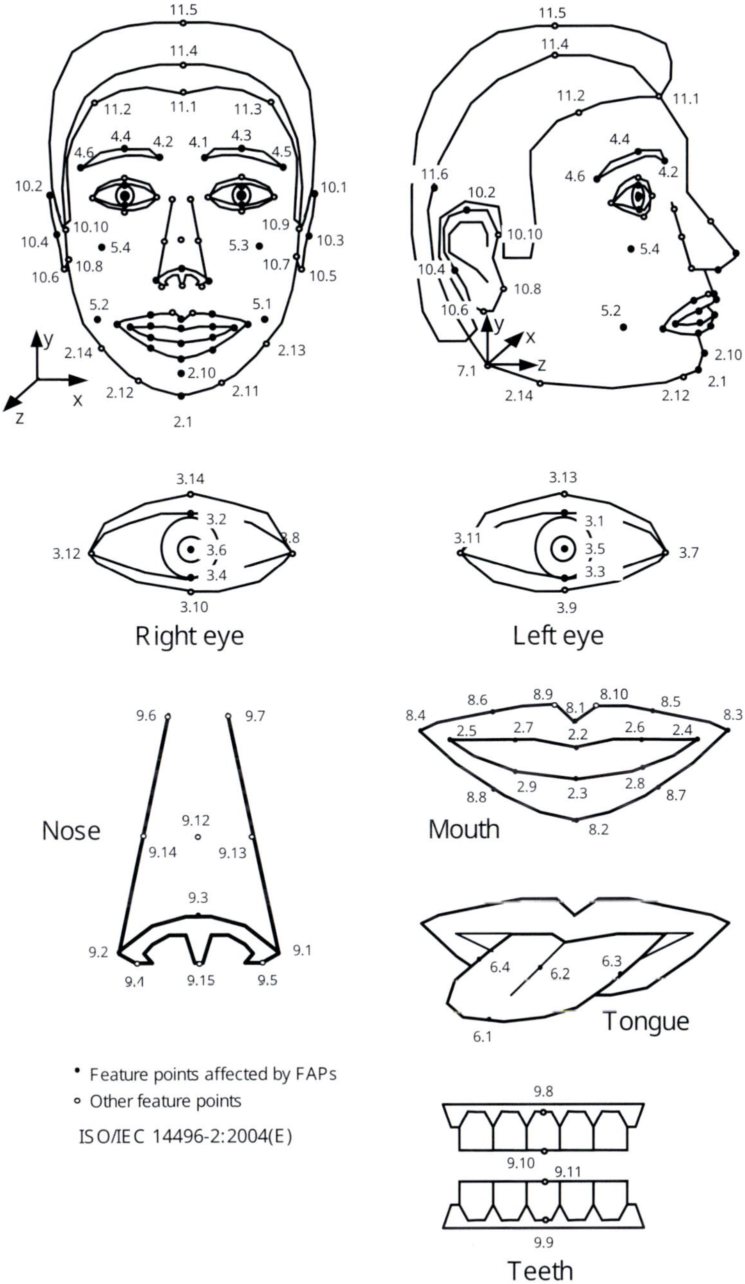

FIGURE 10.10

Feature points corresponding to the MPEG-4 facial definition parameters (FDPs) [37,38].

computing the difference in the measurements between the feature points in the image and the projected feature points from the synthetic setup, the pseudoinverse of the Jacobian indicates how to change the parametric values to reduce the measurement differences.

10.3.2 Blend-shapes and 3DMMs

Previously, in Chapter 7, we discussed how we can use the concept of morphing to go between different facial expressions simply by interpolating mesh vertices between mesh keyframes (see Chapter 7, Algorithm 7.5). Using meshes as keyframes are interchangeably called blend-shapes, morph targets, and sometimes shape-keys in different software packages. The idea is simply that you start with a base neutral face mesh and move the vertices around to achieve different key expressions. Each key can be considered as an entirely separate mesh with the exact same topology as the base. Interpolating between these keyframes over time achieves animation. We briefly discussed morphable models (3DMMs) for facial animation (FLAME [40,41], ICT-FaceKit [42,43], and Table 10.2). Although these are mostly intended for research purposes, they provide a good starting point for exploring the use of 3DMMs for facial animation. Recently, Gaussian Splatting has been used with blend-shapes to capture expressions from monocular video [44]. Figure 10.11a–g shows a blend-shape based character created using the Headshot2 plugin (and manual tweaks) for Reallusion's Character Creator from the reference image (Figure 10.11a) and live performance capture (Figure 10.11h–k).

10.3.3 Tools for creating faces

Although any 3D modeling package such as Blender [45] or ZBrush [46] can be used to create polygonal models of faces, there are specific solutions such as FaceBuilder [47] and Headshot2 for Reallusion's Character Creator [13] that are dedicated to creating high-quality animatable faces. Similarly, Unreal's Metahuman [12] creator allows for the creation of faces from blend-shapes that work in the Unreal engine and they have built-in workflows for fitting a metahuman identity to a 3D scan. To create a 3D scan of your face, you can use photogrammetry (e.g., Reality Capture [48]), or other mobile techniques that use LiDAR such as Scaniverse [49] or Heges [50]. Also, premade animated assets are now available from venues such as 3DScanstore [51] who specialize in creating high-quality retopologized faces/bodies acquired from high-quality photogrammetry.

10.3.4 Textures

Texture maps are very important in facial animation. Most objects created by computer graphics techniques have a plastic or metallic look, which, in the case of facial animation, seriously detracts from the believability of the image. Texture maps can give a facial model a much more organic look and can give the observer more visual

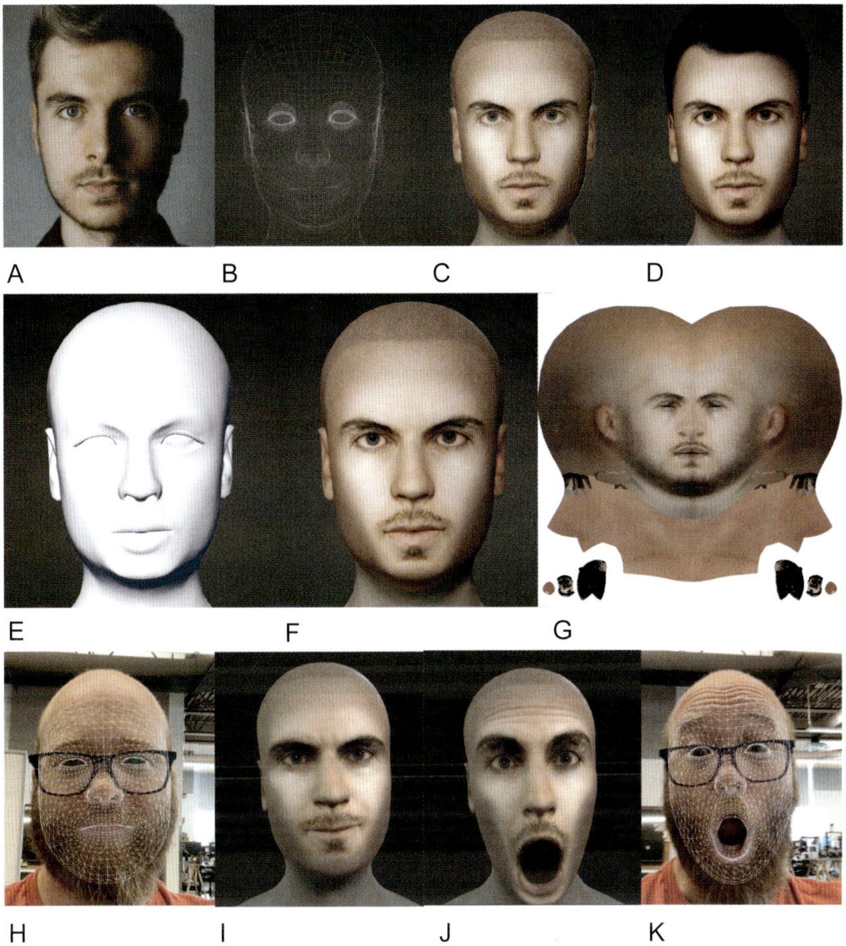

FIGURE 10.11

(a) Reference image. (b) Wireframe mesh. (c) Textured mesh with wireframe. (d) With hair. (e) Diffuse render mesh. (f) Final textured face. (g) Unwrapped diffuse texture. (h–k) Tracking expressions. Reallusion Character Creator mobile companion app (LIVE Face)

cues when interacting with the images. The texture map can be taken directly from a person's head; however, it must be registered with the geometry. The lighting situation during digitization of the texture must also be considered.

Laser scanners are capable of collecting information on intensity as well as depth, resulting in a high-resolution surface with a matching high-resolution texture. However, once the face deforms, the texture no longer matches exactly. Because the scanner revolves around the model, the texture resolution is evenly spread over

Table 10.2 FACS and ICT-FaceKit

FACS	ICT-FaceKit Shapes	FACS	ICT-FaceKit Shapes
AU1 Inner brow raiser	browInnerUp_L + browInnerUp_R	AU20 Lip stretcher	mouthStretch_L + mouthStretch_R
AU2 Outer brow raiser	browOuterUp_L + browOuterUp_R	AU22 Lip funneler	mouthFunnel
AU4 Brow lowerer	browDown_L + browDown_R	AU24 Lip pressor	mouthPress_L + mouthPress_R
AU6 Cheek raiser	cheekSquint_L + cheekSquint_R	AU27 Mouth stretch	jawOpen
AU5 Upper lid raiser	eyeWide_L + eyeWide_R	AU28 Lip suck	mouthRollLower + mouthRollUpper
AU7 Lid tightener	eyeSquint_L + eyeSquint_R	AU29 Jaw thrust	jawForward
AU9 Nose wrinkler	noseSneer_L + noseSneer_R	AU30 Jaw sideways (left)	jawLeft
AU10 Upper lip raiser	mouthShrugUpper	AU30 Jaw sideways (right)	jawRight
AU11 Nasolabial deepener	mouthUpperUp_L + mouthUpperUp_R	AU33 Cheek blow	cheekPuff_L + cheekPuff_R
AU12 Lip corner puller	mouthSmile_L + mouthSmile_R	AU45 Blink	eyeBlink_L + eyeBlink_R
AU14 Dimpler	mouthDimple_L + mouthDimple_R	AU61 Eyes turn left	eyeLookOut_L + eyeLookIn_R
AU15 Lip corner depressor	mouthFrown_L + mouthFrown_R	AU62 Eyes turn right	eyeLookOut_R + eyeLookIn_L
AU16 Lower lip depressor	mouthLowerDown_L + mouthLowerDown_R	AU63 Eyes up	eyeLookUp_L + eyeLookUp_R
AU17 Chin raiser	mouthShrugLower	AU64 Eyes down	eyeLookDown_L + eyeLookDown_R
AU18 Lip pucker	mouthPucker		

the head. However, places are missed where the head is self-occluding (at the ears and maybe the chin) and at the top of the head.

Texture maps can also be created from photographs by simply combining top and side views using pixel blending where the textures overlap [52]. Lighting effects must be taken into consideration, and because the model is not captured in the same process as the texture map, registration with a model is an issue. Using a sequence of images from a video can improve the process.

10.4 Faces: animating

Attempts to animate the face raise the questions: What are the primitive motions/models of the face, and how many degrees of freedom do we need for proper animation? How do we capture/create animations for these models?

10.4.1 Facial rigs

Facial rigs are common ways to animate and deform face mesh models. A simple facial rig in Blender can be seen in Figure 10.12 using the default Rigify add-on (built-in). Once the mesh is rigged and weight painted it can be deformed to create blend-shapes for expressions.

10.4.2 Parameterized models

As introduced in the discussion of FACS, parameterizing the facial model according to primitive actions and then controlling the values of the parameters over time is one of the most common ways to implement facial animation. Abstractly, any possible or imaginable facial contortion can be considered as a point in an n-dimensional space of all possible facial poses. Any parameterization of a space should have complete coverage and be easy to use. Complete coverage means that the space reachable by (linear) combinations of the parameters includes all (at least most) of the interesting points in that space. Of course, the definition of the word *interesting*

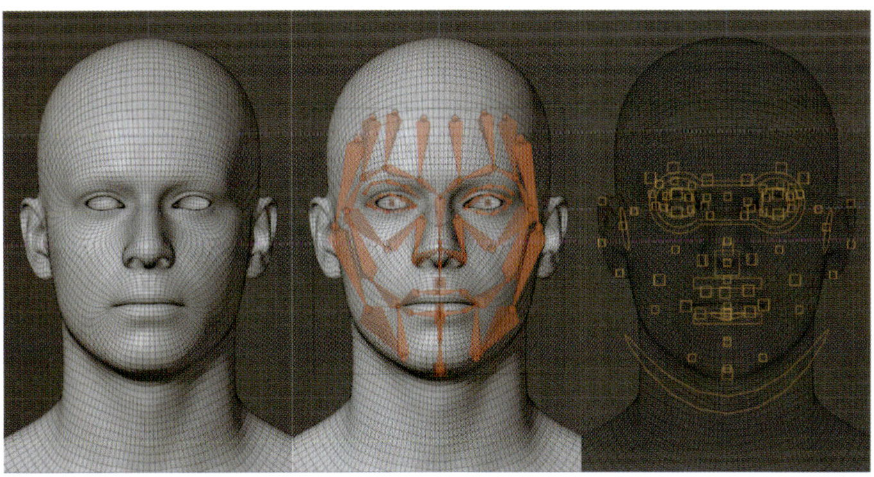

A B C

FIGURE 10.12

(a) Base Mesh from 3D Scan Store. (b) With Bones. (c) With Rigify (Blender) animation rig.

may vary from application to application, so a generally useful parameterization includes as much of the space as possible. For a parameterization to be easy to use, the set of parameters should be as small as possible, the effect of each parameter should be independent of the effect of any other parameter, and the effect of each parameter should be intuitive. Of course, in something as complex as facial animation, attaining all of these objectives is probably not possible, so determining appropriate trade-offs is an important activity in designing a parameterization. Animation brings an additional requirement to the table: the animator should be able to generate common, important, or interesting motions through the space by manipulating one or just a few parameters.

The most popular parameterized facial model is credited to Parke [1,29,35] and has already been discussed in terms of creating facial models based on the so-called conformational parameters of a generic facial model. In addition to the conformational parameters, there are *expression parameters*. Examples of expression parameters are upper-lip position, eye gaze, jaw rotation, and eyebrow separation. Figure 10.13 shows a diagram of the parameter set with the (interpolated) expression parameters identified. Most of the parameters are concerned with the eyes and the mouth, where most facial expression takes place. With something as complex as the face, it is usually not possible to animate interesting expressions with a single parameter. Experience with the parameter set is necessary for understanding the relationship between a parameter and the facial model. Higher level abstractions can be used to aid in animating common motions.

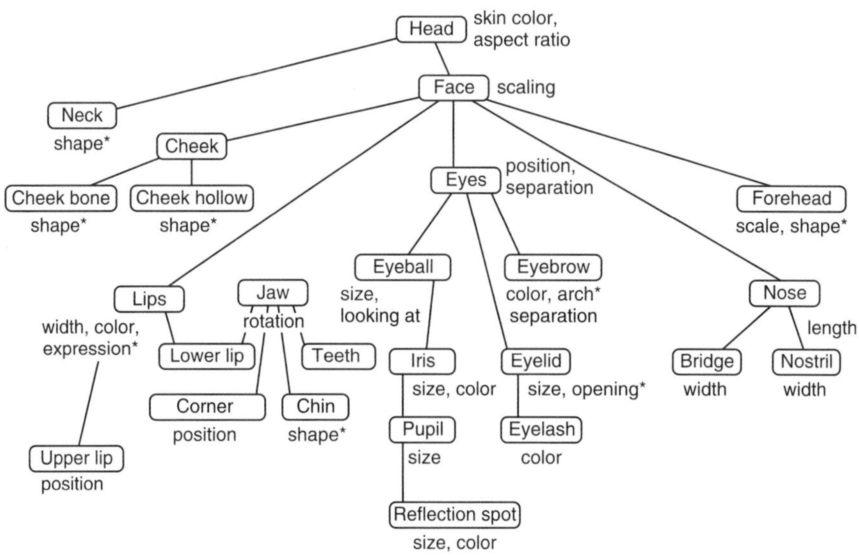

FIGURE 10.13

Parke model. *Indicates interpolated parameters [29].

10.4.3 Blend-shapes

The simplest approach to facial animation is to define a set of key poses, also called *blend-shapes* (e.g., Figure 10.7). Facial animation is produced by selecting two of the key poses and interpolating between the positions of their corresponding vertices in the two poses.

This restricts the available motions to be the interpolation from one key pose to another. To generalize this a bit more, a weighted sum of two or more key poses can be used in which the weights sum to 1. Each vertex position is then computed as a linear combination of its corresponding position in each of the poses whose weight is nonzero. This can be used to produce facial poses not directly represented by the keys. However, this is still fairly restrictive because the various parts of the facial model are not individually controllable by the animator. The animation is still restricted to those poses represented as a linear combination of the keys. If the animator allows for a wide variety of facial motions, the key poses quickly increase to an unmanageable number.

10.4.4 Muscle models

Parametric models encode geometric displacement of the skin in terms of an arbitrary parametric value. Muscle-based models, such as those demonstrated in [53], are more sophisticated, although there is wide variation in the reliance on a physical basis for the models. There are typically three types of muscles that need to be modeled for the face: linear, sheet, and sphincter. The *linear muscle* is a muscle that contracts and pulls one point (the *point of insertion*) toward another (the *point of attachment*). The *sheet muscle* acts as a parallel array of muscles and has a line of attachment at each of its two ends rather than a single point of attachment as in the linear model. The *sphincter muscle* contracts a loop of muscle. It can be thought of as contracting radially toward an imaginary center. The user, either directly or indirectly, specifies muscle activity to which the facial model reacts. Three aspects differentiate one muscle-based model from another: the geometry of the muscle-skin arrangement, the skin model used, and the muscle model used.

The main distinguishing feature in the geometric arrangement of the muscles is whether they are modeled on the surface of the face or whether they are attached to a structural layer beneath the skin (e.g., bone or tissue [31]). The former case is simpler in that only the surface model of the face is needed for the animation system (Figure 10.14). The latter case is more anatomically correct and thus promises more accurate results, but it requires much more geometric structure in the model and is therefore much more difficult to construct (Figure 10.15).

The model used for the skin will dictate how the area around the point of insertion of a (linear) muscle reacts when that muscle is activated; the point of insertion will move an amount determined by the muscle. How the deformation propagates along the skin as a result of that muscle determines how rubbery or how plastic the surface will appear. The simplest model to use is based on geometric distance

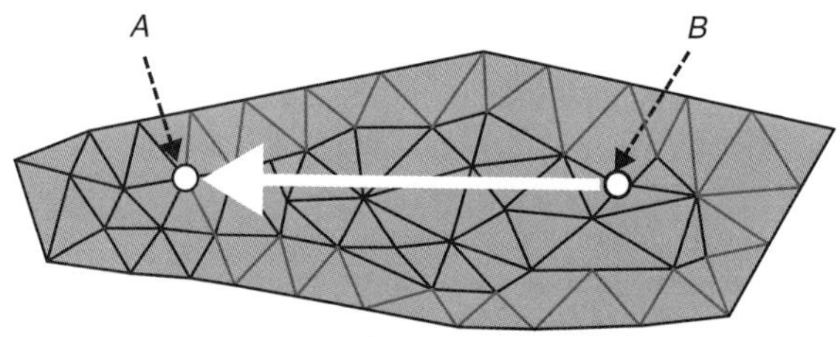

FIGURE 10.14

Part of the surface geometry of the face showing the point of attachment (a) and the point of insertion (b) of a linear muscle; point B is pulled toward point A.

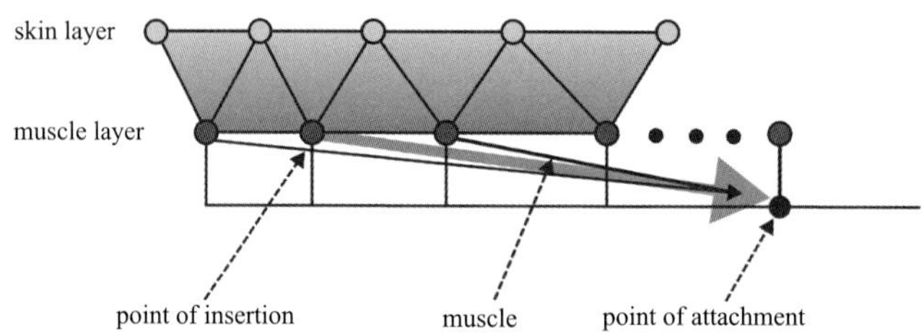

FIGURE 10.15

Cross section of the trilayer muscle as presented by Parke and Waters [29]; the muscle only directly affects nodes in the muscle layer.

from the point and deviation from the muscle vector. For example, the effect of the muscle may attenuate based on the distance a given point is from the point of insertion and on the angle of deviation from the displacement vector of the insertion point. See Figure 10.16 for sample calculations. A slightly more sophisticated skin model might model each edge of the skin geometry as a spring and control the propagation of the deformation based on spring constants. The insertion point is moved by the action of the muscle, and this displacement creates restoring forces in the springs attached to the insertion point, which moves the adjacent vertices, which in turn moves the vertices attached to them, and so on (Figure 10.17). The more complicated Voigt model treats the skin as a viscoelastic element by combining a spring and a damper in parallel (Figure 10.18). The movement induced by the spring is damped as a function of the change in length of the edge.

The muscle model determines the function used to compute the contraction of the muscle. The alternatives for the muscle model are similar to those for the skin, with the distinction that the muscles are active elements, whereas the skin is composed of passive elements. Using a linear muscle as an example, the displacement of the insertion point is produced as a result of muscle activation. Simple models for the muscle will simply specify a displacement of the insertion point based on activation amount. Because, in the case of the orbicularis oris, muscles

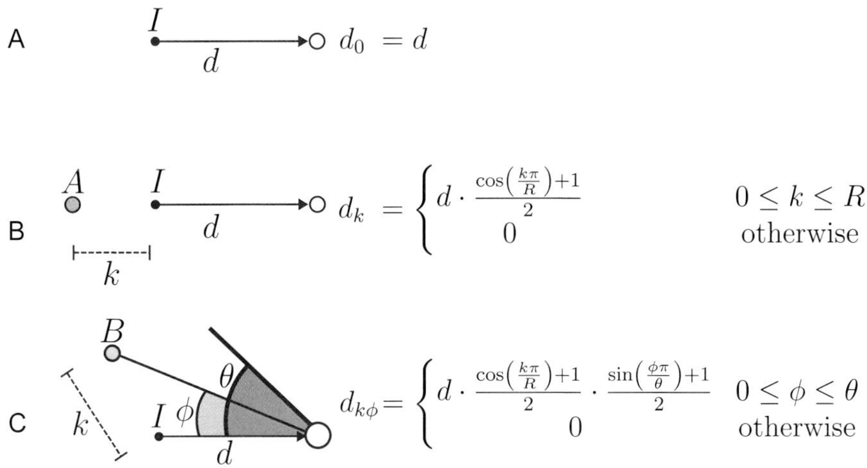

FIGURE 10.16

Sample attenuation: (a) Insertion point I is moved d by muscle. (b) Point A is moved d_k based on linear distance from the insertion point. (c) Point B is moved $d_{k\varphi}$ based on the linear distance and the deviation from the insertion point displacement vector.

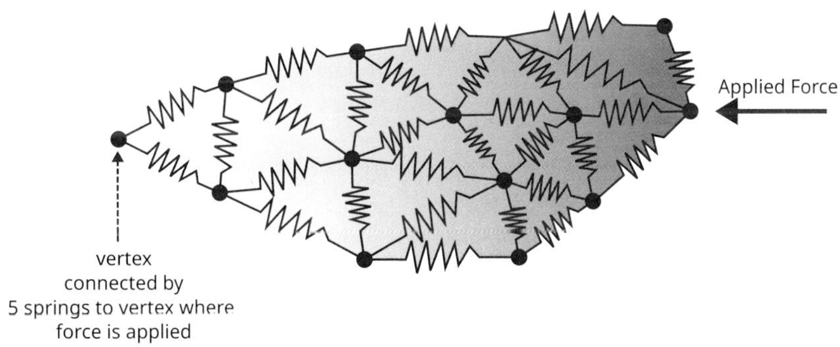

FIGURE 10.17

Spring mesh as skin model; the displacement of the insertion point propagates through the mesh according to the forces imparted by the springs.

are attached to other muscles, care must be taken in determining the skin displacement when both muscles are activated.

More physically accurate muscle models will compute the effect of muscular forces. The simplest dynamic model uses a spring to represent the muscle. Activating the muscle results in a change of its rest length so as to induce a force at the point of insertion. More sophisticated muscle models include damping effects.

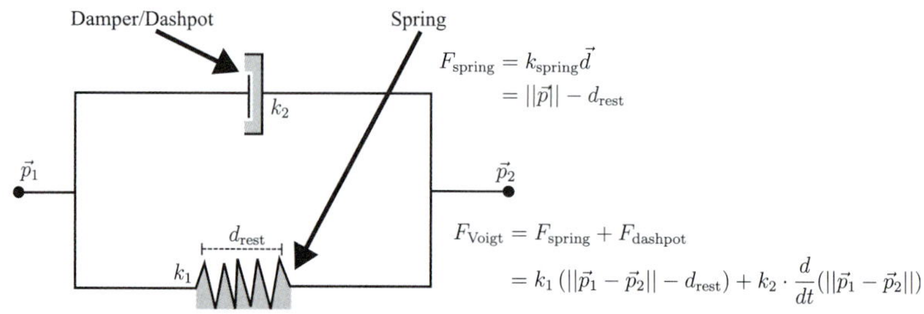

FIGURE 10.18

Voigt viscoelastic model; the motion induced by the spring forces is damped. Variables k and n are spring and damper constants, respectively; and d_i is the rest length for the spring.

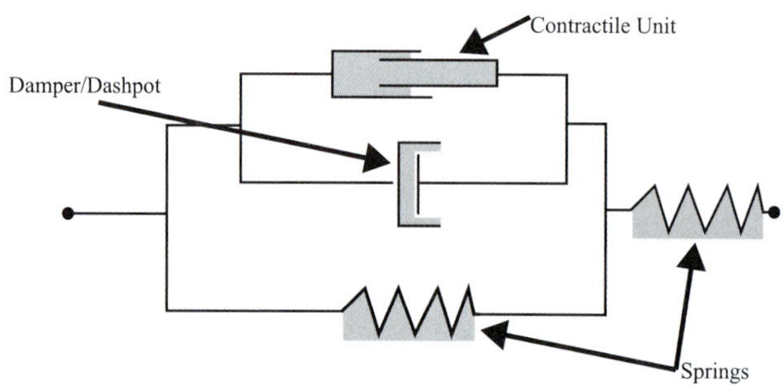

FIGURE 10.19

Hill's model for the muscle.

A muscle model developed by clinical observation is shown in Figure 10.19. However, spring-based facial muscles often result in a computationally expensive approach, and jiggling of the skin can be difficult to control.

10.4.5 Expressions

Facial expressions are a powerful means of communication and are the basis for most facial animation. Any facial animation system will provide for a basic set of expressions. A commonly used set is happy, angry, sad, fear, disgust, and surprise. To achieve such expressions, we can create a number of blend-shapes using specialized software (e.g., Reallusion's Character Creator, or Unreal MetaHuman Creator) or retopologizing 3D scans. Because blend-shapes can be parameterized with a single weight/strength parameter, we can drive them with facial motion capture on mobile devices. See Figure 10.11h–k for an example within Character Creator and the companion LIVE Face app.

10.4.6 Capturing facial movements

Once you have a model, we need to still rig/animate it! Motion capture to the rescue. The standard approach is to place markers on the performer's face and use software to track the markers, transfer them to known locations on a predefined animation rig, and solve for the appropriate deformation that results in these marker locations. Such solutions include Naturalpoint's Optitrack Expression, which is marker-based motion capture that works well with FACS-based pipelines, and Vicon's Carapost [54], which enables motion capture of faces and is used in many industries. Open source solutions such as [55] use machine learning models to find and fit a known model to images and can be streamed to Game Engines and animation software. Unity's ARKit Face Tracking solution [56] and Unreal Engines' Live Link [57] allows you to use your mobile phone and easily control your character's facial rig with the captured movement.

10.5 Faces: lip sync

10.5.1 Articulators of speech

Speech is a complex process and not even completely understood by linguists. Involved in the production of speech are the lungs, the vocal folds, the velum, lips, teeth, and tongue. These articulators of speech constitute the *vocal tract* (Figure 10.20). The lungs produce the primary air flow necessary for sound production. Sound is a sensation produced by vibrations transmitted through air. The various sounds of speech are produced primarily by controlling the frequency, amplitude, and duration of these vibrations. Vibrations are generated by either the vocal folds in the throat or by the tongue in the oral cavity, or by lips. When vibration is produced by the vocal folds, the sound is called *voiced*. For example, the "th" sound in "then" is voiced whereas the "th" of "thin" is not voiced. The sound travels up into either the nasal cavity (e.g., "n") or the oral cavity depending on the configuration of the velum. In the oral cavity, the sound is modified by the configuration of the lips, jaw, and tongue with certain frequencies resonating in the cavity. In addition, the tongue and lips can vibrate by either partially obstructing the air flow or by completely stopping and then releasing it. If the air flow is relatively unrestricted, then the sound is considered a vowel; otherwise it is a consonant. If the air flow is completely stopped and then released (e.g., "t," "d") then it is referred to as a *stop*. If the air flow is partially restricted creating a vibration (e.g., "f," "th") then it is referred to as a *fricative*.

The fundamental frequency of a sound is referred to as F0 and is present in voiced sounds [58]. Frequencies induced by the speech cavities, called *formants*, are referred to as F1, F2, ... in order of their amplitude. The fundamental frequency and formants are arguably the most important concepts in processing speech.

Although most of this activity is interior and therefore not directly observable, it can produce motion in the skin that may be important in some animation. Certainly it

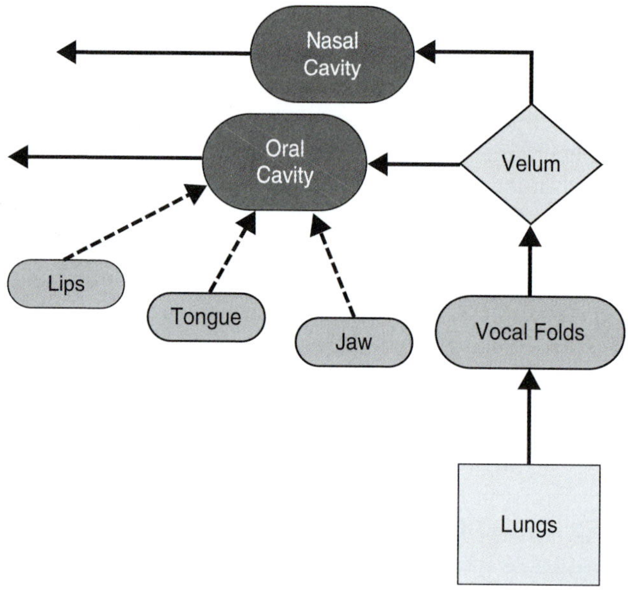

FIGURE 10.20

Schematic of air flow through the vocal tract. Lungs produce air flow. Vocal folds may vibrate. Velum deflects air flow to either nasal cavity or oral cavity. Harmonics of vibrations initiated by vocal folds may be reinforced in the oral cavity depending on its configuration; vibrations may be initiated in the oral cavity by lips or tongue. *Dashed lines* show agents that modify oral cavity configuration.

is important to correctly animate the lips and the surrounding area of the face. Animating the tongue is also usually of some importance.

Some information can be gleaned from a time-amplitude graph of the sound, but more informative is a time-frequency graph with amplitude encoded using color. Using these *spectrographs*, trained professionals can determine the basic sounds of speech.

10.5.2 Phonemes and visemes

In trying to understand speech and how a person produces it, a common approach is to break it down into a simple set of constituent, atomic sound segments. The most commonly used segments are called *phonemes*. Although the specific number of phonemes varies from source to source, there are generally considered to be around 42 phonemes.

The corresponding facial poses that produce these sounds are referred to as *visemes*. Visemes that are similar enough can be combined into a single unique viseme and the resulting set of facial poses can be used (Figure 10.21), for example, as blend-shapes for a simple type of lip-sync animation.

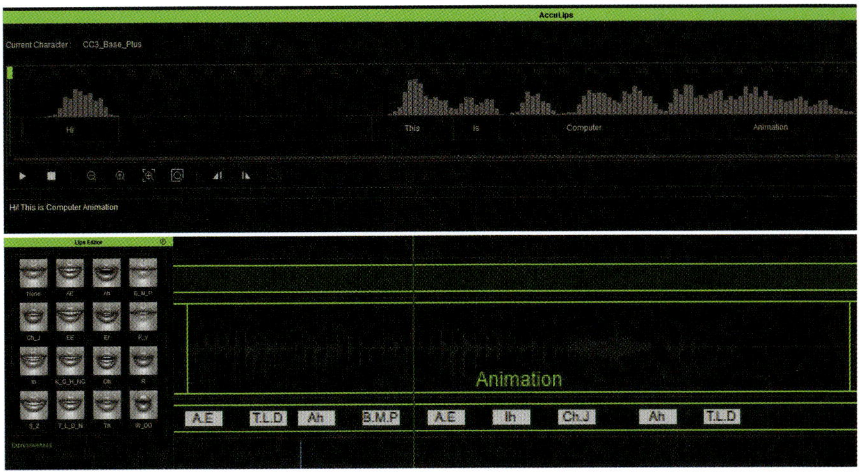

FIGURE 10.21

Visemes for lip-synching in Reallusion iClone8 showing how audio/text is broken down into phonetic lip shapes that can be assigned to the animation timeline.

However, the sounds and associated lip movements are much more complex than can be represented by simply interpolating between static poses. Within the context of speech, a phoneme is manifested as variations of the basic sound. These variations of a phoneme are called *allophones* and the mechanism producing the variations is referred to as *coarticulation*. Although the precise mechanism of coarticulation is a subject for debate, the basic reason for it is that the ideal sounds are slurred together as phonemes are strung one after the other. Similarly, the visemes of visual speech are modified by the context of the speech in which they occur. The speed at which speech is produced and the physical limitations of the speech articulators result in an inability to attain ideal pronunciation. This slurs the visemes together and, in turn, slurs the phonemes.

10.5.3 Coarticulation

One of the complicating factors in automatically producing realistic (both audio and visual) lip-sync animation is the effect that one phoneme has on adjacent phonemes. Adjacent phonemes affect the motion of the speech articulators as they form the sound for a phoneme. The resulting subtle change in sound of the phoneme produces what is referred to as an allophone of the phoneme. This effect is known as *coarticulation*. Lack of coarticulation is one of the main reasons that lip-sync animation using blend-shapes appears unrealistic. Although there have been various strategies proposed in the literature to compute the effects of coarticulation, Cohen and Massaro [59] have used weighting functions, called *dominance functions*, to perform a priority-based blend of adjacent phonemes. King and Parent [60] have modified and extended the idea to animation song. Pelachaud et al. [21] cluster phonemes based on deformability and use a look-ahead procedure that applies forward and backward coarticulation rules. Other approaches include the use of constraints [61], physics [62,63], rules [64], and syllables [65]. None has proven to be a completely satisfying solution for automatically producing realistic audiovisual speech.

10.5.4 Prosody

Another complicating factor to realistic lip-sync animation is changing neutral speech to reflect emotional stress. Such stress is referred to as *prosody*. Effects of prosody include changing the duration, pitch, and amplitude of words or phrases of an utterance. This is an active area of research (e.g., [64–68]).

10.6 Chapter summary

A wide range of approaches can be used to model and animate the face. Which approach to use depends greatly on how realistic the result is meant to be and what kind of control the animator is provided. Results vary from cartoon faces to parameterized surface models to skull-muscle-skin simulations. Realistic facial animation remains one of the interesting challenges in computer animation. Facial animation presents interesting challenges. As opposed to most other areas of computer animation, the foundational science is largely incomplete. This, coupled with the complexity inherent in modeling facial anatomy as well as combating the uncanny valley phenomenon, makes realistic facial animation an ongoing area of research.

References

[1] Parke FI. A parametric model for human faces. The University of Utah; 1974.
[2] Ahlberg J. CANDIDE-3—an updated parameterized face. 2001.
[3] The Uncanny Valley: The Original Essay by Masahiro Mori - IEEE Spectrum." [Online]. Available: https://spectrum.ieee.org/the-uncanny-valley. [Accessed 29 July 2024].
[4] Pollick FE. In search of the uncanny valley. In: Daras P, Ibarra OM, editors. User centric media. Berlin, Heidelberg: Springer; 2010. p. 69–78. https://doi.org/10.1007/978-3-642-12630-7_8.
[5] Diel A, Weigelt S, Macdorman KF. A meta-analysis of the uncanny valley's independent and dependent variables. ACM Trans. Hum.-Robot Interact. 2021;11(1):1:1–1:33. https://doi.org/10.1145/3470742.
[6] Zhang J, Li S, Zhang J-Y, Du F, Qi Y, Liu X. A literature review of the research on the uncanny valley. In: Rau P-LP, editor. Cross-cultural design. User experience of products, services, and intelligent environments. Cham: Springer International Publishing; 2020. p. 255–68. https://doi.org/10.1007/978-3-030-49788-0_19.

[7] Higgins D, Egan D, Fribourg R, Cowan B, McDonnell R. Ascending from the valley: can state-of-the-art photorealism avoid the uncanny? In: ACM symposium on applied perception 2021. New York, NY, USA: Association for Computing Machinery; 2021. p. 1–5. https://doi.org/10.1145/3474451.3476242. SAP '21.

[8] Hepperle D, Ödell H, Wölfel M. Differences in the uncanny valley between head-mounted displays and monitors. In: 2020 international conference on cyberworlds (CW); 2020. p. 41–8. https://doi.org/10.1109/CW49994.2020.00014.

[9] Tinwell A. The uncanny valley in games and animation. CRC Press; 2014.

[10] Assaf R, Kunz S, Teixeira L. The presence of the uncanny valley between animation and cinema: a communication approach. In: Multidisciplinary perspectives on new media art. IGI Global; 2020. p. 97–118. https://doi.org/10.4018/978-1-7998-3669-8.ch005.

[11] Li D, Yi X. Analysis of the uncanny valley theory and the effect of character realism. Science 2022;6(3):334–7.

[12] "MetaHuman | Realistic Person Creator," Unreal Engine. [Online]. Available: https://www.unrealengine.com/en-US/metahuman. [Accessed 26 July 2024].

[13] AI 3D Head Generator | Headshot 2 | Character Creator," AI 3D Head Generator | Headshot 2 | Character Creator. [Online]. Available: https://www.reallusion.com/character-creator/headshot/. [Accessed 26 July 2024].

[14] Song SW, Shin M. Uncanny Valley effects on chatbot trust, purchase intention, and adoption intention in the context of E-commerce: the moderating role of avatar familiarity. Int. J. Human–Computer Interact. 2024;40(2):441–56. https://doi.org/10.1080/10447318.2022.2121038.

[15] Vallis C, Wilson S, Gozman D, Buchanan J. Student perceptions of AI-generated avatars in teaching business ethics: we might not be impressed. Postdigital Sci. Educ. 2024; 6(2):537–55. https://doi.org/10.1007/s42438-023-00407-7.

[16] Lee M, McMillan D, Torre I, Fischer JE, Ruitenburg Y. Between trust and identity: form, function, and presentation. In: Proceedings of the 6th ACM conference on conversational user interfaces. CUI '24. New York, NY, USA: Association for Computing Machinery; 2024. p. 1–4. https://doi.org/10.1145/3640794.3669999.

[17] Davies C, Miron R. Facial anatomy, skin biology, and the effects of aging. 2020. p. 9–25.

[18] Zarins U. Anatomy of facial expressions. In: Anatomy for sculptors. Anatomy next, incorporated; 2019 [Online]. Available: https://books.google.ca/books?id=8UV5zQEACAAJ.

[19] Standring S, editor. Gray's anatomy: the anatomical basis of clinical practice. 42 ed. New York: Elsevier; 2021 [Online]. Available: https://www.clinicalkey.com.au/dura/browse/bookChapter/3-s2.0-C20170037291. [Accessed 29 July 2024].

[20] Ekman P, Friesen WV. Facial action coding system. 2019. https://doi.org/10.1037/t27734-000.

[21] Pelachaud C, Badler NI, Steedman M. Generating facial expressions for speech. Cogn. Sci. 1996;20(1):1–46. https://doi.org/10.1207/s15516709cog2001_1.

[22] Calzolari S, Strada F, Bottino A. The quest for believability: exploring FACS adaptations for emotion facial expressions in virtual humans. In: 2024 IEEE gaming, entertainment, and media conference (GEM); 2024. p. 1–6. https://doi.org/10.1109/GEM61861.2024.10585460.

[23] Wibowo H, Firdausi F, Suharso W, Kusuma WA, Harmanto D. Facial expression recognition of 3D image using facial action coding system (FACS). TELKOMNIKA Telecommun. Comput. Electron. Control 2019;17(2). https://doi.org/10.12928/telkomnika.v17i2.9304.
[24] Cuculo V, D'Amelio A. OpenFACS: an open source FACS-based 3D face animation system. In: Zhao Y, Barnes N, Chen B, Westermann R, Kong X, Lin C, editors. Image and graphics. Cham: Springer International Publishing; 2019. p. 232−42. https://doi.org/10.1007/978-3-030-34110-7_20.
[25] van der Struijk S, Huang H-H, Mirzaei MS, Nishida T. FACSvatar: an open source modular framework for real-time FACS based facial animation. In: Proceedings of the 18th international conference on intelligent virtual agents. Iva '18. New York, NY, USA: Association for Computing Machinery; 2018. p. 159−64. https://doi.org/10.1145/3267851.3267918.
[26] Krumhuber EG, Tamarit L, Roesch EB, Scherer KR. FACSGen 2.0 animation software: generating three-dimensional FACS-valid facial expressions for emotion research. Emotion 2012;12(2):351−63. https://doi.org/10.1037/a0026632.
[27] Amini R, Lisetti C. HapFACS: an open source API/software to generate FACS-based expressions for ECAs animation and for corpus generation. In: 2013 humaine association conference on affective computing and intelligent interaction; 2013. p. 270−5. https://doi.org/10.1109/ACII.2013.51.
[28] Facial Action Coding System (FACS) - A Visual Guidebook - iMotions." [Online]. Available: https://imotions.com/blog/learning/research-fundamentals/facial-action-coding-system/. [Accessed 26 July 2024].
[29] Parke FI, Waters K. Computer facial animation. CRC press; 2008.
[30] Waters K. Physical model of facial tissue and muscle articulation derived from computer tomography data, 1808; 1992. p. 574−83. https://doi.org/10.1117/12.131110.
[31] Waters K, Terzopoulos D. Modelling and animating faces using scanned data. J. Vis. Comput. Animat. 1991;2(4):123−8. https://doi.org/10.1002/vis.4340020405.
[32] "Hierarchical B-spline refinement | ACM SIGGRAPH Computer Graphics." [Online]. Available: https://dl.acm.org/doi/10.1145/378456.378512. [Accessed 26 July 2024].
[33] DeRose T, Kass M, Truong T. Subdivision surfaces in character animation. In: Proceedings of the 25th annual conference on Computer graphics and interactive techniques. SIGGRAPH '98. New York, NY, USA: Association for Computing Machinery; 1998. p. 85−94. https://doi.org/10.1145/280814.280826.
[34] Muraki Shigeru. Volumetric shape description of range data using "Blobby Model". SIGGRAPH Comput. Graph 1991;25(4):227−35. https://doi.org/10.1145/127719.122743.
[35] Parke FI. Computer generated animation of faces. In: Proceedings of the ACM annual conference, 1; 1972. p. 451−7.
[36] DeCarlo D, Metaxas D, Stone M. An anthropometric face model using variational techniques. In: Proceedings of the 25th annual conference on Computer graphics and interactive techniques. SIGGRAPH '98. New York, NY, USA: Association for Computing Machinery; 1998. p. 67−74. https://doi.org/10.1145/280814.280823.
[37] Face animation parameter. Wikipedia; 2023 [Online]. Available: https://en.wikipedia.org/w/index.php?title=Face_Animation_Parameter&oldid=1170479292. [Accessed 26 July 2024].
[38] 14:00-17:00, "ISO/IEC 14496-2:2004," ISO. [Online]. Available: https://www.iso.org/standard/39259.html. [Accessed 26 July 2024].

[39] (archive) COVEN, "COVEN: Collaborative Virtual Environments," COVEN: Collaborative Virtual Environments. [Online]. Available: https://web.archive.org/web/20050422065820/https://coven.lancs.ac.uk/mpeg4/index.html. [Accessed 26 July 2024].
[40] Li T, Bolkart T, Black MJ, Li H, Romero J. Learning a model of facial shape and expression from 4D scans. ACM Trans. Graph. 2017;36(6):194:1−194:17. https://doi.org/10.1145/3130800.3130813.
[41] FLAME. [Online]. Available: https://flame.is.tue.mpg.de/index.html. [Accessed 26 July 2024].
[42] Li R, et al. Learning Formation of physically-based face attributes. 2020.
[43] ICT-VGL/ICT-FaceKit. Python. ICT-VGL; 2024 [Online]. Available: https://github.com/ICT-VGL/ICT-FaceKit. [Accessed 26 July 2024].
[44] Ma S, Weng Y, Shao T, Zhou K. 3D Gaussian blendshapes for head avatar animation. In: ACM SIGGRAPH 2024 conference papers. SIGGRAPH '24. New York, NY, USA: Association for Computing Machinery; 2024. p. 1−10. https://doi.org/10.1145/3641519.3657462.
[45] B. Foundation, "blender.org - Home of the Blender project - Free and Open 3D Creation Software," blender.org. [Online]. Available: https://www.blender.org/. [Accessed 26 July 2024].
[46] M. S. 2023 for M. C. GmbH, "ZBrush - The all-in-one-digital sculpting solution," Home of ZBrush [Online]. Available: https://pixologic.com. [Accessed 26 July 2024].
[47] FaceBuilder for blender | KeenTools. [Online]. Available: https://keentools.io/products/facebuilder-for-blender. [Accessed 26 July 2024].
[48] RealityCapture - 3D models from photos and/or laser scans. [Online]. Available: https://www.capturingreality.com/. [Accessed 01 August 2024].
[49] Scaniverse - 3D scanner - gaussian splatting - LiDAR. [Online]. Available: https://scaniverse.com/. [Accessed 26 July 2024].
[50] Model scanned by the iPhone X scanner app Heges - 3D model by marek simonik - sketchfab. [Online Video]. Available: https://sketchfab.com/models/48197ad84a7145b983e4ed6a2ab169c0/embed?autostart=1&camera=0. [Accessed 26 July 2024].
[51] Head scans [Online]. Available: https://www.3dscanstore.com/3d-head-models. [Accessed 26 July 2024].
[52] Akimoto T, Suenaga Y. 3D facial model creation using generic model and front and side views of face. IEICE Trans. Inf. Syst. 1992;E75-D(2):191−7.
[53] Muscles and tissue [Online]. Available: https://www.sidefx.com/docs/houdini/muscles/index.html. [Accessed 02 August 2024].
[54] Kejian Z, He X, Dai Y, Cai L. Research on face feature acquisition based on motion capture. J. Phys. Conf. Ser. 2018;1087:062038. https://doi.org/10.1088/1742-6596/1087/6/062038.
[55] Pattke M. JimWest/MeFaMo. Python; 2024 [Online]. Available: https://github.com/JimWest/MeFaMo. [Accessed 26 July 2024].
[56] About ARKit face tracking | ARKit face tracking | 1.1.0-preview.6. [Online]. Available: https://docs.unity3d.com/Packages/com.unity.xr.arkit-face-tracking@1.1/manual/index.html#technical-details. [Accessed 01 August 2024].
[57] Live link in unreal engine | unreal engine 5.4 documentation | Epic developer community," Epic Games Developer. [Online]. Available: https://dev.epicgames.com/

documentation/en-us/unreal-engine/live-link-in-unreal-engine. [Accessed 01 August 2024].
[58] Lemmetty S. Review of speech synthesis technology. 1999.
[59] Cohen MM, Massaro DW. Modeling coarticulation in synthetic visual speech. In: Thalmann NM, Thalmann D, editors. Models and techniques in computer animation. Tokyo: Springer Japan; 1993. p. 139–56. https://doi.org/10.1007/978-4-431-66911-1_13.
[60] King SA, Parent RE. Animating song. Comput. Animat. Virtual. Worlds 2004;15(1): 53–61. https://doi.org/10.1002/cav.7.
[61] Edge JD, Maddock S. Constraint-based synthesis of visual speech. In: ACM SIGGRAPH 2004 sketches; 2004. p. 55.
[62] Albrecht I, Haber J, Seidel H. Speech synchronization for physics-based facial animation. Presented at the international conference in central europe on computer graphics and visualization. 2002 [Online]. Available: https://www.semanticscholar.org/paper/Speech-Synchronization-for-Physics-Based-Facial-Albrecht-Haber/a12c0aa3c181808dd40f1bcd051153be15d30c93. [Accessed 26 July 2024].
[63] Somasundaram A. A facial animation model for expressive audio-visual speech. USA: phd, Ohio State University; 2006.
[64] Cassell J, et al. Animated conversation: rule-based generation of facial expression, gesture & spoken intonation for multiple conversational agents. In: Proceedings of the 21st annual conference on Computer graphics and interactive techniques. SIGGRAPH '94. New York, NY, USA: Association for Computing Machinery; 1994. p. 413–20. https://doi.org/10.1145/192161.192272.
[65] Kshirsagar S, Magnenat-Thalmann N. Visyllable based speech animation. Comput. Graph. Forum 2003;22(3):631–9. https://doi.org/10.1111/1467-8659.t01-2-00711.
[66] Byun M, Badler NI. FacEMOTE: qualitative parametric modifiers for facial animations. In: Proceedings of the 2002 ACM SIGGRAPH/Eurographics symposium on Computer animation. SCA '02. New York, NY, USA: Association for Computing Machinery; 2002. p. 65–71. https://doi.org/10.1145/545261.545272.
[67] Breen D, Lin M, Cao Y, Faloutsos P, Pighin FH. Eurographics/siggraph symposium on computer animation. Unsupervised learning for speech motion editing. 2003 [Online]. Available: https://www.semanticscholar.org/paper/Eurographics-siggraph-Symposium-on-Computer-(2003)-Breen-Lin/1c8ab86f0624b93853eed3875cf13b4d1c321d97. [Accessed 26 July 2024].
[68] J. D. Edge and S. Maddock, "Expressive visual speech using geometric muscle functions," Citeseer.

CHAPTER

Fluids, liquids, and gases 11

Among the most difficult graphical objects to model and animate are those that are not defined by a static, rigid, topologically simple structure. Many of these complex forms are found in nature. They present especially difficult challenges for those intent on controlling their motion. In some cases, special models of a specific phenomenon will suffice. We begin the chapter presenting special models for water, clouds, and fire that approximate their behavior under certain conditions. These models identify salient characteristics of the phenomena and attempt to model those characteristics explicitly. Such approaches are useful for a specific appearance or motion, but for a more robust model, a more rigorous scientific approach is needed. As far as computational science is concerned, all of the phenomena mentioned earlier fall under the classification of *fluids* and computing their motion is called *computational fluid dynamics* (CFD). The basics of CFD are given at the end of this chapter.

Many of the time-varying models described in this chapter represent work that is state of the art. It is not the objective here to cover all aspects of recent research. The basic models are covered, with only brief reference to the more advanced algorithms.

11.1 Specific fluid models

Fire, smoke, and clouds are gaseous phenomena that have no well-defined surface to model. They are inherently volumetric models, although surface-based techniques have been applied with limited success. For example, water when relatively still has a well-defined surface; however, water changes its shape as it moves. In the case of ocean waves, features on the water's surface move, but the water itself does not travel. The simple surface topology can become arbitrarily complex when the water becomes turbulent. Splashing, foaming, and breaking waves are complex processes best modeled by particle systems and volumetric techniques, but these techniques are inefficient in nonturbulent situations. In addition, water can travel from one place to another, form streams, split into separate pools, and collect again. In modeling these phenomena for purposes of computer graphics, programmers often make simplifying assumptions to limit the computational complexity and model only those features of the physical processes that are visually important in the specific situation of interest. The growing interest in simulating fluids has resulted in a number of tools that use various techniques, some which are more suited towards real time than accuracy, see Table 11.1.

Computer Animation. https://doi.org/10.1016/B978-0-443-13512-5.00011-2

11.1.1 Models of water

Water presents a particular challenge for computer animation because its appearance and motion take various forms (see [1], [2], [3], [4]). Water can be modeled as a still, rigid-looking surface to which ripples can be added as display attributes by perturbing the surface normal using bump mapping (see [5]). Alternatively, water can be modeled as a smoothly rolling height field in which time-varying ripples are incorporated into the geometry of the surface (see [6]). In ocean waves, it is assumed that there is no transport of water even though the waves travel along the surface in forms that vary from sinusoidal to cycloidal (see [7], [8].)[1] Breaking, foaming, and splashing of the waves can be added on top of the base model in a postprocessing step (see [7], [8]). The transport of water from one location to another adds more computational complexity to the modeling problem (see [9]).

Representation

Let's first define what we mean by "water" for animation purposes. There are a number of different ways we can represent "water" ranging from simple to complex, including the use of textures, meshes, grids, particles, and volumes. Each of these has advantages and disadvantages that should be considered depending on the use cases (i.e., accuracy of simulation, interactivity, and graphical fidelity).

Approach 1: planar textures

Let's say we wish to represent a pond, ocean, or lake that exhibits undulating waves and ripples emanating from a single specific source. A simple approach would be to just use a semitransparent plane with appropriate textures (possibly multiple). This is not very exciting or dynamic, however. We can improve it slightly by adding animation to the texture coordinates (UVs) to scale the texture and blend multiple textures moving in different directions to confuse the eye. Another improvement would be to add additional vector offsets to the texture coordinates with a sinusoid to simulate wave movement. Finally, we can sample from a normal map during rendering (pixel/fragment shader) to add "bumps" where the wave crests and troughs should appear. This can provide a decent approximation in a pinch but at oblique angles appears entirely flat (because it is a planar surface).

Approach 2: meshes

Using a 3D mesh to represent the water surface, we can leverage the same ideas as before while enabling height displacement. Meshes contain a set of vertices and edges to define the topology. We can offset each vertex with a function that changes over time to displace these vertices temporally. Simple waves can be modeled as sinusoids, so we can start with a planar grid (X-Y) and set the height of each vertex using the appropriate wave function (Figures 11.1 and 11.2).

---

[1] A *cycloid* is the curve traced out by a point on the perimeter of a rolling disk.

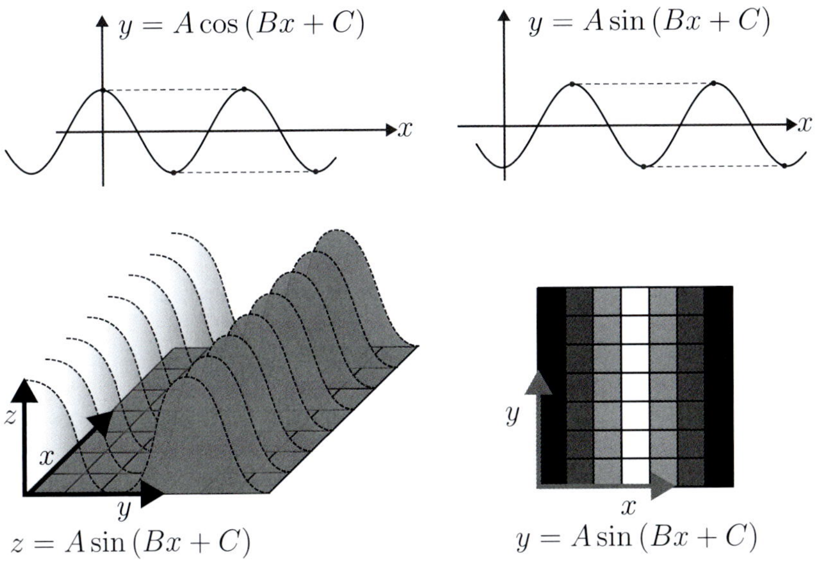

FIGURE 11.1

Visualizing simple waves using sinusoids in 1D *(top)*, 2D *(bottom right)* and 3D *(bottom left)*.

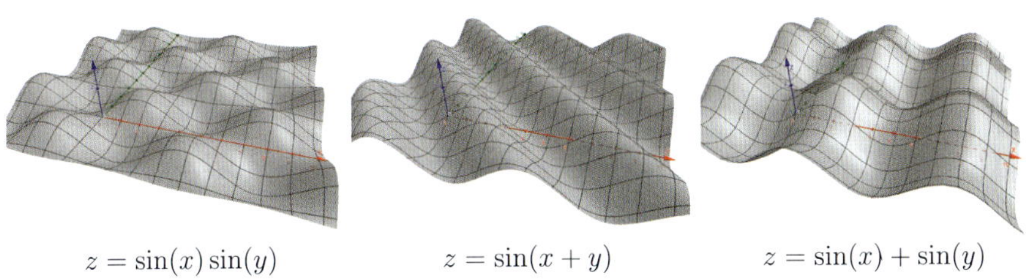

FIGURE 11.2

Combining sinusoids in various ways as a height function of an XY grid.

> **Aside: Sinusoids**
>
> We can define simple 2D sine/cosine waves generally as: $y = A\sin(Bx + C)$, where (x, y) are the coordinates, A is the amplitude/height, B controls the "frequency" or how close the crests/troughs are, and C is the "phase" or translational offset from the origin. Because sin and cos are the same but with different phases C, we can use them interchangeably. See Figures 11.3 and 11.4.

In Figure 11.5a–b, we see that if you offset the vertices on the vertical axis by a sinusoid, you simulate simple "waves." This method doesn't look great yet though. A slightly better method is shown in Figure 11.5c (and Figure 11.6) where each vertex "rides" around on a circle whose radius is set to the amplitude of the wave.

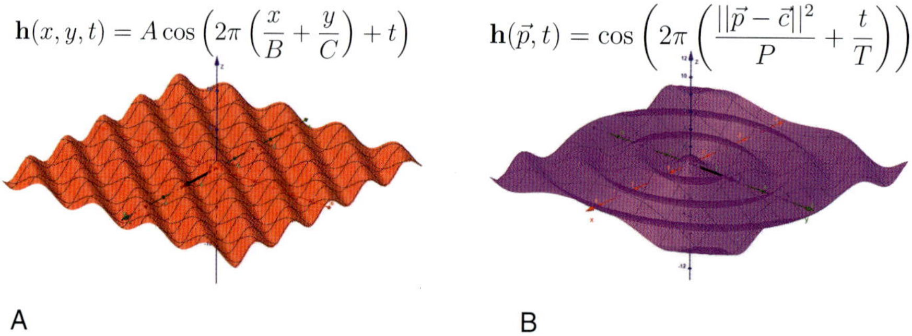

FIGURE 11.3

Examples of height functions for 3D waves. (a), A is the height/amplitude, B controls spacing/frequency, C controls angle of rotation, t is the current animation time. (b) Single ripple emanating from location $\overrightarrow{c}$, $\overrightarrow{p} = (x, y)$ is a point on the grid, t is the animation time, P controls frequency, T controls speed.

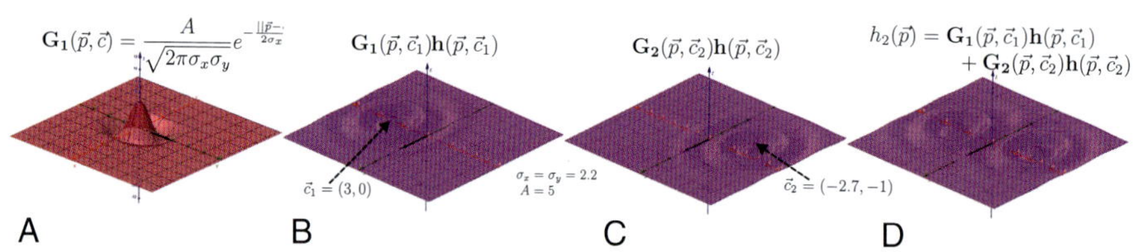

FIGURE 11.4

Combining two ripples and blending with a Gaussian function: (a) the Gaussian blend function; (b) Ripple 1 modulated by Gaussian; (c) Ripple 2 modulated by Gaussian; (d) Sum of modulated ripples, weight factors could be used to emphasize one over the other.

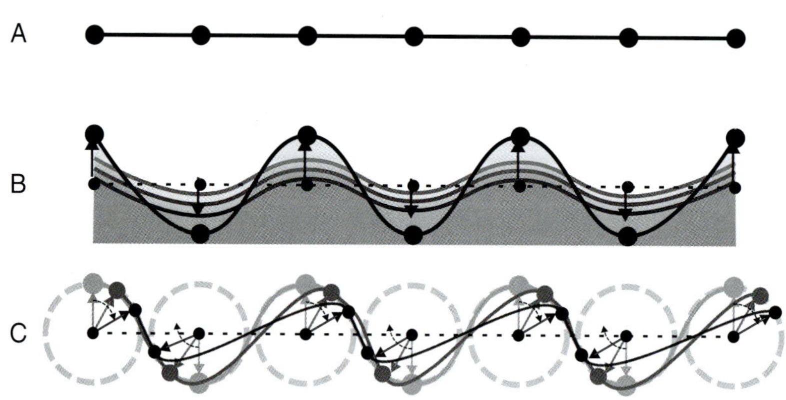

FIGURE 11.5

Mesh deformation for water surface: (a) initial vertices/samples (b) vertical displacement using sinusoid (c) trochoidal displacement (Gerstner wave) method by moving vertices on an implicit circle to cause more realistic undulation. Note that each circle may have different radii and rotation speeds enabling a high degree of dynamic control over the wave function.

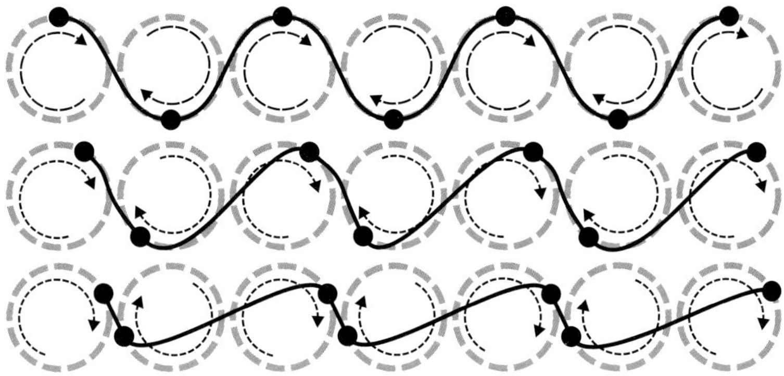

FIGURE 11.6

Demonstration of how trochoidal waves rotate vertices creating undulation: (a) initial; (b) step 1; (c) step 2.

In each simulation step, the vertex moves not only upward and downward but also laterally simulating an "undulating" motion. This technique is the basis of "Gerstner waves" or trochoidal waves (see [10]).

In Figure 11.7, we demonstrate this method in Unity (see [11]), where a mesh is modified using trochoidal sinusoids and uses clever texturing/rendering techniques to create the illusion of depth, foam, and glossiness. In particular, the example shown uses normal mapping, UV-scrolling with multiple layers, a "foam" noise texture sampled and blended when the normal is within a threshold range, and the use of the "scene depth" node controls the transparency and finally the wave simulation is used to displace each vertex in the vertex shader.

Approach 3: liquid volumes

Meshes only represent the "surface" of the water. This doesn't allow us to capture the nuances of density and changing velocities of varying parts of the liquid. Other properties such as viscosity and surface tension are desired for some accurate liquid animations. This can be done using volumetric methods that divide space up into

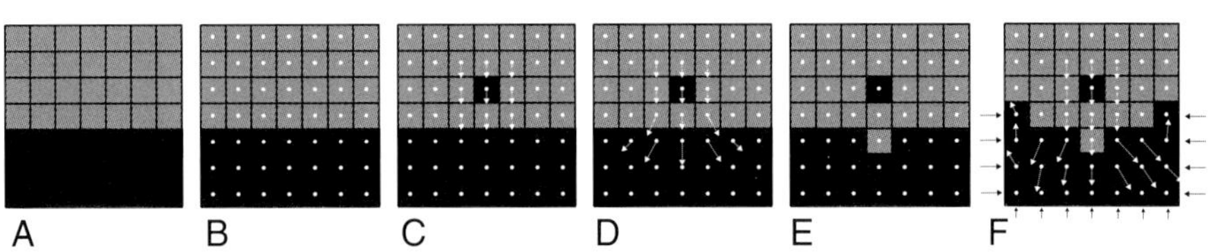

FIGURE 11.7

Example of how the stable fluid algorithm using Navier-Stokes works: (a) initial density; (b) initial velocity; (c) velocity source/force added to velocity field; (d) velocity projection and advection (solve for cell velocity given fluid properties and propagate); (e) density diffusion and advection (solve for density given velocity); (e) update velocity based on boundary conditions.

discrete "volumes" of space that have an assigned density and velocity. Simulation methods derived from Navier-Stokes equations (see [12]) can be used to move the density in the volume taking into account the physical properties of each cell. In particular, the Stam (see [13]) stable fluids algorithm can be applied in both two-dimensional (2D) and three-dimensional (3D) effectively. A simplified 2D example is shown in Figure 11.8, and the results of the various stages of the algorithm are shown in Figure 11.9. Figure 11.10 shows additional examples of this algorithm. This is quite computationally intensive depending on the resolution desired for the 3D simulation volume. Particle-based methods are commonly used in animation software (e.g., Blender). In these methods, many particles are used to represent a "narrow band" of the volume around the surface of the liquid. A lower-resolution volume is used to store liquid properties (density/velocity). These particles sample from this volume, are simulated, and the results propagated back into the volume for the next iteration. This hybrid approach (or FLIP for FLuid Implicit Particle approach [14]) is effective at achieving real-time performance and high accuracy. Examples of this approach can be seen in Figure 11.11, wire frames are shown in Figure 11.12, and sample volume velocity can be seen in Figure 11.13; Figure 11.14 shows the particles themselves used for simulation.

Still waters and small-amplitude waves

The simplest way to model water is merely to assign the color blue to anything below a given height. If the *y*-axis is "up," then color any pixel blue (with, for example, an illumination model that uses a consistent normal) in which the world space coordinate of the corresponding visible surface has a *y*-value less than some given constant. This creates the illusion of still water at a consistent "sea level." It is sufficient for placid lakes and puddles of standing water. Equivalently, a flat

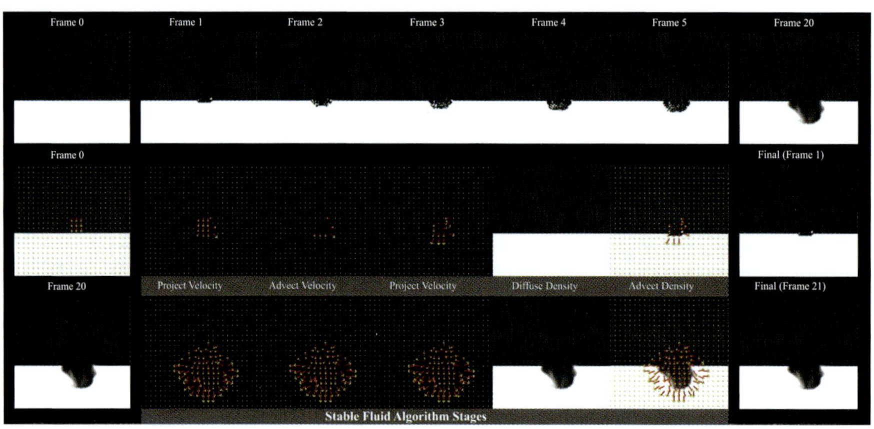

FIGURE 11.8

Demonstration of stable fluid algorithm implementation. *Top:* Final animation frames. *Middle:* Algorithm steps between frame 0 and 1. *Bottom:* Algorithm steps between frame 20 and 21.

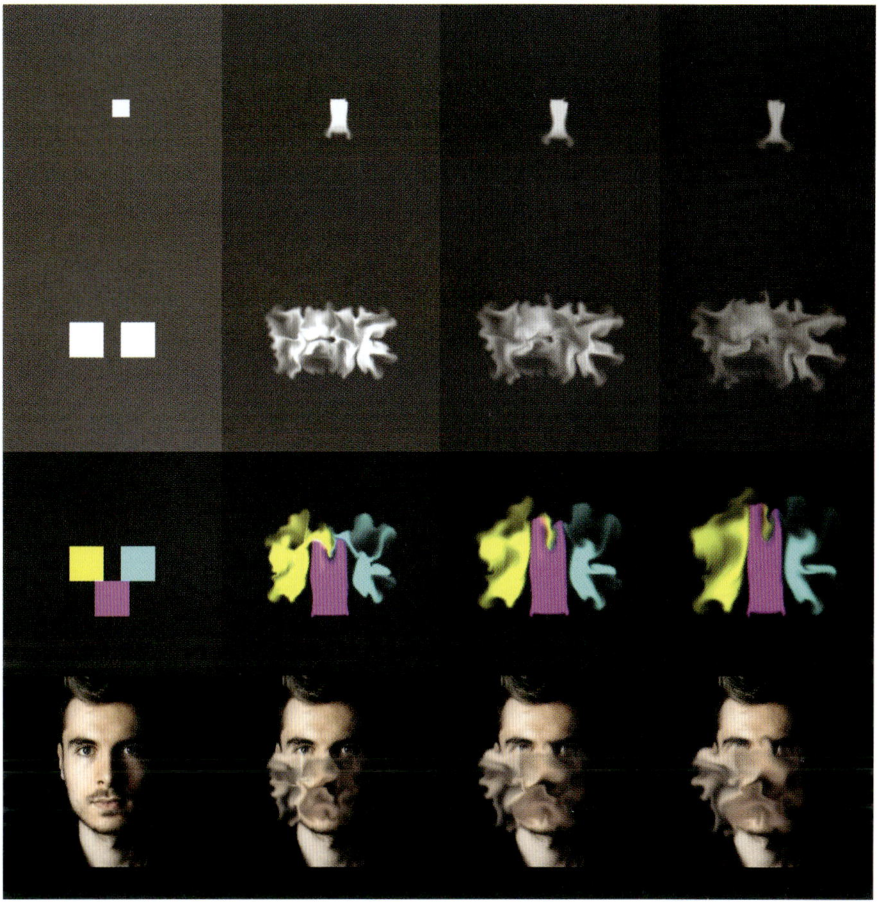

FIGURE 11.9

More examples of stable fluids manipulating. *Top:* Density initialized with downward velocity. *Second:* Two sources initialized with outward velocity. *Third:* RGB density fields (three separate fields) with three sources each (from before but with middle initialized with upward velocity). *Bottom:* Second row density field initialized with RGB color density sampled from an image.

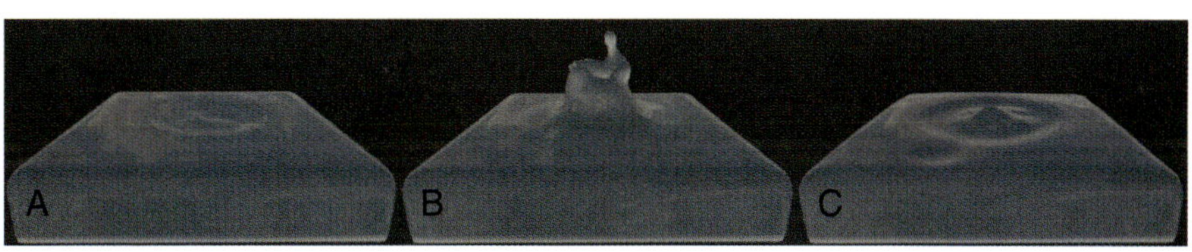

FIGURE 11.10

Example of 3D fluid simulation in Blender using FLIP fluids: (a) initial; (b) object dropped into middle and fluid splashes; (c) afterward, fluid settles due to surface tension and diffusion showing ripples.

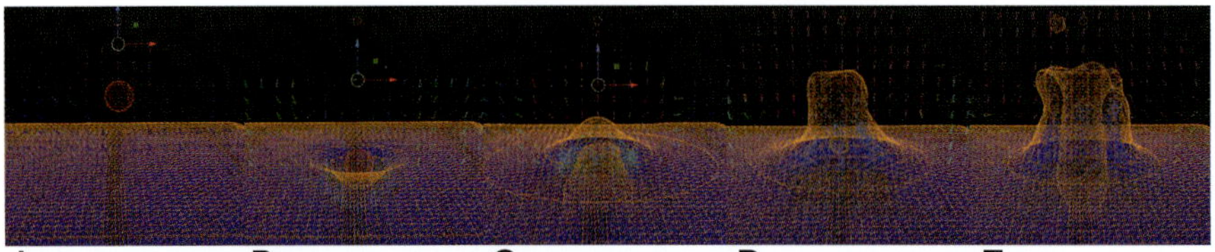

FIGURE 11.11

3D Fluid example in Blender showing mesh wire frame and simulation progression with grid cell velocity indicated.

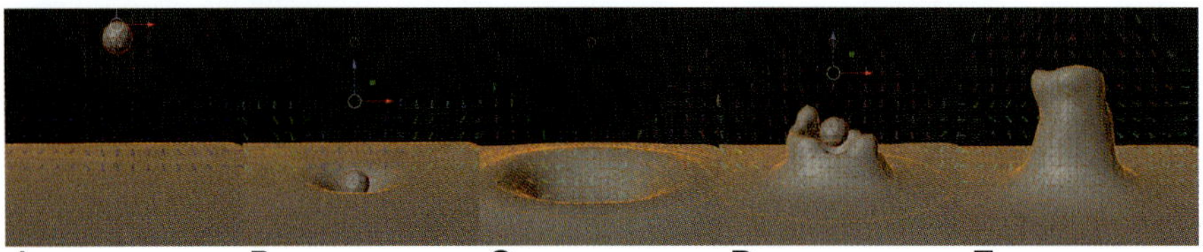

FIGURE 11.12

3D Fluid example in Blender showing solid mesh and grid cell velocity.

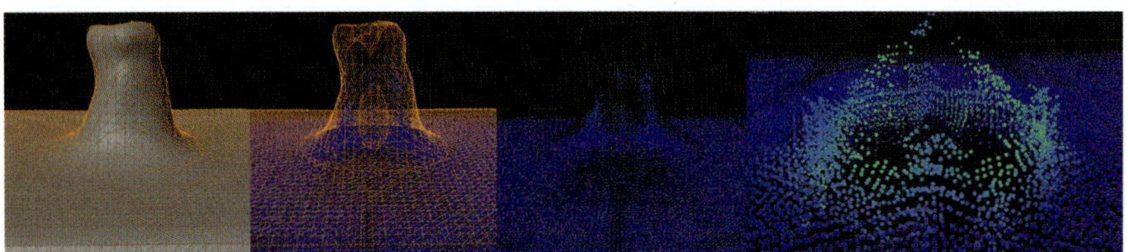

FIGURE 11.13

3D Fluid example in Blender: (a) solid; (b) showing how internal structures can form during simulation; (c) displaying particles from FLIP simulation; (d) closeup on particles

blue plane perpendicular to the y-axis and at the height of the water can be used to represent the water's surface. These models, of course, do not produce any animation of the water.

Normal vector perturbation (the approach employed in bump mapping) can be used to simulate the appearance of small amplitude waves on an otherwise still body of water. To perturb the normal, one or more simple sinusoidal functions are used to modify the direction of the surface's normal vector. The functions are parameterized in terms of a single variable, usually relating to distance from a source point. It is not necessarily the case that the wave starts with zero amplitude at the source. When standing waves in a large body of water are modeled, each function usually has a constant amplitude. The wave crests can be linear, in which case all the waves

FIGURE 11.14

3D Fluid example in Unity. *Top:* Water mesh shown with UV scrolling direction indicated *(left)*, UV map on frame 1 *(middle)* and UV map on frame 10 *(right)*. *Second:* No waves, only UV scrolling and normal map *(left)*, vertex displacement using wave displacement function *(middle)*, additional foam noise texture *(right)*. *Third:* UV map. *Fourth:* Solid. *Bottom:* Wire frame and parameters *(right)*.

generated by a particular function travel in a uniform direction, or the wave crests can radiate from a single user-specified or randomly generated source point. Linear wave crests tend to form self-replicating patterns when viewed from a distance. For a different effect, radially symmetrical functions that help to break up these global patterns can be used. Radial functions also simulate the effect of a thrown pebble or raindrop hitting the water (Figure 11.15). The time-varying height for a point at which the wave begins at time zero is a function of the amplitude and wavelength of the wave (Figure 11.16). Combining the two, Figure 11.17 shows the height of a point at some distance d from the start of the wave. This is a two-dimensional function relative to a point at which the function is zero at time zero. This function can be

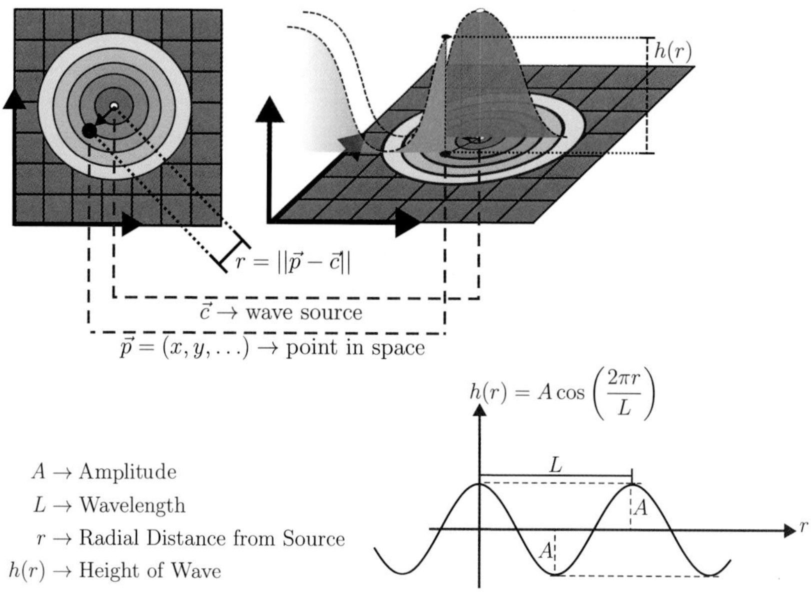

FIGURE 11.15

Radially symmetric standing wave.

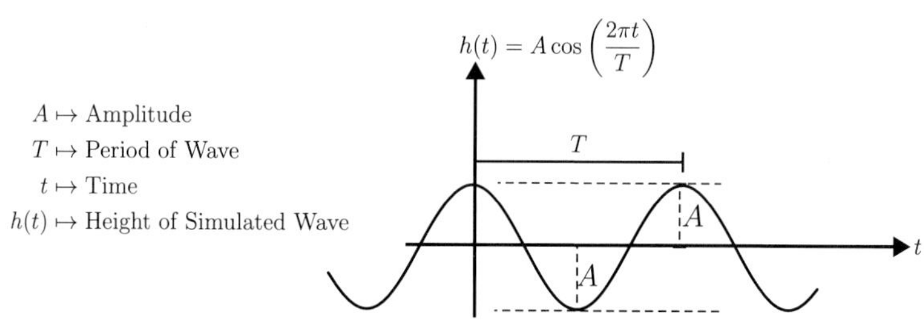

FIGURE 11.16

Time-varying height.

rotated and translated so that it is positioned and oriented appropriately in world space. Once the height function for a given point is defined, the normal to the point at any instance in time can be determined by computing the tangent vector and forming the vector perpendicular to it. These vectors should then be oriented in world space, so the plane they define contains the direction that the wave is traveling.

Superimposing multiple sinusoidal functions of different amplitudes and with various source points (in the radial case) or directions (in the linear case) can generate interesting patterns of overlapping ripples. Typically, the higher the frequency of the wave component, the lower the amplitude. Notice that these do not change the geometry of the surface used to represent the water (e.g., a flat blue

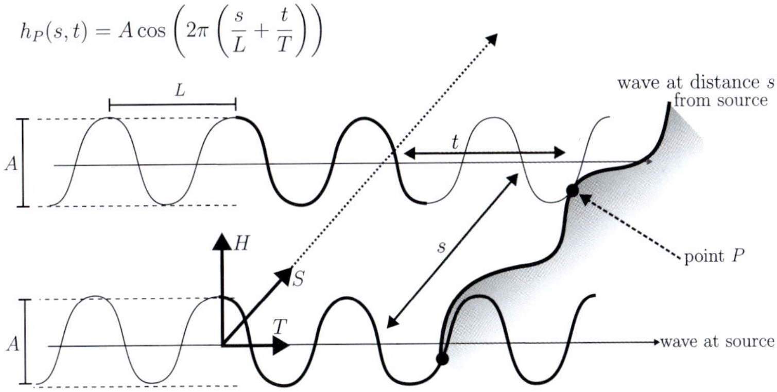

FIGURE 11.17

Time-varying function at point *P*.

plane) but are used only to change the shading properties. Also notice that it must be a time-varying function that propagates the wave along the surface.

The same approach used to calculate wave normals can be used to modify the height of the surface (e.g., [15]). A mesh of points can be used to model the surface of the water and the heights of the individual points can be controlled by the overlapping sinusoidal functions. Either a faceted surface with smooth shading can be used or the points can be the control points of a higher-order surface such as a B-spline surface. The points must be sufficiently dense to sample the height function accurately enough for rendering. Calculating the normals without changing the actual surface creates the illusion of waves on the surface of the water. However, whenever the water meets a protruding surface, like a rock, the lack of surface displacement will be evident. See Figures 11.18 and 11.19 for a comparison between a water surface modeled by normal vector perturbation and a water surface modeled by a height field. An option to reduce the density of mesh points required is to use only the low-frequency, high-amplitude functions to control the height of the surface points and to include the high-frequency, low-amplitude functions to calculate the normals (Figure 11.20).

The anatomy of waves

A more sophisticated model must be used to model waves with greater realism, one that incorporates more of the physical effects that produce their appearance and behavior. Waves come in various frequencies, from tidal waves to capillary waves, which are created by wind passing over the surface of the water. The waves collectively called wind waves are those of most interest for visual effects. The sinusoidal form of a simple wave has already been described and is reviewed here in a more appropriate form for the equations that follow. In Equation 11.1, the function $f(s, t)$ describes the amplitude of the wave in which s is the distance from the source point, t is a point in time, A is the maximum amplitude, C is the propagation speed,

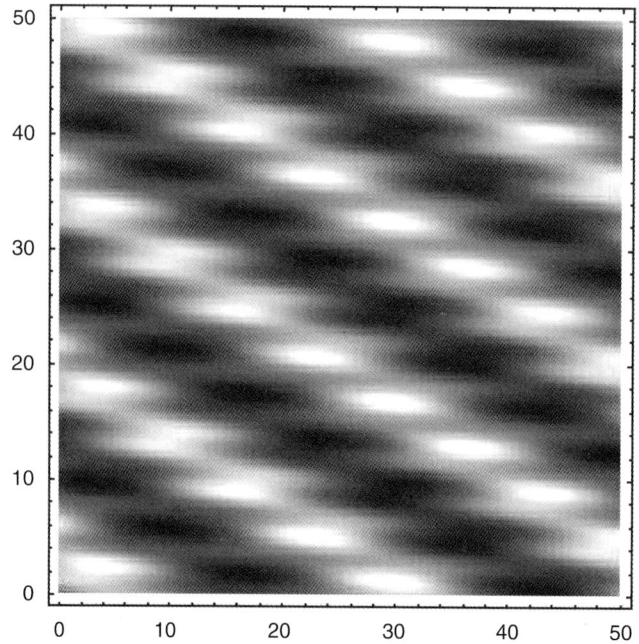

FIGURE 11.18

Superimposed linear waves of various amplitudes and frequencies.

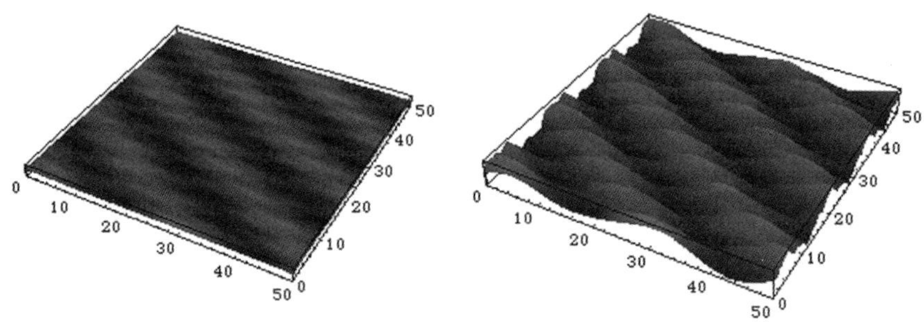

FIGURE 11.19

Normal vector displacement versus height displacement.

and L is the wavelength. The period of the wave, T, is the time it takes for one complete wave to pass a given point. The wavelength, period, and speed are related by the equation $C = L/T$.

$$f(s,t) = \cos^{-1}\left(\frac{2\pi(s - Ct)}{L}\right) \tag{11.1}$$

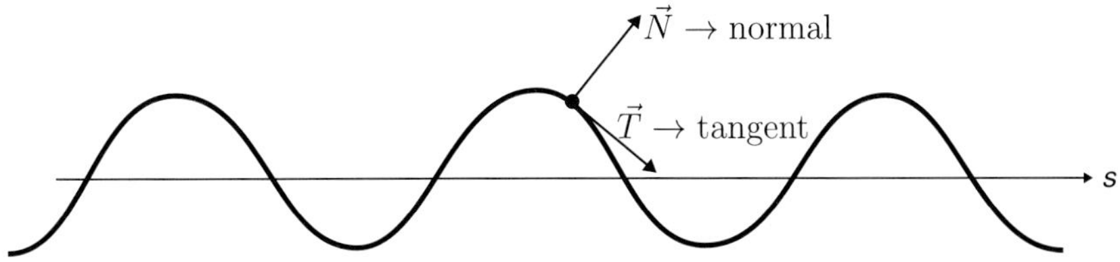

$$h_P(s,t) = A\cos\left(2\pi\left(\frac{s}{L}+\frac{t}{T}\right)\right)$$

$$\frac{d}{ds}h_P(s,t) = -\left(\left(A\frac{2\pi}{L}\right)\sin\left(2\pi\left(\frac{s}{L}+\frac{t}{T}\right)\right)\right)$$

$$\vec{T} = \left(1, \frac{d}{ds}h_P(s,t), 0\right)$$

$$\vec{N} = \left(-\frac{d}{ds}h_P(s,t), 1, 0\right)$$

FIGURE 11.20

Normal vector for two-dimensional wave function.

The motion of the wave is different from the motion of the water. The wave travels linearly across the surface of the water, whereas a particle of water moves in nearly a circular orbit (Figure 11.21). While riding the crest of the wave, the particle will move in the direction of the wave. As the wave passes and the particle drops into the trough between waves, it will travel in the reverse direction. The steepness, S, of the wave is represented by the term H/L, where H is defined as twice the amplitude.

Waves with a small steepness value have basically a sinusoidal shape. As the steepness value increases, the shape of the wave gradually changes into a sharply crested peak with flatter troughs. Mathematically, the shape approaches that of a cycloid.

In an idealized wave, there is no net transport of water. The particle of water completes one orbit in the time it takes for one complete cycle of the wave to pass. The average orbital speed of a particle of water is given by the

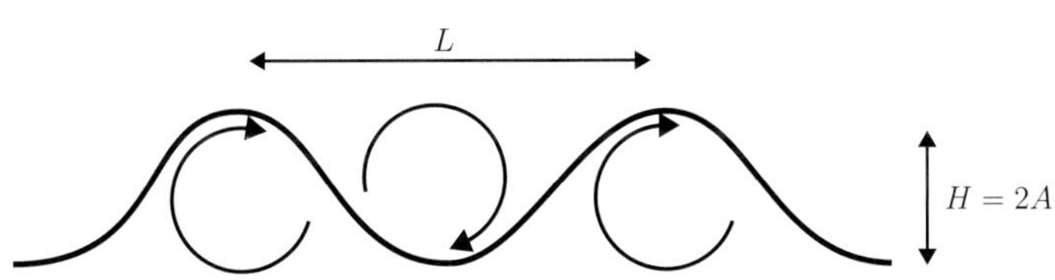

FIGURE 11.21

Circular paths of particles of water subjected to waves.

circumference of the orbit, pH, divided by the time it takes to complete the orbit, T (see Equation 11.2).

$$Q_{\mathrm{ave}} = \frac{\pi H}{T} = \frac{\pi H C}{L} = \pi S C \tag{11.2}$$

If the orbital speed, Q, of the water at the crest exceeds the speed of the wave, C, then the water will spill over the wave, resulting in a breaking wave. Because the average speed, Q, increases as the steepness, S, of the wave increases, this limits the steepness of a nonbreaking wave. The observed steepness of ocean waves, as reported by Peachey (e.g., [8]), is between 0.5 and 1.0.

A common simplification of the full CFD simulation of ocean waves is called the Airy model, and it relates the depth of the water, d, the propagation speed, C, and the wavelength of the wave, L (see Equation 11.3).

$$C = \sqrt{\frac{g}{k}\tanh(\kappa d)} = \sqrt{\frac{gL}{2\pi} \times \tanh\left(\frac{2\pi d}{L}\right)} \quad \text{where } L = CT \tag{11.3}$$

In Equation 11.3, g is the acceleration of a body due to gravity at sea level, 9.81 m/sec^2, and $k = 2\pi/L$ is the spatial equivalent of wave frequency. As the depth of the water increases, the function $\tanh(kd)$ tends toward one, so C approaches $gL/2\pi$. As the depth decreases and approaches zero, $\tanh(kd)$ approaches kd, so C approaches $\sqrt{gd}$. Peachey suggests using *deep* to mean $d > L/4$ and *shallow* to mean $d < L/20$.

As a wave approaches the shoreline at an angle, the part of the wave that approaches first will slow down as it encounters a shallower area. The wave will progressively slow down along its length as more of it encounters the shallow area. This will tend to straighten out the wave and is called *wave refraction*.

Interestingly, even though speed (C) and wavelength (L) of the wave are reduced as the wave enters shallow water, the period, T, of the wave remains the same and the amplitude, A (and, equivalently, H), remains the same or increases. As a result, the orbital speed, Q (see Equation 11.2), of the water remains the same. Because orbital speed remains the same as the speed of the wave decreases, waves tend to break as they approach the shoreline because the speed of the water exceeds the speed of the wave. The breaking of a wave means that water particles break off from the wave surface as they are "thrown forward" beyond the front of the wave.

Modeling ocean waves

The description of modeling ocean waves presented here follows Peachey (e.g., [8]). The ocean surface is represented as a height field, $y = f(x, z, t)$, where (x, z) defines the two-dimensional ground plane, t is time, and y is the height. The wave function f is a sum of various waveforms at different amplitudes (see Equation 11.4).

$$f(x, z, t) = \sum_{i=1}^{n} A_i W_i(x, z, t) \tag{11.4}$$

The wave function, W_i, is formed as the composition of two functions: a wave profile, w_i, and a phase function, $\theta_i(x, z, t)$, according to Equation 11.5. This allows the description of the wave profile and phase function to be addressed separately.

$$W_i(x,z,t) = \omega_i(\text{fraction}[\theta_i(x,z,t)]) \tag{11.5}$$

Each waveform is described by its period, amplitude, source point, and direction. It is convenient to define each waveform, actually each phase function, as a linear rather than radial wave and to orient it so the wave is perpendicular to the x-axis and originates at the source point. The phase function is then a function only of the x-coordinate and can then be rotated and translated into position in world space.

Equation 11.6 gives the time dependence of the phase function. Thus if the phase function is known for all points x (assuming the alignment of the waveform along the x-axis), then the phase function can be easily computed at any time at any position. If the depth of water is constant, the Airy model states that the wavelength and speed are also constant. In this case, the aligned phase function is given in Equation 11.7.

$$\theta_i(x,y,t) = \theta_i(x,y,t_0) - \frac{t - t_0}{T_i} \tag{11.6}$$

$$\theta_i(x,y,t) = \frac{x_i}{L_i} \tag{11.7}$$

However, if the depth of the water is variable, then L_i is a function of depth and u_i is the integral of the depth-dependent phase-change function from the origin to the point of interest (see Equation 11.8). Numerical integration can be used to produce phase values at predetermined grid points. These grid points can be used to interpolate values within grid cells. Peachey (e.g., [8]) successfully uses bilinear interpolation to accomplish this.

$$\theta_i(x,y,t) = \int_0^x \theta_i'(u,z,t)du \tag{11.8}$$

The wave profile function, wi, is a single-value periodic function of the fraction of the phase function (see Equation 11.5) so that $w_i(u)$ is defined for $0.0 \le u \le 1.0$. The values of the wave profile function range over the interval [1, 1]. The wave profile function is designed so that its value is one at both ends of the interval (see Equation 11.9).

$$\omega_i(0,0) = \omega_i(1.0) = 1.0 \tag{11.9}$$

Linear interpolation can be used to model the changing profile of the wave according to steepness. Steepness *(H/L)* can be used to blend between a sinusoidal function (see Equation 11.1) and a cycloid-like function (see Equation 11.10) designed to resemble a sharp-crested wave profile. In addition, wave asymmetry is introduced as a function of the depth of the water to simulate effects observed in waves as they approach a coastline. The asymmetry interpolant, k, is defined as the ratio between the water depth, d, and deep-water wavelength, L_i (see Eq. 11.11). When k is large, the wave profile is handled with no further modification. When k

is small, u is raised to a power to shift its value toward the low end of the range between zero and one. This has the effect of stretching out the back of the wave and steepening the front of the wave as it approaches the shore.

$$\omega_i(u) = 8\left|u - \frac{1}{2}\right|^2 - 1 \tag{11.10}$$

$$\begin{aligned} L_i^{\text{deep}} &= \frac{gT_i^2}{2\pi} \\ k &= \frac{d}{L_i^{\text{deep}}} \end{aligned} \tag{11.11}$$

As the wave enters very shallow water, the amplitudes of the various wave components are reduced so the overall amplitude of the wave is kept from exceeding the depth of the water.

Spray and foam resulting from breaking waves and waves hitting obstacles can be simulated using a stochastic but controlled (e.g., Gaussian distribution) particle system. When the speed of the water, Q_{average}, exceeds the speed of the wave, C, then water spray leaves the surface of the wave and is thrown forward. Equation 11.2 indicates that this condition happens when $\pi S > 1.0$ or, equivalently, $S > 1.0/\pi$. Breaking waves are observed with steepness values less than this (around 0.1), which indicates that the water probably does not travel at a uniform orbital speed. Instead, the speed of the water at the top of the orbit is faster than at other points in the orbit. Thus a user-specified spray-threshold steepness value can be used to trigger the particle system. The number of particles generated is based on the difference between the calculated wave steepness and the spray-threshold steepness.

For a wave hitting an obstacle, a particle system can be used to generate spray in the direction of reflection based on the incoming direction of the wave and the normal of the obstacle surface. A small number of particles are generated just before the moment of impact, are increased to a maximum number at the point of impact, and are then decreased as the wave passes the obstacle. As always, stochastic perturbation should be used to control both speed and direction.

For a more complete treatment of modeling height-field displacement-mapped surface for ocean waves using a fast Fourier transform description, including modeling and rendering underwater environmental effects, the interested reader is directed to the course notes by Tessendorf (e.g., [16]).

Finding its way downhill

One of the assumptions used to model ocean waves is that there is no transport of water. However, in many situations, such as a stream of water running downhill, it is useful to model how water travels from one location to another. In situations in which the water can be considered a height field and the motion is assumed to be uniform through a vertical column of water, the vertical component of the velocity can be ignored. In such cases, differential equations can be used to simulate a wide range of convincing motion [9]. The Navier-Stokes equations (which describe flow through a volume) can be simplified to model the flow.

To develop the equations in two dimensions, the user parameterizes functions that are in terms of distance x. Let $z = h(x)$ be the height of the water and $z = b(x)$ be the height of the ground at location x. The height of the water is $d(x) = h(x) - b(x)$. If one assumes that motion is uniform through a vertical column of water and that $v(x)$ is the velocity of a vertical column of water, then the shallow-water equations are as shown in Equations 11.12 and 11.13, where g is the gravitational acceleration. Equation 11.12 considers the change in velocity of the water and relates its acceleration, the difference in adjacent velocities, and the acceleration due to gravity when adjacent columns of water are at different heights. Equation 11.13 considers the transport of water by relating the temporal change in the height of the vertical column of water with the spatial change in the amount of water moving.

$$\frac{\partial v}{\partial t} + v\frac{\partial v}{\partial x} + g\frac{\partial h}{\partial x} = 0 \tag{11.12}$$

$$\frac{\partial d}{\partial t} + \frac{\partial}{\partial x}(vd) = 0 \tag{11.13}$$

These equations can be further simplified if the assumptions of small fluid velocity and slowly varying depth are used. The former assumption eliminates the second term of Equation 11.12, whereas the latter assumption implies that the term d can be removed from inside the derivative in Equation 11.13. These simplifications result in Equations 11.14 and 11.15.

$$\frac{\partial v}{\partial t} + g\frac{\partial v}{\partial x} = 0 \tag{11.14}$$

$$\frac{\partial d}{\partial t} + d\frac{\partial v}{\partial x} = 0 \tag{11.15}$$

Differentiating Equation 11.14 with respect to x and Equation 11.15 with respect to t and substituting for the cross-derivatives results in Equation 11.16. This is the one-dimensional wave equation with a wave velocity $\sqrt{gd}$. As Kass and Miller [9] note, this degree of simplification is probably not accurate enough for engineering applications.

$$\frac{\partial^2 h}{\partial t^2} + gd\frac{\partial^2 h}{\partial x^2} \tag{11.16}$$

This partial differential equation is solved using finite differences. The discretization, as used by Kass and Miller [9], is set up as in Figure 11.22, with samples of v positioned halfway between the samples of h. The authors report a stable discretization, resulting in Equations 11.17 and 11.18. Putting these two equations together results in Equation 11.19, which is the discrete version of Equation 11.16.

$$\frac{\partial h_i}{\partial t} = \left(\frac{d_{i-1} + d_i}{2\Delta x}\right)\bigg|_{v_{i-1}} - \left(\frac{d_i + d_{i+1}}{2\Delta x}\right)v_i \tag{11.17}$$

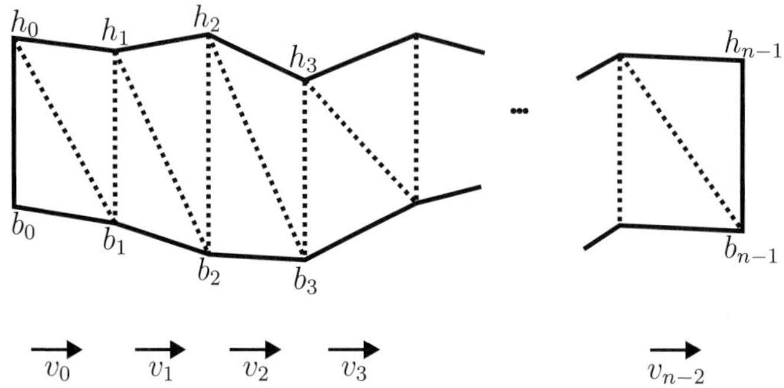

FIGURE 11.22

Discrete two-dimensional representation of height field with water surface *h*, ground *b*, and horizontal water velocity *v*.

$$\frac{\partial v_i}{\partial t} = \frac{(-g)(h_{i+1} - h_i)}{\Delta x} \tag{11.18}$$

$$\frac{\partial^2 h_i}{\partial t^2} = -g\left(\frac{d_{i-1} + d_i}{2(\Delta x)^2}\right)(h_i - h_{i-1}) + g\left(\frac{d_i + d_{i+1}}{2(\Delta x)^2}\right)(h_{i+1} - h_i) \tag{11.19}$$

Equation 11.19 states the relationship of the height of the water surface to the height's acceleration in time. This could be solved by using values of h_i to compute the left-hand side and then using this value to update the next time step. As Kass and Miller (see [9]) report, however, this approach diverges quickly because of the sample spacing.

A first-order implicit numerical integration technique is used to provide a stable solution to Equation 11.19. Numerical integration uses current sample values to approximate derivatives. Explicit methods use approximated derivatives to update the current samples to their new values. Implicit integration techniques find the value whose derivative matches the discrete approximation of the current samples. Implicit techniques typically require more computation per step, but, because they are less likely to diverge significantly from the correct values, larger time steps can be taken, thus producing an overall savings.

Kass and Miller (see [9]) find that a first-order implicit method (Equations 11.20 and 11.21) is sufficient for this application. Using these equations to solve for $h(n)$ and substituting Equation 11.19 for the second derivative ($\ddot{h}(n)$) results in Equation 11.22.

$$\dot{h}(n) = \frac{h(n) - h(n-1)}{\Delta t} \tag{11.20}$$

$$\ddot{h}(n) = \frac{\dot{h}(n) - \dot{h}(n-1)}{\Delta t} \tag{11.21}$$

$$\begin{aligned} h_i(n) = {} & 2h_i(n-1) - h_i(n-2) \\ & -g(\Delta t)^2 \frac{d_{i-1} + d_i}{2\Delta x^2}(h_i(n) - h_{i-1}(n)) \\ & +g(\Delta t)^2 \frac{d_{i-1} + d_i}{2\Delta x^2}(h_{i+1}(n) - h_i(n)) \end{aligned} \tag{11.22}$$

Assuming d is constant during the iteration, the next value of h can be calculated from previous values with the symmetric tridiagonal linear system represented by Equations 11.23–11.25.

$$Ah_i(n) = 2h_i(n-1) + h_i(n-2) \tag{11.23}$$

$$A = \begin{bmatrix} e_0 & f_0 & 0 & 0 & 0 & 0 & 0 \\ f_0 & e_0 & f_i & 0 & 0 & 0 & 0 \\ 0 & f_i & e_2 & \ldots & 0 & 0 & 0 \\ 0 & 0 & \ldots & \ldots & \ldots & 0 & 0 \\ 0 & 0 & 0 & \ldots & e_{n-3} & f_{n-3} & 0 \\ 0 & 0 & 0 & 0 & f_{n-3} & e_{n-2} & f_{n-2} \\ 0 & 0 & 0 & 0 & 0 & f_{n-2} & e_{n-1} \end{bmatrix} \tag{11.24}$$

$$e_0 = 1 + g(\Delta t)^2 \left(\frac{d_0 + d_1}{2(\Delta x)^2} \right)$$

$$e_0 = 1 + g(\Delta t)^2 \left(\frac{d_{i-1} + 2d_i + d_{i+1}}{2(\Delta x)^2} \right) \quad \text{where } 0 < i < n-1$$

$$e_{n-1} = 1 + g(\Delta t)^2 \left(\frac{d_{n-2} + d_{n-1}}{2(\Delta x)^2} \right)$$

$$f_i = -\left(g(\Delta t)^2 \left(\frac{d_i + d_{i+1}}{2(\Delta x)^2} \right) \right) \tag{11.25}$$

To simulate a viscous fluid, Equation 11.23 can be modified to incorporate a parameter that controls the viscosity, thus producing Equation 11.26. The parameter τ ranges between 0 and 1. When $\tau = 0$, Equation 11.26 reduces to Equation 11.3.

$$Ah_i(n) = h_i(n-1) + (1-\tau)(h_i(n-1) - h_i(n-2)) \tag{11.26}$$

Volume preservation can be compromised when $h_i < b_i$. To compensate for this, search for the connected areas of water $\left(h_j < b_j \text{ for } j = i, i+1, \ldots, i+n\right)$ at each iteration and compute the volume. If the volume changes from the last iteration then distribute the difference among the elements of that connected region. The algorithm for the 2D case is shown in Figure 11.23.

FIGURE 11.23

An example of cirrus and cirrostratus clouds at sunset.

(Reproduced with permission from David S. Ebert, 1998).

Extending the algorithm to the 3D case considers a 2D height field. The computations are done by decoupling the two dimensions of the field. Each iteration is decomposed into two subiterations, one in the x-direction and one in the y-direction.

11.1.2 Modeling and animating clouds

Most any outdoor daytime scene includes some type of clouds as a visual element. Clouds can form a backdrop for activity in the foreground, in which case they may be slow moving or even still. Clouds can be used as an area of activity allowing planes to fly around or through them or, as fog, cars to drive through them. Clouds viewed from afar have certain characteristics that are much different from clouds that are viewed close up. From a distance, they exhibit high level opaque appearance features that transparently disappear upon inspection at a closer distance. Cloud formations can inspire, impart calm, be ominous and foreboding, or produce magnificent sunsets. Distant clouds can have a puffy opaque appearance, often resembling familiar shapes of, for example, various animals or other common objects. Other clouds have a layered or fibrous appearance. Whereas some cloud formations viewed from a distance might appear as a stationary backdrop or slow moving rigid formations, storm clouds can form relatively quickly and can appear threatening in a manner of minutes. Complex atmospheric processes form clouds. These processes can be modeled and animated to show the formation of storms, hurricanes, and inclement weather (Figures 11.24 and 11.25).

Clouds are naturally occurring atmospheric phenomena. They are composed of visible water droplets or ice crystals suspended in air, and are formed by moisture droplets adhering to dust particles. When moisture is added to the air and/or the temperature of the air decreases, clouds can form. In either case, moisture in the air condenses into droplets because the air cannot transparently hold that amount

FIGURE 11.24

An example of a cumulus cloud.

(Reproduced with permission from David S. Ebert, 1997.)

of water at that temperature. Clouds occur at a variety of altitudes. Some clouds can be found at 60,000 feet, whereas others can be as low as ground level. Although typically one thinks of clouds as high in the sky, fog phenomena are just very low-level clouds. In addition, a single cloud formation can start near the surface and extend upward as much as 10,000 feet.

Anatomy of clouds and cloud formation

Clouds are categorized according to their altitude, their general shape, and whether they carry moisture (e.g., see [17]). The naming convention combines a standard set of terms that describe the altitude, shape, and moisture of the cloud.

Altitude
Cirrus/cirro: high clouds (by itself, it refers to high-level fibrous clouds) Altus/alto: middle clouds Otherwise: low-level clouds
Shape
Cumulus/cumulo: puffy (Latin for "stack") Stratus/strato: layer (Latin for "sheet")
Moisture
Nimubs/nimbo: water bearing

Certain types of clouds can typically be found at certain elevations. For example, high-level clouds are cirrus, cirrostratus, and cirrocumulus; mid-level clouds are altocumulus, altostratus, and nimbostratus; low-level clouds are cumulonimbus, stratocumulus, stratus, and cumulus. Clouds typified by vertical development are fair weather cumulus and cumulonimbus. Other cloud names less frequently

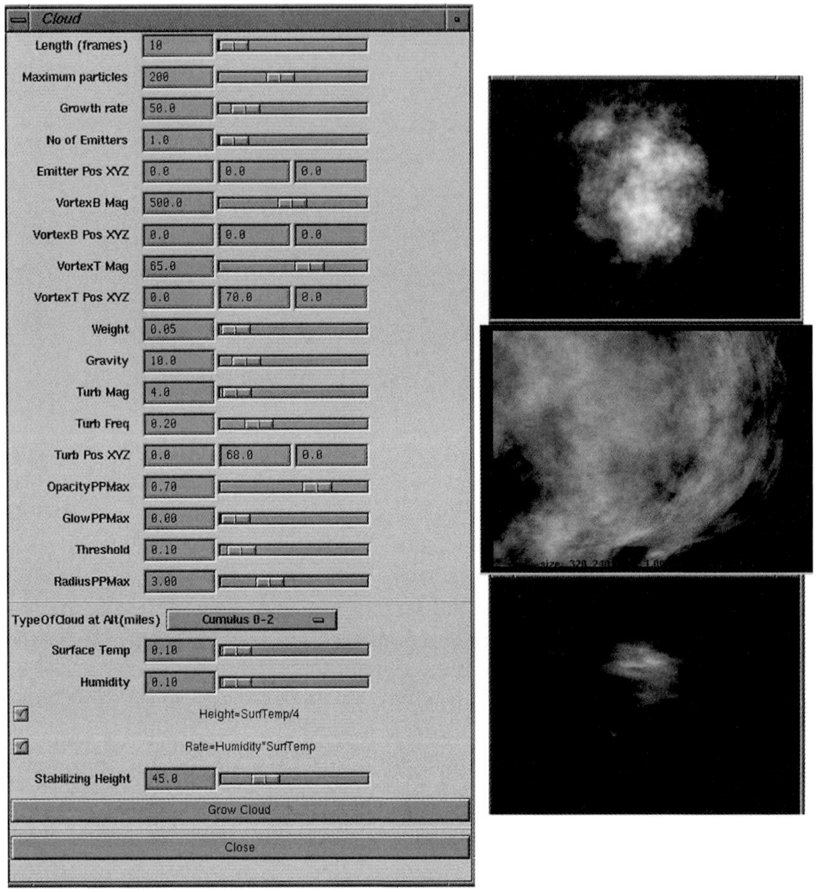

A GUI used to control cloud formation B Example clouds

FIGURE 11.25

(A) An example of cloud dynamics GUI and (B) example images created in Maya.

(Reproduced with permission from © 1999 Rchi Gartha.)

encountered include contrails, billow clouds, mammatus, orographic, and pileus clouds.

Clouds are formed by low-level processes such as particles in the air, turbulence, wind shear, and temperature gradients combined with a significant moisture content. The basic moisture cycle consists of the following: transpiration → evaporation → condensation → precipitation → transpiration.

The processes that form clouds consist of adding moisture to the air or cooling the air. In either case the moisture content becomes higher than what can be handled transparently by the air. As a result, water droplets form and cling to dust particles in the air. The cooling of an air mass is often due to an air mass rising in altitude; air tends to cool as it rises and loses pressure. The cause for this rise is usually due to something forcing the air mass upward: the traveling air mass encounters an incline like a mountain slope; the air mass travels up and over a colder, denser air mass (a warm front); and a cold, dense air mass forces its way underneath the warmer air mass and raises the warm air mass (a cold front). The air mass temperature can also be cooled by the cooling of the earth's surface, often creating fog or other low-level clouds. Adding moisture to the air mass is often accomplished by water evaporating at the earth's surface underneath the air mass.

Cloud models in computer graphics

Over the years, clouds have been quite a challenge for both rendering and animation, so many shortcuts and approaches have been used to provide aesthetically pleasing approximations ranging from simple background painting and traditionally animating them to layered sprites to highly accurate volumetric simulations and recently to real-time solutions leveraging the computational power of the graphics processing unit (GPU) in game engines.

Although modeling clouds as a single, static background painting can be effective in some animations, limited cloud animation can be done cost effectively. This can be a texture mapped sprite. Layering sprites in depth and moving (i.e., panning) the camera around introduces parallax and animation effects can be introduced using animated sprites. Tools like Houdini and EmberGen are specialized in simulating fluids and gases and can export either volumetric data bases (VDBs) or sprite sheets.

For more control and added visual realism, appropriately shaded geometric primitives can be used as cloud building blocks. Two-dimensional primitives can be used for distant clouds, whereas 3D primitives give a greater sense of distance and depth when viewed from various angles and are appropriate for more immersive environments. The primitives can be moved relative to one another and scaled up or down, providing easy control for an animator. Although not physically based, this approach can produce effective visuals if the primitives are carefully designed.

The use of such building blocks was pioneered in 1984 by Geoffrey Gardner (see [18], [19]) and the general approach is still an attractive way to model clouds. Gardner's technique uses a sky plane that is parallel to the ground plane and some distance above it. Ellipsoids are used as the cloud building blocks and are positioned by the user relative to the sky plane. The ellipsoid surface is textured (as described in the next paragraphs) and then mapped onto a sky plane. Gardner also uses these textured ellipsoids to build full 3D cloud models, which allows for a full 3D effect as the viewing angle changes relative to the ellipsoids. Notice, however, that the texturing function is not defined on the interior of the ellipsoid shells, so the visuals associated with flying into a cloud are not supported. In addition to clouds, Gardner also used this approach, with suitable modification to the texture function, to model other environmental features such as trees and hills as in Figure 11.26.

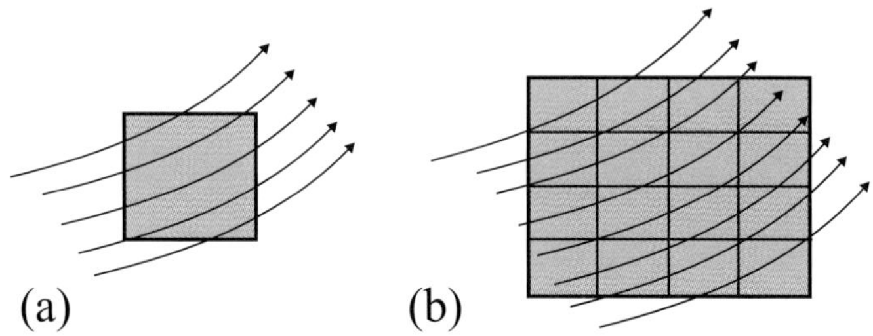

FIGURE 11.26

Grid-based method. (a) Gas flowing through an individual cell. (b) Grid of cells.

The surface texturing function is based on the sum of two weighted sums of sine waves, defined to produce a pseudorandom cloud-like texture. The two sets of sine waves are orthogonal to each other. In each set, each frequency is twice the frequency of its predecessor and has an amplitude of one over radical two times its predecessor. In addition, the phase shift of each frequency is based on its position in the other dimension. A user-defined threshold is set so that any lesser texture value is considered totally transparent. To remove any discontinuities that might arise at the ellipsoid boundary, a monotonically decreasing attenuation function is defined to have a value of one at the middle of the ellipsoid and zero at the boundary. This is used to scale the texture function so that final function values scale down to zero as they approach the limit of the ellipsoid. This creates a cloud primitive that is generally in the shape of an ellipsoid, but whose texture feathers away close to the boundary, thus avoiding any noticeable discontinuities in the shading.

Surface-based textures, such as those used by Gardner, are sufficient for clouds viewed from a distance and represented on a sky plane or viewed from a distance, but to accommodate close viewing and even immersion in the clouds, such as that encountered in current flight simulators and games, a volumetric approach must be taken.

Volumetric approaches define a density value for any point in space. Volumes are rendered by considering the entire line of sight through the volume. This makes realistic shading more difficult because it depends on the accumulated shading of each point along the line of sight inside the cloud. Each point along the light of sight has a certain density that controls its opacity/transparency. Each of these points along the line of sight reflects the light that gets to it from a light source. Direct illumination from the light source is light that filters through the cloud on a line from the light source directly to the point in question. Indirect illumination from the light source is light that comes from the light source by way of reflections off of nearby points in the cloud. This in turn means that the illumination of nearby points must be known to know how much light they reflect. Usually only one or two levels of such reflections are considered to make shading computations tractable. Mathematically, the shading is an integration along the line of sight and illumination is integration along lines from each light source. Indirect lighting is integration from all directions.

For most applications, these integrals can be computed using appropriate discrete approximations or, in some cases, ignored altogether. In any case, the illumination is computationally expensive and not a topic here. The interested reader is directed to the book *Texturing and Modeling: A Procedural Approach*, edited by David Ebert (e.g., see [20]).

The same building block approach to cloud formation can be taken with the volumetric approach, as with the ellipsoid shells of Gardner. See Figure 11.27 for an example of work by David Ebert. At the heart of Ebert's volumetric approach are implicitly defined density functions that provide high-level organization of the cloud, combined with turbulence functions that provide the fine detail.

The implicit function used here is really a sum of individual spherical implicit functions. Each of these spherical functions maps a point in space to a density based on the point's distance from the sphere's center and a density function. One property of the density function is that it is one at its center and monotonically decreases to zero at its outermost edge, which is called its *radius of influence*. In addition, it has a slope of one at its radius of influence, allowing it to blend smoothly with other primitives. A commonly used density function is a sixth-degree polynomial in terms of distance that the point is from the center, but a third-degree polynomial in terms of distance squared, thus avoiding the cost of the square root of the distance calculation (Equation 11.27). The implicit function for the cloud is a weighted sum of these individual implicit functions (Equation 11.28). See Chapter 12.1 for more discussion on implicit functions and surfaces. The use of these implicit density functions provides the macrostructure for the cloud formation, allowing an animator to easily form the cloud with simple high-level controls.

$$F(r) = -\frac{4}{9}\frac{r^6}{R^6} + \frac{17}{9}\frac{r^4}{R^4} - \frac{22}{9}\frac{r^2}{R^2} + 1 \tag{11.27}$$

$$D(p) = \sum_i w_i F(|p - q|) \tag{11.28}$$

To introduce some pseudorandomness into the density values, the animator can procedurally alter the location of points before evaluating the density function. This perturbation of the points should be continuous with limited high-frequency components to avoid aliasing artifacts in the result. The perturbation should also avoid unwanted patterns in the final values.

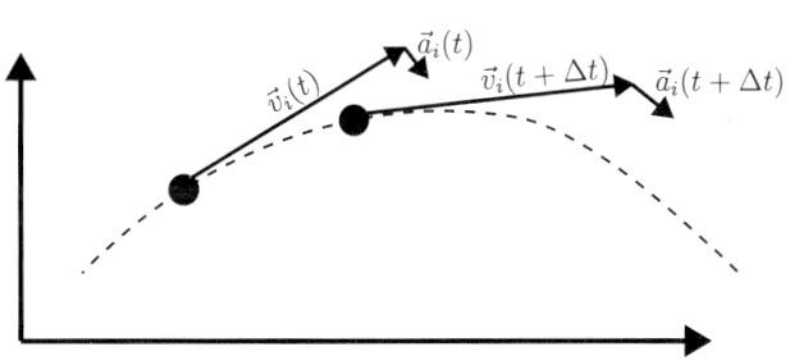

FIGURE 11.27

Particle-based method. Particles move based on fluid velocity/acceleration equations.

The microstructure of the clouds is provided by a procedural noise and turbulence-based density function (see the Appendix). This is blended with the macrostructure density to produce the final values for the cloud density. Various cloud types can be modeled by modifying the primitive shapes, their relative positioning, the density parameters, and the turbulence parameters. See Figures 11.24 and 11.25 for examples.

The building block approach allows the clouds to be animated either at the macro or the micro level. Cloud migration can be modeled by user-supplied scripts or simplified particle system physics can be used. Internal cloud dynamics can be modeled by animating the texture function parameters, in the case of Gardner-type clouds, or turbulence parameters in the case of Ebert.

11.1.3 Modeling and animating fire

Fire is a particularly difficult and computationally intensive process to model. It has all the complexities of smoke and clouds and the added complexity of very active internal processes that produce light and motion and create rapidly varying display attributes. Fire exhibits temporally and spatially transient features at a variety of granularities. The underlying process is that of combustion—a rapid chemical process that releases heat (i.e., is *exothermic*) and light accompanied by flame. A common example is that of a wood fire in which the hydrocarbon atoms of the wood fuel join with oxygen atoms to form water vapor, carbon monoxide, and carbon dioxide. As a consequence of the heated gases rising quickly, air is sucked into the combustion area, creating turbulence.

Recently, impressive advances have been made in the modeling of fire. At one extreme, the most realistic approaches require sophisticated techniques from CFD and are difficult to control (e.g., [21]). Work has also been performed in simulating the development and spread of fire for purposes of tracking its movement in an environment (e.g., [22], [23]). These models tend to be only global, extrinsic representations of the fire's movement and less concerned with the intrinsic motion of the fire itself. Falling somewhere between these two extremes, procedural image generation and particle systems provide visually effective, yet computationally attractive, approaches to fire.

Procedurally generated image

A particularly simple way to generate the appearance of fire is to procedurally generate a 2D image by coloring pixels suggestive of flames and smoke. The procedure iterates through pixels of an image buffer and sets the palette indices based on the indices of the surrounding pixels. Modifying the pixels top to bottom allows the imagery to progress up the buffer. Using multiple buffers and the alpha (transparency) channel, a limited 3D effect can be achieved.

Particle system approach

One of the first and most popularly viewed examples of computer-generated fire appears in the movie *Star Trek II: The Wrath of Khan* (e.g., [24]). In the sequence referred to as the *genesis effect*, an expanding wall of fire spreads out over the surface of the planet from a single point of impact. The simulation is not a completely convincing model of fire, although the sequence is effective in the movie. The model uses a two-level hierarchy of particles. The first level of particles is located at the point of impact to simulate the initial blast; the second level consists of concentric rings of particles, timed to progress from the central point outward, forming the wall of fire and explosions.

Each ring of second-level hierarchy consists of a number of individual particle systems that are positioned on the ring and overlap to form a continuous ring. The individual particle systems are modeled to look like explosions. The particles in each one of these particle systems are oriented to fly up and away from the surface of the planet. The initial position for a particle is randomly chosen from the circular base of the particle system. The initial direction of travel for each particle is constrained to deviate less than the ejection angle away from the surface normal.

Other approaches

Various other approaches have been used in animations with varying levels of success. Two-dimensional animated texture maps have been used to create the effect of the upward movement of burning gas, but such models are effective only when viewed from a specific direction. Using a two-dimensional multiple planes approach adds some depth to the fire, but viewing directions are still limited. Stam and Fiume (see [21]) present advection-diffusion equations to evolve both density and temperature fields. The user controls the simulation by specifying a wind field. The results are effective, but the foundation mathematics are complicated and the model is difficult to control.

11.2 Computational fluid dynamics

Gases and liquids are referred to collectively as *fluids*. The study of methods to compute their behavior is called computational fluid dynamics (CFD).

Fluids are composed of molecules that are constantly moving. These molecules are constantly colliding with one another and with other objects. The molecular motion transports measurable amounts of fluid properties throughout the fluid. These properties include such things as density, temperature, and momentum. In CFD, the assumption is that the fluid is a continuous medium in the sense that these properties are well defined at infinitely small points of the fluid and that the property values are smoothly varying throughout the fluid. This is called the *continuity assumption*.

Modeling gaseous phenomena (smoke, clouds, and fire) is particularly challenging because of their ethereal nature. Gas has no definite geometry, no definite topology. Gas is usually treated as *compressible*, meaning that density is spatially variable and computing the changes in density is part of the computational cost. Liquids are usually treated as *incompressible*, which means the density of the material remains constant. In fact, the equations in Section 11.1.1 were derived from the CFD equations.

In a *steady-state flow*, the motion attributes (e.g., velocity and acceleration) at any point in space are constant. Particles traveling through a steady-state flow can be tracked similarly to how a space curve can be traced out when the derivatives are known. *Vortices*, circular swirls of material, are important features in fluid dynamics. In steady-state flow, vortices are attributes of space and are time invariant. In time-varying flows, particles that carry a nonzero vortex strength can travel through the environment and can be used to modify the acceleration of other particles in the system by incorporating a distance-based force.

11.2.1 General approaches to modeling fluids

There are three approaches to modeling gas: grid-based methods (*Eulerian formulations*), particle-based methods (*Lagrangian formulations*), and hybrid methods. The approaches are illustrated here in two dimensions, but the extension to three dimensions should be obvious.

Grid-based method

The grid-based method decomposes space into individual cells, and the flow of the gas into and out of each cell is calculated (Figure 11.28). In this way, the density of gas in each cell is updated from time step to time step. The density in each cell is used to determine the visibility and illumination of the gas during rendering. Attributes of the gas within a cell, such as velocity, acceleration, and density, can be used to track the gas as it travels from cell to cell.

The flow out of the cell can be computed based on the cell velocity, the size of the cell, and the cell density. The flow into a cell is determined by distributing the

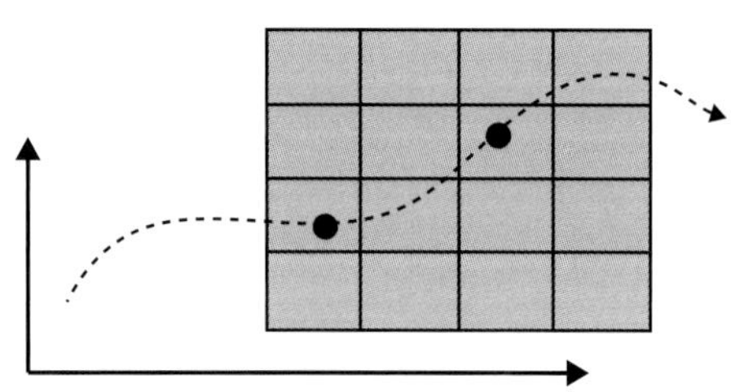

FIGURE 11.28

Hybrid method. Particles sample grid for volume density and velocity to determine movement during simulation.

densities out of adjacent cells. External forces, such as wind and obstacles, are used to modify the acceleration of the particles within a cell.

The rendering phase uses standard volumetric graphics techniques to produce an image based on the densities projected onto the image plane. Illumination of a cell from a light source through the volume must also be incorporated into the display procedure.

The disadvantage of this approach is that if a static data structure for the cellular decomposition is used, the extent of the interesting space must be identified before the simulation takes place to initialize the cells that will be needed during the simulation of the gas phenomena. Alternatively, a dynamic data structure that adapts to the traversal of the gas through space could be used, but this increases the complexity of the simulation.

Particle-based method

In the particle-based method, particles or globs of gas are tracked as they progress through space, often with a standard particle system approach (Figure 11.29). The particles can be rendered individually, or they can be rendered as spheres of gas with a given density. The advantage of this technique is that it is similar to rigid body dynamics and therefore the equations are relatively simple and familiar. The equations can be simplified if the rotational dynamics are ignored. In addition, there are no restrictions imposed by the simulation setup as to where the gas may travel. Particles are assigned masses, and external forces can be easily incorporated by updating particle accelerations and, subsequently, velocities. The disadvantage of this approach is that a large number of particles are needed to simulate a dense expansive gas and that to display the surface of a liquid, the boundary between fluid and nonfluid must be reconstructed from the particle samples. Recent techniques (such as FLIP fluids, see [14]) generalize on the idea of using rigidly defined particles to include a particle that represents a distribution of fluid mass in the surrounding area.

Hybrid method

Some models of gas trace particles through a spatial grid. Particles are passed from cell to cell as they traverse the interesting space (Figure 11.28). The display attributes of individual cells are determined by the number and type of particles

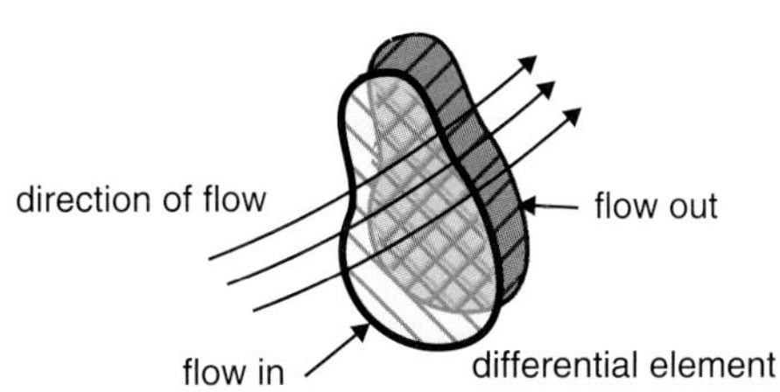

FIGURE 11.29

Differential element used in Navier-Stokes.

contained in the cell at the time of display. The particles are used to carry and distribute attributes through the grid, and then the grid is used to produce the display.

11.2.2 Computational fluid dynamics equations

In developing the CFD calculations, the volume occupied by a small (*differential*) fluid element is analyzed. Differential equations are created by describing what is happening at this element. (Figure 11.29).

The full CFD equations consist of equations that state, in a closed system, the following:

- Mass is conserved.
- Momentum is conserved.
- Energy is conserved.

When expressed as equations, these are the *Navier-Stokes* (NS) equations. The NS equations are nonlinear differential equations. There are various simplifications that can be made to make the NS equations more tractable. For most graphics applications, energy conservation is ignored. Another common simplification used in graphics is to assume the fluid is nonviscous. These assumptions result in what are called *Euler equations* [6]. By ignoring energy conservation and viscosity, the Euler equations describing the conservation of mass and conservation of momentum can be readily constructed for a given flow field. When dealing with liquids (as opposed to a gas), another useful assumption is that the fluid is incompressible, which means that its density does not change.

Conservation of mass

Conservation of mass is expressed by the *continuity equation* (see [25]). The underlying assumption of the conservation of mass is that mass is neither created nor destroyed inside of the fluid. The fluid flows from location to location and, if compressible, can become more dense or less dense at various locations. To determine how the total mass inside of an element is changing, all of the sources and sinks in the element have to be added up. The *divergence* of a flow field describes the strength of the source or sink at a location; the divergence for a field, $\mathbf{F} = f(x, y, z) \mapsto (F_x, F_y, F_z)$, is defined as the sum of the partial derivatives of the vector field (Equation 11.29), which is a useful metric that represents how the vector field is changing at a given point in space. If div $\mathbf{F} < 0$ the field is contracting at that point, at div $\mathbf{F} > 0$ the field is expanding, and div $\mathbf{F} = 0$ represents a linear flow at this point.

$$\text{div } \mathbf{F} = \nabla \cdot \mathscr{F} = \frac{\partial F_x}{\partial_x} + \frac{\partial F_y}{\partial_y} + \frac{\partial F_z}{\partial_z} \tag{11.29}$$

If no mass is created or destroyed inside the element, then it is reasonable that the total divergence within the element must be equal to the flow differences across the element at the x, y, and z boundaries. This is stated by the *divergence theorem*: the integral of the flow field's divergence over the volume of the element is the same as the integral of the flow field over the element's boundary. So, instead of worrying about all the sources and sinks inside of the element, all that has to be computed is the flow at the boundaries.

For now, for a given 3D element, consider only flow in the x direction. To make the discussion a bit more concrete, assume that the fluid is flowing left to right, as x increases, so that the mass flows into an element on the left, at x, and out of the element on the right, at $x + dx$. In the following equations, ρ is density, p is pressure, A is the area of the face perpendicular to the x-direction, V is the volume of the element, and the element dimensions are $dx \times dy \times dz$. To compute the mass flowing across a surface, multiply the density of the fluid times area of the surface times the velocity component normal to the surface, v_x in this case. The conservation of mass equation states that the rate at which mass changes is equal to the difference between mass flowing into the element and the mass flowing out of the element (Equation 11.30). The notation for a value at a given location is $(value)|_{\text{location}}$ or, when appropriate, $(value)|_{\text{location surface}}$.

$$-\frac{\partial(\rho V)}{\partial t} = (\rho v_x A)|_{x+dx} - (\rho v_x A)|_x \qquad (11.30)$$

Replace the volume, V, and area, A, by their definitions in terms of the element dimensions (Equation 11.31).

$$-\frac{d(\rho\, dx\, dy\, dz)}{dt} = (\rho\, v_x\, dy\, dz)_{x+dx} - (\rho\, dy\, dz)|_x \qquad (11.31)$$

Divide through by $dx\, dy\, dz$ (Equation 11.32).

$$-\frac{\partial \rho}{\partial t} = \left.\frac{\rho v_x}{dx}\right|_{x+dx} - \left.\frac{\rho v_x}{dx}\right|_x \qquad (11.32)$$

Replace the finite differences by their corresponding differential forms (Equation 11.33).

$$-\frac{\partial \rho}{\partial t} = \frac{\partial(\rho v_x)}{\partial x} \qquad (11.33)$$

Finally, include flow in all three directions (Equation 11.34).

$$-\frac{\partial \rho}{\partial t} = \frac{\partial(\rho v_x)}{\partial x} + \frac{\partial(\rho v_y)}{\partial y} + \frac{\partial(\rho v_z)}{\partial z} \qquad (11.34)$$

If ∇ is used as the gradient $\nabla \mathbf{F} = \left(\frac{\partial \mathbf{F}}{\partial x}, \frac{\partial \mathbf{F}}{\partial y}, \frac{\partial \mathbf{F}}{\partial z}\right)$ operator, then a common notation is to define the divergence operator as in Equation 11.35.

$$\nabla \cdot \mathbf{F} = \left(\frac{\partial}{\partial x}, \frac{\partial}{\partial y}, \frac{\partial}{\partial z}\right) \cdot (F_x, F_y, F_z) = \frac{\partial \mathbf{F}}{\partial x} + \frac{\partial \mathbf{F}}{\partial y} + \frac{\partial \mathbf{F}}{\partial z} \qquad (11.35)$$

Using the divergence operator in Equation 11.34 produces Equation 11.36.

$$-\frac{\partial \rho}{\partial t} = \nabla \cdot (\rho v) \tag{11.36}$$

If the fluid is incompressible, then the density does not change. This means that $\frac{\partial \rho}{\partial t}$ is zero and the constant density can be divided out, resulting in Equation 11.37.

$$0 = \nabla \cdot v \tag{11.37}$$

Conservation of momentum

The momentum of an object is its mass times its velocity. The momentum of a fluid is its density times the volume of the fluid times the average velocity of the fluid.

A change in momentum $\frac{d(mv)}{dt}$ must be induced by a force (i.e., $f = ma = m\frac{dv}{dt}$). The force in the element of a flow field is either a global force, such as viscosity and gravity, or a change in pressure across the element, $\frac{dp}{dx}$. As noted previously, effects of viscosity are commonly ignored to simplify the equations; we will also ignore gravity for now.

For an element, the change in momentum is the change of momentum inside the element plus the difference between the momentum entering the cell and the momentum leaving the element. The mass inside the cell is ρV, and thus the momentum inside the element is $\rho V v$. The rate of change of momentum inside the element is $\frac{\partial()}{dt}$.

Given a 3D element, consider flow only in the x-direction. The mass flowing out one surface is density × area of the surface times velocity in the x-direction, v_x. The momentum out one surface is the mass flowing out the surface times its velocity, $\rho A v_x v$. The force on the element in the x-direction is the pressure difference across the element from x to $x + dx$. The force is equal to the negative of the change in momentum (Equation 11.38).

$$-\left(p|_{x+dx}^{A} - p|_{x}^{A}\right) = \frac{\partial(\rho V v)}{\partial t} + \left((\rho v_x A)v|_{x+dx} - (\rho v_x A)v|_x\right) \tag{11.38}$$

Following the steps above in developing the conservation of mass equation by replacing the area, A, with its definition in terms of element dimensions, $dydz$, replacing the volume, V, with $dx\,dy\,dz$, dividing through by $dx\,dy\,dz$, and putting everything in differential form gives Equation 11.39.

$$-\frac{\partial p}{\partial x} = \frac{\partial(\rho v_x v)}{\partial x} + \frac{\rho v}{\partial t} \tag{11.39}$$

Now, considering flow in all three directions, and separating out momentum only in the x direction, produces Equation 11.40.

$$-\frac{\partial p}{\partial t} = \frac{\partial\left(\rho v_x^2\right)}{\partial x} + \frac{\partial\left(\rho v_x v_y\right)}{\partial y} + \frac{\partial\left(\rho v_x v_z\right)}{\partial z} + \frac{\partial\left(\rho v_x\right)}{\partial t} \tag{11.40}$$

If desired, viscosity and other forces can be added to the pressure differential force on the left-hand side of the equation. Similar equations can be derived for the y and z directions.

11.2.3 Grid-based approach

The basic process for computing fluid dynamics using a grid-based (Eulerian) approach is to do the following:

- Discretize the fluid continuum by constructing a grid of cells that, collectively, cover the space occupied by the fluid and at each node (cell), the fluid variables (e.g., density and velocity) are approximated and used to initialize the grid cells.
- Create the discrete equations using the approximate values at the element.
- Numerically solve the system of equations to compute new values at the cells using a Newton-like method for the large, sparse system of equations at each time step.

Before solving these equations, boundary conditions must be set up to handle the cells at the limits of the domain. For example, the *Dirichlet boundary condition*, which sets solution values at the boundary cells, is commonly used. The CFD equations, set up for each cell of the grid, produce a sparse set of matrix equations. There are various ways to solve such systems. For example, LU decomposition and Conjugate Gradient solvers are often used. Efficient, accurate methods of solving symmetric and asymmetric sparse matrices, such as these, are the topic of ongoing research. Thankfully, in computer animation believability is more of a concern than accuracy, so approximate techniques typically suffice.

Stable fluids

Stam presents a method that solves the full NS equations that is easy to implement and allows real-time user interaction (see [13]). Although too inaccurate for engineering, it is useful in computer graphics applications. In particular, the procedures are designed to be stable and fairly accurate while still producing interesting visuals computationally efficiently. These algorithms operate on a velocity vector field and density field. The velocity field moves the density values around.

Density update

Density values are moved through the density grid assuming a fixed velocity field over the time step. The density equation (Equation 11.41) states that density (ρ) changes over time according to density sources (s), the diffusion of the density at some specified rate (k), and advection of the density according to the velocity field ($\mathbf{u}$).

$$-\frac{\partial \rho}{\partial t} = s = k\nabla^2\rho - (\mathbf{u} \cdot \nabla)\rho \tag{11.41}$$

In implementing stable fluids, density is kept in an array of scalars. The first term, *s*, is an array of density sources set by user interaction or by the environment. These are used to initialize the new density grid at each time step. The second term diffuses the density from each cell to its adjacent cells. The diffusion of the grid can be solved by relaxation. The third term advects the density according to the velocity field.

To diffuse, each cell is updated by a weighted average of its four neighbors added to the original value. Each neighboring value is multiplied by a where $a = dt \times diff \times N \times N$, where *diff* is a user-supplied parameter, and N is the resolution of the grid. This sum is added to the cell's original value and then this sum is divided by $1 + 4a$.

To advect, the position is interpolated backward according to the velocity field. In the simplest case, the velocity vector at the particle position is accessed and linearly stepping backward according to the selected time step, making sure to clamp within the grid boundaries. The density is then bilinearly interpolated from nearby values, and this interpolated value is used as the density of the position.

The velocity update

The change of the velocity over time is given by Equation 11.42 and is due to external forces *(f)*, diffusion of the velocities, and self-advection.

$$\frac{\partial \mathbf{u}}{\partial t} = f + \mu \nabla^2 \mathbf{u} - (\mathbf{u} \cdot \nabla)\mathbf{u} \tag{11.42}$$

The velocity is kept in an array of vectors. The first term, *f,* adds in external forces from the user or environment. The second term allows for the diffusion of the velocity, and the third term allows the velocity to be carried along by the velocity field.

These equations are implemented by the sequence: add force, advect, diffuse, and project. The projection step is to adjust the density so that mass is preserved.

The simulation

The simulation is conducted by updating the contributions from density forces and external forces, then stepping the velocity field a step in time, taking the density field a step in time, then drawing the density.

11.2.4 Particle-based approaches including smoothed particle hydrodynamics

As previously noted, particle-based approaches have the advantage of being intuitive, easy to program, and fast to execute—at the expense of accuracy. However, for computer graphics and animation, accuracy is a common sacrifice. The basic idea is to model the fluid by a mass of particles. A simple particle system can be used, but the rigid nature of standard particles means that a massive amount of particles has to be used to create the impression of a fluid. In cases of modeling a gas or a spray of liquid this can be effective, but in cases where it is useful to represent a liquid's surface (e.g., for display) this approach is problematic.

To give a better impression of a cohesive fluid, spherical implicit surfaces, often referred to as *metaballs*, can be used in place of rigid particles. Because metaballs allow for the reconstruction of smooth intersections between particles, this approach can produce a gooey-like appearance similar to crunchy peanut butter. Metaballs have the ability to generate organic, blobby shapes but fall short of being able to model liquids effectively. Although this is an improvement over rigid particles, it still takes a very large number of particles to produce a smooth surface. In addition, metaballs lack any physical characteristics that make them suitable for effectively representing liquids.

For a more principled approach and one that produces a smoother surface, smooth particle hydrodynamics (SPH), developed for astrophysics, does a better and faster job of rendering a liquid from a collection of particles. The SPH particle is similar to that in a typical particle system and is represented by its position and velocity. An SPH particle, similar to an implicit surface particle, has a density function that contributes to a field value over its area of influence. The difference is that each SPH particle has a mass and density and each SPH particle also carries and distributes its mass over an area. The SPH particle has a kernel function that plays the role of a metaball's density function. The main difference between an SPH particle and an implicitly defined sphere is that one of the kernel's parameters is its support distance, which is a function of its mass. It should be noted that there are different ways to model particles and compute values in SPH and that the material here follows the work of Muller et al. (see [26], [27]). The interested reader can refer to these papers for more details.

In implementing the fluid dynamics using SPH particles, the main concerns are about conserving mass and updating the fluid particle representation over time due to the forces on the particles.

An additional practical consideration is how to display the fluid—how to reconstruct the fluid from the particle definition at any one point in time for display—and, especially for liquid, how to identify its surface. Similar to a standard particle system, at any one point in time a particle has a position and a velocity and is subject to various forces. The forces considered are those captured in the CFD equations—the pressure gradient and viscosity of the fluid, as well as environmental forces such as gravity. In addition, in the case of liquids, a surface tension force can be modeled.

An SPH particle carries an additional property of mass. This mass is distributed through space according to a smoothing kernel function. In fact, any property of the fluid can be distributed through space using a smoothing function. A property, s, at any given location, r, can be computed using Equation 11.43. In particular, the density can be computed from Equation 11.43, resulting in Equation 11.45. The gradient of a property and the Laplacian of a property, useful in computer pressure gradient and viscosity, can be computed using Equation 11.44.

$$s(r) = \sum_j m_j \frac{s_j}{\rho_j} W_h(r - r_j) \tag{11.43}$$

$$\begin{aligned} \nabla s(r) &= \sum_j m_j \frac{s_j}{\rho_j} \nabla W_h(r - r_j) \\ \nabla^2 s(r) &= \sum_j m_j \frac{s_j}{\rho_j} \nabla^2 W_h(r - r_j) \end{aligned} \tag{11.44}$$

$$\rho(r) = \sum_j m_j W_h(r - r_j) \rho_s(r) = \sum_j m_j W_h(r - r_j) \tag{11.45}$$

The use of particles guarantees that mass is conserved as long as the mass of a particle does not change and as long as particles are not created or destroyed. Updating the fluid according to CFD principles is affected by migration of particles through space due to the forces modeled by the CFD equations. First, the density at a location is computed using Equation 11.44.

Then the pressure is computed using the ideal gas state equation $p = k(\rho - \rho_0)$, where ρ_0 is the rest density for water and k is a constant in the range of 100 to 1000. Forces derived directly by SPH are not guaranteed to be symmetric, so symmetric versions of the force equations are then computed (Equation 11.46):

$$\begin{aligned} f_{\text{pressure}}(r_i) &= -\sum_j M_j \frac{p_i + p_j}{2\rho_j} \nabla W(r_i - r_j, h) \\ f_{\text{gravity}}(r_i) &= \rho_i \mathbf{g} \\ f_{\text{viscosity}}(r_i) &= \mu \sum_j M_j \frac{v_j - v_i}{\rho_j} \nabla^2 W(r_i - r_j, h) \end{aligned} \tag{11.46}$$

Quantities in the particle field can be computed at any given location by the use of a radial, symmetric, smoothing kernel. Smoothing kernels with a finite area of support are typically used for computational efficiency. Smoothing kernels should integrate to 1, which is referred to as *normalized*. Different smoothing kernels can be used when computing various values as long as the smoothing kernel has the basic properties of being normalized and symmetric. As examples, the kernels used in the work being followed here are a general purpose kernel (Equation 11.47), a kernel for pressure to avoid a zero gradient at the center (Equation 11.48), and a kernel for the viscosity (Equation 11.49) and its corresponding Laplacian (Equation 11.50). In this work, a LeapFrog integrator is used to compute the accelerations from the forces.

$$W_{\text{poly6}}(r, h) = \frac{315}{64\pi h^9} \begin{cases} (h^2 - r^2) & 0 \le r \le hb \\ 0 & \text{otherwise} \end{cases} \tag{11.47}$$

$$W_{\text{spiky}}(r, h) = \frac{15}{\pi h^6} \begin{cases} (h - r)^3 & 0 \le r \le h \\ 0 & \text{otherwise} \end{cases} \tag{11.48}$$

Table 11.1 Tools for Simulating Fluids

Game Engines		Animation Packages	
2D Fluids [28]	Godot (Addon)	Blender [34]	Built-in, FLIP, APIC
Fluid Frenzy [29]	Unity (Addon)	Houdini [35]	Built-in, FLIP
InfiniRIVER [30]	Unity (Addon)	Maya [36]	Built-in, Navier-Stokes, Grid,
Niagara Fluids [31] [32]	Unreal (Built-in)	EmberGen, LiquiGen [37]	Fire, Smoke, Explosions, Water, Liquids, Real time, FLIP
Flip Fluids [33]	Blender (Addon)	Lumenstory [38]	Liquid Specialized Anim Studio
		RealFlow [39]	Standalone, plugin for Maya, 3DS Max, Cinema4d

Engineering Simulation Software for Computational Fluid Dynamics				
Autodesk CFD [40]	Ansys [41]	Simscale [42]	Solidworks [43]	Sim-Flow [44]

SDKs		
OpenVDB [45]	Chaos Phoenix [46]	NVidia PhysX [47], Flex [48], Flow [49], Omniverse [50]

$$W_{\text{viscosity}}(r,h) = \frac{15}{2\pi h^3} \begin{cases} -\dfrac{r^3}{2h^3} + \dfrac{r^2}{h^2} + \dfrac{h}{2r} - 1 & 0 \le r \le hb \\ 0 & \text{otherwise} \end{cases} \tag{11.49}$$

$$\nabla^2 W_{\text{viscosity}}(r,h) = \frac{45}{\pi h^6}(h-r) \tag{11.50}$$

11.3 Chapter summary

Most of the techniques discussed in this chapter are still the subject of research efforts. Water, smoke, clouds, and fire share an amorphous nature, which makes them difficult to model and animate. Approaches that incorporate a greater amount of physics have been developed recently for these phenomena. As processing power becomes cheaper, techniques such as CFD become more practical (and more desirable) tools for animating water and gas, but convenient controls for such models have yet to be developed.

11.4 Exercises

Beginner

B1. Plot a sinusoidal wave using Desmos or Geogebra (or similar) with the following properties:

- Amplitude = 2 units, Length between Crests = 3 units, Speed = 1.5 units/sec
- Amplitude = 2.5 units, Length between Crests = 1 units, Speed = 0.25 units/sec
- Amplitude = 5 units, Length between Crests = 1.4 units, Speed = 0.01 units/sec

B2. Use Blender to create a fluid simulation with an object dropping from above into the liquid and demonstrate the following substances:

- Water (low viscosity)
- Honey (high viscosity)
- Create your own substance!

B3. Use a simulation tool such as Houdini or EmberGen to simulate clouds in 3D

Intermediate

I1. Implement the 2D stable fluid algorithm shown in Stam (see [3], [13]) and demonstrate it with different velocities and densities.

I2. Read [16] and implement their "choppy" wave method in a game engine.

I3. In the GDC (game developers conference) Vault, find the talk "Water Technology of Uncharted" from GDC 2012, watch the video and follow along with their slides. Take notes on how they use Gerstner-style waves, level of detail, and mesh-blending to effectively create amazing realtime water effects.

Advanced

A1. Adapt the 2D stable-fluid algorithm to 3D and implement it in Unity (or similar). Hint: you will need to use CUDA for efficiency and lower resolution volumes, but ComputeShaders are the best bet here. Render the volume using marching cubes (use an existing implementation). Can you add interactivity to the volume?

References

[1] Foster N, Metaxas D. Realistic animation of liquids. Graphical models and image-processing. Academic Press 1996;58(5):471−83.

[2] Fournier P, Habibi A, Poulin P. Simulating the flow of liquid droplets. In: Booth K, Fournier A, editors. Graphics interface '98; 1998. p. 133−42. ISBN 0-9695338-6-1.

[3] Stam J. Stable fluids. In: Rockwood A, editor. Computer graphics. Proceedings of SIGGRAPH 99, annual conference series. Los Angeles, Calif: Addison-Wesley Longman; 1999. p. 121–8. ISBN 0-20148-560-5.
[4] Weimer H, Warren J. Subdivision schemes for fluid flow. In: Rockwood A, editor. Computer graphics. Proceedings of SIGGRAPH 99, annual conference series. Los Angeles, Calif: Addison-Wesley Longman; 1999. p. 111–20. ISBN 0-20148-560-5.
[5] Blinn J. Simulation of wrinkled surfaces. In: Computer graphics. Proceedings of SIGGRAPH 78, 12(3). Atlanta, Ga; 1978. p. 286–92.
[6] NASA. Euler equations. NASA; 2024. grc.nasa.gov/WWW/K-12/airplane/eulereqs.html. [Accessed April 2025].
[7] Fournier A, Reeves W. A simple model of ocean waves. In: Evans DC, Athay RJ, editors. Computer graphics. Proceedings of SIGGRAPH 86, 20(4). Dallas, Tex; 1986. p. 75–84.
[8] Peachey D. Modeling waves and surf. In: Evans DC, Athay RJ, editors. Computer graphics. Proceedings of SIGGRAPH 86, 20(4). Dallas, Tex; 1986. p. 65–74.
[9] Kass M, Miller G. Rapid, stable fluid dynamics for computer graphics. In: Baskett F, editor. Computer graphics. Proceedings of SIGGRAPH 90, 24(4). Dallas, Tex; 1990. p. 49–57. ISBN 0-201-50933-4.
[10] Wiegel RL, Johnson JW. Elements of wave theory. Coast Eng Proc 2010;1. 2–2.
[11] BitGem. URP stylized water shader - proto series. 2024. Unity Asset Store, VFX/Shaders.
[12] Temam R. Navier–Stokes equations: theory and numerical analysis, 343. American Mathematical Society; 2024.
[13] Stam J. Real-time fluid dynamics for games. Proceedings of the game developer conference 2003;18(11).
[14] Brackbill JU, et al. Flip: a low-dissipation, particle-in-cell method for fluid flow. Comput Phys Commun 1988;48(1):25–38. https://doi.org/10.1016/0010-4655(88)90020-3.
[15] Max N. Vectorized procedural models for natural terrains: waves and islands in the sunset. In: Computer graphics. Proceedings of SIGGRAPH 81, 15(3). Dallas, Tex; 1981. p. 317–24.
[16] Tessendorf J. Simulating Ocean water. In: SIGGRAPH 2002 course notes #9 (simulating nature: realistic and interactive techniques). ACM Press; 2002.
[17] WeatherOnline Ltd.. Weather facts: cloud types. WeatherOnline Ltd.; 2024. www.weatheronline.co.uk/reports/wxfacts/Cloud-types.html. [Accessed April 2025].
[18] Gardner G. Simulation of natural scenes using textured quadric surfaces. In: Computer graphics. Proceedings of SIGGRAPH 84, 18(3). Minneapolis, Minn; 1984. p. 11–20.
[19] Gardner G. Visual simulation of clouds. In: Barsky BA, editor. Computer graphics. Proceedings of SIGGRAPH 85, 19(3). San Francisco, Calif; 1985. p. 297–303.
[20] Ebert D, Musgrave K, Peachey D, Perlin K, Worley S. Texturing and modeling: a procedural approach. Cambridge, Massachusetts: AP Professional; 1998.
[21] Stam J, Fiume E. Depicting fire and other gaseous phenomena using diffusion processes. In: Computer graphics. Proceedings of SIGGRAPH 95), in annual conference series. Los Angeles, Calif: ACM SIGGRAPH; 1995. p. 129–36.
[22] Bukowski R, Sequin C. Interactive simulation of fire in virtual building environments. In: Whitted T, editor. Computer graphics. Proceedings of SIGGRAPH 97, annual conference series. Los Angeles, Calif: Addison-Wesley; 1997. p. 35–44. ISBN 0-89791-896-7.
[23] Rushmeier H, Hamins A, Choi M. Volume rendering of pool fire data. IEEE Comput Graph Appl 1995;15(4):62–7.
[24] Paramount. Star Trek II: the Wrath of khan (film). 1982.

[25] Engineers Edge. Continuity equation—fluid flow. Engineers Edge; 2024. engineersedge.com/fluid_flow/continuity_equation.htm. [Accessed April 2025].
[26] Muller M, Charypar D, Gross M. Particle-based fluid simulation for interactive applications. In: Eurographics/SIGGRAPH symposium on computer animation; 2003.
[27] Muller M, Schirm S, Teschner M. Interactive blood simulation for virtual surgery based on smoothed particle hydrodynamics. Techno Health Care 2004;12(1):25–31.
[28] MaruoPle. Godot fluid water 2D simulator. 2024. Github, godot-v4-fluid-water-2D-simulator.
[29] F. Byte, "Fluid frenzy", Addon, Unity Asset Store, VFX/Shaders, assetstore.unity.com. [Accessed April 2025].
[30] ARTnGAME, Infiniriver, Unity Asset Store, Tools/Particles-effects, assetstore.unity.com. [Accessed April 2025].
[31] Epic Games, "Getting started with 3D gas systems", Unreal documentation, tutorial. https://dev.epicgames.com/community/learning/tutorials/4Oov/unreal-engine-niagara-fluids-getting-started-with-3d-gas-systems. [Accessed April 2025].
[32] Epic Games, "Liquid simulation in unreal engine 5", Unreal documentation, tutorial. https://dev.epicgames.com/community/learning/tutorials/bOmn/liquid-simulation-in-unreal-engine-5-i-animated-creature-simulation-tutorial-i-niagara-fluids. [Accessed April 2025].
[33] RLGUY, "FlipFluids", Blender Market, Addon. https://blendermarket.com/products/flipfluids. [Accessed April 2025].
[34] Blender, "Fluid", Blender Documentation. https://docs.blender.org/manual/en/latest/physics/fluid. [Accessed April 2025].
[35] SideFX, "Liquids", Houdini Documentation. https://www.sidefx.com/docs/houdini/fluid/. [Accessed April 2025].
[36] Autodesk, "Fluid effects", Maya Documentation 2024. https://help.autodesk.com/view/MAYAUL/2025/ENU/?guid=GUID-8FF11EBA-9FDA-4933-B7EB-F08EE1A44284. [Accessed April 2025].
[37] JangaFX, "EmberGen". jangafx.com/software/embergen/. [Accessed April 2025].
[38] Lumenstory, "Fluid animation", lumenstory.com/fluid/. [Accessed April 2025].
[39] RealFlow, realflow.com/. [Accessed April 2025].
[40] Autodesk CFD, "Simulation software for engineering complex liquid, gas, and air systems". autodesk.com/products/cfd. [Accessed April 2025].
[41] Ansys Fluent, "Fluid simulation software". ansys.com/products/fluids/ansys-fluent. [Accessed April 2025].
[42] Simscale, "Cloud-based engineering platform for fluid dynamic simulation", simscale.com/product/cfd/. [Accessed April 2025].
[43] Solidworks, solidworks.com/product/solidworks-flow-simulation. [Accessed April 2025].
[44] Sim-Flow, sim-flow.com/download/cfd-simulation-software/. [Accessed April 2025].
[45] OpenVDB, openvdb.org/. [Accessed April 2025].
[46] Chaos Phoenix, www.chaos.com/phoenix. [Accessed April 2025].
[47] NVidia, "PhysX", SDK, developer.nvidia.com/physx-sdk. [Accessed April 2025].
[48] NVidia, "FleX", SDK, developer.nvidia.com/flex. [Accessed April 2025].
[49] NVidia, "Flow", SDK, Github, https://github.com/NVIDIAGameWorks/Flow. [Accessed April 2025].
[50] NVidia, "Fluid-Dynamics", Omniverse Documentation, Extensions, docs.omniverse.nvidia.com. [Accessed April 2025].

CHAPTER

The future of animation 12

12.1 Animating liquids, cloth, and elastic bodies

As seen previously, animating and simulating liquids have come a long way. However, advancements in the field are continuing to improve computational speed/efficiency and simulation fidelity for various materials. For example, [1] developed a method that allows for the simulation of viscous fluids (like honey) that rely on adequately balancing the pressure and internal stresses. In their paper they demonstrate the ability to simulate a "liquid rope coil" in honey or thick oils, a phenomenon that standard approaches are unable to adequately address. In [2], a solver is developed that addresses the issue of simulating multiple fluids with varying densities. Imagine water and oil in a single container, when it flows through an opening in the container the fluids should ultimately create a new liquid where they are not mixed (still separated).

12.1.1 Elastic deformation

The standard approaches to deformation using a lattice (or cage) has been implemented in standard animation tools. For example, in Blender bones can be assigned as "bendy-bones" that creates an implicit lattice along the bone (as seen in the previous chapters), which can be used to imitate soft-bodies or enhance squashing/stretching. However, current limitations include nonphysically plausible deformations such as shearing and lack of accuracy for maintaining object volumes. In [3], a new method for deforming objects based on cage deformation is developed. Their method reduces the typical shearing artifacts and enables the volume to be maintained during deformation thus producing physically plausible deformations. In a separate contribution,[4] the standard Green's functions, used for elastic and soft body simulation, are decomposed into a finite sum of spherical harmonics that can represent directional, radial, and material-dependent terms. This enables the development of plausible sculpting brushes that can be used to control real-time deformations.

Computer Animation. https://doi.org/10.1016/B978-0-443-13512-5.00012-4

12.2 Animating faces

Probably one of the most important parts of the human body to animate properly is the human face. Even subtle inaccuracies in muscle movement and lip-sync can make the animation seem implausible due to the uncanny valley phenomenon. Improvements in this area are rapidly progressing by leveraging machine learning and deep learning methods. For instance, AvatarMAV[5] is a fast 3D head avatar reconstruction method using Motion-Aware Neural Voxels. AvatarMAV models both the facial appearance and expressions in a model that corresponds one-to-one with standard 3DMMs. Leveraging improvements in neural radiance fields, NOFA (NeRF-based One-shot Facial Avatar Reconstruction)[6] reconstructs a high-fidelity photorealistic 3D facial avatar using a single reference image. Their method leverages the generative prior of a 3D GAN (generative adversarial network) and an efficient encoder-decoder network to reconstruct the neural volume of a source image, and a second compensation network to complement facial details. They demonstrate that a fine-grained control over facial dynamics and expressions is possible using a controllable deformation warp field. Another exciting neural model, LatentAvatar,[7] is an expressive neural head avatar driven by latent expression codes learned in an end-to-end and self-supervised manner without templates. This method is able to perform expressive reenactment between varying subjects and is able to capture challenging expressions and the subtle movement of teeth and even eyeballs. Meta research has been investigating generative models for 3D faces based on few-shot training over the past few years as it is seen as the holy grail for telepresence in VR. They developed their Pixel Codec Avatars (PiCA)[8] and showed that they can accurately generate photorealistic expressions and novel views of different genders and skin tones efficiently enabling use in VR headsets.

Probably one of the most exciting recent developments is Neural Face Rigging (NFR).[9] NFR is a deep-learning approach for automatic rigging and retargeting of 3D models of human faces in the wild. NFR is the first approach to provide realistic and controllable deformations of in-the-wild face meshes without the manual creation of blend-shapes or correspondence and can produce realistic facial deformations. The method utilizes a deformation autoencoder trained using two data sources: a linear 3DMM with interpretable control parameters (i.e., FACS), and 4D captures of real faces for fine details.

12.2.1 Audio-/text-driven animation

Once you have a face that can animate expressions, one needs to consider how to perform lip-sync effectively or drive the animation using existing (or synthesized) audio as input. GestureDiffuCLIP[10] is a neural network framework for synthesizing realistic, stylized co-speech gestures with flexible style control. A Contrastive Language Image Pretraining (CLIP)-guided mechanism extracts style representations from text, motion clips, or videos. It presents a gesture-transcript alignment mechanism to generate valid gestures. VisemeNet[11] is an approach using deep-learning to produce animator-centric speech motion curves to drive a standard FACS-based facial animation rig. It demonstrates automatic real-time lip-synchronization from audio that integrates seamlessly into existing animation pipelines.

12.3 Animating full bodies

Faces are important, but so is the rest of the body! The future for representing and animating the full body will include the use of parametric morphable models such as SMPL,[12] and even more recently HACK (Head-And-neCK),[13] a novel parametric model for constructing the head and cervical region of digital humans, personalized and anatomically consistent controls. The use of anatomically consistent learned parametric models will allow animators to more easily create variations to character movement that is accurate and physically plausible, thus reducing the amount of work required to create or tweak characters. For video games, this may ultimately enhance customizability and personalization whereby parameters such as mass and weight will accurately influence the movement of the character. Imagine games where your customized avatar ages over time and the animation reflects the characters' well-being and age.

12.3.1 Volumetric video

Volumetric video (VV), a fusion of video and depth sensor data, provides a new medium for video games and interactive media for capturing spatial performances. Differing from standard 3D generative models, VV's goal is to be as general as possible to capture all static and dynamic objects within a volume of space. Although the capture technology differs considerably from traditional 2D recordings, VV can still be considered a "video," albeit where each frame consists of a textured 3D model. A recent survey of the technology, tools, and limitations can be found here.[14] The initial concept, dubbed "virtualized reality,"[15] used an array of cameras to capture a volume of space and employed multiview stereo algorithms to generate 3D representations of each video frame. This resulted in a captured volume that could be viewed from any viewpoint. Because the final output was sequences of 3D models, they could be implanted and rendered into new virtual environments to be viewed in any context. The technology has evolved in a number of different directions each focusing on the promise of photo-realistic capture of performances. Recent machine learning (ML) approaches to VV performance capture[16,17,18] are showing promise in creating photorealistic dynamic avatars from single view video streams, albeit adding a human-only limitation. Another exciting advancement in this field is the combination of VV to generate photorealistic likeness in combination with a rigid skeletal rig. In [19], the authors develop a framework to drive a photorealistic volumetric avatar while leveraging both the structural rig as a parametric model and sparse image inputs simultaneously.

12.3.2 Neural representations

Other ML approaches to generating and animating characters from video have recently been demonstrated. For example, CharacterGen[20] efficiently generates 3D characters using a transformer-based, generalizable sparse-view reconstruction approach. NeRF reconstruction approaches have been extended to video, such as in HumanRF,[21] which is a 4D dynamic neural scene representation that captures full-body appearance in motion from multiview video input, and enables playback from novel, unseen viewpoints. Their method enables the capture of temporally coherent reconstructions of human actors for long sequences. Similarly, Avatar-ReX,[22] generates a NeRF-based full-body avatar from video data. The learned avatar provides expressive control of the body, hands and the face, and supports real-time animation and rendering.

The limitations of NeRF approaches have been that ultimately the output is a point cloud rendered using a neural differentiable rendering approach. Standard pipelines for games and tools for animation generally have been based around triangular meshes. Advances such as in [23] are exciting. MeshAvatar represents the avatar with an explicit triangular mesh extracted from an implicit SDF field, complemented by an implicit material field conditioned on given poses. This enables physics-based rendering to accurately decompose geometry and texture from video and they show that their method can learn mesh-based avatars with high-quality geometry and plausible material decomposition. Because the output is a high-quality mesh, it is controllable with a rig and inherently supports editing, manipulation, and relighting.

12.3.3 Generative/procedural motion generation

Finally, an important aspect for animating non-player-characters in video games is to develop systems that can generate plausible animations from a set of environmental and character-rig constraints. One approach to this has been Motion-Matching,[24] which performs an efficient search through a database of poses to find plausible transitions that optimize a smoothness function. This approach was improved upon[25] and also using a machine learning approach.[26] Recently, a new generative approach to motion-matching (GMM)[27] that leverages generative models to efficiently "mine" a diverse motion database using a single (or few) examples. GenMM does not require extensive prior learning/training and can synthesize high-quality complex motions quickly (fractions of a second). Another approach using training is CALM[28] (Conditional Adversarial Latent Models). CALM is an approach to generating diverse and directable game characters. Using an imitation learning approach, the method learns a representation capturing the complexity and diversity of human movement and enables direct control. The approach learns a control policy and a motion encoder jointly that reconstructs key characteristics of a given motion. Once trained, the character can be controlled using standard video game controls.

12.4 Chapter summary

What does the future hold for animation technology? There are now many different approaches to photorealistic animation of human performances, many of which will ultimately find their way into standard animation tools over the next few years. Embracing the new machine learning paradigm will be key to advancing the field. Just as we are seeing generative AI tools make their way into image processing tools such as Adobe Photoshop, we will soon see tools that provide abilities to more easily capture and prototype animations from video, edit these animations using natural language, enabling animators to focus on more interesting details that these approaches still struggle with such as intricate details of hand movement, eye movement, especially with characters that are non-human and non-photorealistic.

References

[1] Panuelos J, Goldade R, Grinspun E, Levin D, Batty C. PolyStokes: a polynomial model reduction method for viscous fluid simulation. SIGGRAPH 2023;2023. https://doi.org/10.1145/3592146.

[2] Kinetic simulation of turbulent multifluid flows | ACM transactions on graphics. [Online]. Available: https://dl.acm.org/doi/10.1145/3658178. [Accessed 22 August 2024].

[3] Somigliana coordinates: an elasticity-derived approach for cage deformation | ACM SIGGRAPH 2023 conference proceedings. [Online]. Available: https://dl.acm.org/doi/abs/10.1145/3588432.3591519. [Accessed 22 August 2024].

[4] Go Green: general regularized green's functions for elasticity | ACM SIGGRAPH 2022 conference proceedings. [Online]. Available: https://dl.acm.org/doi/10.1145/3528233.3530726. [Accessed 22 August 2024].

[5] Xu Y, Wang L, Zhao X, Zhang H, Liu Y. AvatarMAV: fast 3D head avatar reconstruction using motion-aware neural Voxels. In: ACM SIGGRAPH 2023 conference proceedings; 2023.

[6] Yu W, et al. NOFA: NeRF-based one-shot facial avatar reconstruction. 2023. https://doi.org/10.48550/arXiv.2307.03441. arXiv:2307.03441.

[7] Xu Y, et al. LatentAvatar: learning latent expression code for expressive neural head avatar. In: ACM SIGGRAPH 2023 conference proceedings; 2023.

[8] Ma S, et al. Pixel codec avatars. In: Proceedings of the IEEE/CVF conference on computer vision and pattern recognition; 2021. p. 64–73.

[9] Qin D, Saito J, Aigerman N, Groueix T, Komura T. Neural face rigging for animating and retargeting facial meshes in the wild. 2023. https://doi.org/10.48550/arXiv.2305.08296. arXiv:2305.08296.

[10] GestureDiffuCLIP: gesture diffusion model with CLIP latents. [Online]. Available: https://pku-mocca.github.io/GestureDiffuCLIP-Page/. [Accessed 22 August 2024].

[11] Zhou Y, Xu Z, Landreth C, Kalogerakis E, Maji S, Singh K. Visemenet: audio-driven animator-centric speech animation. ACM Trans Graph 2018;37(4). https://doi.org/10.1145/3197517.3201292.

[12] Loper M, Mahmood N, Romero J, Pons-Moll G, Black MJ. In: SMPL: a skinned multi-person linear model, 34(6); 2015. p. 248. https://doi.org/10.1145/2816795.2818013.

[13] Zhang L, et al. HACK: learning a parametric head and neck model for high-fidelity animation. 2023. https://doi.org/10.48550/arXiv.2305.04469. arXiv:2305.04469.
[14] Jin Y, Hu K, Liu J, Wang F, Liu X. From capture to display: a survey on volumetric video. 2023. https://doi.org/10.48550/arXiv.2309.05658. arXiv:2309.05658.
[15] Kanade T, Narayanan PJ, Rander P. Virtualized reality: concepts and early results. In: Proceedings IEEE workshop on representation of visual scenes (in conjunction with ICCV'95); 1995. p. 69–76. https://doi.org/10.1109/wvrs.1995.476854.
[16] Guo C, Jiang T, Chen X, Song J, Hilliges O. Vid2Avatar: 3D avatar reconstruction from videos in the wild via self-supervised scene decomposition. In: Computer vision and pattern recognition (CVPR); 2023. https://doi.org/10.48550/arxiv.2302.11566.
[17] Xiu Y, Yang J, Cao X, Tzionas D, Black MJ. ECON: explicit clothed humans obtained from normals. In: Proc. Of the IEEE/CVF conference on computer vision and pattern recognition (CVPR); 2022. https://doi.org/10.48550/arxiv.2212.07422.
[18] Li Z, Zheng Z, Zhang H, Ji C, Liu Y. AvatarCap: animatable avatar conditioned monocular human volumetric capture. In: European conference on computer vision (ECCV); 2022. https://doi.org/10.48550/arxiv.2207.02031.
[19] Remelli E, et al. Drivable volumetric avatars using texel-aligned features. In: International conference on computer graphics and interactive techniques; 2022. https://doi.org/10.1145/3528233.3530740.
[20] CharacterGen: efficient 3D character generation from single images. [Online]. Available: https://charactergen.github.io/. [Accessed 22 August 2024].
[21] Işık M, et al. HumanRF: high-fidelity neural radiance fields for humans in motion. ACM Trans Graph TOG 2023;42(4):1–12. https://doi.org/10.1145/3592415.
[22] Zheng Z, Zhao X, Zhang H, Liu B, Liu Y. AvatarRex: real-time expressive full-body avatars. ACM Trans Graph TOG 2023;42(4).
[23] Chen Y, Zheng Z, Li Z, Xu C, Liu Y. MeshAvatar: learning high-quality triangular human avatars from multi-view videos. 2024 [Online]. Available: https://arxiv.org/abs/2407.08414.
[24] Clavet S, and others. Motion matching and the road to next-gen animation. Proc GDC 2016:4.
[25] Häfliger A, Kurabayashi S. Dynamic motion matching: context-aware character animation with subspaces ensembling. In: 2021 IEEE international symposium on multimedia (ISM); 2021. p. 115–22. https://doi.org/10.1109/ISM52913.2021.00028.
[26] Learned motion matching | ACM Trans Graph. [Online]. Available: https://dl.acm.org/doi/abs/10.1145/3386569.3392440. [Accessed 05 July 2022].
[27] Li W, Chen X, Li P, Sorkine-Hornung O, Chen B. Example-based motion synthesis via generative motion matching. ACM Trans Graph TOG 2023;42(4). https://doi.org/10.1145/3592395.
[28] Tessler C, Kasten Y, Guo Y, Mannor S, Chechik G, Peng XB. CALM: conditional adversarial latent models for directable virtual characters. In: ACM SIGGRAPH 2023 conference proceedings. SIGGRAPH '23. New York, NY, USA: Association for Computing Machinery; 2023. https://doi.org/10.1145/3588432.3591541.

Background Information and Techniques

1. Vectors and matrices

A *vector* is a one-dimensional list of values. This list can be shown as a row vector or a column vector (e.g., Eq. 1). In general, a matrix is an n-dimensional array of values. For purposes of this book, a matrix is two-dimensional (e.g., Eq. 2).

$$\begin{bmatrix} a & b & c \end{bmatrix} \begin{bmatrix} a \\ b \\ c \end{bmatrix} \tag{1}$$

$$\begin{bmatrix} a & b & c \\ d & e & f \\ g & h & i \end{bmatrix} \tag{2}$$

Matrices are multiplied together by taking the ith row of the first matrix and multiplying each element by the corresponding element of the jth column of the second matrix and summing all the products to produce the i,jth element. When computing $C = AB$, where A has v elements in each row and B has v elements in each column, an element C_{ij} is computed according to Equation 3.

$$\begin{aligned} C_{ij} &= A_{i1}B_{1j} + A_{i2}B_{2j} + A_{i3}B_{3j} + \ldots + A_{iv}B_{vj} \\ &= \sum_{k=1}^{v} A_{ik}B_{kj} \end{aligned} \tag{3}$$

The "inside" dimension of the matrices must match in order for the matrices to be multiplied together. That is, if A and B are multiplied and A is a matrix with U rows and V columns (a $U \times V$ matrix), then B must be a $V \times W$ matrix; the result will be a $U \times W$ matrix. In other words, the number of columns (the number of elements in a row) of A must be equal to the number of rows (the number of elements in a column) of B. As a more concrete example, consider multiplying two 3×3 matrices. Equation 4 shows the computation for the first element.

$$AB = \begin{bmatrix} A_{11} & A_{12} & A_{13} \\ A_{21} & A_{22} & A_{23} \\ A_{31} & A_{32} & A_{33} \end{bmatrix} \begin{bmatrix} B_{11} & B_{12} & B_{13} \\ B_{21} & B_{22} & B_{23} \\ B_{31} & B_{32} & B_{33} \end{bmatrix} = \begin{bmatrix} A_{11}B_{11} + A_{12}B_{21} + A_{13}B_{31} & \cdots & \cdots \\ \cdots & \cdots & \cdots \\ \cdots & \cdots & \cdots \end{bmatrix} \tag{4}$$

The transpose of a vector or matrix is the original vector or matrix with its rows and columns exchanged (e.g., Eq. 5). The *identity matrix* is a square matrix with ones along its diagonal and zeros elsewhere (e.g., Eq. 6). The *inverse* of a square matrix when multiplied by the original matrix produces the identity matrix (e.g., Eq. 7). The *determinant* of a 3×3 matrix is formed as shown in Equation 8. The determinant of matrices greater than 3×3 can be defined recursively. First, define an element's *submatrix* as the matrix formed when removing the element's row and column from the original matrix. The determinant is formed by considering any row, element by element. The determinant is the first element of the row times the determinant of its submatrix, minus the second element of the row times the determinant of its submatrix, plus the third element of the row times the determinant of its submatrix, and so on. The sum is formed for the entire row, alternating additions and subtractions.

$$\begin{bmatrix} a & b & c \\ d & e & f \end{bmatrix}^T = \begin{bmatrix} a & d \\ b & e \\ c & f \end{bmatrix} \tag{5}$$

$$I = \begin{bmatrix} 1 & 0 & 0 \\ 0 & 1 & 0 \\ 0 & 0 & 1 \end{bmatrix} \tag{6}$$

$$MM^{-1} = M^{-1}M = I \tag{7}$$

$$\begin{vmatrix} a & b & c \\ d & e & f \\ g & h & i \end{vmatrix} = a(ei - fh) - b(di - fg) + c(dh - eg) \tag{8}$$

1.1 Inverse matrix and solving linear systems

The inverse of a matrix is useful in computer graphics to represent the inverse of a transformation and in computer animation to solve a set of linear equations. There are various ways to compute the inverse. One common method, which is also useful for solving sets of linear equations, is *LU* decomposition. The basic idea is that a square matrix, for example, a 4 × 4, can be decomposed into a lower triangular matrix times an upper triangular matrix. How this is done is discussed later in this section. For now, it is assumed that the *LU* decomposition is available (Eq. 9).

$$
\begin{aligned}
A &= \begin{bmatrix} A_{11} & A_{12} & A_{13} & A_{14} \\ A_{21} & A_{22} & A_{23} & A_{24} \\ A_{31} & A_{32} & A_{33} & A_{34} \\ A_{41} & A_{42} & A_{43} & A_{44} \end{bmatrix} \\
&= LU = \begin{bmatrix} L_{11} & 0 & 0 & 0 \\ L_{21} & L_{22} & 0 & 0 \\ L_{31} & L_{32} & L_{33} & 0 \\ L_{41} & L_{42} & L_{43} & L_{44} \end{bmatrix} \begin{bmatrix} U_{11} & U_{12} & U_{13} & U_{14} \\ 0 & U_{22} & U_{23} & U_{24} \\ 0 & 0 & U_{33} & U_{34} \\ 0 & 0 & 0 & U_{44} \end{bmatrix}
\end{aligned} \tag{9}
$$

The decomposition of a matrix A into the L and U matrices can be used to easily solve a system of linear equations. For example, consider the case of four unknowns (x) and four equations shown in Equation 10. Use of the decomposition permits the system of equations to be solved by forming two systems of equations using triangular matrices (Eq. 11).

$$
\begin{aligned}
A_{11}x_1 + A_{12}x_2 + A_{13}x_3 + A_{14}x_4 &= b_1 \\
A_{21}x_1 + A_{22}x_2 + A_{23}x_3 + A_{24}x_4 &= b_2 \\
A_{31}x_1 + A_{32}x_2 + A_{33}x_3 + A_{34}x_4 &= b_3 \\
A_{41}x_1 + A_{42}x_2 + A_{43}x_3 + A_{44}x_4 &= b_4
\end{aligned}
$$

$$
\begin{bmatrix} A_{11} & A_{12} & A_{13} & A_{14} \\ A_{21} & A_{22} & A_{23} & A_{24} \\ A_{31} & A_{32} & A_{33} & A_{34} \\ A_{41} & A_{42} & A_{43} & A_{44} \end{bmatrix} \begin{bmatrix} x_1 \\ x_2 \\ x_3 \\ x_4 \end{bmatrix} = \begin{bmatrix} b_1 \\ b_2 \\ b_3 \\ b_4 \end{bmatrix} \tag{10}
$$

$$
\begin{aligned}
&Ax = b\\
&Ax = b\\
&(LU)x = b\\
&L(Ux) = b\\
&Ux = y\\
&Ly = b
\end{aligned}
\tag{11}
$$

This solves the original set of equations. The advantage of doing it this way is that both of the last two equations resulting from the decomposition involve triangular matrices and therefore can be solved trivially with simple substitution methods. For example, Equation 12 shows the solution to $Ly = b$. Notice that by solving the equations in a top to bottom fashion, the results from the equations of previous rows are used so that there is only one unknown in any equation being considered. Once the solution for y has been determined, it can be used to solve for x in $Ux = y$ using a similar approach. Once the LU decomposition of A is formed, it can be used repeatedly to solve sets of linear equations that differ only in right-hand sides, such as those for computing the inverse of a matrix. This is one of the advantages of LU decomposition over methods such as Gauss-Jordan elimination.

$$
\begin{aligned}
&Ly = b\\
&\begin{bmatrix} L_{11} & 0 & 0 & 0\\ L_{21} & L_{22} & 0 & 0\\ L_{31} & L_{32} & L_{33} & 0\\ L_{41} & L_{42} & L_{43} & L_{44} \end{bmatrix} \begin{bmatrix} y_1\\ y_2\\ y_3\\ y_4 \end{bmatrix} = \begin{bmatrix} b_1\\ b_2\\ b_3\\ b_4 \end{bmatrix}\\
&\text{First row:} \quad L_{11}y_1 = b_1\\
&y_1 = b_1 = L_{11}\\
&\text{Second row:} \quad L_{21}y_1 + L_{22}y_2 = b_2\\
&y_2 = (b_2 - (L_{21}y_1))/L_{22}\\
&\text{Third row:} \quad L_{31}y_1 + L_{32}y_2 + L_{33}y_3 = b_3\\
&y_3 = (b_3 - (L_{31}y_1 - L_{32}y_2))/L_{33}\\
&\text{Fourth row:} \quad L_{41}y_1 + L_{42}y_2 + L_{43}y_3 + L_{44}y_4 = b_4\\
&y_4 = (b_4 - (L_{41}y_1) - (L_{42}y_2) - (L_{43}y_3))/L_{44}
\end{aligned}
\tag{12}
$$

The decomposition procedure sets up equations and orders them so that each is solved simply. Given the matrix equation for the decomposition relationship, one can construct equations on a term-by-term basis for the A matrix. This results in N^2 equations with $N^2 + N$ unknowns. As there are more unknowns than equations, N elements are set to some arbitrary value. A particularly useful set of values is $L_{ii} = 1.0$. Once this is done, the simplest equations (for A_{11}, A_{12}, etc.) are used to establish values for some of the L and U elements. These values are then used in the more complicated equations. In this way the equations can be ordered so there is only one unknown in any single equation by the time it is evaluated. Consider the case of a 4 × 4 matrix. Equation 13 repeats the original matrix equation for reference, and Equation 14 shows the resulting sequence of equations in which the underlined variable is the only unknown.

$$\begin{bmatrix} 1 & 0 & 0 & 0 \\ L_{21} & 1 & 0 & 0 \\ L_{31} & L_{32} & 1 & 0 \\ L_{41} & L_{42} & L_{43} & 1 \end{bmatrix} \begin{bmatrix} U_{11} & U_{12} & U_{13} & U_{14} \\ 0 & U_{22} & U_{23} & U_{24} \\ 0 & 0 & U_{33} & U_{34} \\ 0 & 0 & 0 & U_{44} \end{bmatrix} = \begin{bmatrix} A_{11} & A_{12} & A_{13} & A_{14} \\ A_{21} & A_{22} & A_{23} & A_{24} \\ A_{31} & A_{32} & A_{33} & A_{34} \\ A_{41} & A_{42} & A_{43} & A_{44} \end{bmatrix} \tag{13}$$

For the first column of A

$$U_{11} = A_{11}$$

$$\underline{L_{21}}\, U_{11} = A_{21}$$

$$\underline{L_{31}}\, U_{11} = A_{31}$$

$$\underline{L_{41}}\, U_{11} = A_{41}$$

(14)

For the second column of A

$$\underline{U_{12}} - A_{12}$$

$$L_{21} U_{12} + \underline{U_{22}} = A_{22}$$

$$L_{31} U_{12} + \underline{L_{32}}\, U_{22} = A_{32}$$

$$L_{41} U_{12} + \underline{L_{42}}\, U_{22} = A_{42}$$

For the third column of A $U_{13} = A_{13}$

$$L_{21} U_{13} + U_{23} = A_{23}$$

$$L_{31} U_{13} + L_{32} U_{23} + U_{33} = A_{33} \; L_{41} U_{13} + L_{42} U_{23} + L_{43}\, U_{33} = A_{43}$$

For the fourth column of A $U_{14} = A_{14}$

$$L_{21} U_{14} + U_{24} = A_{24}$$

$$L_{31} U_{14} + L_{32} U_{24} + U_{34} = A_{34}$$

$$L_{41} U_{14} + L_{42} U_{24} + L_{43} U_{34} + U_{44} = A_{44}$$

Notice a two-phase pattern in each column in which terms from the U matrix from the first row to the diagonal are determined first, followed by terms from the L matrix below the diagonal. This pattern can be generalized easily to matrices of arbitrary size [16], as shown in Equation 15. The computations for each column j must be completed before proceeding to the next column.

$$
\begin{aligned}
U_{ij} &= A_{ij} - \sum_{K=1} L_{ik} U_{kj} && \text{for } i = 1, \ldots, j \\
L_{ij} &= \frac{1}{U_{ij}} \left(A_{ij} - \sum_{k=1}^{j-1} L_{ik} U_{kj} \right) && \text{for } i = j+1, \ldots, n
\end{aligned}
\tag{15}
$$

So far this is fairly simple and easy to follow. Now comes the complication—*partial pivoting*. Notice that some of the equations require a division to compute the value for the unknown. For this computation to be numerically stable (i.e., the numerical error less sensitive to particular input values), this division should be by a relatively large number. By reordering the rows, one can exert some control over what divisor is used. Reordering rows does not affect the computation if the matrices are viewed as a system of linear equations; reordering obviously matters if the inverse of a matrix is being computed. However, as long as the reordering is recorded, it can easily be undone when the inverse matrix is formed from the L and U matrices.

Consider the first column of the 4×4 matrix. The divisor used in the last three equations is U_{11}, which is equal to A_{11}. However, if the rows are reordered, then a different value might end up as A_{11}. So the objective is to swap rows so that the largest value (in the absolute value sense) of $A_{11}, A_{21}, A_{31}, A_{41}$ ends up at A_{11}, which makes the computation more stable. Similarly, in the second column, the divisor is U_{22}, which is equal to A_{22} $(L_{21}U_{12})$. As in the case of the first column, the rows below this are checked to see if a row swap might make this value larger. The row above is not checked because that row was needed to calculate U_{12}, which is needed in the computations of the rows below it. For each successive column, there are fewer choices because the only rows that are checked are the ones below the topmost row that requires the divisor.

There is one other modification to partial pivoting. Because any linear equation has the same solution under a scale factor, an arbitrary scale factor applied to a linear equation could bias the comparisons made in the partial pivoting. To factor out the effect of an arbitrary scale factor when comparing values for the partial pivoting, one scales the coefficients for that row, just for the purposes of the comparison, so that the largest coefficient of a particular row is equal to one. This is referred to as *implicit pivoting*.

When performing the decomposition, the values of the input matrix can be replaced with the values of L and U (Figure 1). Notice that the diagonal elements of the L matrix do not have to be stored because they are routinely set to one. If row exchanges take place, then the rows of the matrices in Figure 1 will be mixed up. For solving the linear system of equations, the row exchanges have no effect

$$\begin{bmatrix} A_{11} & A_{12} & A_{13} & A_{14} \\ A_{21} & A_{22} & A_{23} & A_{24} \\ A_{31} & A_{32} & A_{33} & A_{34} \\ A_{41} & A_{42} & A_{43} & A_{44} \end{bmatrix} \Rightarrow \begin{bmatrix} U_{11} & U_{12} & U_{13} & U_{14} \\ L_{21} & U_{22} & U_{23} & U_{24} \\ L_{31} & L_{32} & U_{33} & U_{34} \\ L_{41} & L_{42} & L_{43} & U_{44} \end{bmatrix}$$

FIGURE 1

In-place computation of the *L* and *U* values assuming no row exchanges.

on the computed answers. However, the row exchanges are recorded in a separate array so that they can be undone for the formation of the inverse matrix. In the code that follows (Figure 2), the *LU* decomposition approach is used to solve a system of linear equations and is broken down into several procedures. These procedures follow those found in *Numerical Recipes* [16].

After the execution of **LUdecomp**, the *A* matrix contains the elements of the *L* and *U* matrices. This matrix can then be used either for solving a linear system of equations or for computing the inverse of a matrix. The previously discussed simple substitution methods can be used to solve the equations that involve triangular matrices. In the code that follows, the subroutine **LUsubstitute** is called with the newly computed *A* matrix, the dimension of *A*, the vector of row swaps, and the right-hand vector (i.e., the *b* in $Ax = b$).

One of the advantages of the *LU* decomposition is that the decomposition matrices can be reused if the only change in a system of linear equations is the right-hand vector of values. In such a case, the routine **LUdecomp** only needs to be called once to form the *LU* matrices. The substitution routine, **LUsubstitute**, needs to be called with each new vector of values (remember to reuse the *A* matrix that holds the *LU* decomposition).

To perform matrix inversion, use the *L* and *U* matrices repeatedly with the *b* matrix holding column-by-column values of the identity matrix. In this way the inverse matrix is built up column by column.

1.2 Singular value decomposition

Singular value decomposition (SVD) is a popular method used for solving linear least-squares problems ($Ax = b$, where the number of rows of *A* is greater than the number of columns). It gives the user information about how ill-conditioned the set of equations is and allows the user to step in and remove sources of numerical inaccuracy.

As with *LU* decomposition, the first step decomposes the *A* matrix into more than one matrix (Eq. 16). In this case, an $M \times NA$ matrix is decomposed into a column-orthogonal $M \times NU$ matrix, a diagonal $N \times MW$ matrix, and an $N \times N$ orthogonal *V* matrix.

$$A = UWV^T \tag{16}$$

```
/*LU Decomposition
* with partial implicit pivoting
* partial means that the pivoting only happens by row
* implicit means that the pivots are scaled by the maximum value in the row
*/

/*===============================================================*/
/*LUdecomp
* inputs: A matrix of coefficients
*   n - dimension of A
* outputs: A matrix replaced with L and U diagonal matrices
  (diagonal   values of L = 1)
*   Rowswaps - vector to keep track of row swaps
*   Val - indicator of odd/even number of row swaps
*/
int LUdecomp(float **A,int n,int *rowswaps,int *val)
{
  float epsilon,*rowscale, temp;
  float sum;
  float pvt;
  int   ipvt;
  int   i,j,k;
  rowscale = (float*)malloc(sizeof(float)*n);

  epsilon = 0.00000000001;  /* small value to avoid division by zero */
  *val = 1;                 /* even/odd indicator (valence) */

  /* initialize the rowswap vector to indicate no swaps */
  for (i=0; i<n; i++) rowswaps[i] = i;

  /* for each row, find largest (in absolute value sense) element and
     record in rowscale */
  for (i=0; i<n; i++) {
    temp = fabs(A[i][0]);
    for (j=1; j<n; j++)
      if (fabs(A[i][j]) > temp) temp = fabs(A[i][j]);
    if (temp == 0) return(-1); /* got a row of all zeros - can't deal
                                  with that */
    rowscale[i] = 1/temp; /* later we need to divide by largest
                             element */
  }

  /* loop through the columns of A (and U) */
  for (j=0; j<n; j++) {
```

FIGURE 2

LU decomposition code.

```
    /* do the rows down to the diagonal - these don't need a
       division        so no swap */
    for (i=0; i<j; i++) {
      sum = A[i][j];
      for (k=0; k<i; k++) sum = sum - A[i][k]*A[k][j];
      A[i][j] = sum;
    }
    /* do the rows from the diagonal down */
    pvt = 0.0;
    ipvt = -1;
    for (i=j; i<n; i++) {
      sum = A[i][j];
      for (k=0; k<j; k++) sum = sum - A[i][k]*A[k][j];
      A[i][j] = sum;
      /* calculate the scaled value for pivoting consideration */
         temp = rowscale[i]*fabs(sum);
         if (temp >= pvt) {ipvt = i; pvt = temp;}
    }

    /* if a better pivot value is found, interchange the rows */
       if (j != ipvt) {
          for (k=0; k<n; k++) {
            temp = A[ipvt][k];
            A[ipvt][k] = A[j][k];
            A[j][k] = temp;
          }
          *val = -(*val);  /* keep track of even/odd number
                              interchanges */
          rowscale[ipvt] = rowscale[j];  /* and record which
                                            was     swapped */
       }
      rowswaps[j] = ipvt;

      if (A[j][j] == 0.0) A[j][j] = epsilon; /* to guard against
                                               divisions by zero */
      /* now the row is ready for division */
      for (i=j+1; i<n; i++) A[i][j] = A[i][j]/A[j][j];
   }
   return 1;
}

/* ================================================================ */
/* LUsubstitute
```

FIGURE 2 cont'd.

```
* inputs: A – matrix holding the L and U matrix values as a result
  of     LUdecomp
*       n – dimension of A
*       Rowswaps – vector holding a record of the row swaps
        performed       in LUdecomp
*       b – vector of right-hand values as in Ax = b
*/
void LUsubstitute(float **A,int n,int *rowswaps,float *b)
{
  int  i,j,ib;
  float  sum;
  int  m;

   /* row swap version */
   ib = -1;
   for (i=0; i<n; i++) {
     m = rowswaps[i];
     sum = b[m];
     b[m] = b[i];
     if (ib != -1) {
        for (j=ib; j<i; j++) sum = sum-A[i][j]*b[j];
     }
     else {
       if (sum != 0.0) ib = i;
     }
     b[i] = sum;
   }

   for (i=n-1; i>=0; i--) {
     sum = b[i];
     for (j=i+1; j<n; j++) sum = sum - A[i][j]*b[j];
       b[i] = sum/A[i][i];
     }
   return;
}
```

FIGURE 2 cont'd.

The magnitude of the elements in the *W* matrix indicates the potential for numerical problems. Zeros on the diagonal indicate singularities. Small values (where *small* is user defined) indicate the potential of numerical instability. It is the user's responsibility to inspect the *W* matrix and zero out values that are small enough to present numerical problems. Once this is done, the matrices can be used to solve the least-squares problem using a back substitution method similar to that used in *LU* decomposition. The code for SVD is available in various software packages and can be found in *Numerical Recipes* [16].

2. Geometric computations

A vector (a one-dimensional list of numbers) is often used to represent a point in space or a direction and magnitude in space (e.g., Figure 3). A slight complication in terminology results because a direction and magnitude in space is also referred to as a *vector*. As a practical matter, this distinction is usually not important. A vector in space has no position, only magnitude and direction. For geometric computations, a matrix usually represents a transformation (e.g., Figure 4).

2.1 Components of a vector

A vector, A, with coordinates (A_x, A_y, A_z) can be written as a sum of vectors, as shown in Equation 17, in which i, j, k are unit vectors along the principal axes, x, y, and z, respectively.

$$A = A_x i + A_y j + A_z k \tag{17}$$

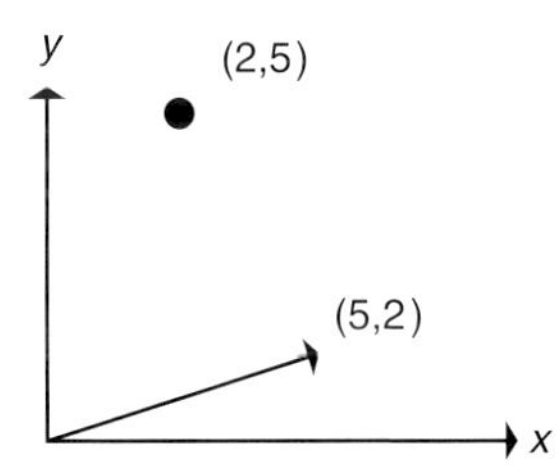

FIGURE 3

A point and vector in two-space.

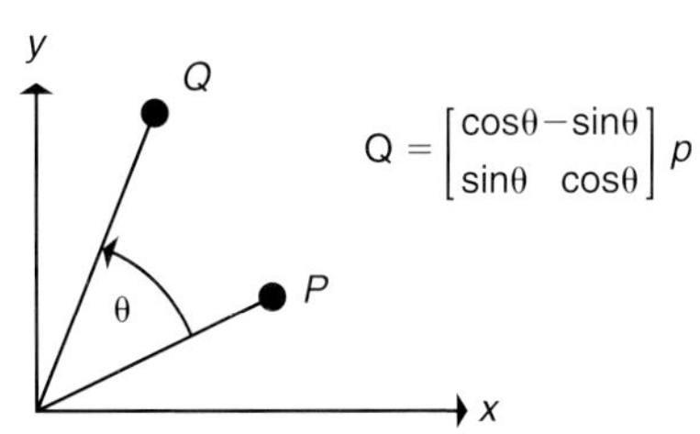

FIGURE 4

A matrix representing a rotation.

2.2 Length of a vector

The *length* of a vector is computed as in Equation 18. If a vector is of unit length, then $|A| = 1.0$, and it is said to be *normalized*. Dividing a vector by its length, forming a unit-length vector, is said to be *normalizing* the vector.

$$|A| = \sqrt{A_x^2 + A_y^2 + A_z^2} \tag{18}$$

2.3 Dot product of two vectors

The *dot product*, or *inner product*, of two vectors is computed as in Equation 19. The computation is commutative (Eq. 20) and associative (Eq. 21). The dot product of a vector with itself results in the square of its length (Eq. 22). The dot product of two vectors, A and B, is equal to the lengths of the vectors times the cosine of the angle between them (Eq. 23, Figure 5). As a result, the angle between two vectors can be determined by taking the arccosine of the dot product of the two normalized vectors (or, if they are not normalized, by taking the arccosine of the dot product divided by the lengths of the two vectors). The dot product of two vectors is equal to zero if the vectors are perpendicular to each other, as in Figure 6 (or if one or both of the vectors are zero vectors). The dot product can also be used to compute the projection of one vector onto another vector (Figure 7). This is useful in cases in which the coordinates of a vector are needed in an auxiliary coordinate system (Figure 8).

$$A \cdot B = A_x B_x + A_y B_y + A_z B_z \tag{19}$$

$$A \cdot B = B \cdot A \tag{20}$$

$$(A \cdot B) \cdot C = A \cdot (B \cdot C) \tag{21}$$

$$A \cdot A = |A|^2 \tag{22}$$

$$A \cdot B = |A||B| \cos\theta \tag{23}$$

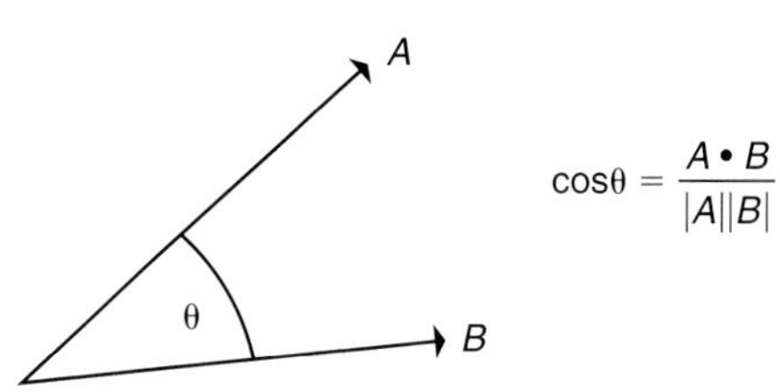

FIGURE 5

Using the dot product to compute the cosine of the angle between two vectors.

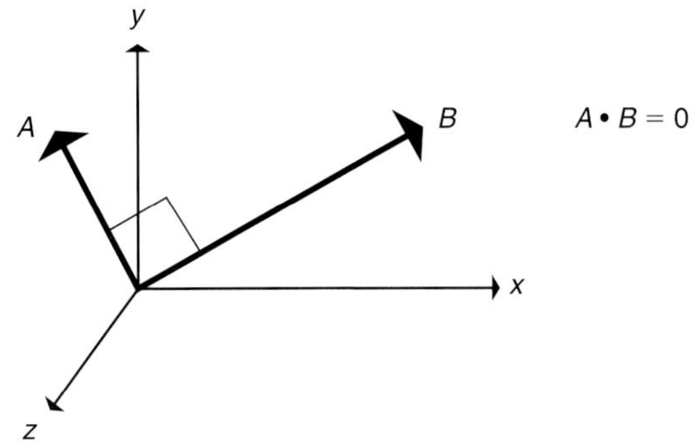

FIGURE 6

The dot product of perpendicular vectors.

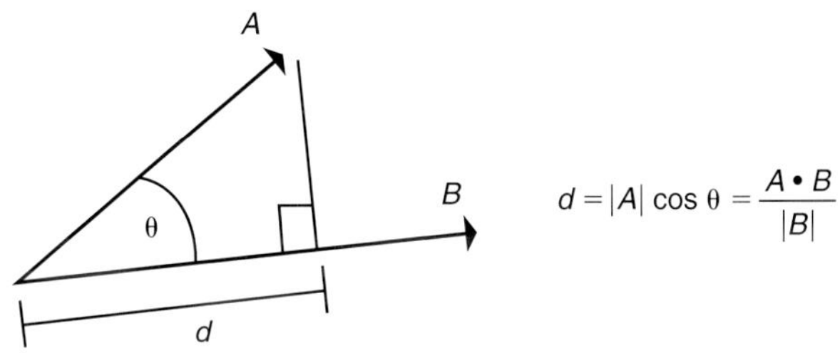

FIGURE 7

Computing the length of the projection of vector *A* onto vector *B*.

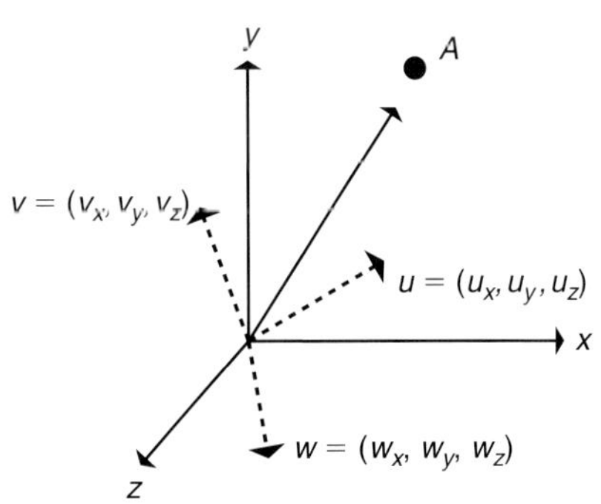

$$A_u = A \bullet u$$
$$A_v = A \bullet v$$
$$A_w = A \bullet w$$
$$A = (A_x, A_y, A_z) = A_u u + A_v v + A_w w$$

FIGURE 8

Computing the coordinates of a vector in an auxiliary coordinate system.

2.4 Cross-product of two vectors

The *cross-product*, or *outer product*, of two vectors can be defined using the determinant of a 3 × 3 matrix as shown in Equation 24, where i, j, and k are unit vectors in the directions of the principal axes. Equation 25 shows the definition as an explicit equation. The cross-product is not commutative (Eq. 26), but it is associative (Eq. 27).

$$A \times B = \begin{vmatrix} i & j & k \\ A_x & A_y & A_z \\ B_x & B_y & B_z \end{vmatrix}_z \tag{24}$$

$$A \times B = \left(A_y B_z - A_z B_y\right) i + \left(A_z B_x - A_x B_z\right) j + \left(A_x B_y - A_y B_x\right) k \tag{25}$$

$$A \times B = -(B \times A) = (-A) \times (-B) \tag{26}$$

$$A \times (B \times C) = (A \times B) \times C \tag{27}$$

The direction of $A \times B$ is perpendicular to both A and B (Figure 9), and the direction is determined by the right-hand rule (if A and B are in right-hand space). If the thumb of the right hand is put in the direction of the first vector (A) and the index finger is put in the direction of the second vector (B), the cross-product of the two vectors will be in the direction of the middle finger when it is held perpendicular to the first two fingers.

The magnitude of the cross-product is the length of one vector times the length of the other vector times the sine of the angle between them (Eq. 28). A zero vector will result if the two vectors are colinear or if either vector is a zero vector (Eq. 29). This relationship is useful for determining the sine of the angle between two vectors (Figure 10) and for computing the perpendicular distance from a point to a line (Figure 11).

$$|A \times B| = |A||B| \sin \theta \tag{28}$$

where θ is the angle from A to B, $0 < \theta < 180$

$$|A \times B| = 0 \text{ if and only if } A \text{ and } B \text{ are colinear,} \tag{29}$$

i.e., $\sin \theta = \sin 0 = 0$, or $A = 0$ or $B = 0$.

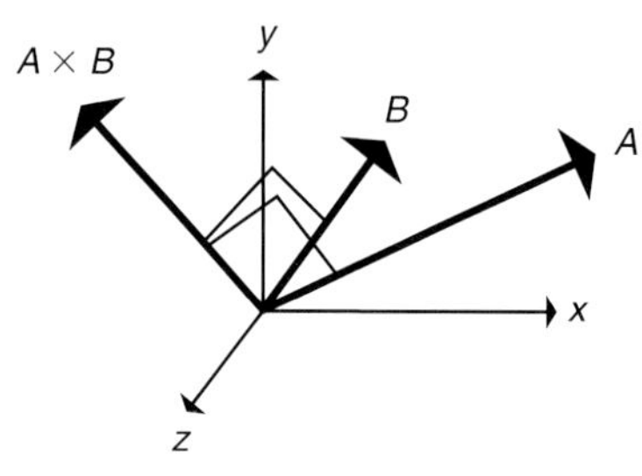

FIGURE 9

Vector formed by the cross product of two vectors

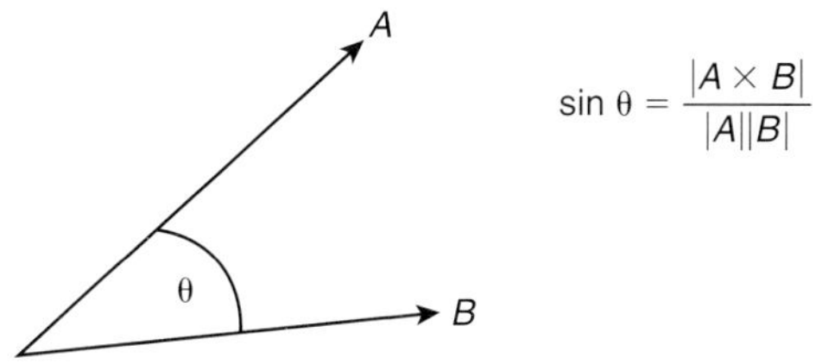

FIGURE 10

Using the cross-product to compute the sine of the angle between two vectors.

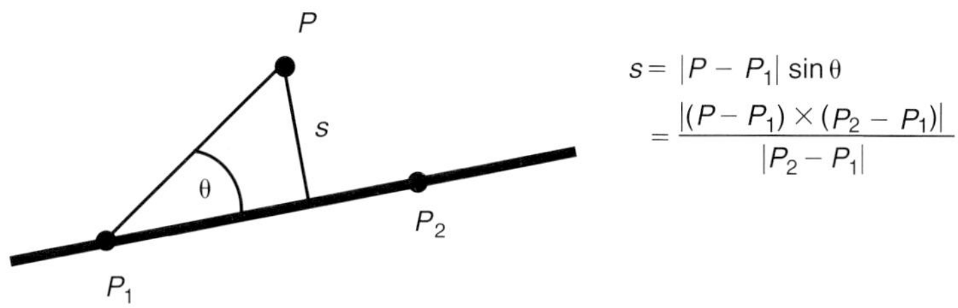

FIGURE 11

Computing the perpendicular distance from a point to a line.

2.5 Vector and matrix routines

Simple vector and matrix routines are given here (Figure 12). These are used in some of the routines presented elsewhere in this appendix.

Vector routines

Some vector routines can be implemented just as easily as in-line code using C's *#define* construction.

2.6 Closest point between two lines in three-space

The intersection of two lines in three-space often needs to be calculated. Because of numerical imprecision, the lines rarely, if ever, actually intersect in three-space. As a result, the computation that needs to be performed is to find the two points, one from each line, at which the lines are closest to each other.

The points P_1 and P_2 at which the lines are closest form a line segment perpendicular to both lines (Figure 13). They can be represented parametrically as points along the lines, and then the parametric interpolants can be solved for by satisfying the equations that state the requirement for perpendicularity (Eq. 30).

$$
\begin{aligned}
&(P_2 - P_1)\cdot V = 0\\
&(P_2 - P_1)\cdot W = 0\\
&(B + tW - (A + sV))\cdot V = 0\\
&(B + tW - (A + sV))\cdot W = 0\\
&t = \frac{-B\cdot V + A\cdot V + sV\cdot V}{W\cdot V}\\
&t = \frac{-B\cdot W + A\cdot W + sV\cdot W}{W\cdot W}\\
&\frac{-B\cdot V + A\cdot V + sV\cdot V}{W\cdot V} = \frac{-B\cdot W + A\cdot W + sV\cdot W}{W\cdot W}\\
&(-B\cdot V + A\cdot V + sV\cdot V)(W\cdot W) = (-B\cdot W + A\cdot W + sV\cdot W)\cdot(W\cdot V)\\
&s = \frac{(A\cdot W - B\cdot W)(W\cdot V) + (B\cdot V - A\cdot V)\cdot(W\cdot W)}{(V\cdot V)(W\cdot W) - (V\cdot W)^2}\\
&t = \frac{(B\cdot V - A\cdot V)(W\cdot V) + (A\cdot W - B\cdot W)(V\cdot V)}{(W\cdot W)(V\cdot V) - (V\cdot W)^2}
\end{aligned}
\tag{30}
$$

```
/* Vector.c */
typedef   struct xyz_struct {
float     x,y,z;
xyz_td;

}
xyz_td     p;

/* ================================================================ */
/* compute the cross product of two vectors */
xyz_td crossProduct(xyz_td v1,xyz_td v2)
{
  xyz_td     p;

  p.x = v1.y*v2.z - v1.z*v2.y;
  p.y = v1.z*v2.x - v1.x*v2.z;
  p.z = v1.x*v2.y - v1.y*v2.x;
  return     p;
}

/* ================================================================ */
/* compute the dot product of two vectors */
float dotProduct(xyz_td v1,xyz_td v2)
```

FIGURE 12

Vector routines.

```
{
  return v1.x*v2.x=v1.y*v2.y+v1.z*v2.z;
}

/* ================================================================== */
/* normalize a vector */
void normalizeVector(xyz_td *v)
{
  float  len;

  len = sqrt(v->x*v->x + v->y*v->y + v->z*v->z);
  v->x /= len;
  v->y /= len;
  v->z /= len;
}

/* ------------------------------------------------------------------ */
/* form the vector from the first point to the second */
xyz_td formVector(xyz_td p1, xyz_td p2)
{
  xyz_td    p;

  p.x = p2.x-p1.x;
  p.y = p2.y-p1.y;
  p.z = p2.z-p1.z;
  return p;
}

/* ================================================================== */
/* compute the length of a vector */
float length(xyz_td v)
{
  return sqrt(v.x*v.x+v.y*v.y+v.z*v.z);
}
```

Matrix Routines

```
/* Matrix.c */

/* ================================================================== */
/* Matrix multiplication */
/* C x B = A */
void Matrix4x4MatrixMult (float **C,float **B,float **A)
{
  int  i,j;
```

FIGURE 12 cont'd.

```
  for (i=0; i<4; i++) {
    for (j=0; j<4; j++) {
      A[i][j] = C[i][0]*B[0][j]+ C[i][1]*B[1][j]+
            C[i][2]*B[2][j]+ C[i][3]*B[3][j];
    }
  }
}

/* ================================================================== */
/* matrix-vector multiplication */
/* N = M x V */
void Matrix4 x 4Vector4Mult (float **M,float *V,float *N)
{
  N[0] = M[0][0]*V[0]+M[0][1]*V[1]+M[0][2]*V[2]+M[0][3]*V[3];
  N[1] = M[1][0]*V[0]+M[1][1]*V[1]+M[1][2]*V[2]+M[1][3]*V[3];
  N[2] = M[2][0]*V[0]+M[2][1]*V[1]+M[2][2]*V[2]+M[2][3]*V[3];
  N[3] = M[3][0]*V[0]+M[3][1]*V[1]+M[3][2]*V[2]+M[3][3]*V[3];
}

/* ================================================================== */
/* vector-matrix multiplication */
/* N = V x M */
void Vector4Matrix4 x 4Mult (float *V,float **M,float *N)
{
  N[0] = M[0][0]*V[0]+M[1][0]*V[1]+M[2][0]*V[2]+M[3][0]*V[3];
  N[1] = M[0][1]*V[0]+M[1][1]*V[1]+M[2][1]*V[2]+M[3][1]*V[3];
  N[2] = M[0][2]*V[0]+M[1][2]*V[1]+M[2][2]*V[2]+M[3][2]*V[3];
  N[3] = M[0][3]*V[0]+M[1][3]*V[1]+M[2][3]*V[2]+M[3][3]*V[3];
}

/* ================================================================== */
/* compute the inverse of a matrix */
void ComputeInverse4 x 4(float **M,float **Minv)
{
  int      rowswaps[4];
  int      val;
  float    b[4];
  int      i,j;
  float**A;

  A = (float **)malloc(sizeof(float *)*4);
  for (i=0; i<4; i++) {
```

FIGURE 12 cont'd.

```
      A[i] = (float *)malloc(sizeof(float)*4);
    }
    for (i=0; i<4; i++) {
      for (j=0; j<4; j++) {
        A[i][j] = M[i][j];
      }
    }

    LUdecomp(A,4,rowswaps,&val);

    for (i=0; i<4; i++) {
      for (j=0; j<4; j++) b[j] = (i==j) ? 1:0;
      LUsubstitute(A,4,rowswaps,b);
      for (j=0; j<4; j++) Minv[j][i] = b[j];
    }
}
```

FIGURE 12 cont'd.

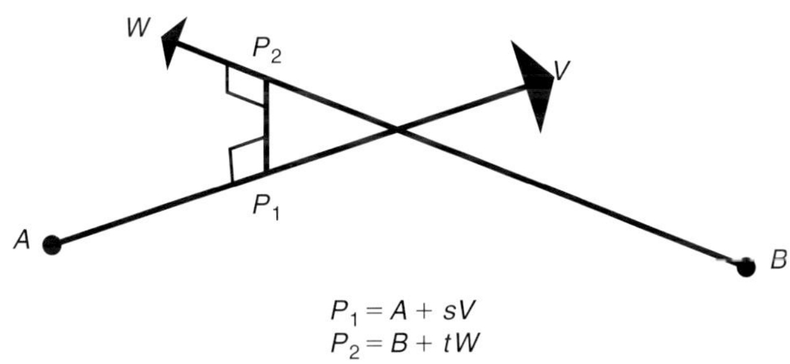

FIGURE 13

Two lines are closest to each other at points P_1 and P_2.

2.7 Area calculations

Area of a triangle

The area of a triangle consisting of vertices V_1, V_2, V_3 is one-half times the length of one edge times the perpendicular distance from that edge to the other vertex. The perpendicular distance from the edge to a vertex can be computed using the cross-product (see Figure 14). For triangles in two dimensions, the z-coordinates are essentially considered zero and the cross-product computation is simplified accordingly (only the z-coordinate of the cross-product is non-zero).

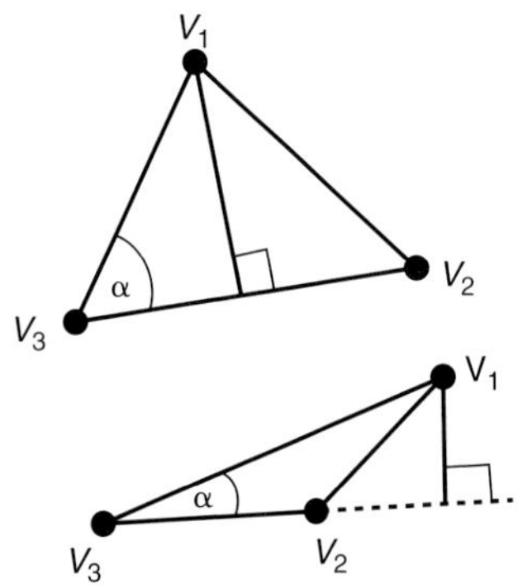

$$\text{Area}(V_1, V_2, V_3) = \frac{1}{2}|V_2 - V_3|\,|V_1 - V_3| \sin\alpha$$
$$= \frac{1}{2}|V_2 - V_3| \frac{|(V_1 - V_3) \times (V_2 - V_3)|}{|V_2 - V_3|}$$
$$= \frac{1}{2}|(V_1 - V_3) \times (V_2 - V_3)|$$

FIGURE 14

Area of a triangle.

The signed area of the triangle is required for computing the area of a polygon. In the two-dimensional case, this is done simply by not taking the absolute value of the z-coordinate of the cross-product. In the three-dimensional case, a vector normal to the polygon can be used to indicate the positive direction. The direction of the vector produced by the cross-product can be compared with the normal (using the dot product) to determine whether it is in the positive or negative direction. The length of the cross-product vector can then be computed and the appropriate sign applied to it.

Area of a polygon

The area of a polygon can be computed as a sum of the signed areas of simple elements. In the two-dimensional case, the signed area under each edge of the polygon can be summed to form the area (Figure 15). The area under an edge is the average height of the edge times its width (Eq. 31, where subscripts are computed modulo $n + 1$).

$$\begin{aligned} \text{Area} &= \sum_{i=1}^{n} \frac{(y_i + y_{i+1})}{2}(x_{i+1} - x_i) \\ &= \frac{1}{2}\sum_{i=1}^{n}(y_i x_{i+1} - y_{i+1} x_i) \end{aligned} \tag{31}$$

The area of a polygon can also be computed by using each edge of the polygon to construct a triangle with the origin (Figure 16). The signed area of the triangle must be used so that edges directed clockwise with respect to the origin cancel out edges directed counterclockwise with respect to the origin. Although this is more computationally expensive than summing the areas under the edges, it suggests a way to compute the area of a polygon in three-space. In the three-dimensional case, one of the vertices of the polygon can be used to construct a triangle with each edge, and the three-dimensional version of the vector equations of Figure 14 can be used.

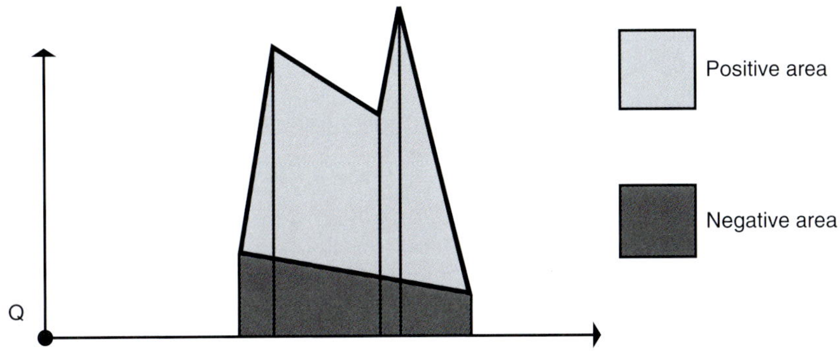

FIGURE 15

Computing the area of a polygon.

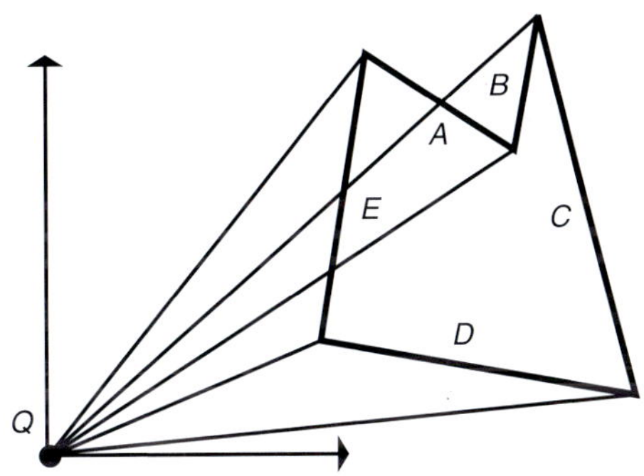

Area of polygon (*A*, *B*, *C*, *D*, *E*) = Area of Triangle (*Q*, *A*)
+ Area of Triangle(*Q*, *B*)
+ Area of Triangle(*Q*, *C*)
+ Area of Triangle(*Q*, *D*)
+ Area of Triangle(*Q*, *E*)

FIGURE 16

The area of a two-dimensional polygon: the edges are labeled with letters, triangles are constructed from each edge to the origin, and the areas of the triangles are signed according to the direction of the edge with respect to the origin. Area of polygon (*A, B, C, D, E*) = Area of Triangle (*Q, A*)

2.8 The cosine rule

The cosine rule states the relationship between the lengths of the edges of a triangle and the cosine of an interior angle (Figure 17). It is useful for determining the interior angle of a triangle when the locations of the vertices are known.

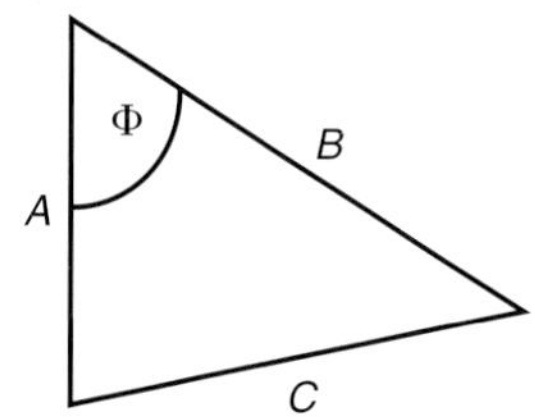

$$|C|^2 = |A|^2 + |B|^2 - 2|A||B|\cos\Phi$$

$$\cos\Phi = \frac{|A|^2 + |B|^2 - |C|^2}{2|A||B|}$$

FIGURE 17

The cosine rule.

2.9 Barycentric coordinates

Barycentric coordinates are the coordinates of a point in terms of weights associated with other points. Most commonly used are the barycentric coordinates of a point with respect to vertices of a triangle. The barycentric coordinates (u_1, u_2, u_3) of a point, P, with respect to a triangle with vertices V_1, V_2, V_3 are shown in Figure 18. Notice that for a point inside the triangle, the coordinates always sum to one. This can be extended easily to any convex polygon by a direct generalization of the equations. However, it cannot be extended to concave polygons.

2.10 Computing bounding shapes

Bounding volumes are useful as approximate extents of more complex objects. Often, simpler tests can be used to determine the general position of an object by using bounding volumes, thus saving computation. In computer animation, the most obvious example occurs in testing for object collisions. If the bounding volumes of objects are not overlapping, then the objects themselves must not be penetrating each other. Planar polyhedra are considered here because the bounding volumes can be determined by inspecting the vertices of the polyhedra. Nonplanar objects require more sophisticated techniques. *Axis-aligned bounding boxes* and bounding spheres are relatively easy to calculate but can be poor approximations of the object's shape. Slabs and *oriented bounding boxes* (OBBs) can provide a

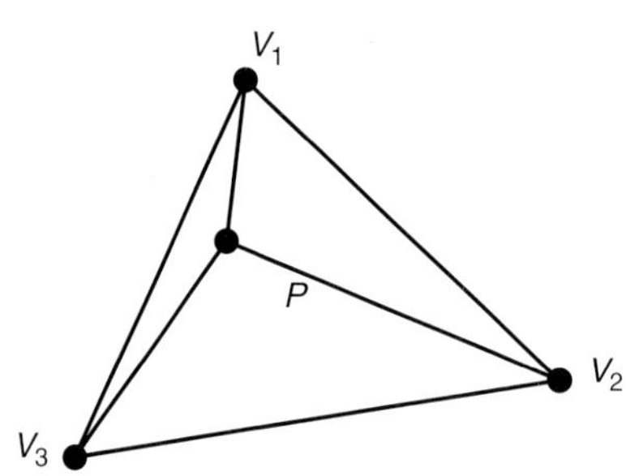

$$u_1 = \frac{\text{Area}(V_1, V_2, V_3)}{\text{Area}(P, V_2, V_3)}$$

$$u_2 = \frac{\text{Area}(P, V_3, V_1)}{\text{Area}(V_1, V_2, V_3)}$$

$$u_3 = \frac{\text{Area}(P, V_1, V_2)}{\text{Area}(V_1, V_2, V_3)}$$

$$P = u_1 V_1 + u_2 V_2 + u_3 V_3$$

FIGURE 18

The barycentric coordinates of a point with respect to vertices of a triangle.

much better fit. OBBs are rectangular bounding boxes at an arbitrary orientation [7]. For collision detection, bounding shapes are often hierarchically organized into tighter and tighter approximations of the object's space. A *convex hull*, the smallest convex shape bounding the object, provides an even tighter approximation but requires more computation.

Bounding boxes

Bounding box typically refers to a boundary cuboid (or rectangular solid) whose sides are aligned with the principal axes. A bounding box for a collection of points is easily computed by searching for minimum and maximum values for the x-, y-, and z-coordinates. A point is inside the bounding box if its coordinates are between min/max values for each of the three coordinate pairs. While the bounding box may be a good fit for some objects, it may not be a good fit for others (Figure 19). How well the bounding box approximates the shape of the object is rotationally variant, as shown in Figure 19B and 19C.

Bounding slabs

Bounding slabs are a generalization of bounding boxes. A pair of arbitrarily oriented planes are used to bound the object. The orientation of the pair of planes is specified by a user-supplied normal vector. The normal defines a family of planes that vary according to perpendicular distance to the origin.

The planar equation $ax + by + cz = d$, (a, b, c) represents a vector normal to the plane. If this vector has unit length, then d is the perpendicular distance to the plane. If the length of (a, b, c) is not one, then d is the perpendicular distance scaled by the vector's length. Notice that d is equal to the dot product of the vector (a, b, c) and a point on the plane.

Given a user-supplied normal vector, the user computes the dot product of that vector and each vertex of the object and records the minimum and maximum values (Eq. 32). The normal vector and these min/max values define the bounding slab. See Figure 20 for a two-dimensional diagram illustrating the idea. Multiple slabs can be used to form an arbitrarily tight bounding volume of the convex hull of the polyhedron. A point is inside this bounding volume if the result of the dot product of it and the normal vector is between the corresponding min/max values for each slab (see Figure 21 for a two-dimensional example).

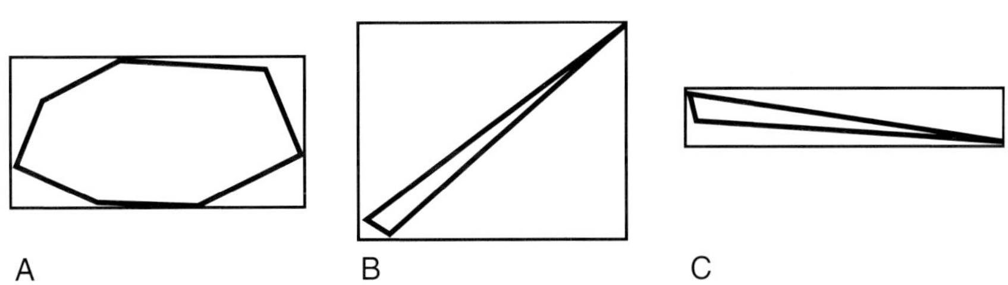

FIGURE 19

Sample objects and their bounding boxes (in two-dimensional).

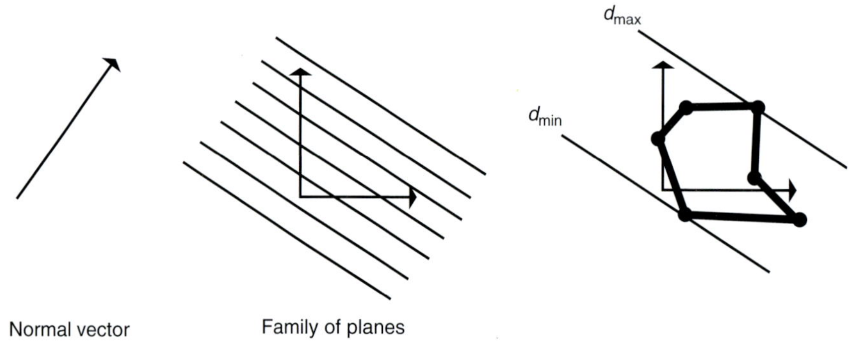

FIGURE 20

Computing a boundary slab for a polyhedron.

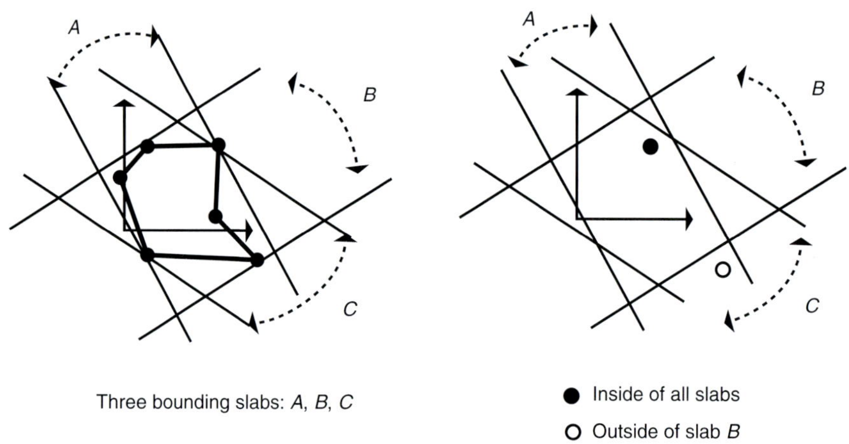

FIGURE 21

Multiple bounding slabs.

$$
\begin{aligned}
p &= (x, y, z) && \text{vertex} \\
N &= (a, b, c) && \text{normal} \\
PgN &= d && \text{computing the planar equation constant}
\end{aligned}
\tag{32}
$$

Bounding spheres

Computing the optimal bounding sphere for a set of points can be expensive. However, more tractable approximate methods exist. A quick and fairly accurate method of computing an approximate bounding sphere for a collection of points is to make an initial guess at the bounding sphere and then incrementally enlarge the sphere as necessary by inspecting each point in the set. The description here follows Ritter [17].

The first step is to loop through the points and record the minimum and maximum points in each of the three principal directions. The second step is to use the maximally separated pair of points from the three pairs of recorded points and create an initial approximation of the bounding sphere. The third step is, for each point in the original set, to adjust the bounding sphere as necessary to include the point. Once all the points have been processed, a near-optimal bounding sphere has been computed (Figure 22). This method is fast and it is easy to implement (Figure 23).

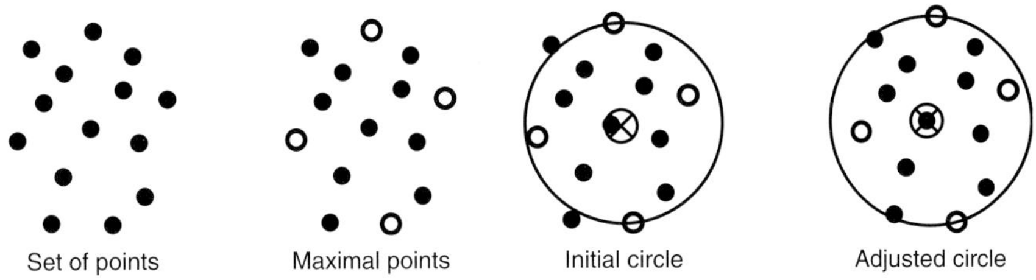

FIGURE 22

Computing a bounding circle for a set of points.

```
/*
** Bounding Sphere Computation
*/
void boundingSphere(xyz_td *pnts,int n, xyz_td *cntr, float *radius)
{
  int    i,minxi,maxxi,minyi,maxyi,minzi,maxzi,p1i,p2i;
  float  minx,maxx,miny,maxy,minz,maxz;
  float  diam2,diam2x,diam2y,diam2z,rad,rad2;
  float  dx,dy,dz;
  float  cntrx,cntry,cntrz;
  float  delta;
  float  dist,dist2;
  float  newrad,newrad2;
  float  newcntrx,newcntry,newcntrz;

  /* step one: find minimal and maximal points in each of 3
     principal    directions */
  minxi = 0; minx = pnts[0].x; maxxi = 0; maxx = pnts[0].x;
  minyi = 0; miny = pnts[0].y; maxyi = 0; maxy = pnts[0].y;
  minzi = 0; minz = pnts[0].z; maxzi = 0; maxz = pnts[0].z;
  for (i=1; i<n; i++) {
    if (pnts[i].x < minx) { minx = pnts[i].x; minxi = i; }
    if (pnts[i].x > maxx) { maxx = pnts[i].x; maxxi = i; }
    if (pnts[i].y < miny) { miny = pnts[i].y; minyi = i; }
```

FIGURE 23

Bounding sphere code.

```
 if (pnts[i].y > maxy) { maxy = pnts[i].y; maxyi = i; }
 if (pnts[i].z < minz) { minz = pnts[i].z; minzi = i; }
 if (pnts[i].z > maxz) { maxz = pnts[i].z; maxzi = i; }
}

/* step two: find maximally separated points from the 3 pairs; use
   to initialize sphere */
/* find maximally separated points by comparing the distance squared
   between points */
dx = pnts[minxi].x - pnts[maxxi].x;
dy = pnts[minxi].y - pnts[maxxi].y;
dz = pnts[minxi].z - pnts[maxxi].z;
diam2x = dx*dx + dy*dy + dz*dz;
dx = pnts[minyi].x - pnts[maxyi].x;
dy = pnts[minyi].y - pnts[maxyi].y;
dz = pnts[minyi].z - pnts[maxyi].z;
diam2y = dx*dx + dy*dy + dz*dz;
dx = pnts[minzi].x - pnts[maxzi].x;
dy = pnts[minzi].y - pnts[maxzi].y;
dz = pnts[minzi].z - pnts[maxzi].z;
diam2z = dx*dx + dy*dy + dz*dz;
diam2 = diam2x; p1i = minxi; p2i = maxxi;
if (diam2y>diam2) { diam2 = diam2y; p1i=minyi; p2i=maxyi; }
if (diam2z>diam2) { diam2 = diam2z; p1i=minzi; p2i=maxzi;}
/* center of initial sphere is average of two points */
cntrx = (pnts[p1i].x+pnts[p2i].x)/2;
cntry = (pnts[p1i].y+pnts[p2i].y)/2;
cntrz = (pnts[p1i].z+pnts[p2i].z)/2;
/* calculate radius and radius squared of initial sphere - from
   diameter squared*/
rad2 = diam2/4;
rad = sqrt(rad2);
printf("maximally separated pair: (%f,%f,%f):(%f,%f,%f),%f\n",
  pnts[p1i].x,pnts[p1i].y,pnts[p1i].z,
  pnts[p2i].x,pnts[p2i].y,pnts[p2i].z,diam2);
printf("initial center: (%f,%f,%f)\n",cntrx,cntry,cntrz);
printf("initial diam2: %f\n",diam2);
printf("initial radius, radius2 = %f,%f\n",rad,rad2);

/* third step: now step through the set of points and adjust
   bounding    sphere as necessary */
for (i=0; i<n; i++) {
  dx = pnts[i].x - cntrx;
```

FIGURE 23 cont'd.

```
dy = pnts[i].y - cntry;
dz = pnts[i].z - cntrz;
dist2 = dx*dx + dy*dy + dz*dz;      /* distance squared of old
                                       center to pnt */
if (dist2 > rad2) {                 /* need to update sphere if this
                                       point is outside old radius*/
   dist = sqrt(dist2);
   /* new radius is average of current radius and distance from
      center to pnt */
   newrad = (rad + dist)/2;
   newrad2 = newrad*newrad;
   printf("new radius = %f\n",newrad);
   delta = dist - newrad;      /* distance from old center to new
                                  center */
   /* delta/dist and rad/dist are weights of pnt and old center to
      compute new center */
   newcntrx = (newrad*cntrx+delta*pnts[i].x)/dist;
   newcntry = (newrad*cntry+delta*pnts[i].y)/dist;
   newcntrz = (newrad*cntrz+delta*pnts[i].z)/dist;

   /* test to see if new radius and center contain the point */
   /* this test should only fail by an epsilon due to numeric
      imprecision */
   dx = pnts[i].x - newcntrx;
   dy = pnts[i].y - newcntry;
   dz = pnts[i].z - newcntrz;
   dist2 = dx*dx + dy*dy + dz*dz;
   if (dist2 > newrad2) {
      printf("ERROR by %lf\n",((double)(dist2))-newrad2);
      printf("  center - radius: (%f,%f,%f) -  %f\n",cntrx,cntry,
                cntrz,rad);
      printf(" New center - radius: (%f,%f,%f)   %f\n",
       newcntrx,newcntry,newcntrz,newrad);

   }
   cntrx = newcntrx;
   cntry = newcntry;
   cntrz = newcntrz;
   rad = newrad;
   rad2 = rad*rad;

  }
}
```

FIGURE 23 cont'd.

```
        *radius = rad;
        cntr->x = cntrx;
        cntr->y = cntry;
        cntr->z = cntrz;
        return;
    }
```

FIGURE 23 cont'd.

Convex hull

The convex hull of a set of points is the smallest convex polyhedron that contains all the points. A simple algorithm for computing the complex hull is given here, although more efficient techniques exist. As this is usually a one-time code for an object (unless the object is deforming), this is a case where efficiency can be traded for ease of implementation. Refer to Figure 24.

1. Find a point on the convex hull by finding the point with the largest y-coordinate. Refer to the point found in this step as P_1.

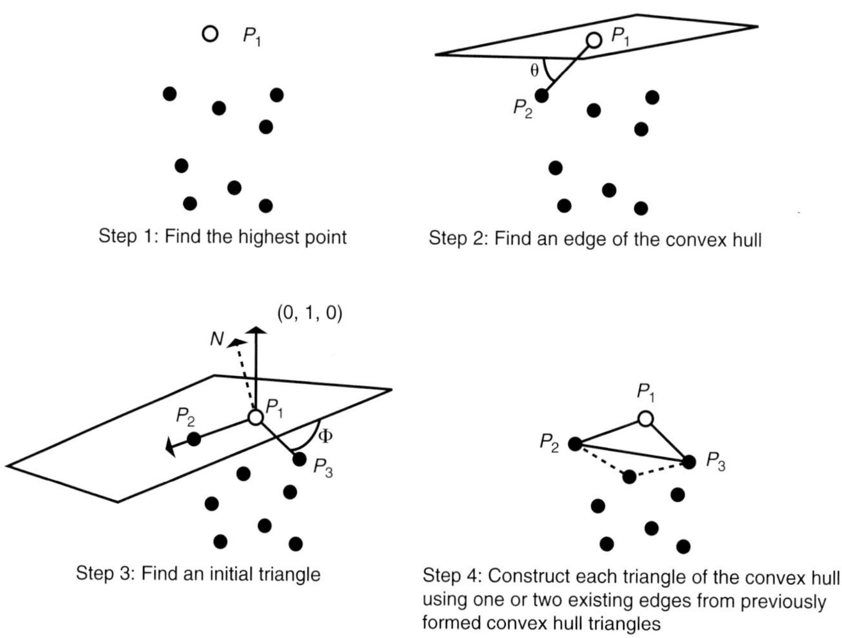

FIGURE 24

Computing the convex hull.

2. Construct an edge on the convex hull by using the following method. Find the point that, when connected with P_1, makes the smallest angle with the horizontal plane passing through P_1. Use L to refer to the line from P_1 to the point. Finding the smallest sine of the angle is equivalent to finding the smallest angle. The sine of the angle between L and the horizontal plane passing through P_1 is equal to the cosine of the angle between L and the vector $(0,\ -1, 0)$. The dot product of these two vectors is used to compute the cosine of the angle between them. Refer to the point found in this step as P_2, and refer to the line from P_1 to P_2 as L.
3. Construct a triangle on the convex hull by the following method. First, construct the plane defined by L and a horizontal line perpendicular to L at P_1. The horizontal line is constructed according to $(L \times (0,\ -1, 0))$. All of the points are below this plane. Find the point that, when connected with P_1, makes the smallest angle with this plane. Use K to refer to the line from P_1 to the point. The sine of the angle between K and the plane is equal to the cosine of the angle between K and the downward-pointing normal vector of the plane. This normal can be computed as $N = (L \times (0, -1, 0)) \times L$ (in right-hand space). Refer to the point found in this step as P_3. The triangle on the convex hull is defined by these three points. A consistent ordering of the points should be used so that they, for example, compute an outward-pointing normal vector $\left(N = (P_3 - P_1) \times (P_2 - P_1),\ N_y > 0.0\right)$ in right-hand space. Initialize the list of convex hull triangles with this triangle and its outward-pointing normal vector. Mark each of its three edges as *unmatched* to indicate that the triangle that shares the edge has not been found yet.
4. Search the current list of convex hull triangles and find an *unmatched* edge. Construct the triangle of the convex hull that shares this edge by the following method. Find the point that, when connected by a line from a point on the edge, makes the smallest angle with the plane of the triangle while creating a dihedral angle (interior angle between two faces measured at a shared edge) greater than 90 degrees. The dihedral angle can be computed using the angle between the normals of the two triangles. When the point has been found, add the triangle defined by this point and the marked edge to the list of convex hull triangles and the unmarked edge. The rest of the unmarked edges in the list must be searched to see if the two other edges of the new triangle already occur in the list. If either of the new edges does not have a match in the list, then it should be marked as unmatched. Otherwise, mark the edge as *matched.* Now, go back through the list of convex hull triangles and look for another *unmatched* edge and repeat the procedure to construct a new triangle that shares that edge. When there are no more *unmatched* edges in the list of convex hull triangles, the hull has been constructed.

Step 4 in the previous algorithm does not handle the case in which there are more than three coplanar vertices. To handle these cases, instead of forming a triangle, form a convex hull polygon for the coplanar points. This is done similarly in two and three dimensions. First, collect all of the coplanar points (all of the points within some epsilon of being coplanar) into a set. Second, initialize the current edge to be the unmatched edge of step 4 and add the first point of the current edge to the set of coplanar points. Third, iteratively find the point in the set of coplanar points that makes the smallest angle with the current edge as measured from the first point of the edge to the second point of the edge to the candidate point. When the point is found, remove it from the set of coplanar points and make the new current edge the edge from the second point of the old current edge to the newly found point. Continue iterating until the first point of the original unmatched edge is found. This will complete the convex hull polygon, which is then added to the list of convex hull polygons; its newly formed edges are processed as in step 4 (see Figure 25).

```
/* ConvexHull.c
 * This code uses a brute force algorithm to construct the convex hull
 * and does not handle more than three coplanar points
 */

#include "Vector.h"

typedef struct conHullTri_struct {
  int   pi[3];
  int   matched[3];
  xyz_td  normal;
  struct conHullTri_struct *next;
} conHullTri_td;

conHullTri_td       *chtList;

/* ============================================================== */
/* CONVEX HULL */
int ConvexHull(xyz_td *pntList,int num,int **triangleList,int *numTriangles)
{
  int       i;
  int       p1i,p2i,p3i,pi;
  xyz_td    yaxis;
  xyz_td    v,n,nn,nnn,v1,v2;
  float     t,t1,t2;
  int       count;
  conHullTri_td *chtPtr,*chtPtrTail,*chtPtrNew,*chtPtrA;
  int         done;
  int         *triList;
  int       dummy,notError;
```

FIGURE 25

Convex hull code.

```
yaxis.x = 0; yaxis.y = 1; yaxis.z = 0;

/* find the highest point */
p1i = 0; t = pntList[0].y;
for (i=1; i<num; i++) {
    if (pntList[i].y > t) { p1i=i; t=pntList[i].y;}
 }

 /* find point that makes minimum angle with horizontal plane */
 p2i = (p1i==0) ? 1:0;
 v = formVector(pntList[p1i],pntList[p2i]);
 normalizeVector(&v);
 t = v.y;
 if (t>0.0) {
    printf(" ERROR - found higher point\n");
    scanf("%d",&dummy);
    return 1;
 }
 for (i=p2i+1; i<num; i++) {
    if (i!=p1i) {
       v = formVector(pntList[p1i],pntList[i]);
       normalizeVector(&v);
       t1 = v.y;
       if (t1 > t) {p2i = i; t = t1;}
    }
 }

 /* find point that makes triangle with minimum angle with horizontal
    plane through edge */
 v1 = formVector(pntList[p1i],pntList[p2i]);

 if ((p1i!=0) && (p2i!=0)) p3i=0;
 else if ((p1i!=1) && (p2i!=1)) p3i=1;
 else p3i=2;
 v2 = formVector(pntList[p2i],pntList[i]);
 n = crossProduct(v2,v1);
 normalizeVector(&n);
 if (n.y < 0) {
    n.x = -n.x; n.y = -n.y; n.z = -n.z;
 }
 for (i=p3i+1; i<num; i++) {
  if ((i!=p1i)&&(i!=p2i)) {
     v = formVector(pntList[p2i],pntList[i]);
```

FIGURE 25 cont'd.

```
            nn = crossProduct(v1,v);
            normalizeVector(&nn);
            if (nn.y < 0) { nn.x = -nn.x; nn.y = -nn.y; nn.z = -nn.z; }
            if (nn.y>n.y) {
            p3i=i;
            n.x = nn.x; n.y = nn.y; n.z = n.z;
          }
        }
      }

      /* compute outward-pointing normal vector in right-hand space for
         clockwise triangle */
      /* recalculate the normal vector */
      v1 = formVector(pntList[p1i],pntList[p2i]);
      v2 = formVector(pntList[p2i],pntList[p3i]);
      n = crossProduct(v2,v1);
      normalizeVector(&n);
      if (n.y<0) {
         n.x = -n.x; n.y = -n.y; n.z = -n.z;
         pi = p1i; p1i = p2i; p2i = pi;
      }

      /* make a convex hull entry */
      count = 1;
      chtPtr = (conHullTri_td *)malloc(sizeof(conHullTri_td));
      if (chtPtr == NULL) {
         printf("unsuccessful memory allocation 1\n");
         scanf("%d",&dummy);
         return 1;
      }
      chtPtr->pi[0] = p1i;
      chtPtr->pi[1] = p2i;
      chtPtr->pi[2] = p3i;
      chtPtr->matched[0] = FALSE;
      chtPtr->matched[1] = FALSE;
      chtPtr->matched[2] = FALSE;
      chtPtr->normal = n;

      /* initialize the convex hull triangle list with the triangle */
      chtList = chtPtr;
      chtPtr->next = NULL;
      chtPtrTail = chtPtr;
```

FIGURE 25 cont'd.

```
/* check and make sure all vertices are 'underneath' the initial
   triangle */
for (i=0; i<num; i++) {
  if ((i!=chtPtr->pi[0]) &&
      (i!=chtPtr->pi[1]) &&
      (i!=chtPtr->pi[2]) ) {
      v = formVector(pntList[chtPtr->pi[0]],pntList[i]);
      t = dotProduct(v,n);
  if (t>0.0) {
      /* ERROR - point above initial triangle */
     printf("ERROR - found a point above initial triangle  (%d)\n",i);
      return 1;
  }
 }
}

/* now loop through the convex hull triangle list and process
   unmatched edges */
done = FALSE;
chtPtr = chtList;
while (chtPtr!=NULL) {
 /* look for first unmatched edge */
 if ((!(chtPtr->matched[0])) ||
    (!(chtPtr->matched[1])) ||
    (!(chtPtr->matched[2])) ) {

    /* set it now as matched, and record 3 points with unmatched as
       first two */
    if (!(chtPtr->matched[0])) {
       p1i=chtPtr->pi[0]; p2i=chtPtr->pi[1]; p3i=chtPtr->pi[2];
       chtPtr->matched[0] = TRUE;
    }
    else if (!(chtPtr->matched[1])) {
     p1i=chtPtr->pi[1]; p2i=chtPtr->pi[2]; p3i=chtPtr->pi[0];
     chtPtr->matched[1] = TRUE;
    }
    else if (!(chtPtr->matched[2])) {
     p1i=chtPtr->pi[2]; p2i=chtPtr->pi[0]; p3i=chtPtr->pi[1];
     chtPtr->matched[2] = TRUE;
    }

    /* get info of triangle of unmatched edge */
    n.x = chtPtr->normal.x;
```

FIGURE 25 cont'd.

```
    n.y = chtPtr->normal.y;
    n.z = chtPtr->normal.z;
    v1=formVector(pntList[p2i],pntList[p1i]);

    /* find new vertex which, with unmatched edge, makes    triangle */
    /* whose normal is closest to normal of triangle of unmatched
       edge */
    pi = -1;
    for (i=0; i<num; i++) {
     if ((i!=p1i)&&(i!=p2i)&&(i!=p3i)) {
        v=formVector(pntList[p1i],pntList[i]);
    /* test to see if point is above triangle */
    t1 = dotProduct(v,n);
    if (t1>0) {
       /* ERROR - point above initial triangle */
      printf("ERROR - found a point above initial triangle   (%d)\n",i);
      return 1;
    }
    /* compute normal of proposed new triangle */
    nn = crossProduct(v,v1);
    normalizeVector(&nn);
    /* test for concave corner */
    nnn = crossProduct(n,nn);
    t2 = dotProduct(nnn,v1);
    if (t2<0.0) {
       printf("ERROR - concave corner found\n");
       return 1;
    }
    /* compute angle made by faces (=angle made by normals)    */
    t1 = dotProduct(n,nn);
    /* printf(" %d: dot product of normals: %f\n",i,t1); */
    /* printf(" normal for comparison: %f %f    %f\n",n.x,n.y,n.z); */
    /* printf(" normal: %f %f %f\n",nn.x,nn.y,nn.z); */
    /* save smallest angle (largest cosine) */
    if (pi==-1) {pi=i; t=t1;}
    else if (t1>t) {pi=i; t=t1;}
   }
}

/* check and make sure all vertices are 'underneath' this    triangle */
v=formVector(pntList[p1i],pntList[pi]);
nn = crossProduct(v,v1);
normalizeVector(&nn);
```

FIGURE 25 cont'd.

```
        for (i=0; i<num; i++) {
         if ((i!=p2i) &&
            (i!=p1i) &&
            (i!=pi) ) {
            v = formVector(pntList[p1i],pntList[i]);
            t = dotProduct(v,nn);
            if (t>0.0) {
             /* ERROR - point above new triangle */
             printf("ERROR - found a point above new triangle   (%d)\n",i);
             return 1;
        }
      }
   }
  /* search for p2i-pi or pi-pi1 already in database - error   condition */
   chtPtrA = chtList; notError = TRUE;
   while ((chtPtrA!=NULL)&&notError) {
    if((chtPtrA->pi[0]==p1i)&&(chtPtrA->pi[1]==pi)) notError =   FALSE;
    else if((chtPtrA->pi[1]==p1i)&&(chtPtrA->pi[2]==pi))  notError = FALSE;
    else if((chtPtrA->pi[2]==p1i)&&(chtPtrA->pi[0]==pi))  notError = FALSE;
    else if((chtPtrA->pi[0]==pi)&&(chtPtrA->pi[1]==p2i))  notError = FALSE;
    else if((chtPtrA->pi[1]==pi)&&(chtPtrA->pi[2]==p2i))  notError = FALSE;
    else if((chtPtrA->pi[2]==pi)&&(chtPtrA->pi[0]==p2i))  notError = FALSE;
    else chtPtrA = chtPtrA->next;
    /* end while */
   if (!notError) {
     printf("ERROR - duplicating edge   (%d,%d,%d)\n",p1i,p2i,pi);
     return 1;
   }

   /* add p1i, p2i, pi */
   count++;
   chtPtrNew = (conHullTri_td *)malloc(sizeof(conHullTri_td));
   if (chtPtrNew == NULL) {
      printf(" unsuccessful memory allocation 2\n");
      return 1;
   }

   chtPtrTail->next = chtPtrNew;
   chtPtrNew->pi[0] = p2i;
   chtPtrNew->pi[1] = p1i;
   chtPtrNew->pi[2] = pi;
```

FIGURE 25 cont'd.

```
chtPtrNew->matched[0] = TRUE;
chtPtrNew->matched[1] = FALSE;
chtPtrNew->matched[2] = FALSE;
chtPtrNew->normal.x = nn.x;
chtPtrNew->normal.y = nn.y;
chtPtrNew->normal.z = nn.z;
chtPtrNew->next = NULL;
chtPtrTail = chtPtrNew;

/* search for p2i-pi or pi-pli already in database in reverse   order */
chtPtrA = chtList;
while (chtPtrA!=NULL) {
 if (!chtPtrA->matched[0]&&(chtPtrA-  >pi[0]==pi)&&(chtPtrA->
    pi[1]==pli)) {
    chtPtrA->matched[0] = TRUE;
    chtPtrNew->matched[1] = TRUE;
 }
 else if (!chtPtrA->matched[1]&&(chtPtrA-  >pi[1]==pi)&&
 (chtPtrA->pi[2]==pli)) {
   chtPtrA->matched[1] = TRUE;
   chtPtrNew->matched[1] = TRUE;
 }
 else if (!chtPtrA->matched[2]&&(chtPtrA-  >pi[2]==pi)&&
 (chtPtrA->pi[0]==pli)) {
   chtPtrA->matched[2] = TRUE;
   chtPtrNew->matched[1] = TRUE;
  }
  else if (!chtPtrA->matched[0]&&(chtPtrA-  >pi[0]==p2i)&&
  (chtPtrA->pi[1]==pi)) {
   chtPtrA->matched[0] = TRUE;
   chtPtrNew->matched[2] = TRUE;
  }
  else if (!chtPtrA->matched[1]&&(chtPtrA-  >pi[1]==p2i)&&
  (chtPtrA->pi[2]==pi)) {
   chtPtrA->matched[1] = TRUE;
   chtPtrNew->matched[2] = TRUE;
  }
  else if (!chtPtrA->matched[2]&&(chtPtrA-  >pi[2]==p2i)&&
  (chtPtrA->pi[0]==pi)) {
   chtPtrA->matched[2] = TRUE;
```

FIGURE 25 cont'd.

```
        vchtPtrNew->matched[2] = TRUE;
       }
       else {
         chtPtrA = chtPtrA->next;
        }
    } /* end while */
  } /* end endif */
  else {
    chtPtr = chtPtr->next;
   }
  }
 triList = (int *)malloc(sizeof(int)*count*3);
 chtPtr = chtList;
 for (i=0; i<count; i++) {
  if (chtPtr==NULL) {
     printf("ERROR: count %d doesn't match data structure\n",count);
     return 1;
    }
    triList[3*i] = chtPtr->pi[0];
    triList[3*i+1] = chtPtr->pi[1];
    triList[3*i+2] = chtPtr->pi[2];
    chtPtr=chtPtr->next;
   }
   *numTriangles = count;
   *triangleList = triList;
  return 0;
 }

 void printCHTlist(conHullTri_td *chtPtr)
 {
 printf("CHT list\n");
 while (chtPtr!=NULL) {
  printf("%d:%d:%d ; %d:%d:%d ; %f,%f,%f\n",
   chtPtr->pi[0],chtPtr->pi[1],chtPtr->pi[2],
   chtPtr->matched[0],chtPtr->matched[1],chtPtr->matched[2],
   chtPtr->normal.x,chtPtr->normal.y,chtPtr->normal.z);
   chtPtr = chtPtr->next;
  }
 }
```

FIGURE 25 cont'd.

3. Transformations

3.1 Transforming a point using vector-matrix multiplication

Vector-matrix multiplication is usually how the transformation of a point is represented. Because a vector is just an $N \times 1$ matrix, vector-matrix multiplication is actually a special case of matrix-matrix multiplication. Vector-matrix multiplication is usually performed by premultiplying a column vector by a matrix. This is equivalent to postmultiplying a row vector by the transpose of that same matrix. Both notations are encountered in the graphics literature, but use of the column vector is more common. The examples in Equations 33 and 34 use a 4×4 matrix and a point in three-space using homogeneous coordinates, consistent with what is typically encountered in graphics applications.

$$\begin{bmatrix} Q_x \\ Q_y \\ Q_z \\ Q_w \end{bmatrix} = Q = MP = \begin{bmatrix} M_{11} & M_{12} & M_{13} & M_{14} \\ M_{21} & M_{22} & M_{23} & M_{24} \\ M_{31} & M_{32} & M_{33} & M_{34} \\ M_{41} & M_{42} & M_{43} & M_{44} \end{bmatrix} \begin{bmatrix} P_x \\ P_y \\ P_z \\ P_w \end{bmatrix} \tag{33}$$

$$\begin{bmatrix} Q_x & Q_y & Q_z & Q_w \end{bmatrix} = Q^T = P^T M^T \& = \begin{bmatrix} P_x & P_y & P_z & 1 \end{bmatrix} \begin{bmatrix} M_{11} & M_{21} & M_{31} & M_{41} \\ M_{12} & M_{22} & M_{32} & M_{42} \\ M_{13} & M_{23} & M_{33} & M_{43} \\ M_{14} & M_{24} & M_{34} & M_{44} \end{bmatrix} \tag{34}$$

3.2 Transforming a vector using vector-matrix multiplication

In addition to transforming points, it is also often useful to transform vectors, such as normal vectors, from one space to another. However, the computations used to transform a vector are different from those used to transform a point. Vectors have direction and magnitude but do not have a position in space. Thus, for example, a pure translation has no effect on a vector. If the transformation of one space to another is a pure rotation and uniform scale, then those transformations can be applied directly to the vector. However, it is not so obvious how to apply transformations that incorporate nonuniform scale.

The transformation of a vector can be demonstrated by considering a point, P, which satisfies a planar equation (Eq. 35). Note that (a, b, c) represents a vector normal to the plane. Showing how to transform a planar equation will, in effect, show how to transform a vector. The point is transformed by a matrix, M (Eq. 36). Because the transformations of rotation, translation, and scale preserve planarity, the transformed point, P', will satisfy some new planar equation, N', in the transformed space (Eq. 37). Substituting the definition of the transformed point, Equation 36, into Equation 37 produces Equation 38. If the transformed planar equation is equal to the original normal postmultiplied by the inverse of the transformation matrix (Eq. 39), then Equation 37 is satisfied, as shown by Equation 40. The transformed normal vector is, therefore, (a', b', c').

$$
\begin{aligned}
&ax + by + cz + d = 0 \\
&\begin{bmatrix} a & b & c & d \end{bmatrix} \begin{bmatrix} x \\ y \\ z \\ 1 \end{bmatrix} = 0
\end{aligned}
\tag{35}
$$

$$
\begin{aligned}
N^T P &= 0 \\
P' &= MP
\end{aligned}
\tag{36}
$$

$$N'^T P' = 0 \tag{37}$$

$$N'^T MP = 0 \tag{38}$$

$$N'^T = N^T M^{-1} \tag{39}$$

$$N^T M^{-1} MP = N^T P = 0 \tag{40}$$

In order to transform a vector (a, b, c), treat it as a normal vector for a plane passing through the origin $[a, b, c, 0]$ and postmultiply it by the inverse of the transformation matrix (Eq. 39). If it is desirable to keep all vectors as column vectors, then Equation 41 can be used.

$$N' = \left(N'^T\right)^T = \left(N^T M^{-1}\right)^T = \left(M^{-1}\right)^T N \tag{41}$$

3.3 Axis-angle rotations

Given an axis of rotation $A = [a_x\ a_y\ a_z]$ of unit length and an angle θ to rotate by (Figure 26), the rotation matrix M can be formed by Equation 42. This is a more direct way to rotate a point around an axis, as opposed to implementing the rotation as a series of rotations about the global axes.

$$
\begin{aligned}
\widehat{A} &= \begin{bmatrix} a_x a_x & a_x a_y & a_x a_z \\ a_y a_x & a_y a_y & a_y a_z \\ a_z a_x & a_z a_x & a_z a_z \end{bmatrix} \\
A^* &= \begin{bmatrix} 0 & -a_z & a_y \\ a_z & 0 & -a_x \\ -a_z & a_x & 0 \end{bmatrix} \\
M &= \widehat{A} + \cos\theta\left(I - \widehat{A}\right) + \sin\theta A^* \\
p' &= MP
\end{aligned}
\tag{42}
$$

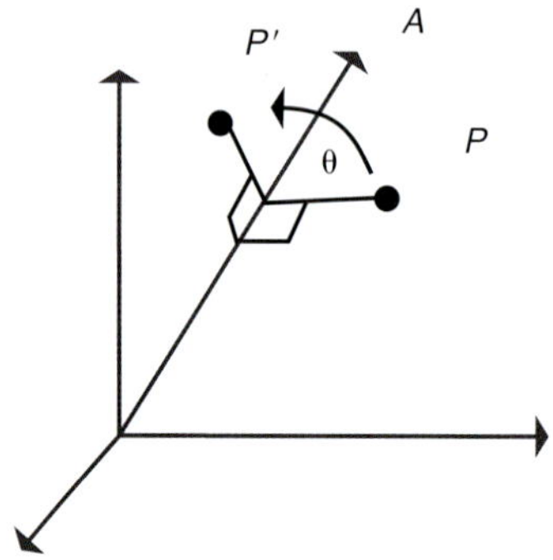

FIGURE 26

Axis-angle rotation.

3.4 Quaternions

Quaternions are discussed in Chapter 2.4. The equations from those chapters, along with additional equations, are collected here to facilitate the discussion.

Quaternion arithmetic

Quaternions are four-tuples and can be considered as a scalar combined with a vector (Eq. 43). Addition and multiplication are defined for quaternions by Equations 44 and 45, respectively. Quaternion multiplication is associative (Eq. 46), but it is not commutative (Eq. 47). The magnitude of a quaternion is computed as the square root of the sum of the squares of its four components (Eq. 48). Quaternion multiplication has an identity (Eq. 49) and an inverse (Eq. 50). The inverse distributes over quaternion multiplication similarly to how the inverse distributes over matrix multiplication (Eq. 51). A quaternion is normalized by dividing it by its magnitude (Eq. 52). Equation 52a is used to compute the quaternion that represents the rotation r such that q represents the halfway rotation between p and r.

$$q = [s, x, y, z] = [s, v] \tag{43}$$

$$[s_1, v_1] + [s_2, v_2] = [s_1 + s_2, v_1 + v_2] \tag{44}$$

$$[s_1, v_1][s_2, v_2] = [s_1, s_2 - v_1 \cdot v_2, s_1 v_2 + s_2 v_1 + v_1 \times v_2] \tag{45}$$

$$(q_1 q_2) q_3 = q_1 (q_2 q_3) \tag{46}$$

$$q_1 q_2 \neq q_2 q_1 \tag{47}$$

$$\|q\| = \sqrt{s^2 + x^2 + y^2 + z^2} \tag{48}$$

$$[s, v][1, (0, 0, 0)] = [s, v] \tag{49}$$

$$\begin{aligned} q^{-1} &= (1/\|q\|)^2 [s, -v] \\ q^{-1} q &= q q^{-1} = [1, (0, 0, 0)] \end{aligned} \tag{50}$$

$$(pq)^{-1} = q^{-1} p^{-1} \tag{51}$$

$$q_{unit} = q/(\|q\|) \tag{52}$$

$$r = 2(p \cdot q) q - p \tag{52a}$$

Rotations by quaternions

A point in space is represented by a vector quantity in quaternion form by using a zero scalar value (Eq. 53). A quaternion can be used to rotate a vector using quaternion multiplication (Eq. 54). Compound rotations can be implemented by premultiplying the corresponding quaternions (Eq. 55), similar to what is routinely done when rotation matrices are used. As should be expected, compounding a rotation with its inverse produces the identity transformation for vectors (Eq. 56). An axis-angle rotation is represented by a unit quaternion, as shown in Equation 57. Any scalar multiple of a quaternion represents the same rotation. In particular, the negation of a quaternion (negating each of its four components, $-q = [-s, -x, y, -z]$) represents the same rotation that the original quaternion represents (Eq. 58).

$$v = [0, x, y, z] \tag{53}$$

$$v' = \mathrm{Rot}(v) = qvq^{-1} \tag{54}$$

$$\begin{aligned} \mathrm{Rot}_q(\mathrm{Rot}_p(v)) &= q(pvp^{-1})q^{-1} \\ &= ((qp)v(p^{-1}q^{-1})) \\ &= ((qp)v(qp^{-1})) \\ &= Rot_{qp}(v) \end{aligned} \tag{55}$$

$$\begin{aligned} \mathrm{Rot}^{-1}(\mathrm{Rot}(v)) &= q^{-1}(qvq^{-1})q \\ &= (q^{-1}q)v(q^{-1}q) = v \end{aligned} \tag{56}$$

$$\mathrm{Rot}_{[0,x,y,z]} = [\cos(\theta/2), \sin(\theta/2)(x, y, z)] \tag{57}$$

$$\begin{aligned} -q &= \mathrm{Rot}_{[-\theta,-x,-y,-z]} \\ &= [\cos(-\theta/2), \sin(-\theta/2)(-(x, y, z))] \\ &= [\cos(\theta/2), -\sin(\theta/2)(-(x, y, z))] \\ &= [\cos(\theta/2), \sin(\theta/2)(x, y, z)] \\ &= \mathrm{Rot}_{[\theta,x,y,z]} \\ &= q \end{aligned} \tag{58}$$

Conversions

It is often useful to convert back and forth between rotation matrices and quaternions. Often, quaternions are used to interpolate between orientations, and the result is converted to a rotation matrix so as to combine it with other matrices in the display pipeline.

Given a unit quaternion $(q = [s, x, y, z], s^2 = x^2 = y^2 = z^2 = 1)$, one can easily determine the corresponding rotation matrix by rotating the three unit vectors that correspond to the principal axes. The rotated vectors are the columns of the equivalent rotation matrix (Eq. 59).

$$M_q = \begin{bmatrix} 1-2y^2-2z^2 & 2xy-2sz & 2xz+2sy \\ 2xy+2sz & 1-2x^2-2z^2 & 2yz-2sx \\ 2xy-2sy & 2yz+2sx & 1-2x^2-2y^2 \end{bmatrix} \quad (59)$$

Given a rotation matrix, one can use the definitions for the terms of the matrix in Equation 59 to solve for the elements of the equivalent unit quaternion. The fact that the unit quaternion has a magnitude of one $\left(s^2 + x^2 + y^2 + z^2 = 1\right)$ makes it easy to see that the diagonal elements sum to $4 = s^2 - 1$.

Summing the diagonal elements of the matrix in Equation 60 results in Equation 61. The diagonal elements can also be used to solve for the remaining terms (Eq. 62). The square roots of these last equations can be avoided if the off-diagonal elements are used to solve for x, y, and z at the expense of testing for a divide by an s that is equal to zero (in which case Eq. 62 can be used).

$$\begin{bmatrix} m_{0,0} & m_{0,1} & m_{0,2} \\ m_{1,0} & m_{1,1} & m_{1,2} \\ m_{2,0} & m_{2,1} & m_{2,2} \end{bmatrix} \quad (60)$$

$$s = \frac{\sqrt{m_{0,0} + m_{1,1} + m_{2,2} + 1}}{2} \quad (61)$$

$$\begin{aligned} m_{0,0} &= 1 - 2y^2 - 2z^2 \\ &= 1 - 2\left(y^2 + z^2\right) \\ &= 1 - 2\left(1 - x^2 - s^2\right) \\ &= -1 + 2x^2 + 2s \end{aligned} \quad (62)$$

$$x = \frac{\sqrt{m_{0,0} + 1 - 2s^2}}{2} \qquad y = \frac{\sqrt{m_{1,1} + 1 - 2s^2}}{2} \qquad z = \frac{\sqrt{m_{2,2} + 1 - 2s^2}}{2} \quad (62a)$$

4. Denavit and Hartenberg representation for linked appendages

4.1 Denavit-Hartenberg notation

The Denavit-Hartenberg (DH) notation is a particular way of describing the relationship of a parent coordinate frame to a child coordinate frame. This convention is commonly used in robotics and often adopted for use in computer animation.

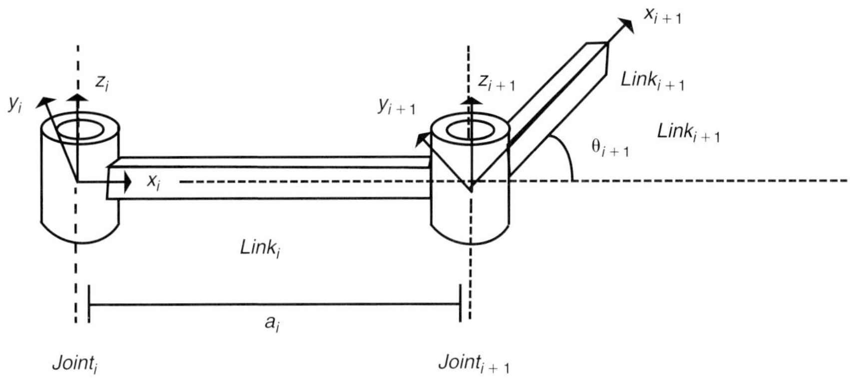

FIGURE 27

DH parameters for planar joints.

Each frame is described relative to an adjacent frame by four parameters that describe the position and orientation of a child frame in relation to its parent's frame. For revolute joints, the z-axis of the joint's frame corresponds to the axis of rotation (prismatic joints are discussed in the next paragraph). The link associated with the joint extends down the x-axis of the frame. First, consider a simple configuration in which the joints and the axes of rotation are coplanar. The distance down the x-axis from one joint to the next is the *link length*, a_i. The *joint angle*, $\theta_i + 1$, is specified by the rotation of the $i + 1$ joint's x-axis, x_{i+1}, about its z-axis relative to the ith frame's x-axis direction, x_i (see Figure 27).

Nonplanar configurations can be represented by including the two other DH parameters. For this general case, the x-axis of the ith joint is defined as the line segment perpendicular to the z-axes of the ith and $i + 1$ frames. The *link twist* parameter, α_i, describes the rotation of the $i + 1$ frame's z-axis about this perpendicular relative to the z-axis of the ith frame. The *link offset* parameter, d_{i+1}, specifies the distance along the z-axis (rotated by α_i) of the $i + 1$ frame from the ith x-axis to the $i + 1$ x-axis (see Figure 28). Notice that the parameters associated with the ith joint do not all relate the ith frame to the $i + 1$ frame. The link length and link twist relate the ith and $i + 1$ frames; the link offset and joint rotation relate the $i - 1$ and ith frames (see Table 1).

Stated another way, the parameters that describe the relationship of the $i + 1$ frame to the ith frame are a combination of ith joint parameters and $i = 1$ joint parameters. The parameters can be paired off to define two *screw transformations*, each of which consists of a translation and rotation relative to a single axis. The offset (d_{i+1}) and angle ($\theta_i + 1$) are the translation and rotation of the $i + 1$ joint relative to the ith joint with respect to the ith joint's z-axis. The length (a_i) and twist (α_i) are the translation and rotation of the $i + 1$ joint with respect to the ith joint's x-axis (see Table 2). The transformation of the $i + 1$ joint's frame from the ith frame can be

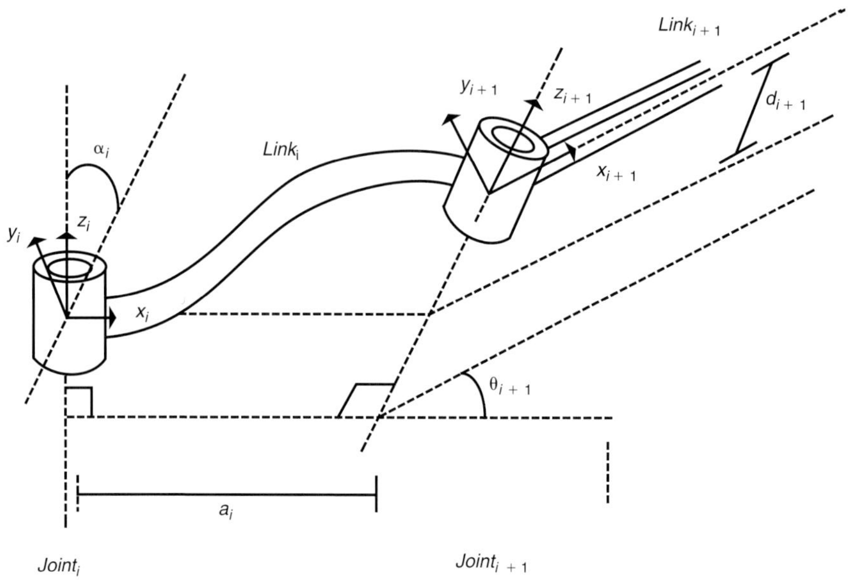

FIGURE 28

DH parameters.

Table 1 DH Joint Parameters for Joint *i*

Name	Symbol	Description
Link offset	d_i	Distance from x_{i-1} to x_i along z_i
Joint angle	y_i	Angle between x_{i-1} and x_i about z_i
Link length	a_i	Distance from z_i to z_{i+1} along x_i
Link twist	a_i	Angle between z_i and z_{i+1} about x_i

Table 2 Parameters That Relate the *i*th Frame and the *i* + 1 Frame

Name	Symbol	Description	Screw Transformation
Link offset	d_{i+1}	Distance from x_i to x_{i+1} along z_{i+1}	Relative to z_{i+1}
Joint angle	$y_i + 1$	Angle between x_i and x_{i+1} about z_{i+1}	Relative to z_{i+1}
Link length	a_i	Distance from z_i to z_{i+1} along x_i	Relative to x_i
Link twist	a_i	Angle between z_i and z_{i+1} about x_i	Relative to x_i

constructed from a series of transformations, each of which corresponds to one of the DH parameters. As an example, consider a point, V_{i+1}, whose coordinates are given in the coordinate system of joint $i+1$. To determine the point's coordinates in terms of the coordinate system of joint i, the transformation shown in Equation 63 is applied.

In Equation 63, T and R represent translation and rotation transformation matrices, respectively; the parameter specifies the amount of rotation or translation, and the subscript specifies the axis involved.

The matrix M maps a point defined in the $i+1$ frame into a point in the ith frame. By forming the M matrix and its inverse associated with each pair of joints, one can convert points from one frame to another, up and down the hierarchy.

4.2 A simple example

Consider the simple three-joint manipulator of Figure 29. The DH parameters are given in Table 3. The linkage is planar, so there are no displacement parameters and no twist parameters. Each successive frame is described by the joint angle and the length of the link.

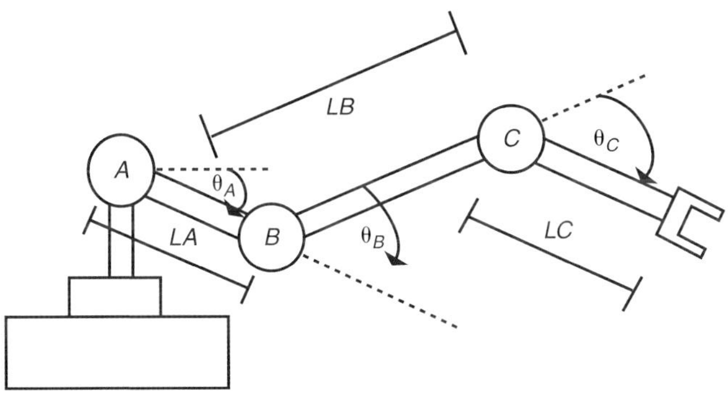

FIGURE 29

Simple manipulator using three revolute joints.

Table 3 Parameters for Three-Revolute Joint Armature

Joint/Parameter	Link Displacement	Joint Angle	Link Length	Link Twist
A	0	θ_A	0	0
B	0	θ_B	LA	0
C	0	θ_C	LB	0

$$V_i = T_x(\alpha_i)R_X(\alpha_i)T_Z(d_i{+}_1)R_Z(\theta_i{+}_1)V_{i+1}$$

$$R_Z(\theta_i{+}_1) = \begin{bmatrix} \cos(\theta_i{+}_1) & (-\sin(\theta_i{+}_1)) & 0 & 0 \\ \sin(\theta_i{+}_1) & \cos(\theta_i{+}_1) & 0 & 0 \\ 0 & 0 & 1 & 0 \\ 0 & 0 & 0 & 1 \end{bmatrix}$$

$$T_Z(d_{i+1}) = \begin{bmatrix} 1 & 0 & 0 & 0 \\ 0 & 1 & 0 & 0 \\ 0 & 0 & 1 & d_{i+1} \\ 0 & 0 & 0 & 1 \end{bmatrix}$$

$$R_X(\alpha_i) = \begin{bmatrix} 1 & 0 & 0 & 0 \\ 0 & \cos(\alpha_i) & -\sin(\alpha_i) & 0 \\ 0 & \sin(\alpha_i) & \cos(\alpha_i) & 0 \\ 0 & 0 & 0 & 1 \end{bmatrix}$$

$$T_X(ai) = \begin{bmatrix} 1 & 0 & 0 & a_i \\ 0 & 1 & 0 & 0 \\ 0 & 0 & 1 & 0 \\ 0 & 0 & 0 & 1 \end{bmatrix}$$

$$V_i = M_i^{i+1} V_i + 1$$

$$M_i^{i+1} = \begin{bmatrix} \cos(\theta_{i+1}) & -\sin(\theta_{i+1}) & 0 & a_i \\ \cos(\alpha_i)\sin(\theta_{i+1}) & \cos(\alpha_i)\cos(\theta_{i+1}) & -\sin(\alpha_i) & (-d_{i+1})\sin(\alpha_i) \\ \sin(\alpha_i)\sin(\theta_{i+1}) & \sin(\alpha_i)\cos(\theta_{i+1}) & \cos(\alpha_i) & d_{i+1}\cos(\alpha_i) \\ 0 & 0 & 0 & 1 \end{bmatrix} \tag{63}$$

4.3 Including a ball-and-socket joint

Some human joints are conveniently modeled using a ball-and-socket joint. Consider an armature with a hinge joint, followed by a ball-and-socket joint followed by another hinge joint, as shown in Figure 30.

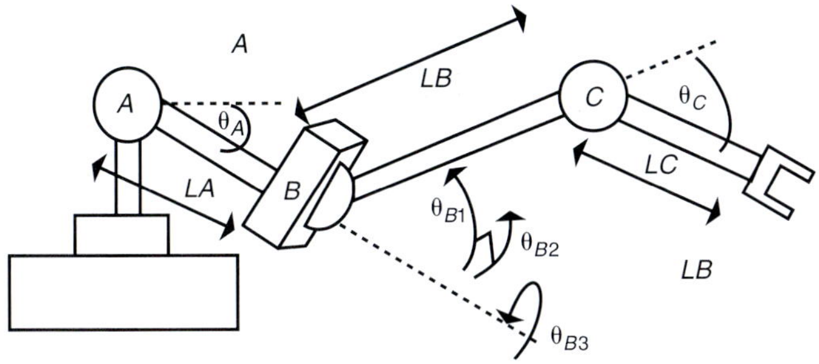

FIGURE 30

Incorporating a ball-and-socket joint.

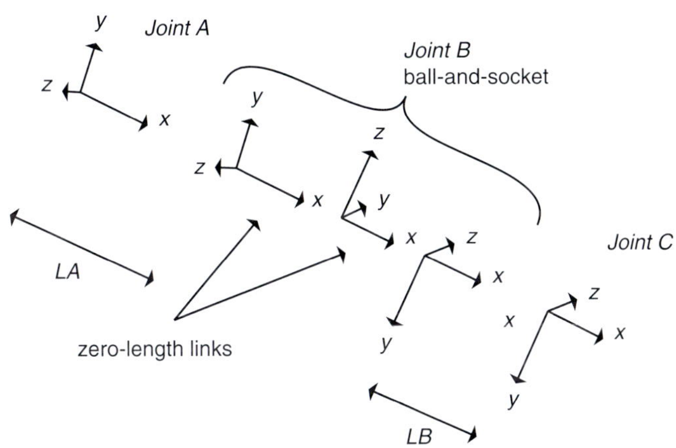

FIGURE 31

Coordinate axes induced by the DH representation of a ball-and-socket joint.

The DH notation can represent the ball-and-socket joint by three single degree-of-freedom (DOF) joints with zero-length links between them (see Figure 31).

Notice that in a default configuration with joint angles set to zero, the DH model of the ball-and-socket joint is in a gimbal lock position (incrementally changing two of the parameters results in rotation about the same axis). The first and third DOFs of that joint are aligned. The z-axes of these joints are colinear because the links between them are zero length and the two link twist parameters relating them are 90 degrees. This results in a total of 180 degrees and thus aligns the axes. As a consequence, the representation of the ball-and-socket joint is usually initialized with the middle of the three joint angles set to 90 degrees (see Table 4).

Table 4 Joint Parameters for Ball-and-Socket Joint

Joint/Parameter	Link Displacement	Joint Angle	Link Length	Link Twist
A	0	θ_A	0	0
B_1	0	θ_{B1}	LA	90
B_2	0	$90 + \theta_{B2}$	0	90
B_3	0	θ_{B3}	0	0
C	0	θ_C	LB	0

4.4 Constructing the frame description

Because each frame's displacement and joint angle are defined relative to the previous frame, a Frame_0 is defined so that the Frame_1 displacement and angle can be defined relative to it. Frame_0 is typically defined so that it coincides with Frame_1 with zero displacement and zero joint angle. Similarly, because the link of the last frame does not connect to anything, the x-axis of the last frame is chosen so that it coincides with the x-axis of the previous frame when the joint angle is zero; the origin of the nth frame is chosen as the intersection of the x-axis of the previous frame and the joint axis when the displacement is zero.

The following procedure can be used to construct the frames for intermediate joints.

1. For each joint, identify the axis of rotation for revolute joints and the axis of displacement for prismatic joints. Refer to this axis as the z-axis of the joint's frame.
2. For each adjacent pair of joints, the ith $-$ 1 and ith for i from 1 to n, construct the common perpendicular between the z-axes or, if they intersect, the perpendicular to the plane that contains them. Refer to the intersection of the perpendicular and the ith frame's z-axis (or the point of intersection of the two axes) as the origin of the ith frame. Refer to the perpendicular as the x-axis of the ith frame (see Figure 32).
3. Construct the y-axis of each frame to be consistent with the right-hand rule (assuming right-hand space).

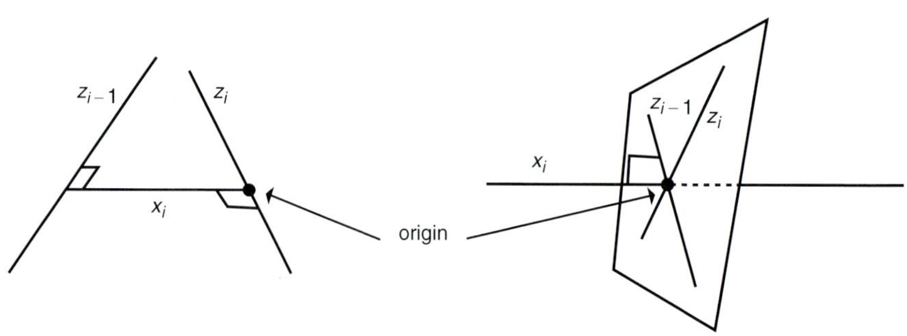

FIGURE 32

Determining the origin and x-axis of the ith frame.

5. Interpolating and approximating curves

This section covers many of the basic terms and concepts needed to interpolate values in computer animation. It is not a complete treatise of curves but an overview of the important ones. While many of the terms and concepts discussed are applicable to functions in general, they are presented as they relate to functions having to do with the practical interpolation of points in Euclidean space as typically used in computer animation applications. For more complete discussions of the topics contained here, see, for example, Mortenson [14], Rogers and Adams [18], Farin [4], and Bartels, Beatty, and Barsky [1].

5.1 Equations: some basic terms

For present purposes, there are three types of equations: *explicit, implicit*, and *parametric*. *Explicit* equations are of the form $y = f(x)$. The explicit form is good for generating points because it generates a value of y for any value of x put into the function. The drawback of the explicit form is that it is dependent on the choice of coordinate axes, and it is ambiguous if there is more than one y for a given x (such as $y = \sqrt{x}$, in which an input value of 4 would generate values of 2 or -2). *Implicit equations* are of the form $f(x, y) = 0$. The implicit form is good for testing to see if a point is on a curve because the coordinates of the point can easily be put into the equation for the curve and checked to see if the equation is satisfied. The drawback of the implicit form is that generating a series of points along a curve is often desired, and implicit forms are not generative. *Parametric equations* are of the form $x = f(t), y = g(t)$. For any given value of t, a point (x, y) is generated. This form is good for generating a sequence of points as ordered values of t are given. The parametric form is also useful because it can be used for multivalued functions of x, which are problematic for explicit equations.

Functions can be classified according to the terms contained in them. Functions that contain only variables raised to a power are *polynomial* functions. If the highest power is one, then the function is *linear*. If the highest power is two, then the function is *quadratic*. If the highest power is three, then it is *cubic*. The highest power of a polynomial function of a single variable is referred to as the *degree* of the polynomial. If the function is not a simple polynomial but rather contains sines, cosines, log, or a variety of other functions, then it is called *transcendental*. In computer graphics, the most commonly encountered type of function is the cubic polynomial.

Continuity refers to how well behaved the curve is in a mathematical sense. For a value arbitrarily close to an x_0 if the function is arbitrarily close to $f(x_0)$, then it has *positional*, or *zeroth-order*, continuity (C^0) at that point. If the slope of the curve (or the first derivative of the function) is continuous, then the function has *tangential*, or *first-order*, continuity (C^1). This is extended to all of the function's derivatives, although for purposes of computer animation the concern is with first-order continuity or, possibly, *second-order*, or *curvature*, continuity (C^2). Polynomials are infinitely continuous.

If a curve is pieced together from individual curve segments, one can speak of *piecewise properties*—the properties of the individual pieces. For example, a sequence of straight line segments, sometimes called a *polyline* or a *wire*, is piecewise linear. A major concern regarding piecewise curves is the continuity conditions at the junctions of the curve segments. A junction has C^0 *continuity*, or is C^0 *continuous*, if one curve segment begins where the previous segment ends. This is referred to as *zeroth-order*, or *positional*, continuity at the junction. If the beginning tangent of one curve segment is the same as the ending tangent of the previous curve segment, then there is *first-order*, or *tangential*, continuity at the junction. The junction is C^1 continuous if it has tangential and positional continuity. If the beginning curvature of one curve segment is the same as the ending curvature of the previous curve segment, then there is *second-order*, or *curvature*, continuity at the junction. The junction is C^2 continuous if it has curvature, tangential, and positional continuity. Typically, computer animation is not concerned with continuity beyond second order.

Sometimes in discussions of the continuity at segment junctions, a distinction is made between *parametric continuity* and *geometric continuity* (e.g., [14]). So far the discussion has concerned parametric continuity. Geometric continuity is less restrictive. First-order parametric continuity, for example, requires that the ending tangent vector of the first segment be the same as the beginning tangent vector of the second. First-order geometric continuity, on the other hand, requires that only the direction of the tangents be the same, and it allows the magnitudes of the tangents to be different. Similar definitions exist for higher-order geometric continuity. One distinction worth mentioning is that parametric continuity is sensitive to the rate at which the parameter varies relative to the length of the curve traced out. Geometric continuity is not sensitive to this rate.

When a curve is constructed from a set of points and the curve passes through the points, it is said to *interpolate* the points. However, if the points are used to control the general shape of the curve, with the curve not necessarily passing through them, then the curve is said to *approximate the points*. *Interpolation* is also used generally to refer to all approaches for constructing a curve from a set of points. For a given interpolation technique, if the resulting curve is guaranteed to lie within the convex hull of the set of points, then it is said to have the *convex hull property*.

5.2 Simple linear interpolation: geometric and algebraic forms

Simple linear interpolation is given by Equation 64 and shown in Figure 33. Notice that the interpolants, $1 - u$ and u, sum to one. This property ensures that the interpolating curve (in this case a straight line) falls within the convex hull of the

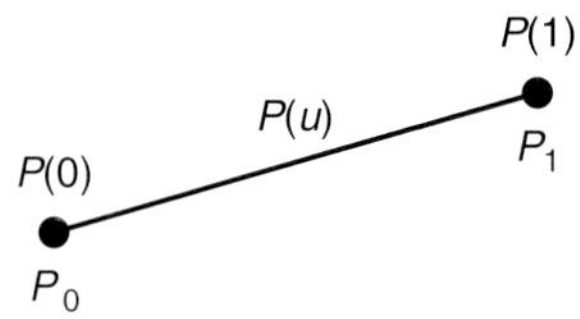

FIGURE 33

Linear interpolation.

geometric entities being interpolated (in this simple case the convex hull is the straight line itself).

$$P(u) = (1 - u)P_0 + uP_1 \tag{64}$$

Using more general notation, one can rewrite Equation 64 as in Equation 65. Here, F_0 and F_1 are called blending functions. This is referred to as the geometric form because the geometric information, in this case P_0 and P_1, is explicit in the equation.

$$P(u) = F_0(u)P_0 + F_1(u)P_1 \tag{65}$$

The linear interpolation equation can also be rewritten as in Equation 66. This form is typical of polynomial equations in which the terms are collected according to coefficients of the variable raised to a power. It is more generally written as Equation 67. In this case there are only linear terms. This way of expressing the equation is referred to as the *algebraic* form.

$$P(u) = (P_1 - P_0)u + P_0 \tag{66}$$

$$P(u) = a_1 u + a_0 \tag{67}$$

Alternatively, both of these forms can be put in a *matrix representation*. The geometric form becomes Equation 68 and the algebraic form becomes Equation 69. The geometric form is useful in situations in which the geometric information (the points defining the curve) needs to be frequently updated or replaced. The algebraic form is useful for repeated evaluation of a single curve for different values of the parameter. The fully expanded form is shown in Equation 70. The curves discussed next can all be written in this form. Of course, depending on the actual curve type, the U (variable), M (coefficient), and B (geometric information) matrices will contain different values.

$$P(u) = \begin{bmatrix} F_0(u) \\ F_1(u) \end{bmatrix} [P_0 P_1] = FB^T \tag{68}$$

$$P(u) = \begin{bmatrix} u & 1 \end{bmatrix} \begin{bmatrix} a_1 \\ a_0 \end{bmatrix} = U^T A \tag{69}$$

$$P(u) = \begin{bmatrix} u & 1 \end{bmatrix} \begin{bmatrix} -1 & 1 \\ 1 & 0 \end{bmatrix} \begin{bmatrix} P_1 \\ P_0 \end{bmatrix} = U^T MB = FB = U^T A \tag{70}$$

5.3 Parameterization by arc length

It should be noted that in general there is not a linear relationship between changes in the parameter u and the distance traveled along a curve (its *arc length*). It happens to be true in the previous example concerning a straight line and the parameter u. However, as Mortenson [14] points out, there are other equations that trace out a straight line in space that are fairly convoluted in their relationship between changes in the parameter and distance traveled. For example, consider Equation 71, which is linear in P_0 and P_1. That is, it traces out a straight line in space between P_0 and P_1. However, it is nonlinear in u. As a result, the curve is not traced out in a nice monotonic, constant-velocity manner. The nonlinear relationship is evident in most parameterized curves unless special care is taken to ensure constant velocity.

$$P(u) = P_0 + ((1-u)u + u)(P_1 - P_0) \tag{71}$$

5.4 Computing derivatives

One of the matrix forms for parametric curves, as shown in Equation 70 for linear interpolation, is U^TMB. Parametric curves of any polynomial order can be put into this matrix form. Often, it is useful to compute the derivatives of a parametric curve. This can be done easily by taking the derivative of the U vector. For example, the first two derivatives of a cubic curve, shown in Equation 72, are easily evaluated for any value of u.

$$\begin{aligned} P(u) &= U^TMB = \begin{vmatrix} u^3 & u^2 & u & 1 \end{vmatrix} MB \\ P'(u) &= U'^TMB = \begin{vmatrix} 3u^3 & 2u & 1 & 0 \end{vmatrix} MB \\ P''(u) &= U''^TMB = \begin{vmatrix} 6u & 2 & 0 & 0 \end{vmatrix} MB \end{aligned} \tag{72}$$

5.5 Hermite interpolation

Hermite interpolation generates a cubic polynomial from one point to another. In addition to specifying the beginning and ending points (P_i, P_{i+1}), the user needs to supply beginning and ending tangent vectors (P'_i, P'_{i+1}) as well (Figure 34).

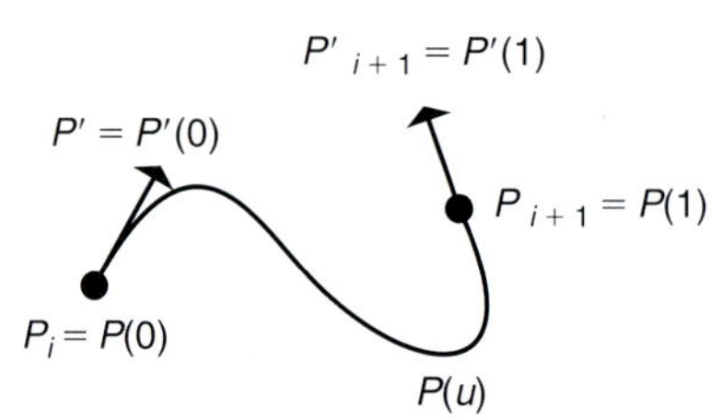

FIGURE 34

Hermite interpolation.

The general matrix form for a curve is repeated in Equation 73, and the Hermite matrices are given in Equation 74.

$$P(u) = U^T MB \tag{73}$$

$$U^T = \begin{bmatrix} u^3 & u^2 & u & 1 \end{bmatrix}$$
$$M = \begin{bmatrix} 2 & -2 & 1 & 1 \\ -3 & 3 & -2 & -1 \\ 0 & 0 & 1 & 0 \\ 1 & 0 & 0 & 0 \end{bmatrix} \tag{74}$$
$$B = \begin{bmatrix} P_i \\ P_{i+1} \\ P_{i+1} \\ P'_i \\ P'_{i+1} \end{bmatrix}$$

Continuity between beginning and ending tangent vectors of connected segments is ensured by merely using the ending tangent vector of one segment as the beginning tangent vector of the next. A composite Hermite curve (piecewise cubic with first-order continuity at the junctions) is shown in Figure 35.

Trying to put a Hermite curve through a large number of points, which requires the user to specify all of the needed tangent vectors, can be a burden. There are several techniques to get around this. One is to enforce second-degree continuity. This requirement provides enough constraints so that the user does not have to provide interior tangent vectors; they can be calculated automatically. See Rogers and Adams [18] or Mortenson [14] for alternative formulations. A more common technique is the Catmull-Rom spline.

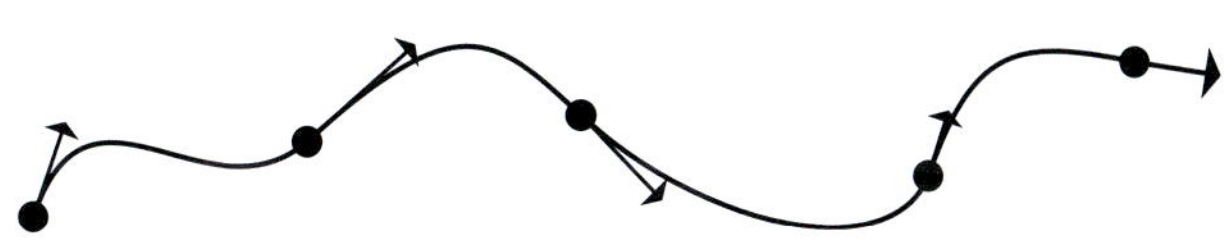

FIGURE 35

Composite Hermite curve.

5.6 Catmull-Rom spline

The Catmull-Rom curve can be viewed as a Hermite curve in which the tangents at the interior control points are automatically generated according to a relatively simple geometric procedure (as opposed to the more involved numerical techniques referred to above). For each interior point, P_i, the tangent at that point, P'_i, is computed as one-half the vector from the previous control point, $P_i - 1$, to the next control point, $P_i + 1$ (Eq. 75), as shown in Figure 36.[1] The matrices for the Catmull-Rom curve in general matrix form are given in Equation 76. A Catmull-Rom spline is a specific type of cardinal spline.

$$P_i' = (1/2)(P_{i+1} - P_{i-1}) \tag{75}$$

$$U^T = \begin{bmatrix} u^3 & u^2 & u & 1 \end{bmatrix}$$
$$M = \frac{1}{2}\begin{bmatrix} -1 & 3 & -3 & 1 \\ 2 & -5 & 4 & -1 \\ -1 & 0 & 1 & 0 \\ 0 & 2 & 0 & 0 \end{bmatrix}$$
$$B = \begin{bmatrix} P_{i-1} \\ P_i \\ P_{i+1} \\ P_{i+1} \end{bmatrix} \tag{76}$$

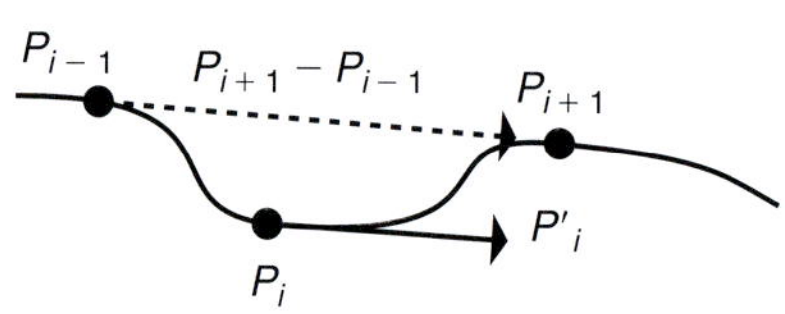

FIGURE 36

Catmull-Rom spline.

[1] Farin [4] describes the Catmull-Rom spline curve in terms of a cubic Bezier curve by defining interior control points. Placement of the interior control points is determined by use of an auxiliary knot vector. With a uniform distance between knot values, the control points are displaced from the point to be interpolated by one-sixth of the vector from the previous interpolated point to the next interpolated point. Tangent vectors are three times the vector from an interior control point to the interpolated point. This results in the Catmull-Rom tangent vector described here.

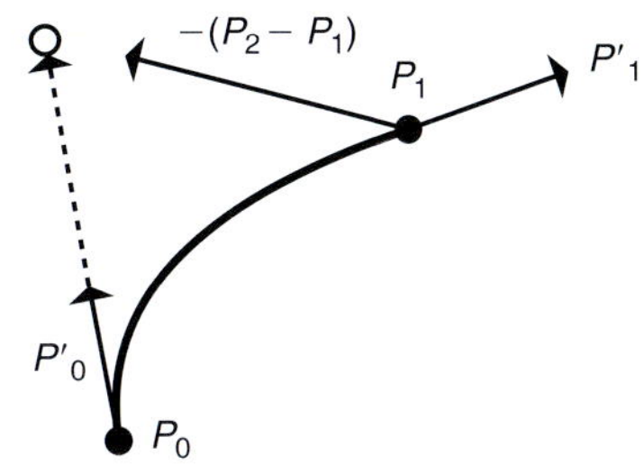

FIGURE 37

Automatically forming the initial tangent of a Catmull-Rom spline.

FIGURE 38

Catmull-Rom spline with end conditions using Equation 77.

For the end conditions, the user can provide tangent vectors at the very beginning and at the very end of the cubic curve. Alternatively, various automatic techniques can be used. For example, the beginning tangent vector can be defined as follows. The vector from the second point (P_1) to the third point (P_2) is subtracted from the second point and used as a virtual point to which the initial tangent is directed. This tangent is computed by Equation 77. Figure 37 shows the formation of the initial tangent curve according to the equation, and Figure 38 shows a curve that uses this technique.

$$P'(0.0) = \frac{1}{2}(P_1 - (P_2 - P_1) - P_0) = \frac{1}{2}(2P_1 - P_2 - P_0) \tag{77}$$

A drawback of the Catmull Rom formulation is that an internal tangent vector is not dependent on the position of the internal point relative to its two neighbors. In Figure 39, all three positions (Q_i, P_i, R_i) for the ith point would have the same tangent vector.

An advantage of Catmull-Rom is that the calculation to compute the internal tangent vectors is extremely simple and fast. However, for each segment the tangent computation is a one-time-only cost. It is then used repeatedly in the computation for each new point in that segment. Therefore it often makes sense to spend a little more time computing more appropriate internal tangent vectors to obtain a better set of points along the segment. One alternative is to use a vector perpendicular to the plane that bisects the angle made by $P_{i-1} - P_i$ and $P_{i+1} - P_i$ (Figure 40). This can be computed easily by adding the normalized vector from P_{i-1} to P_i with the normalized vector from P_i to P_{i+1}.

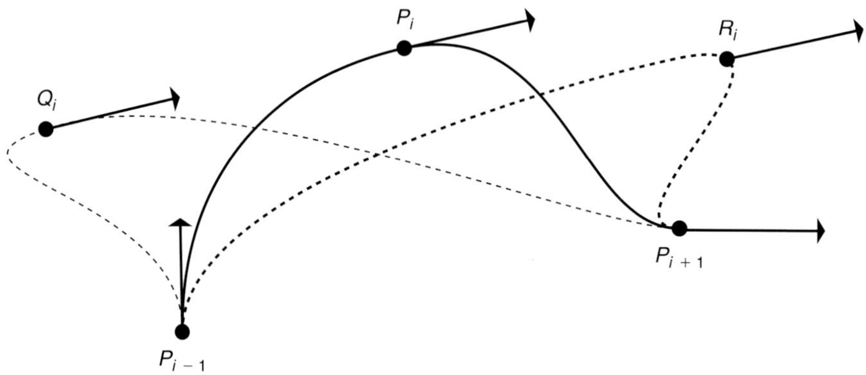

FIGURE 39

Three curve segments, (P_{i-1}, P_i, P_{i+1}), (P_{i-1}, Q_i, P_{i+1}), and (P_{i-1}, R_i, P_{i+1}), using the standard Catmull-Rom form for computing the internal tangent.

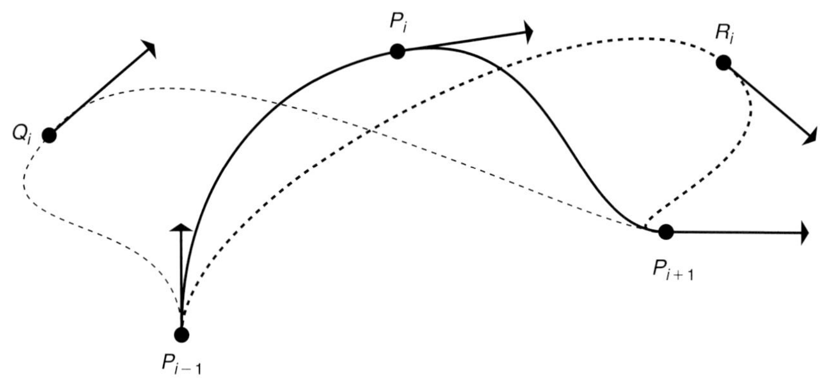

FIGURE 40

Three curve segments, (P_{i-1}, P_i, P_{i+1}), (P_{i-1}, Q_i, P_{i+1}), and (P_{i-1}, R_i, P_{i+1}), using the perpendicular to the angle bisector for computing the internal tangent.

Another modification, which can be used with the original Catmull-Rom tangent computation or with the previously mentioned bisector technique, is to use the relative position of the internal point (P_i) to independently determine the length of the tangent vector for each segment it is associated with. Thus a point P_i has an ending tangent vector associated with it for the segment from P_{i-1} to P_i as well as a beginning tangent vector associated with it for the segment P_i to P_{i+1}. These tangents have the same direction but different lengths. This relaxes the C^1 continuity of the Catmull-Rom spline and uses G^1 continuity instead. For example, an initial tangent vector at an interior point is determined as the vector from P_{i-1} to P_{i+1}. The ending tangent vector for the segment P_{i-1} to P_i is computed by scaling this initial tangent

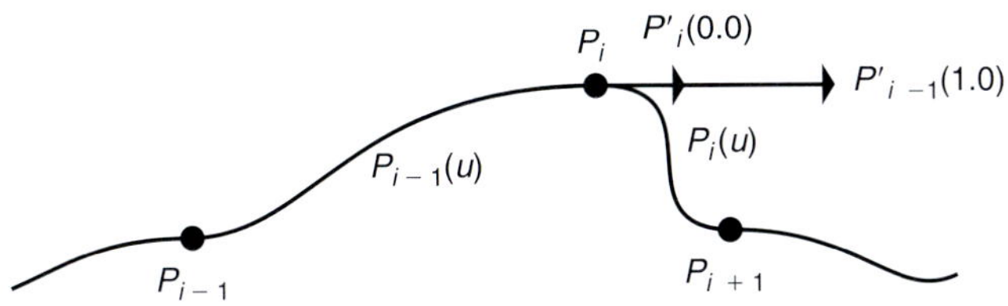

FIGURE 41

Interior tangents based on relative segment lengths.

vector by the ratio of the distance between the points P_i and P_{i-1} to the distance between points P_{i-1} and P_{i+1}. Referring to the segment between P_{i-1} and P_i as $P_{i-1}(u)$ results in Equation 78. A similar calculation for the beginning tangent vector of the segment between P_i and P_{i+1} results in Equation 79. These tangents can be seen in Figure 41. The computational cost of this approach is only a little more than the standard Catmull-Rom spline and seems to give more intuitive results.

$$P'_{i-1}(1.0) = \frac{|P_i - P_{i-1}|}{|P_{i+1} - P_{i-1}|}(P_{i+1} - P_{i-1}) \tag{78}$$

$$P'_i(0.0) = \frac{|P_{i+1} - P_i|}{|P_{i+1} - P_{i-1}|}(P_{i+1} - P_{i-1}) \tag{79}$$

5.7 Four-point form

Fitting a cubic segment to four points (P_0, P_1, P_2, P_3) assigned to user-specified parametric values (u_0, u_1, u_2, u_3) can be accomplished by setting up the linear system of equations for the points (Eq. 80) and solving for the unknown coefficient matrix. In the case of parametric values of 0, 1/3, 2/3, and 1, the matrix is given by Equation 81. However, with this form it is difficult to join segments with C^1 continuity.

$$P(u) = \begin{bmatrix} u^3 & u^2 & u & 1 \end{bmatrix} \begin{bmatrix} m_{0,0} & m_{0,1} & m_{0,2} & m_{0,3} \\ m_{1,0} & m_{1,1} & m_{1,2} & m_{1,3} \\ m_{2,0} & m_{2,1} & m_{2,2} & m_{2,3} \\ m_{3,0} & m_{3,1} & m_{3,2} & m_{3,3} \end{bmatrix} \begin{bmatrix} P_0 \\ P_1 \\ P_2 \\ P_3 \end{bmatrix}$$

$$\begin{bmatrix} P_0 \\ P_1 \\ P_2 \\ P_3 \end{bmatrix} = \begin{bmatrix} u_0^3 & u_0^2 & u_0 & 1 \\ u_1^3 & u_1^2 & u_1 & 1 \\ u_2^3 & u_2^2 & u_2 & 1 \\ u_3^3 & u_3^2 & u_3 & 1 \end{bmatrix} \begin{bmatrix} m_{0,0} & m_{0,1} & m_{0,2} & m_{0,3} \\ m_{1,0} & m_{1,1} & m_{1,2} & m_{1,3} \\ m_{2,0} & m_{2,1} & m_{2,2} & m_{2,3} \\ m_{3,0} & m_{3,1} & m_{3,2} & m_{3,3} \end{bmatrix} \begin{bmatrix} P_0 \\ P_1 \\ P_2 \\ P_3 \end{bmatrix} \tag{80}$$

$$M = \frac{1}{2}\begin{bmatrix} -9 & 27 & -27 & - \\ 18 & -45 & 36 & -9 \\ -11 & 18 & -9 & 2 \\ 2 & 0 & 0 & 0 \end{bmatrix} \tag{81}$$

5.8 Blended parabolas

Blending overlapping parabolas to define a cubic segment is another approach to interpolating a curve through a set of points. In addition, the end conditions are handled by parabolic segments, which is consistent with how the interior segments are defined. Blending parabolas results in a formulation that is very similar to Catmull-Rom in that each segment is defined by four points, it is an interpolating curve, and local control is provided. Under the assumptions used here for Catmull-Rom and the blended parabolas, the interpolating matrices are identical.

For each overlapping triple of points, a parabolic curve is defined by the three points. A cubic curve segment is created by linearly interpolating between the two overlapping parabolic segments. More specifically, take the first three points, P_0, P_1, and P_2, and fit a parabola, $P(u)$, through them using the following constraints: $P(0.0) = P_0, P(0.5) = P_1, P(1.0) = P_2$. Take the next group of three points, P_1, P_2, P_3, which partially overlap the first set of three points, and fit a parabola, $R(u)$, through them using similar constraints: $R(0.0) = P_1, R(0.5) = P_2, R(1.0) = P_3$. Between points P_1 and P_2 the two parabolas overlap. Reparameterize this region into the range [0.0, 1.0] and linearly blend the two parabolic segments (Figure 42). The result can be put in matrix form for a cubic curve using the four points as the geometric information together with the coefficient matrix shown in Equation 82. To interpolate a list of points, this matrix is used by varying U as in previous examples.

$$M = \frac{1}{2}\begin{bmatrix} -1 & 3 & -3 & 1 \\ 2 & -5 & 4 & -1 \\ -1 & 0 & 1 & 0 \\ 0 & 2 & 0 & 0 \end{bmatrix} \tag{82}$$

End conditions can be handled by constructing parabolic arcs at the very beginning and very end (Figure 43). For example, referring to the first three points as p_0, p_1, and p_2, Equation 83 can be used to solve for the constants of the parabolic equation $P(u) = au^2 + bu + c$.

FIGURE 42

Parabolic blend segment.

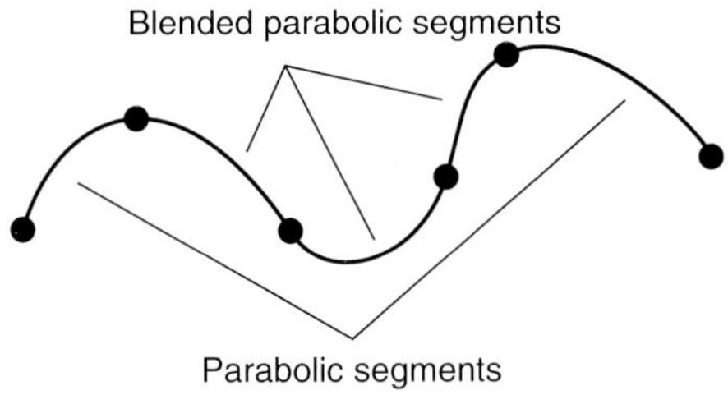

FIGURE 43

Multiple parabolic blend segments.

$$\begin{aligned} P(0) &= c = p_0 \\ P(0.5) &= a(0.5)^2 + b(0.5) + c = p_1 \\ P(1.0) &= a + b + c = p_2 \end{aligned} \tag{83}$$

This form assumes that all points are equally spaced in parametric space. Often it is the case that even spacing is not present. In such cases, relative chord length can be used to estimate parametric values. The derivation is a bit more involved [18], but the final result can still be formed into a 4 × 4 matrix and used to produce a cubic polynomial in the interior segments.

5.9 Bezier interpolation/approximation

A cubic Bezier curve is defined by the beginning point and the ending point, which are interpolated, and two interior points, which control the shape of the curve. The cubic Bezier curve is similar to the Hermite form. The Hermite form uses beginning and ending tangent vectors to control the shape of the curve; the Bezier form uses auxiliary control points to define tangent vectors. A cubic curve is defined by four points: P_0, P_1, P_2, and P_3. The beginning and ending points of the curve are P_0 and P_3, respectively. The interior control points used to control the shape of the curve and define the beginning and ending tangent vectors are P_1 and P_2 (see Figure 44). The coefficient matrix for a single cubic Bezier curve is shown in Equation 84. In the cubic case, $P'(0) = 3(P_1 - P_0)$ and $P'(1) = 3(P_3 - P_2)$.

$$M = \begin{bmatrix} -1 & 3 & -3 & 1 \\ 3 & -6 & 3 & 0 \\ -3 & 3 & 0 & 0 \\ 1 & 0 & 0 & 0 \end{bmatrix} \tag{84}$$

Continuity between adjacent Bezier segments can be controlled by colinearity of the control points on either side of the shared beginning/ending point of the two curve segments where they join (Figure 45). In addition, the Bezier curve form

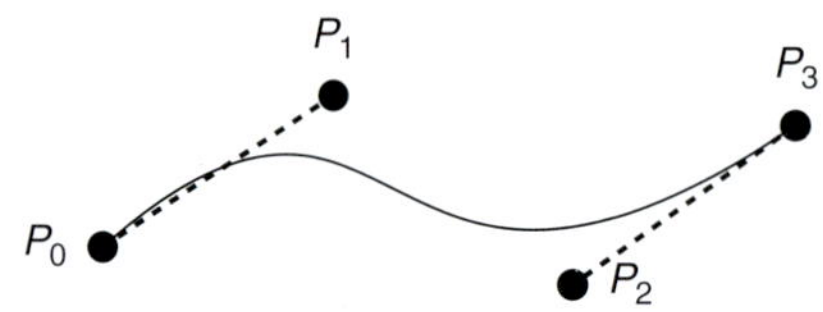

FIGURE 44

Cubic Bezier curve segment.

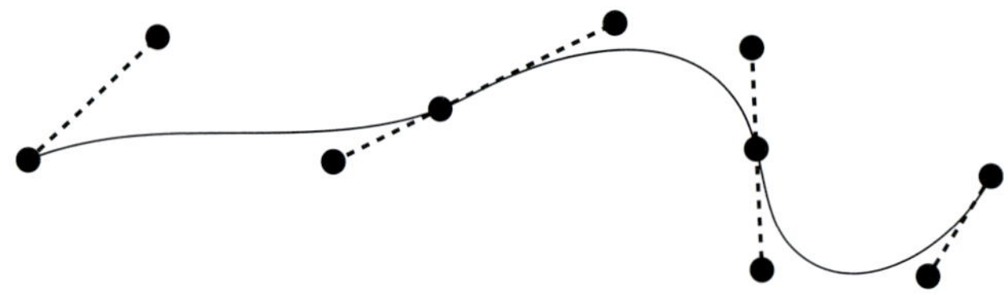

FIGURE 45

Composite cubic Bezier curve showing tangents and colinear control points.

allows one to define a curve of arbitrary order. If three interior control points are used, then the resulting curve will be quartic; if four interior control points are used, then the resulting curve will be quintic. See Mortenson [14] for a more complete discussion.

5.10 De Casteljau construction of Bezier curves

The de Casteljau method is a way to geometrically construct a Bezier curve. Figure 46 shows the construction of a point at $u = 1/3$. This method constructs a point u along the way between paired control points (identified by a "1" in Figure 46). Then points are constructed u along the way between points just previously constructed. These new points are marked "2" in Figure 46. In the cubic case, in which there were four initial points, there are two newly constructed points. The point on the curve is constructed by going u along the way between these two points. This can be done for any values of u and for any order of curve. Higher-order Bezier curves require more iterations to produce the final point on the curve.

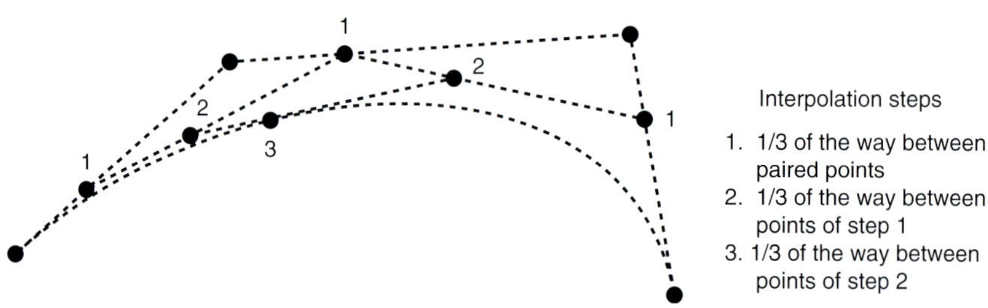

FIGURE 46

De Casteljau construction of a point on a cubic Bezier curve.

5.11 Tension, continuity, and bias control

Often an animator wants better control over the interpolation of keyframes than the standard interpolating splines provide. For better control of the shape of an interpolating curve, Kochanek [11] suggests a parameterization of the internal tangent vectors based on the three values: tension, continuity, and bias. The three parameters are explained by decomposing each internal tangent vector into an incoming part and an outgoing part. These tangents are referred to as the left and right parts, respectively, and are notated by T^L and T^R for the tangents at P_i.

Tension controls the sharpness of the bend of the curve at P_i. It does this by means of a scale factor that changes the length of both the incoming and outgoing tangents at the control point (Eq. 85). In the default case, $t = 0$ and the tangent vector is the average of the two adjacent chords or, equivalently, half of the chord between the two adjacent points, as in the Catmull-Rom spline. As the tension parameter, t, goes to one, the tangents become shorter until they reach zero. Shorter tangents at the control point mean that the curve is pulled closer to a straight line in the neighborhood of the control point (see Figure 47).

$$T_i^L = T_i^R = (1-t)\frac{1}{2}((P_{i+1} - P_i) + (P_i - P_{i-1})) \tag{85}$$

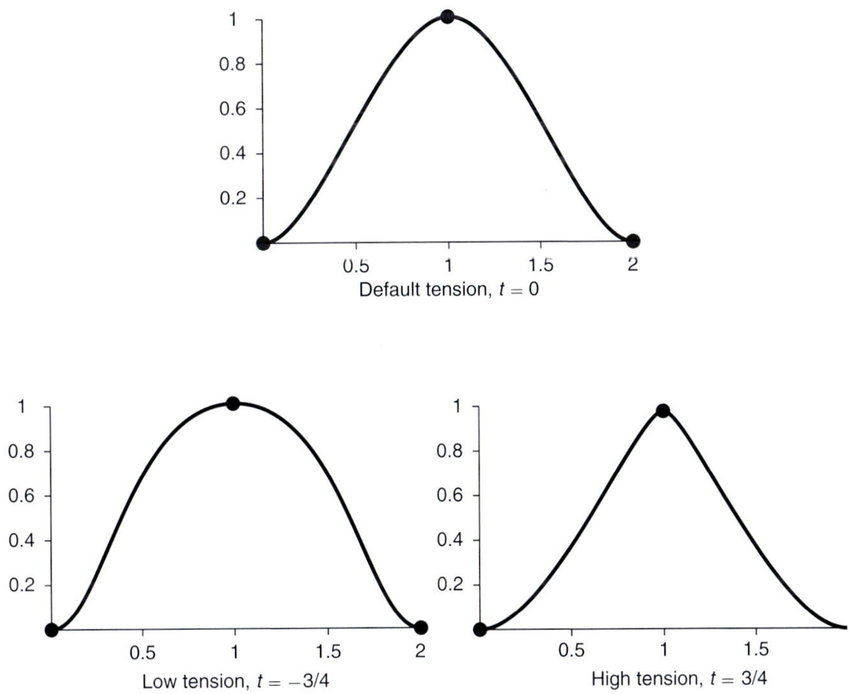

FIGURE 47

The effect of varying the tension parameter.

The continuity parameter, c, gives the user control over the continuity of the curve at the control point where the two curve segments join. The incoming (left) and outgoing (right) tangents at a control point are defined symmetrically with respect to the chords on either side of the control point. Assuming default tension, c blends the adjacent chords to form the two tangents, as shown in Equation 86.

$$\begin{aligned} T_i^L &= \frac{1-c}{2}(P_i - P_{i-1}) + \frac{1+c}{2}(P_{i+1} - P_i) \\ T_i^R &= \frac{1+c}{2}(P_i - P_{i-1}) + \frac{1-c}{2}(P_{i+1} - P_i) \end{aligned} \tag{86}$$

The default value for continuity is $c = 0$, which produces equal left and right tangent vectors, resulting in continuity at the joint. As c approaches -1, the left tangent approaches equality with the chord to the left of the control point and the right tangent approaches equality with the chord to the right of the control point. As c approaches $+1$, the definitions of the tangents reverse themselves, and the left tangent approaches the right chord and the right tangent approaches the left chord (see Figure 48).

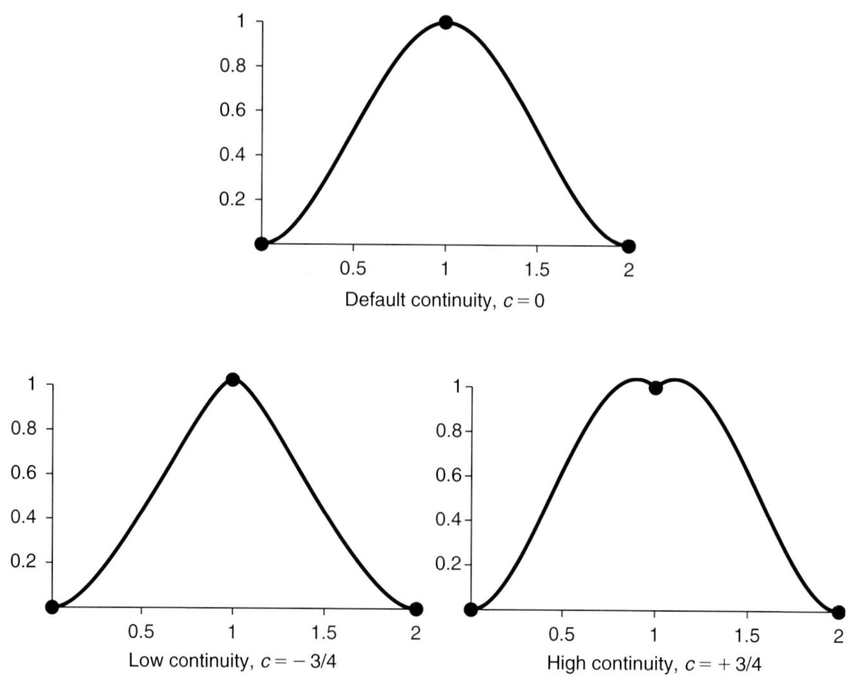

FIGURE 48

The effect of varying the continuity parameter (with default tension).

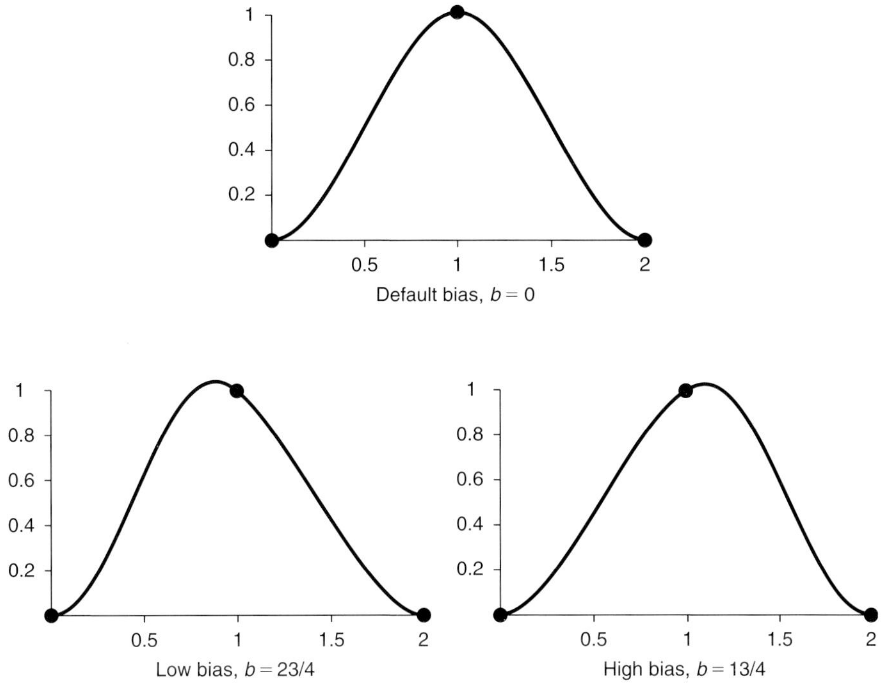

FIGURE 49

The effect of varying the bias parameter (with default tension and continuity).

Bias, b, defines a common tangent vector, which is a blend between the chord left of the control point and the chord right of the control point (Eq. 87). At the default value ($b = 0$), the tangent is an even blend of these two, resulting in a Catmull-Rom type of internal tangent vector. Values of b approaching -1 bias the tangent toward the chord to the left of the control point, while values of b approaching $+1$ bias the tangent toward the chord to the right (see Figure 49).

$$T_i^R = T_i^L \frac{1+b}{2}(P_i - P_{i-1}) + \frac{1-b}{2}(P_{i+1} - P_i) \tag{87}$$

The three parameters, tension, continuity, and bias, are combined in Equation

$$T_i^R = \frac{((1-t)(1+c)(1+b))}{2}(P_i - P_{i-1}) + \frac{((1-t)(1-c)(1+b))}{2}(P_{i+1} - P_i)$$
$$T_i^L = \frac{((1-t)(1-c)(1+b))}{2}(P_i - P_{i-1}) + \frac{((1-t)(1+c)(1-b))}{2}(P_{i+1} - P_i) \quad (88)$$

5.12 B-splines

B-splines are the most flexible and useful type of curve, but they are also more difficult to grasp intuitively. The formulation includes Bezier curves as a special case. The formulation for B-spline curves decouples the number of control points from the degree of the resulting polynomial. It accomplishes this with additional information contained in the *knot vector*. An example of a *uniform knot vector* is [0, 1, 2, 3, 4, 5, 6, . . . , $n+k-1$], in which the knot values are uniformly spaced apart. In this knot vector, n is the number of control points and k is the degree of the B-spline curve. The parametric value varies between the first and last values of the knot vector. The knot vector establishes a relationship between the parametric value and the control points. With replication of values in the knot vector, the curve can be drawn closer to a particular control point up to the point where the curve actually passes through the control point.

A particularly simple, yet useful, type of B-spline curve is a uniform cubic B-spline curve. It is defined using four control points over the interval zero to one (Eq. 89). A compound curve is generated from an arbitrary number of control points by constructing a curve segment from each four-tuple of adjacent control points: (P_i, P_{i+1}, P_{i+2}, P_{i+3}) for $i = 1, 2 \ldots, n-3$, where n is the total number of control points (Figure 50). Each section of the curve is generated by multiplying the same 4 × 4 matrix by four adjacent control points with an interpolating parameter between zero and one. In this case, none of the control points is interpolated.

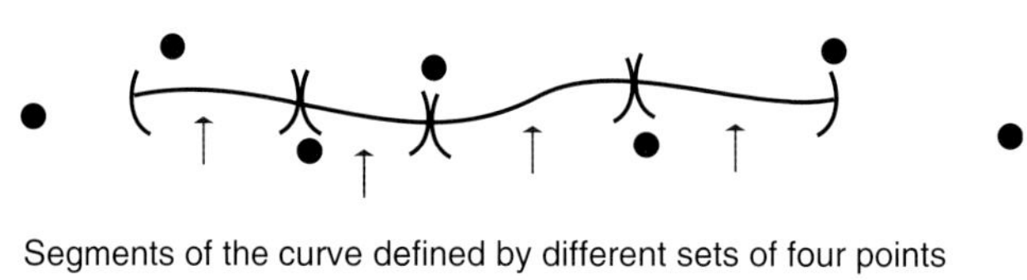

FIGURE 50

Compound cubic B-spline curve.

$$P(u)=\frac{1}{6}\begin{bmatrix} u^3 & u^2 & u & 1 \end{bmatrix}\begin{bmatrix} -1 & 3 & -3 & 1 \\ 3 & -6 & 3 & 0 \\ -3 & 0 & 3 & 0 \\ 1 & 4 & 1 & 0 \end{bmatrix}\begin{bmatrix} P_i \\ P_{i+1} \\ P_{i+2} \\ P_{i+3} \end{bmatrix} \tag{89}$$

Nonuniform rational B-splines (NURBs) are even more flexible than basic B-splines. NURBs allow for exact representation of circular arcs, whereas Bezier and nonrational B-splines do not. This is often important in modeling, but for purposes of animation, the basic uniform cubic B-spline is usually sufficient.

5.13 Fitting curves to a given set of points

Sometimes it is desirable to interpolate a set of points using a Bezier formulation. The points to be interpolated can be designated as the endpoints of the Bezier curve segments, and the interior control points can be constructed by forming tangent vectors at the vertices, as with the Catmull-Rom formulation. The interior control points can be constructed by displacing the control points along the tangent lines just formed. For example, for the segment between given points b_i and b_{i11}, the first control point for the segment, c_i^1, can be positioned at $b_i + (1/3)\ (b_{i+1} - b_{i-1})$. The second control point for the segment, c_i^2, can be positioned at $b_{i+1} - (1/3) \bullet (b_{i+2} - b_i)$ (see Figure 51).

Other methods exist. Farin [4] presents a more general method of constructing the Bezier curve and, from that, constructing the B-spline control points. Both Farin [4] and Rogers and Adams [18] present a method of constructing a composite Hermite curve through a set of points that automatically calculates internal tangent vectors by assuming second-order continuity at the segment joints.

6. Randomness

Introducing controlled randomness in both modeling and animation can often produce more interesting, realistic, natural-looking imagery. Noise and turbulence functions are often used in textures but also can be used in modeling natural phenomena such as smoke and clouds. The code for noise and turbulence that follows is from Peachey's chapter in Ebert [3]. Random perturbations are also useful in human-figure animation to make the motion less "robotic" looking. There are various algorithms proposed in the literature for generating random numbers; Gasch's [6] is presented at the end of this section.

6.1 Noise

The *noise* function uses a table of pseudorandom numbers between 1 and 1 to represent the integer lattice values. The table is created by *valueTableInit* the first time that *noise* is called. Lattice coordinates are used to index into a table of

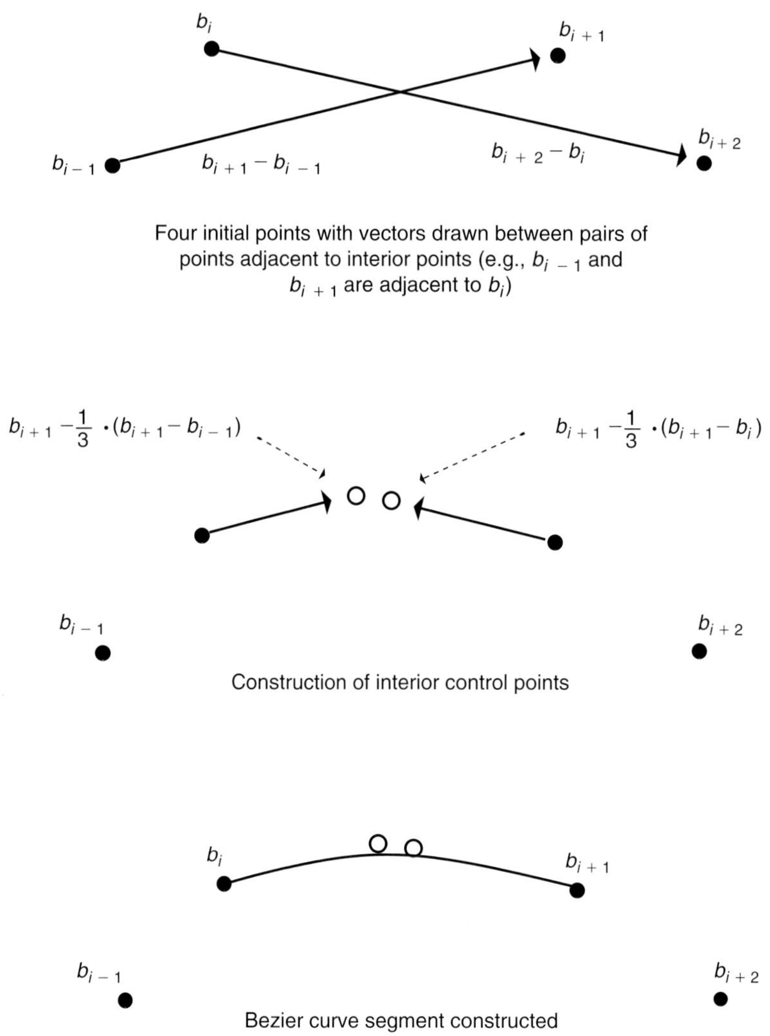

FIGURE 51

Constructing a Bezier segment that interpolates points.

pseudorandom numbers. A simple function of the coordinates, such as their sum, is used to compute the index. However, this can result in unwanted patterns. To help avoid these artifacts, a table of random permutation values is used to modify the index before it is used. A four-point spline is used to interpolate among the lattice pseudorandom numbers (*FPspline*).

```
#define TABSIZE              256

#define TABMASK              (TABSIZE-1)

#define PERM(x)              perm[(x)&TABMASK]

#define INDEX(ix,iy,iz)      PERM((ix) +PERM((iy)+PERM(iz)))
#define FLOOR(x)             (int)(x)
/* PERMUTATION TABLE */

static unsigned char perm[TABSIZE] ={

225, 155, 210, 108, 175, 199, 221, 144, 203, 116, 70, 213, 69, 158, 33, 252, 5, 82,
173,

133, 222, 139, 174, 27, 9, 71, 90, 246, 75, 130, 91, 191, 169, 138, 2, 151, 194, 235,
81, 7,

25, 113, 228, 159, 205, 253, 134, 142, 248, 65, 224, 217, 22, 121, 229, 63, 89, 103,
96,

104, 156, 17, 201, 129, 36, 8, 165, 110, 237, 117, 231, 56, 132, 211, 152, 20, 181,
111,

239, 218, 170, 163, 51, 172, 157, 47, 80, 212, 176, 250, 87, 49, 99, 242, 136, 189,
162,

115, 44, 43, 124, 94, 150, 16, 141, 247, 32, 10, 198, 223, 255, 72, 53, 131, 84, 57,
220,

197, 58, 50, 208, 11, 241, 28, 3, 192, 62, 202, 18, 215, 153, 24, 76, 41, 15, 179,
39, 46,

55, 6, 128, 167, 23, 188, 106, 34, 187, 140, 164, 73, 112, 182, 244, 195, 227, 13,
35, 77,

196, 185, 26, 200, 226, 119, 31, 123, 168, 125, 249, 68, 183, 230, 177, 135, 160,
180, 12,

1, 243, 148, 102, 166, 38, 238, 251, 37, 240, 126, 64, 74, 161, 40, 184, 149, 171,
178, 101,

66, 29, 59, 146, 61, 254, 107, 42, 86, 154, 4, 236, 232, 120, 21, 233, 209, 45, 98,
193, 114,

78, 19, 206, 14, 118, 127, 48, 79, 147, 85, 30, 207, 219, 54, 88, 234, 190, 122, 95,
67, 143,

109, 137, 214, 145, 93, 92, 100, 245, 0, 216, 186, 60, 83, 105, 97, 204, 52

};

#define RANDNBR ww (((float)rand())/RAND_MASK) float valueTab[TABSIZE];

/* ================================================*/==

/* VALUE TABLE INIT */

/* initialize the table of pseudorandom numbers */ void valueTableInit(int seed)

{
```

```
  float *table =valueTab; int i;
  srand(seed);
  for (i=0; i<TABSIZE; i++)
    *(table++) =1.0 -2.0*RANDNBR;
}
/* ===================================================*/==
/* LATTICE function */
/* returns a value corresponding to the lattice point */ float lattice(int ix, int iy,
int iz)
{
  return valueTab[INDEX(ix,iy,iz)];
}
/* ===================================================*/==
/* NOISE function */
float noise(float x, float y, float z)
{
  int ix,iy,iz; int i,j,k; float fx,fy,fz;
  float xknots[4],yknots[4],zknots[4]; static int initialized =0;
  if (!initialized) { valueTableInit(665); initialized =1;
  }
  ix =FLOOR(x);
  fx =x - ix;
  iy =FLOOR(y);
  fy =y - iy;
  iz =FLOOR(z);
  fz =z-iz;
  for (k=-1; k<=2; k++){
    for (j=-1; j<=2; j++){
      for (i=-1; i<=2; i++) [i+1] =lattice(ix+i,iy+j,iz+k);
      yknots[j+1] =spline(fx,xknots);
    }
    zknots[k+1] =spline(fy,yknots);
```

```
  }
  return spline(fz,zknots);
}
#define FP00 -0.5
#define FP01 1.5
#define FP02 -1.5
#define FP03 0.5
#define FP10 1.0

  #define FP11 -2.5
  #define FP12 2.0
  #define FP13 -0.5
  #define FP20 -0.5
  #define FP21 0.0
  #define FP22 0.5
  #define FP23 0.0
  #define FP30 0.0
  #define FP31 1.0
  #define FP32 0.0
  #define FP33 0.0
  /* ==================================================*/==
  float spline(float u,float *knots)
  {
    float c3,c2,c1,c0;
    c3 = FP00*knots[0] + FP01*knots[1] + FP02*knots[2] + FP03*knots[3]; c2 = FP10*knots[0]
    + FP11*knots[1] + FP12*knots[2] + FP13*knots[3]; c1 = FP20*knots[0] + FP21*knots[1] +
    FP22*knots[2] + FP23*knots[3]; c0 = FP30*knots[0] + FP31*knots[1] + FP32*knots[2] +
    FP33*knots[3]; return ((c3*u +c2)*u +c1)*u +c0;
  }
```

6.2 Turbulence

Turbulence is a stochastic function with a "fractal" power spectrum [3]. The function is a sum of amplitude-varying frequencies. As frequency increases, the amplitude decreases.

```
/* TURBULENCE */

float turbulence (float x, float y, float z)

{

  float f;

  float value =0;

  for (f =MINFREQ; f < MAXFREQ; f *=2) value +=fabs(noise(x*f, y*f, z*f))/f; return
  value;

}
```

6.3 Random number generator

This random number generator returns a random number in the range 0 to 999999999. An auxiliary routine would map this number into an arbitrary range of integers.

```
int r[100]; /* "global" pseudorandom table -- */

/* must be visible to rand and init_rand */

/* =====================================================*/==

/* RAND */

/* return a random number in the range 0 to 999999999 */ int rand (void)

{

  int i =r[98]; int j =r[99]; int k;

  int t;

  if ((t =r[i] 2 r[j]) < 0) t +=1000000000 L;

  r[i] =t; r[98]--; r[99]--;

  if (r[98] ==0) r[98] =55;

  if (r[99] ==0) r[99] =55; k =r[100] % 42 +56; r[100] =r[k];

  r[k] =t; return(r[100]);

}

/* ====================================================*/==

/* INIT RAND */

/* seed the random number table */ void init_rand (char *seed)
```

```
{
  char buf[101]; int i, j, k;
  if (strlen(seed) > 85) return(0);
  sprintf(buf, "aEbFcGdHeI%s", seed); while (strlen(buf) < 98) strcat(buf, "Q");
  for (i =1; i < 98; i++) r[i] =buf[i] * 8171717 +i * 997;
  i =97; j =12;
  for (k =1; k < 998; k++){ r[i] -=r[j];
    if (r[i] < 0) r[i] +=1000000000; i--; j--;
    if (i ==0) i=97; if (j ==0) j=97;
  }
  r[98] =55;
  r[99] =24;
  r[100] =77;
}
/* ==========================================================*/==
/* RAND INT */
/* return a random int between a and b */
/* assumes init_rand already called. */ int rand_int(int a, int b)
{
  return (a +rand() % (b - a +1));
}
```

7. Physics primer

Physically based motion is a limited simulation of physical reality. This can be as simple or as complex as the implementation requires. In the following sections are some of the equations of importance in simple physics simulation that can be found in any one of several standard texts. *The Mechanical Universe* [5] is used as the source for the brief discussion that follows.

7.1 Position, velocity, and acceleration

The fundamental equation relating position, distance, and speed is shown in Equation 90. This can be used to control the positioning of an object for any particular frame of the animation because the frame number is tied directly to time (Eq. 91). The average velocity of a body is the distance moved divided by the time it took to move, as stated by Equation 92. Notice that the unit of velocity is distance per time, for example, feet/second.

$$\text{distance} = \text{speed} \times \text{time} \tag{90}$$

$$\text{time} = \text{frameNumber} \times \text{timePerFrame} \tag{91}$$

$$\text{average Velocity} = \text{distanceTraveled}/\text{time} \tag{92}$$

For this discussion, distance as a function of time is $s(t)$; the average velocity from time $t1$ to $t2$ is $(s(t2) - s(t1))/(t2 - t1)$. The instantaneous velocity is determined by moving $t2$ closer and closer to $t1$. In the limiting case this becomes the derivative of the distance function with respect to time. Similarly, the average acceleration of an object is the change in velocity divided by the time it took to effect the change. This is presented in Equation 93, where $v(t)$ is a function that gives the velocity of the object at time t. Notice that the unit of acceleration is velocity per time or distance per time, for example, feet/second.[2] In the same way, instantaneous acceleration is the derivative of $v(t)$ with respect to time (Eq. 94). In the case of motion due to gravity, g is the acceleration due to gravity—a constant that has been measured to be 32 feet/second^2 or 9.8 meters/second^2 (Eq. 95).

$$a_{ave} = (v(t_2) - v(t_1)) \,/\, (t_2 - t_1) \tag{93}$$

$$a(t) = v'(t) = s''(t) \tag{94}$$

$$\begin{aligned} a(t) &= g \\ v(t) &= gt \\ s(t) &= (1/2)gt^2 \end{aligned} \tag{95}$$

7.2 Circular motion

Circular motion is important in physics and arises for a variety of phenomena, including the movement of planets and robotic armatures. Circular motion is easily specified by using polar coordinates. The position of a particle orbiting the origin at a distance r can be described using Equation 96. Here, i and j are orthonormal unit vectors (at right angles to each other and unit length) and $p(t)$ is the positional vector of the particle. In a constant radius circular orbit, $\theta(t)$ varies as a function of time, and the distance r is constant. During uniform circular motion, $\theta(t)$ changes at a constant rate, and *angular velocity* is said to be constant. Angular velocity is referred to here as $\omega(t)$ (Eq. 97). As for constant-velocity linear motion, in which the distance equals speed multiplied by time, for constant angular velocity the angle equals angular velocity multiplied by time (Eq. 98). If $\theta(t)$ is measured in radians and time in seconds, then $\omega(t)$ is measured in radians per second. To simplify the following equations, the functional dependence on time will often be omitted when the dependence is obvious from the context.

$$p(t) = (r\cos(\theta(t)))i + (r\sin(\theta(t)))j \tag{96}$$

$$\frac{d}{dt}\theta(t) = \omega(t) \tag{97}$$

$$\theta(t) = \omega t \tag{98}$$

Taking the derivative of Equation 96 with respect to time gives the instantaneous velocity (Eq. 99). Notice that the velocity vector, $v(t)$, is perpendicular to the position vector, $p(t)$. This can be demonstrated by taking the dot product of the two vectors $v(t)$ and $p(t)$ and showing that it is identically zero.

$$v(t) = \frac{dp}{dt} = ((-r)\omega\sin(\omega t))i + (-r\omega\cos(\omega t))j \tag{99}$$

Computing the length of $v(t)$ shows that $|v| = r\omega$ and, therefore, that the velocity is independent of t (i.e., constant). Notice, however, that a constant circular motion still gives rise to an acceleration. Taking the derivative of Equation 99 produces Equation 100, which is called the centripetal acceleration. The centripetal acceleration resulting from uniform circular motion is directed radially inward and has constant magnitude. With the equation for the length of $v(t)$ from earlier, the magnitude of the acceleration can be written using Equation 101.

$$\begin{aligned} a(t) &= \frac{dv}{dt} = (-\omega^2)((r\cos(\omega t))i + (-r\sin(\omega t))j) \\ &= (-\omega^2)p(t) \end{aligned} \tag{100}$$

$$a = v^2/r \tag{101}$$

For any particle in a rigid mass undergoing a rotation, that particle is undergoing the same rotation about its own center. In addition, if the particle is displaced from the center of rotation, then it is also undergoing an instantaneous positional translation as a result of its circular motion (Figure 52).

7.3 Newton's laws of motion

It is useful to review Newton's laws of motion. The first law is the principle of inertia. The second law relates force to the acceleration of a mass (Eq. 102). In another form, this law relates force to change in momentum (Eq. 103), where momentum is mass times velocity ($m \bullet v$). The third law states that when an object pushes with a force on another object, the second object pushes back with an equal but opposite force. It is important to note that the force F used here is considered to be the sum of all external forces acting on an object. Force is a vector quantity, and

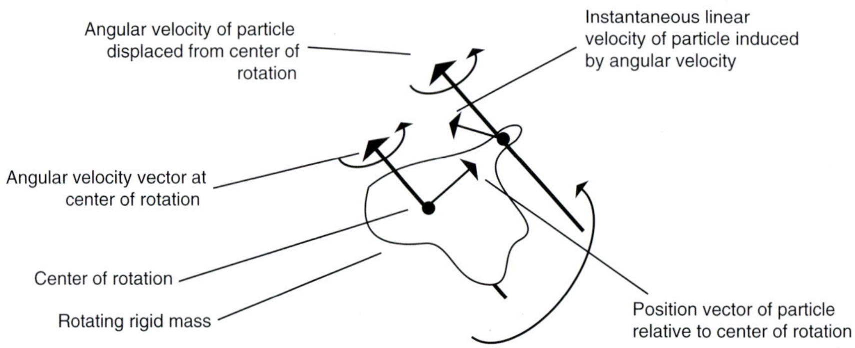

FIGURE 52

Motion of particle in a rotating rigid mass.

these equations really represent three sets of equations, one for each coordinate (Eq. 104). Newton's laws of motion are stated as follows:

> **First Law:** If no force is acting on an object, then it will not accelerate. It will maintain a constant velocity.
> **Second Law:** The change of motion of an object is proportional to the forces applied to it.
> **Third Law:** To every action there is always opposed an equal and opposite reaction.

$$F = ma \tag{102}$$

$$F = \frac{d}{dt}(mv)$$

$$F_x = ma_x \tag{103}$$

$$F_x = ma_y$$

$$F_x = ma_z \tag{104}$$

7.4 Inertia and inertial reference frames

An *inertial frame* is a frame of reference (e.g., a local coordinate system of an object) in which the principle of inertia holds. Any frame that is not accelerating is an inertial frame. In an inertial frame one observes the laws of motion and has no way of determining whether one is at rest or moving in an "absolute" sense. (But then, what is "absolute"?)

7.5 Center of mass

The center of mass of an object is that point at which the object is balanced in all directions. If an external force is applied in line with the center of mass of an object, then the object moves as if all the mass were concentrated at the center ("c" in Figure 53).

7.6 Torque

The tendency of a force to produce circular motion is called *torque*. Torque is produced by a force applied off-center from the center of mass of an object (Figure 54) and is computed by Equation 105.

$$\tau = r \times F \tag{105}$$

It is important to note that *torque* refers to a specific axis of rotation and is perpendicular to both r and F in Figure 54. The same force can exert different torques about different axes of rotation if it is applied at different locations on an object. A given torque vector for a rigid body is position independent. That is, for any particle in a rigid mass, the particle is undergoing that same torque.

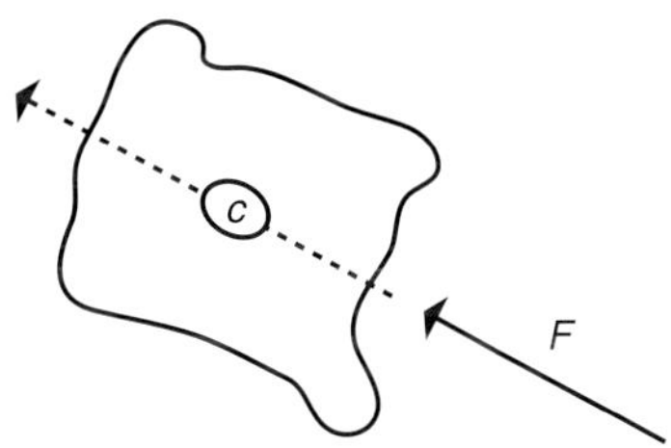

FIGURE 53

Center of mass.

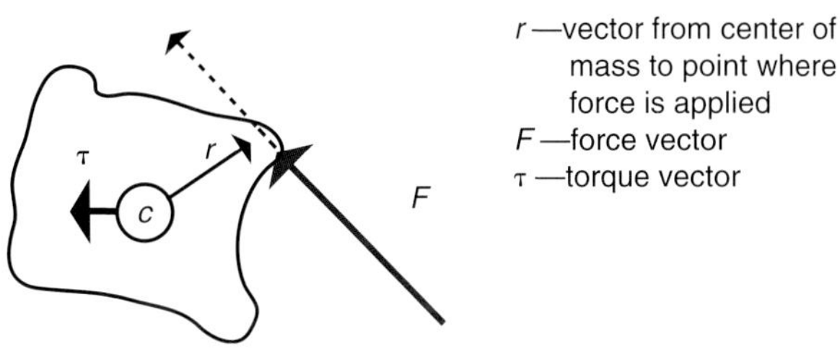

FIGURE 54

Applying a force off-center induces a torque.

7.7 Equilibrium: balancing forces

In the absence of acceleration, there is no change in the motion of an object (Newton's first law). In such cases, the net force and the torque acting on a body vanish (Eqs. 106 and 107). There may be forces present, but the vector sum is equal to zero.

$$\Sigma F = 0 \tag{106}$$

$$\Sigma \tau = 0 \tag{107}$$

7.8 Gravity

Equation 108 is Newton's law of universal gravitation. It calculates the force of gravity between two masses (m_1 and m_2) whose centers of mass are a distance r apart. G is the universal gravitational constant equal to 6.67×10^{-11} Newton meter^2/kilogram.^{2} When two objects are not touching, each acts on the other as if all its mass were concentrated at its center of mass. When an object is on (or near) the earth's surface, the distance of the object to the center of mass of the earth, the mass of the earth, and the gravitational constant of Equation 108 can all be combined to produce the object's acceleration (Eq. 109). This acceleration is usually denoted as g.

$$F = G\frac{m_1 m_2}{r^2} \tag{108}$$

$$a = \frac{F}{m_{\text{object}}} = G\frac{m_{\text{earth}}}{(\text{radius}_{\text{earth}})^2} = 9.8\text{m} / \text{s}^2 = 32\text{f} / \text{s}^2 = g \tag{109}$$

7.9 Centripetal force

Centripetal force is any force that is directed inward, toward the center of an object's motion (centripetal means *center seeking*). In the case of a body in orbit, gravity is the centripetal force that holds the body in the orbit. Consider a body, such as the moon, with mass M_m and a distance r away from the earth. The unit vector from the earth to the moon is R. The earth has a mass M_e. Equation 110 calculates the force vector that results from gravity. The acceleration induced by a circular orbit always points toward the center (centripetal), as in Equation 111. As previously shown, the acceleration due to circular motion has magnitude v^2/r (Eq. 100). This can be used to solve for velocity (Eq. 112).

$$F = -G\frac{M_m M_e}{r^2}R \tag{110}$$

$$\begin{aligned} a &= F/M_m \\ a &= \left((-GM_e)/r^2\right)R \\ a &= \left(-v^2/r\right)R \\ a &= \left(-GM_e/r^2\right)R \end{aligned} \tag{111}$$

$$v = \sqrt{(GM_e)/r} \tag{112}$$

7.10 Contact forces

Gravity is one of the four fundamental forces (gravity, electromagnetic, strong, and weak) that act at a distance. Another important category is contact forces. The tension in a wire or rope is an example of a contact force, as is the compression in a rigid rod. These forces arise from the complex interactions of electric forces that tend to keep atoms a certain distance apart. The empirical law that governs such forces, and that is familiar when dealing with springs, is Hooke's law (Eq. 113). Variable x is the change from the equilibrium length of the spring, k is the spring constant, and F is the restoring force of the spring to return to rest length. The constant k is a measure of the stiffness of the spring; the larger k is, the more sensitive the spring is to motion away from the rest position.

$$F = -kx \tag{113}$$

Another example of contact force, known as the *normal force*, is the result of repulsion between any two objects pressed against each other. It arises from the repulsion of the atoms of the two objects. It is always perpendicular to the surfaces, and its magnitude is proportional to how hard the two objects are pressed against each other. When objects in motion come in contact, an *impulse force* due to collision is produced. The impulse force is a short-duration force that is applied normal to the surface of contact on each of the two objects. Calculation of the impulse force due to collision is discussed in Chapter 5, Section 5.6.3. Other important examples of contact forces are friction and viscosity.

Friction

Friction arises from the interaction of surfaces in contact. It can be thought of as resulting from the multitude of collisions of molecules caused by the unevenness of the surfaces at the microscopic level.

The frictional force works against the relative motion of the two objects. Frictional forces from a surface do not exceed an amount proportional to the normal force exerted by the surface on the object. This is stated in Equation 114, where s is the coefficient of static friction and f_N is the normal force (component of the force that is perpendicular to the surface). Variable s varies according to the two materials that are in contact.

$$f_s = sf_N \tag{114}$$

The frictional forces acting between surfaces at rest with respect to each other are called *forces of static friction*. For a force applied to an object sitting on another object that is parallel to the surfaces in contact, there will be a specific force at which the block starts to slip. As the force increases from zero up to that threshold force, the lateral force is counteracted by an equal force of friction in the opposite direction. Once the object begins to move, *kinetic friction* acts on the object and approximately obeys the empirical law of Equation 115, where k is the coefficient of kinetic friction and f_N is the force normal to the surface. Kinetic friction is typically less than static friction. The force of kinetic friction is always opposite to the velocity of the object.

$$f_k = kf_N \tag{115}$$

Viscosity

The resistive force of an object moving in a medium is *viscosity*. It is another contact force and is extremely difficult to model accurately. When an object moves at low velocity through a fluid, the viscosity is approximately proportional to the velocity (Eq. 116); K is the constant of proportionality, which depends on the size and the shape of the object, and n is the coefficient of viscosity, which depends on the properties of the fluid. The coefficient of viscosity, n, decreases with increasing temperature for liquids and increases with temperature for gases. Stokes's law for a sphere of radius R is given in Equation 117.

$$F_{\text{vis}} = -Knv \tag{116}$$

$$K = 6\pi R \tag{117}$$

An object dropping through a liquid attains a constant speed, called the limiting or terminal velocity, at which gravity, acting downward, and the viscous force, acting upward, balance each other and there is no acceleration (e.g., Eq. 118 for a sphere). Terminal velocity is given by Equation 119. In a viscous medium, heavier bodies fall faster than lighter bodies. For spherical objects falling at a low velocity in a viscous medium, not necessarily at terminal velocity, change in momentum is given by Equation 120.

$$mg = 6\pi Rnv \tag{118}$$

$$v = (mg)/(6\pi Rn) \tag{119}$$

$$m\frac{dv}{dt} = mg - 6\pi Rnv \tag{120}$$

7.11 Centrifugal force

Consider an object (a frame of reference) that rotates in uniform circular motion with respect to a post (an inertial frame) because it is held at a constant distance by a rope. Relative to the inertial frame, each point in the uniformly rotating frame has centripetal acceleration expressed by Equation 121; r is the distance of the point from the axis of rotation, R is the unit vector from the inertial frame to the rotating frame, and v is the speed of the point. The tension in the rope supplies the force necessary to produce the centripetal acceleration. Relative to the rotating frame (not an inertial frame), the frame itself does not move and therefore the *centrifugal* force necessary to counteract the force supplied by the rope is calculated by using Equation 122.

$$a = -\frac{v^2}{r}R \quad (121)$$

$$F_c = -(ma) = -\frac{mv_2R}{r} \quad (122)$$

7.12 Work and potential energy

For a constant force of magnitude F moving an object a distance h parallel to the force, the work W performed by the force is shown in Equation 123. If a mass m is lifted up so that it does not accelerate, then the lifting force is equal to the weight (mass gravitational acceleration) of the object. Because the weight is constant, the work done to raise the object up to a height h is presented in Equation 124. Energy that a body has by virtue of its location is called *potential energy*. The work in this case is converted into potential energy.

$$W = Fh \quad (123)$$

$$W = mgh \quad (124)$$

7.13 Kinetic energy

Energy of motion is called *kinetic energy* and is shown in Equation 125. The velocity of a falling body that started at a height h is calculated by Equation 126. Its kinetic energy is therefore calculated by Equation 127.

$$K = \frac{1}{2}mv^2 \quad (125)$$

$$v^2 = 2gh \quad (126)$$

$$K = \frac{1}{2}mv^2 = mgh \quad (127)$$

7.14 Conservation of energy

Potential plus kinetic energy of a closed system is conserved (Eq. 128). This is useful, for example, when solving for an object's current height (current potential energy) when its initial height (initial potential energy), initial velocity (initial kinetic energy), and current velocity (current kinetic energy) are known.

$$U_a + K_a = U_b + K_b \quad (128)$$

7.15 Conservation of momentum

In a closed system, total momentum (mass times velocity) is conserved. This means that it does not change (Eq. 129) and that the momenta of all objects in a closed system always sum to the same amount (Eq. 130). This is useful, for example, when solving for velocities after a collision when the velocities before the collision are known.

$$\frac{d}{dt}((m_1 v_1 + m_2 v_2 + \ldots + m_n v_n)) = 0 \tag{129}$$

$$m_1 v_1 + m_2 v_2 + \ldots + m_n v_n = \text{constant} \tag{130}$$

7.16 Oscillatory motion

In some systems, the stability of an object is subject to a linear restoring force, F. The force is linearly proportional (using k as the constant of proportionality) to the distance x the object has been displaced from its equilibrium position (Eq. 131). Associated with this force is the potential energy (Eq. 132) that results from the object's displacement. These systems have the property that, if they are disturbed from equilibrium, the restoring force that acts on them tends to move them back into equilibrium. When disturbed from equilibrium, they tend to overshoot that point when they return, due to inertia. Then the restoring force acts in the opposite direction, trying to return the system to equilibrium. The result is that the system oscillates back and forth like a mass on the end of a spring or the weight at the end of a pendulum.

$$F = -kx \tag{131}$$

$$U = \frac{1}{2}kx^2 \tag{132}$$

Combining the basic equations of motion (force equals mass times acceleration) with Equation 131, one can derive the differential equation for oscillatory motion. This equation is satisfied by the displacement function $x(t)$ (Eq. 133).

$$\begin{aligned} F &= ma \\ F &= -kx \\ a &= \frac{d^2x}{dt} \\ m\frac{d^2x}{dt} &= -kx \\ \frac{d^2x}{dt} &= -kx/m \end{aligned} \tag{133}$$

7.17 Damping

The damping force can be modeled after Stokes's law, in which resistance is assumed to be linearly proportional to velocity (Eq. 134). This is usually valid for oscillations of sufficiently small amplitude. The damping force opposes the motion. The constant, k_d, is called the *damping coefficient*. Adding the damping force to the spring force produces Equation 135. Dividing through by m and collecting terms results in Equation 136, where $b = k_d/m$ and $a^2 = k/m$.

$$F_d = -k_d \frac{dx}{dt} \tag{134}$$

$$m\frac{d^2x}{dt} = -kx - k_d\frac{dx}{dt} \tag{135}$$

$$\frac{d^2x}{dt} + b\frac{dx}{dt} + a^2x = 0 \tag{136}$$

If there is a spring force but no damping, the general solution can be written as $x = C + \cos(a\,t + \theta_0)$. If there is damping but no spring force, the general solution turns out to be $x = C + e^{-bt} + D$, with C and D constant. If both the spring force and the damping force are present, the solution takes the form shown in Equation 137.

$$\begin{aligned} &x = Ce^{-bt}\cos(dt + \theta_0) \\ &\text{where } d = \sqrt{a^2 - \frac{b^2}{4}} \\ &\text{for } b < 2a \end{aligned} \tag{137}$$

7.18 Angular momentum

Angular momentum is the rotational equivalent of linear momentum and can be computed by Equation 138, where r is the vector from the center of rotation and p is momentum (mass velocity). The temporal rate of change of angular momentum is equal to torque (Eq. 139). Angular momentum, like linear momentum, is conserved in a closed system (Eq. 140).

$$L = r \times p \tag{138}$$

$$\tau = \frac{dL}{dt} \tag{139}$$

$$\Sigma L_i = \text{constant} \tag{140}$$

7.19 Inertia tensors

An *inertia tensor*, or *angular mass*, describes the resistance of an object to a change in its angular momentum [5] [13]. It is represented as a matrix when the angular mass is related to the principal axes of the object (Eq. 141). The terms of the matrix describe the distribution of the mass of the object relative to a local coordinate system (Eq. 142). For objects that are symmetrical with respect to the local axes, the off-diagonal elements are zero (Eq. 143). For a rectangular solid with mass M and dimensions a, b, and c along its local axes, the inertia tensor at the center of mass is given by Equation 144. For a sphere with radius R and mass M, the inertia tensor is given by Equation 145. If the inertia tensor is known at one position by I, then the inertia tensor I' for parallel axes at a new position (X, Y, Z) relative to the original position is calculated by Equation 146. If the inertia tensor for one set of axes is known by I, then the inertia tensor for a rotated frame is calculated by Equation 147, where R is the rotation matrix describing the rotated frame relative to the original frame.

$$\mathrm{I} = \begin{bmatrix} I_{xx} & -I_{xy} & -I_{xz} \\ -I_{yx} & I_{yy} & -I_{yz} \\ -I_{zx} & -I_{zy} & I_{zz} \end{bmatrix} \tag{141}$$

$$\begin{aligned} I_{xx} &= \int (y^2 + z^2)dm \\ I_{yy} &= \int (x^2 + z^2)dm \\ I_{zz} &= \int (x^2 + y^2)dm \\ I_{xy} &= \int xydm \\ I_{xz} &= \int xzdm \\ I_{yz} &= \int yzdm \end{aligned} \tag{142}$$

$$I = \begin{bmatrix} I_{xx} & 0 & 0 \\ 0 & I_{yy} & 0 \\ 0 & 0 & I_{zz} \end{bmatrix} \tag{143}$$

$$I = \frac{1}{12} \begin{bmatrix} M(b^2 + c^2) & 0 & 0 \\ 0 & M(a^2 + c^2) & 0 \\ 0 & 0 & M(a^2 + b^2) \end{bmatrix} \tag{144}$$

$$= \frac{2MR^2}{5} \begin{bmatrix} 1 & 0 & 0 \\ 0 & 1 & 0 \\ 0 & 0 & 1 \end{bmatrix} \tag{145}$$

$$I_{\text{translated}} = \begin{bmatrix} I_{xx} + M(Y^2 + Z^2) & -I_{xy} - MXY & -I_{xz} - MXZ \\ -I_{xy} - MXY & I_{yy} + M(X^2 + Z^2) & -I_{yz} - MXYZ \\ -I_{xz} - MXZ & -I_{yz} - MZYX & I_{zz} + MX^2 + Y \end{bmatrix} \tag{146}$$

$$I_{\text{rotated}} = RI_{\text{object}}R^{-1} \tag{147}$$

8. Numerical integration techniques

Numerical integration is useful for finding the arc length of the curve, updating arbitrary function values using derivative information, and specifically updating the position of an object over time. A useful technique for arc length computation is Gaussian quadrature. With regard to general function value updating, Runge-Kutta, explicit Euler integration, and implicit Euler integration are discussed. Huen, Verlet, and Leapfrog integration are covered specifically in the context of position update using a known acceleration. As with many numerical techniques, Press et al. [16] is an extremely valuable reference.

8.1 Function integration for arc length computation

Given a function $f(x)$, Gaussian quadrature can be used to produce an arbitrarily close approximation to the integral of the function between two values, $\int_a^b f(x)$, if the function is sufficiently well behaved [16]. Gaussian quadrature approximates the integral as a sum of weighted evaluations of the function at specific values (abscissas). The number of evaluations controls the error in the approximation. In its general form, Gaussian quadrature incorporates a multiplicative function, $W(x)$, which can condition some functions for the approximation (Eq. 148). Gauss-Legendre integration is a special case in which $W(x) = 1.0$, and it results in Equation 149. The code in Figure 55 for $n = 10$ duplicates that used in Chapter 4, Section 4.3.1 for computing arc length. Figure 56 gives the code for computing Gauss-Legendre weights and abscissas for arbitrary n.

$$\int_a^b (W(x)f(x))dx \cong \sum_{i=1}^{n} w_i f(x_i) \tag{148}$$

$$\int_a^b f(x)dx \cong \sum_{i=1}^{n} wf(x_i) \tag{149}$$

8.2 Updating function values

Integrating ordinary differential equations (ODEs) in computer animation typically means that the derivative function f' is available and that a numerical approximation to the function f is desired. For example, in a physically based simulation, the time-varying acceleration of an object is computed from the object's mass and the forces acting on the object in the environment. From the acceleration (the derivative function), the velocity (the function) is numerically calculated over time. Similarly, once the time-based velocity function is known (the derivative function), the time-varying position of the object (the function) can be calculated numerically.

```
/* ---------------------------------------------------------------------
INTEGRATE FUNCTION
use gaussian quadrature to integrate square root of given function in
the given interval */
double integrate_func(polynomial_td *func,interval_td *interval)
{
  double x[5]={.1488743389,.4333953941,.6794095682,.8650633666,.9739065285};
  double w[5]={.2966242247,.2692667193,.2190863625,.1494513491,.0666713443};
  double length, midu, dx, diff;
  int i;
  double evaluate_polynomial();
  double u1,u2;

  u1 = interval->u1;
  u2 = interval->u2;

  midu = (u1+u2)/2.0;
  diff = (u2-u1)/2.0;
  length = 0.0;
  for (i=0; i<5; i++) {
    dx = diff*x[i];
    length += w[i]*(sqrt(evaluate_polynomial(func,midu+dx)) +
    sqrt(evaluate_polynomial(func,midu-dx)));
  }
  length *= diff;
  return (length);
}
```

FIGURE 55

Gauss-Legendre integration for $n = 10$.

The simple form of an ordinary differential equation involves a first-order derivative of a function of a single variable. In addition, it is usually the case that conditions at an initial point in time are known and that the numerical integration is used in a simulation of a system as time moves forward. Such problems are referred to as *initial value problems*.

The (explicit) Euler method

The *Euler method* is the most basic technique used for solving such simple ODE initial value problems. It is shown in Equation 150, where h is the time step such that $x_{n+1} = h + x_n$. This method is not symmetrical in that it uses information at the beginning of the time step to advance to the end of the time step. The derivative at the beginning of the time step produces the vector, which is tangent to the curve representing the function at that point in time. The tangent at the beginning of the interval is used as a linear approximation to the behavior of the function over the

```
/* GAUSS-LEGENDRE */

#define EPSILON 0.00000000001
/* calculate the weights and abscissas of the Gauss-Legendre n-point form */
void gaussWeights(float a, float b, float *x, float *w, int n)
{
  int i,j,m;
  float p1,p2,p3,p;
  float z,z1;
  float xave,xdiff;

  m = (n+1)/2;
  xave = (b+a)/2;
  xdiff = (b-a)/2;
  for (i = 0; i<m; i++) {
    z = cos(PI*((i+1)-0.25)/(n+0.5));
    do {
      p1 = 1.0;
      p2 = 0.0;
      for (j=0; j<n; j++) {
        p3 = p2;
        p2 = p1;
        p1 = ((2*(j+1) - 1.0)*z*p2-j*p3)/(j+1);
      }
      pp = n*(z*p1-p2)/(z*z-1);
      z1 = z;
      z = z1-p1/pp;
    } while (fabs(z-z1) > EPSILON);
    x[i] = xave - xdiff*z;
    x[n-1-i] = xave + xdiff*z;
    w[i] = 2.0*xdiff/((1.0-z*z)*pp*pp);
    w[n-1-i] = w[i];
  }
}
```

FIGURE 56

Computing Gauss-Legendre weights and abscissas.

entire interval (Figure 57). The Euler method is neither stable nor very accurate. Other methods, such as Runge-Kutta, are more accurate for equivalent computational cost.

$$y_{n+1} = y_n + hf'(x_n, y_n) \tag{150}$$

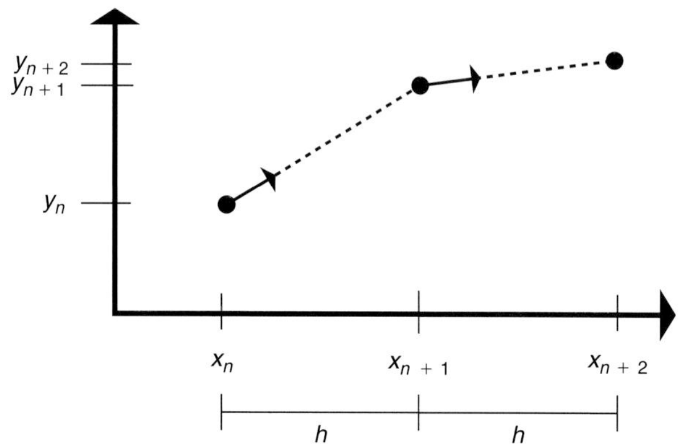

FIGURE 57

The Euler method.

Runge-Kutta

Runge-Kutta is a family of methods that is symmetrical with respect to the interval. The *second-order Runge-Kutta*, or *midpoint method*, is mentioned in Chapter 5, Section 5.6.3 in the discussion of physically based simulations. A half-step, using the explicit Euler method, is taken and the derivative is evaluated. This derivative is then used to update the original value (see Eq. 151).

$$y_{n+1} = y_n + f'\left(x_n + \frac{h}{2}, y_n + \frac{h}{2} f'(x_n, y_n)\right) \tag{151}$$

One of the most useful methods is *fourth-order Runge-Kutta* [16], shown in Equation 152 and Figure 58. It is referred to as a fourth-order method because its error term is on the order of the interval h to the fifth power. The advantage of using the method is that although each step requires more computation, larger step sizes can be used, resulting in an overall computational savings.

$$\begin{aligned}
k_1 &= hf'(x_n, y_n) \\
k_2 &= hf'\left(x_n + \frac{h}{2}, y_n + \frac{k_1}{2}\right) \\
k_3 &= hf'\left(x_n + \frac{h}{2}, y_n + \frac{k_2}{2}\right) \\
k_4 &= hf'(x_n + h, y_n + k_3) \\
y_{n+1} &= y_n + \frac{k_1}{6} + \frac{k_2}{3} + \frac{k_3}{3} + \frac{k_4}{6} + O(h^5)
\end{aligned} \tag{152}$$

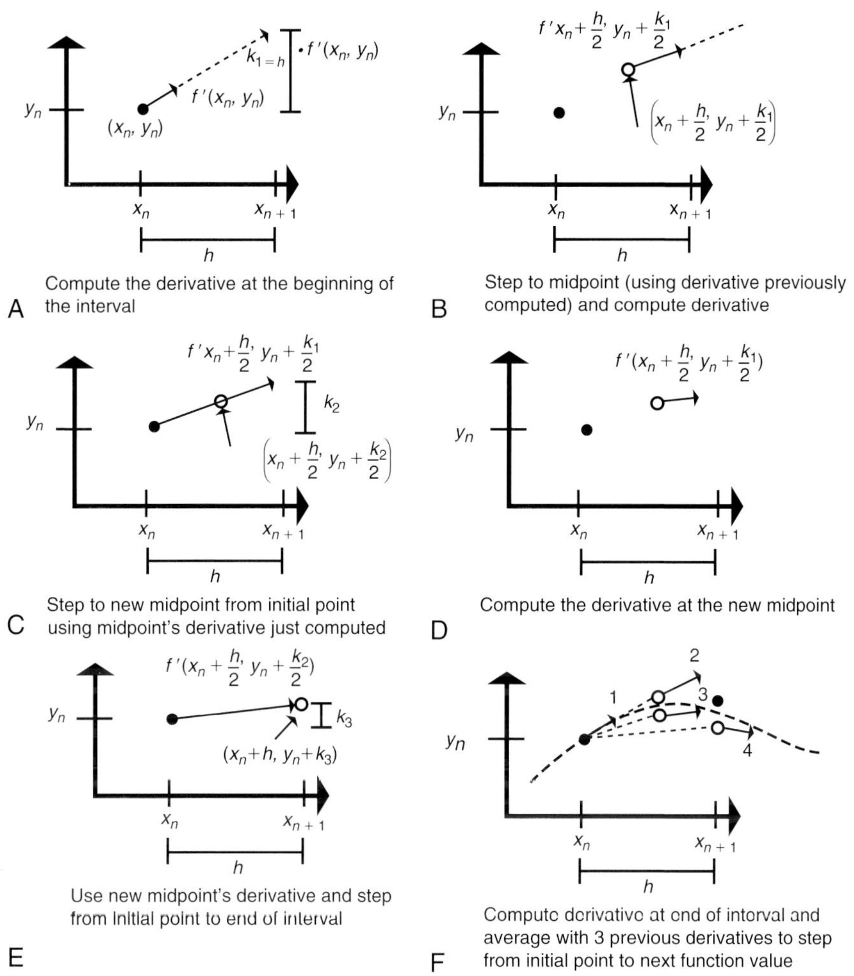

FIGURE 58

The steps in computing fourth-order Runge-Kutta.

The implicit Euler method

The explicit Euler method updates the function value using the derivative at the current value. The danger with the implicit method is that if the time step is too large, the updated function values can be a poor approximation to the actual function. The implicit method, for comparison, finds a new position whose derivative can update the current value to the new value (Eq. 153).

$$y_{n+1} = y_n + hf'\left(x_{n+1}, y_{n+1}\right) \tag{153}$$

This requires solving an equation to find such a y_{n+1} using, for example, a Newton-Raphson method. It takes more time to take a step using the implicit Euler method but because this technique is more stable than explicit Euler, large time steps can be taken and, thus, an overall computational savings can often be achieved.

The semi-implicit Euler method

The *semi-implicit Euler method* is derived from the implicit Euler method by approximating the y_{n+1} term used in evaluating the derivative by an explicit Euler step, thus resulting in Equation 154.

$$y_{n+1} = y_n + hf'(x_{n+1}, y_n + hf'(x_n, y_n)) \tag{154}$$

The semi-implicit Euler method offers more stability than explicit Euler and is computationally much less expensive than implicit Euler.

8.3 Updating position

The next three methods are discussed specifically in the context of updating position from velocity and/or acceleration over a time period\Δt.

The Heun method

The *Heun method* of integration, also called the *improved Euler method*, augments the basic Euler method. The Euler method takes the derivative at the current position to update to the next position. The Heun method takes the derivative at the position computed by the basic Euler method and averages it with the first-computed derivative and uses the average to update the position (Eq. 155). This is a common integration method used in physics texts.

$$\begin{aligned} v(t_{i+1}) &= v(t_i) + a(t_i)\Delta t \\ x(t_{i+1}) &= x(t_i) + \frac{1}{2}(v(t_i) + v(t_{i+1}))\Delta t \\ x(t_{i+1}) &= x(t_i) + v(t_i)\Delta t + \frac{1}{2}a(t_i)\Delta t^2 \end{aligned} \tag{155}$$

The Verlet method

Verlet integration is used to update the position directly from acceleration without explicitly calculating velocity. Essentially, the difference between the current position and the previous position is used as velocity. This vector is updated by acceleration and added to the current position to generate the next position (see Eq. 156).

$$x(t_{i+1}) = 2x(t_i) - x(t_{i-1}) + a(t_i)\Delta t^2 \tag{156}$$

The Leapfrog method

The *Leapfrog method* is unique in its temporal symmetry. It can be run forward in time or backward in time and it will trace out the same path. Position and acceleration are evaluated on the interval while velocity is evaluated on the half interval relative to the position (see Eq. 157).

$$x(t_{i+1}) = x(t_i) + v\left(t_{i+\frac{1}{2}}\right)\Delta t$$
$$v\left(t_{i+\frac{3}{2}}\right) = v\left(t_{i+\frac{1}{2}}\right) + a(t_{i+1})\Delta t \tag{157}$$

9. Optimization

As the field of computer graphics and computer animation matures, more complex and mathematically sophisticated techniques are being used. An increasingly important mathematical tool is *optimization*, also known as *mathematical programming.*[2] This discussion is intended for the reader who is well versed in computer graphics and familiar with the basics of calculus but who has not had much, if any, exposure to mathematical techniques involving optimization and who might be a bit intimidated whenever discussion turns that direction. Optimization is a complex and expansive topic, and finds application in control theory, chemistry, meteorology, VLSI CAD, geophysics, power grid design, and many others. A complete treatment is beyond the scope of the current discussion and the interested reader should follow up with material from the graphics literature (e.g., [27] [28]) or the mass of material on optimization in general (e.g., [29]) or in the literature concerning a specific application of interest.

In computer graphics, optimization finds application in areas such as surface fitting, decimation, inverse kinematics, motion capture data editing, physically based motion, and path construction. These tasks have certain features in common. For example, problems in these areas usually have a large parameter space. Geometric problems that define vertex placement or selection can have tens of thousands of vertices and, of course, triple the number in coordinate values. Animation problems might have a relatively small set of parameters, such as velocity or torque, but require the values for these parameters over thousands of frames of animation. The resulting high-dimensional parameter space can be too complex for an animator to easily set the parameters and produce the desired motion. The other common feature is that the function that evaluates the parameters to find the "best" values

[2] The term "programming" refers to the US military's use of the term "program" as applied to logistics, the problem domain for the first early optimization techniques, referring to a well-defined procedure for doing something (i.e., linear programming), and has nothing to do with computer programming.

is not an analytic function; rather, it is a rather computationally expensive procedure. Thus techniques that require fewer function evaluations are preferred.

Optimization is finding the optimal, or best, value among a set of alternatives. For the current discussion, the minimum function value is sought over the space spanned by the function's parameters. For example, in Equation 158, the minimum value is 1.

$$\min_{x \in \Re^n} f(x) \tag{158}$$

Alternatively, optimization can also be expressed in terms of finding the values for a set of input parameters that minimize (or maximize) a function's single output value. For example, in Equation 159, the input value that corresponds to the function's minimum is 0.

$$\operatorname*{argmin}_{x \in \Re^n} f(x) \tag{159}$$

The number of parameters and their possible values define the search space. The input parameters may be *unconstrained*, as in "x in reals," or the optimization problem may be *constrained*, as in "x greater than 0." The constraints can include equality as well as inequality constraints (Eq. 160).

$$\begin{aligned} &\text{minimize } f(\mathrm{X}) \\ &\text{Subject to } c_i(\mathrm{X}) = 0 \; i = 1, 2, \ldots, k_{eq} \\ &\text{Subject to } \widehat{c}_j\,(\mathrm{X}) = 0 \; j = 1, 2, \ldots, k_{le} \end{aligned} \tag{160}$$

The function, *f*, can be anything that is able to be evaluated given values for its input parameters. As mentioned, in computer graphics applications, the function is often not analytically defined because the function is actually an arbitrarily complex procedure that produces a value such as the time it takes to get somewhere, or a motion that minimizes the maximum torque during some task.

This discussion of optimization will often consider minimizing a function, although it obviously does not matter whether we are trying to minimize or maximize something—a function to be maximized uses the same principles as a function to be minimized, or, if desired, a function to be maximized can be negated and the resulting function considered for minimization. Numerical optimization is often used in situations in which the function is not analytic and an exhaustive search over the parameter space is not feasible because the function is very expensive to evaluate, or because the parameter space is very large, or both.

Optimization techniques can be characterized by the type of function, the type of input parameters, the number and type of constraints, the type of the output value(s), and so forth. The function can be analytic, comprised of mathematical operations that can be evaluated given the input values. The function might, or might not, be continuous and differentiable. The input parameters and/or function value might be reals or could be restricted to integer values (*integer programming*) or might be a mixture of integers and reals (*mixed programming*). The function can be relatively simple to compute or it can be computationally expensive to evaluate. The derivative might have similar variations. There might be constraints on the values that the input parameters can have (*constrained optimization*), and the function might have multiple output values. Because optimization can be applied in a variety of situations under a variety of assumptions, strategies come in many forms. As a result, optimization does lend itself to a nice single taxonomy.

9.1 Analytic Solution

Many approaches to optimization are merely extensions of basic calculus taught in high school physics or calculus class. A basic analytic approach usually involves finding the optimal input x^* that minimizes (or maximizes) a function $f(x)$ by computing a solution to $f'(x^*) = 0$ where the second derivative at x indicates a minimum ($f''(x^*) > 0$) or a maximum ($f'(x^*) < 0$). In this case, optimization needs to find the roots of the first derivative.

If $f''(x) > 0$ for all x, then the function is considered *convex*. Convex means that the function's slope is always increasing. This is important because it means that, assuming $f'(x)$ is negative at negative infinity, it will increase until it reaches zero and that, once $f'(x) = 0$, it will continue to increase as x increases; that is, it will never go back down to zero. This means that $f(x^*)$ is a minimum ($f'(x^*) = 0$ and $f''(x^*) > 0$) and there is no other minimum because $f'(x)$ will never get back down to zero; that is, x^* is a *global* minimum of the function. Similarly, if $f''(x) < 0$ for all x, then the function is *concave* and x^* is a global maximum. It should be pointed out that if the derivative function is not easily available or computable, then approximations to the derivative by finite differencing can be used with a corresponding degree of inaccuracy. Functions that are not convex do not necessarily have a global minimum. In such cases, the initial guess is important as this will dictate which, if any, minimum is found.

9.2 Numerical methods

At the risk of oversimplifying the area, there are two basic approaches to numerical optimization. The first simply randomly samples values of the function and adaptively samples more often in areas of the parameter space where lower values are found. This approach is usually used for functions in a high dimensional space where there are many local optima, so the random sampling hopes to uncover the global optimum or at least an acceptable near-global optimum. This is guaranteed to succeed only in the limit (i.e., taking an infinite number of samples). The second approach to numerical optimization uses knowledge about local trends of the function value to search in a particular direction. The direction is based on derivatives of the function or finite difference approximations to the derivative. The derivative indicates which direction to follow to reduce (or increase) the function value. The local minimum (maximum) is found when the derivative is equal to zero and the second derivative is positive (negative).

Gradient information can be used to direct the search of parameter space to drive the function to a minimum or drive the derivative to zero. In cases where $f'(x) = 0$ cannot be solved analytically, numerical techniques can be used to find its zero values. The Taylor series expansion of a function $g(x + dx)$ is shown in Equation 161 using the big O notation as a function of x^2 to represent the error term when using the first two terms as an approximation to $g(x + dx)$.

$$g(x+dx) = g(x) + g'(x)dx + O\left(dx^2\right) \tag{161}$$

If $x0$ is an initial guess, $x1 = x0 - a*g'(x0)$ can be computed if $g'(x)$ can be computed or is estimated. With the objective of driving the value of $g()$ to zero with successive guesses, the Taylor approximation (without the error term) is set to zero and rearranged to get Equation 162. Thus a succession of guesses is generated using Equation 163.

$$\begin{aligned} 0 &= g(x) + g'(x)dx \\ dx = x_1 - x_0 &= -\frac{g(x)}{g'(x)} \end{aligned} \tag{162}$$

$$x_n = x_{n-1} - \frac{g(x)}{g'(x)} \tag{163}$$

In the current case, $f'(x) = g(x)$. If x is multidimensional, as it usually is in computer graphics applications, then $g(x)$ is the gradient of f(x) (Eq. 164) and $g'(x)$ is the inverse of the Hessian (Eq. 165), but the same strategy holds and becomes Equation 166.

$$\nabla f(\mathrm{x}) = \left[\frac{\partial f}{\partial x_1}(\mathrm{x}), \frac{\partial f}{\partial x_2}(\mathrm{x}), \ldots, \frac{\partial f}{\partial x_n}(\mathrm{x})\right] \tag{164}$$

$$H(x) = \left[\frac{\partial^2 f}{\partial x_i \partial x_j}(\mathrm{x})\right] \tag{165}$$

$$\mathrm{x}_n = \mathrm{x}_{n-1} - \left[Hg(\mathrm{x}_{n-1})\right]^{-1} \nabla g(\mathrm{x}_{n-1}) \tag{166}$$

The negative of gradient is used because the gradient points in the direction of the greatest increase. This is called the *gradient descent method.*

It has been shown that always taking steps in the direction of the gradient can lead to situations that converge very slowly. Therefore taking steps in directions orthogonal to previous steps helps the convergence. This is called the *conjugate gradient method.*

An alternative way to approach the minimization problem is to fit a quadratic approximation to the function f at x, and then solve the quadratic equation for its minimum point and use that in the next iteration. The Taylor series expansion of G is shown in Equation 167.

$$f(x+dx)=f(x)+f'(x)(dx)+f''(x)\frac{(dx)^2}{2}+O\left((dx)^3\right) \quad (167)$$

The quadratic approximation can be easily solved for the minimum value. This is used as the next guess for the minimum and the procedure iterates. In this way, steps are taken toward the minimum of the function using the first and second derivative of the objective function.

So far, constraints on the parameter space have not been considered, and this is called unconstrained optimization. Often, there are constraints on valid input values, such as greater than zero.

Hard and soft constraints, equality constraints, and inequality constraints

The simplest constrained optimization is when the function is linear and the constrains are linear, which is referred to as linear programming. Think of a panel that is tilted representing the linear objective function, and a frame consisting of 2×4s, the constraints, bounding a region of the board. A well-known method of solving a linear programming problem is the simplex method. Essentially, this method says that the constrained minimum must occur at a corner point of the frame. The simplex method progresses from corner to corner, always going in a direction that reduces the objective function.

Nonlinear, constrained optimization is where things get interesting—and complicated. One strategy is to take a step in parameter space to reduce the objective function regardless of the constraints, followed by a step to restore constraint satisfaction.

A different common method for considering constraints is to incorporate constraints in the objective function. This adds a dimension to the parameter space. Assume $f(x)$ is the objective function and $g(x) - c = 0$ is a constraint. The new objective function is shown in Equation 168, where λ is an unknown constant called the *Lagrange multiplier*. Differentiating produces Equation 169. To deal with more complex constraint situations, *sequential quadratic programming* can be used.

$$\text{minimize}\, f(\mathrm{X}) + \lambda(c(\mathrm{X}) - d) \quad (168)$$

$$\frac{\partial F(\mathrm{X})}{\partial \mathrm{X}} = \nabla f(\mathrm{X}) + \lambda \nabla c(\mathrm{X}) = 0$$

$$\frac{\partial F(\mathrm{X})}{\partial \lambda} = c(\mathrm{X}) - d = 0 \quad (169)$$

If evaluation of the derivative of the function is expensive or unavailable, or if the parameter space is expansive with many local minima, the parameter space can be randomly sampled.

Completely random sampling is blended with increased sampling in areas where low values are found. Early sampling favors randomness while later sampling favors sampling in low value areas. Maintaining some randomness ensures that the global minimum will be found in the limit.

This is the basis for the approaches such as *genetic algorithms* and *genetic programming*. They are generally simple to program, but with finite resources do not guarantee convergence on the optimum. They are very useful when finding "good" values are sufficient.

10. Standards for moving pictures

When producing computer animation, one must decide what format to use for storing the sequence of images. Years ago the images were captured on film by taking pictures of refresh vector screens or by plotting the images directly onto the film. This was a long and expensive process requiring single-frame film cameras and the developing of nonreusable film stock. The advent of frame buffers and video encoders made recording on videotape a convenient alternative. With today's cheap disks, memory, and CPU cycles, all-digital desktop video production is a reality. While the entertainment industry is still based on film, most of the rest of computer animation is produced using digital images intended to be displayed on a raster-scan device in such forms as broadcast video, DVD video, animated Web banners, and streaming video. This section is intended to give the reader some idea of the various standards used for recording moving pictures. Standards related to the digital image are emphasized.

10.1 In the beginning, there was analog

Before the rise of digital video, the two common formats for moving pictures were film and (analog) video. Over the years there have been almost a hundred film formats. The formats differ in the size of the frame, in the placement, size, and number of perforations, and in the placement and type of audio tracks [15]. Silent film is played at 16 frames per second (fps). Some sound film is played at 18 fps, but 24 fps is more common. Film played at 24 fps is typically doubly projected; that is, each frame is displayed twice to reduce the effects of flicker.

Some of the film sizes (widths) are listed in Table 5. Note that there are often several formats for each film size. Only the most popular film formats are listed here. See the Web pages of Norwood [15] and Rogge [19] for more information. With the rise of desktop video production, film is less of an issue for home-brew computer animation, although it remains useful for conventional animation and, of course, is still the standard medium for display of feature-length films in theaters, although even this is starting to change.

Broadcast video standard

In 1941, the National Television Standards Committee (NTSC) established 525-line, 60.00 Hz field rate, 2:1 interlaced monochrome television in the United States. In

Table 5 Film Formats

Film Width	Notes
8 mm	An old format, introduced in 1932, 8 mm is used for inexpensive home movies. Cameras for regular 8 mm are no longer manufactured. Regular 8 mm uses 16 mm stock, which is recorded on both sides after flipping the film in the camera. This allows the 16 mm film stock to be split down the middle to produce two 8 mm reels. The frame is 0.192 × 0.145". Super-8 was introduced in 1965 as an improvement over regular 8 mm. The perforations (the holes in the film stock used to advance and register the film) were made smaller and the frame size was increased to 0.224 × 0.163". The film was placed into cassettes instead of on the reels of regular 8 mm film.
16 mm	16 mm is used for television and low-budget theatrical productions. It was introduced in 1923 and has a frame size of 0.404 × 0.295".
35 mm	35 mm has been a standard film size since the turn of the twentieth century [19]. It first became popular because it could be derived from the original 70 mm film made by Kodak. It is the standard for theatrical work as well as television. The *standard academy frame*, the most popular of several 35 mm formats, is 0.864 × 0.630".
65 mm	65 mm was the standard format for large-format cinematography. It is now gaining in popularity in special-venue and "ride" films.
70 mm	70 mm film is often a blow-up print of 35 mm film, produced for improved audio, better registration, and less grain of the release print. With better sound technology (e.g., digital) and the advent of multiplex theaters with smaller screen sizes, there is less demand for this type of 70 mm film. However, IMAX uses 70 mm film (69.6 × 48.5 mm) that is run at 24 fps.

1953, 525-line, 59.94 Hz field rate, 2:1 interlaced, composite color television signals were established as a standard. The image is displayed top to bottom, with each scanline displayed left to right. *2:1 interlaced* refers to the scanning pattern, with the information on the odd scanlines followed by the information on the even scanlines. Each set of scanlines is referred to as a *field*; there are two fields per *frame*. This standard is typically referred to by the initials of the committee—NTSC. Broadcast video in the United States must correspond to this standard. The standard sets a specific duration for a horizontal scanline, a frame time, the amplitude and duration of the various sync pulses, and so on. Home video recording units typically generate much sloppier signals and would not qualify for broadcast. There are encoders that can strip old sync signals off a video signal and re-encode it so that it conforms to broadcast quality standards. There are a total of 525 scanline times per frame time in the NTSC format. The number of frames transmitted per second is 29.97. There is a 2:1 interlace of the scanlines in alternate fields. Of the 525 total scanline times, approximately 480 contain picture information. The remainder of the scanline times are occupied by the overhead involved in the scanning pattern: the time it takes the beam to go from the end of one scanline to the beginning of the next and the time it takes for the beam to go from the bottom of the image to

Table 6 Video Format Comparison [10]

Standard	Lines	Scan Pattern	Field Rate (Hz)	Aspect Ratio
NTSC	525	2:1 interlaced	59.94	4:3
PAL	625	2:1 interlaced	50	4:3
SECAM	625	2:1 interlaced	50	4:3

the top. The aspect ratio of a 525-line television picture is 4:3, so equal vertical and horizontal resolutions are obtained at a horizontal resolution of 480 times 4/3, or 640 pixels per scanline. PAL and SECAM are the other two standards in use around the world (Table 6). They differ from NTSC in specifics like the number of scanlines per frame, the field rate, and the frequency of the color subcarrier, but both are interlaced raster formats. One of the reasons that television technology uses interlaced scanning is that, when a camera is providing the image, the motion is updated every field, thus producing smoother motion.

Black-and-white signal

A black-and-white video signal is basically a single line that has the sync information and intensity signal (luminance) superimposed on one signal. The vertical and horizontal sync pulses are negative with respect to a reference level, with vertical sync a much longer pulse than horizontal sync. On either side of the sync pulses are reference levels called the front porch and the back porch. The active scanline interval is the period between horizontal sync pulses. During the active scanline interval, the intensity of the signal controls the intensity of the electron beam of the monitor as it scans out the image.

Incorporating color into the black-and-white signal

When color came on the scene in broadcast television, engineers were faced with incorporating the color information in such a way that black-and-white television sets could still display a color signal and color sets could still display black-and-white signals. The solution is to encode color into a high-frequency component that is superimposed on the intensity signal of the black-and-white video.

A reference signal for the color component, called the *color burst*, is added to the back porch of each horizontal sync pulse, with a frequency of 3.58 MHz. The color is encoded as an amplitude and phase shift with respect to this reference signal. A signal that has separate lines for the color signals is referred to as a *component* signal. A signal such as the color TV signal with all of the information superimposed on one line is referred to as a *composite* signal.

Because of the limited room for information in the color signal of the composite signal, the TV engineers optimized the color information for a particular hue they considered most important: white skin tone. Because of that, the RGB information has to be converted into a different color space: YUV. Refer to Figure 59. *Y* is

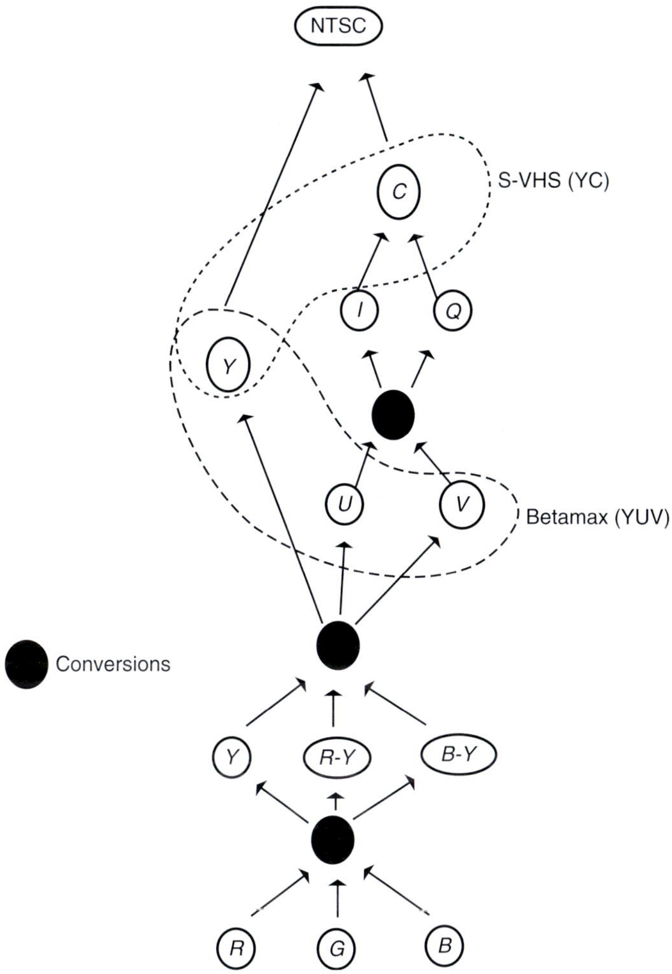

FIGURE 59

Video signal.

luminance and is essentially the intensity information found in the black-and-white signal. It is computed by Equation 170.

$$Y = 0.299R + 0.587G + 0.114B \tag{170}$$

The U and V of television are scaled and filtered versions of B-Y and R-Y, respectively. U and V are used to modulate the amplitude and phase shift of the 3.58 MHz color frequency reference signal. The phase of this chroma signal, C, conveys a quantity related to hue, and its amplitude conveys a quantity related to color saturation. In fact, the I and Q stand for "in phase" and "quadrature," respectively. The

NTSC system mixes *Y* and *C* together and conveys the result on one piece of wire. The result of this addition operation is not theoretically reversible; the process of separating luminance and color often confuses one for the other (e.g., the appearance of color patterns seen on TV shots of people wearing black-and-white seersucker suits).

Videotape formats

The size and speed of the tape and the encoding format contribute to the quality that can be supported by a particular video format. Common tape sizes are 1/2″, 3/4″, 1″, and 2″. The first two sizes are of cassette tapes, and the other two are of open reel tapes. One-half inch supports consumer-grade formats (e.g., VHS, S-VHS, and the less popular Betamax), 3/4″ is industrial strength (U-Matic), and 1″ and 2″ are professional broadcast-quality formats. One inch is the newer technology and has replaced some 2″ systems.

The common 1/2″ video formats are VHS and S-VHS. S-VHS is a format in which the *Y* and *C* signals are kept separate when played back, thus avoiding the problems created when the signals are superimposed. All video equipment actually records signals this way, but S-VHS allows the *Y* signal (luminance) to be recorded at a higher resolution than color. The color information is recorded with the same fidelity as on VHS. In addition, the sound is encoded differently than on regular VHS, also resulting in greater fidelity. The advantages of S-VHS are especially pronounced when it is played back on an S-VHS—compatible television.

10.2 In the digital world

Full-color (24 bits per pixel), video resolution (640×480), video rate (30 fps) animation requires approximately 1.6 gigabytes of information per minute of animation when stored as uncompressed RGB images. The problem is how to store and play back the animation. Various trade-offs must be considered when choosing a format, including the amount of compression, the time it takes for the compression/decompression, and the color and spatial resolution supported. The objective here is to provide an overview of the terminology, the important issues, and the most popular standards in recording animation. The discussion is at the level of consumer-grade technology and is not intended for professionals involved in the production of high-quality digital material.

Digital video sometimes refers specifically to digital versions of video to be broadcast for reception by television sets. In some literature, this is also referred to as *digital TV* (DTV), which is the term used here. On the other hand, *digital video* (DV) is also used in the sense of computer-generated moving images intended to be played back on an RGB computer monitor. DV is used here to specifically denote material intended to be displayed by a computer. These two categories of digital representations, DTV and DV, have much in common. One of the most important common issues is the use of compression/decompression (codec) technology described in the following paragraphs.

Standards related to DTV have two additional concerns. First, the standards are concerned with images that will be encoded for broadcast. As a result, they rarely deal directly with RGB images. When destined for television, digital images are at least partially encoded in a format related to the broadcast video standard (NTSC) soon after they leave the camera (e.g., YUV). DTV has the advantage of encoding a better image (480p) in less bandwidth than its analog counterpart. As a result, DTV can broadcast additional information in the bandwidth given a channel.

Digital images synthesized for playback on a computer are typically generated as RGB images, compressed for storage and transmission, and then decompressed for playback on RGB monitors. Second, DTV standards are concerned with an associated recording format of the images and audio on tape; tape is the common storage medium for broadcast video studios. Because images for computer playback are typically stored digitally on a hard disk or removable disk, DV standards do not cover tape formats. However, there are DV standards for file formats and for digital movies. Digital movie formats organize the image and audio data into tracks with associated timing information.

Compression/decompression

The recent explosion in multimedia applications, especially as a result of the Web, has led to the development of a variety of compression/decompression schemes [25]. After the frames of an animation are computed, they are compressed and stored on a hard disk or CD-ROM. When playback of the animation is requested, the compressed animation is sent to the compute box, using disk I/O or over the Web, where the frames are decompressed and displayed. The decompression and playback can take place in real time as the data is transmitted. In this case, it is referred to as *streaming video*. If the decompression is not fast enough to support streaming video, the compressed animation is transmitted in its entirety to the compute box, decompressed into the complete animation, and then played back. In either case, the compression not only saves space on the storage device but also allows animation to be transferred to the computer much faster. Several of the codecs are proprietary and are used in workstation-based video products. The different schemes have various strengths and weaknesses and thus involve trade-offs, the most important of which are compression level, quality of video, and compression/decompression speed [21].

The amount of compression is usually traded off for image quality. With some codecs, the amount of compression can be set by a user-supplied parameter so that, with a trial-and-error process, the best compression level for the particular images at hand can be selected. Codecs with greater compression levels usually incorporate interframe compression as well as intraframe compression. *Intraframe compression* means that each frame is compressed individually. *Interframe compression* refers to the temporal compression possible when one processes a series of similar still images using techniques such as image differencing. However, when one edits a sequence, interframe compression means that more frames must be decompressed and recompressed to perform the edits.

The quality of the video after decompression is, of course, a big concern. The most fundamental feature of a compression scheme is whether it is *lossless* or *lossy*. With lossless compression, in which the final image is identical to the original, only nominal amounts of compression can be realized, usually in the range of 2:1. The codecs commonly used for video are lossy to attain the 500:1 compression levels necessary to realize the transmission speeds for pumping animations over the Web or from a CD-ROM. To get these levels of compression, the quality of the images must be compromised. Various compression schemes might do better than others with such image features as edges, large monochrome areas, or complex outdoor scenes. The amount of color resolution supported by the compression is also a concern. Some, such as animated GIF format, support only 8-bit color.

The compression and decompression speed is a concern for obvious reasons, but decompression speed is especially important in some applications, for example, streaming video. On the other hand, real-time compression is useful for applications that store compressed images as they are captured. If compression and decompression take the same amount of time, the codec is said to be *symmetric*. In some applications such as streaming video, it is acceptable to take a relatively long time for compression as long as the resulting decompression is very fast. In the case of unequal times for compression and decompression, the codec is said to be *asymmetric*. To attain acceptable decompression speeds on typical compute boxes, some codecs require hardware support.

A variety of compression techniques form the basis of the codec products. Run-length encoding is one of the oldest and most primitive schemes that have been applied to computer-generated images. Whenever a value repeats itself in the input stream, the string of repeating values is replaced by a single occurrence of the value along with a count of how many times it occurred. This was sufficient for early graphic images, which were simple and contained large areas of uniform color. This technique does not perform well with today's complex imagery. The Lempel-Ziv-Welch (LZW) technique was developed for compressing text. As the input is read in, a dictionary of strings and associated codes is generated and then used as the rest of the input is read in. Vector quantization simply refers to any scheme that uses a sample value to approximate a range of values. YUV-9 is a technique in which the color is undersampled, so that, for example, a single color value is recorded for each 4×4 block of pixels. Discrete cosine transform (DCT) is a very popular technique that breaks a signal into a sum of cosine functions of various frequencies at specific amplitudes. The signal can be compressed by throwing away low-amplitude and/or high-frequency components. DCT is an example of the more general wavelet compression in which the form of the base component function can be selected according to its properties. *Fractal compression* is based on the fact that many signals are self-similar under scale. A section of the signal can be composed of transformed copies of other sections of the signal. This is applied to rectangular blocks of the image. In fact, most of the compression schemes break the image into blocks and then compress the blocks.

Codecs employ one or more of the techniques mentioned earlier. The names of some of the more popular codecs are Video I, RLE, GIF, Motion JPEG, MPEG, Cinepak, Sorenson, and Indeo 3.2. Microsoft products are Video I and RLE. Video I employs DCT compression, and RLE uses run-length encoding. GIF is an 8-bit color image compression scheme based on the LZW compression. JPEG uses DCT compression. Motion JPEG (MJPEG) is simply the application of JPEG for still images applied to a series of images. The compression/decompression is symmetric and is done in 1/30 of a second. JPEG compression can introduce some artifacts into some images with hard edges. The Moving Pictures Expert Group (MPEG) standards were designed specifically for digital video. MPEG uses the same algorithms as JPEG for intraframe compression of individual frames, called I-frames. MPEG then uses interframe compression to create B (bidirectional) and P (predicted) frames. MPEG allows quality settings to specify the amount of compression to use [24] and can be set individually for each frame type (I, P, B). MPEG-1 is designed for high-quality CD video, MPEG-2 is designed for high-quality DVD video, and MPEG-4 is designed for low-bandwidth Web applications [22].

Cinepak and Sorenson are products initially targeted for the Apple Mac world, although Cinepak is now available for the PC. Cinepak uses block-oriented vector quantization. Sorenson uses YUV compression with 4×4 blocks and employs interframe compression [20]. Indeo 3.2 is an Intel product that also uses block-oriented vector quantization. Cinepak and Indeo are highly asymmetric, requiring on the order of 300 times longer for compression than for their efficient decompression. Indeo also incorporates color blending and run-length encoding into its scheme.

Digital video formats

The codec products (as opposed to the underlying codec techniques) used for DV have an associated file format. Some formats also include timing information, the ability to animate overlay images (sprites), and the ability to loop over a series of frames. MPEG and MJPEG are both common DV formats. GIF89a-based animation (animated GIF) is basically a number of GIF images stored in one file with interframe timing information but no interframe compression. Compressing continuous-tone images can result in color banding. The compression does well on line drawings but not on complex outdoor scenes. GIF animations can use delta frames, which, for example, overlay images on a previously transmitted background. This saves retransmitting static information for some animations. As used here, *movie format* refers to a format that is codec independent and that can handle audio as well as imagery. Both Quicktime (MOV) and Video for Windows (AVI) [2] are movie formats designed as open codec architectures. Any codec can be used with these standards as long as a compatible plug-in is available. Cinepak has been a standard codec used with Quicktime, but Quicktime can also accommodate other codecs such as Sorenson and JPEG [24]. Quicktime organizes data into tracks and includes timing information. Video for Windows from Microsoft uses Video I and RLE as standard codecs but can also accommodate others. Video for Windows allows interleaving of image and audio information.

Digital television formats

Most of the DTV formats are based on sampling scaled versions of the color difference signals (*B-Y*, *R-Y*). Luminance and the scaled color difference signals are referred to as YUV. Common formats are D1, D2, D3, D5, D6, Digital Betacam, Ampex DCT, Digital8, DV, DVCam, and DVCPRO. When digitally sampled, the YUV signals are referred to as YCrCb. A typical sampling scheme is 4:2:2, in which the color difference signals (Cr, Cb) are sampled at half the sampling rate of luminance (*Y*) in the horizontal direction. 4:1:1 sampling means that the color difference signals are also sampled at half the rate in the vertical direction, resulting in one-quarter of the luminance sampling.

The D1 standard was developed when the broadcast television industry thought it would make the composite analog—to—component digital transition in one fell swoop. But that did not happen because the cost was prohibitive. D1 uses YUV coding, so-called 4:2:2, which means that the *U* and *V* components are horizontally subsampled 2:1. Luminance is sampled at 13.5 MHz, resulting in 720 samples per picture width. There is no compression other than undersampling the chroma information. Aggregate data rate is roughly 27 megabytes per second (MB/s). The D2 standard was developed as a low-cost alternative to D1. D2 is a composite NTSC digital format (i.e., digitized NTSC). The composite signal is sampled at four-times-color-subcarrier, about 14.318 MHz at one byte per sample (aggregate data rate, of course, 14.318 MB/s). It has all the impairment of NTSC but the reliability and performance of digital. It uses the same 3/4″ cassette as D1. As with D1, D2 uses no compression other than undersampling the chroma information. Other uncompressed digital formats include D3, D5, and D6. D3 is a composite format that uses 1/2″ tape. D5 is a component format that uses 1/2″ tape. D6 is a component high-definition television (HDTV) format.

Common compressed DTV formats include Digital Betacam, Ampex DCT, and Digital8 [9]. Digital Betacam uses 1/2″ tapes similar to the Betacam SP format with 2:1 compression based on DCT. Ampex DCT is a proprietary format; the *DCT* in its name stands for Digital Component Technology and not the compression scheme. The trio of DV, DVCam, and DVCPRO are similar formats using DCT compression. Depending on image content, the encoder decides whether to compress two fields separately or as a unit. Digital8 is a consumer-grade version of the DV format but uses cheaper Hi8 tapes. Newer formats include W-VHS, Digital S, Betacam SX, Sony HDD-1000, and D-VHS.

High-definition television and wide-screen format

In the United States the Grand Alliance was created by the Federal Communications Commission to develop the American HDTV specification. It is most commonly based on the MPEG-2 codec [8]. The basic idea behind HDTV is to increase the percentage of the visual field occupied by the image [12]. HDTV is a type of DTV.

Currently, there are two popular wide-screen HDTV formats: 720p and 1080i. The number refers to how many scanlines there are in an image. The "p" in 720p refers to progressive scan; the "i" in 1080i refers to interlaced scan. NTSC-format television has an aspect ratio (ratio of width to height) of 4:3, whereas the widescreen format more closely matches that found in movie theaters and is 16:9.

11. Camera calibration

For digitally capturing motion from a camera image, one must have a transformation from the image coordinate system to the global coordinate system. This requires knowledge of the camera's intrinsic parameters (focal length and aspect ratio) and extrinsic parameters (position and orientation in space). In the capture of an image, a point in global space is projected onto the camera's local coordinate system and then mapped to pixel coordinates. To establish the camera's parameters, one uses several points whose coordinates are known in the global coordinate system and whose corresponding pixel coordinates are also known. By setting up a system of equations that relates these coordinates through the camera's parameters, one can form a least-squares solution of the parameters [23].

Calibration is performed by imaging a set of points whose global coordinates are known and identifying the image coordinates of the points and the correspondence between the two sets of points. This results in a series of five-tuples (x_i, y_i, z_i, c_i, r_i) consisting of the three-dimensional global coordinates and two-dimensional image coordinates for each point. The two-dimensional image coordinates are a mapping of the local two-dimensional image plane of the camera located a distance f in front of the camera (Eq. 171). The image plane is located relative to the three-dimensional local coordinate system (u, v, w) of the camera (Figure 60). The imaging of a three-dimensional point is approximated using a pinhole camera model. The three-dimensional local coordinate system of the camera is related to the three-dimensional global coordinate system by a rotation and translation (Eq. 172); the origin of the camera's local coordinate system is assumed to be at the focal point of the camera. The three-dimensional coordinates are related to the two-dimensional coordinates by the transformation to be determined. Equation 173 expresses the relationship between a pixel's column and row number and the global coordinates of the point. These equations are rearranged and set equal to zero in Equation 174. They can be put in the form of a system of linear equations (Eq. 175) so that the unknowns are isolated (Eq. 176) by using substitutions common in camera calibration (Eqs. 176 and 177). Temporarily dividing through by t_3 ensures that $t_3 \neq 0.0$ and therefore that the global origin is in front of the camera. This step results in Equation 178, where A' is the first 11 columns of A; B' is the last column of A; and W' is the first 11 rows of W. Typically, enough points are captured to ensure an overdetermined system. Then a least-squares method, such as singular value decomposition, can be used to find the W' that satisfies Equation 179. W' is related to W by Equation 180, and the camera parameters can be recovered by undoing the

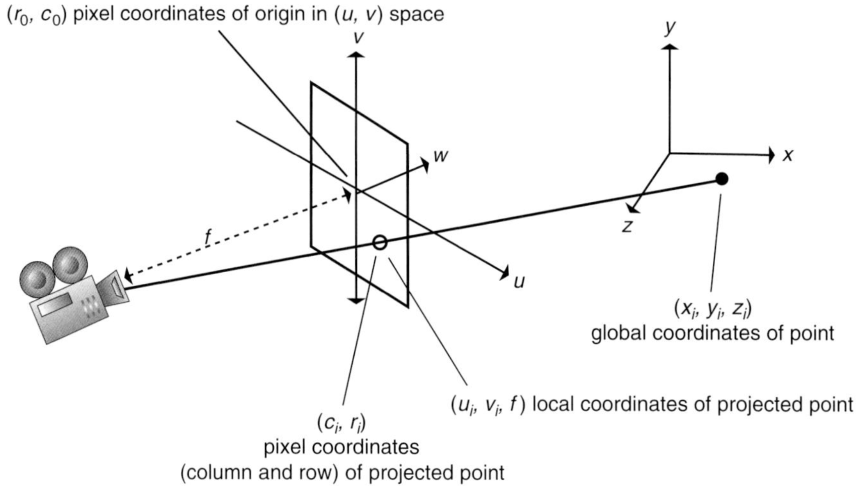

FIGURE 60

Coordinate systems used in the projection of a global point to pixel coordinates.

substitutions made in Equation 176 by Equation 181. Because of numerical imprecision, the rotation matrix recovered may not be orthonormal, so it is best to reconstruct the rotation matrix first (Eq. 182), massage it into orthonormality, and then use the new rotation matrix to generate the rest of the parameters (Eq. 183).

$$c_i - c_0 = s_u u_i$$

$$r - r_0 = s_v v_i \tag{171}$$

$$\begin{bmatrix} u_i \\ v_i \\ f \end{bmatrix} = R \begin{bmatrix} x_i \\ y_i \\ z_i \end{bmatrix} + T$$

$$R = \begin{bmatrix} R_0 \\ R_1 \\ R_2 \end{bmatrix} = \begin{bmatrix} r_{0,0} & r_{0,1} & r_{0,2} \\ r_{1,0} & r_{1,1} & r_{1,2} \\ r_{2,0} & r_{2,1} & r_{2,2} \end{bmatrix} \tag{172}$$

$$T = \begin{bmatrix} t_0 \\ t_1 \\ t_2 \end{bmatrix}$$

$$\frac{u_i}{f} = \frac{c_i - c_0}{s_u f} = \frac{c_i - c_0}{f_u} = \frac{R_0 \cdot [x_i y_i z_i] + t_0}{R_2 \cdot [x_i y_i z_i] + t_2}$$
$$\frac{v_i}{f} = \frac{r_i - r_0}{s_v f} = \frac{c_i - c_0}{f_v} = \frac{R_1 \cdot [x_i y_i z_i] + t_1}{R_2 \cdot [x_i y_i z_i] + t_2} \tag{173}$$

$$(c_i - c_0)(R_2 \cdot [x_i y_i z_i] + t_2) - f_u(R_0 \cdot [x_i y_i z_i] + t_0) = 0$$
$$(r_i - r_0)(R_2 \cdot [x_i y_i z_i] + t_2) - f_v(R_1 \cdot [x_i y_i z_i] + t_1) = 0 \tag{174}$$

$$AW = 0 \tag{175}$$

$$\begin{bmatrix} -x_1 & -y_1 & -z_1 & 0 & 0 & 0 & r_1x_1 & r_1y_1 & r_1z_1 & -1 & 0 & r_1 \\ 0 & 0 & 0 & -x_1 & -y_1 & -z_1 & c_1x_1 & c_1y_1 & c_1z_1 & 0 & -1 & c_1 \\ \cdots & \cdots & \cdots & \cdots & \cdots & \cdots & \cdots & \cdots & \cdots & \cdots & \cdots & \cdots \\ -x_1 & -y_n & -z_n & 0 & 0 & 0 & r_nx_n & r_ny_n & r_nz_n & -1 & 0 & r_n \\ 0 & 0 & 0 & -x_n & -y_n & -z_n & c_nx_n & c_ny_n & c_nz_n & 0 & -1 & c_n \end{bmatrix}$$

$$W_0 = f_u R_0 + c_0 R_2 = [w_0 w_1 w_2]^T$$
$$W_3 = f_v R_1 + r_0 R_2 = [w_3 w_4 w_5]^T$$
$$W_6 = R_2 = [w_6 w_7 w_8]^T$$
$$w_9 = f_u t_0 + c_0 t_2$$
$$w_{10} = f_v t_1 + r_0 t_2$$
$$w_{11} = t_2 \tag{176}$$

$$W = [w_0 w_1 w_2 w_3 w_4 w_5 w_6 w_7 w_8 w_9 w_{10} w_{11}]^T \tag{177}$$

$$A'W' + B' = 0 \tag{178}$$

$$\min_{w} \|A'W' + B'\| \tag{179}$$

$$W = \begin{bmatrix} W_0 \\ W_3 \\ W_6 \\ W_9 \\ W_{12} \\ W_{15} \end{bmatrix} = \frac{1}{\|W_6'\|} \times \begin{bmatrix} W_0' \\ W_3' \\ W_6' \\ W_9' \\ W_{10}' \\ 1 \end{bmatrix} \tag{180}$$

$$
\begin{aligned}
c_0 &= W_0^T W_6 \\
r_0 &= W_1^T W_6 \\
f_u &= -\|W_0 - c_0 W_6\| \\
t_0 &= (W_9 - c_0)/f_u \\
t_1 &= (W_{10} - r_0)/f_v \\
t_2 &= w_{11} \\
R_0 &= (w_0 - c_0 W_6)/f_u \\
R_1 &= (w_3 - r_0 W_6)/f_v \\
R_2 &= W_6
\end{aligned} \tag{181}
$$

$$
\begin{aligned}
R_0 &= (W_0{}' - c_0 W_6{}')/f_u \\
R_1 &= (W_3{}' - r_0 W_6{}')/f_v \\
R_2 &= W_6
\end{aligned} \tag{182}
$$

$$
\begin{aligned}
c_0 &= W_0^T R_2 \\
r_0 &= W_1^T R_2 \\
f_u &= -\|W_0 - c_0 R_2\| \\
f_v &= \|W_3 - r_0 R_2\| \\
t_0 &= (W_9 - c_0)/f_u \\
t_1 &= (W_{10} - r_0)/f_v \\
t_2 &= w_{11}
\end{aligned} \tag{183}
$$

Given an approximation to a rotation matrix, $\widetilde{R}$, the objective is to find the closest valid rotation matrix to the given matrix (Eq. 184). This is of the form shown in Equation 185, where the matrices C and D are notated as shown in Equation 186. To solve this, define a matrix B as in Equation 187. If $q = (q_0, q_1, q_2, q_3)^T$ is the eigenvector of B associated with the smallest eigenvalue, R is defined by Equation 188 [26].

$$\min\|\widehat{R} - R\| \tag{184}$$

$$\|R \cdot C - D\| \tag{185}$$

$$
\begin{aligned}
C &= [C_1, C_2, C_3] \\
D &= [D_1, D_2, D_3]
\end{aligned} \tag{186}
$$

$$
\begin{aligned}
B &= \sum_{i=1}^{3} B_i^T B_i \\
B_i &= \begin{bmatrix} 0 & (C_i - D)^T \\ D_i - C_i & \lfloor D_i - C_i \rfloor_x \end{bmatrix}
\end{aligned} \tag{187}
$$

$$[(x,y,z)]x^{*}=\begin{bmatrix}0 & -z & y\\ -z & 0 & -x\\ -y & x & 0\end{bmatrix}$$

$$R=\begin{bmatrix}1-2\left(q_2^2+q_3^2\right) & 2(q_1q_2-q_0q_3) & 2(q_1q_3+q_0q_2)\\ 2(q_1q_2+q_0q_3) & 1-2\left(q_1^2+q_3^2\right) & 2(q_3q_2+q_0q_1)\\ 2(q_1q_3+q_0q_2) & 2(q_3q_1+q_0q_2) & 1-2\left(q_1^2+q_2^2\right)\end{bmatrix} \quad (188)$$

References

[1] Bartels R, Beatty J, Barsky B. An Introduction to Splines for Use in Computer Graphics and Geometric Modeling. San Francisco: Morgan-Kaufmann; 1987.

[2] Dixon D. AVI Formats. http://www.manifest-tech.com/pc_video/avi_formats/avi_formats.htm; 2001.

[3] Ebert D, editor. Texturing and Modeling: A Procedural Approach. 2nd ed. Boston: AP Professional; 1998.

[4] Farin G. Curves and Surfaces for Computer Aided Design. Orlando, Fla: Academic Press; 1990.

[5] Frautsch S, Olenick R, Apostol T, Goodstein D. The Mechanical Universe: Mechanics and Heat, the Advanced Edition. Cambridge: Cambridge University Press; 1986.

[6] Gasch S. 0.5.12.0 Source Code. http://wannabe.guru.org/alg/node136.html; 2001.

[7] Gottschalk S, Lin M, Manocha D. OBB Tree: A Hierarchical Structure for Rapid Interference Detection. In: Rushmeier H, editor. Computer Graphics. Proceedings of SIGGRAPH 96, Annual Conference Series. New Orleans, La: Addison-Wesley; 1996. p. 171–80. ISBN 0-201-94800-1.

[8] Hromas D. Digital Television: The Television System of the Future.... http://www.cgg.cvut.cz/xhromas/dtv/; 2001.

[9] Iisakkila M. Video Recording Formats. http://www.hut.fi/u/iisakkil/videoformats.html; 2001.

[10] King BTV. Systems: A Comparison. http://www.ee.surrey.ac.uk/Contrib/WorldTV/-compare.html; 2001.

[11] Kochanek D. Interpolating Splines with Local Tension, Continuity and Bias Control. In: Computer Graphics. Proceedings of SIGGRAPH 84, vol. 18(3). Minneapolis: Minn.; 1984. p. 33–41.

[12] Kuhn K. HDTV Television—an Introduction: EE 498. http://www.ee.washington.edu/conselec/CE/kuhn/hdtv/95x5.htm; 2001.

[13] Madsen N. Three Dimensional Dynamics of Rigid Bodies. http://www.eng.auburn.edu/users/gflowers/me232/class_problems/angmom.html; 2001.

[14] Mortenson M. Geometric Modeling. New York: John Wiley & Sons; 1985.

[15] Norwood S. rec.arts.movies.tech: Frequently Asked Questions (FAQ) Version 2.00. http://www.redballoonnet/snorwood/faq2.html; 2001.

[16] Press W, Flannery B, Teukolsky S, Vetterling W. Numerical Recipes: The Art of Scientific Computing. Cambridge: Cambridge University Press; 1986.

[17] Ritter J. An Efficient Bounding Sphere. In: Glassner A, editor. Graphics Gems. New York: Academic Press; 1990. p. 301−3.

[18] Rogers D, Adams J. Mathematical Elements for Computer Graphics. New York: McGraw-Hill; 1976.

[19] Rogge M. More Than One Hundred Years of Film Sizes. http://www.xs4all.nl/wichm/filmsize.html;January; 2001.

[20] Sorenson Media. Sorenson Video Tutorial: Sorenson Video Compression. http://www.sorenson.com/Sorenson-Video/tutorial/page03.html; 2001.

[21] Speights II L. Video Compression Methods (Codecs). http://home.earthlink.net/radse/Page9.html; 2001.

[22] Terrain Interactive. Index of Codecs for Video, CD, DVD, and Audio. http://www.terran.com/CodecCentral/Codecs/index.html; 2001.

[23] Tuceryan M, Greer G, Whitaker R, Breen D, Crampton C, Rose E, et al. Calibration Requirements and Procedures for a Monitor-Based Augmented Reality System. IEEE Trans Vis Comput Graph 1995;1(3):255−73.

[24] Vahlenkamp HGFDL. Visualization Guide: Animation Formats. http://www.manifest-tech.com/pc_video/avi_formats/avi_formats.htm; 2001.

[25] Waggoner B. Technology: A Web Video Guide to Codecs. http://www.dv.com/webvideo/2000/0900/waggoner0900.html; 2001.

[26] Weng J, Cohen P, Herniou M. Camera Calibration with Distortion Models and Accuracy Evaluation. IEEE Trans Pattern Anal Mach Intell 1992;14(10):965−80.

[27] Zordan V. Solving Computer Animation Problems with Numeric Optimization. GVU Technical Report GIT-GVU-02−13. Georgia Institute of Technology 2002.

[28] Velho L, Carvalho P, Gomes J, de Figueiredo L. Mathematical Optimization in Computer Graphics and Vision. New York: Morgan Kaufmann; 2008.

[29] Bradley S, Hax A, Magnanti T. Applied mathematical Programming. New York: Addison Wesley; 1977.

Index

Note: Page numbers followed by f indicate figures, t indicate tables, and b indicate boxes.

D

N

W

Y

Z